Ecuador
and the Galápagos Islands

by David L. Pearson and Les Beletsky

Illustrated by:
Priscilla Barrett
David Beadle
David Dennis
Dan Lane
John Myers
John O'Neill
John Sill
Andy Woodham

Interlink Books

An imprint of Interlink Publishing Group, Inc.
Northampton, Massachusetts

This edition first published 2010 by

INTERLINK BOOKS
An imprint of Interlink Publishing Group, Inc.
46 Crosby Street, Northampton, Massachusetts 01060
www.interlinkbooks.com

Library of Congress Cataloging-in-Publication Data
Pearson, David (David L.)
Ecuador and the Galapagos Islands / by David L. Pearson and Les Beletsky ;
illustrated by Priscilla Barrett ... [et al.].
p. cm.—(The traveller's wildlife guides)
Includes bibliographical references and index.
ISBN 978-1-56656-530-1
1. Animals—Ecuador. 2. Animals—Galapagos Islands. 3. Natural
history—Ecuador. 4. Natural history—Galapagos Islands. I. Beletsky, Les,
1956- II. Barrett, Priscilla. III. Title. IV. Series.
QL245.P43 2004
590'.9866—dc22
2004004350

Printed and bound in China

To request our complete 40-page full-color catalog,
please call us toll free at **1-800-238-LINK,** visit our website at
www.interlinkbooks.com, or write to
Interlink Publishing
46 Crosby Street, Northampton, MA 01060
e-mail: info@interlinkbooks.com

CONTENTS

PREFACE

This book and others in the series are aimed at environmentally conscious travellers for whom some of the best parts of any trip are glimpses of wildlife in natural settings; at people who, when speaking of a journey, often remember days and locations by the wildlife they saw: "That was where we watched the monkeys," and "That was the day we saw the hawk catch a snake." The purpose of this book is to heighten enjoyment of a trip and enrich wildlife sightings by providing you with information to identify several hundred of the most frequently encountered animals and plants of Ecuador and the Galápagos, along with up-to-date information on their natural history, behavior, and conservation. Your skills at recognizing many of the species you see on your travels through Ecuador will be greatly enhanced with this book's color illustrations of 87 species of amphibians and reptiles, 70 mammals, more than 320 birds, 20 insects and arthropods, and with its line drawings of common plants characteristic of each major habitat type.

The idea to write this book grew out of our own travel experiences and frustrations. First and foremost, we found that we could not find a single book to take along on a trip that would help identify all the types of animals and plants that interested us. There are bird and mammal field guides and plant identification handbooks, but their number and weight quickly accumulate until you need an extra suitcase just to carry them. Thus, the idea: create a single guide book that travellers could carry to help them identify and learn about the different kinds of animals and plants they were most likely to see. Also, in our experience with guided tours, we've found that guides vary tremendously in their knowledge of nature and wildlife. Many, of course, are fantastic sources of information on the ecology and behavior of animals and plants. Some, however, know only about certain kinds of animals, birds, for instance. And many others, we found, knew precious little about any animals or plants, and what information they did tell their groups was often incorrect.

Last, like most ecotravellers, we are concerned about the threats to many species as their natural habitats are damaged or destroyed by people; when we travelled, we wanted current information on the conservation statuses of species we encountered. This book provides the traveller with conservation information on many of the species pictured or discussed in the book.

A few administrative notes: because this book has an international audience, we present measurements in both metric and English system units. The scientific classification of common species by now, you might think, would be pretty much established and unchanging; but you would be wrong. These days, what with molecular methods to compare species, classifications of various species groups that were first worked out during the 1800s and early 1900s are undergoing radical changes. Many bird groups, for instance, are being reclassified after comparative studies of their DNA. The research is so new that many biologists are still arguing about the results. We cannot guarantee that all the classifications that we use in the book are absolutely the last word on the subject, or that we have been wholly consistent in the classifications we used. However, for most users of this book, such minor transgressions are probably too esoteric to be of much significance.

Finally, we have tried to make the style of writing interesting and readable, but at the same time challenging and precise. We have tried to avoid terse, dry, textbook prose, and in so doing may offend some of our professional colleagues with narratives that include anthropomorphisms – providing plants and animals with human characteristics – but we do so in fun. Plants and animals do not, of course, reason and think like humans. If you do not appreciate our sense of humor, please ignore those sections; you should still have remaining a solid natural history guide to Ecuador.

We need to acknowledge the help of a large number of people in producing this book. First, much of the information we use is gleaned from published sources, and we owe the authors of these books and scientific papers a great deal of credit; their names and the titles of their publications are listed in the References and Additional Reading section on page 248. We are especially indebted to Greg Vigle (Arizona State University, or ASU) for his writing of the amphibian chapter and for editing the reptile chapter. In addition, every section was read and critiqued by at least one outside expert in that field, and their comments and corrections greatly increased the accuracy of the book. These experts included: Martha Crump (Northern Arizona University) and Jim Collins (ASU), amphibians; Mike Moore (ASU) and Brian Sullivan (ASU-West), reptiles; Dave Stejskal (Field Guides, Inc., Austin, Texas), birds; Andrew Smith (ASU) and Steve Gaulin (University of Pittsburgh), mammals; Phil DeVries (University of Oregon), Sacha Spector (University of Connecticut), and Dennis Paulson (University of Puget Sound, Tacoma, Washington), arthropods; Les Landrum (ASU), plants; and Dave Middleton (naturalist, author and photographer, Bennington, Vermont) and John Alcock (ASU), Galápagos. In Ecuador we must thank several who helped smooth out logistics and travel, provided encouragement, and over the last 30 years became good friends: Jaime Buestán, Miguel Moreno, Oswaldo Muñoz, Ronald Navarrete, Antonio Perrone, Mercedes Rivadeneira, and Danilo Silva. Nancy Pearson not only graciously suffered extended periods of neglect during the writing process of this book but she actually volunteered to read the entire manuscript from the point of view of an ecotraveller. Her comments were numerous and enlightening. Dave Middleton, Nancy Pearson and Pancho Enríquez provided the excellent habitat photos. D. Ahrenholz, J. Alcock, L. Aviles, E.M. Fisher, G.O. Krizek, D. Nunnallee, D. Paulson, N. Pearson, R. Radtke, E.S. Ross, and S. Spector provided the beautiful arthropod photos. We wish also to thank the artists who produced the marvelous illustrations: David Beadle (birds), Priscilla Barrett (mammals), David Dennis (amphibians and reptiles), Dan Lane (birds), John Myers (plants), John O'Neill (birds), John Sill (birds), and Andy Woodham (fish). Also thanks to the individuals who provided reference photographs that assisted the artists in their work, and to the museums that lent the artists pictures or specimens: Louisiana State University Museum of Natural History (Baton Rouge), The British Museum of Natural History (London), and Academy of Natural Sciences (Philadelphia).

Please let us know of any errors, opinions on the book, and suggestions for future editions. We are interested in hearing of your wildlife travel experiences. Write care of the publisher or e-mail: ECOTRAVEL8@aol.com

Chapter 1

ECOTOURISM: TRAVEL FOR THE ENVIRONMENTALLY CONCERNED

- *What Ecotourism Is and Why It's Important*
- *How Ecotourism Helps; Ecotravel Ethics*
- *Conservation and Ecotourism in Ecuador*

What Ecotourism Is and Why It's Important

Ecotourism or *ecotravel* is travel to (usually exotic) destinations specifically to admire and enjoy wildlife and undeveloped, relatively undisturbed natural areas, as well as indigenous cultures. The development and increasing popularity of eco-tourism is a clear outgrowth of escalating concern for conservation of the world's natural resources and *biodiversity* (the different types of animals, plants, and other life forms found within a region). Owing mainly to people's actions, animal species and wild habitats are disappearing or deteriorating at an alarming rate. Because of the increasing emphasis on the importance of the natural environment by schools at all levels and the media's continuing exposure of environmental issues, people have enhanced appreciation of the natural world and increased awareness of environmental problems globally. They also have the very human desire to want to see undisturbed habitats and wild animals before they are gone, and those with the time and resources increasingly are doing so.

But that is not the entire story. The purpose of ecotravel is twofold. Yes, people want to undertake exciting, challenging, educational trips to exotic locales – wet tropical forests, wind-blown deserts, high mountain passes, mid-ocean coral reefs – to enjoy the scenery, the animals, the nearby local cultures. But the second major goal of ecotourism is often as important: the travellers want to help conserve the very places – habitats and wildlife – that they visit. That is, through a portion of their tour cost and spending into the local economy of destination countries – paying for park admissions, engaging local guides, staying at local hotels, eating at local restaurants, using local transportation services, etc. – ecotourists help to preserve natural areas. Ecotourism helps because local people benefit economically as much or more by preserving habitats and wildlife for continuing use by ecotravellers than they could by "harvesting" the habitats for short-term gain. Put another way, local people can sustain themselves better economically by participating in ecotourism than by, for instance, cutting down rainforests for lumber or hunting animals for meat or the pet trade.

Preservation of some of the Earth's remaining wild areas is important for a number of reasons. Aside from moral arguments – the acknowledgment that we share the planet with millions of other species and have some obligation not to be the continuing agent of their decline and extinction – increasingly we understand that conservation is in our own best interests. The example most often cited is that botanists and pharmaceutical researchers each year discover another wonder drug or two whose base chemicals come from plants that live, for instance, only in tropical rainforest. Fully one-fourth of all drugs sold in the USA come from natural sources – plants and animals. About 50 important drugs now manufactured come from flowering plants found in rainforests, and, based on the number of plants that have yet to be cataloged and screened for their drug potential, it is estimated that at least 300 more major drugs remain to be discovered. The implication is that if the globe's rainforests are soon destroyed, we will never discover these future wonder drugs, and so will never enjoy their benefits. Also, the developing concept of *biophilia*, if true, dictates that, for our own mental health, we had better preserve much of the wildness that remains in the world. Biophilia, the word coined by Harvard biologist E. O. Wilson, suggests that because people evolved amid rich and constant interactions with other species and in natural habitats, we have deeply ingrained, innate tendencies to affiliate with other species and actual physical need to experience, at some level, natural habitats. This instinctive, emotional attachment to wildness means that if we eliminate species and habitats, we will harm ourselves because we will lose things essential to our mental well-being.

If ecotourism contributes in a significant way to conservation, then it is an especially fitting reprieve for rainforests and other natural habitats, because it is the very characteristic of the habitats that conservationists want to save, wildness, that provides the incentive for travellers to visit and for local people to preserve.

How Ecotourism Helps; Ecotravel Ethics

To the traveller, the benefits of ecotourism are substantial (exciting, adventurous trips to stunning wild areas; viewing never-before-seen wildlife); the disadvantages are minor (sometimes, less-than-deluxe transportation and accommodations that, to many ecotravellers, are actually an essential part of the experience). But what are the actual benefits of ecotourism to local economies and to helping preserve habitats and wildlife?

The pluses of ecotourism, in theory, are considerable:

1   Ecotourism benefits visited sites in a number of ways. Most importantly from the visitor's point of view, through park admission fees, guide fees, etc., ecotourism generates money locally that can be used directly to manage and protect wild areas. Ecotourism allows local people to earn livings from areas they live in or near that have been set aside for ecological protection. Allowing local participation is important because people will not want to protect the sites, and may even be hostile toward them, if they formerly used the now-protected site (for farming or hunting, for instance) to support themselves but

are no longer allowed such use. Finally, most ecotour destinations are in rural areas, regions that ordinarily would not warrant much attention, much less development money, from central governments for services such as road building and maintenance. But all governments realize that a popular tourist site is a valuable commodity, one that it is smart to cater to and protect.

2 Ecotourism benefits education and research. As people, both local and foreign, visit wild areas, they learn more about the sites – from books, from guides, from exhibits, and from their own observations. They come away with an enhanced appreciation of nature and ecology, an increased understanding of the need for preservation, and perhaps a greater likelihood to support conservation measures. Also, a percentage of ecotourist dollars are usually funnelled into research in ecology and conservation, work that will in the future lead to more and better conservation solutions.

3 Ecotourism can also be an attractive development option for developing countries. Investment costs to develop small, relatively rustic ecotourist facilities are minor compared with the costs involved in trying to develop traditional tourist facilities, such as beach resorts. Also, it has been estimated that, at least in some regions, ecotourists spend more per person in the destination countries than any other kind of tourists.

A conscientious ecotraveller can take several steps to maximize his or her positive impact on visited areas. First and foremost, if travelling with a tour group, is to select an ecologically-committed tour company. Basic guidelines for ecotourism have been established by various international conservation organizations. These are a set of ethics that tour operators should follow if they are truly concerned with conservation. Travellers wishing to adhere to ecotour ethics, before committing to a tour, should ascertain whether tour operators conform to the guidelines (or at least to some of them), and choose a company accordingly. Some tour operators in their brochures and sales pitches conspicuously trumpet their ecotour credentials and commitments. A large, glossy brochure that fails to mention how a company fulfills some of the ecotour ethics may indicate an operator that is not especially environmentally concerned. Resorts, lodges, and travel agencies that specialize in ecotourism likewise can be evaluated for their dedication to eco-ethics.

Basic ecotour guidelines, as put forth by the United Nations Environmental Programme (UNEP), the International Union for Conservation of Nature (IUCN), and the World Resources Institute (WRI), are that tours and tour operators should:

1 Provide significant benefits for local residents; involve local communities in tour planning and implementation.
2 Contribute to the sustainable management of natural resources.
3 Incorporate environmental education for tourists and residents.
4 Manage tours to minimize negative impacts on the environment and local culture.

For example, tour companies could:

1 Make contributions to the parks or areas visited; support or sponsor small, local environmental projects.
2 Provide employment to local residents as tour assistants, local guides, or local naturalists.
3 Whenever possible, use local products, transportation, food, and locally owned lodging and other services.

4   Keep tour groups small to minimize negative impacts on visited sites; educate ecotourists about local cultures as well as habitats and wildlife.

5   When possible, cooperate with researchers; for instance, Costa Rican researchers are now making good use of the elevated canopy walkways in tropical forests that several ecotour facility operators have erected on their properties for the enjoyment and education of their guests.

Committed ecotravellers can also adhere to the ecotourism ethic by disturbing habitats and wildlife as little as possible, by staying on trails, by being informed about the historical and present conservation concerns of destination countries, by respecting local cultures and rules, and even by actions as simple as picking up litter on trails.

Ecotourism, of course, is not a perfect remedy for threatened habitats and wildlife. Some negatives have been noticed, such as overuse of trails and the disruption of the natural behavior of wildlife when ecotourists intrude into their domains. On balance, however, most experts agree that in many situations, in most parts of the world, responsible ecotourism can have a positive role in conservation.

Conservation and Ecotourism in Ecuador

As you might expect, Ecuador, with one of the densest human populations in South America and a poverty rate hovering between 30% and 40%, faces a host of environmental problems and disasters waiting to happen. The list includes deforestation at a high rate to accommodate hungry colonists in search of new agricultural fields and cattle pastures, logging companies interested in quick profits but not in conservation, introduction of domestic animals that compete with native species, and misdirected government environmental policies. Oil currently dominates most political decisions; its economic power usually has its way. A trans-Andean oil duct built in 1971 to last 20 years still functions at full capacity but now with frequent ecologically disastrous breaks, fires and explosions. Not only has the pipeline's environmental pollution increased but the danger to people living along or near it has skyrocketed, literally and figuratively. Banana and African Oil Palm plantations have replaced large stands of native vegetation. This reduction of plant diversity over broad areas to basically one species limits the number of birds, insects and other animals that can live there. If that weren't bad enough, the use of herbicides, fungicides and insecticides to control a few agricultural pest species that exist in the region is overwhelming and unregulated. These poisons not only affect the agricultural crops but they flow into nearby waterways to contaminate everything downstream, eventually reaching coastal estuaries and the ocean. On the Pacific coast, mangroves have been almost completely destroyed (up to 80%, by some estimates) in some areas to build holding ponds in which shrimp are raised commercially – never mind that the shrimp larvae to sustain this commerce come from the estuaries and mangrove swamps that are being destroyed. If these human-caused problems aren't bad enough, their impact is multiplied by what seems to be a constant parade of natural disasters – floods from heavy rains, earthquakes in which entire villages disappear, droughts that dry up reservoirs involved with generating the nation's electricity supply, and volcanoes that erupt and destroy homes and lives. These uncontrollable forces serve to leave Ecuador often staggering from one economic crisis to another – in a constant state of emergency. With these huge problems, it's easy to consider environmental protection a low priority and conservation measures a luxury.

Behind all this pessimism, however, there is hope. Numerous non-government organizations (NGOs), largely staffed by energetic, young Ecuadoreans with a dream, are in many areas holding their own against environmental destruction. Environmental awareness is increasingly being taught in local schools and discussed on television and in newspapers. Politicians are slowly being pressured into at least claiming their advocacy for *green* (environment-enhancing) policies and programs. It is now less unusual to hear that they have taken a stand that benefits the environment. One of the strongest and most rapidly growing forces to benefit the environment in Ecuador is ecotourism. As its economic weight and effect on the country's GDP becomes more obvious, it is being heard and its needs and desires heeded – sometimes even when they run counter to those of oil companies and plantation owners. Groups of NGOs, tourist agencies, and indigenous peoples are working together to solidify their power and convince the government that ecotourism is an important part of Ecuador's future. Your trip to Ecuador to experience its natural wonders is a statement in itself that will benefit Ecuador's environment. If you want to be more than passively involved, however, use your influence to actively help Ecuador and its environment. If you see tour agencies, lodge operators, or officials following procedures or policies that run counter to the principle of ecotourism as a sustainable use of resources, say something to them. Also, seek out Ecuadorean and international non-profit NGOs that run on donations and make contributions.

Chapter 2

ECUADOR: GEOGRAPHY AND HABITATS

- *Geography and Climate*
- *Vegetation Patterns*
- *Major Habitats and Common Plant Species*

Geography and Climate

Ecuador (Map 1, p. 7) is a small country (270,678 sq km, 104,500 sq miles) about the size of Colorado or Italy. But what it lacks in size it more than makes up for in geographic variety. There are seven main geographical regions in Ecuador (Map 2, p. 29): The wet north coastal region, the arid south coastal region (also known as *Tumbesiana*), the western Andean slopes (*Chocó*), the eastern Andean slopes, the high Andean region (*Sierra*), the Amazonian region (called *El Oriente* because it includes the eastern part of Ecuador), and the Galápagos Island region. With more than 11 million people, Ecuador has the dubious honor of being the most densely populated country (35 people per sq km) in South America. This human population, however, is not uniformly distributed. The coast has 46% of the country's inhabitants and is the site of Ecuador's largest city, Guayaquil, with a population of more than 1.8 million. The Sierra has 49% of the population and features the second largest city, and capital, of Ecuador, Quito, with more than 1.4 million. The remaining 5% lives in the Oriente, which makes up more than a quarter of the country's land area.

The coastline is made up of long white-sand beaches interrupted in a few areas by large estuaries at the mouths of rivers emptying into the ocean. Here freshwater and seawater mix to produce mangrove forests and fertile breeding areas for fish, birds and many marine invertebrates. The rivers associated with these streams flow from the mountains and are relatively narrow in the north and south, but in the central coastal plain meandering rivers have formed extensive flat valleys that become immense swamps in the rainy season. In the north, rainfall is seasonal but annual totals range from 1300 to 3000 mm (50 to 120 in). In the south, the cool Humboldt Current in the ocean just off-shore reaches its northern limits, and cool air passes from the sea over the hot land. As this air warms it expands and sucks moisture out of the atmosphere, producing a desert, dry for all but the short rainy season (usually about March). This southern area has given rise to many unique plant and animal species and is called Tumbesiana. Annual rainfall in the south coast ranges from less than 500 to 1300 mm (20 to

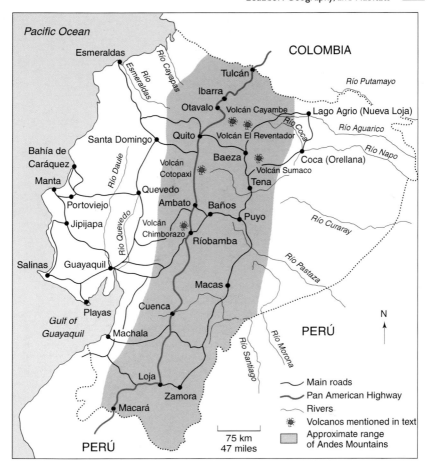

Map I Ecuador, showing main cities and towns, main roads, rivers and volcanoes mentioned in the text.

50 in). During unusual years, when the cold Humboldt Current is forced south by the warmer equatorial currents (El Niño), the temperature difference between the ocean and the land changes and rainfall on the entire coast increases dramatically – sometimes by 5 to 10 times the normal amount. The coastal plain rises abruptly into the heights of the west slope of the Andes Mountains. As moisture-laden air rises up these slopes, it cools and condenses as rainfall and fog throughout the year. This area has many unique plants and animals and is called the Chocó region. A similar area of steep slopes with high rainfall and fog occurs on the eastern side of the Andes.

The Andean region runs north to south the entire length of the country (Map 2, p. 29). The highest parts of the range are the western and eastern ridge of mountains, which are separated by a narrow plateau (*inter-Andean valley*), 2000 to 3000 m (6600 to 10,000 ft) high and 10 to 20 km (6 to 13 miles) wide. The two ridges are about 3000 to 4000 m (10,000 to 13,000 ft) high and are accented by towering, snow-covered volcanoes in the shape of symmetrical cones. Many of them are over 5000 m (16,500 ft) high and the highest one, Chimborazo, reaches 20,700 ft (6310 m).

The Amazonian lowlands (below 300 m, 1000 ft, elevation) east of the Andes cover more than 25% of Ecuadorean territory, and they are called *El Oriente*, or "the East." Rivers draining this tremendous area flow southeast to meet the Río Amazon or one of its main tributaries in Perú or Brazil. From the eastern base of the Andes, the terrain toward the east is flat and interrupted only by small hills (*colinas*) as far as the horizon. Seasonality is less distinct here and consists of a rainy and rainier season. Most precipitation is produced as water vapor rises above the forest canopy and cools to fall back down again as rainfall. Only a small proportion of rain for this region comes on storm fronts from the Atlantic and Caribbean.

The Galápagos Island region (officially the Archipélago de Colón) is a group of 13 major islands, 6 lesser islands, and 42 named islets in the Pacific Ocean 600 miles (970 km) from the continental coast (Map 3, p. 35). These islands were either formed as submarine volcanoes that eventually built up sufficient lava and ash to emerge from the ocean, or were raised as solid blocks from the sea floor by movements in the molten inner layers of the Earth's crust. Rainfall is highly seasonal here (wettest from January to April) and the effects of El Niño years are usually felt here first, as the ocean's temperature rises dramatically and rainfall increases to turn these normally brown islands emerald green.

Visitors should keep in mind that, even during rainy parts of the year, seldom does it rain all day. A typical pattern on the Andean slopes and lowland forests, for instance, is sunny mornings but afternoon showers. Some average annual rainfall values are as follows (see Map 1, p. 7, for locations): for the town of Portoviejo, average rainfall = 437 mm (17 in) and driest months are June to December; for Salinas, 107 mm (4 in) and April to February; Guayaquil, 997 mm (39 in) and July to December; Ibarra, 637 mm (25 in) and June to August; Quito, 1236 mm (49 in) and June to August; Limoncocha (just east of the town of Coca), 3244 mm (128 in) and there are no dry months; Puyo, 4412 mm (174 in) and there are no dry months; La Toma – Catamayo (just west of Loja), 390 mm (15 in) and May to August; Galápagos, about 630 mm (25 in) and June to December. Also remember that, in contrast to temperate regions, where season largely determines temperature, in tropical Ecuador, elevation has the most important effect – the lower you are, the warmer you will be.

Vegetation Patterns

The most striking thing about tropical habitats is their high degree of species diversity. Temperate forests in Europe or North America often consist of only a few tree species. The norm in tropical forests is to find between 50 and 200 tree species within the area of a few hectares or acres. In fact, sometimes it is difficult to find two individuals of the same species within visual distance of each other. Ecologists say tropical areas have a much higher *species richness* than temperate regions – for plant life, as well as for some animals such as insects and birds. Ecuador has one of the richest floras in the world, with more than 20,000 species of plants. Some 4500, or 23%, of these plants are *endemic* (they occur nowhere else in the world) to Ecuador (see Close-up, p. 86).

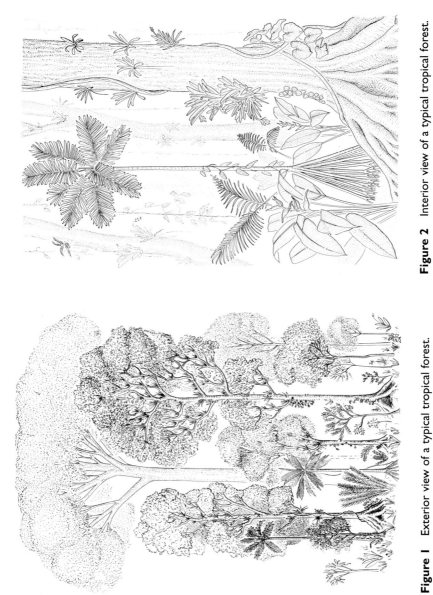

Figure 2   Interior view of a typical tropical forest.

Figure I   Exterior view of a typical tropical forest.

During first visits to tropical forests, people from Europe, North America, and other temperate-zone areas are usually impressed with the richly varied plant forms, many of which are not found in temperate regions. Although not every kind of tropical forest includes all of them, you will usually see a number of highly typical plant forms and shapes.

Tree Shape and Forest Layering

Many tropical trees grow to great heights, straight trunks rising many meters (yards) before branching. Tropical forests often appear layered, or *stratified,* and several more or less distinct layers of vegetation can sometimes be seen. A typical tropical forest has a surface herb layer (ground cover), a low shrub layer, one or more lower levels of shorter trees, and a higher, or *canopy,* tree layer (Figure 1). In reality, there are no formal layers – just various species of trees that grow to different, characteristic, maximum heights. Lone, very tall trees that soar high above their neighbors are sometimes referred to as *emergents* and are characteristic of tropical forests. Trees whose *crowns,* or high leafy sections, are in the often continuous upper layer are part of the *canopy.* Many of the crowns of tropical trees in the canopy are characteristically shaped and look like umbrellas (Figure 1). Those in the next highest layers form the *subcanopy.* Shrubs, bushes and short or baby trees make up the *understory* (Figure 1). The *leaf litter* on the forest floor is a variable layer that during the dry season accumulates many dry leaves, uneaten fruits and fallen branches. However, it becomes very thin during the rainy season, when warm temperatures and moist humidity permit fungi, insects and bacteria to quickly break down this organic material into chemicals and nutrients. They in turn are taken up immediately by the shallow root systems of the trees and shrubs.

Large-leaved Understory Plants

Tropical forests often have dense concentrations of large-leaved understory shrubs and herbs (Figures 1 and 2). Several plant families are usually represented: (1) Aroids, family Araceae, include plants such as *Dieffenbachia,* or Dumb Cane, and climbers such as *Monstera, Philodendron* (Figure 9), and *Syngonium;* (2) Marantas, family Marantaceae, including *Calantha insignis,* the Rattlesnake plant, which is an herb whose flattened yellow flowers resemble a snake's rattle; (3) *Heliconia* (Figure 10), family Heliconiaceae, which are large-leaved perennial herbs. The large leaves of these understory plants at least partially function to help gather the meager sunlight that makes its way though the canopy and subcanopy, so that adequate photosynthesis can take place to maintain the plant.

Tree Roots

Any northerner visiting a tropical forest for the first time quickly stops in his or her tracks and stares at the bottoms of trees. The trunks of temperate zone trees may widen a bit at the base but they more or less descend straight into the ground. Not so in the tropics, where many trees are *buttressed* – roots emerge and descend from the lower section of the trunk and spread out around the tree before entering the ground (Figure 2). The buttresses appear as narrow vertical ridges attached to the sides of a trunk. In older trees they are big and deep enough to hide a person (or a coiled snake!). The function of buttresses is believed to be tree support and, indeed, buttressed trees are highly wind resistant and difficult to blow down. But whether increased support is the primary reason that buttressing evolved is an open question, one that plant biologists study and argue over (increased fire resistance is another hotly argued possible explanation). Another unusual root structure associated with the tropics is *stilt*, or *prop, roots*. These are roots that seem to raise the trunk of a tree off the ground. They come off the tree some distance from the bottom of the trunk and grow out and down, entering the ground at various distances from the trunk (Figure 2). Stilt roots are characteristic of trees, such as mangroves, that occur in habitats covered with water during parts of the year, and many palms. Aside from anchoring a tree, functions of stilt roots are controversial.

Climbers and Stranglers

Tropical trees are often conspicuously loaded with hanging vines (Figures 1 and 2). Vines, also called *climbers, lianas,* and *bush-ropes*, are species from a number of plant families that spend their lives associated with trees. Some ascend or descend along a tree's trunk, perhaps loosely attached; others spread out within a tree's leafy canopy before descending toward the ground, free, from a branch. Vines are surprisingly strong and difficult to break; many older ones grow less flexible and more woody, sometime reaching the diameter of small trees. Common vines that climb trees from the ground up are Philodendrons and those of the genus *Monstera*.

Epiphytes

Epiphytes are plants that grow on other plants (usually trees) but do not harm their "hosts" (Figure 2). They are not parasites – they do not burrow into the trees to suck out nutrients; they simply take up space on trunks and branches. Ecologically, we would call the relationship between a tree and its epiphytes *commensal*: one party to the arrangement, the epiphyte, benefits – it gains growing space – and the other party, the tree, is unaffected. Epiphytes harm trees probably only when an epiphyte load becomes so heavy that the branch bearing it breaks off. How do epiphytes grow if they are not rooted in the host tree or the ground? Epiphyte roots that grow along the tree's surface capture nutrients from the air – bits of dust, soil, and plant parts that breeze by. Eventually, by collecting debris, each epiphyte develops its own bit of soil, into which it is rooted. Epiphytes are especially numerous and diverse in middle and higher-elevation rainforests, where persistent cloud cover and mist provide them ideal growing conditions. *Orchids*, with their striking flowers that attract bees and wasps for pollination, are among the most famous kinds of epiphytes. *Bromeliads*, restricted to the Americas, are common epiphytes with sharply pointed leaves that grow in a circular pattern, creating a central tank, or *cistern*, in which collects rain water, dust, soil, and plant materials. Recent studies of bromeliads show that these cisterns function as small aquatic ecosystems, with a number of different animals – insects, worms, snails, among others – making use of them. Several groups of amphibians are known to spend parts of their life cycles in these small pools (pp. 52, 57), and a number of species of tiny birds nest in bromeliads. (Not all bromeliads are epiphytes; some grow on the ground as largish, spiny plants, such as *Puya* (Figure 3) in the páramo, as well as pineapple (Figure 11).) Other plants that grow as epiphytes are mosses and ferns.

Palms

The trees most closely associated with the tropics worldwide are *palms*. Being greeted by palm trees upon exiting a jet is a sure sign that you have arrived in a warm climate. In fact, it is temperature that probably limits palms mainly to tropical and subtropical regions. They grow from a single point at the top of their stems, and so are very sensitive to frost; if that part of the plant freezes, the plant dies. Almost everyone recognizes palms because, for trees, they have unusual forms: they have no branches, but all leaves (which are quite large and called *fronds*) emerge from the top of the single trunk; and their trunks are usually of the same diameter from base to top. Many taller palms have stilt roots propping them up. Some palms have no trunks, but grow as small understory plants. Coconut Palms *Cocos nucifera*, (Figure 7), found throughout the world's tropical beaches, occur along Ecuador's coast, and a number of other palm species are quite common.

Major Habitats and Common Plant Species

Using associations of particular plant species, several broad habitats can be distinguished in Ecuador. Each habitat consists of large numbers of unique plant species that characterize and make it different from other habitats. Often, some animal species are also associated with each of these habitats. Below are brief descriptions of Ecuador's major habitats and listings of some of the more abundant and recognizable types of vegetation that visitors are almost sure to see. Note that many plants occur in more than one habitat type, so although a tree like *Cecropia* (Figure 5), for instance, occurs throughout Ecuador's Pacific lowland forests, it and related species are also found in the Amazon and up to middle elevations on some mountain slopes. Some common plants do not have English names. Forests that are pristine and have not been cut down by humans are called *primary forests*. Forests that have grown up in areas where humans earlier cut down the primary forest are called *secondary forests*.

Lowland Wet Forest

Ecuador's lowland wet forests both in the north coast and in the Amazon are classic tropical rainforests with emergent trees and deciduous or evergreen canopy trees reaching 40 to 55 m (130 to 180 ft) in height. Canopy trees have broad crowns and sub-canopy trees broad or round crowns. Tree buttresses are very common and often extend high up on trunks. Palms are abundant, often with stilt roots. The ground in these forests is either mostly bare or sparsely covered with a herb layer. Vines and epiphytes are usually abundant. Biologically, these kinds of forests are probably the richest habitats on Earth – supporting the most species of both plants and animals per unit area (more plant species probably support greater animal richness).

In the Amazonian region, the forest is made up of numerous patches of forest types, many types often occurring within a small area. Tall, cathedral-like tree species grow on higher ground that is never flooded by rising rivers, called *tierra firme*. Different types of trees grow in areas closer to rivers, areas that are more frequently flooded during the rainier season.

Some common, recognizable trees and shrubs of Ecuador's lowland wet forests are:

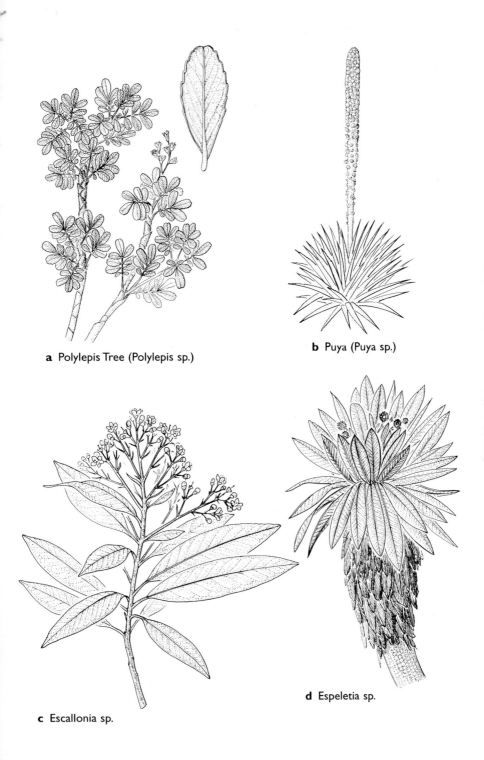

a Polylepis Tree (Polylepis sp.)

b Puya (Puya sp.)

c Escallonia sp.

d Espeletia sp.

Figure 3

a Podocarpus sp.

b Alder tree (Alnus acuminata)

c Treefern (Cyathea sp.)

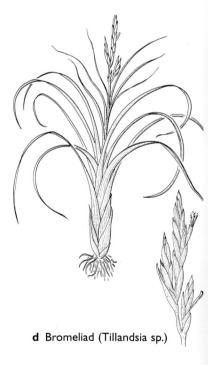

d Bromeliad (Tillandsia sp.)

Figure 4

a Bamboo (Chusquea sp.)

b Mauritia Palm

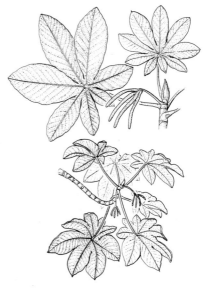

d Amazonian Cecropia (Cecropia sp.)

c Swamp aroid (Montrichardia sp.)

Figure 5

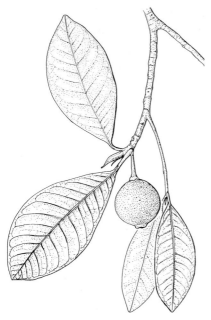

a Strangler Fig (Ficus crassiuscula)

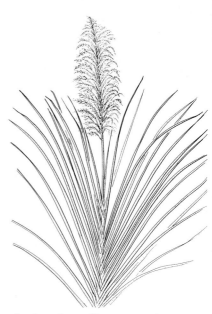

b Caña Brava (Gynerium sp.)

c Willow (Salix humboldtiana)

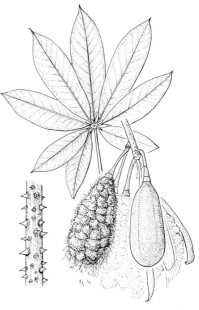

d Giant Kapok Tree (Ceiba pentandra)

Figure 6

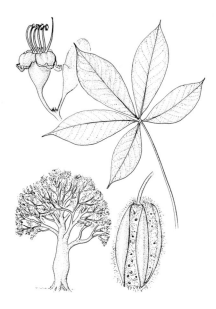

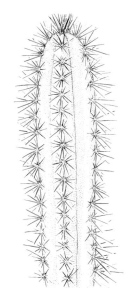

a Bottle-trunk Ceiba (Ceiba trichistandra)

b Cordón Columnar Cactus (Pilosocereus tweedyanus)

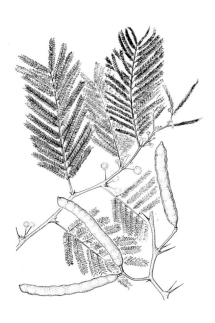

d Coconut Palm (Cocos nucifera)

c Acacia sp.

Figure 7

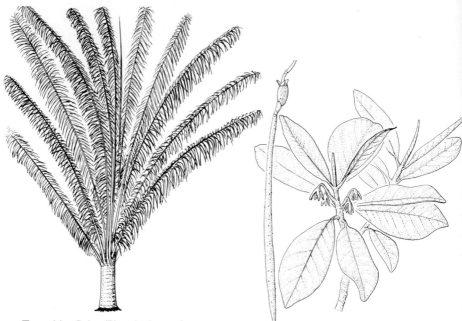

a Tagua Nut Palm (Phytelephas sp.)

b Red Mangrove (Rhizophora mangle)

c Black Mangrove (Avicennia germinans)

d Palo Santo (Bursera graveolens)

Figure 8

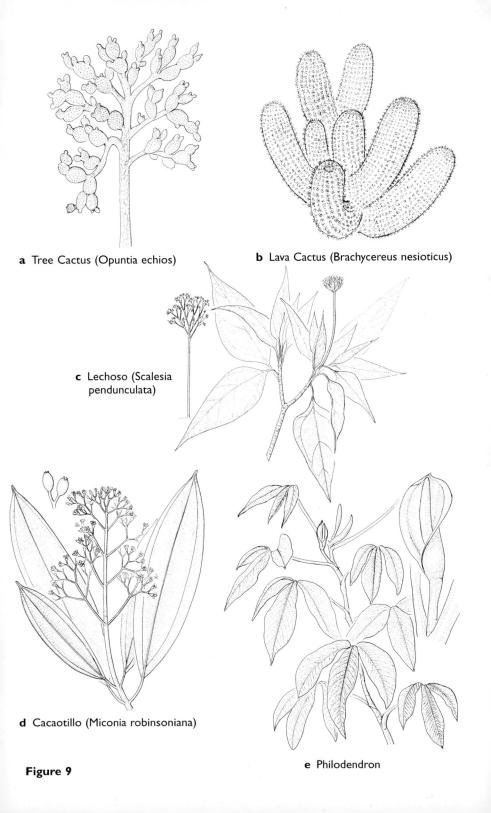

a Tree Cactus (Opuntia echios)

b Lava Cactus (Brachycereus nesioticus)

c Lechoso (Scalesia pendunculata)

d Cacaotillo (Miconia robinsoniana)

e Philodendron

Figure 9

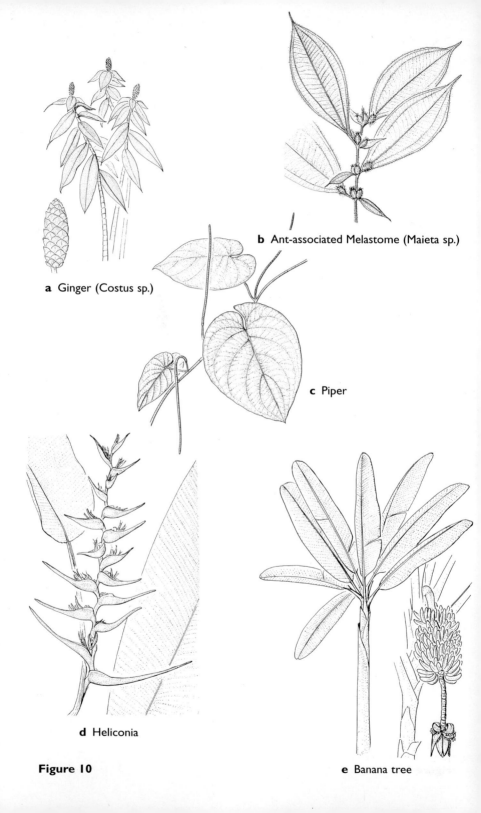

a Ginger (Costus sp.)

b Ant-associated Melastome (Maieta sp.)

c Piper

d Heliconia

e Banana tree

Figure 10

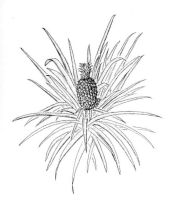

a Pineapple plant

b Sugar cane

c Papaya tree

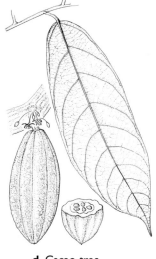

d Cacao tree

e African Oil Palm

Figure 11

Ceiba pentandra: Ceiba, or Kapok, are massive, often epiphyte-laden, trees, large enough to be emergents, with broad, flat crowns (Figure 6). Frequently they are the only trees left standing when pastures are cleared. The canopy towers constructed at several lodges in the Oriente are all built on massive Ceibas that emerge above the rest of the canopy. Fibrous kapok from seeds is used to stuff cushions and furniture.

Strangler Fig (*Ficus crassluscula*): Seed remains of a strangler fig fruit are defecated by a bird or monkey high in the branches of another tree. Here the seed sprouts, the fig tree starting out as an epiphyte. Its leaves grow out to photosynthesize the sun's energy and quickly produce its own canopy (Figure 6). Then it sends its roots down the trunk of the host until they form the veneer of a trunk and eventually reach the ground and burrow in. As it continues to grow, the fig eventually outcompetes the host tree for sunlight and nutrients, and kills the host, which it no longer needs for support.

Philodendron: The large, vaguely heart-shaped leaves of this semi-epiphytic climber/vine on trees are unmistakable (Figure 9).

Costus: Ginger is unique. It grows in a spiral-staircase stem, often a meter or more high (Figure 10). It is common in moister areas on the forest floor, and its flowers are bright and conspicuous, growing from a tiny pineapple-like base. Because its flowers bloom one at a time over several weeks, hummingbirds and insects can rely upon the presence of the nectar and pollen at the same place, so they can form daily routes of flower visitation, or "traplines" (see p. 131). The fruits that form from pollinated flowers also ripen sequentially so that tinamous and rodents, which eat the fruits, learn to return to the site every day for another prize.

Ant-associated Melastome (*Maieta* sp.): The species of the family of melastomes are among the most common in the undergrowth and easiest to recognize. The pattern of parallel cross veins on the leaves running perpendicular to long veins is unique. Species of the genus *Maieta* have distinctive hollow swellings at the base of each leaf that are covered with thick white hairs (Figure 10). Ants use these hollow areas as homes and apparently protect the leaves of the plant from being eaten by many herbivorous insects.

Piper: A very common and widespread genus of tropical forest understory shrubs, with more than 120 species represented in Ecuador. The Spanish name is Candela, after the candle-like, erect, flowering structures. Bats (p. 186), instead of insects or birds, act as pollinators on many of these shrubs. Usually 2 to 3 m (6 to 10 ft) high; occurs at elevations up to 2000 m (6500 ft). Figure 10. Black pepper is harvested from a species in this family.

Heliconia: A genus of striking flowering plants that is characteristic of tropical forests in the Americas; about 70 species occur in Ecuador. They grow within forests along streams and in sunny gaps, around clearings, and in disturbed areas such as roadsides and overgrown agricultural fields. *Heliconia* (Plantanillo, in Spanish) have very large, banana-tree-like leaves and their flowering structures are red, orange and yellow, large and flat, resembling nothing so much as lobster claws. *Heliconia* are pollinated by hummingbirds (p. 130) and occur up to elevations of 2000 m (6500 ft). Figure 10.

Amazon River Edges and Cochas

Near the edge of rivers in the Oriente grows a forest type adapted to maturing quickly in clearings created by the water's scouring action. The fast-growing plants include the hollow *Cecropia*, five-meter high grasses (*caña brava*) and willows. These plants also predominate on islands in the larger rivers. Other types of forest vegetation are associated with the meandering river systems that are more common in eastern parts of Ecuador. As a meander forms, the momentum of the water continuously cuts out the banks on the outside of the curve. Eventually, the meander becomes U-shaped. Then, as the water continues to undercut the banks, the two tails of the "U" come closer and closer until, in a surge, the river cuts through the top of the "U". The meander is completely cut off from the river except at highest flood levels. In Ecuador, these cut-off meanders form lakes called *cochas*. A cocha no longer has a constant current to scour out accumulated tree trunks, sand, and floating vegetation. The cocha slowly fills in, and a series of forest types replace each other in an often predictable sequence. Floating lily pads and grasses die and accumulate to form soils that give more terrestrial plant species a hold. *Cecropia* gives way to semiterrestrial species such as Mauritia Palm and Chonta Palm, which in turn give way to flood forest species.

Some common, recognizable trees and shrubs of Ecuador's Amazonian river edges and cochas are:

Mauritia Palm: These large palms (12 to 20 m, 40 to 65 ft) have fan-shaped leaves and grow in pure stands (*aguajales*) along the edges of cochas and in low moist areas of the forest (Figure 5). They are home to several unique Ecuadorean bird species such as the Point-tailed Palmcreeper and Zig-zag Heron.

Swamp aroid (*Montrichardia* sp.): Related to Philodendron, this tall, almost tree-like plant forms dense stands in swampy areas and along small rivers of the Oriente (Figure 5). It is a favorite food of the Hoatzin (p. 100), and apparently this bird gets its highly distasteful flesh from chemicals found in this plant.

Cecropia: These are conspicuous trees as *pioneer* species – they grow very quickly in disturbed areas of a forest, particularly in large, sunny gaps or clearings. Generally they are thinnish trees with very large, umbrella-like leaves. Most Cecropias harbor teeming colonies of stinging ants in their hollow trunks, and these ants end up protecting the tree from herbivores (or ecotravellers foolish enough to lean a hand on the Cecropia's trunk) by defending their nest site and food source. The Cecropias grow at low and middle elevations over much of Ecuador (Figure 5).

Caña Brava (*Gynerium* sp.): An early succession cane-grass about 5 m (15 ft) high, it grows in dense stands along Amazonian river banks and low river islands recently scoured by floods (Figure 6). The caña brava on these river islands often forms the bulk of a unique habitat to which more than ten species of birds are restricted.

Willow (*Salix humboldtiana*): This small species of willow occurs along white-water rivers in the mid-elevations of the Andes but also descends to the Amazon lowlands. Here it is common in pure stands on sand bars and low islands of larger rivers (Figure 6) .

Tropical Dry Forest

The southern coastal plain south to the Perúvian border is largely tropical dry forest. Here, little or no rain falls six months of the year, and the vegetation is adapted to a dry climate and short rainy season. Trees lose their leaves, roots go deep, cactus is common, and most of the tall trees are along the rivers (called *gallery* or *riparian forest*). These lowland dry forests consist of relatively low, mostly deciduous, trees, usually in two layers, one 20 to 30 m (60 to 100 ft) high with large, broad crowns, and one 10 to 20 m (30 to 60 ft) high, more evergreen, with small crowns. Tree buttressing is relatively uncommon in dry forests. Vines are often present. Epiphytes are uncommon, but when present, bromeliads are the most conspicuous. The shrub layer is dense, ground cover sparse. These forests are not as species-rich as wet forests. Dry forest land also makes for excellent agriculture, and because of this, many of these forests throughout Latin America have been cleared. Because dry forests have a more open, less dense, structure than wet forests, wildlife viewing in them is often far superior.

Some common, recognizable trees of tropical dry forests are:

Bottle-trunk Ceiba (*Ceiba trichistandra*): During the dry season, the bulging, green and bottle-like trunks of these immense trees are leafless and obvious on hillsides with otherwise withered vegetation (Figure 7). During the rainy season their leaves quickly grow out and the cotton-like fruit attracts parrots and other seed-eating birds and monkeys.

Cordón Columnar Cactus (*Pilosocereus tweedyanus*): Looking much like the more familiar Saguaro cactus of Arizona, these tall cactus (Figure 7) rise above most of the short vegetation and bushes of the driest parts of coastal Ecuador. During the rainy season, they are often overgrown by vines of Morning Glory flowers.

Acacia sp.: These thorny desert trees are often the only leafy tree available during the dry season. They provide shade and cover for many animals as well as nectar when their flowers are open (Figure 7).

Mangrove and Coastal Vegetation

Where fresh or brackish water is predictable, such as along estuaries, mangroves are common and form another floral region distinct from tropical dry forest. Mangroves also grow in estuarine areas of the Galápagos.

Some common, recognizable trees of Ecuador's coast are:

Coconut Palm (*Cocos nucifera*): Throughout the Indo-Pacific, this species is restricted to the seashore, where its giant floating seed washes up. Its trunk is typically curved, and the coconut fruit is one you have to watch out for – it hangs heavily overhead waiting to drop (Figure 7).

Tagua Nut Palm (*Phytelephas* sp.): The fruits of this short palm (Figure 8) are very hard and have served as the basis for a booming cottage industry. White, with an ivory-like texture, they are carved into pleasing shapes and forms and sold to tourists.

Mangroves: These are relatively short tree species of several unrelated plant families. They have in common the fact that they grow in areas exposed to salt water, usually around bays, lagoons, and other protected coastal infoldings. Common mangrove species are the Red Mangrove, *Rhizophora mangle* (Figure 8) and the Black Mangrove, *Avicennia germinans* (Figure 8).

Mid-elevation Cloud Forest

On both slopes of the Andes, small changes in altitude can produce major changes in rainfall, cloudiness, and temperature. Many plant species adapted to a specific combination of rain, sunshine and temperature thus can only occur in a narrow range of elevations. Numerous distinct floral regions run in narrow altitudinal belts north and south along the length of the Andes. Rainfall is supplemented by dense clouds of fog that form regularly as the water vapor rising from the lowlands cools and condenses. The trees here are typically covered with thick layers of epiphytes – moss, orchids and bromeliads. Large patches of alders grow in areas disturbed by landslides. These rainforests are mixed deciduous and evergreen in their lower reaches and uniformly evergreen in higher areas. Canopy height generally declines as elevation increases, being at between 30 and 40 m (100 to 130 ft) at lower levels and 20 to 30 m (60 to 100 ft) at higher elevations. These forests generally have two tree layers, canopy and subcanopy, and abundant vines. Tree buttressing is common in forest on mountains' lower slopes, but uncommon in higher-elevation areas.

Some common and recognizable plants of cloud forests are:

Podocarpus: This ancient relative of pine trees has remnant populations in the higher elevations of the Andean slopes. Some of the species grow over 44 m (145 ft) tall and are found in pure stands. Other species are found as sparsely-distributed individuals within montane forests and are not quite so tall (Figure 4).

Alnus acuminata: This alder is very similar to alder species from North America and Europe, but it is the only one found in South America. You will most likely see it on old landslides and clearings between 460 and 800 m (1500 and 2500 ft) altitude on either slope of the Andes. Here it grows in large pure stands until replaced by slower-growing but more shade-tolerant species (Figure 4).

Treeferns (*Cyathea* sp.): These plants are just what they sound like – very large ferns that attain the height of trees – some up to 20 m (65 ft) tall. They are common in many of Ecuador's forested habitats, from coastal areas to high elevations, being especially prevalent in some of the highest elevation rainforests (Figure 4).

Bromeliads: These pineapple relatives usually grow as epiphytes high up in the canopy, perched on top of the larger branches of trees. The bases of the long, narrow but thick leaves interconnect to form a tank which holds up to 5 liters (a gallon) of water. The beautiful flowers of bromeliads are often showy and bright red or pink (Figure 4).

Bamboo (*Chusquea* sp.): These tall woody grasses grow in dense stands and are often 5 m (16 ft) tall (Figure 5). You are most likely to see them in moist protected gullies (*quebradas*) on both eastern and western slopes of the Andes, but they also grow in lowland forest areas with poor drainage. Bamboos produce their seed-like fruits at long intervals of 10 or more years, and the entire population chooses the same year to flower. They then die. It is unknown how they synchronize their flowering over wide areas. Many species of insects, birds and mammals are tightly associated with these bamboo stands. When the stand dies, these animals must quickly disperse and find another stand in which to live – not an easy undertaking if all the stands in a wide area have died at the same time.

High-altitude and Páramo

Higher on the Andes' slopes, the moisture levels drop off and the temperature falls considerably. Multitudes of low bushes form impenetrable fortresses for birds and mammals. In protected gullies (*quebradas*) temperate forests grow, the most intriguing inhabitant of which is a tree in the rose family called *Polylepis*. Above the *Polylepis* forests, shrubs and trees quickly disappear to form a wet, grassy area called *páramo*. Here the cold windy conditions influence the evolution of plants that hug the ground; in some ways, the páramo resembles an Alaskan tundra scene. Páramo eventually gives way to glacial scree of bare gravel and rocks just below the permanent snow-line at about 5500 m (18,000 ft).

Some common, recognizable trees and shrubs of Ecuador's highlands and páramo are:

Polylepis Tree (*Polylepis* sp.): Its shaggy red bark is a signal of the presence of an entire community of plants and animals that are almost solely associated with groves of this high altitude tree species (Figure 3).

Puya (*Puya* sp.): This high altitude plant, typical of the páramo, is a terrestrial bromeliad, that is, it grows on the ground, not as an epiphyte like most of its relatives. During the flowering season, the tall, white and spike-like flower grows to more than 3 m (10 ft) above its thin, spiny leaves (Figure 3).

Escallonia sp.: This bush is evergreen with clusters of small leaves. It is abundant and distinctive in moist páramo areas. Its small greenish flowers are formed together in long and slender racemes (elongated structures each with multiple flowers) that hang down (Figure 3).

Espeletia sp.: This high Andean páramo herb is related to the sunflower and is a distinctive member of the habitat (Figure 3).

Galápagos Islands

The vegetation habitats of the Galápagos Islands are highly varied not only within a single island but from island to island. The main islands are characterized by deep green mangroves on the ocean's edge, and a low arid zone with *xerophytic* (dry tolerant) shrubs and yellowish tree cacti from the coast to about 180 m (600 ft) elevation. An intermediate altitudinal zone (to 550 m, 1800 ft) is dominated by waxy-leafed *Scalesia* forests. The next higher and more humid zone has many low shrubs (Cacaotillo) of the genus *Miconia*. In the most elevated and humid areas there are ferns, grasslands and distinctive trees adapted to low sunlight and foggy conditions.

Some common, recognizable trees and shrubs of the Galápagos are:

Palo Santo (*Bursera graveolens*): This is the most common tree in the dry areas of the islands. It grows to 12 m (40 ft) tall, and during the rainy season produces its leaves and small whitish flowers. During the dry season it loses its leaves, and the pale grey bark of its trunk and branches makes it appear dead (Figure 8).

Tree Cactus (*Opuntia echios*): These tall (12 m, 40 ft) relatives of the beaver-tail cactus have evolved on the islands into a complex of species and forms (Figure 9). On some islands the spines are missing while on others they cover the trunk and branches. Herbivory from tortoises has been suggested as the pressure to keep the spines. On those islands with no historical tortoise populations, the tree cactus tend not to have spines.

Lava Cactus (*Brachycereus nesioticus*): This pioneer species is among the first plants to grow on fresh lava flows. Their flowers open only at night (Figure 9).

Lechoso (*Scalesia pendunculata*): Growing as a shrub or tree depending on moisture and elevation, this plant is one of the most variable on the islands (Figure 9).

Cacaotillo (*Miconia robinsoniana*): At mid-elevations throughout the more mountainous islands, this bush is most obvious when its brilliant pink and lavender flowers appear at the beginning of the rainy season. It is a member of the melastome family, and the parallel cross veins on its leaves are diagnostic (Figure 9).

Pastures, Farms, and Plantations

Agriculture in Ecuador is split between traditional small family farms of, usually, 5 to 10 hectares (12 to 25 acres), which are still plentiful, and large corporate plantations. Family farms generally grow several crops, and plantations, single crops. The biggest export crops are cacao (chocolate) (Figure 11), coffee (café), bananas (plátano or banano) (Figure 10), oil palm (Figure 11), and sugar (Figure 11). Cacao, native to Mexico, was Ecuador's first major export crop. Banana trees, with their large leaves and yellow fruit, have an Asian origin. They occur in gardens, but mostly on plantations along the Pacific Coast. Sugar cane (caña), grown in several regions of Ecuador but particularly in the Pacific lowlands, is a perennial grass that may have originated in the New Guinea region. Pineapple plants (Figure 11) are bromeliads, and are Neotropical in origin. They are grown mainly in the Amazon lowlands and Pacific coastal area. Other common crops are corn (maiz), rice (arroz), and papaya (Figure 11).

Chapter 3

PARKS AND RESERVES: BRIEF DESCRIPTIONS

- *Moist Coastal Lowlands*
- *Arid Coastal Lowlands*
- *Western Slope of Andes*
- *Highlands*
- *Eastern Slope of Andes*
- *Oriente (Amazon Lowlands)*
- *Galápagos Islands*

We chose to include the parks and reserves described below primarily because they are the ones most often visited by ecotravellers in Ecuador – by people who come on organized tours and also those who travel independently. See Map 2 (p. 29) for park locations. The animals profiled in the color plates are keyed to parks and reserves in the following way: the profiles list the Ecuadorean regions (MCL, Moist coastal lowlands; ACL, Arid coastal lowlands; WSA, West slope of the Andes; HAP, Highlands and páramo; ESA, East slope of the Andes; AMA, Amazon lowlands; and GAL, Galápagos Island Archipelago) in which each species is likely to be found, and the parks listed below are arranged by the regions. Visitors who stay at lodges or resorts in the same regions as the parks listed below can expect to encounter similar types of habitats and wildlife as described for these parks and preserves. Tips on increasing the likelihood of seeing mammals, birds, reptiles, or amphibians are given in the introductions to each of those chapters. For more particulars on planning your trip to Ecuador, choosing which areas to visit, places to stay, and transportation, we suggest you use *The New Key to Ecuador and the Galápagos* by D. Pearson and D. Middleton, Ulysses Press, Berkeley, California. It was written as a companion guide to this one, and covers in detail planning and logistics for the ecotraveller. The most reliable map of roads and locations of interest to ecotravellers is *Kevin Healey's Travel Map of Ecuador*, no. 278, International Travel Maps, 345 West Broadway, Vancouver, BC, Canada V5Y 1PB.

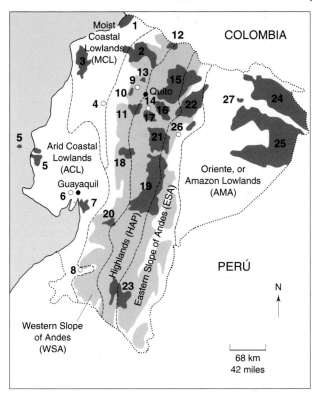

Moist Coastal Lowlands (MCL)
1 Cayapas – Mataje Ecological Reserve
2 Cotacachi – Cayapas Ecological Reserve
3 Mache – Chindul Ecological Reserve
4 Río Palenque Science Center

Arid Coastal Lowlands (ACL)
5 Machalilla National Park
6 Cerro Blanco Forest Reserve
7 Manglares Churute Ecological Reserve
8 Puyango Petrified Forest Reserve

Western Slope of Andes (WSA)
9 Maquipicuna Biological Reserve
10 Mindo – Nambillo Forest Reserve
11 Los Ilinizas Ecological Reserve

Highlands (HAP)
12 El Ángel Ecological Reserve

13 Pululahua Geobotanical Reserve
14 Pasochoa Reserve
15 Cayambe – Coca Ecological Reserve
16 Antisana Ecological Reserve
17 Cotopaxi National Park
18 Chimborazo Faunal Reserve
19 Sangay National Park
20 El Cajas National Park

Eastern Slope of Andes (ESA)
21 Llanganates National Park
22 Sumaco–Napo Galeras National Park
23 Podocarpus National Park

Oriente (Amazon Lowlands, AMA)
24 Cuyabeno Faunal Reserve
25 Yasuní National Park
26 Jatun Sacha Forest Reserve
27 Limoncocha Biological Reserve

Map 2 Ecuador, showing locations of parks and reserves and the six regions used in the book to specify species ranges. Lightly shaded area shows extent of higher-elevation habitats (1200 m, 4000 ft, and higher).

Moist Coastal Lowlands (MCL; the northern Pacific Coast region)

Cayapas-Mataje Ecological Reserve. In 1995, Ecuador declared 51,317 hectares (126,711 acres) of coastal mangroves on the Colombian border as an ecological reserve. This area also includes a small portion of lowland humid forests near its eastern boundary. With the massive destruction of mangroves along the entire coast of Ecuador, mainly for construction of artificial lagoons for commercial shrimp farming, any attempt to save what little remains is encouraging. This reserve is home for what are claimed to be the tallest mangroves in the world – some reaching over 50 m (160 ft) in height! It is also one of the last strongholds in Ecuador of the American Crocodile. Access to much of the reserve is by motorized canoe from San Lorenzo or Borbón.

Cotacachi-Cayapas Ecological Reserve. Created in 1968, this reserve has 204,420 hectares (510,000 acres). It includes habitat types that range from lowland humid forest at 30 m (100 ft) elevation, to Chocó forest with one of the highest diversity of plant species known in the world, to páramo at 4939 m (16,200 ft) on the top of Volcán Cotacachi. Access to the lower parts of the reserve are from Borbón. The high altitude parts of the reserve, such as the Laguna de Cuicocha, can be entered from the towns of Cotacachi and Ibarra.

Mache-Chindul Ecological Reserve. Ecuador's newest national reserve, its 100,000 hectares (247,000 acres) were declared under the protection of the state in 1997. Together with 3000 hectares (7410 acres) of the privately owned Bilsa Biological Station, this area protects the largest remnant of humid lowland coastal forest remaining in Ecuador. Although its elevation in the low coastal ranges of the Mache and Chindul Mountains does not exceed 900 m (3000 ft) in altitude, much of its flora and fauna is typical of the Chocó at much higher elevations on the western slopes of the Andes. Several species of birds, mammals and trees that have been eliminated from or are very rare in other parts of Ecuador have viable populations here. The central part of this reserve is open during the dry season from June to November via a gravel road from Quinindé. During the rainy season it is inaccessible except by foot or by mule.

Río Palenque Science Center. This private reserve of 100 hectares (250 acres) of humid lowland forest was established in 1970 by the University of Florida in Miami. It has a long history of extensive biological research and is thus one of the best known natural sites in all of coastal Ecuador. It is now completely surrounded by African Oil Palm plantations and other agriculture, so its small size has led to unstable populations of many plants and animals. However, more than 360 species of birds still occur here, as well as 350 species of butterflies. The trail and road system make observations fairly easy. The entrance to the reserve is south of Santo Domingo on the main highway to Guayaquil.

Arid Coastal Lowlands (ACL; the southern Pacific Coast region)

Machalilla National Park. Declared a national park in 1979, its 55,059 hectares (136,000 acres) represent the only national park on the entire coast of Ecuador. It protects tropical dry forest, coastal marine habitats and humid fog forest on the isolated tops of the highest mountains within its boundaries. The park is divided into three physically separated units: a small northern unit includes coastal scrub and the driest part of the park; a larger southern unit includes a few small islands just offshore as well as a mainland dry forest rising to small patches of fog forest at 800 m (2640 ft); and a final unit, Isla de la Plata, an island 40 km (25 miles) offshore and sharing many characteristics with the Galápagos Islands, including the only other known site on which the Waved Albatross (Plate 90) nests. You can get to most lowland habitats in the park by vehicle. The fog forests must be hiked to on relatively easy trails from Agua Blanca. Isla de la Plata has charter boats going to it regularly from Puerto Cayo and Puerto Lopez. From June to October, this boat trip is also popular for seeing several species of whales and dolphins.

Cerro Blanco Forest Reserve. This private reserve of tropical dry forest in the low Chongon Hills is only 20 minutes west of downtown Guayaquil. Yet it boasts healthy populations of two species of monkeys and over 200 species of birds, including one of the last nesting areas in Ecuador for the Great Green Macaw. Its 2530 hectares (8725 acres) have numerous trails that meander through moist quebradas or climb to the tops of the low hills. The reserve is owned and supported by the largest cement company in Ecuador and administered by the Pro-bosque Foundation. The nearby Chongon Reservoir and the Río Hondo mangroves offer very different aquatic and marine habitats.

Manglares Churute Ecological Reserve. Only an hour south of Guayaquil, this is one of the most extensive and accessible areas of mangroves remaining on the coast. It was established in 1979 and now includes 35,042 hectares (86,500 acres), of which 8100 hectares (20,000 acres) are mangroves. The rest is tropical dry forest on coastal mountains rising to 900 m (3000 ft) and large freshwater swamps in the back of the mangrove section. The flora and fauna of each of these three sections is quite different. Flamingoes and dolphins are in the mangroves, and the only coastal population of Horned Screamers (Plate 18) is in the swamps. The mountain-tops tend to be moister with more clouds, and two species of monkeys and several species of birds find themselves at the southern end of their distributions here. The reserve is on the main highway between Guayaquil and Machala, and buses or private cars can get you here easily for a day's wandering on the trails. To best explore the mangroves, a boat and guide can be hired from the reserve office.

Puyango Petrified Forest Reserve. No other place in the hemisphere except Petrified Forest National Park in northern Arizona, USA, can offer what this reserve does. Immense petrified logs litter the forest floor, and there are smaller fossils of plants and animals everywhere. The tropical dry forest habitat is also full of living endemic species of plants and animals unique to Tumbesiana. Many of them are easier to see here than in any other part of Ecuador. Although only 2690 hectares (6645 acres) are included in the reserve, additional forest habitat stretches east and south. The reserve is only an hour and a half from the cities of Santa Rosa or Machala on excellent paved and gravel roads.

Western Slope of Andes (WSA)

Maquipicuna Biological Reserve. Despite being so close to Quito, this 4050-hectare (10,000-acre) private reserve has been protected from development by rushing rivers and steep terrain. An additional 4100 hectares (10,120 acres) of secondary growth serve as a buffer zone around the reserve. The habitats include subtropical forests at 1000 m (3300 ft) to intact cloud forests at 3000 m (9900 ft). Besides accommodating ecotravellers, the Maquipicuna Foundation encourages research, education and local environmental work. The reserve entrance is only an hour and a half from Quito.

Mindo-Nambillo Forest Reserve. This private reserve is one of the most popular among ecotravellers because of its proximity to Quito (two hours) and its incredible diversity of wildlife and plants. Over 400 species of birds have been recorded here, including several leks of the outrageously colorful Cock-of-the-Rock (Plate 53). The forest reserve has 14,170 hectares (35,000 acres), and includes pristine subtropical forests to cloud forests and páramo at its highest elevations. You can visit here on a long day trip from Quito or stay overnight at one of the several comfortable lodges in the town of Mindo. The nearby Bella Vista Reserve also has accommodations for ecotravellers and access to different types of cloud forest.

Highlands (HAP; highlands and páramo)

El Ángel Ecological Reserve. One of the least visited of the national reserves, El Ángel is a jewel for anyone who wants to experience untrammeled páramo. It was established in 1992 and includes 15,715 hectares (38,800 acres) of spectacular highland habitat. It is home for the only population of Andean Condors (Plate 23) left in northern Ecuador. The best way to see this habitat is on a several-day trek. The border city of Tulcán is the access point for any trip into the reserve.

Pululahua Geobotanical Reserve. This crater reserve was created in 1978 and is a flat-bottomed valley 13 by 15 km (8 by 9 miles) and 600 m (1980 ft) deep. Its 3383 hectares (8250 acres) include the entire caldera of an extinct volcano. You can view it from an observation point at the rim of the crater, or you can hike down into the caldera on a trail full of switch-backs and scrub vegetation typical of dry sub-páramo. The reserve is only 30 minutes from central Quito.

Pasochoa Reserve. The Fundación Natura in Quito administers this private reserve of 404 hectares (1000 acres) at 4200 m (13,860 ft) elevation and just southeast of Quito's city limits. The entrance, at the bottom of the slopes of the extinct volcano, Cerro Pasochoa, begins with bamboo stands and the hiking paths pass through epiphyte-covered trees until you climb out onto páramo. This type of forest once covered much of the area now taken over by the city of Quito, and it is the closest and largest patch of natural forest remaining in the area.

Cayambe-Coca Ecological Reserve. This huge reserve was established in 1970, and its 403,103 hectares (995,664 acres) cover altitudes from 800 m (2640 ft) on the eastern slopes of the Andes to nearly 6000 m (19,800 ft) in the high páramo of the spectacular volcano Cayambe. Almost 100 lakes traverse the high altitude part of the reserve, and trekking is the best way to experience its environment. The reserve entrances here are from the towns of Cayambe and Olmedo. The lower stretches of the reserve are accessible from several places along the main road between Quito and Lago Agrio, but the most popular is the trail up the smoldering volcano El Reventador – just opposite the beautiful San Rafael Waterfall area.

Antisana Ecological Reserve. This reserve is significant in several ways. Not only does it provide refuge for one of the largest concentrations of Andean Condors (Plate 23) left in Ecuador, but it also provides much of Quito's drinking water. Officially recognized as a national reserve only in 1994, its 120,000 hectares (296,400 acres) are now some of the most rigorously protected natural areas in Ecuador. The snow-covered top of Antisana is at 5758 m (18,886 ft), and it is entirely included in the reserve. The boundaries extend down to 300 m (984 ft) elevation on the eastern slopes, where healthy populations of Spectacled Bears (Plate 79) and Mountain Tapirs still exist.

Cotopaxi National Park. This spectacular mountain and park are visited by more tourists than any other of Ecuador's mainland parks – and for good reason. Not only is it arguably the most beautiful mountain in the country, it is only one and a half hours south of Quito on excellent roads. Much of the park interior is accessible by well-maintained gravel roads. It was declared a national park in 1975 and covers 33,393 hectares (82,480 acres) of páramo and snow-covered slopes. The Cotopaxi summit at 5897 m (19,342 ft) is the most popular destination for mountain climbers in Ecuador. If you want get away from the more popular tourist areas in the park, hundreds of kilometers of trails lead to remote areas on the eastern side of the park.

Chimborazo Faunal Reserve. The tallest peak in Ecuador at 6310 m (20,700 ft), Chimborazo's peak is also the farthest point of land from the center of the Earth. In 1987, 58,560 hectares (144,643 acres) were set aside to provide some measure of protection for the dry and moist páramo habitat surrounding the snow-covered slopes and peak. Because it is not a national park, however, there is no infrastructure for tourists. The advantage is that there are also not many tourists. You can hike in virtually any part of the reserve without restriction. You approach the reserve from either Ambato or Riobamba.

Sangay National Park. This large park (517,725 hectares, 1,278,780 acres) was established in 1992 and, logistically, is really two parks. The upper elevations of the park with páramo and three peaks above 5000 m (16,400 ft) are only accessible from the Baños and Riobamba areas. The lower parts of the park (900 m, 2950 ft) include extensive cloud forest and can only be reached from above Macas. The size of the park and its diversity of habitats make it one of the richest areas in terms of number of species of plants and animals in Ecuador and perhaps the world. To see it, however, you will have to plan for back-packing trips of a week or more.

El Cajas National Park. First officially established in 1979 as a national recreation area, this park's growing popularity among both national and foreign tourists and the need for more vigorous protection caused the government to raise its status to that of a national park in 1997. Its 28,808 hectares (71,156 acres) include 232 alpine lakes and extensive moist páramo habitat. The park's visitor center is at 3870 m (12,771 ft) elevation and is only 25 km (16 miles) from the city center of

Cuenca. The private Manzon Cloud Forest Reserve is adjacent to El Cajas and protects a beautiful cloud forest area.

Eastern Slope of Andes (ESA)

Llanganates National Park. A new (1995) and yet undeveloped national park, this area of more than 200,000 hectares (494,000 acres) protects vast stretches of highland forest on the eastern slopes of the central Andes. Its upper limits are accessible from Latacunga and Ambato, but the lower parts of the park cannot be reached short of mounting an expedition.

Sumaco-Napo Galeras National Park. The beautiful centerpiece of this newly (1994) established national park is the volcano Sumaco. It rises 3732 m (12,240 ft) out of the western edge of the Amazon lowlands, separated from the main Andean chain. The lack of infrastructure and access roads means this park is not a one-day trip. The pristine subtropical and cloud forests that cover the flanks of Sumaco are only going to be seen by tourists willing to invest a minimum of a week camping and exploring this immense, virtually trail-less area (205,249 hectares, 506,965 acres).

Podocarpus National Park. Founded in 1982, this large (146,280 hectares, 361,311 acres) park is one of the most biologically spectacular yet tourist-accessible parks in Ecuador. With elevations varying from 3600 m (11,808 ft) to 600 m (2000 ft), it incorporates moist páramo to upper Amazonian habitats. By some estimates there are more than 700 species of birds here and more than 4000 species of plants, including several species of its namesake, the ancient conifer relative *Podocarpus* (Figure 4). Access to the upper elevations are within 45 minutes of Loja, and the lower elevation areas are within 20 minutes of Zamora. The interpretive centers, trails and camping areas are handy and easy to use, whether for a day trip or for an extended back-packing adventure.

Oriente (Amazon Lowlands; AMA)

Cuyabeno Faunal Reserve. This huge reserve (603,380 hectares, 1,490,348 acres) was first established in 1979. After years unsuccessfully fighting oil companies and colonists, the government, in 1994, adjusted its borders to avoid inroads of civilization. Five groups of indigenous people live within the reserve and continue to hunt and fish using traditional methods. Ecotourists, however, are becoming a more important base of the local economy. The low elevation (250 m, 820 ft) and flat terrain hold a mixture of flooded forest, cochas and tierra firme forest. Fully a third of all the species of birds found in the entire Amazon Basin occur here. Large mammals, fish and clouds of butterflies are also common. Access to the reserve is from the oil-boom town of Lago Agrio, and several comfortable lodges are available within the reserve. Canoe expeditions are a popular way to see the more remote parts of the reserve.

Yasuní National Park. This immense area was declared a national park in 1979. Now the largest reserve or park in Ecuador, it covers 982,000 hectares (2,425,540 acres) of lowland forest with many lakes and rivers. Much of it is still relatively unknown biologically, and almost any level of adventure travelling is possible here. Five luxury ecotraveller lodges are on its borders, but if you want to see more remote areas, several tour companies organize canoe and hiking expeditions into the interior. The thrill of expecting a jaguar around every curve in the river is almost as exciting as actually seeing one. At this park, this type of expectation is not unreasonable.

Jatun Sacha Forest Reserve. This private reserve was founded in 1986 by several North American biologists who wanted to preserve a piece of Amazonian lowland forest that was quickly disappearing. The area of protected forest (now 1619 hectares, 4000 acres) constantly grows as adjacent land is purchased through the non-profit foundation they also founded. This reserve is dedicated to scientific research, environmental education, conservation and ecotourism. It has a grid of well-marked trails, educational center, and detailed lists of plants and animals found there. It can be reached from Quito by a six-hour drive, and there are comfortable lodges near the reserve and in the nearby towns of Misahuallí and Tena.

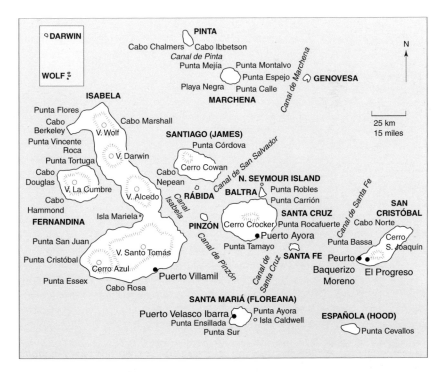

Map 3 Galápagos Islands, which are located 970 km (600 miles) from mainland Ecuador. (cabo = cape; cerro = hill; puerto = harbor; punta = point; V. = volcán = volcano).

Galápagos Islands (GAL)

Galápagos Islands National Park. In 1959, on the 100th year anniversary of the publication of Darwin's *On the Origin of Species*, all of the Galápagos Islands, except settled areas such as Puerto Ayora and Puerto Baquerizo Moreno, were declared a national park. With its abundance of wildlife, easy access and logistics, it is the most popular destination for ecotravellers to Ecuador. Arrival is by passenger jet from Quito and Guayaquil, and then ecotravellers are transferred to ships of various sizes to visit the islands for 5 to 14 days.

Galápagos Marine Resources Reserve. Established in 1986, this reserve extended protection to all animals and plants 15 nautical miles out into the ocean around each island. Within this area, cruise ship pollution, colonization, and international fisheries are now legally controlled.

Chapter 4

HOW TO USE THIS BOOK: ECOLOGY AND NATURAL HISTORY

- *What is Natural History?*
- *What is Ecology and What Are Ecological Interactions?*
- *How to Use This Book*
    Information in the Family Profiles
    Information in the Color Plate Sections

What is Natural History?

The purpose of this book is to provide ecotravellers with sufficient information to identify many common plant and animal species and to learn about them and the families to which they belong. Information on the lives of plants and animals is known generally as *natural history*. More specifically, we can define it as the study of plants' and animals' natural habits, including especially their ecology, distribution, classification, and behavior. This kind of information is important to know for a variety of reasons: researchers need to know natural history as background on the species they study, and wildlife managers and conservationists need natural history information because their decisions about managing animal populations must be partially based on it. More relevant for the ecotraveller, natural history is simply interesting. People who appreciate plants and animals typically like to watch them, touch them when appropriate, and know as much about them as they can.

What is Ecology and What Are Ecological Interactions?

Ecology is the branch of the biological sciences that studies the interactions between living things (animals and plants) and their physical environment and with each other. Broadly interpreted, these interactions take into account almost everything we find fascinating about plants and animals – what nutrients they need and how they get them, how and when they breed, how they survive the rigors of extreme climates, why they are large or small, or dully or brightly colored, and many other facets of their lives.

A plant or animal's life, in some ways, is the sum of its interactions with other plants and animals – members of its own species and others – and with its environment. Of particular interest are the numerous and diverse ecological interactions that occur between different species. Most can be placed into one of several general categories, based on how two species affect each other when they interact; they can have positive, negative, or neutral (that is, no) effects on each other. The relationship terms below are used in the book to describe the natural history of various plants and animals.

Competition is an ecological relationship in which neither of the interacting species benefit. Competition occurs when individuals of the same or different species use the same resource – a certain type of food, nesting holes in trees, etc. – and that resource is in insufficient supply (*limiting resource*) to meet all their needs. As a result, both species are less successful than they could be in the absence of the interaction (that is, if the other were not present).

Predation is an ecological interaction in which one species, the *predator*, benefits, and the other species, the *prey*, is harmed. Most people think of predation as something like a mountain lion eating a deer, and they are correct; but predation also includes such things as a wasp killing a caterpillar or an insect eating a seed.

Parasitism, like predation, is a relationship between two species in which one benefits and one is harmed. The difference is that in a predatory relationship, one animal kills and eats the other, but in a parasitic one, the parasite feeds slowly on the *host* species and usually does not kill it. There are internal parasites, like protozoans and many kinds of worms, and external parasites, such as leeches, ticks, and mites. Even a deer munching on the leaves of a bush can be considered a type of parasitism.

Some of the most intriguing ecological relationships are *mutualisms* – interactions in which both participants benefit. Plants and their pollinators engage in mutualistic interactions. A bee species, for instance, obtains a food resource, nectar or pollen, from a plant's flower; the plant it visits benefits because it is able to complete its reproductive cycle when the bee transports pollen to another plant. In Ecuador, numerous plants, such as the undergrowth bush *Maieta* (Figure 10), exhibit mutualism with the ants that live in them: the ants obtain food (the plants produce sugar for them) and shelter from the plant and in return, the ants defend the plants from plant-eating insects. Sometimes the species have interacted so long that they now cannot live without each other; theirs is an *obligate* mutualism. For instance, termites (Plate 85) cannot by themselves digest wood. Rather, it is the single-celled animals, protozoans, that live in their gut that produce the digestive enzymes that digest wood. At this point in their evolutionary histories, neither the termites nor their internal helpers can live alone.

Commensalism is a relationship in which one species benefits but the other is not affected in any obvious way. For example, epiphytes (p. 11), such as orchids and bromeliads, that grow on tree trunks and branches obtain from trees some shelf space to grow on, but, as far as anyone knows, neither hurt nor help the trees. A classic example of a commensal animal is the Remora, a fish that attaches itself with a suction cup on its head to a shark, then feeds on scraps of food the shark leaves behind. Remora are commensals, not parasites – they neither harm nor help sharks, but they benefit greatly by associating with sharks. Cattle Egrets (Plate 16) are commensals – these birds follow cattle, eating insects and other small animals that flush from cover as the cattle move about their pastures; the cattle, as far as we know, couldn't care one way or the other (unless they are concerned about that certain loss of dignity that occurs when the egrets perch not only near them, but on them as well.)

A term many people know that covers some of these ecological interactions is *symbiosis*, which means living together. Usually this term suggests that the two interacting species do not harm one another; therefore, mutualisms and commensalisms are the symbiotic relationships discussed here.

How to Use This Book

The information here on animals is divided into two sections: the *plates*, which include artists' color renderings of various species together with brief identifying and location information; and the *family profiles*, with natural history information on the families to which the pictured animals belong. The best way to identify and learn about Ecuadorean animals may be to scan the illustrations before a trip to become familiar with the kinds of animals you are likely to encounter. Then when you spot an animal, you may recognize its general type or family, and can find the appropriate pictures and profiles quickly. In other words, it is more efficient, upon spotting a bird, to be thinking, "Gee, that looks like a flycatcher," and be able to flip to that part of the book, than to be thinking, "Gee, that bird is partly yellow" and then, to identify it, flipping through all the animal pictures, searching for yellow birds.

Information in the Family Profiles

Classification, Distribution, Morphology. The first paragraphs of each profile generally provide information on the family's classification (or *taxonomy*), geographic distribution, and *morphology* (shape, size, and coloring). Classification information is provided because it is how scientists separate plants and animals into related groups, and often it enhances our appreciation of various species to know these relationships. You may have been exposed to classification levels sometime during your education, but if you are a bit rusty, a quick review may help: *Kingdom* Animalia: all the animal species detailed in the book are members of the animal kingdom. *Phylum* Chordata, *Subphylum* Vertebrata: all the species in the book with backbones and an internal skeleton are vertebrates. The arthropods, including insects, spiders, and crabs, lack a backbone or internal skeleton, and they are placed in the broad category of Invertebrata. *Class*: the book covers several vertebrate classes: Amphibia (amphibians), Reptilia (reptiles), Aves (birds), and Mammalia (mammals); and invertebrate classes: Insecta (insects), Decapoda (crabs). *Order*: each class is divided into several orders, the members of each order sharing many characteristics. For example, one of the mammal orders is Carnivora, the carnivores, which includes mammals with teeth specialized for meat-eating – dogs, cats, bears, raccoons, weasels. *Family*: Families of animals are subdivisions of each order that contain closely related species that are very similar in form, ecology, and behavior. The family Canidae, for instance, contains all the dog-like mammals – coyote, wolf, fox, dog. Animal family names end in *-dae*; subfamilies, subdivisions of families, end in *-nae*. *Genus*: Further subdivisions; within each genus are grouped species that are very closely related – they are all considered to have evolved from a common ancestor. *Species*: the lowest classification level; all members of a species are similar enough to be able to breed and produce living, fertile offspring.

Example:	Classification of the Chestnut-mandibled Toucan (Plate 45):
Kingdom:	Animalia, with more than 2 million species
Phylum:	Chordata, Subphylum Vertebrata, with about 47,000 species
Class:	Aves (birds), with about 9000 species
Order:	Piciformes, with about 400 species; includes honeyguides, woodpeckers, barbets, and toucans
Family:	Ramphastidae, with about 40 species; all the toucans
Genus:	*Ramphastos*, with 11 species; one group of toucans
Species:	*Ramphastos swainsonii*, known to its friends as Chestnut-mandibled Toucan

Some of the family profiles in the book actually cover animal orders, while others describe families or subfamilies.

Species' distributions vary tremendously. Some species are found only in very limited areas, whereas others range over several continents. Distributions can be described in a number of ways. An animal can be said to be *Old World* or *New World*; the former refers to the regions of the globe that Europeans knew of before Columbus – Europe, Asia, Africa; and the latter refers to the Western Hemisphere – North, Central, and South America. Ecuador falls within the part of the world called the *Neotropics* by biogeographers – scientists who study the geographic distributions of living things. A Neotropical species is one that occurs within southern Mexico, Central America, South America, and/or the Caribbean Islands. The terms *tropical*, *temperate*, and *arctic* refer to climate regions of the Earth; the boundaries of these zones are determined by lines of latitude (and ultimately, by the position of the sun with respect to the Earth's surface). The tropics, always warm, are the regions of the world that fall within the belt from 23.5 degrees North latitude (the Tropic of Cancer) to 23.5 degrees South latitude (the Tropic of Capricorn). The world's temperate zones, with more seasonal climates, extend from 23.5 degrees North and South latitude to the Arctic and Antarctic Circles, at 66.5 degrees North and South. Arctic regions, more or less always cold, extend from 66.5 degrees North and South to the poles. The positions of Ecuador and its Galápagos Islands with respect to these zones are shown in Map 4.

Several terms help define a species' distribution and describe how it attained its distribution:

Range. The particular geographic area occupied by a species.

Native or *Indigenous*. Occurring naturally in a particular place.

Introduced. Occurring in a particular place owing to people's intentional or unintentional assistance with transportation, usually from one continent to another; the opposite of native. For instance, pheasants were initially brought to North America from Europe/Asia for hunting, Europeans brought rabbits and foxes to

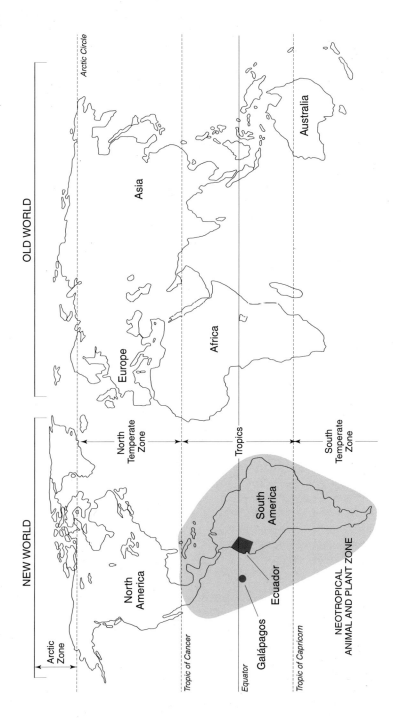

Map 4 Map of the Earth showing the position of Ecuador and its Galápagos Islands; Old World and New World zones; tropical, temperate, and arctic regions; and the Neotropical animal and plant life zone.

Australia for sport, and the British brought European Starlings and House Sparrows to North America.

Endemic. A species, a genus, an entire family, etc., that is found in a particular place and nowhere else. Galápagos Finches are endemic to the Galápagos Islands; nearly all the reptile and mammal species of Madagascar are endemics; all species are endemic to Earth (as far as we know).

Cosmopolitan. A species that is widely distributed throughout the world.

Ecology and Behavior. In these sections, we describe some of what is known about the basic activities pursued by each group. Much of the information relates to when and where animals are usually active, what they eat, and how they forage.

Activity Location – *Terrestrial* animals pursue life and food on the ground. *Arboreal* animals pursue life and food in trees or shrubs. Many arboreal animals have *prehensile* tails, long and muscular, which they can wrap around tree branches to support themselves as they hang to feed or to move about more efficiently. *Cursorial* refers to animals that are adapted for running along the ground. *Fossorial* means living and moving underground.

Activity Time – *Nocturnal* means active at night. *Diurnal* means active during the day. *Crepuscular* refers to animals that are active at dusk and/or dawn.

Food Preferences – Although animal species can usually be assigned to one of the feeding categories below, most eat more than one type of food. Most frugivorous birds, for instance, also nibble on the occasional insect, and carnivorous mammals occasionally eat plant materials.

> Herbivores are predators that prey on plants.
> Carnivores are predators that prey on animals.
> Insectivores eat insects.
> Granivores eat seeds.
> Frugivores eat fruit.
> Nectarivores eat nectar.
> Piscivores eat fish.
> Omnivores eat a variety of things.
> Detritivores, such as vultures, eat dead stuff.

Breeding. In these sections, we present basics on each group's breeding particulars, including type of mating system, special breeding behaviors, durations of egg incubation or *gestation* (pregnancy), as well as information on nests, eggs, and young.

Mating Systems – A *monogamous* mating system is one in which one male and one female establish a pair-bond and contribute fairly evenly to each breeding effort. In *polygamous* systems, individuals of one of the sexes have more than one mate (that is, they have harems): in *polygynous* systems, one male mates with several females, and in *polyandrous* systems, one female mates with several males.

Condition of young at birth – *Altricial* young are born in a relatively undeveloped state, usually naked of fur or feathers, eyes closed, and unable to feed themselves, walk, or run from predators. *Precocial* young are born in a more developed state, eyes open, and soon able to walk and perhaps feed themselves.

Notes. These sections provide interesting bits and pieces of information that do not fit elsewhere in the account, including associated folklore.

Status. These sections comment on the conservation status of each group, including information on relative rarity or abundance, factors contributing to population declines, and special conservation measures that have been implemented. Because this book concentrates on animals that ecotravellers are most likely to see – that is, on more common ones – few of the profiled species are immediately threatened with extinction. The definitions of the terms that we use to describe degrees of threat to various species are these: *Endangered* species are known to be in imminent danger of extinction throughout their range, and are highly unlikely to survive unless strong conservation measures are taken; populations of endangered species generally are very small, so they are rarely seen. *Threatened* species are known to be undergoing rapid declines in the sizes of their populations; unless conservation measures are enacted, and the causes of the population declines identified and halted, these species are likely to move to endangered status in the near future. *Vulnerable to threat*, or *near-threatened,* are species that, owing to their habitat requirements or limited distributions, and based on known patterns of habitat destruction, are highly likely to be threatened in the near future. Several organizations publish lists of threatened and endangered species, but agreement among the lists is not absolute.

Where appropriate, we also include threat classifications from the Convention on International Trade in Endangered Species (CITES) and the United States Endangered Species Act (ESA) classifications. CITES is a global cooperative agreement to protect threatened species on a worldwide scale by regulating international trade in wild animals and plants among the 130 or so participating countries. Regulated species are listed in CITES Appendices, with trade in those species being strictly regulated by required licenses and documents. CITES Appendix I lists endangered species; all trade in them is prohibited. Appendix II lists threatened/vulnerable species, those that are not yet endangered but may soon be; trade in them is strictly regulated. Appendix III lists species that are protected by laws of individual countries that have signed the CITES agreements. The USA's Endangered Species Act works in a similar way – by listing endangered and threatened species, and, among other provisions, strictly regulating trade in those animals. The International Union for Conservation of Nature (IUCN) maintains a "Red List" of threatened and endangered species that often is more broad-based and inclusive than these other lists, and we refer to the Red List in some of the accounts.

Information in the Color Plate Sections

Pictures. Among amphibians, reptiles, and mammals, males and females of a species usually look alike, although often there are size differences. For many species of birds, however, the sexes differ in color pattern and even anatomical features. If only one individual is pictured, you may assume that male and female of that species look exactly or almost alike; when there are major sex differences, both male and female are depicted. The animals shown on an individual plate, in most cases, have been drawn to the correct scale relative to each other.

Name. We provide the common English name for each profiled species and the scientific, or Latin, name. Often, in Ecuador, the local name for a given species varies regionally. For some species, there is no agreed-upon Spanish name; for a few, there is no English name.

ID. Here we provide brief descriptive information that, together with the pictures, will enable you to identify most of the animals you see. The lengths of amphibians given in this book are usually their snout–vent lengths (SVLs). The vent is the opening on their bellies that lies approximately where the rear limbs join the body, and through which sex occurs and wastes exit. Therefore, long tails of salamanders are not included in the reported length measurements, and frogs' long legs are not included in theirs. Reptile lengths are total lengths, including tails. For mammals, size measures given are generally the lengths of the head and body, but do not include tails. Birds are measured from tip of bill to end of tail. For birds commonly seen flying, such as seabirds and hawks, we provide wingspan (wingtip to wingtip) measurements, if known. For most birds, we use to describe their sizes the terms: *very large* (more than 1 m, 3 ft); *large* (49 cm to 1 m, 1.6 to 3 ft); *mid-sized* (20 to 48 cm, 8 in to 1.5 ft); *small* (10 to 19 cm, 3.5 to 7 in); and *tiny* (less than 10 cm, 3.5 in).

Habitat/Region. In these sections we list the regions and habitat types in which each species occurs and provide symbols for the habitat types each species prefers. A species said to occur on the *Andean slopes* occurs in the area between the higher mountains and the coastal lowlands to the west or the Amazon region to the east (see Map 2, p. 29). In general, *low elevation* refers to between 0 and 500 m (0 and 1600 ft) above sea level; *middle elevation* means between 500 and 1200 m (1600 and 4000 ft), and *higher elevation* means greater than 1200 m (4000 ft).

Explanation of habitat symbols:

   =   Lowland wet forest.

   =   Lowland dry forest.

   =   Highland forest and cloud forest. Includes middle elevation and higher elevation wet forests and cloud forests.

   =   Highland páramo (wet, grassy areas above treeline).

   =   Forest edge and streamside. Some species typically are found along forest edges or near or along streams; these species prefer semi-open areas rather than dense, closed, interior parts of forests. Also included here: open woodlands, tree plantations, and shady gardens.

   =   Pastureland, non-tree plantations, savannah (grassland with scattered trees and shrubs), gardens without shade trees, roadside. Species found in these habitats prefer very open areas.

   =   Freshwater. For species typically found in or near lakes, streams, rivers, marshes, swamps.

   =   Saltwater/marine. For species usually found in or near the ocean or ocean beaches.

REGIONS (see Map 2, p. 29):

MCL   Moist coastal lowlands
ACL   Arid coastal lowlands
WSA   Western slope of the Andes
HAP   Highlands and páramo
ESA   Eastern slope of the Andes
AMA   Amazon lowlands (the Oriente)
GAL   Galápagos Island Archipelago

Example

Plate 45e

Chestnut-mandibled Toucan
Ramphastos swainsonii
ID: Large (61 cm, 2 ft); black body with
bright yellow throat and upper breast;
huge dark brown bill with large yellow
stripe covering most of top half; distinctive
voice a loud yelping call distinguishes it
from the very similar Chocó Toucan.

HABITAT: Lowland primary and tall
secondary forest.

REGION: MCL

Chapter 5

AMPHIBIANS

by Greg Vigle

- *Introduction*
- *General Characteristics and Classification of Amphibians*
- *Seeing Amphibians in Ecuador*
- *Family Profiles*
- *Environmental Close-Up 1: Frog Population Declines: Amphibian Armageddon or Alarmist Absurdity?*

Introduction

Fossils indicate that the first *amphibians* appeared during the middle of the Paleozoic Era, about 365 million years ago. They evolved from fish that had lungs and thus could breathe air, and also had fins formed into stubby lobes; these characteristics allowed them to survive for brief periods on land. The word "amphibian" refers to an organism that can live in two worlds, and that is as good a definition of amphibians as any: most stay in or near the water, but many spend at least portions of their lives on land. Approximately 4700 species of living amphibians are known today, separable into three main groups. The largest group, with about 4100 species, is the *frogs* (Order Anura, "without tails," which includes *toads*), followed by the *salamanders* (Order Caudata, the "tailed" amphibians) with 430 species, and a little-known group, the *caecilians* (suh-SEAL-ians, Order Gymnophiona), with some 170 species. The amphibian fauna of Ecuador currently totals about 460 species, of which only 6 are salamanders, 20 are caecilians, and the remainder frogs and toads.

General Characteristics and Classification of Amphibians

Most amphibians, like their fish ancestors, still depend on water to reproduce. This ancient necessity is perhaps the most striking characteristic of modern amphibians. Most frogs and toads have *external fertilization* – sperm and eggs meet outside the body, in aquatic sites such as in lakes, ponds, and streams, although many species of salamanders and caecilians have *internal fertilization*. Most species pass through the aquatic portion of their "two-world" lifestyle only as eggs and free-swimming larvae (*tadpoles*), but some are fully aquatic as adults, and others lay eggs in moist areas on land and never venture near standing water. Water is also essential for amphibians because nearly all species have thin skin that needs to be kept wet for respiration. Thus, even species that never actually immerse themselves in water require a humid environment, or they dry out and perish.

Salamanders are generally small slender creatures with smooth skin, four limbs, and a long tail, although a few aquatic species have only rudimentary stubs for legs or no legs at all (they resemble eels). Salamanders occur in a great range of sizes, including some species that are among the smallest known terrestrial vertebrate animals, with body lengths of less than 1.5 cm (0.6 in), and one giant Asian species that can grow to 2 m (6.5 ft) long. Like other amphibians, their skin is permeable to water and air, and for this reason they all inhabit moist environments. Familiar salamanders of North America and Europe typically live their lives on the ground. They forage for invertebrate prey such as insects, worms, and spiders in leaves and under rocks or decaying logs, often near streams in moist forests. Some, however, are fully aquatic while others live in trees (*arboreal*) or underground (*fossorial*). Most species secrete poisons from the skin as a defense against predators, and some are very brightly colored to warn of this toxicity. Compared with other amphibians, most salamanders have developed advanced breeding habits, including some with internal fertilization via a special sperm "packet," or *spermatophore*, inserted into the body of the female during mating.

Although salamanders are represented by many species in North America and Europe, and are also diverse in Central America, there are very few species in South America (or anywhere in equatorial regions). The six species known from Ecuador are all *lungless salamanders* (Family Plethodontidae, the largest salamander group, with 270 species in North, Central and South America), and most are inhabitants of lowland rainforest. As they have no lungs, respiration takes place solely through the skin. All Ecuadorean salamanders have heavily webbed front and hind feet, and spend their lives moving around on leaves up to 2 m (6.5 ft) above the ground, foraging for insects and other small, moving prey. Most are active only at night, descending to the forest floor to sleep during the day safely hidden in moist leaf litter. Little is known about most Ecuadorean species, although if they are like others in the family, they breed via internal fertilization with spermatophores, their eggs are deposited away from water, and the parents guard the eggs, which develop directly into tiny salamanders. The ECUADOREAN SALAMANDER (Plate 1), dull gray to reddish-brown and reaching a length of 10 cm (4 in), is the largest species in Ecuador. Other species in Ecuador are very similar but slightly smaller, and range in color from light tan to dark brown.

Most people are unaware that a third group of amphibians exists, and still fewer have ever seen a representative. *Caecilians* bear no obvious resemblance to other amphibians. Instead, they look like large worms, lacking limbs throughout their lives. Another reason that caecilians are so poorly known is that they are found exclusively in tropical regions (in Africa, Asia, and Central and South America) and most species live underground, although a few are aquatic; the only time you are likely to see the underground ones is following heavy rain, when soil becomes so saturated that they must rise to the surface to breathe. The RINGED BLUE CAECILIAN (Plate 1), like many species, is pale blue, with lighter blue rings (formed by shallow folds in the skin) running the length of the body; all caecilians have these rings. Both the head and tail ends are very blunt, the head distinguished by the obvious jawline and dark eyespots visible just under the skin. The Ringed Blue Caecilian grows to some 50 cm (20 in) in length and about 1.5 cm (a half inch) in diameter, but most are smaller. All caecilians are essentially blind (why have eyes if you always live underground?), finding their way around by special sensory "tentacles" – small fleshy projections on the snout. They feed opportunistically on insects, worms and other ground-dwelling prey. Caecilians have sophisticated breeding habits involving internal fertilization, with eggs in some species undergoing development inside the mother's body and emerging as tiny but fully formed baby caecilians. A few species have aquatic tadpoles.

Frogs and *toads* all have four limbs as adults, with rear limbs much larger than front limbs (making most of them strong jumpers), and some have poisonous skin secretions to protect them from predators. Many are brightly colored. Males have distinctive mating calls, vocalizing to attract females. Almost all adult frogs and toads are predatory carnivores. The exception is a Brazilian frog that eats fruit. Probably all Ecuadorean species breed via external fertilization in which the male mounts the back of the female and holds on to her tightly with his front legs (*amplexus*). As she releases her eggs into the water or nest, he releases his sperm over them.

Seeing Amphibians in Ecuador

With 460 of the world's 4700 living amphibians, tiny Ecuador has nearly 10% of the world's species. In fact, Ecuador has one of the highest diversities of amphibians of any place its size on Earth (see Close-up, p. 86). With luck and some perseverance, you could see 20 or 30 species in a three-week trip. The specific examples discussed and profiled in this chapter should allow you to identify any amphibian you find, at least to its family or genus.

Unlike birds and mammals, which usually can be observed only from a distance, it is often possible to approach amphibians closely. Indeed, for many species this is necessary if you hope to identify them. However, all wildlife in Ecuador is protected by law, and without scientific permits you are not allowed legally to catch amphibians for even a few minutes. Studying them from a few centimeters away should be adequate for comparisons to the pictures and characters we describe in the text.

There are several good ways to find amphibians. The first is simply to search along the ground in the forest during the day, especially near small forest streams, and look for frogs and toads hopping about. The second is potentially more rewarding; with a flashlight, you can carefully search the tops of leaves at night between 1 and 2 m (3 and 6 ft) above the ground, where small *treefrogs, rainfrogs,* and *salamanders* are active. With some patience, you are likely to encounter at least a small sampling of these nocturnal, arboreal creatures. You can try this along an undisturbed primary (old growth) forest trail or any forest edge area (such as the forest edge surrounding the lodge at which you are staying). By far the best way to see a good diversity of rainforest frogs is to locate at night a small temporary pond (often found along forest edges, in swampy areas, and near rivers) where multiple species are calling loudly. Many call from perches over the water, others while floating in the pond. When large numbers of frogs are calling, such *breeding aggregations* are usually obvious; the racket they make can be heard from some distance away. If you find a shallow pond during the day (when the frogs will be sleeping), look for tadpoles swimming in the water. You can then return with a light after dark to look for adults. Be warned, however, that even at a pond where many frogs can be heard calling, the arboreal ones may be very difficult to see. At some temporary ponds up to a dozen species can be active at one time.

Family Profiles

1. Toads

Although many people think of frogs and *toads* as two distinct groups, the common name "toad" is used for species in several families of frogs. The quintessential toad family, however, is the Bufonidae – a worldwide group of about 400 species. Most of these toads have thick, dry skin that permits them a more terrestrial life than that of many frogs. Toads tend to have short, squat bodies with relatively short limbs, a broad rounded snout (often with distinct bony crests between the eyes), and often are colored dull olive to dark brown. The skin on the upper surface of the body has scattered wart-like raised bumps, and in most species there is a pair of large "warts" (*parotoid glands*) on the shoulder area of the back, one behind each eye. As a group, toads have perhaps the widest range of sizes of any family of frogs, from tiny species less than 2 cm (1 in) in length as adults, to the MARINE or GIANT TOAD (Plate 1), which grows nearly to the size of a dinner plate (20 cm, 8 in).

Ecuador is home to about 35 toad species. Most that you are likely to see resemble the familiar species found in temperate zone areas, but there is one odd group, well represented in Ecuador, that bears little resemblance to their more ordinary cousins. These are the *stubfoot toads* of the genus *Atelopus*, with some 18 species in the country. They are mostly found at higher elevations on the Andean slopes, including some ranging up to 3700 m (12,000 ft). Stubfoot toads have long slender bodies and limbs, pointed snouts, and feet formed into roughly triangular-shaped paddles, often with extensive thick webbing of the toes. Many, such as the RÍO PESCADO STUBFOOT TOAD (Plate 1), are very brightly colored, with patterns of black and yellow or green. All stubfoots in Ecuador are small, ranging from 2 to 3.5 cm (0.8 to 1.4 in).

Natural History

Ecology and Behavior

Terrestrial toads spend much of their time hopping around on the ground where they forage for invertebrate prey (and just about any other animal small enough to eat). Their thicker, drier skin protects them more from water loss than the thin, moist skin of their more aquatic relatives, giving them the freedom to live away from water and often in very dry places that would quickly kill the average frog. Their parotoid glands, which secrete a noxious milky poison that can be fatal to potential predators, also protect them in this life away from water. The dark brown color typical of most toads helps them blend in with the soil and dead leaves on the forest floor. Many of the ordinary brown varieties inhabit lowland forests and are nocturnal, but some are active by day and others are active both day and night.

Some stubfoot toads, such as the RÍO PESCADO STUBFOOT TOAD, have a distinctly different way of life. They live around streams, and often move about or sleep on leaves or branches. A number of Ecuadorean species are often found sitting atop rocks protruding from steep, fast-moving cloud forest streams. The bright colors of many species warn of potent toxins secreted by the glands in the skin. Species found at high elevations are usually terrestrial and diurnal.

Most toads must return to the water to breed, and for this reason many species, such as the TRUANDO TOAD (Plate 1) and SOUTH AMERICAN COMMON TOAD (Plate 1), live near forest streams. The MARINE TOAD inhabits more open areas such as weedy clearings and forest edges, although juveniles are also found in forests. You will most likely encounter this species as it sits just at the edge of a light's illumination at night, attracted by the insects flying into the light. Look for what appears to be a low dark rock.

Breeding

Toads as a group have a great variety of breeding strategies. A few species lay eggs on land, the embryos passing their tadpole stage in the safety of the egg and then hatching directly into small toads (called *direct development*). Most, however, lay their eggs in water, with the eggs hatching into free-swimming tadpoles that later transform into toads. Male toads call from locations in or near water to attract females. The male grasps the female, and while riding on her back in the water he deposits his sperm over her eggs as she releases them into the water. One peculiar breeding characteristic unique to toads is their habit of laying eggs in long strings, as opposed to the clumps of eggs produced by most frogs. The eggs are held together by a jelly-like substance that may contain toxins to protect developing eggs from predators, and it is sometimes used to glue them to a submerged object such as a rock or log. The MARINE TOAD breeds in a wide variety of temporary and permanent bodies of water, each female producing 8000 to 20,000 eggs and then abandoning them. Female TRUANDO and SOUTH AMERICAN COMMON TOADS lay 500 to 2500 eggs in forest streams or temporary ponds.

The breeding habits of many South American toads are poorly known, and this is especially true for the stubfoot toads. One interesting aspect is that their tadpoles are equipped with a large suction-cup on the belly with which they attach themselves to rocks in swiftly flowing streams. Without this suction device, the tadpoles might soon be washed downstream into larger, more predator-filled channels before they could complete their development.

Notes

Folktales suggest that handling toads causes warts, but this is not true; warts are caused by viruses. Several toad species are known to have been used by indigenous peoples of the Neotropics for medicinal and ritualistic purposes. The toxic gland secretion of the MARINE TOAD, for instance, is often one of the ingredients of a complex soup of substances concocted by Haitian witch doctors to induce near-death comas and to create "zombies." The skin secretions of one Mexican species (*Bufo alvarius*) contain powerful hallucinogenic chemicals. Toads were prominent icons in both ancient Mayan and Aztec cultures, as demonstrated by images of them found on unearthed sculptures and engravings at archaeological sites. One *shaman* (a native spiritual guide and healer) from the Amazonian lowlands of Ecuador reported the use of scrapings from the inside of toad skins as a cure for human skin sores.

Status

Although none of Ecuador's toads is officially considered threatened, many populations of stubfoot toads are declining drastically. As with most amphibians, the conditions of most of their populations are not well known. Several species of toads from Chile, Mexico, Puerto Rico, Costa Rica, and the USA mainland are now considered threatened or endangered. At the other end of the spectrum, a few species of amphibians have become pests through introduction into areas where they are not native. The MARINE TOAD has been widely introduced into sugar-cane-growing areas around the world as a control on pest insects. Among other places, it has become established in parts of Australia and southern Florida (USA), where it has multiplied to huge numbers and threatens many native species. In addition, these large toads frequently cause the death of pet dogs and cats, which, when they attack the toads, can receive a fatal mouthful of poison.

Profiles

Río Pescado Stubfoot Toad, *Atelopus balios*, Plate 1c
Truando Toad, *Bufo haematiticus*, Plate 1d
Marine Toad, *Bufo marinus*, Plate 1e
South American Common Toad, *Bufo typhonius*, Plate 1f

2. Rainfrogs

Species in the Family Leptodactylidae are commonly known as *rainfrogs*. They are distributed throughout South and Central America and the Caribbean; a few species occur as far north as the southern USA. With more than 900 species, and new ones being discovered each year, the rainfrogs are by far the most diverse family of tropical frogs. Ecuador is home to nearly 200 species, most of which live in restricted habitats and have small ranges within the country. There are two major types of rainfrogs, and you can distinguish them by body size, shape, and lifestyle. The largest species, usually terrestrial, are those in the genus *Leptodactylus*, such as the SMOKY JUNGLE FROG (Plate 2), which reaches lengths of 18 cm (7 in). *Leptodactylus* frogs superficially resemble common North American frogs such as *bullfrogs* or *leopard frogs*, usually being tan to brown with varying patterns of large spots or bands on a stout body, and with relatively short limbs. The head is broad and rounded, and most species have prominent folds of skin on each side of the upper body. There are no expanded discs on the tips of the toes, the front feet lack webbing, and the hind feet have only slight webbing. Species in the other main group, genus *Eleutherodactylus*, are small (2 to 7 cm, 1 to 2.5 in), patterned with various dull shades of yellow, tan, gray, brown, or even black, and usually arboreal. Some, such as the ORANGE-GROIN RAINFROG (Plate 2), have brightly colored spots that you can see only when the frog extends its legs. Most *Eleutherodactylus* have distinctly expanded discs on toes of both the front and hind feet, which provide a firm grip on leaves and branches. These toes lack webbing and are slender and delicate. Many species have color patterns that vary greatly from one individual to the next, making identification difficult. The genus *Eleutherodactylus* contains more than 600 of the 900 rainfrog species, and most of them are smaller than species of the genus *Leptodactylus*.

Natural History

Ecology and Behavior

Leptodactylus rainfrogs are restricted to lowland rainforests, and all are nocturnal and terrestrial; many frequent low-lying marshy areas and temporary ponds. SMOKY JUNGLE FROGS typically are found in large holes on the forest floor. Males sporadically emit a distinctive and very loud "whooop" call. This species is one of only a few amphibians found in Ecuador on both sides of the Andes. These frogs are opportunistic feeders that eat just about any animal that they can catch and swallow, including many types of invertebrates, and small amphibians and reptiles.

You can find the myriad *Eleutherodactylus* rainfrogs in every major region of Ecuador except in the southwestern deserts and the Galápagos Islands. These frogs are especially diverse and abundant in lowland rainforests on both sides of the Andes, and in moist cloud forests on the eastern and western slopes. Each area has its own distinct set of species, including high-elevation páramo, where some *Eleutherodactylus* are found at elevations up to 4000 m (13,000 ft). Although some lowland and cloud forest species are diurnal leaf-litter dwellers, the majority are nocturnal and arboreal, and can be found at night sitting on leaves of plants between 1 and 3 m (3 to 10 ft) above the ground. They eat mostly invertebrate prey. These small frogs are themselves preyed upon by bats and other small mammals, as well as by a variety of nocturnal tree snakes, and even by larger invertebrates such as tarantulas.

Breeding

Most of the large *Leptodactylus* rainfrogs (as well as the majority of species in most of the 50 or so other genera in the family), breed in standing bodies of water where mating pairs construct a foam nest. The foam is made by the male while the pair is mating (in *amplexus*). With the male mounted on the back of the female and holding on to her tightly with his front legs, he kicks his feet and stirs a mixture of water and air with the eggs, jelly and sperm as they are released. This whitish froth, or foam, floats on the surface of the water and helps protect the developing eggs from predators. The eggs hatch into tadpoles, which complete their development in the water. Each female produces hundreds or thousands of eggs at a time. The smaller *Eleutherodactylus* rainfrogs have direct development of the young. They typically produce only a few eggs (10 to 30), but with a higher energy investment in each egg the eggs are proportionally much larger than *Leptodactylus* eggs. *Eleutherodactylus* rainfrogs exhibit an amazing reproductive adaptation that allows them to breed in the complete absence of standing water. Males of most species call from their leaf perches to attract the larger females, and during mating the fertilized eggs are deposited in a moist secluded place – for instance, in a cavity of a decaying log, or tucked between the leaves of a bromeliad plant. They remain there for about 30 to 60 days, depending on the species, eventually completing their development and hatching out as tiny but fully formed froglets. This mode of reproduction reduces the threat of predation by fish or other aquatic predators on the larvae. Some rainfrogs breed sporadically throughout the year in lowland and cloud forest habitats, and, as their name suggests, breeding activities are most intense following heavy rain. However, because we know so little about the breeding habits of most species, it is hard to make generalizations.

Notes

Rainfrogs, like most amphibians, secrete chemicals of varying degrees of toxicity from glands in their skin. These poisons usually have an offensive odor, which, along with their toxicity, discourages predators. The substances probably also have anti-fungal properties that combat growth of harmful fungus on the always-moist skin of the frogs. The large SMOKY JUNGLE FROG has a potent poison, "leptodactylin," after the genus name *Leptodactylus*. Its effects include blocking some neuromuscular activity and over-stimulating parts of the nervous system. Although this odoriferous poison is unpalatable to most predators, some native people eat the Smoky Jungle Frog after removing the toxic skin.

Status

We know little about what constitutes normal, healthy population sizes and distributions for most rainfrog species. Some are known from only a handful of speci-mens (or even a single specimen) collected from one place. Many have been discovered so recently that there are no historical records with which to compare their current statuses. No Ecuadorean rainfrog is officially classed as threatened or endangered, but given the rapid deforestation that has occurred in some areas of the country, and the very limited ranges known to be occupied by some species, it is likely that some are threatened, and, indeed, that some extinctions are now occurring.

Profiles

Western Lowlands Rainfrog, *Eleutherodactylus achatinus*, Plate 2a
Andean Slopes Rainfrog, *Eleutherodactylus w-nigrum*, Plate 2b
Common Páramo Rainfrog, *Eleutherodactylus unistrigatus*, Plate 2c
Orange-groin Rainfrog, *Eleutherodactylus croceoinguinis*, Plate 2d
Lance Rainfrog, *Eleutherodactylus lanthanites*, Plate 2e
Smoky Jungle Frog, *Leptodactylus pentadactylus*, Plate 2f
Peter's Mudpuddle Frog, *Physalaemus petersi*, Plate 3a

3. Treefrogs

The *treefrogs*, family Hylidae, are a large group of about 700 species, with a nearly worldwide distribution; they are most abundant and diverse in the American tropics. Because many species have bright colors and equally bright, large eyes, they have joined "celebrity" animals such as parrots, monkeys, and the Jaguar, as popular icons associated with Neotropical forests. Stable moisture and temperature conditions prevalent in tropical forests have allowed treefrogs, over evolutionary time, to ascend into at least the lower levels of the forest, where they go about their lives leaping and climbing on leaves and branches. About 100 species occur in Ecuador.

Most treefrogs are small and have extremely long, slender arms and legs relative to their body size, and large feet with varying amounts of webbing. The toes are tipped with expanded "discs" that have pads on the bottom; these provide a firm grip as the frogs move about on leaves and branches. Bodies are typically tear-drop-shaped, with a slender waist and large, broad head and snout. Although most of the species you are likely to encounter in Ecuador are between 2.5 and 5 cm (1 and 2 in) long, adults of various species range in length from 1.7 cm (half an inch) to 15 cm (6 in). Color patterns vary greatly. Some species are clad in shades of light green or patterned with darker green to dark brown. Other species are very brightly colored, much like their distant relatives, the *poison-dart frogs*. One group of treefrogs, the *leaf frogs* (genus *Phyllomedusa*), can be recognized by their exceedingly long limbs and opposed thumbs and first toes (usually without webbing), and their normally slow movements.

Natural History

Ecology and Behavior

As their name suggests, most treefrogs are arboreal creatures, spending much of their time climbing and jumping among leaves and branches of shrubs and trees. Most live in lower vegetation 1 to 3 m (3 to 10 ft) above the ground. They forage at night for invertebrate prey, sleeping away the daylight hours in bromeliad plants or wedged between forked branches or leaves. There are exceptions; some species are terrestrial and others mostly aquatic. One group of treefrogs (found in Ecuador, though rarely) feeds almost exclusively on other small frogs. Many treefrogs can change colors with respect to time of day, often being lighter when they are sleeping (perhaps to camouflage them better among the leaves) and darker at night when they are active.

Breeding

Treefrogs have the widest array of reproductive strategies of any single family of frogs, ranging from species that reproduce in the standard amphibian way by mating and depositing eggs in large bodies of water, to remarkable specialists that brood their eggs in a protective pouch on the mother's back. The latter are restricted to the tropics, and one Ecuadorean example is the HORNED MARSU-PIAL TREEFROG (Plate 3), which takes its name from this pouch-brooding type of reproduction. Another common mode of reproduction is for mating and egg-laying to occur on leaves above pools of standing water. For example, in the TIGER STRIPED LEAF FROG (Plate 5), males call (a soft "cluck") from perches over temporary ponds, attracting females. The frogs *amplex* (mate) on a leaf overhanging the water and then the female, using glue-like skin secretions of mucus, attaches the clutch of about 60 eggs to a leaf. She then folds the leaf into a protective "cocoon," again using "glue" from her skin. The cocoon provides a sealed environment to protect eggs during their development, and may also contain toxins to deter potential predators. The eggs hatch into tadpoles within 10 days or so. The young wriggle out of the folded leaf and drop into the water below, where they complete their development into small frogs. Other treefrogs, such as the TWO-LINED TREEFROG (Plate 3), deposit eggs on leaves over water, but do not seal them within a folded leaf. The CHRISTMAS TREEFROG (Plate 3) and RED-SKIRTED TREEFROG (Plate 5) take an easier approach and simply lay their eggs in small ponds. A few species lay their eggs in "arboreal" water, small pools that accumulate in the central parts, or cisterns, of bromeliad plants, or in depressions and cavities of tree limbs and trunks. Others, such as MIYATA'S JEWELED TREEFROG (Plate 3), have been discovered so recently, or are so rarely seen, that biologists have yet to learn how they breed.

The moistness and relatively constant temperatures of tropical rainforests permit treefrogs to exploit the terrestrial and arboreal world with less danger of drying out, or perishing from extreme heat or cold. But, being amphibians, most must return to the water to breed, and the forces of natural selection have shaped their breeding such that each species has its own special way. One major driving force involved is the danger of predation on eggs or tadpoles, particularly by fish.

In response to this threat, many treefrog species breed only in temporary ponds. These ponds are formed when low-lying areas fill with rainwater, and because of the ephemeral nature of these pools, fully aquatic creatures such as fish cannot survive in them. Treefrog eggs and tadpoles, however, safe from fish predators, develop rapidly into froglets and move to the safety of their adult arboreal life before the pools dry.

The number of eggs produced by each species is highly variable. Some, particularly those that lay their eggs directly in water, produce large numbers (up to 2000 or more per clutch), while others produce far fewer (especially those that lay eggs on leaves over water). In areas with distinct wet and dry seasons, most treefrogs breed during the wet season; in less seasonal environments, such as in the eastern lowlands of Ecuador, treefrogs breed sporadically year-round with breeding activities most intense after heavy rain.

The diversity of breeding strategies and sites used by treefrogs may help reduce competition for breeding sites. If all of the treefrog species in one place bred only in temporary ponds, all at the same time, the ponds could become so choked with tadpoles that all food could be eaten and starvation could ensue. In many cases, the competition for breeding sites between treefrog species – particularly closely related species – may have helped force species to breed at different times of the night (even if at the same pond), or at different times of the year.

Notes

Adult treefrogs, like other frogs, have several ways to avoid or escape predation, including rapid jumping to flee, cryptic coloring that allows them to blend into their environment, loud, startling screams or squawks given when grabbed by predators, and poisons in their skin. Some species are cryptic but not poisonous, some are cryptic and also poisonous, some are brightly colored and poisonous (the bright colors presumably functioning as warning coloration), and others brightly colored but not poisonous (presumably to mimic brightly colored poisonous frogs, to fool predators). Many treefrogs (and other types of frogs) have bright colors on usually concealed surfaces of limbs and body that are only visible when the limbs are extended. The appearance of these bright color patches, called *flash coloring*, when a frog first moves to escape danger, presumably startles predators. The predators naturally then focus on the bright colors, which immediately disappear when a frog assumes a sitting position.

Status

Although no treefrog outside of Australia is officially recognized as threatened, we have so little information on their populations that it is impossible to determine the statuses of most species. Given the present high rate of forest clearing and disturbance, some species undoubtedly are in trouble, particularly those with small ranges or very specialized habitat requirements.

Profiles

Horned Marsupial Treefrog, *Gastrotheca cornuta*, Plate 3b
Two-lined Treefrog, *Hyla bifurca*, Plate 3c
Christmas Treefrog, *Hyla punctata*, Plate 3d
Miyata's Jeweled Treefrog, *Hyla miyatai*, Plate 3e
Triangle Treefrog, *Hyla triangulum*, Plate 3f
Red-skirted Treefrog, *Hyla rhodopepla*, Plate 5a
Tiger-striped Leaf Frog, *Phyllomedusa tomopterna*, Plate 5b

4. Poison-dart Frogs

The *poison-dart* frogs of the family Dendrobatidae are, among amphibians, second only to treefrogs in their popularity as tropical forest poster animals. These small frogs have striking large eyes, and the bright colors of some species warn predators of their extraordinary toxicity. The 170 species are restricted to the warm tropical climates of Central and South America. Ecuador is home to about 55 species, many of them *endemic* – found nowhere else. Poison-dart frogs, in fact, typically have very restricted ranges.

Poison-dart frogs are small, with adults ranging from little more than 1.5 cm (half an inch) to about 5 cm (2 in). Most species have a short head and snout, and usually the tip of the snout has a straight, flat edge, with the top and sides joined at a sharp angle. Body and limbs are fairly short and stout, and the toes end with expanded tips that are usually rectangular in shape. Toes of the front feet lack webbing, and toes of the back feet can be partially webbed, although most species have no webbing at all.

The most striking characteristic of many poison-dart frogs is their spectacularly bright coloration, with colors spanning the rainbow in amazing patterns. Some species, such as the orange HARLEQUIN POISON-DART FROG (Plate 4), have only one color on the upper surface of the body (over a darker background), but some, such as the RUBY POISON-DART FROG (Plate 4), have two or more. The colors often have a metallic shine that makes them appear almost as if there is a light illuminating them from inside the frog's body. Some species, such as the SPOT-LEGGED POISON-DART FROG (Plate 4) and RED-ARMED POISON-DART FROG (Plate 4), have bright colors restricted to their limbs or to surfaces where the limbs attach to the body. Some species have a blue mottled pattern on their bellies, over a background of black or white. In many, the deep blue on the underside has a rich and vibrant metallic shine.

However, fully half of the frogs in the family Dendrobatidae have no bright colors. These are frogs in the genus *Colostethus*, such as the WESTERN DRAB POISON-DART FROG (Plate 4). Their colors range from dull tan to dark brown, often with pale cream to yellowish stripes along the upper and/or lower sides of the head and body. The undersides of most are colored cream to pale yellow or tan, some with a spotted pattern on a darker background. These frogs, although similar in habits to others in the family, do not produce highly toxic skin secretions. A few drab species can be found at elevations up to 2500 m (8000 ft), and many more up to 1500 m (5000 ft). Most of the more colorful species are found in lowland rainforest (although a few also occur at higher elevations).

Natural History

Ecology and Behavior
Virtually all species of poison-dart frogs live on the floor of moist forests. They hop about in the leaf litter during the daytime, foraging for invertebrates such as insects. Although they eat a wide variety of insects, ants and termites make up at least two-thirds of their diet. Many sleep at night on low vegetation, usually less than a meter (3 ft) above the ground, although some (especially the drab species) may also be active at night. The brightly colored species can be especially abundant in primary forest valleys drained by small streams, and some also inhabit more open forest or swampy areas (usually in association with a thick layer of leaf litter on the forest floor). The drab species are very poorly known, and have a

reputation for being wary and secretive (not surprising considering their lack of potent skin toxins and warning colors). Drab species inhabit a wider variety of habitats and elevations than do colorful species, but nearly all poison-dart frogs show strong affinities for living near water, especially streams, owing to their unique reproduction.

The neon glow of the colorful species of poison-dart frogs sends a clear warning understood by most potential predators in the tropical forest: Danger! Stay Away! Poison-dart frogs have some of the brightest colors of any frogs, and also probably the most toxic poisons. The poisons are fat-soluble alkaloids secreted by the skin. They affect nerves and muscles, causing paralysis. One explanation for the source of their poisons involves the frog's food. When poison-dart frogs are removed from their forest environment and fed a human-concocted diet (of, say, baby crickets or mealworms), instead of their natural diet of forest ants, they soon lose their toxicity. Something in their natural diet of ants is necessary for the frogs to produce their own poisons, without which they become defenseless.

Breeding

The ways in which poison-dart frogs reproduce are unlike those of most other groups of frogs because, depending on the species, either the male or the female or rarely both guard and care for their offspring. This behavior is well documented in a number of species, and reflects a complex partnership more typical of birds or mammals. In some species the male calls from his territory to attract a female. When a receptive female appears, he leads her to an appropriate mating and egg-laying spot. After mating, one or the other of the parents guards the eggs, and when the eggs hatch into tiny tadpoles, the guarding parent scoops the tadpoles onto his or her back for transport to a nearby stream or pool. The partner that does the carrying varies from species to species, and sometimes even among individual couples of the same species. (Tadpole-carrying was discovered early in the study of poison-dart frogs, when biologists were surprised to collect specimens with tadpoles adhering to their backs.) Most poison-dart frogs care for their young only until the tadpole stage, after which the tadpoles are left to develop on their own in a stream or pond. A few species go one step further by depositing (or transporting) their tadpoles into water-filled bromeliad plants or other small standing pools of water in trees. In several species the female actually lays infertile eggs into her bromeliad "nursery" for the growing tadpoles to feed on. Almost all of the drab poison-dart frog species also guard eggs and carry tadpoles to water. Based on observations of a few well-studied species, poison-dart frogs produce very small numbers (6 to 20) of relatively large eggs and may breed throughout the year.

Notes

The name "poison-dart frog" refers to the fact that some groups of indigenous people in Latin America use the frogs to poison their blowgun darts for hunting. Only a few species in southern Central America and northern South America are actually known to be used to poison blowgun darts. For all but one species, the blowgun hunters impale a hapless frog on a sharp stick, and then slowly roast it over a flame to provide the maximum amount of irritation, and thus also the maximum secretion of poison. The frothy poison is spread on the business ends of the darts, which are then used to rapidly debilitate even large prey such as monkeys. The most poisonous species of dart-frog was discovered only about 20 years ago in northwestern Colombia, and was named *Phyllobates terribilis* (the Terrible Yellow Poison-dart Frog) because of the extraordinary toxicity of its poison. One group of native people uses *P. terribilis* to poison darts, but unlike other species, the bright yellow frog is spared death by slow roasting. This species is so toxic that the human hunter only needs to rub his dart tip briefly on the back of a frog, and enough poison is transferred to kill just about anything; frogs are then released unharmed. The poison from this frog is in fact one of the most potent natural toxins found on Earth – each small frog has enough poison to kill over 10 people! The hunters know how toxic it is, and unlike other species, they only handle these yellow frogs with leaves, avoiding direct contact with their skin. As an additional safety factor, many indigenous people place the poison just in back of the tip, so that an accidental nick on the hand won't have dire consequences for the hunter.

Status

Many species of poison-dart frogs are currently threatened. However, as is the case with other tropical frog groups, very little is known about the populations of most species. The fact that many species have very restricted ranges makes poison-dart frogs especially susceptible to habitat destruction or over-collecting. Because of this, and because of their beauty and popular appeal, all poison-dart frogs are CITES Appendix II listed.

Profiles

Harlequin Poison-dart Frog, *Dendrobates histrionicus*, Plate 4a
Amazonian Poison-dart Frog, *Dendrobates ventrimaculatus*, Plate 4b
Spot-legged Poison-dart Frog, *Epipedobates pictus*, Plate 4c
Ruby Poison-dart Frog, *Epipedobates parvulus*, Plate 4d
Red-armed Poison-dart Frog, *Epipedobates erythromos*, Plate 4e
Western Drab Poison-dart Frog, *Colostethus infraguttatus*, Plate 4f

5. Other Frogs

There are additional groups of frogs that, although not represented by many species in Ecuador, you may see during your trip to Ecuador. The family Ranidae, or *true frogs*, has a nearly worldwide distribution, but the family's sole representative in Ecuador is the AMAZON BULLFROG (Plate 5). This frog is noteworthy because it is quite large and seen often in lowland forests. Amazon Bullfrogs, which resemble North American bullfrogs and can grow to 13 cm (5 in) in length, are medium to dark green, with fully webbed rear feet (but no webbing on the front feet), prominent external ear discs, and distinct folds of skin on the upper sides of the body.

The *glass frogs*, Family Centrolenidae, are an interesting group of about 120 species found only in Central and South America, with some 30 species known from Ecuador. These tiny frogs, usually less than 2.5 cm (1 in) long, have transparent skin on the undersides of the body and limbs, which in many species reveals the internal organs (including beating heart) and bones. The upper surface of the body is usually pale green, often with distinct spots and specks that can be white, yellow, blue, or brown. Glass frogs closely resemble treefrogs in body form, with long limbs and large feet (usually at least partially webbed); toes are tipped by expanded discs.

Narrow-mouthed frogs, Family Microhylidae, contrary to what the family name suggests, are not tiny treefrogs. With about 315 species and a nearly worldwide distribution, most narrow-mouthed frogs are almost comical in appearance, with rotund bodies, short stubby limbs, and tiny pointed heads. Fewer than a dozen species are known from Ecuador. If you spot a small (usually less than 5 cm, 2 in), dull gray to dark brown, smooth-skinned frog that resembles a tiny beach ball with legs and pointed head, hopping about on the ground, you probably have found a narrow-mouthed frog.

Another frog family represented by only a single species in Ecuador is also one of the most bizarre on Earth. The PIPA, or SURINAM, FROG (Family Pipidae, 30 species in Africa and South America) looks like it has been run over by a truck. Dark brown, it has an extremely flattened, oval body with equally flattened limbs. The hind feet are completely webbed and the front feet end in web-less, uniform-length, straight toes. This strange frog is completely aquatic. It inhabits ponds and swamps in the Amazon lowlands and is virtually helpless on land.

Natural History

Ecology, Behavior, and Breeding

The AMAZON BULLFROG is found in lowland forests on both sides of the Andes mountains, and is active mostly at night in or near ponds, lakes, streams, and swamps. Like North American bullfrogs, they will eat just about anything smaller than themselves. You are most likely to encounter this frog in association with a breeding chorus of *treefrogs* and *rainfrogs* at a temporary pond, or other small forest or forest edge pond. It breeds in the most ordinary frog way, mating and depositing a large number of eggs (5000 to 7000) directly into the water. Amazon Bullfrogs are strong jumpers with powerful leg muscles; spotting one can be easy, but getting close to one is not!

Glass frogs are found in many regions of Ecuador, including lowland forests and the cloud forests on both sides of the Andes (one species occurs up to 3000 m, 10,000 ft, elevation). Most shun disturbed areas and are usually found only in the vicinity of small streams in primary (old growth) forest. Many of the cloud forest species seem to have a preference for spray zones at the edges of small cascading mountain waterfalls. As far as is known, all species are nocturnal and arboreal, and feed on a wide variety of small invertebrates. Glass frogs are noteworthy for their general rarity and extremely restricted ranges, with some species known only from a few individuals collected within very small areas. Lowland species, such as the REGAL GOLDEN GLASS FROG (Plate 5), are somewhat more common and widespread, but even these seem to live exclusively along small streams and are rarely seen except when breeding. Males, often during light rain, call for females from vegetation directly above a stream, where mating occurs. Females then deposit a clutch of 15 to 30 eggs on the surface of a leaf. In some species the male then stands guard over the eggs until they hatch into tiny tadpoles. The tadpoles drop into the stream below and complete their development into frogs.

Narrow-mouthed frogs are usually nocturnal and can be found on the floor of lowland forests on both sides of the Andes. They prefer primary forest, although some can occasionally be found in secondary (recently cut) forest and along forest edges. Many species seem to feed almost exclusively on ants, although other invertebrate prey, such as beetles, may also be eaten. Most are burrowers, and two species (one Ecuadorean, one North American) are known to share burrows happily with large tarantula spiders. It is believed that the frogs eat ants that prey upon tarantula eggs, and thus the tarantulas, which certainly do attack and eat other kinds of frogs, benefit from this arrangement and refrain from attacking the narrow-mouthed frogs. How the tarantulas recognize these helpful frogs is a mystery, but it probably involves smell.

It is easiest to see narrow-mouthed frogs when they congregate to breed at small forest ponds, especially during or immediately following heavy rain. Males call from the edge or the surface of the water to attract females; mating occurs in the water and females deposit 100 to 600 eggs, which hatch into tadpoles that later develop into frogs. One group deposits a very small number of eggs (5 to 10) in water-filled bromeliad plants, where the tadpoles (which apparently do not feed; they have no suitable mouth parts) develop safely into frogs. Worldwide, narrow-mouthed frogs employ a broad array of breeding strategies, including a few species with direct development.

The SURINAM FROG is found in Ecuador only in the Amazon lowlands, and probably only in the easternmost areas. The only fully aquatic frog in Ecuador, and one of only a few such aquatic frogs known, its flattened body and heavily webbed feet serve it well for its daily routine of capturing and eating small fish. The reproductive habits of this group are equally unique; pairs mate in the water, in a twisting motion in which the eggs are glued, in a sticky mass, to the back of the female. Further embrace by the male ensures that the eggs (about 80 per clutch) are well pressed into the soft skin on the back of the female, after which the skin grows rapidly around the eggs. Safely embedded in the mother's back, the eggs travel with her until they hatch into fully formed froglets about 15 weeks later. A bit grotesque, perhaps, but it works.

Status

No species of the four frog families considered here is threatened or endangered in Ecuador, but most of the species are too poorly known to make informed decisions as to status. The glass frogs are the most likely to be threatened because of their extremely restricted ranges, specialized habitats, and preference for undisturbed forests and clean water.

Profiles

Fleischmann's Glass Frog, *Hyalinobatrachium fleischmanni*, Plate 5c
Regal Golden Glass Frog, *Cochranella midas*, Plate 5d
Amazon Bullfrog, *Rana palmipes*, Plate 5e
Bassler's Narrow-mouthed Frog, *Chiasmocleis bassleri*, Plate 5f

Environmental Close-up 1:
Frog Population Declines: Amphibian Armageddon or Alarmist Absurdity?

The Problem

Recently, there has been an outpouring of articles and stories about amphibians in the popular and scientific media, bearing titles such as The Silence of the Frogs, Where Have All the Frogs Gone?, Why Are Frogs and Toads Croaking?, Playing it Safe or Crying Frog?, and Chicken Little or Nero's Fiddle? What's stimulating all the silly titles? The issue traces back a few years, to 1989 to be precise, to a conference in Britain attended by many of the world's leading scientists who study reptiles and amphibians in the wild. Gabbing in the hallways of the convention center, as scientists will do, relating stories about their research and the respective species that they study, they noticed a common thread emerging: many of the populations of frogs, toads, and salamanders that had been monitored for at least several years seemed to be declining in numbers, often drastically. Where some species had been common 20 years before, they were now rare or near extinction. Suspecting that something important was afoot, the scientists met formally the next year in California to discuss the subject, compare notes, and try to reach some preliminary conclusions or, minimally, to phrase some preliminary questions. Such as: (1) Are amphibian populations really declining over a broad geographic area? Or are the stories just that – anecdotal accounts concerning a few isolated populations that, even if they are in decline, do not portend a general trend? (2) If amphibian population declines are, in fact, a general phenomenon, are they over and above those of other kinds of animals (many of which, after all, given the alarming rate of natural habitat destruction occurring over the globe, are also thought to be declining – albeit usually at a gentler pace than that ascribed to the amphibian drops); that is, is the amphibian decline a special case, happening for a reason unrelated to general loss of biodiversity? and (3) If there really is a generalized worldwide amphibian problem, why is it happening?

Most of the conferring scientists agreed that a widespread pattern of amphibian declines was indicated by available data: there were reports from the USA, Central America, the Amazon Basin, the Andes, Europe, and Australia. They speculated about two possible main causes. First, that habitat loss – continued destruction of tropical forests, etc. – was almost certainly contributing to general declines in population sizes of amphibians and other types of animals. That is, that amphibian declines could be at least partly attributed to worldwide biodiversity loss. Second, that owing to their biology, amphibians were doubtless more sensitive than other groups to pollution, especially acid rain (rain that is acidified by various atmospheric pollutants, chiefly from engine emissions, leading to lake and river water being more acidic). Amphibians are more vulnerable to this kind of pollution than, say, reptiles, because of their thin, wet skins, through which they breathe and through which polluting chemicals may gain entry to their bodies, and also owing to their highly exposed and so vulnerable early life stages – eggs and tadpoles in lakes, ponds, and streams. Changes in the acidity of their aquatic environments, or even changes in water temperature, are known to have dire consequences for egg and larval (tadpole) development – and therefore such changes could be the main culprits behind amphibian declines. Plainly, if the reproduction of amphibians were compromised, population numbers would plunge precipitously. Although it sounded a bit far-fetched, some scientists also suggested that the increased bombardment of the Earth by ultraviolet (UV) light, a direct result of the thinning, protective atmospheric ozone layer, might likewise be taking a disproportionate toll on biologically vulnerable amphibians. (Indeed, recent studies have proved to the satisfaction of some, but not all, scientists that increased UV light in natural situations destroys frog eggs and can interact chemically with diseases and acid rain to increase amphibian mortality rates.)

The Controversy

As might be expected, not all herpetologists agree that pollution, UV light, or some other environmental factor is currently exerting lethal effects worldwide on frogs and salamanders. Some biologists point out that the amphibians that they study in some of the world's most pristine environments, having little or no detectable pollution, also have experienced catastrophic population crashes. One of the prime examples is a Costa Rican resident, the Golden Toad. It had been monitored for many years in the same five breeding ponds in one nature reserve, and until the late 1980s, more than 1500 adults had bred each year in the ponds; but from 1988 through 1990, fewer than 20 individuals could be found each year and the toad is now thought to be close to extinction. In total, populations of 20 of the approximately 50 frog species that inhabit the reserve crashed dramatically during the late 1980s and, as of 1996, still had not recovered. Pollution was probably not a factor, although UV light and weather could have had effects – average water temperature had risen a bit and there was a decrease in rainfall during the late 1980s.

Still other scientists, those who study natural size oscillations in animal populations, point out that science is aware of many animals whose populations cycle between scarcity and abundance. For instance, several small rodents of the arctic tundra, voles and lemmings, are famous for one year being at low population densities (a few per acre or hectare) but three or four years hence, being at very high densities (thousands per acre or hectare, so many that it's difficult to walk without stepping on them). These biologists point out that, unless those sounding the alarm of amphibian declines can show that the declines are not part of natural cycles, it is too early to panic. Further, that the only way to know about possible natural population cycles is to monitor closely amphibian populations during long-term studies, which at present, are few and far between.

The side of the debate that takes the amphibian declines as established fact and suspects an anthropogenic cause (scientific jargon for people-caused), while agreeing that long-term studies are necessary, believes that it would be a grave mistake to wait for the conclusions of those studies, 10 or 20 years down the road, before decisions are reached about whether amphibians are declining on a broad scale and what to do about it – because at that point, they believe, it will be too late to do anything but record mass extinctions.

The Future

What will happen now is that the controversy will continue as long-term population studies are conducted. In one novel approach, current populations of frogs and toads in California's Yosemite National Park were compared with notes on their population sizes from a survey conducted in 1915; all seven native species were found to have declined, but the causes are unclear. A group of Australian researchers proposed in 1996 that the catastrophic declines in frogs in eastern Australian rainforests were caused by an unknown virus or fungus – a rapidly spreading, water-borne, epidemic disease. They further suspect that the same disease has spread over the past 15 or 20 years from continent to continent, perhaps in water transported with aquarium fish, and, in concert with pollution and other environmental stresses that make amphibians more vulnerable to diseases, may be responsible for the worldwide amphibian die-offs. The virus or fungus may even be spread on the shoes of researchers and ecotravellers, thus explaining why some newly discovered frog populations succumb to disease shortly after being discovered. This is a controversial idea, and other scientists will have to test it before it is widely accepted as a correct explanation. However, recent work in Panama shows that many frogs there are dying of a protozoan disease, and findings from Central America and Australia prove that a fungus is killing many frogs in those regions, supporting disease explanations for amphibian declines.

A major problem is that, even if the scientific consensus right now was that disease, fungi, pollution, and the increased incidence of UV light were harming amphibians around the world, the will and resources are currently lacking to do anything about it on the massive scale that conservation would require. Unless people's world view changes, preservation of amphibians and reptiles, save special cases like sea turtles (p. 69), will always lag behind preservation efforts made on the behalf of the "cuddlies" – birds and mammals. The best hope is that the recent conservation emphasis on preserving entire ecosystems, rather than particular species, will eventually benefit the disappearing amphibians.

One positive element of the amphibian declines, if it can be called that, is that some scientists have suggested that if it is determined that amphibians are particularly sensitive to pollutants, then perhaps they can be used as indicators of environmental health: ecosystems with healthy amphibian populations could be deemed relatively healthy, those with declining amphibians could be targeted for hasty improvement. As one biologist phrased it, amphibians could be used as "yardsticks for ecosystem vitality," just as canaries in cages indicated to the coal miners who carried them something of vital importance about their environments.

Chapter 6

REPTILES

Edited by Greg Vigle

- *Introduction*
- *General Characteristics and Classification of Reptiles*
- *Seeing Reptiles in Ecuador*
- *Family Profiles*
- *Environmental Close-Up 2: Endemism and High Species Diversity: Why Ecuador?*

Introduction

Reptiles are among the most intriguing animals in Ecuador. Their fascinating colors, shapes and behavior pique the interest of many biologists – amateur and professional alike – and ecotravellers who spot them and watch them carefully are in for an exciting treat. Except in the Galápagos (p. 229), however, you will have to look hard and be lucky to see more than a few representatives of this group. To avoid predation, most reptiles are inconspicuous and often flee from the approach of humans. Exceptions are reptiles that achieve a great deal of safety by being very large – crocodiles and iguanas for instance. Also, some small lizards can be quite common along forest trails. Although it seems obvious that lizards are "dinosaur-like," a major controversy swirls around their true origin. Many scientists now see birds and not present-day reptiles as the most direct descendants of dinosaurs. Regardless of the details, early reptiles gave rise in some form or another to all modern reptiles, birds and mammals.

General Characteristics and Classification of Reptiles

Reptiles have been around for a long while, arising, so the fossil evidence tells us, during the late portion of the Paleozoic Era, some 300 million years ago. Today more than 7000 species live in almost all regions of the Earth, with a healthy contingent in the American tropics. Ecuador has about 410 species, of which 235 are snakes, 135 are lizards, and the remainder turtles and crocodilians. Chief reptile traits include: (1) their skin is covered with tough scales, which cuts down significantly on water loss from their body surface. The development of this trait permitted animals for the first time to remain for extended periods on dry land, and most of today's reptiles are completely terrestrial (whereas most amphibians lack a tough skin and must remain in or near water or moist places, lest they dry out); (2) they have a much more efficient heart and blood system than those of amphibians. This increased efficiency allows for a high blood pressure and the sustained muscular activity required for land-living. The crocodilians even have a completely four-chambered heart that is otherwise found only in birds and mammals; (3) although some reptiles lay eggs and others have live births, all have a blood supply connection between the mother and the embryo to conduct nutrients to the developing young and waste products away from it. This increased involvement of the parent in the development of the young (parental care), much of it inside the mother, means that unlike amphibians, reptiles do not have to return to the water to deposit their eggs; their terrestrial life is assured. In addition, the young are much better protected against predators and the elements.

Reptile biologists (herpetologists) recognize three major groups alive today: the *turtles* and *tortoises* (land turtles) constitute one group, with about 260 species worldwide. Some turtles live wholly on land, the *sea turtles* live out their lives in the oceans (coming ashore only to lay eggs), but most turtles live in lakes and ponds. Some eat plants, some are carnivorous, and others eat both plants and animals. Turtles are easily distinguished by their unique body armor – tough plates that cover their back and belly, creating wrap-around shells into which head and limbs are retracted when danger looms. The *crocodiles* and their relatives, large predatory carnivores that live along the shores of swamps, rivers, and estuaries, constitute a small second group of about 20 species. Last, and currently positioned as the world's most abundant reptiles, the 3300 *lizard* species and 3500 *snakes* comprise a third group (lizards and snakes have very similar skeletal traits, indicating a close relationship).

Lizards walk on all four limbs, except for a few that are legless. Most are ground-dwelling animals, but many also climb when the need arises; a fair number spend much of their lives in trees. Almost all are capable of moving quite rapidly. Most lizards are insectivorous, but some, especially larger ones, eat plants, and several prey on amphibians, other lizards, mammals, birds, and even fish. Ecologists suspect that the ecological success of lizards is due primarily to a combination of their efficient predation on insects and other small animals as well as their low daily energy requirements. They rely primarily on external sources of heat like the sun to raise their internal temperature enough to be active. When it gets too hot they use behavior like seeking shade to lower their internal temperature so they can again be active. However, when the external temperature falls too much, instead of burning up stored energy to maintain their body temperature, they just let their internal temperature drop and become inactive. Their cooled bodies go into a resting state that needs little energy. In some ways, this can be considered an advantage over birds and mammals, which must continually seek food to maintain constant body temperatures.

Most Ecuadorean lizards are insectivorous, also opportunistically taking other small animals such as spiders and mites. Lizards employ two main foraging strategies. Some, such as the small whiptail lizards, are *active searchers*. They move continually while looking for prey, for instance nosing about in the leaf litter of the forest floor. *Sit-and-wait* predators, highly camouflaged, remain motionless on the ground or on tree trunks or branches, waiting for prey to happen by. When they see a likely meal – perhaps a caterpillar or a beetle – they reach out to snatch it if it is close enough or dart out to chase it down. Many lizards are territorial, defending territories from other members of their species with displays, such as bobbing up and down on their front legs and raising their head crests. Lizards are especially common in deserts and semi-deserts, but they are numerous in other habitats as well. They are active primarily during the day, except for many of the gecko species, which are nocturnal.

Snakes probably evolved from burrowing lizards, and all are limbless. Snakes are all carnivores, but their methods of capturing prey differ. Several groups of species have evolved glands that manufacture toxic venom, which is injected into prey through the teeth. The venom immobilizes and kills the prey, which is then swallowed whole. Other snakes strike out at and then wrap themselves around their prey, constricting the animal until it suffocates. The majority of snakes are nonvenomous, seizing prey with their mouths and relying on their size and strong jaws to subdue it. Snakes have no eardrums for hearing, but they can detect ground vibrations through their bodies. They generally rely most on vision and smell to locate prey, although members of two families have thermal sensor organs on their heads that detect the heat of prey animals.

The success of snakes is at least partially attributable to their ability to devour prey that is larger than their heads (their jaw bones are highly mobile and can be moved easily out of their socket joints on the cranium to accommodate large prey as it is swallowed). This unique ability provides snakes with two great advantages over other animals: because they eat large items, they have been able to reduce the frequency with which they need to search for and capture prey; and owing to this, they can spend long periods hidden and secluded, safe from predators. Like lizards, snakes use either active searching or sit-and-wait foraging strategies.

Snakes are themselves prey for hawks and other predatory birds, other snakes, as well as for some mammals. While many snakes are quite conspicuous against a solid color, being decorated with bold and colorful skin patterns, against their normal backdrops, such as a leaf-strewn forest floor, they are highly camouflaged. They rely on their cryptic coloration, and sometimes on speed, to evade predators. Within a species male and female snakes usually look alike, although in some there are minor differences between the sexes in traits such as variation in color patterns or the sizes of their scales.

Seeing Reptiles in Ecuador

Unlike on the Galápagos (p. 229), where you will readily see reptiles, most species on the mainland are shy and often exceedingly difficult to observe. They spend most of their time concealed or still. Few vocalize like birds or frogs, so you cannot use sound to find them. The superb cryptic coloration of snakes means that snakes probably will see more of you than you will of them. Because of the difficulty people have seeing snakes before getting very close to them, the rule for exploring any area known to harbor venomous snakes or any area for which you are unsure, is never, NEVER to place your hand or foot anywhere that you cannot see first. Do not climb rocks or trees, do not clamber over rocks where your hands or feet sink into holes or crevices; do not reach into bushes or trees. Walk carefully along trails and, although your attention understandably wanders as new sights and sounds are taken in, try to watch your feet and where you are going. In more than 30 years of work in Ecuador, however, we have seen few venomous snakes.

If you want to see reptiles, there are a few ways to increase the chances. Knowing about activity periods helps. Lizards and many snakes are active during the day, but some snakes are active at night (often arboreally on low vegetation). Thus, a night walk with flashlights that is organized to find amphibians might also yield some reptile sightings. For instance, many small lizards sleep on leaves above the ground, in the same places where treefrogs are active. In lowland rainforest, many lizards are active by day on tree trunks, and also in sunny areas near forest edges. Weather is also important – snakes and lizards are often more active in sunny, warm weather. If all else fails, one may look for small snakes and lizards by carefully moving aside rocks and logs with a robust stick or with one's boots, although such adventures are not for the faint-hearted. Because there are some venomous snakes that are difficult to identify correctly, all snakes spotted on your trip are best observed from a safe distance.

Family Profiles

1. Crocodilians

Remnants of the age when reptiles ruled the world, today's crocodilians (*alligators, caimans,* and *crocodiles*), when seen in the wild, generally inspire awe, respect, a bit of fear, and a great deal of curiosity. Recent classification schemes include a total of 22 species, distributed over most tropical and subtropical areas of the world. Five are found in Ecuador, but only one is common enough for most visitors to see. The SPECTACLED CAIMAN (Plate 6) is probably the most abundant crocodilian in the New World and can be found in both the eastern and western lowlands of Ecuador. This species is mid-sized, reaching a length of about 2.5 m (8 ft), but another species, the BLACK CAIMAN (Plate 6), found only in the eastern lowlands, can reach a length of 6 m (18+ ft). In contrast to these larger caimans, the DWARF CAIMAN (Plate 6) is a forest-dwelling species that only grows to about 1 m (3 ft) in length. The AMERICAN CROCODILE is also found in Ecuador, but only in isolated areas of protected mangroves along the coast, and it is rarely seen. Ecuador's caimans occupy inland swamps, creeks, ponds, lakes, and rivers.

Natural History

Ecology and Behavior
Although not amphibians, crocodilians are amphibious animals. They usually move slowly over land but in short bursts can cover ground rapidly. Most of their time is spent in the water. They are easiest to see, however, as they bask in the sunshine along banks of rivers, streams, and ponds. Crocodilians in the water are largely hidden, resembling floating logs. This unassuming appearance allows them to move close to shore and seize animals that come to the water to drink. Crocodilians are meat-eaters, but they also relish carrion. The foods taken depend on their age and size. Juvenile caiman eat primarily aquatic insects; adults prey on fish and amphibians. Young AMERICAN CROCODILES feed on small aquatic

and terrestrial vertebrates; adults specialize on fish and turtles. Crocodilians often forage at night, when they can be seen on the surface of the water; their eyes reflect red when shone with a bright light.

Caiman sometimes excavate burrows along waterways, into which they retreat to escape predators and, when water levels fall too low, to *aestivate*, (sleep until water conditions improve). Crocodilians may use vocal signals extensively in their behavior, but their sounds have been little-studied. It is known that juveniles give alarm calls when threatened, and that parents respond by coming quickly to their rescue.

Crocodilians have some of the most developed parental care of any reptile. Nests are guarded, and one or both parents often help hatchlings free themselves from the nest. In some species, parents also carry hatchlings to the nearest water. Females may also remain with the young for up to two years, protecting them. This complex parental care in crocodilians is sometimes mentioned by scientists who study dinosaurs to support the idea that dinosaurs may have exhibited complex social and parental behaviors. Crocodilians are long-lived animals, many surviving 60+ years in the wild.

Somewhat surprisingly, crocodilians are prey for several animals. Young, very small caiman are eaten by a number of predators, including birds such as herons, storks, egrets and anhingas, and a variety of mammals such as JAGUARS (Plate 81). Large adults apparently have only two enemies: people and large anaconda snakes. Cases of cannibalism have been reported.

Breeding
During courtship, male crocodilians often defend aquatic territories, giving displays with their tails – up-and-down and side-to-side movements – that probably serve both to defend the territory from other males and to court females. Typically the female makes the nest by scraping together grass, leaves, twigs, and sand or soil, into a pile near the water's edge. She then buries 20 to 30 eggs in the pile that she, and sometimes the male, guard for about 70 days until hatching. Nests of the DWARF CAIMAN are usually located near termite mounds in the forest. As in the turtles and some lizards, the sex of developing crocodilians is determined largely by the temperature of the ground around the eggs (see p. 71); males develop at relatively high temperatures, females at lower ones. Caiman young from a single brood may remain together in the nest area for up to 18 months. Breeding seasons for crocodilians vary, especially for caiman, with nesting observed during both wet and dry parts of the year.

Notes
Larger caiman are potentially dangerous to people, but they are not considered particularly aggressive species. Caiman are usually inoffensive, most being below a size where they try to eat land mammals; local people may even unconcernedly swim near them.

Owing to their predatory nature and large size, crocodilians play large roles in the history and folklore of many cultures, going back at least to ancient Egypt, where a crocodile-headed god was known as Sebek. The Egyptians apparently welcomed crocodiles into their canals, possibly as a defense from invaders. It may have been believed by Egyptians and other African peoples that crocodiles caused blindness, probably because the disease called river blindness results from infestation with a river-borne parasitic roundworm. To appease the crocodiles during canal construction, a virgin was sacrificed to the reptiles. Indeed, providing crocodiles with virgins seems to have been a fairly common practice among several cultures, showing a preoccupation with these animals (and with virgins). Even today, carvings of crocodiles are found among many relatively primitive peoples, from South America to Africa to Papua New Guinea. The ancient Olmecs of eastern Mexico also had a crocodile deity.

Status

Most crocodilian species worldwide were severely reduced in numbers during the 20th century. Several were hunted almost to extinction for their skins. In the USA, hunting almost caused AMERICAN ALLIGATORS to become extinct. In 1961 hunting alligators was made illegal, but poaching continued. Thanks to the 1973 Endangered Species Act, which gave protection to these alligators, they have returned to most of the areas from which they were eliminated. Crocodile and alligator farms (with captive-bred stock) and ranches (wild-caught stock) in many areas of the world now permit skins to be harvested while wild animals are relatively unmolested. Many of the Latin American crocodilians were hunted heavily during the first half of the 20th century. Today, only the SPECTACLED CAIMAN is hunted in large numbers, particularly in the Pantanal region of Brazil. In fact, all crocodilians are listed by the international CITES agreements, preventing or highly regulating trade in their skins or other parts, and their numbers have been steadily rising during the past 20 years. However, most of the 22 crocodilian species are still threatened or endangered. The AMERICAN CROCODILE, once common on the coast of Ecuador, is now rare, due primarily to replacement of its mangrove habitat with shrimp-raising ponds. It and the BLACK CAIMAN are both considered by the IUCN Red List to be threatened in Ecuador.

Profiles

Spectacled Caiman, *Caiman crocodilus*, Plate 6a
Black Caiman, *Caiman niger*, Plate 6b
Dwarf Caiman, *Paleosuchus trigonatus*, Plate 6c

2. Turtles

It is a shame that *turtles* are rarely encountered in the wild (at least at close range) because they are intriguing to watch, and they are generally innocuous and inoffensive. It is always a pleasant surprise to stumble across a turtle on land, perhaps laying eggs, or to discover a knot of them basking in the sunshine on rocks or logs along a river's edge or in the middle of a pond. The 260 living turtle species are usually grouped into 12 families that can be divided into three types by their typical habits and body forms. Two families comprise the *sea turtles*, ocean-going animals whose females come to shore only to lay eggs. The members of nine families, containing most of the species, live in freshwater habitats – lakes and ponds – except for the *box turtles*, which live on land (*terrestrial*). Finally, one family contains the *land tortoises*, which, as their name suggests, are all terrestrial.

Turtles all have the same basic body plan: bodies encased in tough shells (made up of two layers – an inner layer of bone and an outer layer of scale-like plates); four limbs, sometimes modified into flippers; highly mobile necks; toothless jaws; and small tails. This body plan must be among nature's best, because it has survived unchanged for a long time; according to fossils, turtles have looked more or less the same for at least 200 million years. Enclosing the body in heavy armor above and below was, apparently, an early solution to the problems vertebrates faced when they first moved onto land. It provides rigid support when outside of buoyant water, a high level of security from drying out, and protection from predators.

Turtles come, for the most part, in a variety of browns, blacks and greens, with olive-greens predominating. They range in size from tiny terrapins 11.5 cm (4.5 in) long to 250-kg (550-lb) GALÁPAGOS TORTOISES (Plate 89) and giant LEATHERBACK SEA TURTLES (Plate 88) that can grow to more than 2 m (6.5 ft) long, 3.6 m (12 ft) across (flipper to flipper), and that weigh 600+ kg (1300+ lb). Leatherbacks are the heaviest turtles and, perhaps except for some very large crocodiles, the heaviest reptiles. In many turtle species, females are larger than males. Ecuador has both marine and freshwater turtles, and tortoises. Two sea turtle and five freshwater families are represented. The single family of land tortoises is represented by the 12 living forms of Galápagos Tortoises (found on the various islands), and one mainland species, the SOUTH AMERICAN YELLOW-FOOTED TORTOISE (Plate 6).

Natural History

Ecology and Behavior

The diet of freshwater turtles changes as they develop. Early in life they are carnivorous, eating almost anything they can get their jaws on – snails, insects, fish, frogs, salamanders, reptiles. As they grow the diet of many changes to herbivory. Turtles are slow-moving on land, but they can retract their heads, tails, and limbs into their shells, rendering them almost impregnable to predators – unless they are swallowed whole, such as by crocodiles. Long-lived animals, individuals of many turtle species typically live 25 to 60 years in the wild. GALÁPAGOS TORTOISES routinely live more than 100 years. As is typical of most, if not all, reptiles, a turtle grows throughout its life.

SNAPPING TURTLES (Family Chelydridae; Plate 6) are large freshwater turtles with long tails, hooked jaws, and aggressive dispositions – they will bite people. They are found mainly in marshes, ponds, lakes, rivers, and streams. They are omnivorous, and often quite inconspicuous: sometimes algae grows on their backs, camouflaging them as they lunge at and snatch small animals that venture near. They remain predatory throughout their lives, even taking birds and small mammals, but they also eat aquatic vegetation.

The *aquatic* (or *pond*) *turtles* of Ecuador (five species in two families: the Emydidae and Pelomedusidae) occupy a variety of habitats. Some spend most of their time in lakes and ponds, but a few leave the water to forage on land. The YELLOW-SPOTTED AMAZON RIVER TURTLE (Plate 6) can most often be spotted sunning itself on logs in the water or on muddy beaches of rivers in remote and undisturbed parts of the eastern lowlands. By far most of the species of land tortoises (Family Testudinidae) in Ecuador are in the Galápagos (p. 229). On the mainland one species, the SOUTH AMERICAN YELLOW-FOOTED TORTOISE, is found on moist forest floors, but only in the eastern lowlands; a very similar tortoise may occur in the western coastal region. Sea turtles (Plate 88) are large reptiles that live in the open oceans, with the result that, aside from their beach nesting habits, relatively little is known of their behavior. Although at least four species are occasionally seen along the mainland coast, your best chance of seeing one of these giants of the sea is in the Galápagos archipelago (p. 230).

If turtles can make it through the dangerous juvenile stage, when they are small and soft enough for a variety of predators to take them, they enjoy very high year-to-year survival – 80% or more of an adult population usually survives from one year to the next. However, there is very high mortality in the egg and juvenile stages. Nests are not guarded, and many kinds of predators, such as crocodiles, lizards, and, especially, armadillos, dig up turtle eggs or eat the hatchlings.

Breeding

Courtship in turtles can be quite complex. In some, the male swims backwards in front of the female, stroking her face with his clawed feet. In the tortoises, courtship seems to take the form of some between-the-sexes butting and nipping. All turtles lay their leathery eggs on land. The female digs a hole in the earth or sand, deposits the eggs into the hole, then covers them over and departs. It is up to the hatchlings to dig their way out of the nest and navigate to the nearest water. Many tropical turtles breed at any time of year.

Although the numbers of eggs laid per nest varies extensively among the Ecuadorean freshwater turtles (from one to about 100), in general, these turtles, specialized for life in the tropics, lay small clutches. The reason seems to be that, because of the continuous warm weather, they need not breed in haste like their northern cousins, putting all their eggs in one nest. The danger with a single nest is that if a predator finds it, a year's breeding is lost. Tropical turtles, by placing only one or a few eggs in each of several nests spread through the year, are less likely to have predators destroy their total annual breeding production. Also, it may pay to lay a few big eggs rather than many small ones because bigger hatchlings can run faster to the water and its comparative safety from predators.

Notes

There is an intriguing relationship between turtle reproduction and temperature that nicely illustrates the intimate and sometimes puzzling connections between animals and the physical environment. For many vertebrate animals, the sex of an individual is determined by the kinds of sex chromosomes it has. In people, if each cell has an X and a Y chromosome, the person is male, and if two Xs, female. In birds, it is the opposite. But in most turtles, it is not the chromosomes that matter, but the temperature at which an egg develops. The facts are these. In most turtles, eggs incubated at constant temperatures above 30 °C (86 °F) all develop as females, whereas those incubated at 24 to 28 °C (75 to 82 °F) become males. At 28 to 30 °C (82 to 86 °F), both males and females are produced. In some species, a second temperature threshold exists – eggs that develop below 24 °C (75 °F) again become females. (In the crocodiles and lizards, the situation reverses, with males developing at relatively high temperatures and females at low temperatures.) The exact way that temperature determines sex is not clear although it is suspected that temperature directly influences a turtle's developing brain. This method of sex determination is also mysterious for the basic reason that no one quite knows why it should exist; that is, is there some advantage of this system to the animals that we as yet fail to appreciate? Or is it simply a consequence of reptile structure and function, some fundamental constraint of their biology?

Status

The ecology and status of populations of most freshwater and land turtles are poorly known, making it difficult to determine whether population numbers are stable or declining. In addition, several species of large river turtles in eastern Ecuador have virtually disappeared from all but the most remote streams and lakes. This rapid decline is due largely to over-harvesting of their eggs, which are buried in sandy river bars. These nests are easily found by local people who then sell the eggs to food markets in regional cities. The YELLOW-SPOTTED AMAZON RIVER

TURTLE and the BIG-HEADED AMAZON RIVER TURTLE, as well as the SOUTH AMERICAN YELLOW-FOOTED TORTOISE, are considered threatened in Ecuador by the IUCN Red List. Worldwide, sea turtles are heavily exploited by people, and almost all of them are threatened. Sea turtle eggs are harvested illegally for food in many parts of the world, including Ecuador, and adults (of some species) are taken for meat and for their skins. Many adults also die accidentally in fishing nets and collisions with boats. One of the sea turtles, the HAWKSBILL, (Plate 88) is the chief provider of tortoiseshell, which is carved for decorative purposes; although officially under international protection, these turtles are still hunted. All sea turtles profiled here are listed as endangered by CITES Appendix I. All forms of the GALÁPAGOS TORTOISE are also listed under CITES Appendix I and USA ESA.

Profiles

South American Yellow-footed Tortoise, *Geochelone denticulata*, Plate 6d
Yellow-spotted Amazon River Turtle, *Podocnemis unifilis*, Plate 6e
Snapping Turtle, *Chelydra serpentina acutirostris*, Plate 6f
Pacific Green Sea Turtle, *Chelonia mydas*, Plate 88a
Hawksbill Sea Turtle, *Eretmochelys imbricata*, Plate 88b
Leatherback Sea Turtle, *Dermochelys coriacea*, Plate 88c
Olive Ridley Sea Turtle, *Lepidochelys olivacea*, Plate 88d
Galápagos Tortoise, *Geochelone nigrita* and *G. hoodensis*, Plate 89a

3. Colubrids: Your Regular, Everyday Snakes

Many people think all *snakes*, particularly tropical varieties, are venomous, and hence, must be avoided at all cost. This "reptile anxiety" is serious when it prevents people who are paying initial visits to tropical forests from enjoying the many splendors around them. Many people it seems, irrespective of geography or culture, recoil from images of snakes and regard the real thing as dangerous, indicating more than anything an ignorance of the facts. In Ecuador the vast majority of snakes are NOT venomous. Also, venomous snakes in the American tropics tend to be nocturnal, secretive, and hard to find, even if you are looking for them. Therefore, with a modicum of caution, visitors can enjoy their days in Ecuador without worrying unduly about venomous snakes. If you do find one, you will likely discover that it is a beautiful organism and worth a look.

The largest group of snakes are those of the Family Colubridae – the *colubrid* snakes. Most of these are non-venomous or, if venomous, dangerous only to small prey, such as lizards and rodents; in other words, they are only mildly venomous. This is a worldwide group comprising over 1500 species, including about three-quarters of the New World snakes. About 150 species occur in Ecuador. Most of the snakes with which people have some familiarity, such as *water, brown, garter, whip, green, rat,* and *king snakes*, among a host of others, are colubrids, which have a wide variety of habits and lifestyles. It is not possible to provide a general physical description of all colubrid snakes because of the great variety of shapes and colors that specialize each for their respective lifestyles. Most people will not get close enough to notice, but an expert could identify colubrids by their anatomy: they have rows of teeth on the upper and lower jaws but they do not have hollow, venom-injecting fangs in front on the upper jaw.

Natural History

Ecology and Behavior

Because colubrids vary so much in their natural history, we will concentrate on the habits of the species illustrated (Plates 7, 8), which are representative of several general types. Typical lifestyles of various colubrids are terrestrial, burrowing, arboreal, and aquatic. Arboreal snakes spend most of their time in trees and shrubs. *Vine snakes* (Plate 7d), for instance, are slender, elegant snakes that inhabit lowland forests in Ecuador, feeding on lizards and frogs taken in trees. Their thin, long bodies look much like vines and if not moving, these snakes are very difficult to see. They rely on their camouflage for both hunting and protection: they freeze in place when alerted to danger. BLUNT-HEADED TREE SNAKES (Plate 7) are also arboreal. They possess exceptional heads – broad and squarish, relative to a long, thin body – and large, bulging eyes. They forage at night for small frogs and lizards that they locate at the very outer layer of leaves and branches of trees and shrubs. Another group of slender nocturnal-arboreal tree snakes are the *snail-eaters* (Plate 7), which, as you might expect, feed on snails (and apparently little else). Both blunt-headed snakes and snail-eaters are lightweight tree snakes, which are slightly flattened sideways, and can move from branch to branch over open gaps that are half the length of their bodies. They hide during the day in trees.

The TROPICAL RAT SNAKE (Plate 8) is common throughout much of the American tropics, inhabiting a variety of habitats in lowland and lower-slope forests. It moves over the ground and sometimes through bushes or shallow water, searching for its varied prey, which includes frogs, lizards, mammals, birds, and perhaps even other snakes. These agile snakes, boldly banded with black and yellow, can be more than 2 m (6.5 ft) in length. Having no venom, they constrict their prey in the same manner as *boas*. Another common terrestrial snake is the CHONTA SNAKE (Plate 8). It has a broad range in the Neotropics in wet and semi-dry lowland areas. Hunting by day or night, Chontas have a varied diet, including other snakes; in fact, they even capture and eat the deadly FER-DE-LANCE (Plate 10) and are appreciated for this habit by knowledgeable local people. Chonta Snakes are also interesting because they subdue their prey with a combination of slow-acting venom and physical constriction.

There are many species of small snakes, such as the BROWN GROUND SNAKE (Plate 8), which live much like worms, inhabiting the thick layer of leaf litter on the forest floor; some also burrow into the soil. However, unlike worms, many climb into low vegetation at night to sleep, and this is where you are most likely to see them. Not surprisingly, they eat mostly worms – the most abundant food in their chosen habitat. The many varieties of *false coral snakes* (Plate 8f) are also terrestrial forest dwellers that inhabit the leaf litter and rotting logs. They are brightly colored to fool predators (they visually mimic venomous *coral snakes*, but in fact have no fangs or venom; see p. 77).

Biologists who study snakes know that temperature regulates a snake's life, and is the key to understanding their ecology. Snakes are cold-blooded animals – they inhabit a world where the outside temperature governs their activity. Unlike the temperature of birds and mammals, their body temperature is determined primarily by how much heat they obtain from the physical environment. Simply put, many can only be active when they gather sufficient warmth from the sun. They have some control over their body temperature, but it is behavioral rather than physiological – they can lie in the sun or retreat to shade to raise or lower their internal temperatures to within a good operating range, but only up to a point: snakes must "sit out" hours or days in which the air temperature is either too high or too low. This dependence on air temperature affects most aspects of snakes' lives, from date of birth, to food requirements, to the rapidity with which they can strike at prey. For instance, in cold weather, snakes are less successful at capturing prey (they move and strike more slowly) and have less time each day when the ambient temperature is within their operating range, and so within the range in which they can forage. On the other hand, their metabolisms are slower when they are cold, which means that they need less food to survive these periods. At lower temperatures, snakes also probably grow slower, reproduce less often, and live longer.

Breeding
Relatively little is known of the breeding particulars of Ecuadorean colubrids. The typical number of eggs per clutch varies from species to species, but some, such as the BLUNT-HEADED TREE SNAKE, lay small clutches of one to three eggs. Most snakes that lay eggs deposit them in a suitable location and depart; the parents provide no care of the eggs or young. However, a few species of these snakes guard their eggs.

Notes
Snakes' limbless condition, their manner of movement, and the venomous nature of some of them, have engendered for these intriguing reptiles fear from people, stretching back thousands of years. Myths about the evil power and intentions of snakes are, as they say, legion. But one need go no farther than the Old Testament, where the snake, of course, plays the pivotal role as Eve's corrupt enticer, responsible for people's expulsion from the Garden of Eden. Because these myths cross so many cultures around the world, sociobiologists have hypothesized that this fear may be instinctive. Some studies of monkey behavior seem to support this possibility. Whether or not this fear is instinctive behavior or learned is controversial. We lean toward the learned behavior argument, based primarily on our visits to grade schools with live snakes in hand. Most grade school kids seem to lack the irrational fear often exhibited by their parents.

Status
None of Ecuador's colubrid snakes are currently considered threatened. On the other hand, most experts will concede that at this time little is known about the biology and population numbers of most of them. Long-term studies are necessary to determine if population sizes are stable or changing. Because individual species of snakes normally are not found in great numbers, the truth is that it will always be difficult to tell when they are threatened. Worldwide, about 30 colubrids are listed as vulnerable, threatened, or endangered. The leading threats are habitat destruction and the introduction by people of exotic animals that prey on snakes at some point in their life cycles, such as Giant Toads, Cattle Egrets, armadillos, and fire ants. Considered a top priority now for research and conservation are the snakes of the West Indies. The islands of the Caribbean have dozens of unique snake species, many of which appear to be declining rapidly in numbers – the result of habitat destruction and predation by mongooses, which were imported to the islands to control venomous snakes.

Profiles

Catesby's Snail-Eater, *Dipsas catesbyi*, Plate 7a
Amazon Snail-Eater, *Dipsas indica ecuadorensis*, Plate 7b
Blunt-headed Tree Snake, *Imantodes cenchoa*, Plate 7c
Lance-headed Vine Snake, *Xenoxybelis argenteus*, Plate 7d
Green Parrot Snake, *Leptophis ahaetulla nigromarginatus*, Plate 7e
Southern Cat-eyed Snake, *Leptodeira annulata*, Plate 7f
South American Sipo, *Chironius multiventris*, Plate 8a
Chonta Snake, *Clelia clelia*, Plate 8b
Tropical Rat Snake, *Spilotes pullatus*, Plate 8c
Amazon Water Snake, *Helicops angulatus*, Plate 8d
Brown Ground Snake, *Atractus major*, Plate 8e
Aesculapian False Coral Snake, *Erythrolamprus aesculapii*, Plate 8f
Galápagos Snake, *Antillophis steindachneri*, Plate 89e

4. Dangerous Snakes and Boas

For convenience, we group together in this section what are usually considered the more dangerous snakes, those that are highly venomous and large ones that kill by squeezing their prey – *anacondas* and *boas*. Anacondas are a kind of boa, and of the entire group, only the ANACONDA (Plate 9) truly could be considered potentially dangerous to adult humans (and then only if you were very much in the wrong place at the wrong time). However, few short-term visitors to Ecuador ever encounter venomous snakes or large constrictors of any kind, because most of these snakes are well camouflaged, secretive in their habits, and/or nocturnal.

Vipers, of the Family Viperidae, comprise most of the New World's poisonous snakes. If you are trying to capture and eat a large animal, without the benefit of legs and feet to grasp it, any way of quickly stopping the prey from wiggling free of your grasp would be advantageous. These snakes have evolved just such a method – a venom-injection mechanism: long, hollow fangs that introduce poison into the prey. The venom is sometimes *neurotoxic*; that is it interferes with nerve function, causing paralysis of the limbs and then respiratory failure. Other venoms are *haemotoxic* and cause hemorrhaging both at the site of the bite and then internally, leading to cardiovascular shock and death. (The answer to the question of why venomous snakes are not harmed by their own venom is that they are immune.) Typically vipers coil prior to striking. They vary considerably in size, shape, color pattern, and lifestyle. Many of the vipers are referred to as *pit-vipers* because they have thermal-sensitive "pits," or depressions, between their nostrils and eyes that are sensory organs. Pit-vipers occur from southern Canada to Argentina, as well as in the Old World. The familiar venomous snakes of North America – *rattlesnakes, copperheads, water moccasins* – are pit vipers, as are most of Ecuador's venomous snakes.

About 15 *viperid* species occur in Ecuador. The deadly FER-DE-LANCE (Plate 10) is abundant in lowland wet forest areas and along watercourses in drier areas. Most individuals are shorter than the maximum length of 2 m (6.5 ft). They are slender snakes with lance- or spear-shaped heads (hence the name, which means "iron spear"). *Palm pit-vipers*, such as the EYELASH PALM PIT-VIPER (Plate 10), are common arboreal snakes of lowland areas. There are several species, all small (as long as 1 m, 3 ft, but most are only half that long) with prehensile tails and large wide heads. Their color schemes vary extensively. BUSHMASTERS (Plate 10), the largest venomous snakes of the Neotropics, inhabit lowland wet forest areas on both sides of the Andes. They are the giants of the pit-vipers, slender, large-headed snakes reaching lengths of 2.5 to 3.6 m (8 to 12 ft), but in most regions are very rare.

The Family Elapidae contains what are regarded as the world's deadliest snakes, the Old World *cobras* and *mambas*. In the Western Hemisphere, the group is represented by the *coral snakes* – small, slender snakes, usually quite gaily attired in bands of red, yellow and black, and, unfortunately, possessed of a very powerful neurotoxic venom. About 20 species, such as LANGSDORFF'S CORAL SNAKE (Plate 9), occur in Ecuador. Coral snakes rarely grow longer than a meter (3 ft). In addition to the coral snakes, *elapids* are also represented in Ecuador by a single species of *sea snake*. The yellow and black PELAGIC SEA SNAKE (Plate 9) is the only New World species of a group of highly venomous marine snakes, most of which inhabit coastal waters around Australia and Southeast Asia. The Pelagic Sea Snake is the world's only snake that occurs in open ocean far from land. Fortunately, all elapids in Ecuador, although having highly toxic venom, are small and have small fangs, making it difficult for them to bite humans effectively.

The Family Boidae, members of which kill by constriction, encompasses about 65 species that are distributed throughout the world's tropical and subtropical regions. They include the Old World pythons and the New World's boas and Anaconda, the pythons and Anaconda being the world's largest snakes. Six boa species are found in Ecuador. One of them, the BOA CONSTRICTOR (Plate 9), occurs over a wide range of habitat types, wet and dry, from sea level up to about 1000 m (3300 ft). This boa reaches lengths of about 5 m (16 ft), but typical specimens are only 1.5 to 2.5 m (5 to 8 ft) long. They have shiny, smooth scales and a back pattern of dark, squarish shapes that provides good camouflage against an array of backgrounds. The Anaconda is probably the largest snake on Earth, known to grow to at least 10 m (33 ft). In general body form it is similar to the Boa Constrictor, but has alternating brown blotches over a tan ground color. The other boas in Ecuador, such as the AMAZON TREE BOA and RAINBOW BOA (Plate 9) are more slender and much smaller, reaching less than 2 m (6.5 ft) in length.

Natural History

Ecology and Behavior

FER-DE-LANCE as adults are terrestrial, but partially arboreal as juveniles. They inhabit moist forests but also some drier areas. They eat birds and mammals such as opossums. Palm pit-vipers at night move through trees and bushes, along vines and twigs, searching for treefrogs, lizards, and birds to eat. Like other pit-vipers (and some other snakes), they can sense the heat radiated by prey animals, which assists their foraging. Searching by heat detection probably works for both warm-blooded prey (birds, mammals) and for cold-blooded (lizards, frogs), as long as the prey is at a higher temperature than its surroundings. BUSHMASTERS are terrestrial snakes that feed chiefly on mammals. They are mainly nocturnal and therefore, even where fairly common, are infrequently seen. In a recent Costa Rican study during which these snakes could be followed closely because they were affixed with radio transmitters, biologists learned that the Bushmaster diet consisted almost entirely of forest rats (such as the *bamboo rat* in Plate 83), rather large rodents. Typically, a Bushmaster would lie in wait for days or even weeks at the same spot on the ground, usually beneath a tree; after capturing a rat, the snake moved to a new site. This lazy, low-energy lifestyle has its advantages; the same study calculated that a single snake would need to eat only about six rats per year to survive!

Coral snakes are usually secretive and difficult to study; consequently relatively little is known about their ecology and behavior in the wild. They apparently forage by crawling along slowly on the ground, intermittently poking their heads into the leaf litter. They eat lizards, amphibians including caecilians (Plate 1), and small snakes, which they kill with their powerful venom. They are often found under rocks and logs, and many probably burrow into the soil for protection, and while foraging. They can be day- or night-active. Sea snakes are entirely marine. The PELAGIC SEA SNAKE swims on the surface of the ocean, feeding on fish. They occasionally wash up on beaches, where they are nearly helpless (their flattened tails are not suitable for movement on land) and die quickly in the hot sun.

Coral snakes hold a special place in snake biology studies because a number of non-venomous or mildly venomous colubrid snakes (p. 72), as well as at least one caterpillar species, mimic the bright, striking coral snake color scheme – alternating bands of red, yellow (or white), and black. In Ecuador alone, at least a dozen species of colubrids imitate – to varying degrees – the color patterns of coral snakes (see Plate 8f for example). The function of the *mimicry* apparently is to take advantage of the quite proper respect many predatory animals show toward the lethal coral snakes. Ever since this idea was first proposed more than a hundred years ago, the main argument against it has been that it implied either that the predators had to be first bitten by a coral snake to learn of their toxicity and then survive to generalize the experience to all snakes that look like coral snakes, or that the predators were born with an innate fear of the coral snake color pattern. It has now been demonstrated experimentally that several bird predators on snakes (motmots, kiskadees, herons, and egrets) need not learn that a coral snake is dangerous by being bitten – they avoid these snakes instinctively from birth. Thus, many snakes have evolved as defensive mechanisms color schemes that mimic that of coral snakes. However, some biologists reject the mimicry hypothesis. They argue that the alternating color bands of the coral snake's body probably function as camouflage and not to warn predators away, and also that the snakes' mammalian predators lack color-vision and therefore could not make use of the patterns to avoid the mimics. Nonvenomous snakes also mimic some of the behavior of poisonous snakes, the most obvious example being that a good many snakes, when threatened, coil up and wiggle the tips of their tails, as do rattlesnakes and some other vipers.

All Ecuadorean boas are mainly nocturnal and arboreal, but they are sometimes active on the ground. The ANACONDA, however, is mostly aquatic, spending its time foraging in or very near large bodies of water or swamps. Boa diets include reptiles, birds, mammals, and, in fact, almost any animal small enough to eat. Prey, recognized by visual, chemical (smell), or heat senses, is seized with the teeth after a rapid, open-mouth lunge. As it strikes, a boa or Anaconda also coils around the prey, lifting it from the ground, and then constricts, squeezing the prey. The prey cannot breathe and suffocates. When the prey stops moving, the snake swallows it whole, starting always with the head.

Breeding

Details of the breeding in the wild of most tropical vipers are not well known. Many of them may follow the general system of North American rattlesnakes, which have been much studied. Females attract males when they are ready to mate by releasing *pheromones* (odor chemicals) into the air and also, through the skin of their sides and back, onto the ground. Males search for females. When one is located, the male accompanies and courts her for several days before mating occurs. Fighting between males for the same female is probably uncommon, because it is rare for two males to locate the same female at the same time. North American rattlers have distinct breeding periods, but many tropical vipers may breed at almost any time of year. Most snakes that lay eggs deposit the eggs in a suitable location and depart; the parents provide no care of the eggs or young. A few snakes guard their eggs.

Unlike the colubrids, most of the vipers give birth to live young. The FER-DE-LANCE has a reputation as a prolific breeder, females giving birth to between 20 and 70 young at a time. Each is about a third of a meter (1 ft) long at birth, fully-fanged with active poison glands, and dangerous. Palm pit-vipers have clutches of up to 20 live young, and the BUSHMASTER, the only egg-laying viperid of the New World, usually produces small clutches of 10 or fewer eggs.

Coral snakes lay eggs, up to 10 per clutch. Most sea snakes give birth to live young in the water. All boas in Ecuador, and the ANACONDA, give birth to live young. Litters vary between 12 and 60.

Notes

All of the venomous snakes discussed in this section, if encountered, should be given a wide berth. Watch them only from a distance. Very few visitors to the tropics, even those that spend their days tramping through forests, are bitten by poisonous snakes. The biology of snake bites is an active area of study. Remember that this venom-delivery system is a highly evolved prey-capture strategy, and only secondarily a defensive mechanism. Venom is apparently energetically costly to produce, and venomous snakes can bite without injecting any venom. They can also vary the amount of venom injected – even if bitten, one does not necessarily receive a fatal dose. Within the same species, the toxicity of a snake's venom can vary geographically, seasonally, and from individual to individual.

The small, pretty coral snakes are rarely seen by people because of their secretive habits. Most are usually quite docile. However, if threatened, some give a scary defensive display: they erratically snap their body back and forth, swing their head from side to side with the mouth open, and bite any object that is contacted. Although their mouths and fangs are small, their venom is very powerful. Be advised not to adhere to rules learned for hiking or camping in North America about how to distinguish, based on coloring, coral snakes from non-venomous mimic snakes; the snakes in South America don't follow the rules. To be safe, keep your distance from all coral-snake-like serpents. Sea snakes are also normally not aggressive, but some are known during breeding periods to attack divers. Owing to their highly toxic venom, they should be avoided, especially if washed up on shore.

Boa personalities appear to vary, but some individuals are notoriously aggressive. Boas may hiss loudly at people, draw their head back with mouth open in a threat posture, and bite. They have large sharp teeth that can cause deep puncture wounds. Therefore, even though boas present no real threat to most people, keeping a respectful distance is advised.

Status

None of Ecuador's vipers or coral snakes is officially considered threatened by people (for once, we can even say that it's the other way around!). Some of the boas may be threatened in some areas of the country by habitat destruction and by capture for the pet trade; otherwise boas seem to do well living near people and are still common in many parts of Ecuador and the rest of the American tropics.

Profiles

Boa Constrictor, *Boa constrictor*, Plate 9a
Amazon Tree Boa, *Corallus hortulanus*, Plate 9b
Rainbow Boa, *Epicrates cenchria*, Plate 9c
Anaconda, *Eunectes murinus*, Plate 9d
Pelagic Sea Snake, *Pelamis platurus*, Plate 9e
Langsdorff's Coral Snake, *Micrurus langsdorffi*, Plate 9f
Fer-de-Lance, *Bothrops atrox*, Plate 10a
Speckled Forest Pit-viper, *Bothriopsis taeniata*, Plate 10b
Eyelash Palm Pit-viper, *Bothriechis schlegelii*, Plate 10c
Bushmaster, *Lachesis muta*, Plate 10d

5. Geckos

Geckos are most interesting organisms because, of their own volition, they have become "house lizards" – probably the only self-domesticated reptile. The family, Gekkonidae, is spread throughout tropical and subtropical areas of the world, 870 species strong. In many regions, geckos have invaded houses and buildings, becoming ubiquitous adornments of walls and ceilings. Ignored by residents, they move around dwellings chiefly at night, munching insects. To first-time visitors from northern climes, however, the way these harmless lizards always seem to position themselves on ceilings directly above one's sleeping area can be a bit disconcerting. About 15 species occur in mainland Ecuador.

Ecuadorean geckos are fairly small lizards, usually gray or brown, with large eyes. They have thin, soft skin, covered usually with small, granular scales that produce a slightly lumpy appearance, and big fingers and toes with well developed claws and broad, specialized pads that allow them to cling to vertical surfaces and even upside-down on ceilings. The way geckos manage these feats has engendered a fair amount of scientific detective work. Various forces have been implicated in explaining the gecko's anti-gravity performance, from the ability of their claws to dig into tiny irregularities on man-made surfaces, to their large toes acting as suction cups, to an adhesive quality of friction. The real explanation appears to lie in the series of minuscule hair-like structures on the bottoms of the finger and toe pads, which provide attachment to walls and ceilings by something akin to surface tension – the same property that allows some insects to walk on water.

Adult geckos mostly report in at only 5 to 10 cm (2 to 4 in) in length, tail excluded; tails can double the length. Because lizard tails frequently break off and regenerate (p. 85), their length varies tremendously; gecko tails are particularly fragile. Lizards, therefore, are properly measured from the tip of their snouts to their vent, the urogenital opening on their bellies, usually located somewhere near to where their rear legs join their bodies. The geckos' 5 to 10 cm length, therefore, is their range of "SVLs," or *snout–vent lengths*.

Natural History

Ecology and Behavior

Although most lizards are active during the day and inactive at night, many gecko species, such as the TURNIPTAIL GECKO (Plate 10) are nocturnal. In natural settings, they are primarily ground dwellers, but, as their behavior in buildings suggests, they are also excellent climbers. Geckos feed on arthropods, chiefly insects. In fact, it is their ravenous appetite for cockroaches and other insect undesirables that render them welcome house guests in many parts of the world. Perhaps the only "negative" associated with house geckos is that, unlike the great majority of lizards, which keep quiet, geckos at night are avid little chirpers and squeakers. They communicate with each other with loud calls – surprisingly loud for such small animals. The various species sound different; the word "gecko" approximates the sound of calls from some Asian species.

Geckos are *sit-and-wait* predators; instead of wasting energy actively searching for prey that is usually highly alert and able to flee, they sit still for long periods, waiting for unsuspecting insects to venture a bit too near, then lunge, grab, and swallow. Geckos rely chiefly on their *cryptic coloration* and their ability to flee rapidly for escape from predators, which include snakes during the day and snakes, owls, and bats at night. When cornered, geckos give threat displays; when seized, they give loud calls to distract predators, and bite. Should the gecko be seized by its tail, it breaks off as a last resort, allowing the gecko time to escape, albeit tail-less; although it causes considerable stress to the animal, the tail often regenerates.

Breeding

Almost all geckos are egg-layers. Mating occurs after a round of courtship, which involves a male displaying to a female by waving his tail around, followed by some mutual nosing and nibbling. Clutches usually contain only one to a few eggs, but a female may lay several clutches per year. There is no parental care – after eggs are deposited, they and the tiny geckos that hatch from them are on their own.

Notes

The world's smallest reptile, at 4 cm (1.5 in) long, is a gecko, the CARIBBEAN DWARF GECKO. As reptile biologists like to say, it is shorter than its name.

Status

More than 25 gecko species are listed by conservation organizations as rare, vulnerable, threatened, or endangered, but they are almost all restricted to the Old World. The MONITO GECKO, found only on Monito Island, off Puerto Rico, is endangered. None of Ecuador's geckos is officially considered threatened, but most are very poorly known.

Profiles

Collared Gecko, *Gonatodes concinnatus*, Plate 10e
Turniptail Gecko, *Thecadactylus rapicauda*, Plate 10f
Amazon Dwarf Gecko, *Pseudogonatodes guianensis*, Plate 11a

6. Iguanas and Relatives

The Iguanidae is a large category of lizards that is considered a single family by some experts but divided into several separate families by others. For convenience, we will consider all of the 750 species in this group as *iguanoids*. They are found only in the New World, with more than 65 in Ecuador. Most of the lizards commonly encountered by ecotravellers or that are on their viewing wish-lists, are members of this group. It includes the very abundant *anolis lizards*, the color-fully-named JESUS CHRIST LIZARD (or BASILISK; Plate 11), and the spectacular, Godzilla-like GREEN IGUANA (Plate 11).

The iguanoids are a rich and varied group of diverse habits and habitats. Many in the family are brightly colored and have adornments such as crests, spines, or throat fans. They range in size from tiny anolis lizards, or *anoles* (Plates 11, 12), only a few centimeters in total length and a few grams in weight, to Green Iguanas, which are up to 2 m (6.5 ft) long. Basilisks (Plate 11), brown lizards with prominent head crests, range up to a meter (3 ft) in length and more than half a kg (1 lb) in weight (most of the length in iguanoid lizards resides in the long, thin tail; hence the paradoxically low weight for such a long animal). *Dwarf iguanas* (Plate 12) are a jumbled group of small to moderate-sized iguanoids; the 35 or so species in Ecuador range from about 7 to 15 cm (3 to 6 in), excluding the tail. Scales on their backs are often overlapping and pointed, yielding a bristly appearance. Some species of small iguanoids (especially anoles) are very common in natural areas in Ecuador and also around human habitations.

Natural History

Ecology and Behavior

You can't mistake the GREEN IGUANA; it's the large one resembling a dragon sitting in the tree near the river. They are common inhabitants of many Neotropical rainforests, in moist areas at low to middle elevations. They are often common in town squares and city parks along the coast. Considered semi-arboreal, they spend most of their time in trees, usually along waterways. They don't move much, and when they do it's often in slow-motion (but they can move very quickly when surprised or threatened). They are herbivores as adults, eating mainly leaves and twigs and, more occasionally, fruit; insects are favorites of youngsters. When threatened, an iguana sitting on a branch out over a river will drop from its perch into the water, making its escape underwater; iguanas are good swimmers. During their breeding season, males establish and defend mating territories on which live one to four females.

BASILISKS are medium to large, active lizards commonly found along watercourses in lowland areas. Often they are very abundant – one study in Central America estimated their numbers to be more than 500 per hectare (200 per acre), although abundance can vary greatly from one site to another. They are semi-arboreal and omnivorous, eating a variety of invertebrate and vertebrate animals (especially hatchling lizards), some flowers, and a good deal of fruit. The name "Jesus Christ lizard" refers to their ability to run over the surface of ponds or streams, really skipping along, for distances up to 20 m (60 ft) or more. They do it in an upright posture, on their rear legs, further inviting the divine comparison. The trick is one of fluid dynamics: some of the force to support the lizard comes from resistance of the water when the large rear feet are slapped onto the surface; the rest of the upward force stems from the compression of the water that occurs as the lizard's feet move slightly downwards into the water (their feet move so rapidly up and down that they are actually pulled from below the surface before the water can close over them). Juveniles are better at water-running than are adults, which, when too heavy to be supported on the surface, escape predation by diving in and swimming underwater.

Anoles are small, diurnal, often arboreal lizards. Many species are represented in Ecuador and many are frequently encountered; others, such as ones that live in the high canopy, are rarely seen. Some are ground dwellers, and others spend most of their time on tree trunks perched head toward the ground, visually searching for insect prey. Many sleep at night on leaves of low vegetation. Anoles are known especially for their territorial behavior. Males defend territories on which one to three females may live. In some species males with territories spend up to half of each day defending their territories from males looking to establish new territories. The defender will roam his territory, perhaps 30 sq m (325 sq ft), occasionally giving territorial advertisements – repeatedly displaying his extended throat sac, or *dewlap*, and performing *push-ups*, bobbing his head and body up and down. Trespassers that do not exit the territory are chased and even bitten. Anoles are chiefly *sit-and-wait* predators on insects and other small invertebrates. Anoles themselves, small and presumably tasty, are frequent prey for many birds (motmots, trogons, and others) and snakes.

Most of the various dwarf iguana species in the wild are diurnal, and ground-dwelling or semi-arboreal, but around buildings they are climbers of walls and fences. Sit-and-wait predators, they eat mainly insects, but some also consume plant materials. They are hunted by several species of hawks and kites, and around human habitations domestic cats take their toll. The THORNYTAIL CANOPY IGUANA (Plate 12) apparently lives only in high treetops, in eastern lowland rainforest.

Breeding

Among GREEN IGUANAS, breeding usually occurs during the early part of the dry season. These large lizards lay clutches that average about 40 eggs. They are laid in burrows that are 1 to 2 m (3 to 6.5 ft) long, dug by the females. After laying her clutch, a female iguana fills the burrow with dirt, giving the site a final packing down with her nose. It has been said that a female digging her nest burrow probably engages in the most vigorous activity performed by these sluggish reptiles.

Female BASILISKS produce clutches of two to 18 eggs several times each year. Smaller, younger females, have fewer eggs per clutch. Eggs hatch in about 3 months. Hatchling lizards, weighing only 2 g, are wholly on their own; in one study, only about 15% of them survived the first few months of life. Anoles and dwarf iguanas are also egg-layers, females depositing small clutches (four to 10 eggs) in secluded moist places in the forest. They breed throughout the year. Anoles may produce eggs every few weeks.

Notes

Even the largest iguanoids are not dangerous. They are not poisonous, and they will not bite unless given no other choice. Large iguanas are hunted by local people for invitation to the dinner table – they definitely do NOT taste just like chicken! Try the meat if it is offered; but it's an acquired taste. The THORNYTAIL CANOPY IGUANA is thought to be terribly poisonous by some indigenous Amazonians, who believe that its spiny tail can inflict a fatal sting; the tail is actually harmless.

Via interactions between the external environment and their nervous and hormonal systems, many iguanoids have the novel ability to change their body color. Such color changes may be adaptations that allow them to be more *cryptic*, to blend into their surroundings, and hence, to be less detectable to and safer from predators. Also, alterations in color through the day may aid in temperature regulation; lizards must obtain their body heat from the sun, and darker colors absorb more heat. The feat is accomplished by moving pigment granules within individual skin cells either to a central clump (causing that color to diminish) or spreading them evenly about the cell (enhancing the color). It is now thought that the stimulus to change colors arises with the physiology of the animal rather than with the color of its surroundings.

Status

None of Ecuador's mainland iguanoids is currently considered threatened. Because GREEN IGUANAS are hunted for meat, they are scarce in some localities. All lizards in the Galápagos Islands are strictly protected by Ecuadorean law.

Profiles

Green Iguana, *Iguana iguana*, Plate 11b
Basilisk, *Basiliscus basiliscus*, Plate 11c
Roof Anole, *Anolis bitectus*, Plate 11d
Goldenscale Anole, *Anolis chrysolepis scypheus*, Plate 11e
Orton's Anole, *Anolis ortonii*, Plate 11f
Prince Anole, *Anolis princeps*, Plate 12a
Amazon Forest Anole, *Anolis trachyderma,* Plate 12b
Guichenot's Dwarf Iguana, *Enyaliodes laticeps*, Plate 12c
Red-eyed Dwarf Iguana, *Enyaliodes microlepis*, Plate 12d
Iridescent Dwarf Iguana, *Ophryoessoides iridescens,* Plate 12e
Thornytail Canopy Iguana, *Uracentron flaviceps*, Plate 12f
Marine Iguana, *Amblyrhynchus cristatus*, Plate 89b
Galápagos Land Iguana, *Conolophus subcristatus*, Plate 89c
Galápagos Lava Lizard, *Tropidurus albemarlensis*, Plate 89d

7. Skinks and Whiptails

The *skinks* are a large family (Scincidae, with about 1100 species) of small and medium-sized lizards with a worldwide distribution. Skinks are easily recognized because they look different from other lizards, being slim-bodied with relatively short limbs, and having smooth, shiny scales that produce a mirrored or satiny look. Many skinks are in the 5 to 9 cm (2 to 4 in) long range, not including the tail, which can easily double an adult's length. The COMMON NEOTROPICAL SKINK (Plate 13), profiled here, is the only species of skink found in Ecuador.

Whiptails, Family Teiidae, are a New World group of about 245 species, distributed throughout the Americas. Most are tropical residents, inhabiting most areas below 1500 m (5000 ft) in elevation. About 50 species occur in Ecuador. The larger species, such as the BLACK TEGU (Plate 13), and PETER'S COMMON AMEIVA (Plate 13) are diurnal sun-baskers, and are often quite abundant and conspicuous along trails, roads, beaches, and in forest clearings. Known for their alert behavior and fast movements, they are often easily spotted but difficult to approach closely. The Black Tegu, found in the eastern lowlands, can reach a length of almost a meter (3 ft). If you surprise one along a trail, it can startle you by making a lot of noise as it crashes through the vegetation to escape. All whiptails have slender bodies, angular, pointed heads and, as their name implies, long, slender, whip-like tails (usually much longer than the body). The scales of the larger conspicuous species are very small, giving them a velvety or shiny appearance. Some whiptails are striped, others are striped and spotted, or irregularly blotched.

There are many smaller species of whiptails in Ecuador, 10 to 15 cm (4 to 6 in) in length, including tail, called *ground teiids*. You find them mostly in rainforest leaf-litter, but they can be secretive and hard to see. Of this group, the BROWN GROUND TEIID (Plate 13) is profiled here; many other small, dull gray to brown species are very similar. The SPINY STREAM TEIID (Plate 13) is a small stream-dwelling specialist that resembles a tiny crocodile, with scales on the upper body formed into curved spines.

Natural History

Ecology and Behavior

Many skinks are found in moist ground habitats such as sites near streams and springs or under wet leaf litter. A few species are arboreal, and some are burrowers. Skink locomotion is surprising: they use their limbs to walk but when the need arises for speed, they move around mainly by making rapid wriggling movements with their bodies, snake-fashion, with little leg assistance. Through evolutionary change, in fact, some species have lost limbs entirely, all movement being snake-fashion. Skinks are day-active lizards, and in the tropics they move around most in the morning hours; they spend the heat of midday in sheltered, insulated hiding places, such as deep beneath the leaf litter. Some skinks are sit-and-wait foragers, whereas others seek their food actively. They consume many kinds of insects, which they grab, crush with their jaws or beat against the ground, then swallow whole. Predators on Ecuadorean skinks include snakes, larger lizards, birds, and mammals such as coati, armadillo, and opossum. Skinks generally are not seen unless searched for. Most species are quite secretive, spending most of their time hidden under rocks, vegetation, or leaf litter. The single species found in Ecuador, diurnal and terrestrial, is most common in semi-open forests.

The larger, sun-basking whiptails actively search for their food, which can include just about any animal small enough to eat. Typically they forage by moving slowly along the ground, poking their nose into the leaf litter and under sticks and rocks and using their sense of smell to locate prey. Although most are terrestrial, many also climb into lower vegetation to hunt. Whiptails have a characteristic gait, moving jerkily forward while rapidly turning their head from side to side. The small ground teiids inhabit leaf litter in more shaded areas and forage for invertebrate prey such as insects; most prefer old growth forest and shun more disturbed areas. The SPINY STREAM TEIID has a lifestyle more like a temperate zone salamander than of a typical lizard, living along shaded forest streams in mud under wet logs, rocks, and among water-soaked leaf litter. The spiny scales possessed by this odd lizard apparently function to hold mud to the skin, which probably serves as both camouflage and as protection from drying out.

Breeding

Skinks are either egg-layers or live-bearers. The COMMON NEOTROPICAL SKINK gives birth to three to five live young, the eggs protected within the mother's body throughout development. They breed sporadically all year. Ecuadorean whiptails may breed throughout the year. They are egg-layers, females producing small clutches that average three to five eggs; individuals produce two or more clutches per year. Among the whiptails, a number of species exhibit what for vertebrate animals is an odd method of reproduction, one that is difficult for us to imagine. All individuals in these species are female; not a male among them. Yet they breed merrily away, by *parthenogenesis*. Females lay unfertilized eggs, which all develop as females that, barring mutations, are all genetically identical to mom. (A few species of fish and many insects also reproduce this way.) Some argue that this *asexual* breeding indicates that the males in the population are a drain on resources and thus a luxury. It is likely that parthenogenetic species arise when individuals of two different but closely-related, sexually reproducing, "parent" species mate and, instead of having hybrid young that are sterile (a usual result, as when horses and donkeys mate to produce sterile mules), have young whose eggs can produce viable females.

Notes

Many lizards, including the skinks, whiptails, and geckos, have a drastic predator escape mechanism: they detach a large chunk of their bodies, leaving it behind for the predator to attack and eat while they make their escape. The process is known as *tail autotomy* – "self removal." Owing to some special anatomical features of the tail vertebrae, the tail is only tenuously attached to the rest of the body; when the animal is grasped forcefully by its tail, the tail breaks off readily. The shed tail then wriggles vigorously for a while, diverting a predator's attention for the instant it takes the skink or whiptail to find shelter. A new tail can grow to replace the lost one, but this loss of a major body part is evidently a major stress on the lizard; tail-deprived individuals often become inactive and sometimes die.

Is autotomy successful as a lifesaving tactic? Some snakes that were caught and dissected had nothing but skinks in their stomachs – not whole bodies, just tails! Also, a very common finding when a field biologist surveys any population of small lizards (catching as many as possible in a given area to count and examine them) is that a hefty percentage, often 50% or more, have regenerating tails; this indicates that tail autotomy is common and successful in preventing predation.

Status

Ecuador's skink and whiptails, as far as is known, are secure; none is presently considered threatened. As is the case for many reptiles and amphibians, however, many species have not been sufficiently monitored to ascertain the true health of populations. Many skinks of Australia and New Zealand regularly appear on lists of vulnerable and threatened animals and several Caribbean skinks and whiptails are endangered. In the USA, Florida's SAND and BLUETAIL MOLE SKINKS (USA ESA listed) and the ORANGE-THROATED WHIPTAIL are considered vulnerable or threatened species.

Profiles

Common Neotropical Skink, *Mabuya mabouya*, Plate 13a
Peter's Common Ameiva, *Ameiva ameiva petersi*, Plate 13b
Emerald-striped Teiid, *Kentropyx pelviceps*, Plate 13c
Black Tegu, *Tupinambis teguixin*, Plate 13d
Spiny Stream Teiid, *Echinosaura horrida*, Plate 13e
Brown Ground Teiid, *Alopoglossus festae*, Plate 13f

Environmental Close-up 2:
Endemism and High Species Diversity: Why Ecuador?

An organism is endemic to a place when it is found only in that place. But the size or type of place referred to is variable: a given species of frog, say, may be endemic to the Western Hemisphere, to a single continent such as South America, to a small mountainous region of Ecuador, or to a speck of an island off Ecuador's coast.

A species' history dictates its present distribution. When it's confined to a certain or small area, the reason is that: (1) there are one or more barriers to further spread (an ocean, a mountain range, a thousand kilometers of tropical rainforest in the way), (2) the species evolved only recently and has not yet had time to spread, or (3) the species evolved long ago, spread long ago, and now has become extinct over all but a remnant part of its prior range. A history of isolation also matters: the longer animals and plants are isolated from their close relatives, the more time they have to evolve by themselves and to change into new, different, and unique groups. The best examples are on islands. Some islands once were attached to mainland areas but continental drift and/or changing sea levels led to their isolation in the middle of the ocean; other islands arose suddenly via volcanic activity beneath the seas. Take the island of Madagascar. Once attached to Africa and India, the organisms stranded on its shores when it became an island had probably 100 million years in isolation to develop into the highly endemic fauna and flora we see today. It's thought that about 80% of the island's plants and animals are endemic – half the bird species, about 800 butterflies, 8000 flowering plants, and essentially all the mammals and reptiles. Most of the world's species of lemurs – small, primitive but cute primates – occur only on Madagascar, and an entire nature tourism industry has been built there around the idea of endemism: if you want to see wild lemurs, you must go there. Other examples of islands with high concentrations of endemic animals abound: Indonesia, where about 15% of the world's bird species occur, a quarter of them endemic; Papua New Guinea, where half the birds are endemic; the Philippines, where half the mammals are endemic; and the Galápagos Islands, where 42% of the resident bird species occur nowhere else in the world.

Recent biological surveys of mainland Ecuador show that this country supports a surprising number of species (some of which are endemic but most of which are not). Ecuador is, in fact, considered one of 10 or so "mega-diversity" countries in the world. Despite its small size, it has more species of animals and plants than some other countries 30 times larger (Table 1, below). Ecuador's high biodiversity is due to several factors:

(1) Virtually all groups of animals and plants (such as lizards, insects, trees and birds) show a pattern of species number related to latitude. The higher latitudes (the north and south poles are at 90° latitude and the equator is at 0° latitude) have few species and as you look at lower and lower latitudes toward the equator the number of species increases. This pattern is called a *latitudinal gradient in species diversity* and is likely caused by an increasing availability of sunlight energy (the energy plants use for photosynthesis, the production of glucose from carbon dioxide and water) as you move toward the equator. Ecuador is on the equator, where the world's greatest species diversity occurs.

(2) Due to Ecuador's *varied topography*, there are a multitude of habitat types, and some highly isolated habitats that act as "biological islands" (for example, inland highland areas surrounded by lower-lying regions – such as high-elevation forest habitats around the isolated volcano Sumaco or the separated mountain range of the Cutucú in southeastern Ecuador). These isolated areas support large numbers of endemic species, and the wide range of habitat types, especially at different altitudes, makes room for many species, endemic and non-endemic, to exist in a relatively small area.

(3) The Amazon area of Ecuador is part of the most species-rich area of the world. To understand the Amazon area's current species diversity, we need to look at its geological history. Over the last 100,000 years or so there have been ten-thousand-year cycles of drought and heavy rainfall. These cycles changed large parts of this immense forest region into grassland-savannah and back to forest over and over again. Because of the Andes Mountains and the shape of the continental coastline, rainfall across that Amazon Basin is not, and probably never has been, uniform. Even today, in the middle of a high rainfall part of the cycle, small pockets of forest with 3 to 4 m (10 to 13 ft) of annual rainfall can be surrounded by forest areas with less than a meter and a half (5 ft) of annual rainfall. During the most severe drought epochs, annual rainfall totals were probably cut by a third or more. Only the high rainfall forest pockets, perpetually wet, were able to maintain themselves against the inroads of fire that changed the drier forest areas to grasslands and savannah. The patches of cool and moist tree areas within a great sea of open grasslands became islands, or *forest refugia*, for the plants and animals adapted to forests. Isolated for tens of thousands of years, many of these populations of plants and animals changed (evolved) into different species and no longer were capable of breeding with members of their former species in other forest refuges. When the drought cycle shifted back to high rainfall, the plants in the forest islands began to expand and reclaim the grassland habitat. Eventually the expansion of these forests brought them again into contact with each other. At the zones of contact where the forests met, they once more formed a continuous forest habitat. The species formed during the period of isolation

Table 1. Number of species of selected animal groups in Ecuador (284,000 sq km, 109,000 sq miles, in area) and in the USA (9.4 million sq km, 3.6 million sq miles), the number of those that are endemic to Ecuador, and a comparison with the number of species worldwide and the number in the USA.

Group	Total no. of species in USA	Total no. of species in Ecuador	Number of species endemic to Ecuador (% endemic)	Approximate no. of species worldwide (% in Ecuador)
Mammals	428	324	25 (8%)	4629 (7%)
Birds	768	1559	37 (2%)	9040 (17%)
Reptiles	261	409	114 (28%)	7000 (6%)
Amphibians	194	460	138 (30%)	4600 (10%)
Butterflies	678	2200	200+ (9%)	24000 (9%)
Tiger Beetles	111	89	34 (38%)	2250 (4%)

could now spread and mix into a newly connected forest, thus greatly enriching the diversity of species. Scientists have been able to discern 15 to 20 Amazonian forest refuges formed at various times throughout the Pliocene and Pleistocene geological periods. The most persistent and largest forest island consistently was the area covering most of present-day eastern Ecuador – the Napo Refuge. Because it has been intact forest for hundreds of thousands of years, it has been a productive area in which new species could evolve and a stable area in which older and now endemic species could persist – yielding an accumulation of species that helps explain the high diversity in the region.

Chapter 7

BIRDS

- *Introduction*
- *General Characteristics and Classification of Birds*
- *Features of Tropical Birds*
- *Seeing Birds in Ecuador*
- *Family Profiles*
- *Environmental Close-Up 3: Frugivory: Animals That Eat Fruit and the Trees That Want Them To*

Introduction

By far the most common vertebrate animals you will see on a visit to just about anywhere at or above the water's surface in Ecuador are birds. Unlike many other terrestrial vertebrates, birds are most often active during the day, visually conspicuous and usually quite vocal as they pursue their daily activities. But why are birds so much more conspicuous than other vertebrates? The reason lies in the essential nature of birds: they fly. The ability to fly is one of nature's premier anti-predator escape mechanisms, and animals that can fly well are released from the danger of being stalked by a large proportion of the predators in an area. Most mortality from predators among tropical birds comes while they are eggs or helpless young in the nest. Once they reach adulthood, their mortality rate by predation falls to very low levels. By being able to escape most predation, they are released from much of the tyranny of natural selection that places a premium on camouflage, unobtrusiveness and shyness. Thus they can be both reasonably conspicuous in their behavior and also reasonably certain of daily survival. Most flightless land vertebrates, tied by gravity to moving in or over the ground or on plants, are easy prey unless they are quiet, concealed, and careful or, alternatively, very large or fierce; many smaller ones, in fact, have evolved special defense mechanisms, such as poisons or nocturnal behavior.

Not only are birds among the easiest animals to watch, but they are among the most beautiful. Experiences with Ecuador's birds will almost certainly provide some of your trip's most memorable naturalistic moments. Your first view of a flock of huge and noisy Blue-and-yellow Macaws flying over the forest tops in the Amazon or a mockingbird saucily sitting on your camera's telephoto lens in the Galápagos will be highlights you will want to share with everyone.

General Characteristics and Classification of Birds

Birds have one trait that they share with no other vertebrates – they have feathers. Feathers evidently evolved from reptilian scales, and they, together with most everything else in and on the bird body, serve to lighten the load and provide the power to make flight possible. The feathers provide an ultralight but durable protective covering. The hollow bones of the skeleton provide a light but sturdy framework to attach powerful flight muscles, especially on the breast. The teeth are replaced by an expanded part of the digestive tract, the gizzard, which along with the reduction and rearrangement of many internal organs makes the center of gravity more aerodynamically positioned. A four-chambered heart together with warm-bloodedness and a super-efficient lung system make possible an accelerated use of energy to sustain the physiologically expensive costs of flight. Finally, the forelimbs have evolved to become sublime wings with spoilers to overcome wing tip air turbulence, ailerons for maneuvering, and such a host of detailed adaptations for flight control that engineers at the Boeing Company can only marvel with envy.

Birds began evolving from reptiles during the Jurassic Period of the Mesozoic Era, perhaps 150 million years ago, and then there was an explosive development of new species during the last 50 million years or so. The development of flight is the key factor behind birds' evolution, their historical spread throughout the globe, and their current ecological success. Flight, as mentioned above, is a fantastic predator evasion technique, but it also permits birds to move over long distances in search of particular foods or habitats, and its development opened up for vertebrate exploration and exploitation an entirely new and vast theater of operations – the atmosphere.

At first glance, birds appear to be highly variable beasts, ranging in size from 135 kg (300 lb) ostriches to 4 kg (10 lb) eagles to 3 g (a tenth of an ounce) hummingbirds. However, when compared with other types of vertebrates, birds are remarkably standardized physically. The reason is that, whereas mammals or reptiles can be quite diverse in form and still function as mammals or reptiles (think how different in form are lizards, snakes, and turtles), if birds are going to fly, the physics of aerodynamics narrowly dictate which shape and form will most efficiently stay in the air. Thus all flying birds have a similar gestalt, or body plan. (The flying mammals, bats, also follow these dictates.) Only birds like ostriches that lost their ability to fly developed very unbird-like body shapes.

Bird classification is one of those areas of science that continually undergoes revision. Currently more than 9000 separate species are recognized worldwide, and they are placed in 2040 genera. These genera are grouped into 170 families, which in turn are grouped into 28 to 30 orders, depending on whose classification scheme you want to follow. The orders are roughly divided into two major groups, the perching (dickie bird) species such as robins, sparrows and jays (Passerines) and all the rest (Non-passerines), which includes everything from penguins, ducks and herons to parrots, kingfishers and hawks. For the purposes of this book we divide birds into various groups: those that are unrelated but occur together in broad habitat types; those that are similar in appearance and might be confused easily; and finally, those that are closely related (and thus often found in similar habitats and also often similar in appearance).

Features of Tropical Birds

The first thing to know about tropical birds is that they are exceedingly diverse. There are many more species of birds in the tropics than in temperate or Arctic regions. For instance, fewer than 700 bird species occur regularly in North America north of Mexico, and about 3300 species occur in the Neotropics (Central and South America). But nearly 1600 species are found in tiny Ecuador – almost half of the species in the Neotropics and close to 15% of all the species in the world!

Tropical birds, like their temperate zone brethren, eat insects, seeds, nectar, fruit and, for the predaceous species, meat. A big difference, however, is the degree of specialization in tropical species. In temperate areas fruit is such a temporary resource that few species can afford to make their living as confirmed *frugivores*, but in many tropical areas fruit is available throughout much of the year, so bird species have evolved bills, digestive systems and behavior that make them experts on finding and eating fruits. Similarly, species that eat insects (*insectivores*), seeds (*granivores*), flower nectar (*nectarivores*) and, to some degree, even the meat-eaters (*carnivores*), have high degrees of specialization.

Mating systems of birds are driven by a pattern of inequality between the sexes. Females generally have the most power to choose mates. Each male is thus left with the task of convincing these picky females that he and he alone is the most appropriate one to father her young. A male can scream this message with louder or prettier songs, longer and more colorful tail feathers, or a combination of sounds, colors and behavioral antics that increase his chances of convincing the female of his gene superiority.

Mating systems range from single territorial males with one female (*monogamy*) to one male having numerous female mates (*polygyny*) and even some cases of a female having numerous male mates (*polyandry*). Among tropcal birds, monogamy apparently is the most common form of mating, although we now know that a lot of extracurricular sneaking around goes on. Monogamous mating is perhaps made most obvious when the males sing on the boundaries of their territories to declare to all the world, but especially to other males of the same species, "Stay out. This is my home and you are not welcome to tarry here." Polygyny is less common but often made obvious by the many bizarre behaviors associated with this mating system. Among polygynous species, males often have to congregate, each strutting his gene superiority so that a female can compare them side by side and make her choice – a beauty contest. This type of congregated male courting is called a *lec* (often spelled *lek*, the original Swedish form). Females in this type of society are usually single working mothers because the father, after mating, has no further contact with his mate or his offspring. Polyandry is the rarest type of mating system, and it is practiced primarily by only two groups of birds in Ecuador, the tinamous and the jacanas. In both cases males guard nests and females dump eggs in each of several males' nests after mating with them.

Breeding seasons in the tropics tend to be longer than in temperate areas but are usually closely tied to the wet season and the abundance of food associated with it, especially heavy concentrations of insect life and ripening fruit. In Ecuador, birds in the tropical dry forests of the southern coast breed primarily from January to March. On the northern coast they breed from November to April. In the mountains they breed from June to September. In the Amazon the breeding season is more ambiguous, with some species breeding almost every month of the year. One notable aspect of bird breeding in the tropics that has long puzzled biologists is that clutches of the small land birds (Passerines) are usually small, most species typically laying only two eggs per nest. Similar birds that breed in temperate zone areas usually have clutches of three to five eggs. Possible explanations are that: (1) small broods attract fewer nest predators; (2) because such a high percentage of nests in the tropics are destroyed by predators, it is not worth putting too much energy and effort into any one nest; and (3) with the increased hours of daylight during the summer breeding season in northern areas, temperate zone birds have more time each day to gather enough food for extra nestlings.

Finally, tropical birds include some of the most gorgeously attired birds in the world. Many have bright, flashy colors and vivid plumage patterns, with some of Ecuador's parrots, toucans, trogons, cotingas, and tanagers, claiming top honors. Why so many tropical birds possess highly colored plumages is unknown, but may be at least partially explained by the presence of a large number of species in which males are under natural selection pressures by female mating choices to have gaudy plumage. Also, although people take more notice of birds with bright, striking plumage colors and patterns, we should point out that, actually, most species in the tropics are dull-colored and visually unremarkable.

Seeing Birds in Ecuador

We chose for illustration and profiling below 322 species that are among Ecuador's most frequently seen birds. The best way to spot these birds is to follow three easy steps:

(1) Look for them at the correct time. You can see birds at any time of the day, but your best chance of seeing them is when they are most active and singing frequently, during early morning and late afternoon. Some species of owls, potoos and nightjars are strictly nocturnal, and the best way to see them is to follow their calls at night and find them in the beam of your flashlight.

(2) Be quiet as you walk along trails or roads, and stop periodically to look around carefully. Not all birds are noisy, and some, even brightly colored ones, can be quite inconspicuous when they are directly above you in the forest canopy. Trogons, for instance, beautiful medium-sized birds with green backs and bright red or yellow bellies, are notoriously difficult to see among branches and leaves. Sometimes sitting or standing quietly, especially along a stream, is the best way to see otherwise shy denizens.

(3) BRING BINOCULARS on your trip. You would be surprised at the number of people who visit tropical areas with the purpose of viewing wildlife and don't bother to bring binoculars. They need not be an expensive pair, but binoculars are essential to bird viewing. If you become excited about wildlife in the middle of your trip and have no binoculars, many of the eco-lodges rent them out by the day.

A surprise to many people during their first trip to a tropical habitat like rainforest is that they do not immediately see or hear hordes of birds upon entering a trail. During large portions of the day, in fact, the forest is mainly quiet, with few birds noticeably active. The birds are there, but many are inconspicuous – small brownish birds near to the ground, and greenish, brownish, or grayish birds in the canopy. A frequent, at first discombobulating experience, is that you will be walking along a trail, seeing few birds, and then, suddenly, a *mixed species foraging flock* with up to 20 or more species swooshes into view, filling the trees around you at all levels – some hopping along the ground, some moving through the brush, some clinging to tree trunks, others in the canopy – more birds than you can easily count or identify – and then, just as suddenly, the flock is gone, moved on in its meandering path through the forest. If the trail system is extensive, sometimes you can move quietly ahead of the flock and let it pass by you again and again. This works especially well for low-moving flocks of antbirds, woodcreepers and flycatchers. High-moving flocks, with birds such as tanagers and cotingas, are much harder to follow and are often best seen from canopy towers built at several jungle lodges throughout the country.

It would be a shame to leave Ecuador without seeing at least some of its spectacular birds, such as macaws, toucans, trogons, and tanagers. If you have trouble locating such birds, be sure and let people around you know of your interest – tourguides, resort employees, park personnel. In Ecuador everyone involved in the tourist industry wants to share the country's richness of natural beauty, and they can either tell you the best places to go for particular birds or send you to someone who knows.

Family Profiles

1. Pelican Allies and Flamingoes

Along Ecuador's rich coasts, as along coasts almost everywhere, *seabirds*, many of them conspicuously large and abundant, reign as the dominant vertebrate animals of the land, air, and water's surface. In Ecuador the pelicans and their relatives are the most conspicuous of these seabirds. Some also penetrate inland even into the Amazon. Many Ecuadorean seabirds commonly seen by visitors from northern temperate areas are the same species or very similar to species found back home. Some, however, are members of groups restricted to the tropics. As a group, seabirds are incredibly successful animals, present often at breeding and roosting colonies in enormous numbers. Their success is largely owed to their incredibly rich food resources – the fish and invertebrate animals (crabs, mollusks, insects, jellyfish) produced in the sea and on beaches and mudflats. The dark side of this abundance of food is that during El Niño years, when the warm but nutrient-poor tropical currents displace the cold nutrient-rich currents, severely depleting food supplies, it is the seabirds that suffer most drastically; some species, in fact, suffer up to 80% mortality rates during these periods.

Five of the birds treated here are members of the Order Pelecaniformes: *Boobies*, in the Family Sulidae (nine species worldwide, five in Ecuador), are large seabirds known for their sprawling breeding colonies on offshore islands and for plunging into the ocean from heights to pursue fish. Boobies have tapered bodies, long, pointed wings, long tails, long, pointed bills, and often, brightly colored feet. The BLUE-FOOTED BOOBY (Plate 14) is the most common species of booby seen from the coast. It and two other species of boobies nest on the Galápagos, where they are more easily seen (see Plate 91). *Frigatebirds*, of the Family

Fregatidae (five species with mainly tropical distributions; two off Ecuadorean shores), are very large soaring birds, mostly black, with long, narrow and pointed wings that span up to 2 m (6 ft) or more, and a long, forked, tail. Males have red throat pouches that they inflate, balloon-like, during courtship displays. Two species occur off the coast of Ecuador, but by far the most abundant is the MAG-NIFICENT FRIGATEBIRD (Plate 14), which you will see flying over every fishing boat and beach area in the country. *Pelicans*, Family Pelecanidae (eight species worldwide, two in Ecuador), are large-headed and heavy-bodied seabirds, and, with their big, saggy throat pouches, are perhaps among the most recognizable of coastal seabirds. The most common species is the BROWN PELICAN (Plate 14). Although usually you will see flocks of pelicans flying low over the water in a long line just off the beach, at bluffs along the beach they often soar to great heights on updrafts. The NEOTROPIC CORMORANT (Plate 14) is a medium-sized bird, usually black, with short legs, long tail, and longish bill with a hooked tip. It is in the family Phalacrocoracidae (28 species worldwide, two in Ecuador). The ANHINGA (Plate 14) of the family Anhingidae (four species worldwide, one in Ecuador) is similar to cormorants, with males all blackish and females and immatures with buffy heads and necks. Their bills, however, are long and thin with a sharp point. They have long tails and very long, thin necks, and when they occasionally soar to great heights with tail and wings spread, they resemble a soaring hawk or eagle with a long neck. The species occurs both in coastal mangroves and in the Oriente.

The final species in this section, the CHILEAN FLAMINGO (Plate 14) of the family Phoenicopteridae (five species worldwide, two in Ecuador), is variously placed in its own order Phoenicopteriformes or placed in with the ducks and geese in the order Anseriformes. It nests on saline lakes of the Peruvian, Chilean and Bolivian Andes above 4000 m (13, 000 ft) elevation and in the lowlands of extreme southern South America. During the Austral (southern hemisphere) winter, June through September, it migrates to the coast, and several hundred individuals reach the south coast of Ecuador every year, especially in the salt lakes near the city of Salinas. The GREATER FLAMINGO (Plate 92) also occurs in Ecuador but only as a resident of the Galápagos Islands (p. 237).

Natural History

Ecology and Behavior

All of these seabirds except the flamingo feed mainly on fish, and they have developed a variety of ways to catch them. Boobies, which also eat squid, plunge dive from 15 m (50 ft) or more above the ocean surface to catch fish in their serrate-edged bills. Unlike almost all other birds, boobies do not have holes or nostrils at the base of the upper bill for breathing. The holes are closed over to keep seawater from rushing into their lungs as they dive deep into the ocean. They have to breath through their mouths. Frigatebirds are often abundant around fishing boats, where they use their superior maneuverability in the air to chase other, smaller birds like terns and boobies, forcing them to drop their freshly caught fish. A frigatebird then swoops down to catch its ill-gotten booty before it touches the water. Unlike all the other seabirds, the frigatebirds never alight on the water. They are airborne all day long except for roosting at night and nesting on islands. They even drink by flying low over the water's surface and sticking their long bill in the water. Occasionally they will stop for a brief respite on the mast of a boat. Pelicans eat fish almost exclusively. Unlike all the other pelicans in the world, the BROWN PELICAN and its much larger but closely related cousin that also occasionally reaches the southern coast of Ecuador, the PERUVIAN PELICAN, plunge dive to catch fish. While underwater the throat sac expands when the pelican opens its bill and is used like a net to scoop up fish up to 30 cm (1 ft) long. Rising to the surface, the pelican then drains the water from its bill pouch and swallows the fish before flying up to plunge dive again. Pelicans appear ungainly as they sit on rocks or on beaches along the coast, but they are excellent fliers. They can use updrafts to soar high above the coastline for hours. At other times a flight of them will pass by just skimming the ocean's surface in a long line or "V" formation. Unlike the other members of their order, which often make distinctive squawks and screeches, particularly on their breeding islands, pelicans are generally silent. Diving from the surface of lakes, rivers, lagoons, and coastal saltwater areas, NEOTROPIC CORMORANTS and ANHINGAS pursue fish underwater, using their large webbed feet for propulsion. Cormorants, which eat crustaceans as well as fish, catch the fish in their hooked bills. They often feed in large groups, especially when fish are concentrated in a small area. They roost and nest together in large colonies, usually in the tops of tall trees, and they move between roosting and feeding-areas in large "V"-shaped flocks. Anhingas are solitary and spear prey underwater on the tips of their sharp bills.

Flamingoes are filter-feeders and use their tongue and open bill to first suck in water laden with microscopic crustaceans and then expel the water through the sieve-like filters on the edges of the closed bill. They usually concentrate in brackish waters that tend to have high densities of these tiny swimming crustaceans.

Breeding

Except for the ANHINGA, all these species nest in large colonies either on isolated islands or, as in the case of the flamingoes, on isolated salt flats, both of which are relatively predator-free. Some breed on ledges, slopes or cliffs (boobies), some in trees (cormorants and anhinga), some on tops of shrubs or bare ground if no vegetation is available (pelicans and frigatebirds). The flamingoes construct mud-sided dikes around their nests in shallow salt lakes. These species are monogamous and both mates share in nest-building, incubation and feeding young. In some groups like the pelicans, the male gathers sticks and stones for the nest, but the female actually constructs the nest. Individuals keep the same mate for several seasons and tend to return to the same site on the same island to nest. BROWN PELICANS lay two or three eggs, which are incubated for 30 to 37 days, but usually only one young is raised successfully. BLUE-FOOTED BOOBY females lay one or two eggs, which are incubated for about 45 days. Only one chick normally survives, often pecking its nest mate to death. MAGNIFICENT FRIGATE-BIRDS lay a single egg that is incubated for about 55 days; both members of the pair share incubating the egg, usually in 12-day shifts. An unguarded nest is likely to be quickly stripped of its sticks and the egg robbed by marauding neighbor frigatebirds. Young remain in and around the nest, totally dependent on the parents for up to 6 months. NEOTROPIC CORMORANTS begin breeding when they are 3 or 4 years old. Two to four eggs are incubated for about 4 weeks, and the young fledge 5 to 8 weeks after hatching.

Notes

Boobies are sometimes called *gannets*, particularly by Europeans. The term *booby* apparently arose because the nesting and roosting birds seemed so bold and fearless toward people, which was considered stupid. Actually the lack of predators on their nesting islands and cliffs meant they had never developed, or alternatively had lost, fear responses to large mammals like humans. Frigatebirds are also known as *man-of-war birds*, both names referring to warships and to the birds' behavior of stealing prey from smaller seabirds *(kleptoparasitism)*; they also steal nesting material from other birds, furthering the image of avian pirates. Anhingas are also known as *darters*, the name derived from the way the birds underwater swiftly thrust their necks forward to spear fish on the points of their bills. Because they often swim with bodies submerged and only long necks and heads above water, they are also often called *snakebirds*. Cormorants have been used for centuries by people in China, Japan and Central Europe as fishing birds. A ring is placed around the cormorant's neck so that it cannot swallow its catch. Then, usually on a long leash, it is permitted to swim underwater to pursue fish. When the bird returns to the surface, it is reeled in, usually with an unswallowable fish clenched in its bill.

Status
None of the seabirds that occur along the shores of mainland Ecuador is considered threatened or endangered. However, years of El Niño can devastate these seabirds so that their populations are reduced to tiny remnant populations within 18 months, the normal length of an El Niño event. In the past these remnant populations have always eventually recovered. However, with the recent technological advances in fishing techniques and equipment, people have been able to so efficiently depress the fisheries in even these hardest of times that the post-El Niño recovery of fish as well as seabird populations could be threatened in the near future. On the Galápagos, several seabird species have extremely small populations and are even more fragile (see Galápagos section for more details).

Profiles
Brown Pelican, *Pelecanus occidentalis*, Plate 14a
Blue-footed Booby, *Sula nebouxii*, Plate 14b and Plate 91c
Magnificent Frigatebird, *Fregata magnificens*, Plate 14c
Neotropic Cormorant, *Phalacrocorax brasilianus*, Plate 14d
Anhinga, *Anhinga anhinga*, Plate 14e
Chilean Flamingo, *Phoenicopterus chilensis*, Plate 14f
Greater Flamingo, *Phoenicopterus ruber*, Plate 92b

2. Gulls and Terns

On the open ocean, over coastal estuaries, on Andean lakes and along Amazonian rivers, the closely related *gulls* and *terns* are often present in large numbers and are among the most obvious birds seen by travellers to Ecuador. They feed on fish and other aquatic and marine invertebrates, and they are often mesmerizing as they dive, swoop and soar in search of their food or in noisy encounters with each other. At rest they perch on sandy beaches and mudflats almost always in flocks of single or mixed species.

These species are all members of the Order Charadriiformes, which also includes the shorebirds (Plate 20). The gulls and terns are in the family Laridae (85 species worldwide, 26 in Ecuador). Terns are smaller, more streamlined forms of gulls. On the coast of Ecuador, several species of terns winter or are transient in migration. The LARGE-BILLED TERN (Plate 15) and the tiny YELLOW-BILLED TERN (Plate 15) are restricted to the large rivers of the Oriente where they are permanent residents. They are noisy and obvious as they fly along a river or roost on isolated sand islands. The BLACK SKIMMER (Plate 15) is closely related to the gulls and terns but is placed in its own family, the Rynchopidae (three species worldwide, one in Ecuador). It is the most bizarre and memorable of all these gull-like species, with its all black body and huge red bill, in which the lower part extends beyond the tip of the upper part. It is usually seen roosting on sand bars in the rivers of the Oriente but is also found in migration along coastal estuaries and occasionally nests along the southern coast. In flight its long, arched wings are distinctive.

Natural History

Ecology and Behavior

These seabirds eat mainly fish and invertebrates. The terns feed primarily on fish which they catch by hovering high over the water and then diving into the water a few inches to grab an unlucky fish that has tarried too long near the surface. Flocks of terns will often concentrate, repeatedly diving on a school of fish forced to the surface by larger, predatory fish. Gulls are less elegant and less choosy in their pursuit of food. They will wade in shallow water to catch opportunistically a wide variety of organisms. They are not above scavenging on dead animals or even in garbage and sewage effluent. The *skimmers* use their peculiar flight and even more peculiar bill to pluck fish and large invertebrates from the water's surface. They fly low over the water with their blade-like bills open and the lower mandible skimming the surface. When they strike a small crustacean or fish, they quickly close the bill and catch it. Frequently they skim a line in the water and then turn to skim back along the same line. On the coast, gulls and terns are frequently pursued by frigatebirds (p. 93), which, even though they are three to 10 times larger than the species they are pursuing, can so easily outmaneuver them in flight, that they can force the tern or gull to regurgitate and drop the morsel they have just caught. The terns on rivers of the Oriente do not have this problem, but the fish are generally not as concentrated or common as on the coast, so they have to work harder to find food than their coastal cousins.

Breeding

As with most seabirds, these gulls and their allies all breed in noisy colonies, usually on an isolated island or remote sand spit. Most of these species are monogamous, male and female sharing brooding and feeding the young. Males often present food to prospective mates in a ritual feeding that apparently provides clues to a female of the male's ability to catch quality prey and as a provider for their offspring. Because they nest on the ground, they have little protection from predators, although they will vigorously dive bomb, peck and defecate on intruders into their nesting colony, human or otherwise. They lay up to four eggs, which are incubated for about 30 days. Young are fed when they push their bills into their parents' throats, in effect forcing the parents to regurgitate food stored in their crops – enlargements of the top part of the esophagus. The low river islands on which the skimmer and two Oriente tern species nest are frequently flooded, and a large proportion of the young drown.

Notes

Most skimmers on the coast do not nest there and are apparently migrants from inland. No one knows the route they use, but it probably involves some high altitude flights over the Andes.

Status

None of these mainland species is threatened, but habitat destruction, pollution and human interference on nesting areas make some populations vulnerable. The more limited ranges and specialized habitats for the ANDEAN GULL, LARGE-BILLED TERN and YELLOW-BILLED TERN, however, make these species more sensitive to increasing water contamination and inroads from growing human populations both along páramo lakes and Amazonian rivers.

Profiles

Gray-headed Gull, *Larus cirrocephalus*, Plate 15a
Gull-billed Tern, *Sterna nilotica*, Plate 15b
Andean Gull, *Larus serranus*, Plate 15c
Large-billed Tern, *Phaetusa simplex*, Plate 15d
Yellow-billed Tern, *Sterna superciliaris*, Plate 15e
Black Skimmer, *Rynchops niger*, Plate 15f

3. Herons and Egrets

Herons and *egrets* are beautiful medium to large-sized wading birds that enjoy broad distributions throughout temperate and tropical regions around the world. Herons, egrets and the more elusive *bitterns* constitute the heron family, Ardeidae, which includes about 60 species. Twenty species occur in Ecuador, most of which breed there. Herons frequent all sorts of aquatic habitats: along rivers and streams, in marshes and swamps, and along lake and ocean shorelines. The difference between what is called an egret and what is called a heron is arbitrary and inconsistent. Generally, however, the term egret is reserved for species that are all white. Most herons and egrets are easy to identify. They are the tallish birds standing upright and still in shallow water or along the shore, staring intently into the water. They have slender bodies, long necks (always folded back in a flattened "S" in flight and sometimes when perched or resting, producing a short-necked, hunched appearance), long, pointed bills, and long legs with long toes. Ecuadorean species range in height from 0.3 to 1.3 m (1 to 4 ft). Most are attired in soft shades of gray, brown, blue, or green, and black or all white. Close-up, many are exquisitely marked with small colored patches of facial skin or broad areas of spots or streaks; the tiger-herons, in particular, are strongly barred or streaked. During the breeding season both sexes of some species acquire long back and head plumes, and leg and bill color become brighter. The bizarre and poorly known BOAT-BILLED HERON (Plate 16) is sometimes placed as a single species in its own family, Cochleariidae, and it occurs from western Mexico south, throughout the Amazon, to northern Argentina.

Natural History

Ecology and Behavior

The CATTLE EGRET (Plate 16) is a recent arrival to Ecuador and is mainly present as a migrant to the Oriente. Unlike all the other herons and egrets, it rarely enters the water but instead, in upland areas, eats insects flushed by the feet of large grazing mammals such as cows. Until recently, the Cattle Egret was confined to the Old World, where it made its living following herds of large mammals such as elephant and buffalo. How it got to the New World is intriguing. Whereas many of the animals that have recently crossed oceans and spread rapidly into new continents have done so as a result of people's intentional or unintentional machinations, these egrets did it on their own. Apparently the first ones to reach the New World were from Africa. Perhaps blown off-course by a storm, they first landed in northern South America in about 1877. Finding the New World to its liking, during the next decades the species spread far and wide, finding abundant food where tropical forests were cleared for cattle grazing. Cattle Egrets have now colonized much of northern South America, Central America, all the major Caribbean islands, and much of the United States. The other herons are mainly sit-and-wait hunters along water edges. Some species wait with infinite patience for prey to move and then strike out in a flash with their bill to grab the fish, frog or crab. The SNOWY EGRET (Plate 16), however, often staggers around in the shallows like a drunken sailor trying to scare up prey that are then easy targets for its bill. The GREEN HERON (Plate 17) is known to use bait like bread stolen from a picnic area to swish in the water and attract fish to within striking range of its bill. The CAPPED HERON (Plate 17), RUFESCENT TIGER-HERON (Plate 16) and the BOAT-BILLED HERON (Plate 16), with its grotesquely large bill, are denizens of small forest streams. They are often so well camouflaged that you can pass close by them in your canoe without noticing them. At day break and again just before sunset they are more likely to be out in the open. The Boat-billed Heron, however, is nocturnal and your best chance of seeing it is by shining a flashlight in the tangled foliage along waterways at night or finding a small group in a protected roost within dense thickets during the day. It uses its huge bill to grope in the water for frogs, fish and shrimp.

Breeding

Most herons are social birds, roosting and breeding in colonies, often several species together. Some, however, like the tiger-herons, are predominantly solitary. Herons are known for their often elaborate courtship displays and ceremonies, which continue through pair-formation and nest-building. Generally the female constructs the nest from sticks presented to her by the male. The nests are in trees, reeds or occasionally on the ground. Both sexes incubate the three to seven eggs for 16 to 30 days, and both feed the young for another 35 to 50 days until they fledge.

Herons and egrets often lay more eggs than the number of chicks they can successfully feed. This seems contrary to our usual view of nature, which we regard as finely tuned through natural selection so that behaviors avoid waste. The likely answer to this puzzle is that this behavior allows a pair to raise the maximum number of offspring every year even if food levels are unpredictable from year to year. Females lay eggs one or two days apart, and start incubating with the first egg. Chicks hatch out at the same intervals, and so the young in a single nest are of different ages and quite different sizes. The largest chicks receive the most food, probably because they can more easily attract the adults and get to the food they regurgitate. The larger chicks on occasion will also kill their smaller siblings (siblicide), especially if food is scarce. If there is sufficient food, the next biggest chicks will also be able to eat often enough to survive. In years of super-abundant food, even the smallest chicks will be able to eat enough. Thus, laying more eggs than can be reared as chicks most years may be to insure that many chicks are raised in the years of abundance.

Notes

All herons have a distinctive comb on the flattened middle toe of each foot. They use it to groom themselves and spread bits of specialized feathers called *powder down* throughout their body surface. Powder down is found in only a very few other birds in the world; its function appears to be to help clean the large body feathers when they become full of fish scales and grime.

Status

Some of Ecuador's herons and egrets are fairly rare, but they are not considered threatened species because they are common in other parts of their ranges, outside the country.

Profiles

Boat-billed Heron, *Cochlearius cochlearius*, Plate 16a
Snowy Egret, *Egretta thula*, Plate 16b
Cattle Egret, *Bubulcus ibis*, Plate 16c
Great Egret, *Ardea alba*, Plate 16d
Rufescent Tiger-heron, *Tigrisoma lineatum*, Plate 16e
Cocoi Heron, *Ardea cocoi*, Plate 17a
Green Heron, *Butorides striatus*, Plate 17b
Capped Heron, *Pilherodius pileatus*, Plate 17c

4. Marsh and Stream Birds

Marsh and stream birds are a collection of unrelated species that share a habitat of standing and running water surrounded by grasses, bushes, trees and other relatively thick vegetation. They do not rely heavily on flight but rather swim in the water or walk on and through vegetation near the water. They tend to be shy and retiring, and they often slink away from danger before a predator (or an approaching canoe with tourists) has a chance to see them.

The *jacanas* (jha-SAH-nahs) form a worldwide family, Jacanidae (eight species worldwide). Only one species, the WATTLED JACANA (Plate 17), is found in Ecuador, and it is common in lowland marshes on both sides of the Andes. It has incredibly long toes for walking on floating vegetation without sinking. Female jacanas are larger than males, and immatures are lighter and streaked. The *rails*, family Rallidae (140 species worldwide, 24 in Ecuador) are often shy and difficult-to-see inhabitants of swampy areas. The large GRAY-NECKED WOOD-RAIL (Plate 17) is common in marshy forested areas throughout the Oriente and the rail you are most likely to encounter. The SUNBITTERN (Plate 18) belongs to the family Eurypigidae, which is represented by only this one species, which occurs from southern Mexico to southern Bolivia. In Ecuador it is found in the lowlands of the northwest and throughout the Oriente. When a Sunbittern's wings are spread, the bars and spots on its wings create a striking "sunburst" pattern. The SUNGREBE (Plate 18) is in the family Heliornithidae, and it is not at all related to grebes but rather is a close cousin to the Sunbittern. It is a small duck-like species that swims under the vegetation hanging low over forested streams. There are two other similar species in the family, one each in tropical Africa and Asia, where they are called *finfoots*. The HOATZIN (Plate 18) is one of the most intriguing and unusual species you will see in the flooded forests and marshes of Amazonian Ecuador. There is only one species in its family, Opisthocomidae (closely related to cuckoos). It is restricted to the upper Amazon and its tributaries. This turkey-sized bird looks for all the world like some prehistoric dinosaur with feathers. The HORNED SCREAMER (Plate 18) belongs to a uniquely South American family related to ducks, Anhimidae, which has two other species in it. This immense bird looks like a plump black and white heron on the ground but like an eagle with long legs when it flies. It has a deep liquid call that carries for miles. It is found throughout the Amazon, but a small population also lives on the south coast of Ecuador near Guayaquil. The SILVERY GREBE (Plate 18) in the Family Podicipedidae (20 species worldwide, three in Ecuador) is a small duck-like species found only in open and marshy lakes of the high altitude páramo in Ecuador. Its small size and thin bill immediately separate it from any of the true ducks that also occur on these high lakes.

Natural History

Ecology and Behavior
The GRAY-NECKED WOOD-RAIL is more often heard than seen from flooded forest and thick river edge. At dawn and dusk several pairs will sing in a chorus together. Their raucous, almost maniacal laughing call, "to-tooky, to-tooky" gradually tapers off until only one individual is left singing. Occasionally this rail emerges briefly into open areas in the early morning or late afternoon. The WATTLED JACANA is common and easy to see in flooded grasslands and open marshy areas. It uses its immensely long toes to walk on floating vegetation and lily pads. Sharp spurs on the wing are used for fighting other jacanas and against predators. The SUNBITTERN lives along forested streams and flooded forest where they walk along searching for insects, crabs, frogs, crayfish and small fish. The SUNGREBE swims in among the roots and overhanging leaves of thick vegetation along lakes and streams, where it feeds on frogs, worms, crustaceans and insects. It runs across the surface of the water and flies low to escape predation, and your best view will probably be as it skitters away from your canoe into the dense vegetation. HOATZINS are usually in loose flocks of five to 10 birds in bushes along the edges of slow-moving streams or forested lakes. They announce their displeasure at your presence with hisses and croaks just before they weakly flap their wings to fly to the next branch over the water. They eat only leaves and have a digestive system similar to a cow's that uses fermentation to digest otherwise undigestible plant parts. You will most likely see the HORNED SCREAMER in grassy marshes as it flies up noisily. Screamers graze on marsh vegetation, and also perch frequently in the tops of trees to make their loud calls. They are strong fliers and can soar to great heights. The SILVERY GREBE feeds in páramo lakes by diving after fish and invertebrates. It can adjust its buoyancy and simply sink out of sight, or it can leap forward out of the water for a more athletic dive.

Breeding
Jacanas are unusual in that they are often polyandrous (one female mates with numerous males). Males each defend small territories from other males, but each female has a larger territory that encompasses two to four male territories. Males build nests of floating, compacted aquatic vegetation, into which the female deposits three or four eggs. The male incubates the nest for 21 to 24 days and then cares for the chicks by himself. Jacanas also are able to move their young chicks in case of flooding or danger by holding them under their closed wings and running to safety. The SUNBITTERN is well known for its spectacular courtship and threat display in which the tail and wings are spread to reveal a sunburst pattern of yellows, blacks and rust colors. It makes a rounded cup-like nest in a tree or bush, and apparently both mates incubate and feed the two or three young. The

SUNGREBE makes a flat nest of sticks and reeds, often on branches of dead trees low over the water. The two to five eggs are incubated by both parents. The male has a unique adaptation to protect the fledged young. In case of danger the small chicks climb into pouches in the skin under the wings and the male dives underwater to escape. The HOATZIN'S two to four young are incubated for 28 days by both parents in a stick nest placed several meters out over the water in a tree branch. Some observations suggest that groups of up to six adults may be involved cooperatively in incubating and feeding the young. When in danger, the young jump from the nest into the water and swim underwater to then clamber up another bush. To facilitate their tree-climbing ability they have an extra, opposable, digit on the naked wing that they use like a hand. This extra digit is lost as the chick matures and its feathers and wings develop so it can fly. The SILVERY GREBE is monogamous and builds a floating nest of aquatic material. This way a rise or fall in the water level of the marshy lake will not affect the safety of the two to six eggs or young. When both adults are away from the nest at the same time, they cover the eggs or chicks with vegetation to keep them warm and camouflaged from potential enemies. Both mates are equally involved in incubation and guarding the striped chicks, which soon leave the nest. The young continue to be dependent on the adults for three to four weeks as they swim around the pond and hide in vegetation at night. HORNED SCREAMERS, like their relatives, geese and swans, mate for life. Their nests are in shallow water and made of sticks and vegetation. The five eggs are incubated for 40 days and screamers are full grown in about 4 months.

Notes

The term "skinny as a rail" refers originally not to a railroad track but to the bird. Rails are extremely flattened from side to side so they can fit into narrow spaces – thus the saying. Hoatzins are large birds with few chances to escape hunters, yet virtually no indigenous peoples use hoatzins for food (although their eggs are often eaten). The reason is that among the plants and leaves they eat is one common aroid plant (*Montrichardia*) that grows along the edges of lakes in Amazonia. It has a thick woody stem and heart-shaped leaves. The leaves contain chemicals that when eaten are absorbed by the muscles and convey a smell and taste not unlike a sewer. Even a starving person would likely turn down a serving of Hoatzin.

Status

The BROWN WOOD-RAIL is considered a threatened species in coastal Ecuador, where it occurs locally in mangroves and on the floor of moist lowland forests. SILVERY GREBE populations in Ecuador have been falling at alarming rates over the last 20 years. Cattle and sheep grazing, pollution and increasing human contact in the páramo are likely the cause. This species, however, is common throughout much of the rest of the Andes south into Argentina. The HORNED SCREAMER populations in Amazonia have also fallen dramatically, probably owing to hunting pressure. The small population on the coast, however, is stable and well protected from hunting by the Churute National Reserve.

Profiles

Gray-necked Wood-rail, *Aramides cajanea*, Plate 17d
Wattled Jacana, *Jacana jacana*, Plate 17e
Sunbittern, *Eurypyga helias*, Plate 18a
Sungrebe, *Heliornis fulica*, Plate 18b

Hoatzin, *Opisthocomus hoazin*, Plate 18c
Horned Screamer, *Anhima cornuta*, Plate 18d
Silvery Grebe, *Podiceps occipitalis*, Plate 18e

5. Ducks

Members of the Family Anatidae, which includes about 150 species of *ducks, geese* and *swans*, are all associated with water. They are distributed throughout the world in habitats ranging from open sea to high mountain lakes. Although abundant and diverse in temperate regions, only a relatively few species migrate to or reside in the tropics. Ducks vary quite a bit in size and coloring, but most share the same major traits: duck bills, webbed toes, short-tails, and long, slim necks. Plumage color and patterning vary, but there is a preponderance within the group of grays and browns, and black and white, although many species have at least small patches of brighter colors. In some species male and female look alike, but in others there is a high degree of difference between the sexes. About 15 species occur in Ecuador, from tidal marshes on the coast to the cold páramo lakes at high elevations, to the Amazon lowlands. The TORRENT DUCK (Plate 19), living in white-water streams on both slopes of the Andes, is the most unusual of the ducks in Ecuador – the male and female are so differently colored that they are often mistaken for separate species.

Natural History

Ecology and Behavior
Ducks eat aquatic plants, small fish and invertebrates, but some, such as the MUSCOVY DUCK (Plate 19) and the ORINOCO GOOSE (Plate 19), regularly graze on grasses, moist upland vegetation and terrestrial insects. More typical is the dabbling feeding behavior of WHITE-CHEEKED PINTAILS (Plate 19) and YELLOW-BILLED PINTAILS (Plate 19), which dip their bills into the water while swimming. Sometimes they will tip their rear ends into the air trying to reach a bit deeper into the water for a morsel, but they do not dive underwater. As their name suggests, TORRENT DUCKS pursue their food of fish underwater in fast-flowing mountain streams. They propel themselves with their feet, dodging large boulders and mastering the powerful currents with ease. They often sit for long periods resting on the top of a large mid-stream boulder.

Breeding
All these ducks except one nest on the ground in protective vegetation near their feeding areas. The MUSCOVY DUCK nests in tree cavities often more than 15 m (50 ft) above the ground. Typically duck nests are lined with downy feathers that the female plucks from her breast. In most species of ducks the female alone performs the duties dealing with nesting and caring for the young. In large species like geese and swans the pair typically mates for life, and both parents are more equally involved in raising the young. The young hatch feathered and able to run within a few minutes (*precocial*); they can swim and feed themselves soon after. The parents' main role is to guard them against predators and teach them how to find food.

Notes
Ducks, geese and swans have been objects of people's attention since ancient times, chiefly as a food source. These birds typically have tasty flesh, are fairly

large and thus economical to hunt, and usually easier and less dangerous to catch than many other animals, particularly large mammals. Owing to their frequent use as food, several wild ducks and geese have been domesticated for thousands of years; Ecuador's native MUSCOVY DUCK, in fact, in its domesticated form is a common farmyard inhabitant in several parts of the world. Wild ducks also adjust well to the proximity of people, to the point of taking food from them – a practice that surviving artworks show has been occurring for at least 2000 years. Hunting ducks and geese for sport is also a long-practiced tradition. As a consequence of these long interactions between ducks and people, and the research on these animals stimulated by their use in agriculture and sport, a large amount of scientific information has been collected on the group; many of the ducks and geese are among the most well known of birds. The close association between ducks and people has even led to a long contractual agreement between certain individual ducks and the Walt Disney Company.

Status

The populations of all the species profiled here have been affected to some degree by hunting pressures. The ORINOCO GOOSE is especially susceptible to people's presence and has disappeared from all but the most isolated rivers in Ecuador. The MUSCOVY DUCK has suffered a similar but not so extreme fate throughout its range in the Neotropics. When these ducks were more common, local hunters would tether a female to a tree and then kill males that came a-courting; with this method, up to 50 males could be lured to their deaths in a single day. The other species are still relatively common in their appropriate habitats.

Profiles

Muscovy Duck, *Cairina moschata*, Plate 19a
Orinoco Goose, *Neochen jubata*, Plate 19b
White-cheeked Pintail, *Anas bahamensis*, Plate 19c
Yellow-billed Pintail, *Anas georgica*, Plate 19d
Torrent Duck, *Merganetta armata*, Plate 19e

6. Shorebirds

Spotting *shorebirds* is usually a priority only for visitors to the Neotropics who are rabid birdwatchers. The reason for the lack of interest is that many shorebirds in Ecuador are visitors from their nesting grounds in North America. Of course, being mostly brown and lacking in reasonably distinguishing characteristics may have something to do with it as well. Nevertheless, it can be a treat watching these fellow travellers in their tropical wintering areas as they forage in meadows, along streams, on mudflats and on sandy ocean beaches. When a large flock, often of several species, rises from a sand bar, it is fun to follow its progress until out of sight. The resident species of shorebirds in Ecuador are intriguing for their combination of similarities to and frequently jarring differences from their migratory cousins. Shorebirds are traditionally placed along with the gulls in the avian Order Charadriiformes. They are global in distribution, and we profile species from four families found in Ecuador. Most shorebirds, regardless of size, have a characteristic "look." They are usually drably colored birds (especially during the nonbreeding months), darker above, lighter below, with long, thin legs for wading through wet meadows, mud, sand, or surf. Depending on feeding habits, bill length varies from short to very long.

The *sandpipers*, Family Scolopacidae, are a worldwide group of approximately 85 species. About 30 species occur in Ecuador, some being quite abundant during much of the year, yet all but a few high altitude species are migrants that nest in the Arctic of North America. However, some nonbreeding individuals can be present in Ecuador any month of the year. Most of the Ecuadorean sandpipers range from 15 to 48 cm (6 to 19 in) long. They are generally slender birds with straight or curved bills of various lengths and live on sandy beaches or mudflats along the coast or in the Amazon. The ANDEAN SNIPE (Plate 20), however, is a species resident in the high altitude Andes. It usually occurs around moist areas with grass, but sometimes in drier areas as well. This is a "heart attack" bird, as the only way you are likely to see it is as it rises up from almost under your feet, startling you, while hiking through grassy páramo.

Plovers, in the Family Charadriidae, are small to medium-sized (15 to 30 cm, 6 to 12 in) shorebirds with short tails and straight, relatively stout, dove-like bills. They are mostly shades of gray and brown but some have bold color patterns such as a broad white or dark band on the head or chest. Worldwide there are more than 60 species. Eleven species occur regularly in Ecuador, seven of which are resident non-migratory species.

The family of the *stilts*, Recurvirostridae, has 10 species worldwide but only one species in Ecuador, the BLACK-NECKED STILT (Plate 20). It congregates in flocks of five to 100 in estuarine ponds and tidal flats along the coast. The flocks are so noisy you often hear them before you can see them. Apparently some of the individuals in Ecuador are migrants from Central America and the Caribbean, but the species also nests in Ecuador, both on the coast of the mainland and in the Galápagos. The most bizarre and unusual of all the families in this shorebird order, the *seedsnipes* (Thinocoridae, four species in western and southern South America) has a sole representative in Ecuador, the RUFOUS-BELLIED SEEDSNIPE (Plate 21). Looking more like the cross between a dove and a quail, this species is common only on the highest mountains between 4500 m (14,750 ft) and just below the snow line. Seedsnipe are so camouflaged they are often hard to see, even when you are right on top of them. Listen for their low whistling calls. They feed on the ground among low vegetation of high páramo, mainly looking for seeds.

Natural History

Ecology and Behavior

Even though shorebirds are all excellent fliers, they spend a lot of time on the ground foraging and resting. When pursued, they often prefer running to flying away. Sandpipers tend to use their bills to probe into the soil or mud for small invertebrates, and different shapes and lengths of bills help the various sandpiper species find different prey even when they are feeding side by side. The plovers use their bills to take prey or even seeds off the soil surface and never probe. Stilts take advantage of their long legs and bill to probe mud in deeper water, sometimes feeding with their heads entirely underwater. The short-legged and short-billed seedsnipes, of course, eat seeds. They also apparently do not drink free-standing water but instead get the water they need from leaves and vegetation they eat. Many shorebirds, especially among the sandpipers, establish winter feeding territories along stretches of beach; they use the area for feeding for a few hours or for the day, defending it aggressively from other members of their species. Many of the sandpipers and plovers are gregarious birds, often seen in large groups, especially when they are travelling. Several species make long migrations over large expanses of open ocean.

Breeding

Most shorebird nests are simply small depressions in the ground in which eggs are placed; some of these are in sand, on gravel or on a grass hummock. Seldom do the adults prepare the nest with more than a few pebbles. In almost all these shorebird families monogamy is the rule, and both parents incubate the eggs. In the seedsnipe, however, the female incubates the eggs while the male stands guard some distance from the nest. Shorebird young are precocial and able to run and feed themselves soon after hatching. Parents usually stay with the young to guard them until they can fly, 3 to 5 weeks after hatching. Adults of many ground-nesting species such as these shorebirds protect their nests and young by performing a "broken wing" display. At the approach of a predator, the adult runs in front of the danger, calling, and dragging one of its wings on the ground as if it is severely injured. The predator sees an easy meal and follows after the adult, which is able to just keep out of the striking range of the predator and leads it away from the young hidden in the nest or in the grass. If this fails, species like stilts fly close to the predator and hassle it until it leaves.

Notes

The manner in which flocks of thousands of birds, particularly shorebirds, fly in such closely regimented order, executing abrupt maneuvers with precise coordination, such as when all individuals turn together in a split second in the same direction, has puzzled biologists and engendered some research. The questions include: What is the stimulus for the flock to turn – is it one individual within the flock, a "leader," from which all the others take their "orders" and follow into turns? Or is it some stimulus from outside the flock that all members respond to in the same way? And how are the turns coordinated? Everything from "thought transference" to electromagnetic communication among the flock members has been advanced as an explanation. After studying films of DUNLIN, a North American and Eurasian sandpiper, flying and turning in large flocks, one biologist has suggested that the method birds within these flocks use to coordinate their turns is similar to how the people in a chorus line know the precise moment to raise their legs in sequence or how "the wave" in a sports stadium is coordinated. That is, one bird, perhaps one that has detected some danger, like a predatory falcon, starts a turn, and the other birds, seeing the start of the flock's turning, can then anticipate when it is their turn to make the turn – the result being a quick wave of turning coursing through the flock.

Status

None of the shorebirds of Ecuador is threatened or endangered. However, a major goal for conservation of shorebirds is the need to preserve critical migratory stopover points – pieces of habitat, sometimes fairly small, that hundreds of thousands of shorebirds settle into mid-way during their long migrations to stock up on food. These *staging areas* are vital for shorebird populations, and several such areas likely exist in Ecuador. These very sites, however, are also heavily threatened from construction of shrimp farms and pollution from herbicide and pesticide runoff from nearby banana plantations.

Profiles

Whimbrel, *Numenius phaeopus*, Plate 20a
Pied Lapwing, *Vanellus cayanus*, Plate 20b
Black-necked Stilt, *Himantopus mexicanus*, Plate 20c

Andean Snipe, *Gallinago jamesoni*, Plate 20d
Spotted Sandpiper, *Actitis macularia*, Plate 20e
Sanderling, *Calidris alba*, Plate 20f
Black-bellied Plover, *Pluvialis squatarola*, Plate 21a
Rufous-bellied Seedsnipe, *Attagis gayi*, Plate 21b

7. Tinamous

The *tinamous* are an interesting group of secretive but very vocal chicken-like birds that are occasionally seen walking on forest trails. However, they represent an ancient group of birds more closely related to ostriches than chickens. The family, Tinamidae, with about 45 species, is confined in its distribution to the Neotropics, from Mexico to southern Chile and Argentina; 16 species occur in Ecuador, from coastal dry forest and high altitude páramo to Amazon rainforest, where most of the species live.

Tinamous are medium-sized birds, 23 to 45 cm (9 to 18 in) long, chunky-bodied, with fairly long necks, small heads, and slender bills. They have short legs and very short tails. The back part of a tinamou's body sometimes appears higher than it should be, a consequence of a dense concentration of rump feathers. Tinamous are attired in understated, protective colors – browns, grays, and olives; often the plumage is marked with dark spots or bars. Male and female look alike, with females being a little larger than males. The three species you are most likely to encounter in Ecuador are all found in lowland primary and secondary forests, and your encounter is most likely to be by ear rather than by eye. The UNDU-LATED TINAMOU (Plate 21) makes one of the most common sounds of secondary forest in the Amazon. The call, two low whistles followed by a longer note slurred upwards, is ubiquitous all day long. If you have patience and can stand still for ten to twenty minutes, you can mimic the whistle and sometimes call in an individual close enough to see it. The slightest movement, however, will send it scurrying away. During the drier seasons, when dry leaves accumulate on the forest floor, you can often detect these birds by the crackling sounds of their feet disturbing the leaves.

Natural History

Ecology and Behavior
Except for the GREAT TINAMOU (Plate 21), which sleeps in trees, tinamous are among the most terrestrial of birds, foraging, sleeping and breeding on the ground. They are very poor at flying, doing so only when alarmed by a predator, and then merely for a short distance. They are better at running along the ground, the mode of location called *cursorial*. The tinamou diet consists chiefly of fruit and seeds, but they will also eat insects and other invertebrates they encounter on the forest floor. Some species use their feet to scratch and dig at the soil to feed on roots and termites. Tinamous often avoid predators by standing still or squatting, easily blending in with the surrounding vegetation. Sometimes they will slowly and quietly, almost ghost-like, walk away from danger. If you get too close to a tinamou, it will fly upwards in a sudden burst of loud wing-beating and fly to a new hiding spot in the undergrowth. In the early evening, one of the most delightful parts of the forest is the serenade of melodious whistles that make tinamous such a characteristic part of Neotropical forests.

Breeding

Tinamous are *polyandrous* (one female mates with several males) just like their Ostrich relatives. Each male has a nest on the ground which he guards and broods. Females wander around choosing a series of males to mate with and dumping a few eggs in each nest. Perhaps this is a way females have of not putting all their eggs in one basket. One nest can have up to 12 eggs deposited by numerous females. Of course each male also mates with numerous females as they make their rounds, so this mating system is *polygynous* as well as polyandrous. The nest itself is seldom more than an indentation in the forest floor, often hidden in a thicket or at the base of a tree.

Notes

Outside of protected areas, all tinamous are hunted extensively for food. Tinamou meat is considered tender and tasty, albeit a bit strange-looking; it has been described variously as greenish and transparent. Many species of tinamous have eggs that are large, with an extremely glossy surface. Their colors are also bright, from purple, green and greenish yellow to rusty. Actually seeing them, you have to wonder how these bright eggs can ever escape the attention of the many nest predators that prowl the forest floor. One hypothesis is that in the nest these shiny eggs act like mirrors, reflecting the surrounding vegetation so that they become virtually invisible.

Status

The tinamous' camouflage coloring and secretive behavior must serve the birds well because, although hunted for food, tinamous apparently maintain healthy populations even in populated countryside. In Ecuador, the species of tinamous that have the greatest reductions in populations are the very large species of the lowlands and the páramo species, both groups of which are the most likely to be hunted extensively.

Profiles

Great Tinamou, *Tinamus major*, Plate 21c
Little Tinamou, *Crypturellus soui*, Plate 21d
Undulated Tinamou, *Crypturellus undulatus*, Plate 21e

8. Guans and Trumpeter

Large, pheasant-like birds strutting about the tropical forest floor or fluttering about in trees and running along high branches, are bound to be members of the guan family, Cracidae. This family, related to pheasants and chickens and distributed from southern Texas to Argentina, contains more than 40 species of *guans*, *chachalacas* and *curassows*. Thirteen species are found in Ecuador.

Ecuadorean guans as a group range in length from 56 to 91 cm (20 to 36 in) – as large as small turkeys – and weigh up to 4 kg (9 lb). They have long legs and long, heavy toes. Many have conspicuous crests. The colors of their bodies are generally drab – gray, brown, olive, or black and white; some appear glossy in the right light. They typically have small patches of bright coloring such as yellow, red, or orange on parts of their bills, cheeks, or on a hanging throat sac called a dewlap. The SPECKLED CHACHALACA (Plate 22) is by far the most common species of this family in Ecuador. At dawn a flock of these pheasant-sized birds in the Amazon will give a chorus of their loud and raucous calls, that with some imagination can be rendered as a rapid "chachalaca" repeated over and over. Then another flock will answer from across the river and the signalling will go back and forth for a half-hour or until it's time to start feeding, usually from the tops of trees in secondary forest or river edges. If you have the great fortune to see a SALVIN'S CURASSOW (Plate 22), count yourself among the lucky. It will be an indication that you are in pristine Amazon forest, as these large, and unfortunately delicious, birds are easily hunted and thus rare in many areas. The female is similar to the black and white male but somewhat smaller. Listen for the series of very low-pitched humming or "booming" noises of the males early in the morning and on moonlit nights.

The GRAY-WINGED TRUMPETER (Plate 22) is similar in appearance to the guans, but it is related instead to the rails and cranes. It is placed in its own small family of three species, Psophiidae; all three are found in different parts of the Amazon Basin. True to its name, this species has a loud deep call that is not unlike an untuned trumpet. When disturbed, trumpeters growl like a dog and thump their body with closed wings. Where they are hunted, trumpeters are very shy, and you will be lucky to see this tall bird slinking away into the undergrowth of primary forest. As it is commonly kept as a pet by local people, you are most likely to see it running around a village bullying the chickens. Trumpeter sexes are similar, both weighing about 1 kg (2.2 lb).

Natural History

Ecology and Behavior
The guans are birds of the forest, and the larger the species, the more it is limited to denser forest. All of the guans roost in trees at night, and some, such as the chachalacas and *piping-guans*, rarely ever descend to the ground. They prefer to eat fruits, seeds and insects from the tree tops. The larger guans spend more time on the forest floor, eating fallen fruits and insects, but they often feed in the tree tops as well. The curassows spend all but their roosting time at night on the ground. The smaller species are often in flocks, but the larger species are more solitary. Trumpeters also feed on the forest floor, scratching with their feet to stir up large insects and looking for fallen fruits. They are almost always in flocks of five to 20 or more individuals moving elegantly along the forest floor, but they do fly to the tree tops to escape danger and roost at night.

Breeding
The guans are all monogamous breeders in which the sexes share reproductive duties. The nest is a simple open construction of twigs and leaves placed in a tree or shrub several meters from the ground. Two to four eggs are incubated for 22 to 34 days. The young leave the nest soon after hatching to hide in surrounding vegetation, where, unlike most species with precocial young, they are fed by the parents. Within a few days the young can fly short distances. The breeding biology of trumpeters is very poorly known. Nests have been reported from large holes in trees and the top of a palm tree. The female apparently incubates the six to eight eggs alone. The black young are covered with streaks and bars of rusty and cinnamon, and they follow one or both parents away from the nest soon after hatching.

Notes
Curassows are frequently kept as pets in local villages, but they are shy birds in captivity. The trumpeters kept as pets, however, quickly become attached to the

owner's home and poultry. They take on the mantle of dominant boss and protector. They readily chase dogs and other wild predators from chickens, and even unfamiliar humans can expect to be challenged with a growl from these birds, which think they are German Shepherds. They are surprisingly affectionate pets, and if you can get close enough to one to scratch it gently on the back of the head, it will follow you for the rest of the day.

Status

A variety of factors converge to assure that the guans will remain a problem group into the foreseeable future. They are chiefly birds of the forests at a time when Neotropical forests are increasingly being cleared. They are desirable game birds, hunted by local people for food. In fact, as soon as new roads penetrate virgin forests in Central and South America, one of the first chores of settlers is to shoot curassows for their dinners. Unfortunately, curassows reproduce slowly, raising only small broods each year. Exacerbating the problem, their nests are often placed low enough in trees and vegetation to make them vulnerable to a variety of predators, including people. In the face of these unrelenting pressures on their populations, guans are among the birds thought most likely to survive in the future only in protected areas, such as national parks. In Ecuador, four species of guans are considered threatened, the RUFOUS-HEADED CHACHALACA and the GREAT CURASSOW in lowland coastal forests, and the BEARDED GUAN and BAUDO GUAN in montane forests of the Andean slopes.

Profiles

Speckled Chachalaca, *Ortalis guttata*, Plate 22a
Spix's Guan, *Penelope jacquacu*, Plate 22b
Blue-throated Piping-Guan, *Pipile cumanensis*, Plate 22c
Salvin's Curassow, *Mitu salvini*, Plate 22d
Gray-winged Trumpeter, *Psophia crepitans*, Plate 22e

9. Vultures

Birds at the very pinnacle of their profession, eating dead animals, *vultures* are highly conspicuous and among the most frequently seen birds both in rural areas and in towns and cities. That they feast on rotting flesh does not reduce the majesty of these large, soaring birds as they circle for hours over fields and forest. They are large birds, generally black or brown, with hooked bills and curious, unfeathered heads whose bare skin is often richly colored in red, yellow, or orange. Male and female vultures look alike, and males are slightly larger than females.

The family of American vultures, Cathartidae, has only seven species, with representatives from Canada to southern Argentina. Five species occur regularly in Ecuador. The ANDEAN CONDOR (Plate 23), with a 3 m (10 ft) wingspan and distinctive wing pattern, unfortunately is no longer common in the high altitude páramo of Ecuador. Only about 100 pairs still occur in the country and they are concentrated primarily in two or three of the better-protected volcano redoubts in the northern and central Andes.

Natural History

Ecology and Behavior

Vultures are carrion eaters of the first order. Most soar during the day in groups looking for and, in the case of some species, smelling for food. They can cover many miles daily in their search for dead and rotting bodies and garbage. With their super eyesight, fine-tuned sense of smell, and ability to cover so much ground each day searching, vultures are nature's most efficient garbage collectors. Apparently their bills and feet are not strong enough to dismember fresh meat. The bare skin of their heads and large nostrils on the bill aid them in avoiding problems of gore accumulating on their heads and interfering with seeing, hearing and breathing.

KING (Plate 23) and GREATER YELLOW-HEADED VULTURES (Plate 23) and ANDEAN CONDORS are usually seen in pairs or solitarily, but the other two species are more social, roosting and foraging in groups of various sizes. BLACK VULTURES (Plate 23), in particular, often congregate in large numbers at feeding places, and it is common to find a flock of them at any village dump. At small to medium-sized carcasses, there is a definite pecking order among the vultures: Black Vultures are dominant to TURKEY VULTURES (Plate 23), and can chase them away; several Black Vultures can even chase away a King Vulture, which is the bigger bird. However, in an area with plenty of food, all three species may feed together in temporary harmony. When threatened, vultures may spit up partially digested carrion, a strong defense against harassment if ever there was one.

Black and Turkey Vultures roost communally, the two species often together. A common observation has been that once an individual finds a food source, other vultures arrive very rapidly to share the carcass. Biologists strongly suspect that the group roosting and feeding behavior of these birds are related, and that the former increases each individual's food-finding efficiency. In other words, a communal roost serves as an information center for finding food.

Breeding
Vultures are monogamous breeders. Both sexes incubate the one to three eggs, which are placed on the ground in protected places or on the floor of a cave or tree cavity. Eggs are incubated for 32 to 58 days. Both sexes feed the young regurgitated carrion for 2 to 5 months until they can fly. Nest predation is very rare, and given the long length of time the apparently helpless nestlings are exposed to danger, the best explanation is that the stench of the carrion and decaying animal flesh around the nest and chicks keep potential predators away.

Notes
Being such large and conspicuous birds, and being carrion-eaters associated with death, guaranteed that vultures would figure prominently in the art and culture of most civilizations. The vultures of Egypt and Old World mythology, however, are actually feather-challenged eagles and only distantly related to the superficially similar New World vultures. Recent comparative studies of DNA suggest that the New World Vultures are more closely related to storks than to hawks and eagles.

Status
Four of the five Ecuadorean species of vultures are common or very common birds. The only Ecuadorean vulture in dire trouble is the ANDEAN CONDOR. As recently as the 1970s, on a clear day you could expect to see five to 20 condors soaring over passes near Quito. Now the entire population in the country is down to about 100 pairs. In Venezuela and Colombia the condor is virtually extinct. Only in the southern part of its range, from Bolivia to Argentina and Chile, does it seem to be holding its own. The main causes of condor declines in the 20th

century were hunting (they were persecuted especially because ranchers believed they ate newborn cattle and other domesticated animals), their ingestion of poisonous lead shot from the carcasses they fed on, and the thinning of their eggshells owing to the accumulation of organochlorine pesticides (DDT) in their bodies.

Profiles

Turkey Vulture, *Cathartes aura*, Plate 23a
Black Vulture, *Coragyps atratus*, Plate 23b
Greater Yellow-headed Vulture, *Cathartes melambrotus*, Plate 23c
King Vulture, *Sarcoramphus papa*, Plate 23d
Andean Condor, *Vultur gryphus*, Plate 23e

10. Hawks, Eagles and Kites

The raptor family, Accipitridae, is an immense group that worldwide includes about 200 species of *hawks, eagles* and *kites*. Species in this family vary considerably in size and in patterns of their generally subdued color schemes, but all are similar in overall form – we know them when we see them. They are fierce-looking birds with strong feet, hooked, sharp claws, or talons, and strongly hooked bills. The plumages of the two sexes are usually similar, but females are larger than males, in some species extremely so. Juvenile raptors often spend several years in subadult plumages that differ in pattern and brightness from the adults.

Natural History

Ecology and Behavior

Although many raptors are common birds, typically they spread themselves out thinly over large areas, as is the case for all top predators (a predator at the pinnacle of the food chain and thus having too few prey available to support large populations of the predator). Some large eagles feeding on monkeys or sloths, such as the HARPY EAGLE, may need a territory of a 1000 sq km (385 sq miles) or more to ensure sufficient food for itself and its nestlings. Most species have developed unique hunting techniques to increase efficiency of prey capture. Among the kites, for instance, the AMERICAN SWALLOW-TAILED KITE (Plate 24) soars over forest canopies and open areas searching for reptiles, especially snakes, sunning themselves in the open. The kite swoops down on a reptile and carries it off to a perch to devour. The SNAIL KITE (Plate 24) has a peculiarly long, narrow and curved bill that enables it to specialize on giant snails that inhabit the marshes. With this bill the kite can easily slip past the otherwise protective door (operculum) that the snail closes across the opening of the shell to protect itself. The bill then extracts the juicy body of the snail like some specialized escargot fork. The DOUBLE-TOOTHED KITE (Plate 24) has an unusual association with monkey troops, and you are most likely to see this kite near active primates. As the monkeys jump from branch to branch they often scare large insects out of hiding. Before these panicked insects can reach refuge, the kite quickly grabs them as they land. Large grasshoppers and katydids are among the most common prey items taken this way by these kites.

Among the hawks, the MANGROVE BLACK HAWK (Plate 25) of coastal Ecuador is highly specialized for its habitat of mangrove swamps, where few other hawks live; it preys on a diet of crabs and fish, especially when they are exposed at low tide. The ROADSIDE HAWK (Plate 25), on the other hand, is a generalist, and eats everything from small birds and mammals to insects and even an occasional lizard or snake. Forest clearings and scrub edges are actually beneficial for this hawk because it has little competition there and these man-made habitats make the type of prey it prefers more common.

Breeding
Many raptors are territorial, a solitary individual or a breeding pair defending an area for feeding and, during the breeding season, for reproduction. Displays that advertise a territory and that also may be used in courtship consist of spectacular aerial twists, loops, and other acrobatic maneuvers. Hawk, eagle and kite nests in general are constructed of sticks that both sexes place in a tree or on a rocky ledge. Some nests are lined with leaves. Usually only the female incubates the one to six eggs for about a month. The male hunts for the female while she sits on the eggs, and after the first chicks hatch out, he continues to give prey to the female, which then tears it up to give in turn to the chicks. When the chicks are a little bigger and the demand for food rises, both mates hunt and feed the chicks directly. The young can fly at 28 to 120 days, bigger species taking longer to fledge than the smaller species.

Notes
Large, predatory raptors have doubtless always attracted people's attention, respect, and awe. Wherever eagles occur, they are chronicled in the history of civilizations. Early Anglo-Saxons were known to hang an eagle on the gate of any city they conquered. Some North American Indian tribes and also Australian Aboriginal peoples deified large hawks or eagles. Several states have used likenesses of eagles as nation symbols, among them Turkey, Austria, Germany, Poland, Russia, and Mexico. Eagles are popular symbols on regal coats of arms and one of their kind, a fish-eater, was chosen as the emblem of the USA (although, as most USA schoolchildren know, Benjamin Franklin would have preferred that symbol to be the Wild Turkey.)

Status
Several of Ecuador's hawks and eagles are considered threatened or endangered, such as the HARPY EAGLE (CITES Appendix I listed) and CRESTED EAGLE (CITES Appendix II), both of which were formerly much more common in Ecuador. The northwest coastal population of Harpy Eagles in Ecuador has been extirpated probably due to hunting and deforestation. However, many of these large raptors enjoy extensive distributions external to the country, ranging from Mexico to northern or central South America, and are more numerous in other regions. The SNAIL KITE (CITES Appendix II) is uncommon in many parts of its range, including most of Ecuador except the southern coast, owing to destruction of its marsh habitats. The GRAY-BACKED HAWK of coastal forests is considered threatened. However, a few hawks adapt well to people's habitat alterations. A case in point is the common ROADSIDE HAWK. It prefers open habitats and, especially, roadsides. It has expanded its range and numbers in Ecuador with deforestation and road-building in areas that previously were large tracts of inaccessible closed forest. Conservation measures aimed at raptors are bound to be difficult to formulate and enforce because the birds are often persecuted for a number of reasons (hunting, pet and feather trade, ranchers protecting livestock) and they roam very large areas. Also, some breed and winter on different continents, and thus need

to be protected in all parts of their ranges, including along migration routes. Further complicating population assessments and conservation proposals, there are still plenty of Neotropical raptor species about which very little is known. For example, for the approximately 80 species of raptors that breed primarily in Central and South America (excluding the vultures), breeding behavior has not been described for 27 species and nests are unknown for 19 species. The typical prey taken by six species is unknown.

Profiles
Gray-headed Kite, *Leptodon cayanensis*, Plate 24a
American Swallow-tailed Kite, *Elanoides forficatus*, Plate 24b
Snail Kite, *Rostrhamus sociabilis*, Plate 24c
Double-toothed Kite, *Harpagus bidentatus*, Plate 24d
Plumbeous Kite, *Ictinia plumbea*, Plate 24e
Mangrove Black Hawk, *Buteogallus subtilis*, Plate 25a
Roadside Hawk, *Buteo magnirostris*, Plate 25b
Puna Hawk, *Buteo poecilochrous*, Plate 25c
Harpy Eagle, *Harpia harpyja*, Plate 25d
Ornate Hawk-eagle, *Spizaetus ornatus*, Plate 25e

11. Falcons and Osprey

Closely related to the hawks, eagles and kites, the *falcons* and their allies, the *forest-falcons* and *caracaras*, are placed in their own family, Falconidae. The family has about 60 species worldwide, 19 in Ecuador. Externally they look like kites and other hawks. The main differences are found in subtle but consistent divergences in internal structures of the skeleton that indicate separate evolutionary branches.

The OSPREY (Plate 26), or Fishing Eagle, occurs worldwide and is the only species in its family, Pandionidae. Its large size, white and black color pattern, peculiarly bowed wing profile in flight, and its obligatory association with water – coastal estuaries to Amazonian rivers – make it easy to recognize. Its loud whistles are frequent, especially when a neighboring Osprey invades its home space. Although it is common throughout lowland and even occasionally highland Ecuador, it has never been recorded breeding in the country. The population is a migratory and nonbreeding one, even though many individuals are present all months of the year.

Natural History

Ecology and Behavior
Typical falcons are best known for their remarkable eyesight and fast, aerial pursuit and capture of moving prey such as flying birds. The PEREGRINE FALCON, which very rarely nests in highland Ecuador, is considered to be the fastest bird in the world, achieving almost 320 km per hour (200 miles per hour) in a steep stoop on prey. For a prey item to be able to avoid or escape this speed of attack seems impossible, yet many if not most potential prey do escape. The success rate of attack is low, and the falcon must often try numerous times before finally catching something to eat or feed to its young. The hunting behavior of falcons has, over evolutionary time, shaped the behavior of their prey animals. Falcons hit perched or flying birds with their talons, stunning the prey and sometimes killing it outright. An individual bird caught unawares has little chance of escap-

ing the rapid, acrobatic falcons. But birds in groups have two defenses. First, each individual in a group benefits because the group, with so many eyes and ears, is more likely to spot a falcon at a distance than is a lone individual, thus providing all in the group opportunities to watch the predator as it approaches and so evade it. This sort of anti-predation advantage may be why some animals stay in groups. Second, some flocks of small birds, such as starlings, which usually fly in loose formations, immediately tighten their formation upon detecting a flying falcon. The effect is to decrease the distance between each bird, so much so that a falcon flying into the group at a fast speed and trying to take an individual risks injuring itself – the "block" of starlings is almost a solid wall of bird; the close formation also makes a single victim more difficult to target. Biologists believe that the flock tightens when a falcon is detected because the behavior reduces the likelihood of an attack.

As suggested by its name, the most typical of the falcons profiled here, the BAT FALCON (Plate 26), hunts at dusk for early-flying bats. During the day it goes after swallows and other birds, but often it also takes large flying insects. The caracaras are all scavengers and nest robbers. The BLACK CARACARA (Plate 26) is especially fond of raiding dense nesting colonies of Yellow-rumped Caciques (Plate 68) for eggs and nestlings. The amount of bare skin on the side of the face of a species is often a reflection of how much scavenging it does. Like the vultures, fewer face feathers on caracaras makes accumulation of gore and blood less likely and the head easier to clean. The LAUGHING FALCON (Plate 26) is a snake specialist, and the forest falcons are almost entirely bird predators. One of the easiest ways to see the elusive forest falcons is to squeak or kiss the back of your hand loudly when you hear one calling nearby. This sound mimics the distress calls of small birds – a call to supper for the forest-falcon.

The OSPREY is the quintessential fisherman. It hovers over the water until a fish rises close enough to the surface. Then the Osprey plunges, sometimes all but the upstretched wings underwater, to grab the fish in its extremely long and sharp talons. The soles of its feet are rough to better hold slippery fish. After emerging from the water and violently shaking itself to rid the feathers of water, it turns the fish head-forward and flies to a nearby dead tree to feast on its bounty.

Breeding
Falcons nest in vegetation, in tree and rock cavities or on a ledge. Some make stick nests, but others make no obvious nest preparation. Incubation of the eggs takes 25 to 35 days and in most species is performed only by the female. (In caracaras both sexes participate in incubation.) The male feeds the female until the chicks hatch, and then both sexes feed the chicks. The nestlings fledge after 25 to 49 days in the nest, but the parents continue to feed the youngsters for several weeks after they fledge, until they are proficient hunters.

Notes
People have had a close relationship with falcons for thousands of years. Falconry, in which captive falcons are trained to hunt and kill game at a person's command, may be the oldest sport, with evidence of it being practiced in China 4000 years ago and in Iran 3700 years ago. One of the oldest known books on a sport is "The Art of Falconry," written by the King of Sicily in 1248. Although falconry is not as widely practiced today, many countries have aficionados who continue the tradition.

Status

At least two of Ecuador's falcons are considered threatened. The ORANGE-BREASTED FALCON (CITES Appendix II) was never common in Ecuador, but now it can be looked for in only a few sites on the east slopes of the Andes and in the Oriente. The PLUMBEOUS FOREST-FALCON is a rare and highly localized species on the west slope of the Andes from southwestern Colombia to Northwestern Ecuador. Little is known of its biology. The RED-THROATED CARACARA formerly was a fairly common resident of northwestern Ecuador, but now is rare there and evidently declining in the Oriente. This species is a specialist on wasp and bee larvae, and insecticide spraying may be affecting both the bird itself as well as the availability of its specialized prey. By contrast, the YELLOW-HEADED CARACARA has expanded recently into the Oriente of Ecuador, probably due to forest felling and the creation of vast open areas – its preferred habitat.

Profiles

Black Caracara, *Daptrius ater*, Plate 26a
Laughing Falcon, *Herpetotheres cachinnans*, Plate 26b
Collared Forest-falcon, *Micrastur semitorquatus*, Plate 26c
Bat Falcon, *Falco rufigularis*, Plate 26d
Osprey, *Pandion haliaetus*, Plate 26e

12. Pigeons and Doves

The *pigeon* family, Columbidae, includes about 255 species worldwide, 27 in Ecuador. It is a diverse group with representatives on every continent except Antarctica. In Ecuador they inhabit environments from desert scrub to lowland rainforest, cloud forest, and páramo. In general the smaller species are called doves and the larger species pigeons, but there is considerable inconsistency.

All pigeons are generally recognized as such by almost everyone, a legacy of people's familiarity with domestic and feral pigeons. Pigeons worldwide vary in size from the dimensions of a sparrow to those of a small turkey; Ecuador's species range in body length from 15 to 35 cm (6 to 14 in). Doves and pigeons are plump-looking birds with compact bodies, short necks, and small heads. Legs are usually fairly short. Bills are small, straight, and slender. Typically there is a swollen bulge (cere) at the base of the bill. Body colors are generally soft and understated grays and browns with an occasional splash of bolder black or white. Some have subtle patches of iridescence, usually on the neck or wings. The female tends to have similar, if somewhat duller plumage to the male.

Natural History

Ecology and Behavior

Most pigeons and doves are at least partially arboreal, but several spend most of their time on the ground. They eat seeds, ripe and unripe fruits, berries and very rarely an insect. They do not have hard bills for seed cracking and thus swallow their food whole. Their chewing is accomplished in the *gizzard*, a muscular portion of the stomach in which food is smashed against small pebbles and other grit eaten from the soil. As they walk on the ground, all species characteristically bob their heads. Camouflage and rapid flight are the two most important anti-predator tactics used by doves. Many species are gregarious to some degree, and some form large flocks during the nonbreeding season.

Breeding

Doves and pigeons are monogamous breeders. Nests are shallow, open affairs of loose twigs, plant stems and roots placed on the ground, rock ledges or in shrubs and trees. Reproductive duties shared by male and female include nest-building, incubating the one or two eggs, and feeding the young. All doves and pigeons feed their young regurgitated *pigeon's milk*, a protein-rich fluid produced by sloughing off cells lining the crop, an enlarged portion of the esophagus otherwise used for food storage. As the chicks grow older the proportion of solid food fed them grows greater until no more pigeon's milk is supplied. Incubation time ranges from 11 to 28 days, depending on species size.

Notes

Although many pigeons today are very common, some species met extinction within the recent past. There are two particularly famous cases. The DODO was a large, flightless pigeon, the size of a turkey, with a large head and strong, robust bill and feet. Dodos lived, until the 17th century, on the island of Mauritius, in the Indian Ocean, east of Madagascar. Reported to be clumsy and stupid (hence the expression, "dumb as a dodo"), but probably just unfamiliar with and unafraid of predatory animals, such as people, they were killed by the thousands by sailors who stopped at the island to stock their ships with food. This caused population numbers to plunge; the birds were then finished off by the pigs, monkeys, and cats introduced by people to the previously predator-free island – animals that ate the Dodos' eggs and young. The only stuffed Dodo in existence was destroyed by fire in Oxford, England, in 1755.

North America's PASSENGER PIGEON, a medium-sized, long-tailed member of the family, suffered extinction because of overhunting and because of its habits of roosting, breeding, and migrating in huge flocks. People were able to kill many thousands of them at a time on the Great Plains in the central part of the USA, shipping the bodies to markets and restaurants in large cities through the mid-1800s. It is estimated that when Europeans first settled in the New World, there were three billion Passenger Pigeons, a population size perhaps never equaled by any other bird, and that they may have accounted for up to 25% or more of the birds in what is now the USA. It took only a little more than 100 years to kill them all; the last one died in the Cincinnati Zoo in 1914. The common ROCK DOVE, the urban pigeon with which everyone who has visited a city or town is familiar, is a native of the Old World. Domesticated for thousands of years and transported around the world by people, feral populations have colonized all settled and many unsettled areas of the Earth. In the wild, they breed and roost in cliffs and caves.

Status

In Ecuador only one species of this family is considered vulnerable, the OCHRE-BELLIED DOVE, a Tumbesian endemic restricted to the coast of southwestern Ecuador and northwestern Perú. Several New World pigeons in other regions, however, are now endangered, some critically so.

Profiles

Band-tailed Pigeon, *Columba fasciata*, Plate 27a
Pale-vented Pigeon, *Columba cayennensis*, Plate 27b
Ruddy Pigeon, *Columba subvinacea*, Plate 27c
Croaking Ground-dove, *Columbina cruziana*, Plate 27d

Black-winged Ground-dove, *Metriopelia melanoptera*, Plate 27e
Eared Dove, *Zenaida auriculata*, Plate 28a
White-tipped Dove, *Leptotila verreauxi*, Plate 28b
Ruddy Quail-dove, *Geotrygon montana*, Plate 28c

13. Parrots

Everyone knows parrots as caged pets, so discovering them for the first time in their natural surroundings is often a strange but somehow familiar experience (like a dog-owner's first sighting of a wild coyote). One has knowledge and expectations of the birds' behavior and antics in captivity, but how do they act in the wild? Along with toucans, parrots are probably the birds most commonly symbolic of the tropics. The 300+ parrot species that comprise the Family Psittacidae (the "P" is silent; try referring to parrots as psittacids to impress your friends and tour guide!) are globally distributed across the tropics with a few species spilling over into the temperate zones. In Ecuador, 47 different species are found, and they occupy habitats from coastal desert to high-altitude forest and the Amazon. Parrot fanciers have their own lexicon of common names that often bear no resemblance to the common names used by ornithologists. In Ecuador the common names most widely used divide this family mainly by size: the sparrow-sized parrotlets are about 10 cm (4 in) long and the smallest of all; the parakeets are long-tailed or short-tailed but small (20 to 30 cm, 8 to 12 in); the parrots are larger (30 to 45 cm, 12 to 18 in); and the macaws are the largest (60 to 100 cm, 24 to 40 in).

Parrots, regardless of size, share a set of distinctive traits that set them apart from all other birds. They are short-necked with a compact and stocky body. All have a short, hooked bill with a hinge on the upper half that provides great mobility for handling food and for clambering around branches and vegetation. Legs are short and feet, with toes that are very dexterous, are highly adapted for grasping. Although most species are green, many depart from this scheme, often in a spectacular fashion, with gaudy blues, reds and yellows. Their raucous calls in flight, usually in flocks, make them easy to see, but when they land in a tree overhead, they can virtually disappear instantaneously. Only the steady rain of discarded fruit parts gives away their presence. Your best view will probably be when a flock suddenly leaves a feeding tree, or when a flock is located loafing and squabbling the afternoon away in an isolated, open tree. To distinguish the various species: listen for differences in their voices; look for the length of the tail; and watch for the way they flap their wings – deep and full strokes or twittering, shallow strokes.

The star attractions of the parrot world in Ecuador are the *macaws*. There are two sizes of macaws; some species, like the CHESTNUT-FRONTED MACAW (Plate 29), are only a bit larger (46 cm, 18 in) than the largest parrots, while others such as the SCARLET MACAW (Plate 29) and the BLUE-AND-YELLOW MACAW (Plate 29) are enormous (90 cm, 35 in). The macaws have the loudest voices of all the parrots here, and you will inevitably hear them long before you see them appear from in back of a line of trees. Their slow but steady wingbeats together with their long tails make them unmistakable.

Natural History

Ecology and Behavior

Parrots are extremely noisy, highly social seed- and fruit-eaters. Some species give their assortment of harsh, often screeching vocalizations throughout the day, others only in flight, and others call from communal roosts mainly before leaving and when arriving. Many species roost in groups for the night, sometimes in the thousands in more protected parts of the forest or on islands. Often several species roost together. During early morning, flocks of parrots leave the roost, moving out to cover the forest in search of fruiting trees. They may travel up to 75 km (45 miles) or more in a day. In the afternoon the flocks begin to head back from all directions to the same roosting site. At certain times of the year, parrots of many species concentrate in huge wheeling flocks around high river banks to eat clay from the soil. A possible explanation for this behavior is that the clay, or the chemicals in it, aids in digestion. Another hypothesis is that clay helps counteract some of the potent toxins present in many fruits. If you can find such a parrot "salt lick," be sure to spend some time there; early morning is usually best.

Parrots use their special locomotory talent to clamber methodically through trees in search of fruits and flowers, using their powerful feet to grasp branches and their bills as, essentially, a third foot. Just as caged parrots, they will hang at odd angles and even upside down, the better to reach some delicious morsel. Parrot feet also function as hands, delicately manipulating food and bringing it to the bill. Parrots feed mostly on fruits and nuts, buds of leaves and flowers, and on flower parts and nectar. They are usually considered frugivores, but careful study reveals that when they attack fruit, it is usually to get at the seeds within. The powerful bill slices open fruit and crushes seeds. As one bird book colorfully put it, "adapted for opening hard nuts, biting chunks out of fruit, and grinding small seeds into meal, the short, thick, hooked parrot bill combines the destructive powers of an ice pick (the sharp-pointed upper mandible), a chisel (the sharp-edged lower mandible), a file (ridged inner surface of the upper mandible), and a vise." (F.G. Stiles and A.F. Skutch 1989) Thick, muscular parrot tongues are also specialized for feeding, used to scoop out pulp from fruit and nectar from flowers. Thus parrots, unlike most frugivorous birds, are not ingesting seeds to eventually disperse them when they defecate. They are, more technically, seed predators. However, some studies suggest that because of the large numbers of uneaten fruit that they drop to the ground, they make available fruits and their seeds to be dispersed by ground frugivores such as tinamous and rodents. These ground-dwelling species are more properly seed dispersers because they eat the pulp and so do not regularly destroy the seeds contained within.

Breeding

In all of the Ecuadorean parrots, the sexes are very similar or identical in appearance; breeding is monogamous and pairing is often for life. Nesting is carried out during the dry season and, for some, into the early wet season. Most species breed in cavities in dead trees, although a few build nests. Macaw nests are almost always placed 30 meters (100 ft) or more above the ground. A female parrot lays two to eight eggs, which she incubates alone for 17 to 35 days while being periodically fed regurgitated food by her mate. The helpless young of small parrots are nest-bound for 3 to 4 weeks, those of the huge macaws, 3 to 4 months. Both parents feed nestlings and fledglings.

Notes

Parrots have been captured for people's pleasure as pets for thousands of years; Greek records exist from 400 bc describing parrot pets. The fascination stems from the birds' bright coloring, their ability to imitate human speech and other sounds (strangely enough, they do not appear to mimic sounds in the wild), their individualistic personalities (captive parrots definitely like some people while disliking others), and their long life spans (up to 80 years in captivity). Likewise, parrots have been hunted and killed for food and to protect crops for thousands of years. Some Peruvian Incan pottery shows scenes of parrots eating corn and being scared away from crops. Historically, people have killed parrots to protect crops – Charles Darwin noted that in Uruguay in the early 1800s, thousands of parakeets were killed to prevent crop damage. Macaws, the largest parrots, are thought to have been raised in the past for food in the West Indies, and macaw feathers were used as ornaments and had ceremonial functions.

Status

Seventy or more parrot species are threatened or endangered worldwide, and at least eight species that occur in Ecuador are currently threatened. The GOLDEN-PLUMED PARROT is associated with cloud forests and a rare coniferous tree, *Podocarpus* (p. 14). Its highly spotty distribution is shrinking due mainly to habitat destruction. The even rarer YELLOW-EARED PARROT is another highland species associated with a locally distributed palm. Both the palm and the parrot are affected by human colonization and clearing of habitat for agriculture. The GREAT GREEN MACAW has been reduced in the country to probably less than 15 surviving pairs, all on the northwest and central coast. However, this species is more numerous in other parts of its range in Central and northern South America. The MILITARY MACAW has a highly disjunct distribution from Mexico to Bolivia, and in Ecuador is found only in widely separated, small areas along the eastern slopes of the Andes. The WHITE-BREASTED PARAKEET, EL ORO PARAKEET, SPOT-WINGED PARROTLET, RUSTY-FACED PARROT and ROSE-FACED PARROT are all smaller species with limited ranges that are considered threatened in Ecuador. The ranges and abundances of some other species, such as the SCARLET MACAW, have been severely reduced during the past 100 years, primarily owing to destruction of forests. Whereas during the early years of this century this macaw was common throughout Amazonian lowland areas, now it is absent from much of the Oriente.

Many Ecuadorean parrot species still enjoy healthy populations and are frequently seen. Unfortunately, however, parrots are subject to three powerful forces that, in combination, take heavy tolls on their numbers: parrots are primarily forest birds, and forests are increasingly under attack by farmers and developers; parrots are considered agricultural pests by farmers and orchardists owing to their seed- and fruit-eating, and are persecuted for this reason; and parrots are among the world's most popular cage birds. Several Ecuadorean species, especially the larger macaws, are prized as pets, and nests of these parrots are often robbed of young for local sale as pets or to international dealers. To get to the young birds, the nest tree, often a dead palm, is cut down. Few of the chicks survive the tree fall, and one of the few cavity nest sites around has been eliminated for renesting. For every macaw that reaches the market place, perhaps 20 to 50 die in the process. Without fast, additional protection, many more Ecuadorean parrots soon will be threatened.

Profiles

Pacific Parrotlet, *Forpus coelestis*, Plate 28d
Cobalt-winged Parakeet, *Brotogeris cyanoptera*, Plate 28e
Blue-and-yellow Macaw, *Ara ararauna*, Plate 29a
Scarlet Macaw, *Ara macao*, Plate 29b
Chestnut-fronted Macaw, *Ara severa*, Plate 29c
White-eyed Parakeet, *Aratinga leucopthalmus*, Plate 29d
Red-masked Parakeet, *Aratinga erythrogenys*, Plate 29e
Dusky-headed Parakeet, *Aratinga weddellii*, Plate 29f
White-breasted Parakeet, *Pyrrhura albipectus*, Plate 30a
Black-headed Parrot, *Pionites melanocephalus*, Plate 30b
Blue-headed Parrot, *Pionus menstruus*, Plate 30c
Orange-winged Parrot, *Amazona amazonica*, Plate 30d
Mealy Parrot, *Amazona farinosa*, Plate 30e

14. Cuckoos and Anis

Many of the *cuckoos* and *anis* (AH-neez) are physically rather plain but behaviorally rather extraordinary. As a group they employ some of the most bizarre breeding practices known among birds. Cuckoos and anis are considered by some to be in the same family, Cuculidae, which, with a total of 130 species, enjoys a worldwide distribution including both temperate and tropical areas; 17 species occur in Ecuador. While the cuckoos are shy and solitary birds of woodlands, forests and dense thickets, anis are bold, obvious and gregarious birds of savannahs, brushy scrub and river edges. Anis make you wonder where they perched before the advent of fences.

Most cuckoos are medium-sized, slender, long-tailed birds. Male and female mostly look alike, attired in plain browns, tans, and grays, often with streaked or spotted patches. Several have alternating white and black bands on their tail undersides. (Many cuckoos of the Old World are more colorful.) They have short legs and bills that curve downwards at the end. The STRIPED CUCKOO (Plate 31) is found commonly in open and cut-over brushlands on the west side of the Andes. Occasionally it will fly up from the ground or low vegetation and sit motionless on a fence post for many minutes. More often, however, you will be made aware of its presence by what must be the most persistent, and sometimes irritating, song of these open areas – two short whistles, the second note higher, and given over and over every two or three seconds throughout the middle of the day. The SQUIRREL CUCKOO (Plate 31) is a large red-brown species of secondary and primary forest throughout the lowlands on both sides of the Andes. Its long tail, with a little imagination resembling a squirrel's tail, is often all you see of it as it runs down a branch.

Anis are conspicuous medium-sized birds, glossy black all over, with iridescent sheens particularly on the head, neck and breast. Their bills are exceptionally large, with humped or crested upper ridges. The SMOOTH-BILLED ANI (Plate 31) is an abundant and obvious bird throughout the cleared areas of lowland Ecuador and on the marshy margins of lakes and rivers in the Oriente. Its all black color, loose and floppy flight, and large bill make it easy to recognize. The GREATER ANI (Plate 31) is a much larger edition with a distinct bluish tinge to the all-black body and a white eye. It occurs mainly along forested streams and lakes of the Oriente, but a few populations are on the coast. When the members of a flock start their loud and discordant vocalizations, it sounds like a boiler factory.

Natural History

Ecology and Behavior

Most of the cuckoos are arboreal. They eat insects, apparently having a special affinity for caterpillars. They even safely consume hairy caterpillars, which are avoided by most other predators because they have painful stinging hairs or even poisons. Cuckoos have been seen snipping off one end of a hairy caterpillar, squeezing the body with the bill and beating it against a branch until the toxic entrails fall out. They then can swallow the remains safely. How they get around the hairs is still a mystery, however. A few cuckoos, such as the GROUND CUCKOO, are ground-dwellers, eating small birds, snakes and lizards as well as insects. They are most often seen around army ant swarms, where they eat large insects as well as small antbirds attracted to the swarm.

The highly social anis forage in groups, usually on the ground. Frequently they feed around cattle, grabbing the insects that are flushed out of hiding places by the grazing mammals. They eat mostly bugs, but also a bit of fruit. Anis live in groups of eight to 25 individuals, each group containing two to eight adults and several juveniles. Each group defends a territory from other groups throughout the year. The flock both feeds and breeds within its territory.

Breeding

Cuckoos in the Old World are highly evolved brood parasites. They build no nests of their own, and the females lay their eggs in the nests of other species (the hosts). Immediately after hatching, cuckoo nestlings push the rightful heirs out of the nest, and the host adults then raise the young cuckoos as their own off-spring. In the New World only a few cuckoo species such as the STRIPED CUCKOO and the PHEASANT CUCKOO are brood parasites. The rest are typically monogamous breeders. The male feeds the female in courtship, especially during her egg-laying period. Both sexes build the plain platform nest that is made of twigs and leaves and placed in a tree or shrub. Both sexes incubate the two to six eggs for about 10 days, and both parents feed the young.

Anis, consistent with their highly social ways, are *communal breeders*. In the most extreme form, all individuals within the group contribute to a single nest, several females laying eggs in it – up to 29 eggs have been found in one nest. Many individuals help build the stick nest and feed the young. Although this behavior would seem to benefit all the individuals involved, the dominant male and female gain the most. Their eggs go in the communal nest last, on top of all the others, which often get buried. Also some females roll eggs out of the nest before depositing their own; thus it pays to be last.

Notes

The name cuckoo comes from the calls made by a common species in Europe, which is also the source of the sounds for cuckoo clocks.

Status

The STRIPED CUCKOO has been expanding its range within Ecuador, it being a species that does well in the forest edge, thicket, and open areas that increasingly are created through deforestation. One species of Ecuadorean cuckoo appears to be highly endangered, the BANDED GROUND-CUCKOO, a Chocó Forest endemic of northwestern Ecuador and southwestern Colombia.

Profiles

Striped Cuckoo, *Tapera naevia*, Plate 31a
Squirrel Cuckoo, *Piaya cayana*, Plate 31b
Smooth-billed Ani, *Crotophaga ani*, Plate 31c
Greater Ani, *Crotophaga major*, Plate 31d

15. Owls and Oilbird

Most *owls* are members of the Family Strigidae, with about 120 species worldwide, 25 in Ecuador. Most species are nocturnal, and they share distinctive features such as large heads with forward-facing eyes, hooked bills, plumpish bodies and sharp claws (talons). They tend to be camouflaged in colors of gray, brown and black. The group includes species that range in size from 15 to 75 cm (6 to 30 in). The sexes are similar, but females tend to be considerably larger. Because it is frequently active during the day, the FERRUGINOUS PYGMY-OWL (Plate 32) is one owl species that you are likely to see. It is the size of a large sparrow, and its high-pitched, staccato whistles are common in scrub areas and forest edges of the lowlands. On the coast and in the mountains, other, similar-looking, species are also active during the day and likely to make themselves fairly obvious by perching out in the open or calling. For owls active at night, try locating them by their call notes and songs. When you locate an owl this way, shine a flashlight on it to see it well. Often owls will sit for a long time on the same perch calling and looking around, even in the bright beam of your flashlight. Note the body size and facial patterns to identify them. Also, watch for the "ear" tufts, which are usually evident on species that have them; but they can also be flattened and difficult to see.

The OILBIRD (Plate 31) is the only species in the Family Steatornithidae. This strange species is 46 cm (18 in) long and has a wingspan of about 90 cm (3 ft). The beak is powerful and hooked with long hair-like feathers at either side. Apparently it is related to both the owls and the nightjars. It is found only in localized areas in northwestern South America from Venezuela to northern Bolivia, usually in immense colonies associated with large caves. There are but a few such caves known in Ecuador, from the highlands near Quito to the lower slopes on both sides of the Andes. Occasionally, dispersing individuals show up in different areas, usually found roosting during the day in a bush or some other vegetation. The warm brown color and silver-white spots are distinctive.

Natural History

Ecology and Behavior

In general, owls occupy a variety of habitats: forests, clearings, fields, grasslands, mountains and marshes. They are considered the nocturnal replacements of the day-active hawks, eagles and falcons. Although most owls hunt at night, some hunt at twilight (*crepuscular* activity) and some during the day. Owls eat a broad range of animals, from small mammals, birds and reptiles to insects and earthworms. Larger owls often develop a taste for smaller owls. Owl vision is good in low light (mainly in black and white, as they are considered to be largely color-blind). In the absence of moonlight and under the cloak of a forest canopy, however, owls hunt using their ears to locate prey. Not only are the ears themselves extremely sensitive but the two ears have different-sized openings. The effect of this asymmetry is comparable to the way you turn your head back and forth to better locate a sound. The owl can locate sounds without turning its head, especially important in flight. In addition, owls have soft flight feathers and a sound baffle of fringed feathers on the leading edge of the wings that provide a cloak of silence during flight; few prey can hear them coming. They swallow small prey whole, but instead of digesting or defecating the hard bones, fur and feathers, they regurgitate these parts in compact *owl pellets*. These gray oblong pellets often accumulate beneath an owl's perch. If you come across some of these pellets, pull them apart to see what the owl has been dining on.

The OILBIRD is one of the few bird species in the world to use bat-like echolocation, a type of sonar, to help it navigate, especially through the pitch black caves it inhabits. It utters clicking noises that echo off the cave walls, ceiling and rocks, and hearing these echoes, an oilbird can avoid the obstacles in its path. Hundreds of birds emerge from their cave entrance every evening to spend the night searching for high-fat-content fruits, like palm fruits. Each night, they fly long distances of up to 50 km (30 miles) from their cave. When they find suitable fruits, they fly up to the fruits and pull them off the tree often without landing. Before the light of dawn they return to the cave to spend the day.

Breeding
Most owls are monogamous breeders. They do not build nests themselves, but either take over nests abandoned by other birds or nest in cavities such as a tree or rock hole. Incubation of the one to 10 eggs is usually conducted by the female alone for 4 to 5 weeks, but she is fed regularly by her mate. Upon hatching, the female broods the young while the male continues to hunt for her and the young. The chicks fledge after 4 to 6 weeks in the nest.

OILBIRDS live permanently in pairs and roost at their nest sites on ledges within their cave all year around. The nest itself is made of droppings and partially digested fruit pulp and is little more than a mound with a slight depression in it. The four eggs are laid over a two-week period, but incubation begins with the first egg and lasts about 34 days. The young hatch at the same interval in which they were laid as eggs, and being fed only fruits (low in proteins), they develop very slowly. After about 70 days the young are very chubby – often weighing much more than the adults. At the end of three or four months they lose weight, develop adult plumage and leave the nest – nearly six months after being laid as eggs.

Notes
The forward-facing eyes of owls are a trait shared with only a few other animals: humans, most other primates, and to a degree, the cats. Eyes arranged in this way allow for almost complete binocular vision (both eyes can see the same object but from a slightly different angle), a prerequisite for good depth perception, which, in turn, is important for quickly judging distances when catching prey. However, owl eyes cannot move much, so owls swivel their heads to look left or right. Owls in many parts of the world, including Ecuador, are considered an omen of bad luck, or even worse, death. Many indigenous people kill owls when they encounter them to avoid any future visits and bad news brought by the owl. Young oilbirds have long been harvested from their caves by people for their fat deposits. Historically their carcasses were boiled down to provide oil for lamps and cooking.

Status
Owls in Ecuador are threatened primarily by forest clearing, but no species are

considered endangered. The OILBIRD has such highly localized colonies, that a single fire or hunter can quickly kill all the birds in an entire cave. In Ecuador the best defense has been to not publicize the location of newly discovered colony sites. Many of the known caves are officially protected, but only on paper.

Profiles

Tropical Screech-owl, Otus choliba, Plate 32a
Crested Owl, Lophostrix cristata, Plate 32b
Spectacled Owl, Pulsatrix perspicillata, Plate 32c
Ferruginous Pygmy-owl, Glaucidium brasilianum, Plate 32d
Black-banded Owl, Ciccaba huhula, Plate 32e
Oilbird, Steatornis caripensis, Plate 31e

16. Nightjars and Potoo

Species of birds known as nightjars are in the Family Caprimulgidae, which has about 70 species worldwide, 19 species in Ecuador. Like their closest relatives the owls, nightjars are primarily nocturnal. They have a very characteristic appearance. In the New World most range in size from 16 to 32 cm (6 to 12 in) long. They have long wings, medium or long tails, and big eyes. Their small, stubby bills enclose big, wide mouths that they open in flight to scoop up flying insects. Many species have bristles around the mouth area, which act as a food funnel. With their short legs and weak feet, they are poor walkers – flying is their usual mode of locomotion. The plumage of these birds is uniformly cryptic: mottled, spotted, and barred mixtures of browns, grays, tans, and black. They often have white patches on their wings or tails that can be seen only in flight. The PAURAQUE (Plate 33) is the most common nightjar in Ecuador.

The closely related potoos are placed in their own family, the Nyctibiidae, with seven species that occur from Mexico south into Argentina. In Ecuador there are five species, but you are likely to find only one of them, the COMMON POTOO (Plate 33). At night, when it is active, it gives a mournful series of long, slow and low descending whistles. The locals often call it madre de la luna (mother of the moon) or alma perdida (lost soul) because of its tendency to sing on full-moon nights and the seeming tragedy emoted by its song. During the day this bird sits on branches, usually out in the open, and with its camouflaged coloring and its bill pointed into the air, it looks like a dead branch.

Natural History

Ecology and Behavior

Most nightjars are night-active birds, with some becoming active at twilight (crepuscular activity). They feed on flying insects, which they catch on the wing, either by forays out from a perched location on the ground or from tree branches, or with continuous circling flight. You can see some species feeding on insects drawn to lights at night. Others you will see only as you flush them from their daytime roost on the ground or in low vegetation. Their camouflage coloring makes them difficult to see, even when you are close to them. The potoos are solitary species that hunt at night for large insects and small birds, lizards and occasionally mammals. A potoo's immense mouth opens like a cavern to catch prey in flight.

Breeding

Nightjars breed monogamously. No nest is built, but instead the female lays her one or two eggs on the ground in a small depression, usually under a bush or a rock. Either the female alone or both sexes incubate the eggs for 18 to 20 days, and both parents feed the young once they hatch. As is typical of many ground-nesting species, regardless of family, nightjars engage in *broken-wing displays* to distract predators from the nest and young. They flop around on the ground, often with one or both wings held down as if injured, making gargling or hissing sounds, all the while moving away from the nest. Potoos build no nest but lay a single egg in a crevice of a large branch or stump, usually high up in a tree. The breeding biology is poorly known, but apparently both sexes are involved with incubation.

Notes

The other names for nightjars are *goatsuckers* or *nighthawks*, both of which are misleading monikers. At twilight some species fly low over the ground near grazing animals, such as goats. The birds often fly right next to the mammals to catch insects being scared up as they walk through the grass. Evidently the assumption was that these birds were after the goats' milk, and a legend was born. These often pointed-winged species of birds were also mistaken for hawks flying around at dusk and at night, when accurate identification was difficult, and the name "nighthawk" has stuck ever since. One of the nightjars, North America's COMMON POORWILL, may be the only bird known actually to hibernate, as some mammals do, during very cold weather. During their dormant state, poorwills save energy by reducing their metabolic rate and their body temperature, the latter by about 22 8C (40 8F).

Status

None of the Ecuadorean nightjars is threatened. In the New World, the WHITE-WINGED NIGHTJAR of Brazil and Paraguay and the PUERTO RICAN NIGHTJAR occur in very limited areas and are endangered.

Profiles

Sand-colored Nighthawk, *Chordeiles rupestris*, Plate 33a
Pauraque, *Nyctidromus albicollis*, Plate 33b
Lyre-tailed Nightjar, *Uropsalis lyra*, Plate 33c
Common Potoo, *Nyctibius griseus*, Plate 33d

17. Swifts and Swallows

Swifts and *swallows* are remarkably similar in appearance and behavior, but they are not closely related. They both rely on the same feeding technique, catching insects on the wing during long periods of sustained flight. Swifts, although superficially resembling swallows, are instead closely related to hummingbirds. There are 80 or so species of swifts (Family Apodidae) worldwide in temperate and tropical areas; 14 species are found in Ecuador, some albeit rarely. Swifts, like swallows, are slender, streamlined birds, with long, pointed wings. They are 9 to 25 cm (3.5 to 10 in) long and have very short legs, short tails or long, forked tails, and very short but broad bills. Swifts' tails are stiffened to support the birds as they cling to vertical surfaces. The sexes look alike: sooty-gray or brown, with white or grayish rumps or flanks. Many are glossily iridescent. The most widespread and among the largest species in Ecuador is the WHITE-COLLARED SWIFT

(Plate 34). Although they nest behind waterfalls high in the mountains, they can be expected anywhere in the lowlands, often in immense and noisy flocks high in the air as they seek insect concentrations. The SHORT-TAILED SWIFT (Plate 34) is a lowland species in the Oriente; its tailless appearance and light gray rump are the best characters to use to distinguish it from several similar species found in the same area. It, however, is usually the most common of these "tailless" swift species.

The swallow family, Hirundinidae, is related to perching birds such as fly-catchers, warblers and sparrows. There are 80 species of swallows worldwide, and 15 species in Ecuador, four of which winter here or pass through on their way to or from North American breeding grounds. Swallows are small, streamlined birds, 11.5 to 21.5 cm (4.5 to 8.5 in) long, with short necks, bills and legs. They have long, pointed wings and, often, forked tails, wonderfully adapted for fast and sustained flight; they have amazing ability to maneuver in the air as they pursue flying insects or chase each other for competitive or amorous intentions. Some are colored in shades of blue, green or black, but many are gray or brown. The sexes look alike, at least to us. On the coast, the GRAY-BREASTED MARTIN (Plate 35) is abundant, often gathering by the thousands at dusk to roost on electric wires.

Natural History

Ecology and Behavior

Among the birds, swifts and swallows represent the pinnacle of flying prowess and aerial pursuit of insects. It seems as if they fly effortlessly all day, circling low over water and land, or flying in seemingly erratic patterns high overhead. Swifts especially are perpetual fliers, rarely roosting except at night, when they come together in large groups to spend the non-flying hours gathered on a vertical cliff face behind a waterfall, inside a hollow tree or among the fronds of a palm tree. They roost on these vertical surfaces clinging with their tiny but sharply-clawed feet and bracing themselves against the sides of the roost with their stiff tail feathers. A swift spends more time airborne than any other type of bird, even copulating in the air in a death-defying tail-spin that gives meaning to the concept of sexual thrills. The name swift is apt as these are the fastest flying birds in level flight, moving along at up to 160 kph (100 mph). Swifts can be told from swallows by their faster, more twittering wingbeats, made possible by an exceptionally short arm bone (the humerus). Some species of swifts hunt every day for insects hundreds of miles from the nesting area. The chicks of swifts have the ability to go into short-term physiological inactivity (*torpor*) during extended periods of inclement weather when no insects are flying. They can endure the lack of food for up to a week by lowering their body temperatures and energetic requirements (and thus their need for food).

Swallows also take insects on the wing as they fly back and forth over water and open areas. Some also eat berries. Swallows perch more frequently than swifts, often resting during the hottest parts of the day on tree branches over water or open areas. Directly after dawn, however, and at dusk, swallows are always airborne. Because swallows depend each day on capturing enough insects, their daily habits are largely tied to the prevailing weather. Flying insects are thick in the atmosphere on warm, sunny days, but relatively scarce on cold, wet ones. Therefore, on good days, swallows can catch their fill of bugs in only a few hours of flying, virtually anywhere. But on cool, wet days, they may need to forage all day to find enough food, and they tend to do so over water or low to the ground, where under such conditions bugs are more available.

Breeding

Swifts are monogamous, and most are colonial breeders, but some nest solitarily. The sexes share nesting chores. Nests are usually attached to vertical surfaces of rocks, tree cavities or palm fronds, depending on the species of swift. The nests consist of plant pieces, twigs and feathers glued together with the birds' saliva. One to six eggs are incubated for 16 to 28 days, with young fledging at 25 to 65 days of age. Swallows are also monogamous; many species breed in dense colonies of hundreds to thousands of pairs. They make nests of mud and some plant material which they attach to vertical surfaces, or they nest in cavities of trees, or tunnel into vertical banks. Both sexes or the female alone incubate the three to seven eggs for 13 to 16 days. Both parents help feed the young for 18 to 28 days, until the young fledge.

Notes

Nests of swifts in some parts of the Old World are almost totally made of saliva, and these nests are harvested to make birds' nest soup. Swallows have a long history of beneficial association with people. In the New World, owing to their insect-eating habits, they have been popular with people going back to the time of the ancient Mayan civilization. Mayans, it is believed, respected and welcomed swallows because they reduced insect damage to crops. In fact, Cozumel (the word refers to swallows), off Mexico's Yucatán Peninsula, is the Island of Swallows. People's alterations of natural habitats, harmful to so many species, are often helpful to swallows, which adopt buildings, bridges, road culverts, road banks, and quarry walls as nesting areas. BARN SWALLOWS in some areas of North America have for the most part given up nesting in anything other than human-crafted structures. The result of this close association is that, going back as far as ancient Rome, swallows have been considered good luck. Superstitions attached to the relationship abound; for example, it is said that the cows of a farmer who destroys a swallow's nest will give bloody milk. Arrival of the first migratory Barn Swallows in Europe is considered a welcoming sign of approaching spring, as is the arrival of CLIFF SWALLOWS at some of California's old Spanish missions.

Status

The WHITE-CHESTED SWIFT, considered threatened, is highly localized in the highlands of southern Colombia and occasionally is seen in Ecuador. So little is known of many species of swifts that we are uncertain of their populations' sizes or vulnerabilities. None of the swallows that breeds or winters in Ecuador is threatened, but the PALE-FOOTED SWALLOW of the eastern slope of the Andes is so local in Ecuador that habitat or nesting site destruction could quickly threaten its status.

Profiles

White-collared Swift, *Streptoprocne zonaris*, Plate 34a
Short-tailed Swift, *Chaetura brachyura*, Plate 34b
Fork-tailed Palm-swift, *Tachornis squamata*, Plate 34c
White-winged Swallow, *Tachycineta albiventer*, Plate 34d
Southern Rough-winged Swallow, *Stelgidopteryx ruficollis*, Plate 34e
Gray-breasted Martin, *Progne chalybea*, Plate 35a
White-banded Swallow, *Atticora fasciata*, Plate 35b

18. Hummingbirds

Hummingbirds are birds of extremes. They are among the most recognized kinds of birds, the smallest of birds, and arguably the most beautiful, albeit on a small scale. Fittingly, much of their biology is nothing short of amazing. Found only in the New World, the hummingbird family, Trochilidae, contains about 330 species, more than 200 of which call Ecuador home! The variety of forms encompassed by the family, not to mention the brilliant iridescence of most of its members, is indicated by the diversity and inventiveness needed by biologists to give descriptive names to these species: emeralds, sunangels, sunbeams, comets, metaltails, fairies, woodstars, woodnymphs, pufflegs, sabrewings, thorntails, thornbills, sicklebills and lancebills. Hummingbirds live in a broad spectrum of habitats from Alaska to southern Argentina. Various species are resident at snow-line in the Andes (4000 m, 13,000 ft) down to deserts and mangrove areas along the coast. All they seem to require to live in a region is a reliable supply of flower nectar and a few insects for protein.

Almost everyone can identify hummingbirds (call them hummers to sound like an expert). They are mostly tiny birds, usually clad in iridescent metallic greens, reds, violets and blues, that whiz by us at high speeds, the smallest of them more resembling big insects than respectable birds. Most hummers are in the range of only 6 to 13 cm (2.5 to 5 in) long, although a few of the larger kinds reach 20 cm (8 in), and they tip the scales at an almost imperceptibly low 2 to 9 g (most being 3 to 6 g) – the weight of a large paper-clip! Bill length and shape vary extensively among species. Many of them have distinctively formed bills to fit precisely into a species or genus of flowers from which that hummingbird species delicately draws its liquid food. Males are usually more colorful than females, and many males have gorgets, bright, glittering throat patches that in the right light are red, violet, green or blue. A little turn of the head, however, will change the reflection to black. Not all hummers are so vividly outfitted, however. One group, called the *hermits* (supposedly because of their solitary ways), has dull greenish-brown and gray plumages. Hummers have tiny legs and feet; in fact, they are included by most ornithologists with the swifts (p. 126) in the avian Order Apodiformes, which means "without feet." With more than 200 species to be seen in Ecuador, we can only begin to introduce you to some of its hummingbirds. The 21 species we have chosen to profile are a cross section of the ranges of sizes, colors and adaptations you can see in various habitats throughout the country. These species are also the ones you are most likely to see and be able to identify by their habitats and distinctive traits.

Natural History

Ecology and Behavior

Because of their many anatomical, behavioral and ecological specializations, hummingbirds have long attracted the research attention of biologists. The outcome is that we know quite a lot about these tiny birds:

(1) Hummers are capable of very rapid, finely controlled, acrobatic flight, more so than any other type of bird. The bones of their wings have been modified to allow for stationary hovering flight as well as the unique ability to fly backwards. Their wings beat in a figure-8-shaped wingstroke and at a speed beyond our ability to distinguish the individual beats – up to 80 times per second. Because

most people see hummers only during the birds' foraging trips, they often appear to be flying continuously, as they zip from flower to flower. They do, however, perch every now and again, providing the best chance to see them well.

(2) Hummingbirds have very fast metabolisms, a necessary condition for small, warm-blooded animals. To pump enough oxygen and nutrient-delivering blood around their little bodies, their hearts beat up to 10 times faster than human hearts – 600 to 1000 times per minute. To obtain sufficient energy to fuel their high metabolism, hummingbirds must eat many times each day. They can starve quickly without almost constant feeding. At night, when they are inactive, they burn much of their available energy reserves and on cold nights, if not for special mechanisms, they would surely starve to death. The chief method to avoid energy depletion on cold nights is to enter into a sleep-like state of *torpor*, during which the body's temperature is lowered to just above that of the outside world, from 17 to 28 8C (30 to 50 8F) below their normal daytime operating body temperature. This torpor means they virtually stop using and needing energy; in effect, they hibernate each night. If you ever find a hummingbird perched as if in a daze early on a cool morning, it is not sick – just not yet warmed up and ready for its active life in the daytime.

(3) All hummingbirds are *nectarivores* – they get most of their nourishment from consuming nectar from flowers (thus the name *chupaflor* in Spanish, which means flower-sucker). They have long, thin bills and specialized tongues, which they can extend far into the long, thin flowers and the nectar, or sugar water, reward that awaits them at the bottom. This is done while the hummingbird hovers, but a few species must land on the flower and even turn their heads upside down to get access to the nectar. The advantage for the flower to provide this nectar reward is that the hummingbird's head must pass by the male parts of the flower, which have pollen on their surfaces. This pollen sticks to the feathers of the hummingbird, and then some of it is jostled to drop off on the female parts of the next flower – thus achieving *pollination*, or sex via an intermediary. Because nectar is primarily a sugar and water solution, hummingbirds need to obtain additional nutrients, such as proteins, from other sources, especially when feeding growing chicks. Thus, they also eat insects and spiders, which they catch in the air or pluck from leaf surfaces or even from spider webs. Some recent studies suggest that these insects make up a much larger proportion of a hummingbird's diet than is generally believed, some going so far as to suggest that some hummingbird species visit flowers more often to catch insects there than to gather nectar.

(4) Hummingbird-pollinated flowers are often shaped to permit only a single or a few species of hummingbirds with the matching shape and length of bill to be able to reach the nectar source. The advantage to the hummingbirds is that insects and other species of hummingbirds cannot compete for the nectar in that species of flower. The advantage to the flower is that these specialized hummingbirds won't be wandering around visiting lots of other species of flowers and dropping pollen in all the wrong places. The specialization ensures that the next flower visited is highly likely to be of the same species, and thus these flowers don't have to produce much extra pollen. They can use that energy instead to make better roots, more leaves, and other useful parts that otherwise might have been sacrificed. Interlopers in this *mutualistic* interaction are a group of pollen-eating mite species. Mites are minuscule arthropods, allied with the spiders and ticks. Some mites may spend their lives on a single plant, feeding and reproducing, but others, perhaps searching for mates or new sites to colonize, try to reach

other plants. Walking to another plant for such a small animal is almost out of the question. What to do? The mites jump onto the bills of hummingbirds when the birds visit flowers and become hitchhikers on the bird, usually hiding in their nostrils. The passengers leap off the bird's bill during a subsequent visit to a plant of the same species that they left, necessary because the mites are specialized for certain plants. Recent research suggests that the passenger mites monitor the scents of flowers to identify the correct type, to know when to get off the bus.

(5) Many hummers are highly aggressive birds, energetically defending individual flowers or feeding territories from all other hummingbirds, regardless of species, as well as from large insects. Not all are territorial, however. Some are *trapline feeders*, repeatedly following a regular route around a large undefended section of the habitat and checking the same series of widely spaced flowering plants for their nectar. Unlike many plants that put out all their flowers at the same time, and then only for a short period, these trapline types of plants put out only one or a few flowers each day, but they continue doing so for several weeks, so the hummingbirds can learn about and depend on this nectar source. Some traplines can be more than a kilometer (0.6 mile) long. Whether a bird defends a territory or not depends on the balance of the costs of energy used and the benefits of energy (in terms of resources) gained. If the flowers in an area are superabundant, providing sufficient food for all, or if the flowers are so spread out that no one hummingbird could possibly defend them all (as in trapline flowers), then owning and defending a territory is not cost-effective. If the opposite is the case, and by keeping away interlopers from a defendable area with limited nectar, a hummingbird can keep more of the nectar for itself, then a territory is worthwhile.

Predators on hummingbirds include small agile hawks and falcons, large frogs and insects such as preying mantises, which ambush the small birds as they feed at flowers. Another hazard is large spider webs, from which sometimes a poor hummingbird cannot extricate itself.

Breeding

Hummingbirds are polygamous breeders in which females do almost all the work. In some species a male in his territory advertises for females by singing squeaky songs. A female enters the territory and, following often spectacular aerial courtship displays, mates. She then leaves the male's territory to nest on her own. Other species are lec breeders, especially some of the hermits. Three to 25 males gather in a cleared area of the forest undergrowth, each with a tiny mating territory in that area in which he sings his squeaky little song in the hope of impressing and attracting a passing female to mate with him. The males spend hours there each day during the breeding season, singing their little hearts out. When a female enters a lec area, she chooses a lucky stud from among the males there and mates with him. A male might spend months at a lec but have only one 15-minute mating interaction with a female, or, if his song is pitiful and unimpressive, mate with no females. Other males, presumably the Placido Domingos and Garth Brooks of the hummingbird-world, attract more females with their songs and mate with many of them in a season. (This is not to imply that Placido and Garth are promiscuous.) The females construct their tiny nests from plant parts, mosses, lichens, feathers, animal hairs and spider webbing. The nests are placed perched on the top of small branches, often attached with spider webbing. Hermits use this spider webbing to weave together the sides of the tip of a large-leafed plant. They then add plant material to construct a nest that hangs on the underside of the leaf, protected from rain and predators. The female lays two eggs, incubates them for 15 to 19 days, and feeds the chicks regurgitated nectar and insects for 20 to 26 days until they fledge.

Notes

Intriguingly, some hummingbirds are as curious about us as we are of them. A common occurrence while following a trail is to be closely approached by a passing hummingbird, which stops in midair to size up the large primate, darts this way and that to view the intruder from all angles, then, its curiosity apparently satisfied, zips off into the forest. You can increase your chances of this type of encounter by wearing a bright red bandanna, or tying it to your pack as you hike. Hummers always seem eager to investigate a new source of nectar, and the red color is usually their cue to a freshly opened flower. Several eco-lodges in the higher elevations have hummingbird feeders on their porches. Dozens of flashy large hummingbirds chase each other to gain access to the sugar water while you sit only a meter or two away. For some reason, these hummingbird feeders do not work well in the lowlands, probably because they attract so many wasps and bees.

Several groups of Indians used colorful, iridescent hummingbird feathers in their wedding ornaments. Hummingbird bodies have a long mythical history in Latin America of being imbued with potent powers as love charms. Having a dead hummer in the hand or pocket is thought by some even today to be a sure way to appear irresistible to a member of the opposite sex. Even powdered hummingbird is sold for this purpose.

Status

At least 30 species of hummers are currently threatened or considered vulnerable to threat. In Ecuador, five are threatened or endangered, including the ESMERALDAS WOODSTAR (Plate 39), LITTLE WOODSTAR, VIOLET-THROATED METALTAIL, TURQUOISE-THROATED PUFFLEG and BLACK-BREASTED PUFFLEG. Several other Ecuadorean species are very uncommon in the country, but are more abundant in other parts of their ranges.

Profiles

Green Hermit, Phaethornis guy, Plate 35c
Long-tailed Hermit, Phaethornis superciliosus, Plate 35d
Little Hermit, Phaethornis longuemareus, Plate 35e
White-tipped Sicklebill, Eutoxeres aquila, Plate 36a
White-necked Jacobin, Florisuga mellivora, Plate 36b
Sparkling Violetear, Colibri coruscans, Plate 36c
Green Thorntail, Popelairia conversii, Plate 36d
Fork-tailed Woodnymph, Thalurania furcata, Plate 36e

Rufous-tailed Hummingbird, Amazilia tzacatl, Plate 37a
Chimborazo Hillstar, Oreotrochilus chimborazo, Plate 37b
Ecuadorean Piedtail, Phlogophilus hemileucurus, Plate 37c
Green-crowned Brilliant, Heliodoxa jacula, Plate 37d
Giant Hummingbird, Patagona gigas, Plate 37e

Collared Inca, Coeligena torquata, Plate 38a
Sword-billed Hummingbird, Ensifera ensifera, Plate 38b
Buff-tailed Coronet, Boissonneaua flavescens, Plate 38c
Gorgeted Sunangel, Heliangelus strophianus, Plate 38d

Booted Racket-tail, Ocreatus underwoodii, Plate 38e
Black-tailed Trainbearer, Lesbia victoriae, Plate 39a
Purple-backed Thornbill, Ramphomicron microrhynchum, Plate 39b
Esmeraldas Woodstar, Acestrura berlepschi, Plate 39c

19. Trogons

Although not as familiar to most people as other gaudy birds such as toucans and parrots, trogons are generally regarded by wildlife enthusiasts as among the globe's most visually impressive and glamorous birds. The Family Trogonidae inhabits tropical and semi-tropical regions throughout the Neotropics, Africa and southern Asia. It consists of about 40 species, all of them colorful, medium-sized birds with compact bodies, short necks and short, almost parrot-like bills. The largest of these species, the quetzals, are the most dazzling. Considering the broad and widely separated geographical areas over which the species of this family are spread, the uniformity of the family's body plan and plumage pattern is striking. Males are consistently more colorful than the females and have metallic or glittering green, blue or violet heads, backs and chests. Their breasts and undersides are contrasting bright red, yellow or orange. The duller females usually have the bright back and head colors replaced with brown or gray, but they share the brightly colored breasts and bellies of the males. The characteristic tail is long and squared off, with horizontal black and white stripes on the underside. Trogons usually sit erect with their distinctive tails pointing straight down to the ground.

Natural History

Ecology and Behavior
You usually see trogons by themselves or occasionally in pairs. In spite of their persistent calls, they are often difficult to locate and see. Their bright colors meld into the colors of the foliage, and except during their fast and darting flight, they tend to sit still for long periods. At a fruiting tree they will fly up to a fruit and grab it in the bill without landing. They take big insects and occasionally small lizards in much the same way. They are probably most easily seen as part of a mixed species feeding flock in the canopy. At these times they move around more and tend to sit out in the open for short periods.

Breeding
Trogons are monogamous, nesting in tree cavities and occasionally in excavations in arboreal ant or termite nests. Generally the female incubates the two or three eggs overnight, and the male takes over during the day. Incubation is 17 to 19 days. Young are tended by both parents, and fledging is at 14 to 30 days.

Notes

The RESPLENDENT QUETZAL of Central America, a large trogon with extremely long tail feathers, is revered and held sacred by several indigenous groups. The skin of trogons and quetzals is so thin that it has been described as being like wet toilet paper. Why is a question no one yet has been able to answer satisfactorily, but it does mean that you are unlikely to ever see trogons fighting with each other; the slightest cut would be severe.

Status

The trogons and quetzals of Ecuador are fairly common, and apparently none are threatened. However, the RESPLENDENT QUETZAL of Central America is considered endangered (CITES Appendix I) because of hunting and continuing destruction of its cloud forest habitat.

Profiles

Golden-headed Quetzal, *Pharomachrus auriceps*, Plate 39d
White-tailed Trogon, *Trogon viridis*, Plate 40a
Collared Trogon, *Trogon collaris*, Plate 40b
Violaceous Trogon, *Trogon violaceus*, Plate 40c
Masked Trogon, *Trogon personatus*, Plate 40d

20. Kingfishers

Kingfishers are handsome, bright birds, and most of Ecuador's are easy to see. Most often found along forest streams, large rivers and lowland lakes, they are included in the worldwide Family Alcedinidae (but the New World species are sometimes split into their own family, Cerylidae). Nearly 100 species occur throughout the world in temperate and tropical areas, and five of the six New World species are found in Ecuador. They range in size from 12 to 46 cm (5 to 16 in), but all are similar in form: large heads with very long, robust, straight bills, short necks, and short legs. Their colors are blue-gray or oily green above with white and chestnut breasts. The largest species in Ecuador, the RINGED KINGFISHER (Plate 41), is loud and obvious on large rivers and lakes of lowlands on both sides of the Andes. Its blue-gray back and head, along with its large size, separate it from the other local kingfishers. It often flies high overhead as it moves from one water area to another, giving its far-carrying "check" call. An oily green back and head is characteristic of the other four species in Ecuador.

Natural History

Ecology and Behavior

New World kingfishers, as the name suggests, are all mainly piscivores, or fish-eaters. Usually seen hunting alone, a kingfisher sits quietly on a low branch over water attentively scanning the water below. When it sees a fish, it swoops down and dives head first into the water, sometimes as deep as 60 cm (24 in) to catch the unwary fish in its bill. If successful, the kingfisher returns to its perch, beats the hapless fish several times on the branch and then swallows it head first. The RINGED KING-FISHER will also hover over the water several seconds before making the plunge. Occasionally they will go after tadpoles and large aquatic insects. Kingfishers have a buzzy and fast flight when moving low over the water's surface.

Kingfishers are highly territorial, noisily defending their territory from other members of the same species with noisy chattering, chasing and fighting. They inhabit lowland forests and waterways, but occasionally the Ringed Kingfisher is found at ponds in cloud forests at 2500 m (8000 ft). The step-wise size differences of Ecuador's five kingfisher species may not be just a coincidence. Because studies show that each smaller kingfisher species tends to catch and eat fish smaller than the next larger species, the graded variation in body size may be a way to reduce potential competition for fish. That one species seldom, if ever, chases an individual of another species from its territory reinforces this hypothesis of reduced competition by having different body and prey sizes.

Breeding

Kingfishers are monogamous breeders that nest in tunnels excavated from vertical or near vertical banks over water. Both mates help defend their territory, and both also help dig the nest tunnel, which can be 0.75 to 1.5 m (2 to 5 ft) deep. Both parents incubate the three to eight eggs for a total of 19 to 26 days. They feed their young increasingly large fish until they fledge at 25 to 38 days old. Fledglings continue to be fed outside the nest by the parents for up to 10 weeks. Eventually the parents expel the young from the territory, and the young must then establish their own. The kingfishers are notoriously bad housekeepers, and the stench of decaying fish and droppings is often your first clue that a nest tunnel is nearby. This very stench, however, may be so overpowering that it overwhelms the delicate olfactory senses of predators and discourages them from entering to eat what would otherwise be easy prey.

Notes

Kingfishers are the subject of a particularly rich mythology, a sign of the bird's conspicuousness and its association throughout history with oceans, lakes, and rivers. The power over wind and waves that was attributed by sailors to the god Halcyon was passed on to the Halcyon bird, or the kingfisher, which became credited with protecting sailors and calming storms. The seven days before and after the winter solstice were thought to be the days when this kingfisher nested and were thus days of peace and calm, the "halcyon" days.

Status

All the New World kingfisher species are moderately common to abundant and none is considered threatened.

Profiles

Ringed Kingfisher, *Ceryle torquata*, Plate 41a
Amazon Kingfisher, *Chloroceryle amazona*, Plate 41b
Green Kingfisher, *Chloroceryle americana*, Plate 41c
Green-and-rufous Kingfisher, *Chloroceryle inda*, Plate 41d
American Pygmy Kingfisher, *Chloroceryle aenea*, Plate 41e

21. Jacamars and Puffbirds

Two interesting and closely related Neotropical families distantly related to kingfishers are the *jacamars* and *puffbirds*. The jacamar family (Galbulidae) includes 18 species, with nine in Ecuador, and the puffbird family (Bucconidae) includes about 30 species, with 19 in Ecuador. Species of both families are generally forest dwellers, mostly in warm lowlands. Jacamars are by far the flashier members of these two families, with most having glittering green and blue backs and heads, and noisy vocalizations. Some have described them as over-sized hummingbirds because of their colors and long, sharp bills. They are, however, much larger than hummingbirds (15 to 31 cm, 6 to 12 in, long) and have distinctly different behavior. Puffbirds are, in contrast, much duller in color – mainly subdued browns and grays or black and white. Their size range is somewhat smaller than that for jacamars, 15 to 28 cm (6 to 11 in). Their bills are moderately long but most are very thick and often end in a small hook.

Natural History

Ecology and Behavior

You are most likely to see jacamars along small forest streams and at forest clearings. Here they sit, usually in pairs or family groups, chattering away, moving their heads back and forth and waiting for a large butterfly, dragonfly, or other tasty insect to fly by. One of them then darts out and deftly snatches the insect out of the air with the tip of its long bill and then returns to a perch, often the same one from which it launched the aerial attack. After slamming the insect against the perch a couple of times, it removes the wings and swallows the body. Quite often you will find a pile of discarded butterfly and other insect wings on a path. This is a good sign for you to look up and search for a jacamar roosting overhead. They often have a series of favorite perches they use through the day, so if it's not there when you first look, check again later.

Most puffbirds are less gaudy and noticeable than jacamars. However, a few species are show-offs, and you have a good chance of seeing them. The WHITE-NECKED PUFFBIRD (Plate 42) is striking with its black and white colors, but you will see it only if you look for it in the canopy, where it often sits on an open branch by itself for an hour or more without moving. If you are visiting one of the canopy towers built in the Oriente of Ecuador, you will have a better possibility of seeing one without straining your neck staring at the tops of trees from the ground. It and most other puffbirds hunt by waiting patiently for a lizard, small snake or large insect to walk or run on a nearby trunk or on the ground. Then the puffbird swoops from its perch and snatches the luckless prey in its bill. The WHITE-FRONTED NUNBIRD (Plate 42) makes itself so obvious, vocally and visually, that you will have a hard time not noticing it. Usually two to six individuals will sit on a branch together high up in a tree and sing their rollicking and raucous song for several minutes, each one trying to sing louder than its neighbor. Apparently the name "nunbird" was applied by some scientist unappreciative of the local chorus of nuns in black and white habit he had to endure in his childhood church. This species hunts for large insects and lizards running on tree trunks and branches in the mid-levels of lowland primary forests of the Oriente and is usually associated with mixed species foraging flocks in the canopy. Its close cousin, the BLACK-FRONTED NUNBIRD, just as common and noisy, is also all dark gray with a red bill, but it lacks the white feathers surrounding the base of the bill. It occurs only in secondary forests and scrubby areas near water in the Oriente. Occasionally a family group of nunbirds will follow a troop of monkeys and catch the large insects scared into flight by movements of the monkeys. The most commonly seen puffbird in Ecuador, and the most bizarre in appearance, is the SWALLOW-WINGED PUFFBIRD (Plate 42). This black, white, and rufous species appears to have no tail. It sits, usually in pairs or small groups, in isolated tree tops in the middle of cleared fields or along large rivers of the Oriente. All of a sudden one or all of the group will fly out a long distance, swoop to catch a small insect in the air and then return to the same perch. Their wings are long and tapered, and misidentifications as swallows are common. Even at rest they resemble husky swallows, or as one wag put it, "like swallows on steroids."

Breeding

Jacamars nest in short, horizontal burrows they dig in steep hillsides or in river banks. Both parents incubate the two to four eggs for a total of 20 to 22 days.

They feed insects to the young for 19 to 26 days until fledging. Little is known about breeding in puffbirds, but some nest in burrows on the forest floor and some in burrows excavated from arboreal termite nests. The WHITE-FRONTED NUNBIRD surrounds its tunnel entrance with sticks to hide the hole. Numerous adults appear to feed the young in a helpers-at-the-nest behavior also known from several other families, such as jays. Both mates share in tunnel excavation, incubation and feeding the young. The SWALLOW-WINGED PUFFBIRD digs vertical nesting tunnels in sandy soil that are up to 2 m (6.5 ft) deep.

Notes
Puffbirds of several species have been called stupid ("bobo") because they often sit still, depending on camouflage, and permit close approach. But these birds actually can be quite stealthy in their behavior and movements; many pass by near forest trails without our noticing – even on popular tourist trails.

Status
The limited range of the COPPERY-CHESTED JACAMAR (Plate 42) in Ecuador and the cutting of much of its habitat has brought some to consider it a threatened species. Among the puffbirds, LANCEOLATED MONKLET populations appear to be declining, and this species may be near-threatened.

Profiles
White-eared Jacamar, *Galbalcyrhynchus leucotis*, Plate 42a
Coppery-chested Jacamar, *Galbula pastazae*, Plate 42b
White-necked Puffbird, *Notharchus macrorhynchos*, Plate 42c
White-chested Puffbird, *Malacoptila fusca*, Plate 42d
White-fronted Nunbird, *Monasa morphoeus*, Plate 42e
Swallow-winged Puffbird, *Chelidoptera tenebrosa*, Plate 42f

22. Motmots

With beautiful coloring but a ridiculous name, motmots, related to the kingfishers, have several distinctive features. The nine species in the Family Momotidae are all Neotropical; four occur in Ecuador. All are found in lowlands on both sides of the Andes. They occur in all types of forest, from primary to flooded, secondary to open orchards, suburban parks and even tropical areas of the southwestern coast. Motmots are colorful, long, slender and medium-sized birds (32 to 48 cm, 16 to 19 in, long). They all have long, broad bills somewhat curved down at the ends and with serrate edges, adapted to grab and hold their animal prey. The most peculiar feature, however, is their tail. In most motmots, two central feather shafts grow much longer than the others. With preening, feather barbs just above the ends of the shafts drop off, producing a short length of naked shaft and an isolated feather patch on the end called a racquet. General motmot colors are soft hues of cinnamon, and the BLUE-CROWNED MOTMOT (Plate 43) adds a black face and blue-green to turquoise head. Its deep, hollow call of "BOO-boop," probably the source of the common name of motmots, is given at 3- to 5-second intervals for long periods. The Blue-crowned is the motmot you will most likely encounter either in primary forests or in cut-over areas almost anywhere in Ecuador below 500 m (1600 ft) elevation.

Natural History

Ecology and Behavior

Motmots are predators on large insects, spiders, and small frogs, lizards and snakes, which they snatch off leaves or from the ground while they are in flight. Typically they perch quietly on tree branches, regularly swinging their long tails from side to side, until they spot a suitable meal moving. They then dart out quickly and seize the prey in their bill, carry it back to their perch and eat it. If the prey is large and struggling, the motmot will thwack it against the branch several times to dispatch it before swallowing it. Motmots are also frugivores, eating small fruits up to the size of plums, which they collect from trees while hovering. You will find motmots almost always by themselves, even though they may pair for the entire year. Pairs tend to separate during the day to feed. They start their daily activities before dawn and continue to well past twilight, after most diurnal birds have gone to bed.

Breeding

Male and female motmots are similar in size and color. Some of their low-key courtship activities include calling back and forth high up in the trees, and holding bits of green leaves in their bills. Motmots are burrow nesters, like their kingfisher cousins. Both male and female help dig the burrow, often placed in the vertical bank of a riverside or road cut. Tunnels can be up to 4 m (13 ft) long, but most are of the order of 1.5 m (4 ft). Both parents incubate the two to four eggs. Young are fed and brooded by male and female for 24 to 30 days, at the end of which the juvenile motmots are able to fly from the burrow entrance.

Notes

Because of the characteristic swinging of the tail from side to side, one common name for motmots in South America is *relojero*, or clock-maker, evidently referring to the pendulum-like ticking of the tail. This group is one of the few in which there are more species in Central America than in South America, and this is likely the result of a different and probably unique historical origin and subsequent movements of this group.

Status

None of Ecuador's motmot species are considered endangered or threatened.

Profiles

Rufous Motmot, *Baryphthengus martii*, Plate 43a
Broad-billed Motmot, *Electron platyrhynchum*, Plate 43b
Blue-crowned Motmot, *Momotus momota*, Plate 43c

23. Barbets and Toucans

The *barbets* and *toucans* are two closely related groups considered as separate families by some experts and as part of the same family by others; both groups are cousins to the woodpeckers. The barbets, have a broad distribution in the tropics of Africa, southern Asia and the Neotropics (Subfamily Capitoninae), with a total of 75 species, seven of which are found in Ecuador. Barbets are colorful, with patches of red, orange, yellow, black and white. Males are generally brighter than females. Several species are known for duet singing between mates. Often one mate sings every other note (an *antiphonal* duet) and the other mate fills in the missing notes in such a perfect, coordinated manner that it sounds like one seamless composition. Ranging in size from 15 to 20 cm (6 to 8 in), barbets are stocky birds with stout but not long bills; they are considerably smaller than toucans. The largest of the barbets in Ecuador, and in the Neotropics, is the TOUCAN BARBET (Plate 44). Its bright colors and loud duet singing are one of the highlights of the cloud forest on the west slope of the Andes. This species is so large and its bill so elongated, that it is almost exactly intermediate in size and bill length between the typical barbet species and the small toucan species. The BLACK-SPOTTED BARBET (Plate 43) is common in the lowland primary and secondary forests of the Oriente. It is frequently in mixed species feeding flocks in the canopy.

Toucans are stunning, and no other word suits them better. Their shape, brilliant color patterns and tropical quintessence make them one of the most popular "poster animals" for the tropical forests of the Americas. Most ecotravellers want to see toucans, and with a little luck, they will. The toucan family, Ramphastidae, has about 40 species, all restricted to the Neotropics. Ecuador has 19 species, including some of the smaller types called *aracaris* (AH-rah-SAH-rees) and *toucanets*. Your first sighting of a toucan in the wild will be exciting – the large size of the bird, the bright colors, the enormous almost cartoonish bill all combine to surpass the toucan of your imagination. If you see it in flight, it will somewhat resemble a flying banana, as it alternately flaps and sails in its undulating flight (smaller species fly more directly with a buzzy flight). The toucans' most distinctive mark, their bill, looks so ungainly and heavy you might wonder how they can maintain their balance perched on a branch or in flight. Actually, the bill is mostly hollow and therefore lightweight.

The large toucans (Plate 45) in Ecuador are all most common in primary forest, but a fruiting tree in secondary (recently cut) forest nearby can easily tempt them. Up high in the cloud forest, the PLATE-BILLED MOUNTAIN-TOUCAN (Plate 45), with its brilliant blue-gray and black plumage, is the largest toucan you will see on the west slopes of the Andes. Also here high in the mountain forests, you can see the small green CRIMSON-RUMPED TOUCANET (Plate 44). The greatest variety of toucans, however, is among the aracaris, with their numerous variations on the theme of yellow breast, dark back and squealing vocalizations. You will usually see them as a flock flying by one at a time in a long procession (moving from tree to tree in "strings"). The most solitary of the species is the GOLDEN-COLLARED TOUCANET (Plate 45). Even though it is common in the primary forests of the Oriente, it is shy and hard to see. Only by its persistent call, which sounds like the tooting of a toy train, does it signal its abundance.

Natural History

Ecology and Behavior
Barbets and toucans live in moist forests from sea level to 3000 m (10,000 ft). You often see barbets in mated pairs among large mixed species foraging flocks in the subcanopy. They commonly eat fruits and seeds, but they also take insects and even small lizards. Almost all toucans are social and gregarious. When they forage at a fruiting tree they reach with their long bills to the outermost fruits, grasp one with the tip of the bill, toss it in the air and swallow it. Toucans also raid other birds' nests to eat eggs and nestlings. Toucans have a mean reputation among smaller birds, and not just because of their nest-robbing proclivities. Apparently toucans take umbrage at other birds feeding in the same fruiting tree

and may at times eat adult birds of small sizes. When a flock of toucans lands in a tree, most of the other birds, even large parrots such as macaws, will quickly abandon the site.

Breeding
Both barbets and toucans nest in tree cavities, either natural cavities or those built originally by woodpeckers. Barbets occasionally use their bills to enlarge holes in softer or dead wood. Nests can be any height above ground up to 30 m (100 ft) or more. Both sexes incubate and feed the two to four young. Both toucans and barbets are apparently monogamous. Some species of toucans like the COLLARED ARACARI seem to breed cooperatively, with numerous helpers at the nest in addition to the mother and the father bringing food to the young. Frugivorous birds such as toucans are critical for dispersing seeds away from the parent trees and helping maintain the healthy plant diversity of these forests.

Notes
The colorful rump and tail feathers of toucans are commonly used to construct the feathered crowns of the Cofan and Shuar people in the Oriente of Ecuador. If someone tries to sell or even give you one of these crowns, however, you must decline; it is against both Ecuadorean and international law to export or even possess them.

Status
Habitat clearing and hunting are the main factors explaining decline of toucan populations in some parts of Ecuador, but none of the species are considered threatened at the present time.

Profiles
Scarlet-crowned Barbet, *Capito aurovirens*, Plate 43d
Black-spotted Barbet, *Capito niger*, Plate 43e
Toucan Barbet, *Semnornis ramphastinus*, Plate 44a
Crimson-rumped Toucanet, *Aulacorhynchus haematopygus*, Plate 44b
Chestnut-eared Aracari, *Pteroglossus castanotis*, Plate 44c
Many-banded Aracari, *Pteroglossus pluricinctus*, Plate 44d
Pale-mandibled Aracari, *Pteroglossus erythropygius*, Plate 44e
Golden-collared Toucanet, *Selenidera reinwardtii*, Plate 45a
Plate-billed Mountain-Toucan, *Andigena laminirostris*, Plate 45b
White-throated Toucan, *Ramphastos tucanus*, Plate 45c
Black-billed Mountain-Toucan, *Andigena nigrirostris*, Plate 45d
Chestnut-mandibled Toucan, *Ramphastos swainsonii*, Plate 45e

24. Woodpeckers

Everyone knows what a woodpecker is, at least by name and perhaps by their cartoon incarnations. They are highly specialized forest birds that occur almost everywhere in the world (even in some places without trees) except Australia, New Zealand and Antarctica. The family, Picidae, includes more than 200 species that range in size from the tiny piculets (9 cm, 3.5 in long) to the largest woodpeckers (50 cm, 20 in). Thirty-five species of various sizes occur throughout Ecuador's diverse habitats. They all share strong, straight and chisel-like bills, very long and barbed tongues, and sharp toes that spread widely for clinging to tree trunks. All but the small piculets also have stiffly reinforced tail feathers that support them as they climb on vertical surfaces. To accommodate the constant banging and drumming with their bills on wood surfaces, they have extra spongy bone at the base of the bill to absorb shock waves. They come in mostly subdued shades of gray, green, black and white, frequently with bars and streaks. Most, however, have bright patches of crimson, especially males.

Natural History

Ecology and Behavior

Woodpeckers are adapted to cling to a tree's bark and move lightly over its surface, listening and looking for insects. They drill holes into bark where they hear insects chewing on the wood and then use their long, often sticky tongues to extract the juicy morsels, which include both adult insects and grubs. Some species, such as YELLOW-TUFTED (Plate 47) and BLACK-CHEEKED WOODPECKERS (Plate 47), commonly act like flycatchers as they sally out from perches high in trees to catch flying insects in the air. Many species also eat fruit, nuts and nectar from flowers. The piculets use the smallest branches of trees and bushes, usually low in the forest, and, lacking a long stiff tail like the other woodpeckers, clamber about pecking on horizontal branches. In flight, woodpeckers typically undulate up and down with an alternating short burst of rapid wing beating; this causes a rise in altitude that is followed by a short period of folded, wing gliding in which altitude is lost. They sleep and rest in cavities they excavate from trees. Woodpeckers use their bills and their pecking ability in three ways: for drilling holes to get insect food; for excavating holes for roosting and nesting; and for *drumming*, that is, extra rapid beats usually on a hollow surface that amplifies the sound for communication to other woodpeckers.

The holes that woodpeckers excavate for their own nests are used over and over again by a plethora of birds and mammals that cannot excavate their own cavities. Some of these interlopers use abandoned woodpecker holes, but others, such as some aracaris, will at times evict woodpeckers from their active cavity. These cavities are vital for protection from nest predators and are thus at a premium. Their availability may affect the population sizes of many species dependent on them. A species or group of species whose presence or absence directly affects the ability of many other species to persist in a habitat is called a keystone species. In this case, the protection of woodpeckers, which can be considered keystone species, is important because their absence would harm a large number of other bird species.

Breeding

Woodpeckers are monogamous, and some live in large social or family groups. Tropical woodpeckers usually remain paired throughout the year. Both mates are involved with the nest excavation, the interior of which they line with wood chips. Both sexes incubate the two to four eggs for 11 to 18 days, males typically taking the night shift. They feed the young 20 to 35 days until fledging. Juveniles remain with the parents outside the nest for several months.

Notes

Woodpeckers often damage trees and buildings in their quest for food and nest sites. They also eat fruits from orchards and gardens and so are considered a pest in some parts of the tropics. The ANDEAN FLICKER, which occurs in the treeless páramo of extreme southern Ecuador, makes its nest and roosting hole in clay banks. The adobe mud huts built by people in this region are perfect for the flicker's tunnel-building behavior but the birds are unappreciated by those living in the dwelling. Often the local people shoot four of these pesky woodpeckers and tie their bodies so that they dangle from each corner of the house – to warn other flickers of the punishment for trespassing.

Status
None of Ecuador's woodpecker species are considered threatened, but several of the larger species in coastal primary forest are declining with continued forest clearing.

Profiles
Ecuadorean Piculet, *Picumnus sclateri*, Plate 46a
Spot-breasted Woodpecker, *Chrysoptilus punctigula*, Plate 46b
Crimson-mantled Woodpecker, *Piculus rivolii*, Plate 46c
Cream-colored Woodpecker, *Celeus flavus*, Plate 46d
Lineated Woodpecker, *Dryocopus lineatus*, Plate 47a
Yellow-tufted Woodpecker, *Melanerpes cruentatus*, Plate 47b
Black-cheeked Woodpecker, *Melanerpes pucherani*, Plate 47c
Crimson-crested Woodpecker, *Campephilus melanoleucos*, Plate 47d

---

All of the bird families considered below are *passerine*, or *perching birds*, members of the Order Passeriformes (see p. 90).

---

25. Woodcreepers

Woodcreepers, Family Dendrocolaptidae, are small to medium-sized brown birds that pursue a mostly arboreal existence. About 50 species are distributed from Mexico to Argentina, 29 in Ecuador. They occur in moist lowland forest, tropical dry and thorn forest, and all the way up in altitude to cloud forests. Although their long stout bills, stiff tail feathers and tree trunk climbing recall woodpeckers, these birds are more closely related to flycatchers; the similarities to woodpeckers are superficial and coincidental – what biologists term evolutionary *convergence*. Most are slender birds that range in size from 20 to 36 cm (8 to 14 in). The sexes look alike, with plumages of various shades of brown, chestnut and tan. Most have spotting, streaking or banding, but different species are confusingly similar and their identification to species is frustrating at best.

Natural History

Ecology and Behavior
Woodcreepers feed by hitching upwards on tree trunks and also horizontally along branches, peering under bark and into moss clumps and epiphytes, using their stout bills to probe and catch prey in tight nooks and crannies. Unlike woodpeckers, they do not drill holes in search of prey or drum with their bills. The foraging procedure among the various species follows a standard theme but with many variations. An individual flies to the base of a tree and then spirals up the trunk, using its stiff tail for support and sharp toenails for purchase on the bark's surface. Near the top of the tree the bird flies down to the base of the next tree and repeats the process. Some species, however, use smaller trees or even bamboo, others tend to stay higher in the canopy, and some frequently follow army ant swarms to catch large insects flying up to escape the horde. In these cases the woodcreepers will hunt from the base of a tree near the ground or some-

times right on the ground. They will also fly out to catch insects on the wing. Usually woodcreepers are solitary but occasionally a pair will forage together. Some species, however, commonly forage in mixed species foraging flocks of the forest undergrowth or the canopy.

Breeding
Most woodcreeper species practice standard monogamy, with the sexes equally sharing nesting chores and care of the young. In some, however, they form no real pair bonds, and after mating, females nest alone. Nests are usually in tree crevices or holes and occasionally in arboreal termite nests. Parents line nests with wood chips. The two or three eggs are incubated for 17 to 21 days and young fledge 18 to 24 days after hatching.

Notes
Some woodcreepers have reputations for being extremely aggressive toward other species, for example, harassing and evicting roosting or nesting woodpeckers from tree cavities.

Status
Most woodcreepers are common to abundant in Ecuador. Species in northwestern forests that are most threatened by habitat destruction have large ranges that extend into Central America, with many healthy populations outside of Ecuador.

Profiles
Olivaceous Woodcreeper, *Sittasomus griseicapillus*, Plate 48a
Wedge-billed Woodcreeper, *Glyphorynchus spirurus*, Plate 48b
Long-billed Woodcreeper, *Nasica longirostris*, Plate 48c
Barred Woodcreeper, *Dendrocolaptes certhia*, Plate 48d
Streak-headed Woodcreeper, *Lepidocolaptes souleyetii*, Plate 48e

26. Ovenbirds

More diverse than the woodcreepers, the ovenbirds are even more difficult to tell apart. There are a mind-numbing 240+ species of this family (Furnariidae) from Mexico to Argentina, with 74 in Ecuador, many of which are differentiated by no more than subtle shades of brown. We profile six species which you can easily identify and which you are most likely to see in various Ecuadorean habitats, from open páramo grasslands and cloud forests of the Anean slopes, to the drier lowlands of coastal Ecuador and the moist forests of the Oriente.

Natural History

Ecology and Behavior
Ovenbirds are all insectivores that mainly glean their resting prey from undersides of leaves and branches. Most ovenbirds live low in their habitats or even on the ground, but a few are regular in the canopy of tall forests. Although dull-colored and unobtrusive in behavior, they are interesting because of the diversity of ecological niches they occupy. They have invaded virtually every habitat in South America. In this remarkable "radiation," the various species have developed such a breadth of adaptations that they have become similar to and behave like unrelated families that occupy those respective niches in other parts of the world. Thus, there are ovenbird "replacements" of thrushes, wheatears, pipits, dippers, larks, wagtails, nuthatches and chickadees (tits).

Breeding

Many ovenbirds appear to mate for life. Virtually all species of ovenbirds use closed nests. Some such as *xenops* make tunnels in vertical banks, others use tree cavities or construct elaborate structures of twigs or mud. The nests of the family's namesake, the several species called *horneros* (genus *Furnarius*), are mind-boggling. They build large domed nests out of clay, sometimes 30 cm (12 in) in diameter. The shape is much like a small-scale replica of the old bread ovens also made of clay and used by early European colonists in the New World. Usually these nests are placed out in exposed areas 1 or 2 m (3 to 6 ft) off the ground. The sun bakes the clay brick hard and few predators can break down its walls. More clever predators, however, try to use the entrance of the nest to gain access to eggs or chicks, but are usually foiled by the large but false tunnel that leads down into the clay mass and then ends abruptly. The actual nest entrance leads up unobtrusively from the fake tunnel.

Notes

The oven-shaped nests of the PALE-LEGGED HORNERO (Plate 49) are a common part of the scenery in coastal Ecuador. They are so durable that each one lasts for years. Often, other species of birds use these cavities for their own nests after the ovenbirds have abandoned them.

Status

Most ovenbirds in Ecuador are common and have extensive ranges. Three species, the HENNA-HOODED FOLIAGE-GLEANER, BLACKISH-HEADED SPINETAIL, and RUFOUS-NECKED FOLIAGE-GLEANER, however, are considered vulnerable because of their extremely small ranges – in this case all are Tumbesian endemics restricted in Ecuador to the south-coastal part of the country. Habitat destruction and brush fires could easily push such species to low populations and even extinction.

Profiles

Bar-winged Cinclodes, *Cinclodes fuscus,* Plate 49a
Pale-legged Hornero, *Furnarius leucopus,* Plate 49b
Andean Tit-spinetail, *Leptasthenura andicola,* Plate 49c
Pearled Treerunner, *Margarornis squamiger,* Plate 49d
Rufous-rumped Foliage-gleaner, *Philydor erythrocercus,* Plate 49e
Streaked Xenops, *Xenops rutilans,* Plate 49f

27. Antbirds

Antbirds are small and medium-sized, often drab inhabitants of the lower parts of the forest. Many are difficult to see, but often they are loud and vocal. The family of antbirds, Formicariidae, has about 200 species, all restricted to the Neotropics, with 93 in Ecuador. The name comes not from their eating ants but from the behavior of some of these species to use army ants to scare up insect prey. Antbirds range in size from 8 to 36 cm (3 to 14 in). The smaller ones are called *antwrens* and *antvireos*. The mid-sized ones are the *antbirds,* and larger species are called *antshrikes, antthrushes* and *antpittas.* In detail these species are quite varied in appearance and body shape. Males are generally colored with understated shades of brown, gray, black and white. Females are generally duller than the males with olive-brown or chestnut predominating. Some species have bright red eyes or patches of bright bare skin around the eye. Some, like the GREAT

ANTSHRIKE (Plate 50) are bold and often emerge from the scrubby bushes to sing and scold. Others, like the TAWNY ANTPITTA (Plate 50), are shy and incredibly difficult to see as they run through undergrowth.

Natural History

Ecology and Behavior

Antbirds generally occur in thick vegetation in secondary and primary forests. A few species run on the forest floor, but most are in low to middle parts of the forest. A very few are up in the canopy. Most species are insectivorous, but some of the larger species also eat fruit, lizards, snakes and frogs. Most species glean for their prey by searching the undersides of leaves and branches. A few hawk for flying insects, and a number always follow army ant swarms (that is, they are *obligate* ant followers). These species wait at the advancing line of army ants as they raid the forest floor (see p. 224). Panicked insects run or fly up from the ant onslaught into the waiting bills of the antbirds. Often several species of antbirds along with woodcreepers and many other bird species jostle each other for the best positions to catch the escaping insects.

Breeding

Many antbirds appear to mate for life. Courtship feeding occurs in some of these birds, males passing food to females prior to mating. Many antbirds build cup nests out of pieces of plants that they weave together. Nests are usually placed in a fork of branches low in a tree or shrub. Some nest in tree cavities. Male and female share nest-building duty, as well as incubation of the two or three eggs and eventually feeding insects to the young. Incubation is 14 to 20 days, and young remain in the nest for nine to 18 days. Some of the obligate ant following species have abbreviated courtship and nesting behavior, apparently to facilitate their following the army ants when these mobile insect colonies move on from their temporary bivouacs in the forest. In some species, family groups remain together, male offspring staying with the parents, even after acquiring mates themselves.

Notes

The strange compound names of these birds, such as antwrens and antshrikes, arose partially because, to the naturalists who first named them, there were obvious parallels in size and, at least superficially, appearance, of these various species to North American, European and Asian wrens and shrikes. These common names are only confusing because some birds similarly named, such as the anttanagers, really are tanagers (p. 160) that follow army ants and are not members of the antbird family. Some ornithologists prefer to consider the ground-dwelling antpittas and anthrushes as their own separate family, Formicariidae, and the "typical" antbirds as the Family Thamnophilidae.

Status

Three Ecuadorean antbirds are presently considered threatened or endangered, the BICOLORED ANTVIREO, the GRAY-HEADED ANTBIRD and the GIANT ANTPITTA. They all have extremely small geographical ranges in isolated higher-elevation forest and thus are extremely vulnerable to forest clearing and habitat destruction.

Profiles

Great Antshrike, *Taraba major*, Plate 50a
Barred Antshrike, *Thamnophilus doliatus*, Plate 50b

White-flanked Antwren, *Myrmotherula axillaris,* Plate 50c
White-plumed Antbird, *Pithys albifrons,* Plate 50d
Black-faced Antthrush, *Formicarius analis,* Plate 50e
Tawny Antpitta, *Grallaria quitensis,* Plate 50f

28. Manakins

The *manakins,* Family Pipridae, are a Neotropical group of about 60 species, with 20 in Ecuador. They are small, compact, stocky passerine birds, 9 to 19 cm (3.5 to 7.5 in) long, with short tails and bills, and two attention-grabbing features: brightly colored plumages and some of the most elaborate courtship displays among birds. Some male manakins are outstandingly beautiful, predominantly glossy black but with brilliant patches of bright orange-red, yellow, or blue on their heads and/or throats. Some have deep blue on their undersides and/or backs. The exotic appearance of male manakins is sometimes enhanced by long, streamer-like tails, up to twice the length of the body, produced by the elongation of two of the central tail feathers. Females, in contrast, are duller and less ornate, usually shades of yellowish olive-green or gray. To accompany the bird's courtship displays, the wing feathers of some species, when moved in certain ways, make whirring or snapping sounds.

The BLUE-CROWNED MANAKIN (Plate 51) is one of the most common species of manakins in the lowland forests of the Oriente and northwestern Ecuador. The males of this species, however, are relatively solitary and rarely form organized mating lecs (see below). The males of the WIRE-TAILED MANAKIN (Plate 51), in contrast, form noisy and active lecs in the lowlands of the Oriente. Listen for their explosive and nasal calls from the understory. Unlike its colorful cousins, both sexes of the relatively large THRUSH-LIKE MANAKIN (Plate 51) are dull. Common in the low undergrowth of primary and secondary humid lowland forests, this species is solitary and does not form lecs. It is most often found by its distinctive whistled song. Some ornithologists think this species is so different that it is better placed in the cotinga family.

Natural History

Ecology and Behavior
Manakins are highly active forest birds, chiefly of warmer, lowland areas, although some range up into cloud forests. Residents of the forest understory, they eat mostly small fruits, which they pluck from bushes and trees while in flight, and they also take insects from the foliage. Largely frugivorous, manakins are important seed dispersers of the fruit tree species from which they feed. The cozy relationships between fruit trees and the birds that feed on them are explored in the Close-Up on p. 168. Manakins are fairly social animals when it comes to feeding and other daily activities, but males and females do not pair. They employ a non-monogamous mating system and, in fact, most of our knowledge about manakin behavior concerns their breeding behavior – how females choose males with which to mate and, in particular, male courting techniques. To use the ornithological jargon, manakins are promiscuous breeders. No pair-bonds are formed between males and females. Males mate with more than one female and females probably do the same. After mating, females build nests and rear young by themselves. Males, singly or in pairs, during the breeding season stake out display sites on tree branches, in bushes, or on cleared patches of the forest

floor, and then spend considerable amounts of time giving lively vocal and visual displays, trying to attract females. An area that contains several of these performance sites is called a *lec*, and thus manakins, along with other birds such as some grouse, some cotingas, and some hummingbirds, are *lecking* breeders.

At the lec, male manakins *dance*, performing elaborate, repetitive, amazingly rapid and acrobatic movements, sometimes making short up and down flights, sometimes rapid slides, twists, and turn-arounds, sometimes hanging upside down on a tree branch while turning rapidly from side to side and making snapping sounds with their wings. The details of a male's dance are *species specific*, that is, different species dance in different ways. Females, attracted to lecs by the sounds of male displays and by their memories of lec locations – the same traditional forest sites are used from one year to the next – examine the energetically performing males with a critical eye and then choose the ones they want to mate with, sometimes making the rounds several times before deciding. In a few species, two and sometimes three males (*duos* and *trios*) join together in a coordinated dance on the same perch. In their dance the males alternate *leapfrog hops* with bouts of slow, *butterfly flight*. In these curious cases, one male is dominant, one subordinate, and only the dominant of the pair eventually gets to mate with interested females. Why the subordinate male appears to help the dominant one obtain matings (are they closely related? Do subordinate males stand to inherit display sites when the dominants die? Do subordinates achieve "stolen" matings with females when the dominants are temporarily distracted?), why the manakins dance at all, and on what basis females choose particular males to become the fathers of their young, are all areas of continuing scientific inquiry.

Breeding
Males take no part in nesting. The female builds a shallow cup nest that she weaves into a fork of tree branches, 1 to 15 m (3 to 50 ft) from the ground. She incubates the one or two eggs for 17 to 20 days, and rears the nestlings herself, bringing them fruit and insects, for 13 to 20 days. Manakins, like most birds that use open, cup-like, nests, often suffer very high rates of nest destruction. In one small study, only about 7% of eggs survived the incubation stage and hatched. Most nests were lost to predators, for which the suspect list is quite lengthy: ground-dwelling as well as arboreal snakes, birds such as motmots, puffbirds, toucans, and jays, large arboreal lizards, and mammals such as opossums, capuchin monkeys, kinkajous, and coatis.

Notes
Colorful manakin feathers were often used by the indigenous peoples of Central and South America for ornamental purposes, especially for clothing and masks used during dances and solemn festivals.

Status
None of the Ecuadorean manakins is currently considered to be threatened.

Profiles
Blue-crowned Manakin, *Pipra coronata,* Plate 51a
Wire-tailed Manakin, *Pipra filicauda*, Plate 51b
Golden-winged Manakin, *Masius chrysopterus*, Plate 51c
White-bearded Manakin, Manacus manacus, Plate 51d
Thrush-like Manakin, *Schiffornis turdinus*, Plate 51e

29. Cotingas

Owing to their variety of shapes, sizes, ecologies, and breeding systems, as well as to their flashy coloring, *cotingas* are usually considered to be among the Neotropic's glamour birds. The Family Cotingidae is closely allied with the manakins and flycatchers and contains about 70 species, with 33 in Ecuador. The cotingas include species from tiny, warbler-sized birds to large, crow-sized birds. Primarily fruit- and insect-eaters, some eat only fruit (which among birds is uncommon). In some species the sexes look alike, but in many the males are stunningly attired in bright spectral colors while the females are plain. There are territorial species that breed *monogamously* and *lecking* species that breed *promiscuously* (see below); all in all a very eclectic family.

Among the Ecuadorean cotingas are *pihas*, *"typical" cotingas*, *umbrellabirds*, and *fruitcrows*, the last two being quite large. Perhaps the only generalizations that apply to these birds is that all have short legs and relatively short, rather wide bills, the better to swallow fruits. Males of some of the group are quite ornate, with patches of gaudy plumage in unusual colors. For instance, some of the typical cotingas are lustrous blue and deep purple, and some are all white; others are wholly black, or green and yellow, or largely red or orange or gray. The ANDEAN COCK-OF-THE-ROCK (Plate 53) is one of the most dramatic species of cotingas in Ecuador, and it is also a lecking species. Twenty to 80 large, bright red and crested males gather to attract rather dull-colored females at historical sites often used for decades. (Males on the western slopes of the Andes are deeper red than the east slope male we have illustrated, and some experts think the two may be separate species.) Males of the almost equally handsome BLACK-NECKED RED-COTINGA (Plate 52) also lec in the extreme eastern lowlands. They are noisy and sometimes easy to see at historical courting sites. The PURPLE-THROATED FRUITCROW (Plate 53) lives in highly social flocks of five to 10 individuals. They seldom leave the canopy of primary lowland forest in the Oriente as well as moist coastal forests of northwestern Ecuador. Listen for its distinctive calls, which are loud and slurred whistles interspersed by rude hacking noises, like someone getting ready to spit. If you try mimicking their whistles, you can often attract them in close to you as they investigate this intruder into their territory. One Ecuadorean cotinga that you will hear over and over in the lowland forest of the Oriente, but probably never see, is the SCREAMING PIHA (Plate 52). Its ear-splitting shrill whistles are given by numerous males from the tops of widely separated, tall trees in primary forest. Their plain gray plumage makes them almost impossible to see, but females are more interested in how individual males sing in their lecs than in how colorful they are.

Natural History

Ecology and Behavior

Cotingas primarily inhabit the high canopy of the forest. They are fruit specialists, a feature of their natural history that has engendered much study. They eat small and medium-sized fruits that they take off trees, often while hovering. Some cotingas, such as fruitcrows and pihas, supplement the heavily frugivorous diet with insects taken from the treetop foliage, but others, particularly the species called *fruiteaters*, feed exclusively on fruit. This dependence creates both problems and benefits (as detailed in the Close-up, p. 168); one consequence is that when young are fed only fruit, the nestling period can be unusually long because rapidly growing nestlings require protein that an all-fruit diet provides only at a low rate. Because of the cotingas' feeding specialization on fruit, they are vital as dispersers of tree seeds. Owing to their high-canopy habits, the precise fruits cotingas go after often are difficult to determine. They feed heavily at palms, laurels, and incense trees, and also at, among others, members of the blackberry/raspberry family.

Breeding

Some cotingas pair up, defend territories from *conspecifics* (individuals of the same species), and breed conventionally in apparent monogamy. But others, such as umbrellabirds, cock-of-the-rocks and pihas, are lecking species, in which males individually stake out display trees and repeatedly perform vocal and visual displays to attract females. Females enter display areas, called lecs, assess the jumping and calling males, and choose the ones they wish to mate with. With this type of breeding, females leave after mating and then nest and rear young alone.

Several species of cotingas are *altitudinal migrants*, breeding in higher-elevation forests but spending the "off" season in lowland forests. Nests, usually placed in trees or bushes, are generally small, open, and inconspicuous, some nest cups being made of loosely arranged twigs, some of mud, and some of pieces of plants. Many species lay only a single egg, some one or two eggs. Incubation is 17 to 28 days and the nestling period is 21 to 44 days, both stages quite long for passerine birds.

Notes

Because they are often dubbed onto the soundtrack of most movies and TV programs with a "jungle" setting, calls of the SCREAMING PIHA likely will be a strangely familiar part of your first hike into Amazonian lowland forest. The sound is now so widely used by the entertainment industry that it could be considered trite – until you stand in the midst of a small group of these males each calling from the top of a different tree. Even from a kilometer (half-mile) away, the sound penetrates the vegetation; if you are directly beneath a calling male, you may well have to hold your hands over your ears to stop the ringing.

Status

Of the Ecuadorean cotingas, only the LONG-WATTLED UMBRELLABIRD is considered threatened. It is a Chocó endemic restricted to uncut forests of the west slope of the Colombian and Ecuadorean Andes. The species is primarily limited now to mid-altitude forests, logging and habitat destruction having severely fragmented its range and disrupted its former altitudinal migration to lowland forests of the coast. Lecs that have been discovered recently have contained only three to six displaying males. The recently discovered CHESTNUT-BELLIED COTINGA (first described by researchers in 1994) is known only from a few high altitude forest sites in the Podocarpus National Park area of southern Ecuador and adjacent northern Perú. Its apparently tiny geographical range makes it vulnerable.

Profiles

Black-necked Red-cotinga, *Phoenicircus nigricollis*, Plate 52a
Plum-throated Cotinga, *Cotinga maynana*, Plate 52b
Red-crested Cotinga, *Ampelion rubrocristata*, Plate 52c
Green-and-black Fruiteater, *Pipreola reifferii*, Plate 52d

Screaming Piha, *Lipaugus vociferans*, Plate 52e
Amazonian Umbrellabird, *Cephalopterus ornatus*, Plate 53a
Purple-throated Fruitcrow, *Querula purpurata*, Plate 53b
Bare-necked Fruitcrow, *Gymnoderus foetidus*, Plate 53c
Masked Tityra, *Tityra semifasciata*, Plate 53d
Andean Cock-of-the-Rock, *Rupicola peruviana*, Plate 53e

30. American Flycatchers

The *American flycatchers* comprise a huge group of passerine birds that is broadly distributed over most habitats from Alaska and northern Canada to the southern tip of South America. The flycatcher family, Tyrannidae, is considered among the most diverse of avian groups. Some experts even combine American flycatchers, manakins (Pipridae) and cotingas (Cotingidae) into one megafamily. With more than 380 species, the flycatchers usually contribute a hefty percentage of the avian biodiversity in every locale. For instance, it has been calculated that flycatchers make up fully one tenth of the land bird species in South America, and perhaps one-quarter of Argentinean species. Even in relatively tiny Ecuador, the group is represented by a healthy contingent of about 200 species.

Flycatchers range in length from 6.5 to 30 cm (2.5 to 12 in). At the smallest extreme are some of the world's tiniest birds, weighing, it is difficult to believe, only some 7 g (1/4 oz). Their bills are usually broad and flat, the better to snatch flying bugs from the air. Tail length is variable, and some species even have long, forked tails, which probably aid the birds in their rapid, acrobatic, insect-catching maneuvers. Most flycatchers are dully turned out in shades of gray, brown, and olive-green, and the sexes are generally similar in appearance. Many species have some yellow in their plumage, and a relatively few are quite flashily attired in, for example, bright expanses of red or vermilion. A great many of the smaller, drabber flycatchers, clad in olives and browns, are extremely difficult to tell apart in the field, even for experienced birdwatchers. One set of frequently seen flycatchers that are easy to see and identify all share bright yellow breasts and some variation on a theme of white eyelines and dark heads. The most likely species of this group of flycatchers you will see in Ecuador include the GREAT KISKADEE (Plate 55), the LESSER KISKADEE (Plate 55), the BOAT-BILLED FLYCATCHER (Plate 55), the SOCIAL FLYCATCHER (Plate 55) and the TROPICAL KINGBIRD (Plate 54). These are all widespread species found in open areas and can be distinguished by presence or absence of rufous coloring in the wings and tail, size of the bill, and habitat. High up in the páramo a group of flycatchers called *ground-tyrants* practices very un-flycatcher-like behavior. They run on long legs in open grassland and rocky areas looking more like thrushes than self-respecting flycatchers. One of the most common species of this group in highland Ecuador is the PLAIN-CAPPED GROUND-TYRANT (Plate 54).

Natural History

Ecology and Behavior

Flycatchers are common over a large array of different habitat types, from snowline in the páramo to lowland moist forests, treeless plains and grasslands, marshes and mangrove swamps. As their name implies, flycatchers are insectivores, obtaining most of their food by employing the classic flycatching technique. They perch motionless on tree or shrub branches or on fences or telephone wires, then dart out in short, swift flights to snatch from the air insects foolhardy enough to enter their field of vision; they then return time and again to the same perch to repeat the process. Many flycatchers also take insects from foliage as they fly through vegetation, and many also supplement their diets with berries and seeds. Some of the larger flycatchers will also take small frogs and lizards, and some, such as the GREAT KISKADEE, consider small fish and tadpoles delicacies to be plucked from shallow edges of lakes and rivers. A few species like the PIRATIC FLYCATCHER (Plate 55) have ceded flycatching to their relatives and are now, as adults, completely frugivorous.

Some flycatchers show marked alterations in their lifestyles as seasons, locations, and feeding opportunities change. Such ongoing capacity for versatile behavior in response to changing environments is considered a chief underlying cause of the group's great ecological success. An excellent example is the EASTERN KINGBIRD'S drastic changes in behavior between summer and winter. Breeding during summer in North America, these black and white flycatchers are extremely aggressive in defending their territories from birds and other animals, and they feed exclusively at that time on insects. But a change comes over the birds during the winter, as they idle away the months in South America's Amazon Basin. There, Eastern Kingbirds congregate in large, nonterritorial flocks with apparently nomadic existences, and they eat mostly fruit.

Breeding

Almost all of the relatively few flycatchers that have been studied inhabit exclusive territories that mated, monogamous pairs defend for all or part of the year. Some forest-dwelling species, however, breed promiscuously: groups of males call and display repeatedly at traditional courting sites called lecs, attracting females that approach for mating but then depart to nest and raise young by themselves. Many flycatchers are known for amazing courtship displays, males showing off to females by engaging in aerial acrobatics, including flips and somersaults. In monogamous species, males may help females build nests. Some build cup nests, roofed nests, or globular hanging nests placed in trees or shrubs, others construct mud nests that they attach to vertical surfaces such as rock walls, and some nest in holes in trees or rocks. Tropical flycatchers generally lay two eggs that are incubated only by the female for 12 to 23 days; nestlings fledge when 14 to 28 days old.

The tody flycatchers construct large, hanging, woven, or "felted," nests that take up to a month or more to build. These nests tend to hang from slender vines or weak tree branches, which provides a degree of safety from climbing nest predators such as snakes and small mammals. Often, however, such efforts are ineffective – nest predation rates are quite high. In response, some of the tody flycatchers purposefully build their nests near to colonies of stinging bees, apparently seeking additional protection from predators. The PIRATIC FLYCATCHER lives up to its name. This scoundrel species drives hard-working caciques, oropendolas and even other flycatchers from their nests and usurps them for its own.

Notes

Flycatchers in Ecuador are notorious because of the difficulty of distinguishing the many similar species in the field. Some can only be readily distinguished by their voices, so if you have feelings of frustration trying to figure this group out, you are not alone.

Status

Three species of flycatchers restricted to Ecuador's coastal lowland forests, the PACIFIC ROYAL FLYCATCHER, the GRAY-BREASTED FLYCATCHER, and the OCHRACEOUS ATTILA, have such small and declining populations that they are considered threatened. Another flycatcher species, the WHITE-TAILED SHRIKE-TYRANT, has become extremely rare and local throughout its range in the high Andes from Ecuador to Argentina. No one understands why its populations seem to be declining so precipitously.

Profiles

Torrent Tyrannulet, *Serpophaga cinerea*, Plate 54a
Common Tody-flycatcher, *Todirostrum cinereum*, Plate 54b
Black Phoebe, *Sayornis nigricans*, Plate 54c
Plain-capped Ground-tyrant, *Muscisaxicola alpina*, Plate 54d
Masked Water-tyrant, *Fluvicola nengeta*, Plate 54e
Tropical Kingbird, *Tyrannus melancholicus*, Plate 54f
Great Kiskadee, *Pitangus sulphuratus*, Plate 55a
Lesser Kiskadee, *Pitangus lictor*, Plate 55b
Boat-billed Flycatcher, *Megarynchus pitangua*, Plate 55c
Social Flycatcher, *Myiozetetes similis*, Plate 55d
Piratic Flycatcher, *Legatus leucophaius*, Plate 55e

31. Jays

Jays are members of the Corvidae, a passerine family of 115 species that occurs just about everywhere in the world – or, as ecologists would say, corvid distribution is *cosmopolitan*. The group also includes the *crows*, *ravens*, and *magpies*. Although on many continents birds of open habitats, jays of the Neotropics are primarily woodland or forest birds. Jays, aside from being strikingly handsome birds, are known for their versatility, adaptability, and for their seeming intelligence. In several ways, the group is considered by ornithologists to be one of the most highly developed of birds. They are also usually quite noisy.

Members of the family range in length from 18 to 77 cm (7 to 30 in), many near the higher end – large for passerine birds. Corvids have robust, fairly long bills and strong legs and feet. Many of them (crows, ravens, rooks, jackdaws) are all or mostly black, but the jays are different, being attired in bright blues, purples, greens, yellows, and white. In corvids, the sexes generally look alike. The COMMON RAVEN is the largest passerine bird in the world, but although its range encompasses several continents, it does not extend to Ecuador. The only representatives of this family in Ecuador are six species of jays, most of which you will see in small family groups.

Natural History

Ecology and Behavior

Jays eat a large variety of foods (and try to eat many others) and so are considered omnivores. They feed on the ground, but also in trees, eating carrion, insects (including some flying ones), fruits and nuts, and also taking bird eggs and nestlings. They are considered to be responsible for a significant percentage of the nest predation on many songbird species, particularly those with open-cup nests.

Bright and versatile, they are quick to take advantage of new food sources and to find food in agricultural and other human-altered environments. Jays use their feet to hold food down while tearing it with their bills. Hiding food for later consumption, *caching*, is practiced widely by the group.

Corvids are usually quite social, Ecuadorean jays being no exception. Most of these species remain all year in small groups of relatives, five to 10 individuals strong. They forage together within a restricted area, or *home range*, and at the appropriate time, breed together on a group-defended territory. Jays are usually raucous and noisy, giving varieties of harsh, grating, loud calls as the foraging flock straggles from tree to tree, but at times they can be amazingly quiet and unobtrusive, especially during the breeding season.

Breeding
Several species of jays raise young cooperatively. Generally the oldest pair in the group breeds and the other members serve only as *helpers*, assisting in nest construction and feeding the young. Courtship feeding is common, the male feeding the female before and during incubation, which she performs alone. Bulky, open nests, constructed primarily of twigs, are placed in trees or rock crevices. Two to 7 eggs are incubated for 16 to 21 days, the young then being fed in the nest by parents and helpers for 20 to 24 days.

Notes
Although considered by many to be among the most intelligent of birds, and by ornithologists as among the most highly evolved, corvid folklore is rife with tales of crows, ravens and magpies as symbols of ill-omen. This undoubtedly traces to the group's frequent all-black plumage and habit of eating carrion, both sinister traits. COMMON RAVENS, in particular, have long been associated in many Northern cultures with evil or death, although these large, powerful birds also figure more benignly in Nordic and Middle Eastern mythology. Several groups of indigenous peoples of Northwestern North America consider the Raven sacred and sometimes, indeed, as a god.

Status
Some of the six species of jays that occur in Ecuador are fairly rare, but none is considered threatened. Many corvids adjust well to people's activities, often expanding their ranges when they can feed on agricultural crops.

Profiles
Turquoise Jay, *Cyanolyca turcosa*, Plate 56a
Violaceous Jay, *Cyanocorax violaceus*, Plate 56b
Green Jay, *Cyanocorax yncas*, Plate 56c
White-tailed Jay, *Cyanocorax mystacalis*, Plate 56d

32. Wrens and Dipper

Wrens are small, brownish species with an active, snappish manner and, characteristically, erect, upraised tails. Most skulk in thick undergrowth, but a few are *arboreal*, staying in trees in more open areas. Approximately 75 wren species comprise the family Troglodytidae, a group that except for one Eurasian species is confined to the Western Hemisphere; 26 species occur in Ecuador. Among other traits, wrens are renowned for their singing ability, vocal duets, and nesting behavior. They range in length from 10 to 22 cm (4 to 9 in) and usually appear mainly in shades of brown or reddish brown, with smaller bits of tan, gray, black, and white. Some of these birds are tiny, weighing in at less than 15 g (half an ounce). Wings and tails are frequently embellished with finely barred patterns. Wrens have rather broad, short wings and owing to this, are considered poor flyers. The sexes look alike.

Dippers are similar to wrens in coloring and chunky shape, but they are specialized for living along fast-flowing streams in mountainous areas, the only truly aquatic family of passerines. The Family Cinclidae has five species worldwide, but only the WHITE-CAPPED DIPPER (Plate 56) occurs in Ecuador. Unmistakable in their habitat, you will usually see them bouncing up and down on their legs (thus the name dipper) on a large boulder in a white-water stream on either slope of the Andes. They fly low over the water in a buzzy flight, but most distinctive is their ability to walk into the water of these rapidly moving streams and forage among underwater rocks and on the stream bottom. The sexes are indistinguishable by color or size.

Natural History

Ecology and Behavior
Most wrens are *cryptically* colored and fairly secretive in their habits as they sneak, hop and poke around the low levels of the forest, and through thickets, grasslands, and marshes, searching for insects. They are completely *insectivorous* or nearly so. Often spending the year living in pairs, they defend territories in which during the breeding season they will nest. The HOUSE WREN (Plate 57) is the same species as in North America and familiar to many. It is ubiquitous throughout Ecuador up to 4000 m (13,000 ft) elevation, except for in undisturbed forested areas. Some of the larger wrens, such as the THRUSH-LIKE WREN (Plate 57) of the Amazon lowlands and the FASCIATED WREN (Plate 57) of the tropical dry forest of coastal southern Ecuador, spend their days higher in the trees in small family flocks, and, owing to their size, are a bit bolder in their movements. Their loud songs also make them obvious. After breeding, wrens will use their nests as roosting places – or "dormitories," as one researcher puts it. Some species actually build specific nests for roosting that are of a different structure than nests for raising young. The vocalizations of wrens have been studied extensively. Especially talented, a pair of the BLACK-CAPPED DONACOBIUS (Plate 57) will call back and forth as they lose sight of each other while foraging in dense marsh grasses of the Oriente, keeping in contact. The mated pairs sing some of the bird world's most complex duets, male and female rapidly alternating in giving parts of one song (as we think of it), so rapidly and expertly that it actually sounds as if one individual utters the entire sequence. Such duets probably function as "keep-out" signals, warning away from the pair's territory other members of the species, and in maintaining the pair-bond between mated birds. The donacobius was thought for a long time to be such a gifted singer that it had to be in the mockingbird family, but subsequent molecular and behavioral studies place it more convincingly with the wrens. The MUSICIAN WREN (Plate 57) has to be heard to be believed. If you hear what sounds like a child learning to whistle in the undergrowth of the Amazonian forest, it is probably this species. It is most easily seen as it participates in undergrowth mixed species for-aging flocks that move low through denser parts of the forest.

Dippers forage primarily for larvae of aquatic insects, but they also take small clams, crayfish and fish. They plunge from a rock or stream bank into the rushing water and use their wings to swim underwater. Their song is a loud trill used to mark territorial boundaries along the stream.

Breeding

The wrens of Ecuador are mainly monogamous, but some like the BLACK-CAPPED DONACOBIUS breed *cooperatively*, with members of the small family group helping out at the single nest of the parents. Nests, generally of woven grass, are placed in vegetation or in tree cavities. They are small but elaborate nests, roofed, with inconspicuous side entrances. Intriguingly, in some species the male builds many more nests on his territory than his mate (or mates, in polygynous species) can use, apparently as a courtship signal, perhaps as an inducement for a female to stay and mate. Only the female incubates the two to five eggs, for 13 to 19 days. Sometimes she is fed by the male during this period. Nestlings are fed by both parents for 14 to 19 days, until fledging.

The single species of dipper in Ecuador constructs a large, domed nest usually on a vertical cliff but sometimes on the underside of a bridge. Apparently monogamous, both sexes participate in nest construction. The nest is primarily of moss and lined with dry leaves and vegetation. The four or five eggs hatch in 16 days and the young are fed by both parents. Each pair is highly territorial and defends a stretch of the stream year-round.

Notes

The HOUSE WREN has one of the most extensive ranges of any bird species in the Western Hemisphere. It nests from North America to throughout South America. One of the reasons for its extensive range is that it often nests in association with people and their structures. These birds root about near and in human settlements, looking for insects. Nests are often placed in crannies and crevices within buildings or other structures. (Many wrens nest in naturally occurring cavities, hence the family name, Troglodytidae, or "cave dweller.")

Underwater swimming of the dipper is made possible by a series of adaptations that include a third eye-lid (*nictitating membrane*), which protects the eye surface underwater, extra dense plumage to protect against buffeting against rocks by the strong currents, and an extra large oil gland at the base of the tail to keep the feathers moisture-proof.

Status

Most of the 25 or so wren species that occur in Ecuador are fairly or very abundant; none is threatened. The dipper is also fairly common, although with its restricted habitat, water pollution could drastically affect its food supply locally and so threaten it in certain areas.

Profiles

White-capped Dipper, *Cinclus leucocephalus*, Plate 56e
Black-capped Donacobius, *Donacobius atricapillus*, Plate 57a
Thrush-like Wren, *Campylorhynchus turdinus*, Plate 57b
Fasciated Wren, *Campylorhynchus fasciatus*, Plate 57c
White-breasted Wood-wren, *Henicorhina leucosticta*, Plate 57d
House Wren, *Troglodytes aedon*, Plate 57e
Musician Wren, *Cyphorhinus aradus*, Plate 57f

33. Thrushes and Mockingbirds

The more than 300 species of thrushes inhabit most terrestrial regions of the world and include some of the most familiar park and garden birds. The family,

Turdidae, has few defining, common features that set its members apart from other groups, as perhaps could be expected; so large an assemblage of species is sure to include a significant amount of variation in appearance, ecology, and behavior. *Thrushes, robins, nightingale thrushes* and *solitaires* of the Western Hemisphere are slender-billed birds that range from 12.5 to 31 cm (5 to 12 in) in length. In Ecuador there are 22 species of this family, some of which are migrants from nesting grounds in North America. Generally they are not brightly colored; instead, they come in drab browns, grays, brown-reds, olive, and black and white. The sexes are very similar in appearance. During their first year of life, young thrushes are clad in distinctively spotted plumages.

Many species of thrushes have adapted to living near humans and benefiting from their environmental modifications. On five continents, a thrush is among the most common and recognizable of garden birds, including North America's AMERICAN ROBIN, Europe's REDWING and BLACKBIRD, and Ecuador's GREAT THRUSH (Plate 58), which is common throughout the highlands, even in the middle of Quito. Thrushes in general are famous for their rich and musical sounds, and one of the champion songsters of the world is the LAWRENCE'S THRUSH (Plate 58). It is easily overlooked in the primary forests of the Amazon, but it is one of the most remarkable mimics in South America. It sings high in the forest all day long, and the song of a single individual may include song phrases of up to 35 other species; with some patience, this songster supreme can usually be found on its favorite perch day after day.

Although superficially similar to the thrushes, the family of *mockingbirds*, Mimidae, is now thought to be most closely related to the starlings. The *mimids*, which also include *thrashers* and *catbirds*, are found only in the New World. These medium-sized birds (20 to 30 cm, 8 to 12 in) have long tails and rather short and rounded wings. Most species have strong, moderately long bills, often down-curved. The species tend toward gray, brown or rufous, often with flashes of white in the tail and wings. There is no distinct difference in the plumages of the sexes. Only a few species actually mimic calls and songs of other species. Of the 30+ species in the family, only the LONG-TAILED MOCKINGBIRD (Plate 58) is found on the mainland of Ecuador. Here it is common and obvious in dry forest and scrub areas of the central and southern coastal lowlands. Experts think that this coastal species is closely related to the complex of mockingbird species on the Galápagos, and it may have been the original colonist to reach the islands.

Natural History

Ecology and Behavior

Many thrushes eat fruits, some are primarily *insectivorous*, and most are at least moderately *omnivorous*. Although generally arboreal birds, many thrushes frequently forage on the ground for insects, other arthropods, and, a particular favorite, delicious earthworms. Some of the thrushes in Ecuador associated with gardens and lawns forage like the familiar thrushes from North America or Europe – they hop and walk along the ground, stopping at intervals, cocking their heads to peer downwards. These birds are residents of many kinds of habitats – deep forest, forest edge, clearings, and other open areas such as shrub areas and grasslands, gardens, parks, suburban lawns, and agricultural areas. Many thrushes are quite social, spending their time during the nonbreeding season in flocks of the same species, feeding and roosting together. Some of the tropical thrushes, like the BLACK-BILLED THRUSH (Plate 58), evidently make seasonal migrations within the Amazon, following changing food supplies.

The mockingbirds feed on fruits, seeds and insects. Many feed on the ground using their curved bills to dig and probe for prey in soft soils and leaf litter. With their long tails and the open habitat they prefer, they are often one of the most conspicuous bird species present. They tend to be highly territorial and often solitary throughout the year.

Breeding
Thrushes breed monogamously, male and female together defending exclusive territories during the breeding season; pairs may associate year round. Nests, usually built by the female and placed in tree branches, shrubs, or crevices, are open and cup-shaped, made of grass, moss, and like materials, and often lined with mud. Two to six eggs (usually two or three) are incubated by the female only for 12 to 14 days. Young are fed by both parents for 12 to 16 days prior to their fledging. The mockingbirds are monogamous, and both sexes participate in building the bulky, open cup-shaped nest of twigs and lining it with hair or grass. It is placed low in a bush or occasionally on the ground. The two to four eggs are generally incubated by the female alone for about two weeks. The chicks are then fed by both parents for another 13 to 19 days until they fledge.

Notes
English colonists in the New World gave the AMERICAN ROBIN, a thrush, its name because it resembled England's common ROBIN, an Old World flycatcher – both birds have reddish breasts. The New World bird, however, is more closely related to Europe's BLACKBIRD, also a common garden bird and a true thrush; and you wonder why common names of birds can be so confusing.

Status
Although several thrushes in many different parts of the world are vulnerable to threat or are now considered threatened, none of the species that breed in Ecuador are in imminent danger. Some of the species called solitaires have suffered recent population declines in accessible areas, probably owing to poaching for the pet trade: these birds are famous in Ecuador for their grand, flute-like songs. The mainland species of mockingbird in Ecuador appears to have adapted well to cultivation and forest clearing and apparently is thriving. In the Galápagos, the CHARLES MOCKINGBIRD has become extinct on the large island of Floreana and now exists on only two small islands.

Profiles
Long-tailed Mockingbird, *Mimus longicaudatus*, Plate 58a
Great Thrush, *Turdus fuscater*, Plate 58b
Lawrence's Thrush, *Turdus lawrencii*, Plate 58c
Black-billed Thrush, *Turdus ignobilis*, Plate 58d
Ecuadorean Thrush, *Turdus maculirostris*, Plate 58e

34. Wood Warblers

More than 110 species of the spritely and often beautiful family of New World *wood warblers* (Parulidae) are found from Alaska to Argentina. In Ecuador, 28 species occur: 14 species that are migrants from nesting grounds in North America, and 14 species that are non-migratory. Most of the migratory species are easy to see as they forage high in trees of secondary and primary forests, but they do little singing on their wintering grounds and for most of their stay in Ecuador are clad in subdued colors that make them difficult to identify. The non-migratory species, in contrast, sing loudly and wear the same plumage all year round. Unfortunately they also tend to skulk in the dense undergrowth, and many of them at their brightest plumage are as dull as the winter plumages of the migratory species. The plumages of both sexes of non-migratory species tend to be similar, but in migratory species, only the males acquire a brilliant summer plumage. Warblers all have thin narrow bills and both migratory and non-migratory species regularly participate in mixed species foraging flocks.

The BLACKBURNIAN WARBLER (Plate 59) is a common migrant species that spends its winter (September to April) in the higher-elevation forests of both slopes. The CANADA WARBLER (Plate 59) is another common winter visitor to Ecuador (October to April) and also spends most of its time in higher-elevation forests, but during migration it can be common in the undergrowth of primary forest in the Oriente lowlands. Found only along forested streams of the lower slopes of the Andes and in the lowlands of the coast and the Oriente, the BUFF-RUMPED WARBLER (Plate 60), resident year-round, is largely terrestrial. Its loud ringing song, buff rump seen in flight, and association with forested streams on both sides of the Andes make it easy to find and identify.

Natural History

Ecology and Behavior

Wood warblers are largely insect eaters. Some species, such as the *redstarts*, sally out like flycatchers to snatch flying insects in the air. Some species probe flowers and buds with their thin bills for insects hiding there. Most species, however, glean insects from undersides of leaves and twigs. The quality of songs among these warblers ranges from loud and clear notes to insect-like trills and buzzes.

The migratory distances for species nesting in North America involve thousands of kilometers. The BLACKPOLL WARBLER, for instance, winters as far south as Bolivia and nests as far north as northern Canada. For many years, North American scientists interested in warblers and many other songbirds concentrated their research on the birds' ecology and behavior during breeding, essentially ignoring the fact that the birds spent more than half of each year wintering in the tropics, many of them in South America. Now, with the realization that the birds' biology during the nonbreeding season is also important for understanding their lives, their ecology and behavior during the winter have become areas of intense interest. Being addressed in research studies are such questions as: Are species that are territorial during breeding also territorial on their wintering grounds, and if so, in what way? Do individual birds return to the same spot in the tropics each year in winter as they do for nesting during the North American spring? Do migratory birds compete for food on their wintering grounds with those species that remain all year in the tropics? Why do the migratory species of warblers have dull plumages on the wintering grounds, and why do the non-migratory species have the same plumage all year around?

Breeding

Most warbler species place their nests in trees or shrubs, but some nest on the ground or in tree cavities. The nest shape is usually an open cup-like structure, but in the tropics many species build a domed nest with an entrance at the side.

They are primarily monogamous, but the females do most if not all the nest construction. The two to four eggs are incubated by the female for about 12 days. After hatching, the chicks are fed by both parents for 8 to 12 days in the nest, and continue to be fed by the parents for a few weeks after leaving the nest.

Status

No warblers that occur in Ecuador are known to be threatened. Two other warblers, however, are now endangered – KIRTLAND'S WARBLER, which breeds in the USA (Michigan) and winters in the Bahamas, and SEMPER'S WARBLER, which occurs only on the Caribbean island of St. Lucia. Kirtland's Warbler, which nests only in stands of young Jack-pine trees, has been victimized by its own specialization on one type of breeding habitat combined with a shrinking availability of that habitat, by destruction of its wintering habitat, and by BROWN-HEADED COWBIRDS, which lay their eggs in the nests of warblers and other species, reducing their reproductive success (see p. 164). It is suspected that mongooses, which were introduced to St. Lucia by people and which are predators on bird nests, play a major role in endangering Semper's Warbler, which nests on or near the ground. Ten to 12 additional American warbler species are probably now at risk, but there is at present insufficient information about their populations to judge their statuses with any certainty. The BACHMAN'S WARBLER, which nested throughout the southeastern USA and wintered in Cuba, apparently became extinct in the 1960s.

Profiles

Blackburnian Warbler, *Dendroica fusca*, Plate 59a
Canada Warbler, *Wilsonia canadensis*, Plate 59b
Spectacled Redstart, *Myioborus melanocephalus*, Plate 59c
Slate-throated Redstart, *Myioborus miniatus*, Plate 59d
Gray-and-gold Warbler, *Basileuterus fraseri*, Plate 59e
Three-striped Warbler, *Basileuterus tristriatus*, Plate 59f
Buff-rumped Warbler, *Phaeothlypis fulvicauda*, Plate 60a

35. Flower-piercers, Conebills and Honeycreepers

This group of species does not fit obviously into any single family, and no two ornithologists seem to agree on who their relatives are. Some experts place the *flower-piercers, conebills* and *honeycreepers* in the tanager family, Thraupidae. Others place them in their own subfamily and related to the finches, Emberizidae. Yet others place some of them with the wood warblers, Parulidae. All these species are associated with flowers, and many of them are very colorful. The flower-piercers occur mainly at higher altitudes on both slopes of the Andes, and they have a peculiar bill that is upturned and hooked at the end. The conebills are also primarily in the higher altitudes, but honeycreepers and *dacnis* are most common in the lowlands. The GIANT CONEBILL (Plate 60) is limited to *Polylepis* forests in the highlands of the Andes. It crawls up and down the reddish trunks of these trees like a nuthatch searching for insects. You will most likely see the dacnis and honeycreepers in high canopy flocks of the lowland forests. An easy way to see them well is from one of the canopy towers constructed by lodges in the Oriente. The BANANAQUIT (Plate 61), which is either lumped into the warbler group or is the only member of its own family, Coerebidae (its classification is controversial), is a tiny yellow and olive/grayish bird with a broad Neotropical distribution: from southern Mexico and the Caribbean to northern Argentina. It is a common species in lowland urban areas and disturbed habitats – so people have been a boon to its spread. In Amazonia its presence indicates that the primary forest has been largely disturbed in the area.

Natural History

Ecology and Behavior
Flower-piercers use their peculiar bills to bore holes into the base of a flower and rob nectar. Unlike more gracious species, such as hummingbirds, that enter the flower properly to reap a reward of nectar, and often obtain a deposit of pollen on the head, flower-piercers bypass the pollination system and cheat the flower by not paying for the nectar reward by spreading pollen. Most large flowers at mid to high altitudes in Ecuador will have small holes in their bottoms, indicating how ubiquitous these cheaters are. Flower-piercers also glean insects from vegetation and eat fruits. Conebills, bananaquits, dacnis and honeycreepers also probe flowers, but only occasionally for nectar. More frequently they are searching for insects. They also commonly eat fruits, and are most easily seen in mixed species foraging flocks moving through the upper parts of the forest.

Breeding
Most species in this group build open, cup-shaped nests of moss and grass. They are presumably monogamous, but little is known about their breeding biology. Unusual among birds, BANANAQUITS build not only breeding nests, but also lighter, domed dormitory nests, which they sleep in individually. Both Bananaquit sexes build the round, domed, breeding nest. Only the female incubates the two or three eggs, for 12 to 13 days. Both parents feed the chicks in the nest for 17 to 19 days by regurgitating food to them.

Status
Some of the species in this group have extremely small geographical ranges, which makes them vulnerable; extensive habitat destruction in these areas could easily threaten these birds. At the present time, however, only the SCARLET-BREASTED DACNIS, a Chocó endemic of extreme northwestern Ecuador and southwestern Colombia, is considered threatened.

Profiles
Masked Flower-piercer, Diglossa cyanea, Plate 60b
Glossy Flower-piercer, Diglossa lafresnayii, Plate 60c
Giant Conebill, Oreomanes fraseri, Plate 60d
Cinereous Conebill, Conirostrum cinereum, Plate 60e
Bananaquit, Coereba flaveola, Plate 61a
Blue Dacnis, Dacnis cayana, Plate 61b
Yellow-bellied Dacnis, Dacnis flaviventer, Plate 61c
Green Honeycreeper, Chlorophanes spiza, Plate 61d
Purple Honeycreeper, Cyanerpes caeruleus, Plate 61e

36. Tanagers

Tanagers comprise a large New World group of beautifully-colored, small passerine birds, most of which are limited to tropical areas. They are among the tropics' most common and visible birds, primarily owing to their habit of associating in *mixed-species foraging flocks* that gather in the open, often near human habitation, to feed in fruit trees, and they are a treat to watch. All told, there are some 230 species of tanagers (Family Thraupidae), the group including the *typical tanagers* and the *euphonias*. Some of the tanagers, such as the SUMMER TANAGER (male all red, female yellow-olive), breed in North America and migrate to winter in Ecuador. Tanagers inhabit all forested and shrubby areas of the American tropics, over a wide range of elevations, and are particularly numerous in wet forests and forest edge areas. Not devotees of the dark forest interior, most prefer the lighter, upper levels of the forest canopy and more open areas; some prefer low, brushy habitat. More than 115 species of tanagers call Ecuador home.

Tanagers vary from 9 to 28 cm (3.5 to 11 in) in length, with most concentrated near the smaller end of the range. They are compact birds with fairly short, thick bills and short to medium-long tails. Tanagers' outstanding physical attribute is their bright coloring – they are strikingly marked with patches of color that traverse the entire spectrum, rendering the group among the most fabulously attired of birds. It has been said of the typical tanagers *(genus Tangara)* that they must "exhaust the color patterns possible on sparrow-sized birds." Yellows, reds, blues and greens predominate, although a relatively few species buck the trend and appear in plain blacks, browns, or grays. The sexes usually look alike. Euphonias are small, stout tanagers, whose appearances revolve around a common theme: males blue-black above, with yellow foreheads, breasts, and bellies; and females all dull olive. We profile typical species found commonly in each of the mainland habitats of Ecuador. They all tend to be relatively easy to distinguish by their color patterns and habitat preference.

Natural History

Ecology and Behavior

Most tanager species associate in mixed-species tanager flocks, usually together with other types of birds. Finding eight or more tanager species in a single group is common. A mixed flock will settle in a tree full of ripe fruit such as berries and enjoy a meal. These flocks move through forests or more open areas, searching for fruit-laden trees and also gleaning for insects. Although most species are arboreal, a few are specialized ground foragers, taking seeds and bugs. Tanagers usually go after small fruits that can be swallowed whole, such as berries, plucking the fruit while perched. After plucking it, a tanager rotates the fruit a bit in its bill, then mashes it and swallows. (Ecologists divide frugivorous birds into *mashers*, such as tanagers, and *gulpers*, such as trogons and toucans, which swallow fruit whole and intact.) One explanation is that mashing permits the bird to enjoy the sweet juice prior to swallowing the rest of the fruit. This fits with the idea that mashers select fruit based partially on taste, whereas gulpers, which swallow intact fruit, do not. Tanagers, as mashing frugivores, sometimes drop the largest seeds from the fruits they consume before swallowing but, nonetheless, many seeds are ingested; consequently, these birds are active seed dispersers (see Close-up, p. 168). Some ecologists believe tanagers to be among the most common dispersers of tropical trees and shrubs, that is, they are responsible for dropping the seeds that grow into the trees and shrubs that populate the areas they inhabit. Euphonias, for example, are crucial for the mistletoe life cycle because, after eating the berries, they deposit their seed-bearing droppings on tree branches, where the seeds germinate, the mistletoe plants starting out there as parasites.

Some tanagers, such as the *ant-tanagers*, are frequent members of mixed-species flocks of the undergrowth (along with antbirds, woodcreepers and others) that spend their days following army ant swarms, feeding on insects that rush from cover at the approach of the devastating ants. Euphonias specialize on mistletoe berries, but eat other fruits and some insects as well. Some tanagers are *altitudinal migrants*, seasonally moving to higher or lower elevation habitats.

Breeding
Most tanagers appear to breed monogamously, although a number of bigamists have been noted (BLUE-GRAY TANAGER, Plate 65, among them). Breeding is concentrated during the transition from dry to wet season, when fruit and insects are most plentiful. In many species, male and female stay paired throughout the year. Males of many species give food to females in nuptial feeding, and during courtship displays make sure that potential mates see their brightly colored patches. Either the female alone or the pair builds a cup nest in a tree or shrub. Two eggs are incubated by the female only for 12 to 18 days and young are fed by both parents for 12 to 18 days prior to their fledging. A pair of tiny euphonias build a nest with a roof and a side entrance, often within a bromeliad plant.

Notes
The word *tanager* comes from the Brazilian Tupi Indian word *tangara*, which is also used as the genus name for a group of tanagers.

Status
Three Ecuadorean tanagers are currently considered threatened or endangered, the YELLOW-GREEN BUSH-TANAGER, MASKED MOUNTAIN-TANAGER and the ORANGE-THROATED TANAGER. All three have highly restricted or disjunct ranges at higher elevations in the Andes. In addition, several of the euphonias are increasingly scarce and the reason may be that, although they are not hunted for the international pet trade, they are prized as cage birds within South American countries.

Profiles
Golden Tanager, *Tangara arthus*, Plate 62a
Blue-and-black Tanager, *Tangara vassorii*, Plate 62b
Beryl-spangled Tanager, *Tangara nigroviridis*, Plate 62c
Orange-eared Tanager, *Tangara calliparaea*, Plate 62d
Bay-headed Tanager, *Tangara gyrola*, Plate 62e
Green-and-gold Tanager, *Tangara schrankii*, Plate 63a
Paradise Tanager, *Tangara chilensis*, Plate 63b
Thick-billed Euphonia, *Euphonia laniirostris*, Plate 63c
White-vented Euphonia, *Euphonia minuta*, Plate 63d
Chestnut-breasted Chlorophonia, *Chlorophonia pyrrhophrys*, Plate 63e

Swallow Tanager, *Tersina viridis*, Plate 64a
Black-backed Bush-Tanager, *Urothraupis stolzmanni*, Plate 64b
Common Bush-Tanager, *Chlorospingus ophthalmicus*, Plate 64c
Golden-crowned Tanager, *Iridosornis rufivertex*, Plate 64d
Grass-green Tanager, *Chlorornis riefferii*, Plate 64e
Blue-winged Mountain-Tanager, *Anisognathus somptuosus*, Plate 65a
Scarlet-bellied Mountain-Tanager, *Anisognathus igniventris*, Plate 65b
Hooded Mountain-Tanager, *Buthraupis montana*, Plate 65c
Palm Tanager, *Thraupis palmarum*, Plate 65d

Blue-gray Tanager, *Thraupis episcopus*, Plate 65e

Silver-beaked Tanager, *Ramphocelus carbo*, Plate 66a
Masked Crimson Tanager, *Ramphocelus nigrogularis*, Plate 66b
Flame-rumped Tanager, *Ramphocelus flammigerus*, Plate 66c
White-shouldered Tanager, *Tachyphonus luctuosus*, Plate 66d
Magpie Tanager, *Cissopis leveriana*, Plate 66e

37. American Orioles and Blackbirds

Diversity is the key to comprehending the *American* orioles and *blackbirds*. The
passerine family Icteridae includes about 95 species, 30 of which occur in
Ecuador. They vary extensively in size, coloring, ecology, and behavior, but they
also partition neatly into very different groups called *blackbirds, caciques (kah-SEE-
kays), cowbirds, grackles, meadowlarks, orioles* (distinct from the unrelated family of
birds called orioles in Eurasia and Africa), and *oropendolas*. These *icterids* range
over most of North, Central, and South America. Distinguishing this varied
assemblage from most other birds is a method for feeding, known as *gaping* – a
bird places its closed bill into crevices or under leaves, rocks or other objects, then
forces the bill open, exposing the previously hidden space to its prying eyes and
hunger. The icterid group inhabits marshes and almost all types of terrestrial habitats, and occupies warm lowland areas, middle elevations, as well as colder,
mountainous regions. Many of these birds have adapted well to human settlements and are common denizens of gardens, parks, and urban and agricultural
areas.

Icterids range in length from 15 to 56 cm (6 to 22 in) – medium to fairly large-
sized birds. Bills are usually sharply pointed and conical. Black is the predominant
plumage color in the group, but many combine black with bright reds, yellows,
or oranges. In some species, the sexes are alike (particularly in the tropical
species), but in others, females look very different than males, often more cryptically outfitted in browns, grays, or streaked plumage. Pronounced size differences
between the sexes, females being smaller, are common; male oropendolas, for
instance, may weigh twice as much as females. Bills and eyes are sometimes
brightly colored. The wide ranges of sizes, shapes, colors, mating systems, and
breeding behaviors of these birds have attracted considerable interest from avian
researchers.

Natural History

Ecology and Behavior
Icterids occur in all sorts of habitat types – woodlands, thickets, grassland,
marshes, forest edges, and the higher levels of closed forests – but they are especially prevalent in more open areas. Their regular occupation of marshes has
always been viewed as interesting, as they are not otherwise obviously adapted for
living in aquatic environments – they do not have webbed feet, for example, nor
are they able to float or dive. They are *omnivorous* and eat a wide variety of foods
including insects and other small animals, fruit and seeds. A common feature of
the group is that although they are primarily seed-eaters *(granivores)* during the
nonbreeding periods, they become *insectivorous* during breeding, and feed insects to
the young. Gaping for food is frequent and will be seen repeatedly if one
observes these birds for any length of time. Oropendolas and caciques join in

mixed-species foraging flocks in the canopy; in a single fruit tree one may see two or more species feeding with several species of tanagers, honeycreepers, and others. Outside of the breeding season, icterids, particularly the blackbirds and grackles, typically gather in large, sometimes enormous, flocks that can cause damage to roosting areas and agricultural crops.

Breeding

Icterid species pursue a variety of breeding strategies. Some, such as the orioles, breed in classically monogamous pairs, male and female defending a large territory in which the hanging pouch nest is situated. The TROUPIAL (Plate 68), however, has the peculiar habit of using recently abandoned colonies of cacique nests and laying its eggs in one of them instead of building its own nest. The caciques and the oropendolas nest in colonies. The members of an oropendola colony weave large, bag-like or pouch-like nests that hang from the ends of tree branches, many on the same tree. In Costa Rica, researchers documented a rare form of non-monogamous breeding. Three to 10 male MONTEZUMA'S OROPENDOLAS establish a colony in a tree (often an isolated one) and defend a group of 10 to 30 females that will mate and nest in the colony. The males engage in fighting and aggressive displays, competing among themselves to mate with the females. The most dominant males (the *alpha* birds) in each colony, usually heavier males, obtain up to 90% of all matings, and therefore, are the fathers of most of the colony's young. Caciques, also with pouch-like nests, breed either solitarily in the forest or in colonies. In one study it was noted that each cacique in a colony tries to locate its nest toward the center of the colony, presumably because there is less of a chance of suffering nest predation at the colony's center.

Breeding colonies of caciques and oropendolas are often located in trees that contain or are near large bee or wasp nests. The wasps or bees swarm in large numbers around the birds' nests. Apparently the birds benefit from this close association because the aggressiveness the stinging insects show toward animals that try to raid the birds' hanging nests offers a measure of protection. Icterid nests range from hanging pouches woven from grasses and other plant materials to open cups lined with mud to roofed nests built on the ground, hidden in meadow grass. Nests are almost always built by females. The female also incubates the two or three eggs, for 11 to 14 days, while the male guards the nest. Nestlings are fed for 10 to 30 days either by both parents (monogamous species) or primarily by the female (polygamous species).

Most of the cowbirds, like some cuckoo species, are *brood parasites*, building no nests themselves. Rather, females, after mating with one or more males, lay their eggs, one in each nest and up to 14 or more per season, in the nests of other species – other icterids as well as species in other families. The host species then incubate and raise these foster young. Some of the cowbirds specialize on icterid hosts – the GIANT COWBIRD (Plate 67) parasitizes only caciques and oropendolas. Its occurrence is apparently restricted only by the presence of colonies of its hosts, various cacique and oropendola species. Some host species have evolved the abilities to recognize cowbird eggs and eject them from their nests, but others have not. The cowbirds benefit from this selfish behavior by being freed from nest-building and tending chores – what must amount to significant savings of energy and also decreased exposure to predators. The host species suffer reproductive harm because a female cowbird often ejects a host egg when she lays her own (when the nest is left unguarded). Also, more often than not, the cowbird's young are larger than the host's own, and are thus able to out-compete them for food brought to the nest by the adult birds. The host's own young often starve or are significantly weakened.

How can brood parasitic behavior arise? Evolutionary biologists posit that one way would be if, long ago, some female cowbirds that built nests had their nests destroyed mid-way through their laying period. With an egg to lay but no nest in which to place it, females in this situation may have deposited the eggs in the nests of other species, which subsequently raised the cowbird young. Alternatively, the nesting behavior of the Troupial, which uses old cacique nests, suggests another possible evolutionary road to brood parasitism: if a female Troupial did not bother to wait for the caciques to finish using their nests before she laid her egg, she could quickly develop a brood parasitic lifestyle.

Notes
"Cacique" is an interesting name for a bird: in Spanish it means "chief" or "boss;" in Mexico, it also has the suggestion of "tyrant;" in Chile and some other parts of South America, it means "one who leads an easy life."

Status
None of the icterids of Ecuador is presently considered threatened. The PALE-EYED BLACKBIRD, however, is known from only a few forested lakes in the western Amazon, and three of these sites, Limoncocha, Kapawi and Tiputini, are in Ecuador. Recent oil exploration, dynamite fishing and habitat destruction on these lakes could easily bring the Ecuadorean population of this species to the brink of extinction. In North America, the BROWN-HEADED COWBIRD, an open country species like all other cowbirds, has been able to expand its range with deforestation. Because it does not regularly penetrate into extensive forests, many forest-dwelling songbird species, especially migrants from South America, were long-protected from this brood parasite. Now, with only small forest remnants (which are readily entered by cowbirds) left throughout much of eastern North America, these other small songbirds have been overwhelmed not only by loss of habitat but also by increased rates of cowbird parasitism. This combination of factors together with habitat destruction in Ecuador may help explain the precipitous decline of some North American species that winter in Ecuador.

Profiles
Peruvian Meadowlark, *Sturnella bellicosa*, Plate 67a
Scrub Blackbird, *Dives warszewiczi*, Plate 67b
Giant Cowbird, *Scaphidura oryzivora*, Plate 67c
Oriole Blackbird, *Gymnomystax mexicanus*, Plate 67d
White-edged Oriole, *Icterus graceannae*, Plate 67e
Troupial, *Icterus icterus*, Plate 68a
Great-tailed Grackle, *Quiscalus mexicanus*, Plate 68b
Yellow-rumped Cacique, *Cacicus cela*, Plate 68c
Crested Oropendola, *Psarocolius decumanus*, Plate 68d
Russet-backed Oropendola, *Psarocolius angustifrons*, Plate 68e

38. Sparrows and Finches

The New World *sparrows* and *finches* are a large, diverse group, totaling about 320 species that include some of South America's most common and visible passerine birds. The group's classification is continually being revised, but here we can consider them to be separate families: the sparrows, *seedeaters*, and *grassquits* in Family Emberizidae, and the *grosbeaks* and *saltators* in Family Cardinalidae. The *siskins* are in the closely related family Fringillidae. These groups are almost *cosmopolitan* in distribution, meaning representatives occur just about everywhere, in all kinds of habitats and climates, from Alaska and northern Canada south to Tierra del Fuego.

Sparrows and finches are generally small birds, 9 to 22 cm (3.5 to 9 in) in length, with relatively short, thick, conical bills, that are specialized to crush and open seeds. In some species, the upper and lower halves of the bill can be moved from side-to-side, the better to manipulate small seeds. Sparrows have relatively large feet that they use in scratching the ground to find seeds. Coloring varies greatly within the group but the plumage of most is dull brown or grayish, with many sporting streaked backs. The sexes generally look alike. We profile 17 species of these birds that are common and easily seen in various habitats throughout Ecuador.

Natural History

Ecology and Behavior

Sparrows and finches are mostly seed-eaters (*granivores*), although many are considered almost *omnivorous*, and even those that specialize on seeds for much of the year often feed insects to their young. Some species also eat fruit. Sparrows in Ecuador mainly inhabit open areas such as grassland, parkland, brushy areas, and forest edge. They are birds of thickets, bushes, and grasses, foraging mostly on the ground or at low levels in bushes or trees. Because many species spend large amounts of time in thickets and brushy areas, they can be quite inconspicuous. Whereas in North America sparrows constitute perhaps the most important group of seed-eating birds, they are less dominant in the Neotropics. Other groups of birds, such as pigeons (p. 116), occupy more of the seed-eating niche in South American countries than do sparrows and, as a consequence, one encounters sparrows much more often in North than in South America.

Most species are strongly territorial, a mated pair aggressively excluding other members of the species from sharply defined areas. In the *typical sparrows*, pairs often stay together all year; other species within the group often travel in small family groups. Sometimes, territories are defended year round and almost all available habitat in a region is divided into territories. The result is that those individuals that do not own territories must live furtively on defended territories, always trying to avoid the dominant territory owner, retreating when chased, and waiting for the day when the owner is injured or dies and the territory can be taken over. Only when one of these *floaters* ascends in the hierarchy to territorial ownership status can he begin to breed. In species that have this kind of territorial system, such as the RUFOUS-COLLARED SPARROW (Plate 71), the "floater" individuals who live secretly on other individual's territories, waiting and watching, were termed by their discoverer an avian *underworld*, and the name has stuck.

Breeding

Most sparrows and finches are monogamous breeders. The female of the pair usually builds a cup-shaped or, more often in the tropics, a domed nest, from grasses, fine roots and perhaps mosses and lichens. Nests are concealed on the ground or low in a shrub or tree. The female alone incubates two or three eggs, for 12 to 14 days. Both male and female feed nestlings, which fledge after 10 to 15 days. Most breeding is accomplished from March through August. Some species, such as the abundant and conspicuous Rufous-collared Sparrow, breed almost continually through the year.

Notes

The New World sparrows and finches have been especially well studied by scientists, and thus they have contributed substantially to our general knowledge of birds. For instance, studies of North America's SONG SPARROW and the Neotropic's RUFOUS-COLLARED SPARROW provided the basis for much of the information we have about avian territoriality and many other kinds of behavior.

Status

The MASKED SALTATOR, TANAGER FINCH and the Tumbesian endemic SAFFRON SISKIN are all considered threatened or near-threatened. The PALE-HEADED BRUSH-FINCH, endemic to a single river valley in the highlands of southern Ecuador, had not been seen since the mid-1960s and was feared extinct, but in late 1998, 10 pairs were rediscovered in the area.

Profiles

Slate-colored Grosbeak, *Pitylus grossus*, Plate 69a
Buff-throated Saltator, *Saltator maximus*, Plate 69b
Red-capped Cardinal, *Paroaria gularis*, Plate 69c
Lesser Seed-finch, *Oryzoborus angolensis*, Plate 69d
Blue-black Grassquit, *Volatinia jacarina*, Plate 69e
Variable Seedeater, *Sporophila americana*, Plate 69f
Yellow-bellied Seedeater, *Sporophila nigricollis*, Plate 70a
Chestnut-bellied Seedeater, *Sporophila castaneiventris*, Plate 70b
Rufous-naped Brush-finch, *Atlapetes rufinucha*, Plate 70c
Plumbeous Sierra-finch, *Phrygilus unicolor*, Plate 70d
Band-tailed Seedeater, *Catamenia analis*, Plate 70e
Collared Warbling-finch, *Poospiza hispaniolensis*, Plate 70f
Rufous-collared Sparrow, *Zonotrichia capensis*, Plate 71a
Saffron Finch, *Sicalis flaveola*, Plate 71b
Hooded Siskin, *Carduelis magellanica*, Plate 71c
Crimson Finch, *Rhodospingus cruentus*, Plate 71d
Southern Yellow Grosbeak, *Pheucticus chrysogaster*, Plate 71e

Environmental Close-up 3:
Frugivory: Animals That Eat Fruit and the Trees That Want Them To

Frugivory From the Animal's Point of View

A key feature of tropical forests, and of the animal communities that inhabit them, is the large number of birds (cotingas, finches, manakins, parrots, orioles, tanagers, toucans, and trogons make up a partial list), mammals, and even some fish that rely on fruit as a diet staple. Frugivory represents a trade-off, each participant – the fruit-bearing tree and the fruit-eating animal – offering the other something of great value (and therefore it is a kind of mutualism – see p. 38). The complex web of relationships between fruit-eaters and fruit-producing trees is particularly interesting because it nicely demonstrates ecological interactions between plant and animal, between food producer and food consumer, between predator and prey, and the mutual dependence sometimes engendered by such relationships.

Benefits of Frugivory for Animals

Most small and medium-sized tropical forest birds, many mammals, and some fish eat either fruits or animals such as insects, or they eat both. But it is the fruit-eating habit that accounts for much of the incredible ecological success of animals in the tropics. For birds, many more species occupy the Earth's tropical areas than temperate zones and, ecologists believe, about 20% of the difference is directly attributable to the tropical birds' superior abilities to exploit fruit resources. In fact, probably 50% of tropical bird biomass (the summed weight of all tropical birds alive at one time) is supported by fruit-eating. You would think, therefore, that fruit must be tremendously profitable "prey" for birds, and in several ways it is:

(1) Fruit is conspicuous. First consider insects as food. Palatable insects are often small and/or inconspicuous; they hide or blend in extremely well with their surroundings. Finding such insects is a chore that takes a lot of time. Ripe fruit, on the other hand, usually attracts attention to itself, being sweet-smelling, brightly colored, and displayed out in the open.

(2) Fruit is easy to stalk, run down, catch, kill, and devour. Insects, as far as we can tell, are absolutely loath to be eaten – they run, hide, and resist to the end; some even spray noxious chemicals at their attackers. Fruit, however, never attempts escape and, in fact, when it is ripe and so most attractive to frugivores, it is most easily separated from the tree that bears it.

The underlying reason for points (1) and (2), which becomes more clear when considering frugivory from the trees' point of view (see below), is that fruits are made to be consumed by animals. It is their *raison d'être*. Owing to this, trees could hardly be expected to make their fruit difficult to locate or pluck. Thus we have a major ecological insight: insects benefit by not being eaten, but unless a fruit is eaten, the plant gains nothing from the effort to produce it.

(3) Fruit is abundant. When a bird locates a tree with fruit, there is often a large amount available for consumption. Thus, meeting a day's nutritional requirements means finding one or, at most, a few, fruit-bearing trees.

(4) Fruit in the tropics is usually available year-round. There are wide-ranging consequences of points (3) and (4) for avian frugivores. That fruit is always available and abundant means that birds can safely specialize on it – evolve special ways to pluck, eat, and digest it – without encountering times of the year when no fruit is available, forcing the birds to search for food that they are ill-equipped to handle. Owing to its abundance, species that concentrate on fruit often are quite successful, meaning that within a given area the numbers of individuals of these species can be quite large. But the greatest influence of frugivory on the lives of birds is that, because fruit is abundant and easy to locate and eat, birds can fulfill nutritional needs in only a few hours, leaving many hours each day available to pursue other activities. In contrast, an avian insectivore or piscivore (specializing on insects or fish, respectively), to survive may have to hunt most of each day.

The abundance of fruit, in fact, probably permitted the evolution of polygamous and promiscuous breeding in tropical birds. Take the manakins and cotingas that breed promiscuously. Males establish display sites on tree branches or on ground courts. Several of these display sites near each other constitute a lec. Females visit lecs, attracted by the males' vocalizations and dancing display antics, compare the males displaying, and choose one or more to mate with. Afterwards, the females go off by themselves to nest and raise their young. At their lecs, male manakins, for instance, spend up to 80% to 90% of daylight hours during the breeding season displaying and trying to attract females (the more they are able to convince to mate with them, the more offspring the males will have in the next generation). The free time frugivory affords permits both the prolonged display time in these breeding systems as well as the requisite ability of females to raise young themselves.

Also, when food is fairly scarce or difficult to locate or catch, to ensure adequate supplies for themselves and their young, birds may need to defend individual territories and struggle to keep out other members of their species. Furthermore, male and female may need to continue their pairing past actual mating because one parent foraging alone cannot provide sufficient food for the young. But establishing a territory to defend the fruit it holds is unnecessary because there is usually fruit enough for all that want it. (In fact, usually birds cannot eat all the fruit that ripens on a tree.) It is far more efficient to forage in groups, to be social feeders, as are toucans and parrots, and so to each day have help in finding trees bearing ripe fruit (sometimes easier said than done because trees within a small area usually do not ripen simultaneously).

Problems of Frugivory

Have birds encountered difficulties in the process of specializing on fruit? Yes, there are some associated problems:

(1) Fruits, although providing plentiful carbohydrates and fats, are relatively low in protein, so these birds, although easily meeting their daily calorie needs, sometimes have "protein deficits" that they must ease by feeding occasionally on insects or other animals (the occasional snail or frog, the odd lizard). Few bird species eat fruit exclusively. The ones that do, such as many cotingas, need make special provision for their all-fruit diet. For instance, because rapidly growing young need good amounts of protein, cotinga nestlings, fed only fruit by their parents, grow relatively slowly, and so spend perhaps 50% more time in the nest than non-frugivorous birds of the same size. Many of these birds nest in

tree cavities where their slow-developing young are better-protected from the many nest predators roaming tropical habitats. Also, some of these birds seek out unusual fruits that are high in proteins and fats, such as avocados.

(2) Eating liquidy fruit pulp means that frugivores consume a lot of water, which is both bulky and heavy, and which must be transported for a time (which uses up energy) and disposed of regularly.

(3) The birds' nutrition comes from the fleshy fruit pulp. The seeds that are eaten incidentally are usually indigestible or even poisonous and must be, like water, carried for a while and then disposed of – either by regurgitation or after being passed through the digestive tract.

(4) When a species specializes on a particular type of fruit, it becomes vulnerable to any temporary or permanent decline in the fruit's availability. (It appears that most avian frugivores avoid such vulnerability by not being overly specialized: in an observational study that followed the feeding habits of 70 fruit-eating species in the tropics, researchers discovered that each bird species consumed, on average, 10 species of fruits.)

Frugivory From the Tree's Point of View

It is clear what birds get from frugivory, but what of the trees, which are picked clean of the fruit that they spend so much time and energy producing? The answer is that the trees, by having birds eat, transport, and then drop their seeds, achieve efficient reproduction – something well worth their investment in fruit. The trees make use of birds as winged, animate, seed dispersal agents.

Why don't trees just let their seeds drop to the ground? It turns out that seeds dropped near the parent most often do NOT survive. They die because they must compete with the much larger parent for sun and other nutrients. Also, specialized insects that eat seeds can more easily find and destroy seeds that are in large accumulations, like under the mother tree. Seeds carried some distance from the parent tree have a better chance of germination and survival, and they will not compete with the parent tree (also, because in the tropics trees of the same species usually do not grow near each other, seeds dropped by birds are unlikely to be regularly competing with any trees of the same species). Furthermore, because they are more spread out, seed predators are less likely to find them. Thus, seed dispersal by birds enhances a parent tree's prospects for successful reproduction, and also allows the tree to colonize new sites.

The tree's use of animal power for seed dispersal is exquisitely fine-tuned. As seeds are being readied, fruit is green, hard, and bitter-tasting – unappealing fare to birds (and to people!). When the seeds mature and are ready for dispersal and germination, the surrounding fruit brightens in color, becomes softer and easier to pluck from the tree, and in a *coup de grâce*, trees inject sugars into fruits, making them sweet and very attractive.

Not all animals attracted to fruits are good seed dispersers. Some, notably the parrots, eat and digest seeds, acting as predators rather than dispersers. These seed destroyers, however, in the course of their movements from branch to branch often knock many fruits out of the canopy that fall to the forest floor. Here, frugivorous animals such as tinamous and agoutis that can't climb trees well await this largesse. They eat the fruit, dispersing seeds later when they defecate, or cache it in the ground for later consumption, where seeds may later germinate.

Ecological Consequences of Frugivory for Birds, Trees, and Ecosystems

As tropical birds have benefited in several ways by specialization on fruit, so too have trees. In fact, ecologists now suspect that together with pollination by insects, bats and birds, seed dispersal by birds and other vertebrate animals was and is responsible for the initial spread and current domination of the Earth by flowering plants. They estimate that upwards of 80% of trees and shrubs in tropical wet forests have their seeds dispersed by animals. These plants provide the nutrients to support large, healthy populations of frugivorous birds and bats. Moreover, the great species diversity of plants in the tropics may be largely linked to frugivorous animals continually eating fruits and spreading seeds into new areas. Such constant dispersal, which also allows continual, healthy genetic mixing, is beneficial for plant populations, always working to decrease the chances that individual species will go extinct. In fact, the more successful a tree species is at being "preyed upon" by birds, the more its seeds will be dropped over a wide area, and the more abundant it will become.

One potential problem for trees, though, is that if their fruit is eaten by only one or two bird species, that strict dependence for seed dispersal brings vulnerability. If the bird that disperses such a specialist tree for some reason declines in abundance and becomes extinct, so too, in short order, will the tree species. Examples of such occurrences are on record. For instance, when Dodo birds (p. 117) were eliminated from the Indian Ocean's island of Mauritius, the tree species for which they were the sole dispersal agents were endangered. (Luckily, turkeys introduced to the island by people seem able to replace the Dodo there as a tree seed disperser.) Most tree species, however, enjoy the seed dispersal services of at least several bird species.

The trade-offs that the birds and trees make, the conflicting strategies to survive and complete their life cycles, are fascinating. Think about it from one evolutionary perspective: the beneficial aspect of the interaction for the tree – having a bird transport its seeds – is the negative aspect for the animal, which has no "desire" to carry seeds from which it gets no benefit. The beneficial aspect for the bird – the fruit pulp that the plant manufactures to attract animals – is the negative part of the interaction for the plant, which loses the energy and nutrients required to make the fruit. Frugivory is one of the tropic's most important and compelling ecological interactions, and one that currently attracts strong interest from ecological researchers. Frugivory may even have been a causative factor in the early evolution of color vision, as the first fruit-eaters that could easily distinguish ripe and unripe fruit plainly would have had advantages over those that could not.

A Fruitful Connection Between Land and Water

The PIRANHA, thanks to cartoons and horror movies, is etched into our minds as a blood-thirsty fish of the Amazon. Here it supposedly reduces large animals, unlucky enough to fall into the water, to nothing but bones within minutes. Although some do eat flesh, their reputations are greatly exaggerated. They do occasionally bite swimmers, but this behavior is very rare in Ecuador. We regularly swim near these intriguing fish, and in 30 years have never had so much as a nibble – except on a fishing line. The biggest threat these fish pose to people may be when freshly caught piranha are flopping around on the bottom of a fisherman's canoe, with bare toes exposed to their sharp teeth.

There are 25 piranha species in the Amazon Basin – some black and others white; a few are red-bellied. Regardless of their reputation, piranhas also eat a lot of fruits floating in the water. All species are primarily frugivores when young, and, even as adults, fruits are a major to occasional part of their diets, depending on the species. Only six species of piranhas (red-bellied species in the genus *Pygocentrus*), however, are primarily flesheaters as adults. Even then the flesh they eat is usually in the form of fins and scales of other fish. In Ecuador, only one species of this red-bellied genus occurs, *Pygocentrus ternetzi* (Figure 12; adult body length 20 to 30 cm, 8 to 12 in).

During the rainier season in Ecuador's Oriente, rivers flood and low forest, dry for most of the year, has up to a meter (3.3 ft) or more of water standing at the bases of the trees. Many of these trees time their flowering and fruiting to coincide with this flooding, their specialized fruits dropping to float in the water below. Fish, including piranhas, swim in among the bases of the trees to devour the fruits or chew at their outer coverings. Many seeds are dropped or pass through the fish digestive system to be defecated somewhere else in the flooded forest. The seeds fall to the forest floor, and if lucky, germinate when the floods recede. Not only does this story dispel the undeserved super-carnivore reputation of piranhas, it also dispels the idea that aquatic and terrestrial systems are very separate. That an aquatic fish serves as a major seed disperser for a terrestrial tree is just one of many examples of how differently we must look at and study this diverse area.

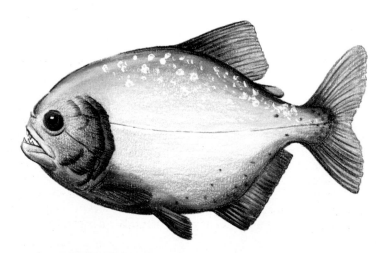

Figure 12 Pirhana, *Pygocentrus* ternetzi.

Chapter 8

MAMMALS

- *Introduction*
- *General Characteristics and Classification of Mammals*
- *Features of Tropical Mammals*
- *Seeing Mammals in Ecuador*
- *Family Profiles*

Introduction

Leafing through this book, you may have noticed that there are many more profiles of birds than mammals. At first glance you might see this as discriminatory, especially because people themselves are mammals and, owing to that direct kinship, are often keenly interested and motivated to see and learn about mammals. What's going on? Aren't mammals as good as birds? Why not include more of them? There are several reasons for the discrepancy – good biological reasons. One is that, even though the tropics generally have more species of mammals than temperate or Arctic regions, the total number of mammal species worldwide, and the number in any region, is almost always much less than the number of birds. In fact, there are only 4629 mammal species in the world, compared with 9040 birds, and that relative difference is reflected in Ecuador's fauna. Another compelling reason not to include more mammals in a book on commonly sighted wildlife, is that, even in regions of South America sporting high levels of mammalian diversity, you will rarely see mammals – especially if you are a short-term visitor. Mammals are delicious fare for any number of predatory beasts (eaten in good numbers by reptiles, birds, other mammals, and even the odd amphibian), but most mammals lack a basic protection from predators that birds possess, the power of flight. Consequently, most have been forced into being active nocturnally, or, if active during daylight hours, they are highly secretive. Birds often show themselves with abandon, mammals do not. An exception is monkeys. They are fairly large and primarily arboreal, which keeps them safe from a number of kinds of predators, and thus permits them to be noisy and relatively conspicuous. A final reason for not including more mammals in the book is that about 130 (40%) of the 324 mammal species occurring in Ecuador are bats. They are for the most part nocturnal animals that, even if you are lucky enough to get good looks at them, are very difficult for anyone other than an expert to identify to species.

General Characteristics and Classification of Mammals

Mammals as a group first arose, so fossils tell us, approximately 245 million years ago, splitting off from the primitive reptiles during the late Triassic Period of the Mesozoic Era, somewhat before the birds did the same thing. Four main traits distinguish mammals from other vertebrates, and each of these traits helped mammals spread into most of the habitats around the world: hair on their bodies which insulates and helps maintain constant internal temperatures as well as protects the skin from injuries; milk production for the young, freeing mothers from having to search for specific foods for their offspring; the bearing of live young instead of eggs, allowing breeding females to be mobile and hence, safer than if they had to guard eggs for several weeks; and advanced brains, with highly integrated sensory systems that contribute to mammals' breadth of survival mechanisms.

Mammals are quite variable in size and form, many being highly adapted – changed through evolution – to specialized habitats and lifestyles: bats specialized to fly, marine mammals specialized for their aquatic world, deer to run swiftly, etc. The smallest mammals are the shrews, tiny insect eaters that weigh as little as 2.5 g (a tenth of an ounce). The largest are the whales, weighing in at up to 160,000 kg (350,000 lb, half the weight of a loaded Boeing 747) – as far as anyone knows, the largest animals that have ever lived.

Mammals are divided into three major groups, primarily according to reproductive methods. The *monotremes* are an ancient group that actually lays eggs and still retains some other reptile-like characteristics. Only four species of them survive: one platypus and three spiny anteaters, and they are found only in Australia and New Guinea. The *marsupials* give birth to live young that are relatively undeveloped. When born, the young crawl along mom's fur to attach themselves to her nipples, usually inside her pouch, where they find milk supplies and finish their development. There are about 240 marsupial species, including kangaroos, koalas, wombats, and opossum, and they are limited in distribution to Australia and the Neotropics (the industrious but road-accident-prone VIRGINIA OPOSSUM also inhabits much of Mexico and the USA). The majority of mammal species are *eutherians* (the "true mammals"). These animals are distinguished from the other groups by having a well developed placenta, which efficiently connects a mother to her developing babies, allowing for long internal development. This trait, which allows embryos to develop to a fairly mature form in safety, and for the female to be mobile until birth, has allowed these mammals to colonize successfully and prosper in many habitats. The true mammals include those with which most people are intimately familiar: rodents, rabbits, cats, dogs, bats, primates, elephants, horses, whales – everything from house mice to ecotravellers. The 4600 species of living mammals are grouped into about 115 families, which are in turn categorized into about 20 orders.

Features of Tropical Mammals

There are several important features of tropical mammals and their habitats that differentiate them from temperate zone mammals. First, tropical mammals face different environmental stresses than do temperate zone mammals, and they respond to stresses in different ways. Many temperate zone mammals, of course, must endure extreme variation within a year; from cold winters with snow and low winter food supplies to hot summers with dry weather and abundant food. Many of them respond with hibernation, staying more or less dormant for several months until conditions improve. Tropical mammals, except in the high altitude páramo, do not encounter such extreme annual changes, but they do face dry seasons, up to 5 months long, that sometimes severely reduce food supplies. For some surprising reasons, they cannot alleviate this stress by hibernating, waiting for the rainy season to arrive with its increased food supplies. When a mammal in Canada or Alaska hibernates, many of its predators leave the area. This is not the case in the tropics. A mammal sleeping away the dry season in a burrow would be easy prey to snakes and other predators. Moreover, a big danger to sleeping mammals would be ... army ants! These voracious insects are very common in the tropics and would quickly eat a sleeping mouse or squirrel. Also, external parasites, such as ticks and mites, which are inactive in extreme cold, would continue to be very active on sleeping tropical mammals, sucking blood and doing considerable damage. Last, the great energy reserves needed to be able to sleep for an extended period through warm weather may be more than any mammal can physically accumulate. Therefore, tropical mammals need to stay active throughout the year. One way they counter the dry season's reduction in their normal foods is to switch food types seasonally. For instance, some rodents that eat mostly insects during the rainy season switch to seeds during the dry; some bats that feed on insects switch to dry-season fruits.

The abundance of tropical fruit brings up another interesting difference between temperate and tropical mammals: a surprising number of tropical mammals eat a lot of fruit, even among the carnivore group, which, as its name implies, should be eating meat. All the carnivores in Ecuador, save the PUMA, JAGUAR and otters, are known to eat fruit. Some, such as the SPECTACLED BEAR, seem to prefer fruit. Upon reflection, that these mammals consume fruit makes sense. Fruit is very abundant in the tropics, available all year, and, at least when it is ripe, easily digested by mammalian digestive systems. A consequence of such frugivory (fruit-eating) is that many mammals have become, together with frugivorous birds, major dispersal agents of fruit seeds, which they spit out or which travel unharmed through their digestive tracts to be deposited in feces far from the mother tree (see Close-up, p. 168). Some biologists believe that, even though the carnivores plainly are specialized for hunting down, killing, and eating animal prey, it is likely that fruit has always been a major part of their diet.

Finally, there are some differences in the kinds of mammals inhabiting tropical and temperate regions. For instance there is only a single Neotropical bear species, distributed sparsely from the highlands of Venezuela to southern Bolivia. There are few social rodents like beavers and prairie dogs and very few rabbit species. On the other hand, some groups occur solely in the tropics and do fabulously there. There are about 50 species of New World monkeys, all of which occur in tropical areas (16 occur in Ecuador). Arboreal mammals such as monkeys and sloths are plentiful in tropical forests, probably because there is a rich, resource-filled, dense canopy to occupy and feed in. Also, the closed canopy blocks light to the ground, which only allows an undergrowth that is sparse and poor in resources, and consequently permits few opportunities for mammals to live and feed there. Bats thrive in the tropics, being very successful both in terms of number of species and in their abundances. Seven families of bats occur in Ecuador, including more than 130 species; only four families and 40 species occur in the entire USA, an area more than 100 times larger than Ecuador's. While most of the North American bats are insect-eaters, the Ecuadorean bats are quite varied in lifestyle, among them being fruit-eaters, nectar-eaters, fish-eaters and even a few that consume other animals or their blood.

The social and breeding behaviors of various mammals are quite diverse. Some are predominantly solitary animals, males and females coming together occasionally only to mate. Others live in family groups. Like birds, female mammals have most of the say in choosing a mate, but unlike most bird species, where both mates are necessary to raise the young and monogamy (one male mates with one female) is thus common, milk production among female mammals usually frees the male from caring for the young. He is better off and more likely to get more of his genes into the next generation by convincing additional females to mate with him. This leads to polygyny (one male mates with a harem of several females) or promiscuity (a sexual free-for-all where dominant males tend to mate with a mind-blurring array of females) as the most common mating systems among mammals. Monogamy is uncommon, but polyandry (one female mates with several males) is even rarer among mammals than birds. Depending on resources like food availability and access to mates, some mammal species are rigorously territorial, others are not.

Seeing Mammals in Ecuador

No doubt about it, mammals are tough to see. You could go for two weeks and, if in the wrong places at the wrong times, see very few of them. A lot of luck is involved – a tapir, a small herd of peccaries, or a porcupine happens to cross the trail just a bit ahead of you, or by chance someone in your group spots a sloth in a tree. We can offer three pieces of mammal-spotting advice: first, if you have time and are a patient sort, stake out a likely looking spot near a stream or watering hole, be quiet, and wait to see what approaches. Second, try taking quiet strolls along paths and trails very early in the morning. At this time, many nocturnal mammals are quickly scurrying to their day shelters. Third, although only for the stout-hearted, try searching with a flashlight at night around field stations or campgrounds. After scanning the ground (for safety's sake as well as for mammals), shine the light toward the middle regions of trees and look for bright, shiny eyes reflecting the light. You will certainly stumble across some kind of mammal or another; then it is simply a matter of whether you scare them more than they scare you. Doing the same thing at night from a canoe can also be a good way to spot eye-shine of mammals in the vegetation along the edge of a stream or forested lake.

Some mammals, of course, you can see more reliably. Monkeys, for instance, are often easy to see in many of Ecuador's national parks, and squirrels and peccaries are frequently sighted in lowland areas both on the coast and in the Oriente. Banish all thoughts right now of ever encountering *El Tigre*, the Jaguar, which is found regularly now only in isolated regions of the coast and Oriente. Even there, however, your chances of encountering one are slim, although their tracks along rivers and lakes are a regular sight in Yasuní National Park.

Family Profiles

1. Opossums

Marsupials are an ancient group, preceding in evolution the development of the *true*, or *placental*, mammals, which eventually replaced the marsupials over most parts of the terrestrial world. Marsupials alive today in the Australian and Neotropical regions therefore are remnants of an earlier time when the group's distribution spanned the Earth. Of the eight living families of marsupials, only three occur in the New World, and only one, the *opossums*, occurs in Ecuador. This family, Didelphidae, is distributed widely over the northern Neotropics (with one member, the VIRGINIA OPOSSUM, reaching far northwards into the USA). Twenty-five species represent the family in Ecuador. They are a diverse group, occupying essentially all of the country's habitats up to about 3300 m (11,000 ft) elevation. Some, such as the COMMON OPOSSUM (also called SOUTHERN OPOSSUM; Plate 72), are abundant and frequently sighted, while others are rarer or shier.

All opossums are basically alike in body plan, although species vary considerably in size. Their general appearance probably has not changed much during the past 40 to 65 million years. Basically, these mammals look like rats, albeit in the case of some, such as the Common Opossum, like large rats. Their distinguishing features are pointed snouts, short legs, a long, often hairless tail, which is usually *prehensile* (that is, opossums can wrap it around a tree branch and hang from it), and large, hairless ears. Opossums come in a narrow range of colors – shades of gray, brown, and black. Male and female opossums generally look alike, but males are usually larger than females of the same age. Females in about half of the species have pouches for their young on their abdomens. Opossum hind feet have five digits each, one digit acting as an opposable thumb.

Natural History

Ecology and Behavior

Most opossums are night-active omnivores, although some also can be seen during the day. Their reputation is that they will eat, or at least try to eat, almost anything they stumble across or can catch; mostly they take fruit, eggs, invertebrates and small vertebrate animals. The COMMON OPOSSUM forages mainly at night, often along ponds and streams, sometimes covering more than a kilometer (half-mile) per night within its *home range*, the area within which it lives and seeks food. Opossums that have been studied are not territorial – they do not defend part or all of their home ranges from others of their species. Some opossums forage mainly on the ground, but most are good climbers and are able to forage also in trees and shrubs; and some species are chiefly arboreal. The WATER OPOSSUM (Plate 72) is semi-aquatic and feeds primarily on fish, crustaceans and large insects it catches in the clear water of streams and lakes at the base of the Andes. Water Opossums are not shy, and if you see a pair of mammalian eyes reflecting light as they move quickly across the water's surface, it is likely to be this species. The female's pouch can be sealed to protect the young from drowning while in the water. The terrestrial BROWN FOUR-EYED OPOSSUM (Plate 72) and the arboreal LONG-FURRED WOOLLY MOUSE OPOSSUM (Plate 72) are both much shier and warier. They concentrate on insects for food, but during times of the year when there are lots of fruit, your best chance to see them is at a fruiting tree. After a night's foraging, an opossum spends the daylight hours in a cave, a rock crevice, or a cavity in a tree or log.

Predators on opossums include owls, snakes, and carnivorous mammals. Some opossums apparently are somewhat immune to the venom of many poisonous snakes. The response of the Common Opossum to threat by a predator is to hiss, growl, snap its mouth, move its body from side to side, and finally, to lunge and bite. They often try to climb to escape. The VIRGINIA OPOSSUM, a common North and Central American species, is famous for faking death ("playing possum") when threatened, but that behavior is rare or absent in the Common Opossum.

The Common Opossum has what can be considered a commensal relationship with people. Throughout its range in northern South America, populations of these opossums are concentrated around human settlements, particularly near garbage dumps, where they feed. They also partake of fruit crops and attack farmyard birds. Consequently, this species of opossum is more likely to be seen near towns or villages than in uninhabited areas. Of course, these opossums pay a price for the easy food – their picture commonly is found in the dictionary under "road kill."

Breeding

Opossums are unsociable animals and usually observed singly. The exception is during the breeding season, when males seek and court females, and two or more may be seen together. Female opossums give birth only 12 to 14 days after mating. The young that leave the reproductive tract are only about 1 cm (a half inch) long and weigh less than half a gram (one-hundreth ounce). These tiny opossums, barely embryos, climb unassisted along the mother's fur toward her nipples. They then grasp a nipple in their mouths, either within the pouch, or, if a species without a pouch like the BROWN FOUR-EYED OPOSSUM or the mouse opossums, directly on her chest. The nipple swells to completely fill the young mouth, essentially attaching it to the mother for about 2 months. Usually more young are born (up to 20) than make it to the nipples to attach correctly. In studies, six young, on average, are found on the females' nipples (they have up to 13 nipples). Following this attached phase, the female continues to nurse her young for another month or more, often in a nest she constructs of leaves and grass in a tree cavity or burrow.

Notes

COMMON OPOSSUMS are known as foul-smelling beasts. Their reputation probably stems from the fact that they apparently enjoy rolling about in fresh animal droppings. Also, when handled, they employ some unattractive defense mechanisms – tending to squirt urine and defecate.

Status

None of Ecuador's opossum species is considered threatened or endangered, although several are very local and uncommon. Opossum meat is not regarded as tasty, so these mammals are rarely hunted for food. Opossums, chiefly COMMON OPOSSUMS, are killed intentionally near human settlements to protect fruit crops and poultry, and unintentionally but frequently by cars.

Profiles

Brown Four-eyed Opossum, *Metachirus nudicaudatus*, Plate 72a
Common Opossum, *Didelphis marsupialis*, Plate 72b

Long-furred Woolly Mouse Opossum, *Micoureus demerarae*, Plate 72c
Water Opossum, *Chironectes minimus*, Plate 72d

2. Anteaters, Sloths, and Armadillos

Anteaters, sloths, and *armadillos* are three types of very different-looking mammals that, somewhat surprisingly, are closely related. The group they belong to is the Order Edentata, meaning, literally, without teeth. However, because all but the anteaters have some teeth, the name is a misnomer. The edentates are New World mammals specialized to eat ants and termites, or to eat leaves high in the forest canopy. Although the edentates might look and behave differently, they are grouped together because they share certain skeletal features and aspects of their circulatory and reproductive systems that indicate close relationships. Because anteaters and sloths are found only in the tropical and semi-tropical forests of Central and South America, they are perhaps the quintessential mammals of the region, the way that toucans and parrots are the quintessential Neotropical birds. If given a choice of mammals, most visitors to Ecuador would probably prefer to see a Jaguar, but it is far more likely that the characteristic Neotropical mammal they spot will be a sloth.

The anteater family, Myrmecophagidae, has four species, all restricted to Neotropical forests, and all are found in Ecuador: the very rare, 2-meter-long (6.5 ft) GIANT ANTEATER (Plate 73) in the eastern lowlands, the NORTHERN TAMANDUA in western Ecuador, the very similar SOUTHERN TAMANDUA (Plate 73) in the Oriente, and the very small PYGMY or SILKY ANTEATER, also in the Oriente. Because the last species is a nocturnal tree-dweller, the only anteater you are likely to see during your trip is one of the tamanduas.

There is nothing else like a sloth. They vaguely resemble monkeys ("deformed monkeys," according to one chronicler), but their slow-motion lifestyle is the very antithesis of most primates' hyperkinetic lives. There are two families of sloths, the two-toed and three-toed varieties, distinguished by the number of claws per foot. There are five sloth species, three of which occur in Ecuador. The two-toed sloths (Family Megalonychidae) weigh about 5 to 8 kg (11 to 17.5 lb) and are active only at night. The much smaller three-toed sloths (Family Brady-podidae, meaning slow-footed) weigh, on average, about 4 kg (9 lb), are pale yel-lowish or brown with a round, white face with dark side stripes, and are active both during the day and the night. Their hair is long and stiff, producing a shaggy look. Long limbs end in feet with three curved claws that they use as hooks to hang from tree branches.

Armadillos are strange ground-dwelling mammals that, probably owing to the armor plating on their backs, are protected from many smaller predators. The family, Dasypodidae, contains about 20 species that are distributed from the southern tip of South America to the central USA, with four species in Ecuador. The endangered GIANT ARMADILLO (Plate 73) (up to 1.5 m (5 ft) in length, including the tail, and weighing about 30 kg, 65 lb), is rare in the lowland forests of the Oriente, but where present, huge holes it makes in the forest floor adver-tise the fact. The uncommon GREAT LONG-NOSED ARMADILLO of the Oriente lowland forests and the abundant NINE-BANDED ARMADILLO (Plate 73) are very similar in appearance (70 cm, 27.5 in, in length, including the tail). Because all the other species are entirely nocturnal, you are most likely to see only the Nine-banded Armadillo, which is often also active during the day. It is also the species that extends into the USA. All these armadillos are grayish or yellowish, with many crosswise plates of hard, horn-like material on their backs (bony plates underlie the outer horny covering).

Natural History

Ecology and Behavior

Anteaters are mammals highly specialized to feed on ants and termites; some also dabble in bees. From an anteater's point of view, the main thing about these social insects is that they live in large colonies, so that finding one often means finding thousands. The anteaters' strong, sharp, front claws are put to use digging into ant colonies in or on the ground, and into termite nests in trees (the very abundant, dark, globular, often basket-ball sized *termitarium* attached to the trunks and branches of tropical trees). Their long, thin snouts are used to get down into the excavation, and their extremely long tongues, coated with a special sticky saliva, are used to extract the juicy insects. The tamanduas and SILKY ANTEATER are largely arboreal. They have prehensile tails for hanging about and moving in trees, allowing them to get to hard-to-reach termite nests. Particular about their food, anteaters don't generally go after army ants or large, stinging ants that might do them harm. Tamanduas rest in hollow trees or other holes during mid-day, but are otherwise active, including nocturnally. They forage both on the ground and in trees, usually solitarily. Each individual's home range, the area in which it lives and seeks food, averages about 70 hectares (170 acres). Anteaters are fairly slow-moving animals and their metabolic rates low because, although ants and termites are plentiful and easy to find, they don't provide a high nutrition, high energy diet. Deceptively placid and shy, anteaters, especially the GIANT ANTEATER, if attacked, can rear back and slash with deadly accuracy and force, using their powerful front legs and sharp claws to disembowel or severely injure enemies.

Sloths are active almost exclusively in trees, feeding on leaves as they hang upside down. "Active" is probably the wrong word to describe their behavior. Sloths, particularly the three-toed ones, move incredibly slowly – so much so that at one time it was mistakenly thought that a sloth spent its entire life moving about slowly in a single tree. Detailed observations have shown that sloths do indeed switch trees, but, on average, only once every two days. When switching, they do not cross open ground, but move between the trees' overlapping branches. This is smart, both because slowly descending to the ground and then climbing another tree would be a waste of time and energy and because a slow-moving sloth on the ground would be easy, defenseless prey for a variety of predators – snakes, large cats, and eagles. (One person clocked a female sloth on the ground as moving only 4.5 m, 14 ft, in a minute – and that was in rapid response to the call of her offspring!) Sloths can swim, however, and you should look for them crossing small rivers.

Besides their slow movements that probably help sloths escape notice from predators searching the canopy, the surface of their hair has many grooves and pits in which algae and fungi readily grow to turn the animal greenish and camouflaged. Not only do sloths support plants on their bodies, they support insects as well. A number of different beetle and moth species spend at least parts of their life cycles living on sloths. One moth species, a "sloth moth," lives as an adult moth in the hair of a sloth, reproducing by laying its eggs in sloth droppings. While the three-toed sloths are docile and non-aggressive, the two-toed sloths are dangerous and can do considerable damage, even in slow motion, with their front claws. All species of sloths apparently come down from their elevated perches only about once per week, to urinate and defecate at the base of a tree. Why they do so, instead of just defecating from the heights, remains a mystery. The three-toed sloths, but not the two-toed sloths, take extra time to dig a small hole, void themselves, and cover the droppings. During this 30-minute period, the animals are vulnerable to predators.

Leaves are notoriously difficult to digest, so a pure diet of leaves provides little nutrition. That means the sloths must eat a lot of them to survive. Sloths have very low metabolic rates and relatively low body temperatures; in fact, at night, sloths save energy by lowering their body temperatures to almost match that of the environment. Sloths are solitary and apparently territorial – only one per tree is permitted (or a female together with her young). Look for sloths in large, leafy trees (particularly Cecropias), as they hang upside down, their hook-like claws grasping the branches. Two-toed sloths will often eat fruits in addition to leaves, so also look for them at night in fruiting trees.

Some armadillos, such as the GIANT ARMADILLO, specialize on ants and termites. This species uses its immense bulk and large claws on its front feet to quickly dig out these insects from their nests in the ground. The NINE-BANDED ARMADILLO, however, is more omnivorous, eating many kinds of insects, small vertebrates, and also some plant parts. Usually they spend the day foraging alone, but several family members may share the same sleeping burrow they have dug out with their sharp claws. They are generally slow-moving creatures that, save for their armor plating, would be easy prey for predators. When attacked, they curl up into a ball so that their armor faces the attacker, their soft abdomens protected at the center of the ball. Few natural predators can harm them. However, like opossums, they are frequently hit on roads by automobiles.

Breeding

Female anteaters bear one offspring at a time, and lavish attention on it. At first the newborn is placed in a secure location, such as in a tree cavity, and the mother returns to it at intervals to nurse. Later, when it is old enough, the youngster rides on the mother's back. After several months, when the young is about half the mother's size, the two part ways. Breeding may be at any time of year. Sloths also produce one young at a time. Following 6 months of pregnancy, the offspring is born. It is then carried about and fed by the mother for about 4 months, at which point it is put down and must forage for itself. Until it is a year old or so, the juvenile forages within its mother's home range; then it moves out on its own. Sloths not only move slowly, they grow slowly. Apparently they do not reach sexual maturity until they are three years old, and they may live for 20 to 30 years. Female armadillos, after 70-day pregnancies, produce several young at a time, usually four. For some unknown reason, each litter of armadillo young arises from a single fertilized egg, so that if a female has four young, they are always identical quadruplets.

Notes

GIANT ANTEATERS are also known as Ant Bears, for obvious reasons. Frequently, three-toed sloths are captured and released into city parks and plazas, where they survive amazingly well.

Status

Overall, the edentate mammals are not doing badly, but all suffer population declines from habitat destruction. One problem in trying to determine the status of their populations is that many are nocturnal, and some of the armadillos spend most of their time in burrows. The result is that nobody really knows the real health of some populations. The GIANT ANTEATER has been exterminated from much of its range in Central and South America. It is fairly common only on the savannahs of Venezuela and Colombia. In Ecuador it survives only in the most remote forests. Tamanduas are found throughout lowland Ecuador but, outside of protected areas, they are sometimes killed as pests by locals. The SILKY ANTEATER is thought to be fairly common, but because their populations naturally are sparse and also because they are so difficult to spot, good information on them is lacking. Ecuador's three sloth species apparently are fairly common, although, again, there is no good information on their populations. Some biologists suspect that three-toed sloths are one of the most abundant larger mammals of Neotropical forests. One sloth, Brazil's MANED THREE-TOED SLOTH, is endangered (CITES Appendix I and USA ESA listed). Armadillos can be common in Ecuador and other parts of their ranges, but because they are hunted for meat, their populations are often sparse around heavily settled areas. NINE-BANDED ARMADILLOS are especially common in coastal Ecuador. The GIANT ARMADILLO is killed for meat, and is now endangered (CITES Appendix I listed) from over-hunting.

Profiles

Brown-throated Three-toed Sloth, *Bradypus variegatus*, Plate 73a
Hoffman's Two-toed Sloth, *Choloepus hoffmanni*, Plate 73b
Giant Armadillo, *Priodontes maximus*, Plate 73c
Nine-banded Armadillo, *Dasypus novemcinctus*, plate 73d
Giant Anteater, *Myrmecophaga tridactyla*, Plate 73e
Southern Tamandua, *Tamandua tetradactyla*, Plate 73f

3. Bats

Because they are so hard to see or hear, *bats* have always been considered foreign, exotic, and mysterious, even in our own backyards. Unlike any other mammals, they engage in sustained, powered flight ("rats with wings," in the memorable phrasing of an unappreciative acquaintance). Bats are active at night and navigate the dark skies chiefly by "sonar," or *echolocation*: by broadcasting ultrasonic sounds – extremely high-pitched chirps and clicks – and then gaining information about their environment by "reading" the echoes. They also use this sonar to locate prey such as flying insects and surfacing fish. Although foreign to people's primate sensibilities, bats, precisely because their lives are so very different from our own, are increasingly of interest to us. In the past, of course, bats' exotic behavior, particularly their nocturnal habits, engendered in most societies not ecological curiosity but fear and superstition.

Bats are widely distributed, inhabiting most of the world's tropical and temperate regions, except for some oceanic islands. With a worldwide total of about 980 species, the bats are second in diversity among mammals only to the rodents. Ecologically, they can be thought of as nighttime replacements for birds, which dominate the daytime skies. Bats of the Neotropics, although often hard to see and, in most cases, difficult for anyone other than experts to identify (because of their great diversity), are tremendously important mammals. Their numbers tell the story: 39% of all Neotropical mammal species are bats, and there are often more species of bats in some Neotropical forests than of all other mammal species combined. Researchers estimate that bats make up most of the mammalian biomass (the total amount of living tissue, by weight) in any given Neotropical region. Of the 324 species of mammals that occur in Ecuador, 130 are bats. We profile 10 species that represent a spectrum of the types of bats you are most likely to encounter.

Bats have true wings that are made of thin, strong, highly elastic membranes that extend from the sides of the body and legs to cover and be supported by the elongated fingers of the arms. (The name of the order of bats, Chiroptera, refers to the wings: *chiro*, meaning hand, and *ptera*, wing.) Other distinctive anatomical features include bodies covered with silky, longish hair; toes with sharp, curved claws that allow the bats to hang upside down and are used by some to catch food; scent glands that produce strong, musky odors; and, in many, very odd-shaped folds of skin on their noses (*noseleaves*) and prominent ears that aid in echolocation. Like birds, bats' bodies have been modified through evolution to conform to the needs of energy-demanding flight: they have relatively large hearts, low body weights, and high metabolisms.

Bats, although they come in a variety of sizes, are sufficiently standardized in form such that all species are easily recognized by everyone as bats. Females in most species are larger than males, presumably so they can fly when pregnant. Bat species in Ecuador weigh 5 to 200 g (0.2 to 7 oz) and have wingspans of 5 to 80 cm (2 to 31 in). Bats tend not to occur above 500 m (1600 ft) elevation, but at night in almost any lowland habitat this group of mammals takes over. At dusk, when it is not yet too dark to see them, some species are already flying over streams and forests. During the night as you walk along a closed forested path, bats frequently will fly past the light beam of your flashlight. They may even brush your body with their wings as they swiftly fly by in hot pursuit of a scrumptious insect. Don't panic. They are harmless, unless you act like an insect. Bats absolutely do NOT make nests in your hair.

Natural History

Ecology and Behavior

Most Neotropical bat species specialize in eating insects (a single individual has been estimated to eat up to 1200 insects per hour!). They use their sonar not just to navigate the night but to detect insects, which they catch on the wing, pick off leaves, or scoop off the ground. Bats use several methods to catch flying insects. Small insects may be captured directly in the mouth; some bats use their wings as nets and spoons to trap insects and pull them to their mouth; and others scoop bugs into the fold of skin membrane that connects their tail and legs, then somersault in midair to move the catch to their mouth. Small bugs are eaten immediately on the wing, while larger ones, such as big beetles, are taken to a perch and dismembered. However, not all species are insectivores. Neotropical bats have also expanded ecologically into a variety of other feeding niches: some specialize in eating fruit, feeding on nectar and pollen at flowers, preying on vertebrates such as frogs or birds, eating fish, or drinking blood.

Bats are highly social animals, roosting and often foraging in groups. They spend the daylight hours in *day roosts*, usually tree cavities, shady sides of trees, caves, rock crevices, or, these days, in buildings or under bridges. Some bats make their own individual roosting sites in trees by biting leaves so that they fold over, making small tents that shelter them from predators as well as from the elements. More than one species of bat may inhabit the same roost, although some species will associate only with their own kind. For most species, the normal resting position in a roost is hanging by their feet, head down, which makes taking flight as easy as letting go and spreading their wings. Many bats leave roosts around dusk and then move to foraging sites at various distances from the roost. Night activity patterns vary, perhaps serving to reduce food competition among species. Some tend to fly and forage intensely in the early evening, become less active in the middle of the night, then resume intense foraging near dawn; others are relatively inactive early in the evening, but more active later on. Bats do not fly continuously after leaving their day roosts, but group together at a *night roost*, a tree for instance, where they rest and bring food. Fruit-eaters do not rest in the tree at which they have discovered ripe fruit, where predators might find them, but they make several trips per night from the fruit tree to their night roost.

If you see any bats on your trip to Amazonian Ecuador, they likely will be LONG-NOSED BATS (Plate 75). They roost in groups up to 30 or more on the underside of logs and banks along rivers and lakes. They hang in a line, evenly spaced but so well camouflaged, you will have to look carefully to see them. They readily take flight in the daytime if you come too close, and fly ahead of your canoe like a flock of large, whitish butterflies. At dusk they begin to feed on tiny insects low over the water. The WHITE-LINED SAC-WINGED BAT (Plate 74) is one of the most frequently encountered bats of Ecuador's lowland forests. By day they roost in groups of five to 50 in hollow trees or caves, rocks, or buildings; they are often seen under overhangs at ecotourist facilities. They leave roosts just before dark to commence their insect foraging, which they do under the forest canopy, usually within 300 m (1000 ft) of their roosts. Individual males defend territories in the day roosts, and they have harems of up to nine females each. After birth, a mother carries her pup each night from the day roost and leaves it in a hiding place while she forages. Pups can fly at about 2 weeks old, but continue to nurse for several months. The GREATER FISHING BAT (Plate 74) is relatively large and orange-colored. Fishing bats (sometimes called bulldog bats) roost in hollow trees and buildings near fresh or salt water. They have very large hind feet and claws that they use to pull fish, crustaceans, and insects from the water's surface. These bats fly low over still water, using their sonar to detect the ripples of a fish just beneath or breaking the water's surface. Grabbing the fish with their claws, they then move it to their mouth, land, hang upside down, and feast. The FALSE VAMPIRE BAT (Plate 74) is the New World's largest bat, with a wingspan of up to 80 cm (2.5 ft). They feed on vertebrates such as birds, rodents, and other bats. (The name originates with the mistaken belief of early European explorers that the largest, meanest-looking bat in the region must be the blood-sucker of which they had heard so many tales.) Some of the animals they prey on weigh as much as they do, but these bats are fierce, with large canine teeth, shearing molars, and powerful jaw muscles. They roost in small groups, usually a pair of adults and their recent offspring. Apparently, False Vampires, although they forage alone, are good family bats: young pups at night are left in the day roost to be guarded by an adult or subadult family member; the returning foragers are greeted with mutual "kissing" when they return (one observer compared it to the mutual muzzle licking and nosing practiced by wolves when they greet one another). Adult "babysitter" bats may be fed by the returning foragers. The COMMON LONG-

TONGUED BAT or NECTAR BAT (Plate 75) is a small bat with a misleading name. Although it can hover for a few seconds at flowers to take pollen or nectar, most of its omnivorous diet consists of fruit and insects. It roosts in large groups in both dry and wet forest habitats. Young use their teeth to cling to their mothers' fur after birth, being carried along during foraging trips; pups can fly on their own at about a month old. The SHORT-TAILED FRUIT BAT (Plate 75) is another small and very common species that lives in large groups, up to several hundred, usually in caves or tree cavities. They are primarily fruit-eaters, but also seasonally visit flowers for nectar. Usually they pick fruit from a tree, then return to a night roost to consume it. After giving birth, females carry their young for a week or two during their nightly foraging; older young are left in the day roost. Because of their abundance and frugivory, these bats are critical dispersers of tree seeds in Neotropical forests. A medium-sized fruit-eater in wet and dry forests, the JAMAICAN FRUIT-EATING BAT (Plate 74) also takes insects and pollen from flowers. It plucks fruit and carries it to a night roost 25 to 200 m (80 to 650 ft) away to eat it. Observers estimate that nightly each bat carries away from trees more than its own weight in fruit. Jamaican Fruit-eating Bats roost in caves, hollow trees, or in foliage. Breeding is apparently polygynous (a single male mates with more than one female), because small roosts are always found to contain one male plus several females (up to 11) and their dependent young.

Vampire bats are the only mammals that feed exclusively on blood; the only true mammalian parasites. Only three living species of these notorious blood-eating vampires are known, and they range from northern Mexico south to Argentina. All three are found in Ecuador, and two of them only eat blood from birds (including poultry if available). The COMMON VAMPIRE BAT (Plate 74), however, specializes on mammalian blood. Day roosts are in hollow trees and caves, and they can be instantly recognized by the accumulation of their tar-like droppings. At night, vampires fly out, using both vision (they have larger eyes and better vision than most bats) and sonar to find victims. They not only fly well and quietly, they use the extra long thumb on their wing like a front foot to allow agile walking, running, and hopping – of great assistance in perching on, feeding on, and avoiding swats by their prey. They use their sharp incisor and canine teeth to bite the awake or sleeping animal, often on the neck, and remove a tiny piece of flesh. An anti-clotting agent in the bat's saliva keeps the small wound oozing blood. The vampire laps up the oozing blood – they do not suck it out. The feeding is reported to be painless (we won't ask how researchers know this, but, with a shudder, we can guess). Because blood is mostly water and proteins, which, unlike fats and carbohydrates, cannot be stored easily, each bat must consume a blood meal (of about half its body weight) at least every 60 hours or starve to death. Vampires breed at any time of the year; older young are fed blood from the mother's mouth for several months until they can get their own. Although they rarely feed on humans, when they do, they prefer biting people at sleep on the nose or toes. If you see the local people sleeping with a basket over their heads and their feet, or if your host insists you sleep under mosquito netting even when there are no mosquitos around, consider taking appropriate protection. If you don't, those scabs on the end of your nose or fingers in the morning will give you great bragging rights back home.

The SUCKER-FOOTED BAT (Plate 75) is a tiny bat with peculiar, circular adhesive cups on its thumbs and feet. It roosts most commonly in small family groups (2 to 9) in rolled up banana or *Heliconia* leaves or fronds. The "sucker" cups adhere to the leaves. When in a few days the leaf matures and unfurls, the family must seek a new home. Interestingly, unlike most bats, the Sucker-foots in their roosts adhere head upwards. They are common in lowland rain forests and gardens and can be a startling surprise as they fly suddenly out of the young rolled leaf you have just disturbed along the trail. During the night they feed on insects in openings of the forest and along rivers. The BLACK MYOTIS (Plate 75) is a common representative of a group of tiny bats that are distributed widely over the Neotropics. They roost in large groups in hollow trees and buildings; males usually roost separately from females and their young. At sunset they leave the roost in search of flying insects, and return just before dawn. Young are carried by the mother for a few days after birth, but are then left behind with other young in the roost when the female leaves to forage. Pups can fly at about 3 weeks of age, are weaned at 5 to 6 weeks, and are reproductively mature at only 4 months.

Bats are beneficial to forests and to people in a number of ways. Many Neotropical plants have bats, instead of bees or birds, as their main pollinators. These species generally have flowers that open at night and are white, making them easy for bats to find. They also give off a pungent aroma that bats can home in on. Nectar-feeding bats use long tongues to poke into flowers to feed on nectar – a sugary solution – and pollen. As a bat brushes against a flower, pollen adheres to its body, and is then carried to other plants, where it falls and leads to cross-pollination. Fruit-eating bats, owing to their high numbers, are important seed dispersers (see Close-up, p. 168), helping to regenerate forests by transporting and dropping fruit seeds onto the forest floor. Also, particularly helpful to humans, bats each night consume enormous numbers of annoying insects.

Bats eat a variety of vertebrate animals; unfortunately for some of them, they play right into the bat's hands ... uh, feet. Some bats that specialize on eating frogs, it has been discovered, can home in on the calls that male frogs give to attract mates. These frogs are truly in a bind: if they call, they may attract a deadly predator; if they do not, they will lack for female company. Some types of bat prey, on the other hand, have developed anti-bat tactics. Several groups of moth species, for instance, can sense the ultrasonic chirps of some echolocating insectivorous bats; when they do, they react immediately by flying erratically or diving down into vegetation, decreasing the success of the foraging bats. Some moths even make their own clicking sounds, which apparently confuse the bats, causing them to break off approaches.

Relatively little is known about which predators prey on bats. The list however, includes birds-of-prey (owls, hawks), snakes, other mammals such as opossums, cats, and (yes) people, and even other bats, such as the carnivorous False Vampire Bat. Squirrel Monkeys actually hunt tent-roosting bats that they find in tree leaves. Tiny bats, such as the 3 to 5 g (0.1 to 0.2 oz) Black Myotis, are even captured and eaten by large spiders and cockroaches. Bats, logically, are usually captured in or near their roosts, where predators can reliably find and corner them. One strong indication that predation is a real problem for bats is that many species reduce their flying in bright moonlight. Bats showing this "lunar phobia" include the Jamaican Fruit-eating Bat and Short-tailed Fruit Bat. On the other hand, others, like the very small White-lined Sac-winged Bat, do not decrease their activity levels under a full moon, perhaps because they hunt mostly in the darker understory of forests.

Breeding

Bat mating systems are diverse. The males of some species have harems of two to five females, but various species employ monogamy, polygyny, and/or promiscuity; the breeding behavior of many species has yet to be studied in detail. Some Ecuadorean species breed at particular times of the year, but others have no regular breeding seasons. Most bats produce a single pup at a time.

Notes

Bats have frightened people for a long time. The result, of course, is that there is a large body of folklore that portrays bats as evil, associated with or incarnations of death, devils, witches, or vampires. Undeniably, it was the bats' alien lives – their activity in the darkness, flying ability, and strange form – and people's ignorance of bats, that were the sources of these superstitions. Many cultures, worldwide, have evil bat legends, from Japan and the Philippines, to Europe, the Middle East, Australia and Central and South America. Many ancient legends tell of how bats came to be creatures of the night. But the association of bats with vampires – blood-sucking monsters – may have originated in recent times with Bram Stoker, the English author who in 1897 published *Dracula* (the title character, a vampire, could metamorphose into a bat). Vampire bats are native only to the Neotropics. Stoker may have heard stories of their blood-lapping ways from travellers, and for his book, melded the behavior of these bats with legends of vampires from India and from Slavic Gypsy culture. Although not all New World cultures imparted evil reputations to bats, it is not surprising, given the presence of vampire bats, that some did. The Mayans, for instance, associated bats with darkness and death; there was a "bat world," a part of the underworld ruled by a bat god, through which dead people had to pass.

Speaking of vampire bats, they presumably are much more numerous today than in the distant past because they now have domesticated animals as prey. Before the introduction of domesticated animals to the Neotropics, vampires would have had to seek blood meals exclusively from wild animals such as deer and peccaries (two species, however, are specialists on bird blood); now they have, over large parts of their range, herds or flocks of large domesticated animals to feed on. In fact, examinations of blood meals reveal that vampire bats in settled areas feed almost exclusively on ranch and farm animals – cattle, horses, poultry, etc. Vampire bats rarely attack people, although it is not unheard of. Out of fear and ignorance, there is a tendency for local people to kill any large bat. Most of these large bats, however, are fruit and insect-eating bats that are critical for pollination, seed dispersal and insect control. Vampire bat eradication can only be justified in agricultural areas, but it must discriminate and leave unharmed all the other bats species in the area as well as vampire bats living away from settled areas. In some regions, bats, especially vampire bats, may transmit rabies. As most of them will bite in self-defense, it's best to avoid handling any bat bare-handed. If you must handle bats, make sure you have your rabies prophylactic shots and wear gloves.

Status

Determining the statuses of bat populations is difficult because of their nocturnal behavior and habit of roosting in places that are hard to census. With some exceptions, all that is known for most Neotropical species is that they are common or not common, widely or narrowly distributed. Some species are known from only a few museum specimens, or from their discovery in a single cave, but that does not mean that there are not healthy but largely hidden wild populations. Because many forest bats roost in hollow trees, deforestation is obviously a primary threat. Eight species of Ecuadorean bats, two of which are from the Galápagos, are considered threatened in the IUCN Red List of Threatened Animals. All the bats profiled are common or, in the case of the FALSE VAMPIRE BAT, naturally fairly rare. Many bat populations in temperate regions in Europe and the USA are known to be declining and under continued threat by a number of agricultural, forestry, and architectural practices. Traditional roost sites have been lost on large scales by mining and quarrying, by the destruction of old buildings, and by changing architectural styles that eliminate many building overhangs, church belfries, etc. Many forestry practices advocate the removal of hollow, dead trees, which frequently provide bats with roosting space. Additionally, farm pesticides are ingested by insects, which are then eaten by bats, leading to death or reduced reproductive success.

Profiles

Greater Fishing Bat, *Noctilio leporinus*, Plate 74a
Jamaican Fruit-eating Bat, *Artibeus jamaicensis*, Plate 74b
Common Vampire Bat, *Desmodus rotundus*, Plate 74c
False Vampire Bat, *Vampyrum spectrum*, Plate 74b
White-lined Sac-winged Bat, *Saccopteryx bilineata*, Plate 74e

Short-tailed Fruit Bat, *Carollia perspicillata*, Plate 75a
Sucker-footed Bat, *Thyroptera tricolor*, Plate 75b
Common Long-tongued Bat, *Glossophaga soricina*, Plate 75c
Long-nosed Bat, *Rhynchonycteris naso*, Plate 75d
Black Myotis, *Myotis nigricans*, Plate 75e

4. Primates

Most people, it seems, find *monkeys* (in Spanish, *monos*) striking, even transfixing, when first encountered, but then responses diverge. Some people adore the little primates and can watch them for hours, whether it be in the wild or at zoos. Others, however, find them a bit, for want of a better word, unalluring – even to the point of making people slightly uncomfortable. It is probably the same characteristic of monkeys that both so attracts people and turns them off, and that is their quasi-humanness. Whether or not we acknowledge it consciously, it is this trait that is the source of all the attention and importance attached to monkeys and apes. They look like us, and, truth be told, they act like us, in a startlingly large number of ways. Aristotle, 2300 years ago, noted similarities between human and nonhuman primates, and Linnaeus, the Swedish originator of our current system for classifying plants and animals, working more than 100 years before Darwin, classed people together in the same group with monkeys. Therefore, even before Darwin's ideas provided a possible mechanism for people and monkeys to be distantly related, we strongly suspected there was a link; the resemblance was too close to be accidental. Given this bond between people and other primates, it is not surprising that visitors to parts of the world that support nonhuman primates are eager to see them and very curious about their lives. Fortunately, Ecuador provides homes for many monkey species, some of them still sufficiently abundant in protected areas to be readily located and observed.

Primates are distinguished by several anatomical and ecological traits. They are primarily arboreal animals. Most are fairly large, very smart, and highly social – they live in permanent social groups. Most have five very flexible fingers and toes per limb. Primates' eyes are in the front of the skull, facing forward (eyes in the front instead of on the sides of the head are required for binocular vision and good depth perception, without which swinging about in trees would be an extremely hazardous and problematic affair), and primates have, for their sizes, relatively large brains. Unlike most other mammals, primates have color vision. Female primates give birth usually to a single, very helpless, infant.

Monkeys are distributed mainly throughout the globe's tropical areas and many subtropical ones, save for the Australian region. They are divided into four groups: (1) *Prosimians* include several families of primitive primates from the Old World. They look the least like people, are mainly small and nocturnal, and include lemurs, lorises, galago (bushbaby), and tarsiers. (2) *Old World Monkeys* (Family Cercopithecidae) include baboons, mandrills, and various monkeys such as rhesus and proboscis monkeys. (3) *New World Monkeys* (Families Callitrichidae and Cebidae) include many kinds of monkeys, marmosets, and tamarins. (4) The *Hominoidea* group contains the gibbons, orangutans, chimpanzees, gorillas, and ecotravellers.

New World monkeys, in general, have short muzzles and flat, unfurred faces, short necks, long limbs, and long tails that are prehensile in some of the larger species – used as fifth limbs for climbing about in trees. They are day-active animals that spend most of their time in trees, usually coming to the ground only to cross treeless space that they cannot traverse within the forest canopy. About 45 species of New World Monkeys are distributed from southern Mexico to northern Argentina, and 16 occur in Ecuador. The New World monkeys are conveniently divided into two major families: the marmosets and tamarins (Family Callitrichidae) and the typical monkeys (Family Cebidae).

The *marmosets* and *tamarins* are tiny to small in size (70 to 600 g, 2.5 to 21 oz) with long tails that are NOT prehensile. Their feet have claws instead of flattened nails, and they typically give birth to twins. Because they are so small, local hunters seldom waste expensive shells on them, and they can be common even in secondary forests near inhabited areas. Only one species of marmoset and three species of tamarins occur in Ecuador, including the enigmatic and very rare GOELDI'S MONKEY, which is sometimes placed by itself in its own family, Callimiconidae. The *"typical" monkeys* are larger (800 to 1500 g, 1.8 to 3.3 lb) and have long tails that in the largest species are prehensile. Their feet have flattened nails, and they give birth to a single young. They are actively hunted and so are among the first native species to disappear from an area after people settle there.

Natural History

Ecology and Behavior
In the lowlands of the Oriente of Ecuador you can find the smallest primate present in the New World, the PYGMY MARMOSET (Plate 76). Its tiny size (14 cm, 5.5 in, long without tail) and shyness would make it difficult to see if it weren't for its foraging habits. Besides foraging for insects under bark and leaves in mature lowland forests of the Oriente, it gouges out small pits in the trunks of trees with its front teeth, usually low down on the trunk. Sap oozes from these wounds, and the marmosets return again and again to lap up the sap and make new holes, sometimes up to a hundred on a single tree. If you can find a tree with these holes, wait quietly below it, and eventually you will be rewarded with the

sight of a single marmoset or small family group jumping to land on the trunk. The home range of a family group is often less than a hectare (2.5 acres), so if you listen carefully near a feeding tree, they can usually be heard somewhere nearby giving their grasshopper type calls and high-pitched whistles.

The three common tamarins in Ecuador are all restricted to the lowlands of the Oriente. All three travel in noisy troops giving chirps and twitters that sound more bird-like than primate-like. They feed in mid levels of the forest and dense vine tangles on fruits, insects, flower nectar and occasionally lizards and birds. The very rare GOELDI'S MONKEY is all black and travels very close to or even on the ground. It is seen most often trailing a troop of other species of tamarins.

Titis are small monkeys (1.2 kg, 2.6 lb) with thickly furred, nonprehensile tails that hang straight down. They travel in small family groups and feed on fruits and frequently on leaves, especially bamboo. They have very small home ranges that often center on a dense tree fall or vine tangle, where they spend the night. Although the DUSKY TITI MONKEY (Plate 76) of lowland (below 850 m, 2800 ft) Amazonian Ecuador is rarely seen, you will almost certainly hear it. The male and female duet early in the morning and at dusk with loud chimpanzee-like whoops that no one can miss. Because of its small home range, small size and retiring behavior, this is often the only monkey species remaining in extensively cleared parts of the forest. Apparently all it needs to prosper is a small patch of trees and some dense tangle to hide in.

The COMMON SQUIRREL MONKEY (Plate 77) lacks a prehensile tail, and with its white eye mask, black snout and large noisy troop behavior is unmistakable throughout the lowlands of the Ecuadorean Amazon. Squirrel monkeys feed on fruits, insects and some leaves and are often found associating with a troop of capuchin monkeys. A troop (five to 40 individuals) usually consists of several adult males and many females and their dependent young, although during non-breeding portions of the year the sexes may separate into uni-sex groups. Squirrel monkeys apparently do not defend exclusive territories: observers have noticed that the home ranges of troops frequently overlap, and they will often tolerate a coalescing of troops into a monstrous supertroop. During a one-month period, a troop may range back and forth over an area (home range) of about 2 sq km (0.8 sq miles). These monkeys are commonly spotted in trees near water – along lake shores, rivers, and swamps.

The WHITE-FRONTED CAPUCHIN (Plate 77) is a larger monkey (2.3 kg, 5 lb) that often travels in large and noisy troops. Its white face and light snout as well as its coiled and semi-prehensile tail distinguish it from other monkeys. The BROWN CAPUCHIN MONKEY of the Oriente lowlands is distinguished by its overall brown color, black cap, tail and legs and a dark vertical line in front of each ear. Capuchins are highly arboreal, but also versatile – they forage over all levels of the forest, from canopy to lower tree trunks, and they also occasionally come to the ground to feed. Their diet is broad, consisting mainly of ripe fruit and insects, but also bird eggs, young birds, baby squirrels, and small lizards. (Although they rarely attack larger animals, one male capuchin was observed to attack a 1.7 m (6 ft) long Green Iguana (Plate 11) and break off and eat the end of its tail.) In one study, a troop was found to consume 20% animal prey (mostly insects), 65% fruit, and 15% green plant material; but insects make up 50% or more of the diet during some periods of the year. Capuchins are very active monkeys, spending 80% or more of daylight hours moving through the forest, foraging in any number of ways, such as looking through leaves and leaf litter, pulling bark off trees, and rolling over sticks and logs. A troop, two to 30 strong (often six to 10), consisting usually of a single adult male plus females and their young, travels an average of about 2 km (1.2 miles) per day, while remaining within a fairly small home range of a few square km (about a square mile). Troops maintain exclusive territories, aggressively defending their turf whenever they meet other troops of the same species at territorial boundaries.

The COMMON WOOLLY MONKEY (Plate 77) is a large species (males regularly weigh more than 10 kg, 22 lb) with a true prehensile tail. The body color can vary from gray to brown, but the face is almost always darker. Woolly monkeys feed mostly on fruit and seeds and occasionally on insects and leaves from the canopy of tall forests of the Oriente. They move in large, noisy troops giving musical trills, barks and whoops, and each troop needs a minimum of 500 hectares (1200 acres) for a home range. This species is considered in Ecuador the most desirable monkey for eating, and this hunting pressure, combined with a female being able to give birth only every other year, makes it especially vulnerable to human pressures. Even when protection is provided, populations take a long time to recover.

The WHITE-BELLIED SPIDER MONKEY (Plate 77) is the longest monkey species in Ecuador, with males reaching up to 1.5 m (5 ft), including the tail. They stay mostly within a forest's upper canopy, rarely descending to the ground, and move quickly through trees using their fully prehensile tail as a fifth limb to climb, swing, and hang. They are known to feed occasionally at night, but they typically feed in the early morning and late afternoon. Spider monkeys eat young leaves and flowers but are especially fond of hard palm fruits. During the day, troops, varying in size from two to 25 or more (groups of 100 or more have been reported), range over wide swaths of forest, but stay within a home range of 2.5 to 4.0 sq km (1 or 2 sq miles). Troops usually consist of an adult male and several females and their dependent offspring. Spider monkeys are commonly observed in small groups, often two animals, but frequently they are members of a larger troop; the troop breaks up daily into small foraging parties, then coalesces each evening at a mutual sleeping tree. The BROWN-HEADED SPIDER MONKEY of Panamá and coastal Colombia barely reaches extreme northwest Ecuador. There are no reliable recent records, but it should be looked for in mid-elevation forests along the Colombian border of the west slope of the Andes.

Howlers inhabit a variety of forest habitats, but prefer lowland forests. On the coast of Ecuador, the MANTLED HOWLER MONKEY (Plate 78) is found in pockets of relatively undisturbed evergreen and river-associated areas of deciduous dry forest. It is the largest monkey found on the coast of Ecuador. The RED HOWLER MONKEY (Plate 78) is relatively common in the Oriente from 1200 m (4500 ft) down into the Amazonian lowlands. Howlers are highly arboreal and rarely come to the ground; typically they spend most of their time in the upper reaches of the forest. In contrast to the other monkey species, howlers are relatively slow-moving and more deliberate in their canopy travels. They eat fruit and a lot of leafy material; in fact, in one study, leaves comprised 64% of their diet, fruit and flowers, 31%. Owing to their specialization on a super-abundant food resource – leaves – their home ranges need not be, and are not, very large. Most troops have 10 to 20 individuals, which are made up of females, associated young, and usually one male in Red Howler troops, and multiple males in Mantled Howler troops. Many people on trails pass directly below howlers without noticing them, because they are slow-moving and often quiet. They are most assuredly not inconspicuous, however, when the males let loose with their incredible lion-like roaring, which is amplified and modulated by a special bony plate over the throat. Their very loud, deep choruses of roars, at dawn, during late afternoon, and, frequently, during heavy rain, are a characteristic and wonderful part of the rainforest environment. (The initial response of a newcomer to the Neotropics, upon being awakened in the morning by howling howlers, is sure to be "Now what the heck is THAT?"). These vocalizations are probably used by the howlers to communicate with other troops, to advertise their locations and to defend them; although troops of these monkeys do not maintain exclusive territories, they do appear to defend current feeding sites. The males' howling can be heard easily at 3 km (1.8 miles) away in a forest or 5 km (3 miles) away across water.

Saki monkeys (Plate 78) are medium sized (up to 2.25 kg, 5 lb) species with long thick hair and nonprehensile tails that are thickly furred. They forage primarily on fruits, seeds and a few leaves, and usually are seen in small family groups of two to four. They wander and feed from the lower canopy down to mid levels of lowland forests in the Oriente and are often hard to see because of their shy and retiring behavior. You are most likely to see sakis along streams and lakes as they sit without moving in a low tree, only their long bushy tails hanging straight down telling you they're not just another tangle of dead leaves.

The *night*, or *owl*, *monkeys* are, as their name suggests, active primarily at night. They are relatively small (1 kg, 2.2 lb) with a two-colored tail tipped in black that is non-prehensile. At night, their large eyes reflect light, and they can only be mistaken for an opossum or Kinkajou, neither of which has the striking black and white facial pattern. They feed mostly on fruits in small family groups. The taxonomy of the night monkeys is controversial, with some scientists identifying up to eight species in Central and South America. In eastern Ecuador the NOISY NIGHT MONKEY (Plate 78) occurs in east slope cloud forests as high as 3000 m (9800 ft) and down into the Amazonian lowlands. Your best chance of seeing it is from a canoe at night as you drift along the edge of a forested lake or stream. Look for eye-shine and listen for its low, distinctive three-note hoots that sound like an owl. Occasionally you can see them in the light late in the afternoon as they begin to forage, usually at forest edges.

A variety of animals prey on Ecuador's monkeys, including Boa Constrictors (Plate 9), birds-of-prey such as eagles (Plate 25), arboreal cats such as Jaguarundi and Margay (Plate 81), and people. Other causes of death are disease (for instance, many monkey populations in the coastal lowlands of Ecuador crashed during the early 1950s because of an outbreak of yellow fever) and parasite infestations, such as that by *botflies*. Botflies lay their eggs on mosquitos, monkeys being exposed when infected mosquitos land on them to feed. Botfly larvae burrow into a monkey's skin and develop there for ten weeks before emerging as adults. Many howlers, for instance, are observed to have severe botfly infestations of their necks, seen as swollen lumps and the holes created when adult botflies emerge from the monkey's body. In one Panamanian study, each member of a howler population had an average of two to five botfly parasites; several monkeys in the study died, apparently of high levels of botfly infestation.

Monkeys are especially crucial elements of rainforest ecosystems because they are seed dispersers for many hundreds of plant species, particularly of the larger canopy trees. Mammals transport seeds that stick to their fur from the producing tree to the places where the seeds eventually fall off. Mammals that are *frugivores* (fruit-eaters) also carry fruit away from a tree, then eat the soft parts and drop the seeds, which may later germinate; or they eat the fruit whole and transport the seeds in their digestive tracts. The seeds eventually fall, unharmed, to the ground and germinate (see Close-up, p. 168). Monkeys, it turns out, are major seed dispersers. For example, in Panamá, a troop of capuchins was estimated to disperse each day more than 300,000 tiny seeds of a single tree species; up to two-thirds of the seeds that passed through the monkeys' digestive systems later germinated (a proportion that was actually higher than seeds that made it to the ground without passing through an animal gut). Monkeys also assist plants in another way: capuchins eat so many insects that they probably have a significant effect in reducing insect damage to trees. Because some monkeys eat leaves, they also harm trees, but reports are very rare of primates stripping all the leaves from trees, killing them. Also, monkeys at times are seed predators. They extract seeds from fruit and chew them, destroying them, and also eat young fruits and nuts that contain seeds too undeveloped ever to germinate.

Most monkey troops are quite noisy as they forage, moving quickly about in trees and also vocalizing. A variety of other animals take advantage of monkey foraging, apparently attracted by the noise-making: squirrel monkeys and the DOUBLE-TOOTHED KITE (Plate 24) regularly follow capuchins, catching large insects that the capuchins scare up as they move. Various ground-dwellers such as agouti (Plate 83) and peccaries (Plate 82) often congregate under foraging troops, feeding on dropped fruit.

Breeding

Female monkeys in Ecuador usually produce a single young (tamarins and marmosets two) that is born furred and with its eyes open. The tamarins, marmosets, and most of the small "typical" monkeys, such as titis, night monkeys and sakis, are monogamous, but the SADDLE-BACKED TAMARIN (Plate 76) appears to be occasionally polyandrous – one female mates with two males (such a rare behavior among mammals that scientists are still amazed). The male of these species carries the young until they are large enough to forage on their own. The other monkeys are polygynous, with a male having a harem of two to five females. The squirrel monkeys, however, are promiscuous, and a male mates with several females in the troop in a sexual scramble. In polygynous and promiscuous species the female carries the young. Squirrel monkeys, which live up to 21 years in captivity, begin reproducing at 3 (females) to 5 (males) years old. The young cling to their mother after birth and are not truly independent until about a year old. Pregnancy is between 160 and 172 days. Mating is during the dry season, with births occurring during the wet season. Female capuchins reach sexual maturity at 3 to 4 years of age, then give birth at 1 to 2 year intervals. Most births occur during the dry season. Young cling to the mother's fur immediately following birth, and are carried by the mothers for 5 to 6 months, until they can travel on their own. Pregnancy is about 180 days. Capuchins live up to 46 years in captivity. Spider monkeys appear to have no regular breeding seasons. Females reach sexual maturity at about 4 years old (males at about 5), then give birth every 2 to 4 years after pregnancies of about 230 days. Young, which weigh about 500 grams (a pound) at birth, are carried by the mother for up to 10 months and are nursed for up to a year. Upon reaching sexual maturity, young females leave their troops to find mates in other troops; males remain with their birth troop. Spider monkeys have lived for 33 years in captivity. Female MANTLED HOWLERS reach sexual maturity at 3 to 4 years of age. They give birth following pregnancies of about

180 days. At 3 months, youngsters begin making brief trips away from their mothers, but until a year old, they continue to spend most of their time on their mother's back; they are nursed until they are 10 to 12 months old. Howlers have survived in the wild for up to 20 years.

Notes

The current range of the RED-BACKED SQUIRREL MONKEY, restricted to fragmented regions on the Pacific coasts of Panama and Costa Rica, is at least 500 km (300 miles) distant from the nearest South American squirrel monkey populations. The discontinuous nature of the distributions is puzzling, and it has led biogeographers to suggest that squirrel monkeys may have arrived in Central America only with the help of people; that is, they may have been introduced there by travellers from South to Central America in Pre-Columbian times.

Owing to their active lifestyles, intelligence, and mischievousness, capuchins are sought after as pets and as "organ-grinder" monkeys; consequently, they are probably the most numerous captive monkeys in North America and Europe. Trade in capuchins for pets, however, is now illegal.

Status

All New World monkeys are listed in CITES Appendix II as species that, although they may not be currently threatened, need to be highly regulated in trade or they could soon become threatened. The IUCN Red List includes three species of Ecuadorean primates – GOELDI'S MONKEY, WHITE-BELLIED SPIDER MONKEY, and BROWN-HEADED SPIDER MONKEY. Main menaces to monkeys are deforestation – elimination of their natural habitats – and poaching for trade and meat. The larger monkeys – especially woolly, spiders and howlers – are often hunted for their meat, and therefore are usually rare near human settlements. CENTRAL AMERICAN SPIDER and MANTLED HOWLER MONKEYS are listed as endangered by CITES Appendix I and USA ESA; however, even given their fragmented populations, both are still fairly abundant in protected areas.

Profiles

Dusky Titi Monkey, *Callicebus moloch*, Plate 76a
Golden-mantled Tamarin, *Saguinus tripartitus*, Plate 76b
Saddle-backed Tamarin, *Saguinus fuscicollis*, Plate 76c
Pygmy Marmoset, *Cebuella pygmaea*, Plate 76d

Common Squirrel Monkey, *Saimiri sciureus*, Plate 77a
White-fronted Capuchin Monkey, *Cebus albifrons*, Plate 77b
Common Woolly Monkey, *Lagothrix lagotricha*, Plate 77c
White-bellied Spider Monkey, *Ateles belzebuth*, Plate 77d

Noisy Night Monkey, *Aotus vociferans*, Plate 78a
Monk Saki Monkey, *Pithecia monachus*, Plate 78b
Red Howler Monkey, *Alouatta seniculus*, Plate 78c
Mantled Howler Monkey, *Alouatta palliata*, Plate 78d

5. Carnivores

Carnivores are ferocious mammals – including the cat that sleeps on your pillow and the dog that takes table scraps from your hand – that are specialized to kill and eat other vertebrate animals. They all share clawed toes and teeth customized to grasp, rip, and tear flesh – witness their large, cone-shaped canines. Most are meat-eaters, but many are at least somewhat omnivorous, taking fruits and other plant materials. Carnivore populations tend to be sparse and individuals notoriously difficult to see at any time. They range in size from weasels 9 cm (3.5 in) long to bears 3 m (10 ft) long. Five families within the Order Carnivora have Ecuadorean representatives: *dogs, bears, raccoons, weasels* and *cats*. Of these, only the raccoon family is unique to the New World; the others are widely represented throughout the Old World as well.

The 36 species in the worldwide dog family (Canidae) include wolves, coyotes, foxes and hunting dogs. They are all highly adapted for running; their feet are arranged so that they bear weight on the toes; and they tend to be highly vocal. The bear family (Ursidae) is made up of eight species of large and robust animals. They have poor eyesight but excellent powers of hearing and smell, and they tend to be highly omnivorous as well as scavengers. The raccoon family (Procyonidae) includes medium-sized species that carry their full weight on the soles of the feet and have long tails, both of which help with maneuverability and balance in their largely arboreal habitats. They are omnivorous and largely nocturnal. The weasel family (Mustelidae) includes weasels, stoats, skunks, minks, wolverines and badgers and is characterized by relatively long bodies, short legs, and walking on the soles of the feet. Most have dense, soft fur and a gland that produces chemicals with powerful odors. Their extremely powerful jaws and sharp teeth can kill large prey quickly. Members of the cat family (Felidae) bear weight on their toes and have retractable claws. They are completely carnivorous and use their extremely sharp and long teeth to dispatch prey with a bite to the back of the head or neck. They tend to have excellent vision, including color vision. They have a short nose and their eyes are set at the front of the head to maximize depth perception.

Natural History

Ecology and Behavior

Dogs. The dogs have five representatives in Ecuador, only three of which you might encounter on your trip, but these encounters will probably be in the form of tracks or *scats* (droppings). The ANDEAN, or CULPEO, FOX (Plate 79) is relatively common in open páramo habitats above 3600 m (12,000 ft). Its long, thin droppings and footprints are common in some areas. It can be quite bold at times and is active day and night. It preys on small mammals and birds, but occasionally scavenges dead animals such as llamas and sheep. The similar-sized GRAY FOX is apparently a relatively recent arrival from North America. Its back and upper side of the tail are gray. It occurs in forest edges at lower elevations in the Andes of northern Ecuador and down the west slope into the upper coastal areas of secondary forest. The SECHURAN FOX is a small and pale species restricted to the coastal deserts of extreme southwestern Ecuador and northwestern Perú; you may see this species at night on secluded roads near the southern city of Arenillas.

Bears. Only one species of bear occurs in South America, the SPECTACLED BEAR (Plate 79), and it is restricted to cloud forests and páramo of the Andes above 1800 m (6000 ft). This large species (200 kg, 440 lb), active both day and night, is solitary and extremely shy. Even some scientists studying it for two or three years have seen nothing of it but tracks, scat, and claw marks on trees. The bears eat mainly tubers, bromeliad buds and other vegetable matter dug out with their powerful claws, but if given the opportunity, they will not turn down a juicy rodent or the chance to scavenge a dead deer or cow. They are usually on the ground but are also amazingly agile tree climbers. Their predilection for corn (maize) sometimes makes them easy to see, as often they will become quite bold around this food source. Unfortunately, local farmers whose corn crops are being raided often shoot bears. These bears live up to 30 years in captivity.

Raccoons. The raccoons make up a New World group of about 15 species (until recently, the Asian Red Panda was thought also to be in this group). Six species occur in Ecuador, but you are only likely to see a few of them. The most visible ones are three species of *coatis*, one each in the Oriente, coastal lowlands, and mid-elevation cloud forests. Although adult males are usually solitary, the females and juveniles of these species in large groups of up to 30 move through the under-growth and mid-levels of trees making barks, whines and other noises. They are immediately recognized by their long tails held vertically as they walk on the ground or along branches. They use their long noses and hand-like fore-paws to investigate every nook and cranny for insects, fruits and small vertebrates. The other frequently seen *procyonid* in Ecuador is the KINKAJOU (Plate 79), which is limited to moist lowland forests of the coasts and the Oriente. Kinkajous are nocturnal, solitary and spend most of their time in trees, foraging for fruits and arboreal vertebrates. Alone among the procyonids, their long, thin tail is fully prehensile, permitting them to grasp branches with it and hang upside down. Your best chance for seeing one is by walking out into the forest at night and looking for their eye-shine reflected in the light of your flashlight. They can often be spotted moving about tree branches at night, making squeaking sounds; several often feed together in a single tree. If you are really lucky, you may catch a glimpse of a CRAB-EATING RACCOON (Plate 79) as you quietly float in a canoe at night along a forested stream or lake in the lowlands of Amazonian Ecuador. This species occurs from Costa Rica to Argentina, but nowhere is it common, and its natural history is poorly known. They are associated with open areas along water and, although omnivores, seem to prefer clams, fish and crabs. They spend the day sleeping in dens, and the best evidence of their presence, short of seeing one, is looking for their small, human-like foot and hand prints in wet mud along water.

Weasels. The weasel family comprises about 70 species of small and medium-sized, slender-bodied carnivores that are distributed globally except for Australia and Antarctica. In Ecuador the family is represented by eight species of weasels, skunks, and otters, but only three are commonly sighted. TAYRA (TIE-rah, Plate 80) are large tree climbers that will often descend to search the ground for a variety of foods – fruit, bird eggs or nestlings, lizards, rodents, rabbits, and insects. Although they are often wary animals, they can be quite bold at times and are among the most frequently sighted of the *mustelids*, especially when attracted to fruits in gardens and orchards. STRIPED HOG-NOSED SKUNKS (Plate 80) are nocturnal and forage solitarily on the ground where they root about a good deal in the leaf litter and soil, looking for insects, snails, and small vertebrates such as rodents and lizards; occasionally they take fruit. Skunks, with their spray defenses (see below), usually move quite leisurely, apparently knowing that they are well protected from most predators. The LONG-TAILED WEASEL (Plate 80) is one of the most fascinating of the mustelids, largely because the same species occurs from Canada all the way south into Bolivia. In the northern part of its range, it turns white in the winter, but in Central and South America it remains the same color year round. This small mammal (30 cm, 1 ft, long) has to be one of the most ferocious for its size in the world. It runs down narrow burrows and captures rodents and rabbits more than ten times its size, but it also eats birds and lizards in open areas of grassland and bushes above 1000 m (3300 ft). It is active both day and night. Your best chance of seeing one is as it stands up on its hind feet in the páramo to survey an area or check on who you are. Weasels are very bold, and if you stand still and squeak like a bird in distress, it is relatively easy to attract them right up to your feet. The GIANT OTTER (Plate 80) once occurred throughout Amazonian South America from Venezuela to northern Argentina, but it is now absent from most of this range. Its huge size (up to 2 m, 6.5 ft, and 34 kg, 75 lb) and noisy vocalizations in family groups of five to eight make it easy to find. Its luxurious pelt makes it a target of intense persecution by people. It remains now only in isolated and highly protected patches of its former range. Otters are active both during the day and at night, hunting in streams, rivers, and ponds for fish and crustaceans such as crayfish. Although otters always remain in or near the water, they spend their inactive time in burrows on land. Adapted with webbed feet, flattened tail and a sleek form for moving swiftly and smoothly through water, they move on land awkwardly, with a duck-like waddle. There are only a few places left in Amazonian Ecuador where you can still hear the haunting whistles, screams and hums of a group of these wondrous animals as they frolic in the water of an isolated stream or lake. If you do experience the sight and sounds of this otter, it will be a memory you will never forget. The smaller NEOTROPICAL OTTER (1 m, 3.3 ft, and 12 kg, 26 lb) is also rare in Ecuador's Oriente. Besides its size, it can be distinguished by its pale belly and rounded but tapering tail.

Cats. Because all six species of cats that occur in Ecuador are fairly rare, some to the point of being endangered, and because of their mainly nocturnal habits, your chances are slim of seeing even a single wild cat on any brief trip. More than likely, all that you will see of cats are traces; some tracks in the mud near a stream or scratch marks on a tree trunk or log. (Although some communication is vocal, cats also signal each other by making scratch marks on vegetation and by leaving urine and feces to scent-mark areas.) In Ecuador the cat species can be divided into two groups – spotted or unspotted. The four spotted species generally are yellowish, tan, or cinnamon on top and white below, with black spots and stripes on their heads, bodies, and legs. The smallest is the ONCILLA, or LITTLE SPOTTED CAT, the size of a small house cat. The largest is the JAGUAR (Plate 81), which is the largest New World cat and weighs between 60 and 120 kg (130 to 260 lb). The two unspotted cats are the mid-sized JAGUARUNDI (Plate 81), which is blackish, brown, gray, or reddish, and the PUMA (Plate 81), or MOUNTAIN LION, which is tan or grayish and almost as large as the Jaguar. The Puma, which occurs from the Arctic Circle of North America to Tierra del Fuego in extreme southern South America, has one of the largest geographical ranges of any animal. Female cats of most species are smaller than males, up to a third smaller in the Jaguar. The cats are finely adapted to prey on vertebrate animals, and hunting methods are extremely similar among the various species. They do not run to chase prey for long distances. Rather, cats slowly stalk their prey or wait in ambush, then capture the prey after pouncing on it or after a very brief, fast chase. Biologists are often impressed by the consistency in the manner that cats kill their prey. Almost always it is with a sharp bite to the neck or head, breaking the neck or crushing the skull. Retractile claws, in addition to their use in grabbing and holding prey, give cats good abilities to climb trees, and some of them are partially arboreal animals, foraging and even sleeping in trees.

Aside from some highly social large cats of Africa, most cats are solitary animals, foraging alone, individuals coming together only to mate. Some species are territorial but in others individuals overlap in the areas in which they hunt. Cats, with their big eyes to gather light, are often nocturnal, especially those of rainforests, but some are also active by day. When inactive, they shelter in rock crevices or burrows dug by other animals. Cats are the most carnivorous of the carnivores, that is their diets are more centered on meat than any of the other families. Little is known of the natural history of forest-dwelling Oncillas beyond that they eat birds and small rodents. MARGAYS (Plate 81) are mostly arboreal forest cats that forage in trees for rodents and birds. OCELOTS (Plate 81) eat rodents, snakes, lizards, and birds. They are probably more common than Oncillas and Margays and, although they are quite secretive, they are the most frequently seen of the spotted cats. Active mainly at night, they often spend daylight hours asleep in trees. They also tend to be the most adaptable to human presence, especially if a chicken coop is involved. *El Tigre*, the Jaguar, can be active day or night. These cats inhabit low and middle elevation forests, hunting for large prey such as peccary and deer, but also monkeys, birds, lizards, even caiman. Jaguarundi are both day and night active, and are usually seen in forests. They eat small rodents, rabbits, and birds. Puma occupy various habitat types from páramo to evergreen forest to desert scrub, and they prey on deer and other large mammals.

Breeding

Most dogs are monogamous and although they often dig their own dens for the young, they are not above taking over a hole made by an armadillo or some other burrowing animal, enlarging and modifying it for their own use. The large litter of young is born naked and blind and fed by both parents even after they emerge from the den. After mating, the fertilized egg of the SPECTACLED BEAR female does not implant in the uterus for several months, a trait apparently held over from its northern cousins, whose semi-hibernation forces them to extend pregnancy so that the young aren't born too early. Spectacled Bears give birth in a den to one to three naked and helpless young. They are cared for by only the mother for the next 3 years or so until the next litter is born. Mortality among the young is extremely high.

Among all the Ecuadorean procyonids, females raise young without help from males. Young are born in nests made in trees. Duration of pregnancy varies from about 65 days in raccoons, to about 75 days in coatis, to about 115 days in KINKAJOUS. Raccoons have three to seven young per litter, coatis, one to five young, and Kinkajous, always only one. Female mustelids give birth in dens under rocks or in crevices, or in burrows under trees. Pregnancy for TAYRA, skunks, and otters usually lasts about 60 to 70 days. Tayra produce an average of two young per litter, skunk, four or five, and otter, two or three. As is true for many of the carnivores, mustelid young are born blind and helpless. Male and female cats of the Neotropics come together only to mate; the female bears and raises her young alone. She gives birth in a den that is a burrow, rock cave, or tree cavity. The young are sheltered in the den while the female forages; she returns periodically to nurse and bring the kittens prey to eat. Most of the cats have one or two young at a time, although PUMA and JAGUAR may have up to four. Pregnancy is about 75 days in the smaller cats, about 100 in the large ones. Juvenile Jaguars remain with their mother for up to 18 months, learning to be efficient hunters, before they go off on their own.

Notes

JAGUAR rarely attack people, who normally are given a wide berth; these cats tend to run away quickly when spotted. Recently there have been widely circulated reports of PUMA attacking people in the USA, but this seems more due to people moving to live in prime Puma habitat, which is increasingly limited, than to a desire on the cat's part for human prey. Cats in Ecuador are sometimes seen walking at night along forest trails or roads. General advice if you happen to stumble across a large cat: do not run because that often stimulates a cat to chase. Face the cat, make yourself large by raising your arms, and make as much loud noise as you can.

Mustelids have scent glands on their backsides that produces a secretion called *musk*, which has a strong, characteristic odor. These secretions are used to communicate with other members of the species by marking territories as well as signal availability for breeding and courtship. In skunks, these glands produce particularly strong, foul-smelling fluids that with startling good aim can be violently squirted in a jet at potential predators. The fluids are not toxic and cannot cause blindness as is sometimes commonly believed, but they can cause temporary, severe irritation of eyes and nose. Most predators that approach a skunk once rarely repeat the exercise.

One facet of mustelid natural history that is particularly helpful to people, though not universally appreciated, is that these carnivores eat a staggering number of rodents. For instance, it has been calculated that weasels each year in New York State eat some 60 million mice and millions of rats. In fact, in the past, TAYRA were kept as pets in parts of South America to protect homes and belongings from rodents.

Status

All of the Neotropical cats are now threatened or actually endangered (MARGAY, ONCILLA, and JAGUAR are listed by CITES Appendix I and USA ESA, as are Central American populations of PUMA, JAGUARUNDI, and OCELOT). Their forest habitats are increasingly cleared for agricultural purposes, they were, and still are to a limited extent, hunted for their skins, and large cats are killed as potential predators on livestock and pets. Jaguar have been eliminated from much of Ecuador and are only present in small numbers in protected areas such as Yasuní National Park and Bilsa Forest Reserve.

Many mustelids in the past were trapped intensively for their fur, which is often soft, dense, and glossy, just the ticket, in fact, to create coats of otter or weasel, mink or marten, sable or fisher. The GIANT OTTER is sufficiently rare to be considered endangered (CITES APPENDIX I, USA ESA, and IUCN Red List). The COLOMBIAN WEASEL, SPECTACLED BEAR and BUSH DOG are also considered threatened species in Ecuador, on the IUCN Red List. TAYRA are common animals that usually do well even where people disturb their natural habitats. Another Ecuadorean mustelid, the GRISON (Plate 80), a grayish and black weasel-like animal, is fairly rare and may be threatened.

Profiles

Spectacled Bear, *Tremarctos ornatus*, Plate 79a
Kinkajou, *Potos flavus*, Plate 79b
Crab-eating Raccoon, *Procyon cancrivorous*, Plate 79c
South American Coati, *Nasua nasua*, Plate 79d
Andean (Culpeo) Fox, *Dusicyon culpaeus*, Plate 79e

Giant Otter, *Pteronura brasiliensis*, Plate 80a
Tayra, *Eira barbara*, Plate 80b
Grison, *Galictis vittata*, Plate 80c
Long-tailed Weasel, *Mustela frenata*, Plate 80d
Striped Hog-nosed Skunk, *Conepatus semistriatus*, Plate 80e

Jaguarundi, *Herpailurus yaguarondi*, Plate 81a
Ocelot, *Leopardus pardalis*, Plate 81b
Margay, *Leopardus wiedii*, Plate 81c
Jaguar, *Panthera onca*, Plate 81d
Puma, *Puma concolor*, Plate 81e

6. Freshwater Dolphins, Manatee and Tapirs

In the Galápagos, as you cruise from island to island, you expect to see *dolphins* (Order Cetacea; Plate 95) riding the bow wave and sporting in the ocean shoals, and you undoubtedly will. In the Amazon, however, the last thing many eco-travellers expect is a dolphin, but wonder of wonders, they are here, too. Two species of freshwater dolphins reach the western limits of their ranges in extreme eastern Ecuador. Here the main channels and tributaries of the Río Napo and Río Aguarico are home to these gentle aquatic mammals. Neither is common in Ecuador, but the PINK RIVER DOLPHIN (Plate 84), restricted to freshwater in the Amazon and Orinoco River basins, is the one you are most likely to see as it rises from under the water to exhale noisily at the surface. Look for it along the edge of a river or in a quiet, isolated lake. It is large (males reach nearly 3 m, 10 ft, in length), has no distinct fin on the back, and is light gray in color (despite the name, it actually shows little pink coloring in Ecuador). The GRAY, or ESTUAR-INE, DOLPHIN is the second smallest cetacean in the world (1.4 m, 4.5 ft), and it is only rarely seen in Ecuador on the Río Napo and Río Aguarico near the Peruvian border. It is gray-brown to bluish and has a distinctively triangular dorsal fin. It occurs along the Amazon and its major tributaries, out the mouth of the Amazon, and along the coast of northern South America to Panamá.

Along with the *dugongs* of the Indian Ocean, the *manatees*, or *sea cows*, form the tropical Order Sirenia. Despite their similarities to seals and cetaceans, they are unrelated to either group and are the only completely aquatic herbivorous mammals in the world. Except for bristles on the snout, they are basically hairless and look like walruses without tusks. They have tiny eyes and back molar teeth that resemble those of elephants. As adaptations for their aquatic life, they have evolved streamlined bodies; their hind feet have developed into a horizontal fluke and their fore-legs into flippers. Only two species of manatees are in the New World tropics. The AMAZONIAN MANATEE (Plate 84), a freshwater species, occurs along the Amazon River and its major tributaries as far west as the Oriente of Ecuador, and is only 2.8 m (9 ft) long. Because of its shy and often nocturnal behavior, it is extremely difficult to see as it feeds on aquatic vegetation in a quiet lake, only infrequently rising with its body in a vertical position to put its snout just above the water's surface to breathe. The larger WEST INDIAN MANATEE (up to 4.5 m, 13 ft, long) does not reach Ecuador and is found in brackish and salt water from Florida to northern Venezuela and coastal Brazil.

Although *tapirs* are only distantly related to either cetaceans or manatees, we include them here because they are almost always associated with swamps, lakes and river edges. They swim well, often with little more than their long snout extending above the water's surface. In fact, if you are going to see one, it will most likely be from a canoe as you come upon a swimming tapir just emerging from the water. There are only four species of tapirs (Family Tapiridae) in the world, three in the New World tropics and one in southeast Asia. All three New World species are found in Ecuador, but no two species occur together. Although they look like they should be related to pigs or hippopotamus, they are actually related to rhinoceros and horses (in the Order Perissodactyla, made up of hoofed animals (*ungulates*) with odd numbers of toes on some of the feet). Tapirs have three toes on the hind feet and four on the front feet. Their peculiarly elongated snout functions somewhat like an elephant's trunk in grasping vegetation to eat. They have excellent hearing and smelling abilities but relatively poor eyesight. They are the largest terrestrial animals in Ecuador, some males weighing up to 300 kg (660 lb). The largest of the three species in Ecuador, BAIRD'S TAPIR, is also the rarest here. It formerly occurred from Central America south along the coast of Colombia and Ecuador to Guayaquil. In Ecuador it is now confined to a few larger remnant forest patches in the northwest. It is the only tapir species in the coastal lowlands up to an altitude of 1800 m (6000 ft) on the west slope of the Andes. The similar and somewhat smaller (250 kg, 550 lb) BRAZILIAN TAPIR (Plate 84) has the widest range of any tapir species in the world and is found throughout South America west of the Andes and north of Argentina. In Ecuador it is the most common species of tapir and is found in isolated areas of forest throughout the lowlands of the Oriente and up to 2000 m (6600 ft) altitude on the east slope of the Andes. This is the species you are most likely to encounter, but that encounter is most likely to consist of distinctive footprints on muddy paths and along sandy river beaches. The most poorly known and smallest tapir species in Ecuador is the MOUNTAIN TAPIR. It has distinctively white-colored lips and is covered with curly hair, the source of its alternative names of WOOLLY and HAIRY TAPIR. It occurs in cloud forest and páramo meadows between 2500 and 4000 m (8000 to 13,000 ft) in Colombia and Ecuador; in Ecuador it is most common on the eastern cordillera of the Andes.

Natural History

Ecology and Behavior

The AMAZONIAN MANATEE in Ecuador feeds mainly at night on aquatic vegetation like floating grasses and water hyacinths. During the dry season when many lakes and small rivers dry up, they may retreat to deeper channels in the main rivers where they fast for several weeks or more. Generally this species is extremely difficult to see, but its impressive production of floating dung (like horse apples) is the best sign of its presence. Manatees usually occur alone except during courtship, but they do communicate with each other by sounds they produce underwater. Individuals take about five to six years to reach sexual maturity.

In Asia and South America, five similar species of dolphins have evolved unique adaptations to live in freshwater. The most widespread of these species in South America, the PINK RIVER DOLPHIN, feeds chiefly on fish as well as other aquatic organisms such as crabs, which they generally catch in deep shady water near the banks of rivers or at points where smaller tributaries enter larger rivers. They use their excellent eyesight to locate prey in clear water, but in turbid water they emit a series of clicking noises, 30 to 80 per second, which they then use as sonar by listening for them to bounce off potential prey items. They use their ability to flex their necks back and forth to broadcast and scan these clicking sounds over a large area. They also give numerous other sounds including a screeching alarm call. During the dry season these dolphins are often confined to the main channels of deep rivers, but during the rainy season, they will pursue fish well into flooded forest areas and swamps. This species tends to occur alone or in pairs, and it rarely jumps out of the water. The second species of dolphin found in Amazonian Ecuador, the GRAY DOLPHIN, is more like typical marine dolphins. They tend to be highly social, sometimes seen in pods of up to 20, but they are shyer than the Pink River Dolphin, and often harder to see. The sound of their blow when reaching the surface to breathe after a dive can barely be heard more than 15 m (50 ft) away. It is much softer than the explosive sounds made by surfacing Pink River Dolphins. This smaller Gray Dolphin, however, is more likely to leap out of the water and make its presence known. It feeds primarily on crabs, prawns and catfish, which it locates underwater at close distances with sonar clicks.

Tapirs are active primarily at night and hide in dense thickets of undergrowth during the day. They browse on leaves and vegetation as well as fruits fallen to the ground. Tapirs follow habitual trails through vegetation, and routinely cross rivers at the same place, thus forming obvious tunnels through the undergrowth and gulleys at river banks where they are most likely to be seen (and shot if being hunted). Individuals use established wallowing areas in which they apply a layer of mud to their skin to help protect them from horseflies and other biting insects that plague them throughout the year. Although generally solitary, tapirs, by using these habitual trails and wallowing areas together with communal defecation sites, at least loosely associate and communicate with each other. They are shy and retiring, and except for grunts of alarm and high whistles during the mating season, are quiet.

Breeding

Dolphins in the Amazon reproduce seasonally, usually giving birth during the flood season. The gestation period is 10.5 months and a single young is produced every two years. The calf is cared for by the mother for almost a year. Manatees give birth to a single calf after a gestation period of 13 months. The calf is dependent on the mother and accompanies her closely for two or more years. Thus, a female only gives birth every three and a half years or more. Tapirs remain together as mated pairs for only a few weeks of courtship and then separate. Occasionally males will fight to the death over a sexually receptive female. Females are entirely responsible for rearing and caring for the young, which have peculiar horizontal stripes and spots. Usually a single but rarely two calves are born after a gestation period of 13 months. The calf remains with the mother for up to a year. This long gestation period and extended care of the young mean a female can reproduce only every 17 months.

Notes

The PINK RIVER DOLPHIN has received considerable attention in the sexual fantasies of local people. In most parts of the Amazon, dolphins are treated with respect and even fear. The local people believe that dolphins turn themselves into beautiful women who seduce innocent men and drown them. Alternatively, the dolphins are often blamed for impregnating unwed mothers. Whatever the source of these folktales, they serve the useful function of protecting the dolphins from being hunted. Manatees, as they floated vertically in the water, were apparently the source of the myth of mermaids. Evidently lonely sailors who had been on board ship way too long imagined these forms to be female humans with fins.

At least two researchers have noted that tapirs, which can become infested with blood-sucking, disease-carrying ticks, have let other mammals – a coati in one case, a tame peccary in the other – approach them and pick and eat the ticks on their bodies. If this occurs regularly, it is a mutualistic association: tapirs obviously benefit because they are freed temporarily from the harmful ticks, and the tick-eaters receive the nutritional value of the bloodsuckers (yech!).

Status

The freshwater dolphins of the Amazon are common and widespread, but water contaminants and fishing with explosive charges have evidently reduced populations in some parts of their range. The IUCN Red List includes the PINK RIVER DOLPHIN as threatened in Ecuador. Both species of New World manatees have been hunted and killed extensively. Their populations have been severely reduced, and they are considered endangered (CITES Appendix 1, USA ESA, and IUCN Red List). Because they are so heavily hunted, tapirs are very shy and cautious animals. This hunting pressure may be forcing them more and more into nocturnal activity, and, together with low population sizes, may explain why they are so rarely seen. Because they are hunted for meat, and also due to deforestation, all three Neotropical tapirs are now rare and considered endangered, listed by both CITES Appendix I and USA ESA.

Profiles

Brazilian Tapir, *Tapirus terrestris*, Plate 84b
Pink River Dolphin, *Inia geoffrensis*, Plate 84c
Amazonian Manatee, *Trichechus inunguis*, Plate 84d

7. Peccaries and Deer

Peccaries and *deer* are the two Neotropical representatives of the Order Artiodactyla, the globally distributed hoofed mammals (*ungulates*) with even numbers of toes on each foot. Other *artiodactyls* are pigs, hippos, giraffes, antelope, bison, buffalo, cattle, gazelles, goats, and sheep. In general, the group is specialized to feed on leaves, grass, and fallen fruit.

Three peccary species comprise the Family Tayassuidae. They are confined in their distributions to the Neotropics, although one species pushes northwards into the southwestern USA, where it is often called JAVALINA; two species, the COLLARED PECCARY (Plate 82) and the WHITE-LIPPED PECCARY (Plate 82), occur in Ecuador on both sides of the Andes. Peccaries are small to medium-sized hog-like animals covered with coarse, bristly, longish hair, with slender legs, large heads, small ears, and short tails. They have enlarged, sharp and pointed, tusk-like canine teeth. The Collared Peccary is the smaller of the two Ecuadorean species, adults typically weighing 17 to 30 kg (35 to 75 lb). They come in black or gray as adults, with a band of lighter-colored hair at the neck that furnishes their name; youngsters are reddish brown or buff-colored. The White-lipped Peccary, named for the white patch of hair on its chin, weighs 25 to 40 kg (55 to 85 lb). Collared Peccaries are more abundant than the White-lipped Peccary, occur in more habitats, and are seen more frequently.

The deer family, Cervidae, has 43 species worldwide, six in Ecuador. Only two, however, are common enough that you are likely to see them, the WHITE-TAILED DEER (Plate 82) and the RED BROCKET DEER (Plate 82). Deer are large mammals with long, thin legs, short tails, and big ears. Males have antlers that they shed each year and regrow. The White-tailed Deer has a remarkably broad distribution from southern Canada to Bolivia. This species does not occur in lowland rain-forests, and in Ecuador it is most common in cleared areas on the Andean slopes at mid-elevations and in river border forests of drier coastal lowlands. South American White-tailed Deer (30 to 50 kg, 65 to 110 lb) are, in general, slightly larger than Red Brocket Deer (24 to 48 kg, 50 to 100 lb), but usually smaller, by a third to a half, than members of their species in the USA and Canada. Very young deer usually have white spots. The Red-brocket Deer, strictly a forest species, is found throughout the lowlands of the Oriente and the coast.

Natural History

Ecology and Behavior

Peccaries are day-active, highly social animals, rarely encountered singly. COL-LARED PECCARIES travel in small groups of three to 25 or so, most frequently six to nine; WHITE-LIPPED PECCARY herds generally are larger, often 50 to 100 or more (smaller herds occur where they are heavily hunted). They travel single file along narrow forest paths, spreading out when good foraging sites are found. These animals are omnivores, but mainly they dig into the ground with their snouts, *rooting* for vegetation. Peccaries feed on roots, underground stems, and bulbs, but also leaves, fruit (the White-lipped Peccary, with extra-strong jaw muscles, is better adapted for eating hard palm fruits), insects, and even small ver-tebrates that they stumble across. Because White-lipped Peccaries are larger than Collared Peccaries and travel in larger groups, they need to wander long distances each day to locate enough food. Like pigs, peccaries often wallow in mud and shallow water, and there is usually a customary wallowing spot within their home ranges, the area within which a group lives and forages. During dry seasons, pec-caries may gather in large numbers near lakes or streams. Because peccaries are hunted by people, they are usually quiet, wary, and therefore, sometimes hard to notice or approach. Besides their tracks, you can detect that a group has just passed by a cloyingly sweaty smell that lingers after them for a half hour or more in the undergrowth of a forest. Peccaries are preyed upon by large snakes such as boas, and by Puma and Jaguar (Plate 81).

Deer eat leaves and twigs from trees and shrubs that they can reach from the ground (*browsing*), and grass (*grazing*). The RED BROCKET DEER, in particular, also eats fruit and flowers, chiefly those that have already fallen to the ground. WHITE-TAILED DEER inhabit open places and forest edge areas, rarely dense for-est, whereas the Red Brocket Deer is a forest species that wanders through terrain with no trails. The large, branched antlers of male White-tails make moving through dense forest a dubious business; male Red Brocket Deer, on the other hand, have short, spike-like, rearwards-curving antlers – plainly better for maneu-vering in their dense jungle habitats. Both White-tailed Deer and Red Brocket Deer are active during daylight hours and also often at night, although Red

Brocket Deer are most commonly seen during early mornings and at dusk. White-tailed Deer travel either solitarily or in small groups, whereas Red Brocket Deer are almost always solitary. Deer are *cud-chewers*. After foraging and filling a special chamber of their stomach, they find a sheltered area, rest, regurgitate the meal into their mouths and chew it well so that it can be digested. Predators on deer include the big cats – Puma and Jaguar; eagles may take young fawns.

Breeding
Female peccaries have either one or two young at a time, born 4 to 5 months after mating. The young are *precocial*, meaning that they can walk and follow their mother within a few days of birth. Deer, likewise, give birth to one or two young that, within a week or two, can follow the mother. Until that time, they stay in a sheltered spot while their mother forages, returning at intervals to nurse them.

Notes
Both species of peccary enjoy reputations for aggressiveness toward humans, but experts agree that the reputation is exaggerated. There are stories of herds pan-icking at the approach of people, stampeding, even chasing people. These are large enough beasts, with sufficiently large and sharp canine teeth, to do damage. If you spot peccaries, err on the side of caution; watch them from afar and leave them alone. Be quiet and they might take no notice of you; their vision appar-ently is poor. If you are charged, a rapid retreat into a tree could be a wise move.

When a WHITE-TAILED DEER detects a predator or person that has not yet spotted the deer, it slinks away with its head and tail down, the white patch under the tail concealed. But when the deer is alarmed – it spots a predator stalking it or hears a sudden noise – it bounds off with its tail raised, its white rump and white tail bottom exposed, almost like a white flag. Animal behaviorists believe that the white is a signal to the deer's party, relatives likely to be among them, that a potential predator has been spotted and that they should flee. Many indige-nous people throughout South America, including in Ecuador, believe that the spirits of their dead relatives reside in deer; many people, therefore, will not hunt or kill deer.

Status
Peccaries were hunted for food and hides long before the arrival of Europeans to the New World, and such hunting continues. COLLARED PECCARIES, CITES Appendix II listed, are still locally common in protected wilderness and more rural areas. WHITE-LIPPED PECCARIES, also CITES Appendix II listed, are less common, and less is known about their populations; they may soon be threat-ened. Deer are likewise hunted for meat, skins, and sport. Deer range widely in Ecuador but, owing to hunting pressures, are numerous only in remote areas. RED BROCKET DEER employ excellent anti-hunting tactics, being solitary animals that keep to dense forests.

Profiles
Collared Peccary, *Tayassu tajacu*, Plate 82a
White-lipped Peccary, *Tayassu pecari*, Plate 82b
Red Brocket Deer, *Mazama americana*, Plate 82c
White-tailed Deer, *Odocoileus virginianus*, Plate 82d

8. Rodents and Rabbit

Rodents and *rabbits* superficially resemble each other with their large, front incisor teeth. They are, however, only distantly related. Rodents (Order Rodentia) are distributed worldwide from the Arctic to the tropics, and they include *mice, rats, squirrels, chipmunks, marmots, gophers, beavers,* and *porcupines.* There are more than 2000 species, representing 44% of the approximately 4629 known mammalian species. More individual rodents are estimated to be alive at any one time than individuals of all other types of mammals combined. Nevertheless many eco-travellers will discover among rodents a paradox: although by far the most diverse and abundant of the mammals, rodents are, with a few obvious exceptions in any region, relatively inconspicuous and rarely encountered. Rodents' near-invisibility to people, particularly in the Neotropics, can be explained best by the facts that most rodents are very small, secretive or nocturnal, and many of them live in subterranean burrows. Of course, many people do not consider it a hardship that rodents are so rarely encountered.

High rodent abundance and diversity is likely related to their efficient, specialized teeth and associated jaw muscles, as well as to their broad, nearly omnivorous, diets. Rodents are characterized by having four large incisor teeth, one pair front-and-center in the upper jaw, one pair in the lower (other teeth, separated from the incisors, are located farther back in the mouth). With these strong, sharp, chisel-like front teeth, rodents "make their living": gnawing (*rodent* is from the Latin *rodere,* to gnaw), cutting, and slicing vegetation, fruit, and nuts, killing and eating small animals, digging burrows, and even, in the case of beavers, imitating lumberjacks.

The Neotropics contain some of the largest and most interesting of the world's rodents, and at least 80 species occur in Ecuador. However, only a few representatives of six families are commonly spotted by visitors, and we profile seven species from these families. Squirrels are members of the Family Sciuridae, a worldwide group of 273 species that occurs on all continents except Australia and Antarctica. The family includes *ground, tree,* and *flying squirrels;* only six species occur in Ecuador. Family Erethizontidae contains the 12 species of New World porcupines, which are distributed throughout the Americas save for the southern third of South America. Five species of these sharp-spined mammals are native to Ecuador. The 78 species of *spiny* or *tree rats* are placed in the Family Echimyidae and are almost all restricted to lowland rainforests. About 20 species occur in Ecuador, but their classification is very poorly known. Three other families that are restricted to tropical America contain a few large rodents that all share an ungulate-type body form with long legs: Family Agoutidae contains the PACA (Plate 83), Family Dasyproctidae includes the *agoutis,* and Family Hydrochaeridae contains a single species, the CAPYBARA (Plate 84), which is the world's largest rodent.

Porcupines generally are fairly large, heavyset rodents (although Ecuador has some small species that weigh only 0.95 kg, 2 lb) with many sharp spines covering their bodies and often the tail. These spines easily break off to embed themselves in the skin of a predator unfortunate or naive enough to try to bite a porcupine. The most common Ecuadorean species, the BICOLOR-SPINED PORCUPINE (Plate 83), weighs 3.4 to 4.7 kg (7.5 to 12 lb) and occurs from lowland forests up to 2500 m (8250 ft) altitude in the foothills on both sides of the Andes. Its body is covered with long, black hair that shrouds most of the short, barbed spines. A long prehensile tail, with bare top, is always curled under rather than over a branch for climbing. It has short limbs and small feet with long, curved claws that aid in gripping and climbing trees. The spiny and tree rats are touted by some experts as the most common terrestrial mammals in the rainforests of Ecuador. Many of them have long bristles or flat spines on the back, but unlike porcupine spines, these are not barbed and do not readily detach. As common as they are, you are likely to encounter only one species, the AMAZON BAMBOO RAT (Plate 83), which has no spines on the back, large eyes and a total length, including the tail, of 65 cm (2 ft). Instead of seeing this large rat, you are much more likely to hear its incessant series of loud quacks given in the middle of the night. You can be forgiven for mistaking these sounds for some loud frog, but they are quite unlike any amphibian in the Amazon: these hollow and ventriloquial sounds are given at increasingly softer levels and more widely spaced intervals until they stop. If you follow the sound, the final approach to the rat itself will be facilitated by its commanding aroma, which has a strong musky component.

BLACK AGOUTI (Plate 83), PACA (Plate 83) and CAPYBARA (Plate 84) are large, almost pig-like rodents, usually brownish, with long legs, short hair, and squirrel-like heads. The Black Agouti weighs only 5 kg (11 lb), but is common in secondary and primary forest throughout the Oriente lowlands of Ecuador. Paca weigh up to 12 kg (26 lb) and are distinguished by the four rows of white spots along their flanks. Two paca species are found in moist lowlands on both sides of the Andes and in cloud forests. The huge Capybara (to 65 kg, 140 lb) is most regularly found throughout the lowlands of the Oriente, usually near rivers or marshes, but historically it also occurred in northwestern Ecuador.

Rabbits, even though they look like rodents, are in a separate order, the Lagamorpha. The group is differentiated from rodents by four instead of two front incisor teeth on the upper jaw, large hind legs, and long ears. Only one species occurs in Ecuador, the BRAZILIAN RABBIT, and it looks for all the world like the cottontail so common throughout North America; it is even in the same genus, *Sylvilagus*. Most ecotravellers to Ecuador will see this species in clearings just below the tree line (3500 m, 12,000 ft), where it is common on both slopes of the Andes.

Natural History

Ecology and Behavior

Rodents are important ecologically primarily because of their great abundance. They are so common that they make up a large proportion of the diets of many carnivores. For instance, in a recent study of Jaguar, it was discovered that rodents were the third most frequent prey of the large cats, after sloths and iguanas. In addition, rodents, owing to their ubiquitousness and numbers, are themselves important predators on seeds and fruit. That is, they eat seeds and seed-containing fruit, digesting or damaging the seeds, rendering them useless to the plants that produced them for reproduction. Of course, not every seed is damaged (some fall to the ground as rodents eat, others pass unscathed through their digestive tracts), and so rodents, at least occasionally, also act as seed dispersers (see Closeup, p. 168). Burrowing is another aspect of rodent behavior that has significant ecological implications because of the sheer numbers of individuals that participate. When so many animals move soil around (rats and mice, especially), the effect is that over several years the entire topsoil of an area is turned, keeping soil loose and aerated, and therefore more suitable for plant growth.

The NORTHERN AMAZON RED SQUIRREL (Plate 83) and the AMAZON DWARF SQUIRREL (Plate 83) are both solitary day-active species, generally seen in trees and, occasionally, foraging on the ground. The large red squirrel typically feeds on fruits and large palm nuts. They are usually found low in the forest and often on the ground or in the understory where they frequently hide (cache) food for later meals by burying it in the ground or placing it in tree cavities. In contrast, the dwarf squirrel's diet is largely made up of insects, spiders and other arthropods it searches out on branches, tangles and other vegetation, from high in the canopy to the forest floor. It also apparently eats bark and fungi. This species is quickly and reliably attracted to squeaking noises that mimic a bird or small mammal in distress. This behavior may indicate that dwarf squirrels, like other insectivorous squirrel species, are also partially carnivorous. Although the natural history of these Ecuadorean species is poorly known, Central American species closely related to the Northern Amazon Red Squirrel are known to have females that defend exclusive living and feeding areas from other females. Males are not territorial; their home ranges, the areas over which they range daily in search of food, overlap those of other males and those of females.

BICOLOR-SPINED PORCUPINES are solitary, nocturnal animals, almost always found in trees. They move slowly along branches, using their prehensile tail as a fifth limb. They feed on leaves, green tree shoots, and fruit. During the day they sleep in tree cavities or on branches hidden amid dense vegetation. They are found mostly in higher-elevation forests. The AMAZON BAMBOO RAT is active only at night and spends the daytime resting in thick tangles of vegetation, usually in or near bamboo thickets. They are almost entirely arboreal and feed in family groups mainly on leaves, shoots and stems. Their calls at night are often in duets.

PACA are usually only active at night, foraging individually for fruit, nuts, seeds, and vegetation. They sleep away daylight hours in burrows. Along with the agouti, they can sit up on their hind legs and eat, holding their food with their front paws, much like a squirrel or rat. Several observers have noted that Paca, although usually terrestrial, will, if startled or threatened, dive into nearby water if available. The smaller agouti are completely terrestrial and naturally day-active, but many populations have become increasingly nocturnal in their habits in areas where they are intensively hunted. They mainly eat seeds and fruit, but also flowers, vegetation, and insects. When threatened or startled, agoutis usually run, giving warning calls or barks as they go, presumably to warn nearby relatives of danger. They make so much noise running through the undergrowth vegetation that it is easy to mistake them for a much larger peccary. In Ecuador, the immense CAPYBARA is always closely associated with river banks, lake edges and forested swamps, and in the dry season it can be found in groups of up to 20, depending on the availability of water. It is normally diurnal, but under human hunting pressure often becomes more active at night. At the slightest hint of danger it leaps into the water and disappears under the surface to emerge far away. If it is present, its huge and distinctive foot prints are common on sandy river beaches and in the mud along lake shores. It feeds largely on aquatic vegetation but also on fruits. These three species, all large and tasty, are preyed on by a variety of mammals and reptiles, including large snakes and such carnivores as Jaguarundi (Plate 81).

Breeding

Relatively little is known of the breeding behavior of most Neotropical tree squirrels and of many other rodents. Tree squirrel nests consist of a bed of leaves placed in a tree cavity or a ball of leaves on a branch or in a tangle of vegetation. One to three young are born per litter, although two is the norm. Females of species closely related to red squirrels have two or three litters per year. Actual mating in this species takes place during sex chases, during which four or more males chase a female for several hours, the female apparently choosing which male or males she mates with. Pregnancy is about 45 days; young nurse for 8 to 10 weeks. Breeding tends to be during the dry season, from late December through March.

Porcupines have one to three young per litter. Pregnancy periods are relatively long, and, as a result, the young are *precocial* – born eyes open and in an advanced state. They are therefore mobile and quickly able to follow the mother. Paca and agouti appear to live in monogamous pairs on territories, although male and female often tend to forage separately. Capybaras are polygynous with a fluid social system depending on how much water there is to spread out into. All three species have precocial young, usually in litters of one or two for the Paca and agouti and up to seven for the Capybara. A day after their birth, a mother agouti leads her young to a burrow where they hide, and to which she returns each day to feed them. Pregnancies for agouti and Paca last 115 to 120 days, and for Capybara 150 days.

Notes

Through the animals' constant gnawing, rodents' chisel-like incisors wear down rapidly. Fortunately for the rodents, their incisors, owing to some ingenious anatomy and physiology, continue to grow throughout their lives, unlike those of most other mammals.

Contrary to folk wisdom, porcupines cannot "throw" their quills, or spines, at people or predators. Rather, the spines detach quite easily when touched, such that a predator snatching a porcupine in its mouth will be impaled with spines and hence, rendered very unhappy. The spines have barbed ends, like fishhooks, which anchor them securely into the offending predator.

PACA, AGOUTI and CAPYBARA meat is considered to be among the most superior of wild meats, because it is tasty, tender, and lacks much of an odor; as such, when it can be purchased in Ecuador, it is very expensive. All three species are favorite game animals throughout their ranges. In Venezuela, Capybara meat is considered to be the holiday meal for Easter dinner, and Capybaras are widely raised in captivity to meet the demand for this market. In the northwestern part of Ecuador, near Esmeraldas, the local people depend heavily on large tree rats as a meat source, which they trap at night in the forest. Some attempts are being made to raise these rats in captivity and farm them as a more dependable resource.

Status

Four of Ecuador's rodents are listed as threatened by the IUCN Red List, all of them mice. Habitat destruction and over-hunting have also caused local elimination of several of the larger species of rodents. One species of porcupine, southeastern Brazil's BRISTLE-SPINED PORCUPINE, is now highly endangered (listed as such by USA ESA).

Profiles

Northern Amazon Red Squirrel, *Sciurus igniventris*, Plate 83a
Amazon Bamboo Rat, *Dactylomys dactylinus*, Plate 83b
Amazon Dwarf Squirrel, *Microsciurus flaviventer*, Plate 83c
Bicolor-spined Porcupine, *Coendou bicolor*, Plate 83d
Black Agouti, *Dasyprocta fuliginosa*, Plate 83e
Paca, *Agouti paca*, Plate 83f
Capybara, *Hydrochaeris hydrochaeris*, Plate 84a

Chapter 9

INSECTS AND OTHER ARTHROPODS

- *Introduction*
- *General Characteristics and Classification of Arthropods*
- *Features of Tropical Arthropods*
- *Seeing Arthropods in Ecuador*
- *Order and Family Profiles*

Introduction

All of the *insects*, together with *spiders, scorpions, centipedes, crabs, shrimps* and *barnacles* are placed together in the megagroup Arthropoda. By some estimates, the *arthropods* of the world make up more than four of every five organisms known and occupy every habitat in the world, including the bottom of the deepest oceans and the ice cap of Antarctica. On the basis of their species numbers, diversity of habitats they inhabit, and the number of individuals, the arthropods must be the most successful group of animals ever to live on Earth.

Among the arthropods, by sheer numbers insects are the dominant group and the one which we emphasize here. They make up over 75% of all the species of animals in the world (by some estimates that means more than 10 million species), and we guarantee that this is one group of animals that you will see, hear and experience no matter where you go in Ecuador. With the word "insect," however, your first reaction may be to conjure up images of scurrying cockroaches, clouds of mosquitos, and childhood memories of disgusting small things with buzzy wings and too many legs. But these stereotypes and prejudices are belied by the facts. Insects and their relatives are a beneficial and integral part of virtually all habitats in Ecuador. Scientists who study insects (entomologists) estimate that less than 5% of all insect species are actually harmful to humans, and most of the rest are directly or indirectly beneficial. To name just a few direct benefits: as pollinators of fruit orchards and grain-crop fields, they help supply a large proportion of the food eaten in North America and Europe; as efficient predators, they keep plague species in check (biological control); and as sensitive barometers of pollution, they provide warning of changes in the environment long before we could see them ourselves (acting as *bioindicators*). Even the herbivorous (plant-eating) insects have become essential to the quality and health of our lives. They often force plants to produce defense chemicals, many of which end up, by coincidence, having a physiological effect on humans – so are the source for many of the medicines we use today. If we want to be honest about it, we should be thanking insects rather than squashing them.

Because of insects' often restricted ranges and high degree of habitat specialization, some scientists suggest that with habitat destruction and forest clearing, it is almost certain that many species of insects in Ecuador and other regions are probably becoming extinct every year – most never having been discovered or described by scientists before their demise. In fact, we know so little about the biology and distribution of most insect species in Ecuador that it is difficult to judge how many are endangered or threatened.

The majority of ecotravellers to Ecuador are most excited about seeing the big hairy and feathered animals. However, the effects of charismatic jaguars, macaws, and others of their ilk, on the habitats they inhabit, while important, is nowhere as significant as those of the humble arthropods. Without the pollination, seed dispersal, insect control, and decomposing of organic material undertaken largely if not uniquely by insects, the habitats we "ooh" and "ahh" over would be much simpler and less diverse and interesting. Some scientists studying fossil evidence of plant evolution have suggested that a major rise of insects in the Cretaceous period (120 million years before present) is directly linked to the abrupt rise of flowering plants at that time through pollination specialization and co-dependency of the plants and insects. Thus, the flowering plants are linked inextricably both in their origin and survival with insects.

For the ecotraveller, many arthropods, especially insects, will provide an additional esthetic quality to enhance a trip to Ecuador. The beautiful butterflies, the dragonflies and beetles, and the bizarre insects to which you can't even begin to put a name, will pique your curiosity and raise your appreciation of Ecuador's wonderful wildlife. The dreaded insects, such as mosquitos, that you might have anticipated with anxiety, will underwhelm you. In comparison to the clouds of mosquitos people become accustomed to in the summer in many parts of the USA or Europe, you will be pleasantly surprised at how few there are on a path in the middle of the Amazon jungle. Except during the rainy season on the coast (January to March) and a few marshy areas of the Oriente, these pests are insignificant. In the cloud forests and highlands, biting insects are even rarer.

General Characteristics and Classification of Arthropods

All arthropods share the characteristics of having a hard outer skeleton, or exoskeleton (*cuticle*), and multi-jointed legs. These legs are variously modified for walking, swimming, feeding, defense, mating and for sensing the environment. The *lobsters, crayfish* and *shrimp* (Class Crustacea) are found primarily in the ocean (but some are in freshwater and a few are on land). They have two pairs of antennae and ten or more pairs of legs. The *spiders, ticks* and *scorpions* (Class Arachnida) are found primarily on land. They have four pairs of walking legs and claw-like mouth parts. Their bodies are divided into a head (*cephalothorax*) and large rear segment (*abdomen*). The *insects* (Class Insecta) are found primarily on land and in freshwater and have two pairs of wings, three pairs of legs and usually jaw-like mandibles. Their bodies are divided into three distinct parts, a head, *thorax* (which bears the legs and wings), and an abdomen. The class is made up of about 26 orders, such as *beetles, flies, butterflies, wasps, true bugs* and *termites*.

Features of Tropical Arthropods

As with most other groups, arthropods, especially insects, are so much more diverse in the tropics than in North America or Europe that it is mind-boggling. What we don't know about these insects is even more overwhelming. On one 5-km (3-mile) path in the Amazon, specialists in butterflies (lepidopterists) found almost 1200 species of butterflies (this doesn't count any of the night-flying moths), many more than are found in all of North America. From a single tree in the Amazon, another biologist found more species of ants than occur in all of England. From the canopy of another tree a researcher collected a kilo (2.2 lb) of insects and spiders, which contained almost 2000 species, but only about 100 of these species were known before or had scientific names; the rest were completely new to science.

Arthropods in Ecuador eat a wide variety of food including leaves, nectar, plant juices, other insects and blood, but few can eat wood. The major component of the tough cell walls that surround plant cells is a sugar-starch called *cellulose*, which is held together by very strong chemical bonds. Every year plants produce 100 billion tons of cellulose worldwide, and it is the most abundant organic compound on Earth. Most herbivorous insects cannot digest these tough cell walls made of cellulose and instead consume the more easily digested ingredients contained inside the plant cells. It turns out that among the few organisms that can actually digest cellulose, especially in its densest form, wood, are termites. In partnership (*mutualism*) with specialized one-celled organisms that occur only in their guts and produce unique enzymes to break down wood, termites have access to an abundant food source with little competition from other organisms. They break otherwise indigestible wood into shorter-chained sugar products that they and other organisms can use and break down further until eventually the chemical chains are so fragmented that they can be taken up through plant roots. As a nutrient, these chemicals are then used to make, among other things, cellulose and wood, and the cycle starts all over again. Termites, therefore, help recycle dead wood that otherwise would accumulate and go unused for many years or even centuries as it weathered slowly away.

Reproductive strategies of arthropods are so diverse and remarkable that they often make bird and mammal mating systems seem simple. Some species have *asexual reproduction*, in which only females are present and eggs mature without the influence of sperm. Other species alternate between asexual and sexual reproduction, but many rely fully on sexual reproduction. Mating behavior includes promiscuity, monogamy, and polyandry, but the most common mating system among arthropods, and insects in particular, is polygyny. Like in the birds, mammals and frogs, female arthropods tend to have most of the say in selecting potential mates, and males are often left then with the problem of communicating to a female just how superior their genes are, so she can choose the best one to father her young. The result is a complex of courtship behavior, spectacular male colors and behavior, lecs, territoriality, and a plethora of other characters – enough to satisfy the programming demands of TV's Discovery Channel for the next thousand years.

Among some insects, the young are like small wingless forms of the adult and are called *nymphs*. They get progressively bigger until they have full wings and reach adult size. In other insect groups, however, the young are completely different from the adults. This young insect is called a *larva*, and it eventually undergoes a sudden transformation (*metamorphosis*) into the adult form. In butterflies, larva are known as *caterpillars*; in flies, *maggots*; in beetles, *grubs*. Most insects spend far more of their lives in these immature stages than as adults, and the change into the adult stage (*emergence*) is often cued for many species simultaneously by the right combination of rain and temperature. For the most part, adults are active during parts of the year that are rainy and warm. Don't worry, however, if your trip to Ecuador doesn't conform to one of these rainy, warm periods; there will be at least a few arthropods active in any habitat during any month of the year.

Seeing Arthropods in Ecuador

It may sound ludicrous to provide advice on how to see arthropods, but most species do not seek out humans or come to them uninvited. Many nocturnal species are attracted to lights at night, and it can be rewarding to study the little beasts flapping around the light outside your cabin or at a fluorescent light at a rural gasoline station. From a canoe or along a trail at night, shine your flashlight on the vegetation, and you will often see small white reflections that are the eyes of *jumping* and *wolf spiders* stalking their insect prey. During the day, look for these night-active spiders on the underside of leaves and the surface of tree trunks, where they spend the day motionless, depending for protection on their abilities to match the background color. Many day-active species concentrate around flowers, rotting fruit and dung. Other species are active only on sandy beaches or rock faces. Some arthropod species such as *cicadas* make their presence known more by sound than sight, and at dusk the sounds of a forest full of cicadas can make sensitive ears ring. Many other insects, however, make more subtle sounds. Listen for *crickets* and *katydids* making their different clicks and churring notes all night long. Because many of these species are so small, it is easy to pass them up as uninteresting. But even if you don't have a microscope or magnifying glass, try looking at these interesting, tiny animals. If you have binoculars, reverse them and carefully look through them backwards. As you get within about 2 cm (1 in) from an insect or spider, it will come into focus and be sufficiently enlarged so you can see lots of detail. You will be amazed at the variety of shapes, forms, and colors you see and at the behaviors you can watch.

Order and Family Profiles

Tens of thousands of species of arthropods occur in Ecuador. Entire guide books could be written on any of the orders and most of the families of Ecuador's insects alone, but there is no room for such detail in a book of this size. Here we focus on 20 species that both represent the range of the common arthropod groups you are likely to see on your trip to Ecuador and have a fairly well-studied natural history.

1. Dragonflies and Damselflies

Relatively large, often colorful, and actively flying during the day, adult *dragonflies* and *damselflies* (Order Odonata) are easy to recognize. Their four elongate wings are folded back at rest in most damselflies and spread out to the side in dragonflies. The large eyes bulge out from the sides of the head, and are widely separated in the front in damselflies but approach or actually touch each other in the front in dragonflies. The antennae are very small and bristlelike. The abdomen is long and slender with finger-like structures at the end, used by the male to clasp the female in copulation. Present-day *odonates* vary in length from 2 to 18 cm (1 to 7 in), but a species that lived 250 million years ago and known only from fossils had a wing spread of 64 cm (2.5 ft)! Adults catch small insects in the air using their legs like a basket. Unlike all other insects, which have their copulatory organs at the end of their abdomen, male odonates have theirs at the front of the abdomen. The two sexes spend considerable time flying together in "tandem" with the male clasping the female. The female may lay her eggs while in tandem with the male or alone, depending on the species, but she always deposits her eggs in or near water. Some species show considerable territoriality, with the male guarding the female while she deposits eggs in his territory. The nymphs live underwater using gills at the end of the abdomen to breathe. They use modified mouth parts to grab small prey items such as tadpoles, small fish, and larvae of other insects. When they eventually grow large enough, the last nymphal stage crawls out of the water on a blade of grass or detritus. The adult, winged form breaks out of the husk of hard exoskeleton that surrounded the nymph and sits quietly just above the surface of the water. Here its soft brown outer surface slowly hardens and takes on color. During this hardening stage, the young adult is especially vulnerable to predation because it cannot fly well.

You will see many dragonflies and damselflies in virtually every habitat in Ecuador, and most will look and behave like ones you have seen in North America or Europe. As a purely Neotropical representative, however, no odonate is more spectacular and different than the huge HELICOPTER DAMSELFLY (Plate 85). There are 19 species of these peculiar damselflies (Family Pseudostigmatidae), and they are all restricted to the tropical lowland forests of South and Central America. On a sunny day in lowland rainforest, especially following a rainy day, these long (15 cm, 6 in), thin damselflies flutter like some small-scale helicopter through the lower and mid levels of vegetation. The four long wings often beat slowly and independently, and their bright yellow or white tips make them obvious and seemingly easy prey for any hungry bird. These damselflies, however, are very maneuverable and almost like magic easily avoid being caught as they rise into the canopy. They search for insects and spiders sitting on leaves, but they also often hover in front of spider webs and pluck out the resident spider when it makes itself obvious. The long abdomen is used to put eggs into hollow bamboo, tree holes, or pineapple-like bromeliads that hold reservoirs of water. Here the nymphs hatch out into the water and feed on mosquito larvae, small frog tadpoles and other odonate nymphs, until they finally emerge from the water as adults. Males of some species defend this larval site for several months, breeding with females that visit them.

Profile
Helicopter Damselfly, *Microstigma rotundatum*, Plate 85a

2. Grasshoppers, Crickets, and Cockroaches

Most of the species of this order (Orthoptera) are large, from 2 to 18 cm (0.8 to 7 in) long. They have front wings that are elongated and thickened like leather. At rest, these thickened wings cover the membranous hind wings. The body is elongated and the antennae are very short to relatively long. Young develop gradually into adults. Some of the best songsters in the insect world are found in this order – especially *grasshoppers* and *crickets*. Sounds are produced by *stridulation*: rubbing a scraper over a filelike ridge that is variously placed on the legs, wings or other body parts. Each species produces a different song. Along with this sound-producing ability, most species have a large ear (tympanum) along the side of the thorax or abdomen. It is used to detect the sounds and distinguish specific rhythms in songs that are used, for instance, for mate attraction or to signal species identity. In some species many males will sing together in a synchronized chorus. Most species feed on plant material like leaves and seeds, but a few eat other insects and others, such as many cockroaches, are scavengers.

Many of the species of BUSH KATYDIDS (Plate 85) have wings that so resemble leaves, that you have to look twice to see it is an insect and not part of the plant on which it is resting. These herbivorous insects are night-active and eat leaves mainly from vegetation in the understory of forests. Quite often adults are attracted to lights at night. To make sounds at night, they have little bumps on the insides of their wings that they rub over each other by moving the closed wings back and forth. Usually males make most of these sounds to attract females, and the song of each species is different. The young nymphs also eat leaves. During the day you can find Bush Katydids sitting in among the leaves of undergrowth shrubs.

Profile
Leaf-mimicking Bush Katydid, *Cycloptera speculata*, Plate 85b

3. Termites

The small insects in the Order Isoptera are the oldest of all social insects and have the most complex societies in the insect world. *Termite* colonies usually have two or three different-sized and shaped individuals (*castes*) within a single species, each having different jobs such as *workers, soldiers,* or *reproductives* (Plate 85). Within the same colony there can be individuals with wings (four and held flat) and those without. More subtly, there can be further specialization within each caste so that some workers do only one task and other workers a different task. Some colonies have *wild-card* nymphs, which, as they grow, perform a variety of tasks but transform into workers, soldiers or reproductives depending on the colony's needs. Males and females also are different castes.

Most, but not all, termites are light-colored, with soft bodies, long and thread-like antennae and a broad connection between the abdomen and thorax. They look somewhat like white ants, but are quite different. Ants have hard, dark bodies, short and bent antennae and usually a narrow waist connecting the abdomen to the thorax. In ants, the castes are exclusively female except for a few male drones, and the young are white grubs that do not work. In termites, the various body forms or castes within a colony are made up of both sexes, and young nymphs are usually workers. Termites must eat the droppings of each other to pass on one-celled organisms that live in their guts and carry the enzymes for breaking down wood (p. 213) – the main food of most termites. Without these helpers, termites would starve. Nests of termites can be completely underground (subterranean), sit on the ground in the form of a hard mud-like cone (termitarium) or be off the ground and attached to the trunk or large branch of a tree (arboreal). The covered tunnels or runways running from these nests to feeding areas are constructed of termite feces; they function to protect the termites from predators and temperature fluctuations.

The common arboreal termite nest in the lowlands of Ecuador is made by the NASUTE TERMITE (Plate 85), named after the soldier caste, which is often called a "nozzle head" for the unique shape of its head. Soldiers and workers may be either males or females, but they are sterile. Fertile queen and king castes carry on reproduction. The soldier of this type of termite squirts a smelly, sticky turpentine-like chemical from the nozzle on its head to cover enemies. This chemical makes it hard for other arthropods, especially enemy ants, to walk or fly and may even be irritating to large predators like anteaters and birds. The workers are more typical in shape and have mandibles. Because the soldiers lack mandibles, the workers must feed them as well as undertake all their other tasks. Some birds such as trogons and puffbirds often hollow out arboreal termite nests and use them as a cavity nest for their own young. Spectacular mass flights of dispersing winged termites often follow a heavy rainfall. At this time they are easy pickings for many birds. Evidently, however, the explosion of dispersing termites is so dense and short-lived that the predators in the area are never abundant enough to eat all of them, no matter how easy they are to catch; many survive to start new colonies. These termites frequently live with a wide variety of ants in the same nest. Whether this togetherness is equally beneficial to both species is not yet known for sure.

Profile
Nasute Termite, *Nasutitermes* sp., Plate 85c

4. Cicadas and Relatives

This order of insects (Homoptera) includes minute species such as *aphids* less than 1 mm (0.04 in) long to *cicadas* more than 5 cm (2 in) long. All are distinguished by mouth parts that have been modified for a piercing-sucking function; in fact they cannot chew. They insert their beak into plants and suck juices from them. The wings at rest are held roof-like over the back.

The EVENING CICADA (Plate 85), as is typical of all cicadas, lives as an adult for only a month or so. Most of its life is spent as a nymph underground sucking plant juices from roots. Nymphs of some species construct large, 15-cm (6-in) high turrets of red clay that cover the moist floor of Amazonian forests. Nymphs develop gradually into adult forms, and the left-over brownish and hollow skin (*exuviae*) of the last stage before the adult is often left hanging on the side of a tree trunk or some other vertical surface. Because adult cicadas are mainly found in the canopy of the forest, you are most likely to see them only when they are attracted to lights at night. Most commonly, however, your encounter with adult cicadas will be auditory. Male cicadas produce sounds, often painfully loud, and each species gives sounds at its own characteristic pitch, intensity and timing. Some species sing in all-male choruses that can become very intense. The sound-producing organs are called *tymbals*, which are thin plates on the side of the abdomen; they are depressed by a pair of large muscles attached to them and then spring back to make a noise. They are depressed and released with extreme rapidity to make the various sounds and pitches. Strangely, these sound producers are located right at the opening of the ears on the side of the abdomen – how can you hear anything with such a noise next to your ear? Most species make their sounds in the late afternoon and early evening.

The PEANUT BUG or LANTERN BUG (Plate 85) is a regular inhabitant of Ecuador's lowland forests. Throughout Central and South America, local legends assert that it is poisonous, but no scientist has ever been able to substantiate anything more than that it looks dangerous. It is quite large (10 cm, 4 in), but during the day hides camouflaged on the trunks of large trees, sometimes in small groups. If a predator is smart enough to recognize it despite the camouflage, the bug has a whole repertoire of additional anti-predator strategies. It can intimidate would-be predators by flashing open its wings to reveal large eye spots that resemble the eyes of an owl or large bird. If that doesn't work, its snake-like head is marked with apparent eyes, mouth and teeth to alarm the predator – never mind that this entire front part of the "head" is a hollow sham. The bug's real eyes and mouth are hidden back at the base of the wings. Finally, if worse comes to worst, there are reports that it can release a foul-smelling defense chemical. The adults apparently suck plant juices in the canopy, but little is known of the nymph stages.

Profiles
Evening Cicada, *Fidicina mannifera*, Plate 85d
Peanut Bug, *Fulgora laternaria*, Plate 85e

5. Antlions

As adults, all the members of this order (Neuroptera) have soft bodies, four membranous wings and long antennae. They are relatively weak fliers and predators on other insects, but some species do not feed at all as adults. Larvae of most species live in the ground, but a few live underwater. The representative of this order that you are most likely to see in Ecuador is the *antlion*. The adults look like dragonflies but have long antennae with knobs on the end (Plate 85). They sometimes come to lights at night. It is the larval form, however, that you will see most commonly. The short and flat larva has enormous mandibles. It excavates a funnel-shaped pit in dry sand and lies in wait at the bottom, often completely buried except for its mandibles. When an insect comes strolling along and accidentally stumbles at the precipitous edge, the antlion flicks sand grains out of the bottom to produce a constant avalanche of sand giving out under the hapless insect. This causes the insect to slide down into the waiting mandibles of the antlion. Crunch!

Profile
Antlion, *Myrmeleon* sp., Plate 85f

6. Beetles

The beetle order (Coleoptera) has more species in it than any other insect order – some estimate more than a million. These species occur in virtually all habitats on land and freshwater, but not in the ocean or in Antarctica. The trait shared by all these species is a front pair of wings hardened into shields (*elytra*) that when the insect is at rest cover the second pair of membranous flight wings and the top of the abdomen. The mandibles of the adults are large and variously used for catching small insect prey, crushing seeds, or chewing wood. The larvae are grubs and often occur in habitats different from those of the adults or have very different behavior.

In the cloud forests and lower páramo areas of Ecuador, the CHAUDOIR'S MONTANE TIGER BEETLE (Plate 86) is a common resident of road cuts and open clay banks. Even on cloudy or foggy days, you can see a few of these large (17.5 mm, 0.7 in) deep blue beetles running at the base of the road cuts or up their vertical faces. On sunny days they will be everywhere. Although they have wings, they rarely fly. They are predators on other arthropods and search for them using their large eyes. With their long legs, they run the prey down, grab them in their monstrous and sharp mandibles, then puree them. If you catch one, watch out for the mandibles; the bite, together with an enzyme they spit up, can really sting. They lay their eggs on near-vertical clay banks, and when the larvae hatch they immediately burrow horizontally into the bank. Then from this tunnel, the larva waits, its head just perfectly filling the mouth of the tunnel, for an ant or some other arthropod to come within striking distance. The larva, aided by hooks on its back, stretches quickly out of the tunnel to grab the prey in its large mandibles. If successful, the larva pulls the prey to the bottom of the tunnel and dismembers it, eventually tossing the inedible parts from the mouth of the tunnel. Almost 90 species of tiger beetles have been found in Ecuador, most of them at lower altitudes, where the beetles often occur on rocks near streams and on sandy river banks, but also on the forest floor.

The GREEN DUNG BEETLE (Plate 86) is attractive to the eye, but its habits may at first be off-putting to more squeamish ecotravellers. The members of this part of the Family Scarabaeidae (most of which are black) are some of the most intensely studied insects in Ecuador. They are crucial in passing nutrients and vital chemicals to the rest of the ecosystem by helping decompose dung. They are also unusual among insects because so many of these species have complex behavior when it comes to constructing nests and caring for their young. Some dung beetles merely eat their way through dung and deposit their eggs below a dung pat in a superficial nest and are called *dwellers*. Other species, the *tunnelers*, dig a vertical tunnel below the dung pat and carry, push and drag dung down into the bottom of the tunnel to avoid competitors and predators. Here the dung is either used as food by the adults or stored as food for eggs laid here. Finally, a large number of dung beetles are *rollers*. Making a ball of dung, they stand on their fore legs, use their hind legs to push and steer the ball, and transport this resource away from the dung pat area before burying it in a suitable location. The female sometimes helps roll this ball, but more often than not she just rides on top of the ball, walking as the world turns under her. At some distance from the original site of the pat, the pair stops and buries the ball. The beetles mate, and the female lays eggs on the section of dung they buried. When the eggs hatch, the larvae are protected underground from predators and competitors and have a dung banquet upon which they can feed and grow. Males of many species have a prominent horn on the tip of their snout that curves back over the head. The horn is used to battle other males over the dung as well as to impress the females that wait to see who wins the dung fight.

Dung is located mainly by smell, and the beetles' feather-shaped antennae act as super sniffers. Particular types of dung, however, are so prized by some beetle species that they also apparently use their eyes to quickly locate this resource as it falls from the canopy. The beetles use a circling flight with ever tighter loops to home in on the prize. Some species of dung beetles will use almost any type of dung they encounter while others are highly specialized on bird dung, monkey dung, cat dung, and even snail and millipede dung. One highly specialized dung beetle rides around near the anus of sloths (p. 179) and waits for a sloth to climb down from the canopy and defecate. The dung of herbivorous animals tends to be rich in carbohydrates and dung of carnivorous animals tends to be rich in nitrogen, and the different needs of various dung beetle species for growing versus daily energy needs for adult beetles influence their choice of repast.

The spectacular and large (6 cm, 2.4 in) HARLEQUIN LONG-HORNED BEE-TLE (Plate 86) is a member of the long-horned beetle family (Cerambycidae), which is characterized by extremely long antennae and a propensity to bore into dead or living tree trunks and branches. Some members of this family are unusual in that they directly produce enzymes that break down plant cellulose. Unlike termites (p. 216) and other cellulose-eating insects, they do not rely on one-celled organisms in their gut to provide the proper enzymes. The bright orange, gray and black coloring of the Harlequin Beetle may function to break up its shape visually, so predators do not notice it easily. The front legs of the male are much longer than those of the female and are used both when copulating and for reaching across gaps to walk from branch to branch. The adults are primarily active during the day. After mating, the female chews a gash in the bark of a tree and places her eggs in it. The young hatch out and tunnel deeper into the tree, producing a maze, or *gallery*, of tunnels. Sometimes their damage can be so extensive that they kill the tree. These beetles carry around a mini-ecosystem on their backs: small herbivorous mites graze on the algae and fungi that grow over the body surface of large adults; tiny predaceous pseudoscorpions, in turn, feed on the mites.

Profiles

Chaudoir's Montane Tiger Beetle, *Pseudoxycheila chaudoiri*, Plate 86a
Green Dung Beetle, *Oxysternon conspicillatum*, Plate 86b
Harlequin Long-horned Beetle, *Acrocinus longimanus*, Plate 86c

7. Butterflies and Moths

The *butterflies* and *moths* (Order Lepidoptera) are perhaps the most easily recognized insect groups in the world. They have four wings, but the hind and fore wing on each side often have a coupling mechanism that makes them look and act like a single huge wing. The characteristic shared by all members of this group, however, is the layer of tiny scales covering the wings. They come off easily, and if you handle the wings of a butterfly, look for the scales on your finger (the scales will look like dust). The adults either do not feed at all or feed on nectar or rotting fruit juices. Their mouthparts are shaped into a long thin proboscis which can be rolled up when not extended for feeding. Males often need extra sodium and other salts for producing sperm, and it is not unusual to see clouds of male butterflies fluttering near and landing on dung, urine, rotting fruit, or even the nose of a basking turtle, to suck up excretions containing these chemicals. Even salt-ladened human sweat can attract beautiful butterflies, so don't swat all the insects that come flying around you. If you attract butterflies day after day, it may be time to take a shower. In general, adult butterflies are active during the day and have thread-like antennae with knobs on the end. Moths are usually active at night and have either thread-like antennae without knobs or large feather-shaped antennae. Larval *lepidopterans* are almost all plant-eating and use large mandibles to chew holes out of the edges of leaves. Many of the major agricultural pests in the world are larval moths. Some lepidopteran species have their own specific food plant species on which they lay eggs and on which their caterpillars feed when they emerge. The brown silken chamber in which the larval moth meta-morphoses into an adult is called a *cocoon*. The chamber of the larval butterfly is called a *chrysalis*; it is ornate and often colorful.

The intense, almost neon-like blue of the first male MENELAUS' MORPHO BUTTERFLY (Plate 86) you see will be a sight you will never forget. There are many species of morphos in Ecuador. Some are duller blue to black, some have females that are very dull, and others, like the one we have illustrated here, have females almost as brilliant as the males. These huge butterflies flap lazily along river edges and forest trails with an up and down movement of the whole body. Apparently entire populations in an area will use the same flight path day after day, so if you see one using a path, just wait and others will eventually fly along the same route. Often you will come across several adults on the ground puddling at a muddy area or sucking rotted fruit or feces. With their wings folded, the highly camou-flaged undersides make them very difficult to see until suddenly they fly up, flash-ing the blue uppersides of the wings. Their major enemies are jacamars (p. 135) and other flycatching birds, and the slow flapping of the wings may help them escape these birds. By making themselves alternately obvious and camouflaged as their wings open and close in flight, and randomly changing directions between wingbeats, they apparently confuse pursuing birds trying to anticipate which direction the morphos will be going when next their wings open up. The large larvae (9 cm, 3.5 in) are red and yellow, and the head is covered with specialized hairs that sting like nettles when broken off by a naive predator.

One of the most common butterfly species you will see low on forest paths in Ecuador is the AURORINA'S CLEAR-WINGED SATYR (Plate 86). Except for the black spots and reddish color at the tail-end of the wings, this butterfly has no scales on its wings, and they are thus transparent. At rest, the red rear ends of the wings together with the black spots give the impression of a head, and this confusion is probably a way of diverting a predator's attention from the real head and direc-tion of escape.

Another common forest butterfly you will see in Ecuador has bold orange and black stripes and is called the *Tiger Butterfly*. In reality this butterfly is not a single species but instead is a jumble of 20 or more confusingly and amazingly similar species of butterflies and moths. This color pattern is common through-out the lowland and lower elevation cloud forests of Ecuador and represents a *mimicry complex*. Within this mimicry complex, MECHANITIS BUTTERFLY (Plate 86) larvae are able to harmlessly absorb and store the nasty chemicals from the specific food plant they eat. When they metamophose into adults, they keep these chemicals in their body and wings. This species represents a distasteful and poisonous species in the tropical subfamily Ithomiinae that serves as an evolutionary *model*. Its bright color pattern and high population levels ensure that naive predators will quickly learn and unambiguously remember that bright orange and black stripes mean a terrible taste, causing vomiting or even worse. Another species, the DISMORPHA BUTTERFLY (Plate 86), shares a similar color pattern and size. It, however, is much rarer and in the cabbage butterfly family, Pieridae, most species of which are the familiar white or sulphur-yellow species we see in our gardens in North America and Europe. This species is not protected by poisons or distastefulness, but instead cheats as a *mimic* of the distasteful species. Because the distasteful model species is more common, the predators have most likely learned to associate any orange-and-black striped butterfly with a very bad gustatory experience, so the rarer but tasty mimic is mistaken for the model species and also avoided. In many cases the males of mimic species are not as similar to the model species as are the females. Perhaps so that females will choose them as mates, the males have to prove their gene superiority by showing they can survive even as imperfect mimics. Alternatively, the males may have to show more clearly just which species they are, so the females don't waste time trying to mate with a confusingly similar male of another species.

Easily mistaken for a swallow-tailed butterfly, the bright metallic green and black LELIUS' URANIA MOTH (Plate 86) is actually a day-flying moth. Besides its spectacular colors, this species is common, often seen puddling along the river's edge of lowland rainforest. It is most famous, however, for its massive migrations, when thousands pass over a river or forest site in a day. The explanation for these massive movements of adults may lie in their food plant, a genus (*Omphalea*) of vine related to the rubber plant. As the larvae of these specialized moths munch away at the leaves of this vine, they apparently "induce" the plant to respond by increasing the levels of toxic chemicals in its leaves. After three or four generations of attack from Urania larvae, the levels of plant toxins become so high that the next generation of moths will not be able to handle them, no matter how specialized they are at detoxifying them normally. At this point the adults somehow recognize the futility of laying their eggs on vines in this area, and they all get up and fly hundreds of kilometers to another area that has not had a concentration of Urania moths feeding on these vines for a long time. To save energy, the plants reduce the level of production of toxins when they are not under attack. The eruptive migrations of Urania occur at a low level every year, but about every 4 to 8 years a super movement occurs that lasts only a few weeks. The adults feed on nectar of leguminous trees and are important pollinators.

Profiles

Menelaus' Morpho Butterfly, *Morpho menelaus*, Plate 86d
Aurorina Clear-winged Satyr, *Cithaerias aurorina*, Plate 86e
Mechanitis Butterfly, *Mechanitis* sp., Plate 86f
Dismorpha Butterfly, *Dismorpha* sp., Plate 86g
Lelius' Urania Moth, *Urania lelius*, Plate 86h

8. Flies

Another very large group of insects is the *flies* (Order Diptera). Their identifying character is the presence of only the front pair of wings. The rear wings have been reduced to small knobs (*halteres*) used for balance in flight. Most adults are small and soft-bodied, and they include many of the biting insects we stereotype as "bad," such as *mosquitos, horseflies, no-seeums*, and *black flies*; only the females bite. Because of their roles in the spread of disease as well as in agricultural plagues, representatives of this group surely rank high as pests. However, many species of flies are critical for such functions as cleaning up rotted bodies, killing other insects and pollinating flowers. Larvae are grub-like and most live in water, where they feed on dead vegetation, decaying animal matter or other larvae.

One of the largest and most intriguing flies in Ecuador is the ROBBER FLY

(Plate 87). Its long body and big eyes are diagnostic. The many species of this fly are all predators and hunt flying insects with a spectacular flight from a perch on the ground or low vegetation. Using its long thin wings for quick acceleration and maneuverability, the robber fly pursues and grabs an insect in the air with its long legs. Then, quickly inserting its pointed mouth parts into a body joint of the prey, it injects a venom to dispatch it. The fly then returns to its perch and sucks the body juices from the dead insect. These robber flies are so tough that they often kill wasps and bees larger than themselves. The long, relatively inflexible wings make a lot of noise when they fly, and with a little practice you can hear a robber fly before you see it. Evidently the extreme acceleration needed to move from rest to fast flight requires these long and noisy wings. Such energy-intensive flights require fairly warm temperatures, so some species of these flies are active in very hot environments such as around river sand bars. Some species are also active in the forest understory, but only on warm and sunny days; on cloudy days and at night they remain inactive. The grub-like larvae live in the ground or in leaf litter and are predators on the larvae of other insects.

Profile
Robber Fly, *Smeryngo* sp., Plate 87a

9. Ants, Wasps, and Bees

Although this group (Order Hymenoptera) is perhaps best known for its stinging females, it contains some of the most beneficial insect species in the world. *Ants* help turn over and aerate soil as well as disperse seeds. Many species of *wasps* are predators on herbivorous insects and function as a major biological control of numerous pest species. *Bees* are important pollinators of many native and agricultural plants. In Ecuador, a steadily rising market for honey has made bees even more economically important. The species with wings have four membranous wings, in which the fore- and hind-wing on each side are fastened together with tiny hooks. The mouthparts are either strong mandibles for chewing or modified into a long tongue for sucking up nectar and other liquid food. In most species the abdomen is attached to the thorax by a narrow waist. The larvae are grub-like and usually cared for in hives or nests. Many species are highly colonial. Sex of an egg is determined by whether or not it has been fertilized by male sperm. If it has been fertilized, it develops into a female, but if not, it develops into a male.

The underground nests of LEAF-CUTTER ANTS (Plate 87) are obvious in the lowland forests. The up to 0.2 hectare (half acre) of exposed clay and mud is completely devoid of undergrowth plants. Up to 5 million individuals live in a single colony. All day long columns of ants carrying small pieces of leaves or flowers enter holes in the ground while others exit. The columns of ants extend from the colony via cleared paths to the trees under attack. Their activity usually ceases at nightfall and during extended rainy periods during the day. The leaf pieces are cut with the sharp mandibles of the large worker caste and carried by them like an umbrella back to the nest. Many of these workers are susceptible to attack by flies and wasps trying to lay eggs on them that will later emerge and consume the worker. With her mandibles occupied carrying the leaf load, she cannot protect herself without dropping the leaf. Instead, small caste ants (*minima*) often ride on top of the leaf where they can challenge approaching danger and keep it at bay. In the nest, special galleries are set aside where the leaf bits are received by other workers. These leaves are not food, but instead they are cleaned, scraped and then added to underground gardens. Here a specialized fungus grows on the leaves and produces a spongy layer that is eaten by the entire ant colony and fed to developing larvae. If a queen ant leaves the nest to start a new colony, she must take a mouthful of the fungus to use as a starter for food in the new colony. This farming behavior is important for the forest because it quickly moves immense amounts of nutrients through the system. The ants are very choosy about which plant species they incorporate into their underground gardens. Apparently the chemicals contained in the leaves of some plant species inhibit fungal growth and are thus avoided by the ants.

There are many species of *army ants*, but the most obvious and well-studied species is BURCHELL'S ARMY ANT (Plate 87). A single colony of this ant can contain more than a million individuals of several castes. Even though they lack eyes, they forage in immense but coordinated raiding columns 3 to 15 m (10 to 50 ft) wide. They swarm across the forest floor, driving escaping animals in front of them, and pouncing on slower insects, spiders and occasionally small lizards; they overpower the prey by sheer numbers and incessant stings. This immense colony is always only temporarily "bivouacked" because they must move on every month or so as their raids reduce the number of prey in the vicinity of the bivouac. The framework of the nest is actually made up of an immense cluster of ants holding on to each other with their mandibles, usually in the hollow of a tree or base of a buttress root. The eggs, larvae, and single queen are all guarded within this unique structure and carry on their normal functions until the colony moves to its next location. You can tell if the army ant column is raiding or moving by what the workers are carrying. If they are carrying white larvae and not dead insect parts, you know it is a relocation column. Males have wings and large eyes, but they are produced in very small numbers, and you are most likely to see them attracted to night lights at the beginning of the rainy season. It is always a good idea to glance down at the trail every once in a while as you walk or stand in the forest, to make sure you are not standing in an army ant column. Otherwise, if you haven't tucked your pants legs inside your socks, you will soon find out by their stings that the ants are there. Although their stings can be painful, army ants, unlike their Hollywood movie portrayal, do not attack and carry off large vertebrates such as humans. The worst thing you can do, however, is to stomp your feet and crush these ants. They use chemicals rather than sight to coordinate their movements, and crushed ants give off a chemical that elicits defensive behavior by the rest of the column. You don't want that. Just calmly but quickly walk away from the column and brush off your pants' legs and shoes (you have of course already tucked your pants' cuffs into the tops of your socks). One good way to find a raiding column is to listen for the growling calls of antbirds (p. 144) around the ants. A large flock of these noisy and obvious birds usually assembles at the head of the raiding column to catch large flying insects trying to escape the ants, but the birds do not eat the ants.

The large (16 to 22 mm, 0.5 to 1 in), all-black CONGA ANT (Plate 87) is probably the most dangerous animal you will encounter during your trip to lowland rainforests in Ecuador. If all you do is see it, count yourself lucky, as the sting of this animal is considered one of the most painful in the entire world – it may even cause hallucinations in some people. Its effect varies considerably from person to person, and we have seen big, husky and macho men crying unashamedly in pain from its sting, while some smaller people, male and female, only felt some pain for a minute or so. Never place your hand on a tree while you rest along a trail, because this is the surest way to encounter the Conga Ant. As a warning for potential enemies, these ants make a noise by scraping body parts together, a sound that you should learn and listen for. Because they are so well protected from predators, several other insect species have evolved similar body shapes to mimic these ants. One, an arboreal tiger beetle, not only looks and walks like a Conga Ant but also *stridulates* using the same sound frequencies as the ant. The nests of this ant are usually in the ground at the base of a tree, and they usually contain fewer than two hundred individuals, one queen and the rest a single caste of workers. They forage, often singly, from the forest floor and undergrowth vegetation all the way up into the canopy. They are active during the daytime in the rainy season and at night during the dry season. Besides hunting live prey, including other insects and occasionally small lizards and birds, they also scavenge dead animals and eat nectar from flowers.

As you walk through a rainforest in the lowlands of Ecuador, you often can hear the low but distinct humming of a large bumblebee-like insect flying lazily through the undergrowth or along the trail. As it gets closer, you will see a large, colorful bee, MERIAN'S ORCHID BEE (Plate 87), investigating nooks and crannies of trees and plants or landing in a wet section of the path to gather mud. If it flies close to you, it is probably only investigating some new smell that has attracted its attention. These bees are docile and do not sting unless severely provoked. They pollinate a wide range of flowers, the males being especially attracted to orchids. Instead of nectar, each orchid species offers a different chemical reward that can smell like wintergreen, vanilla, bubble gum, eucalyptus oil or cinnamon. Evidently the males need this chemical to combine into a particular smell that attracts females. When the male enters the orchid flower to get to the chemical, it has to lean against a part of the interior of the blossom that has a sticky packet of pollen (*pollinarium*), and, depending on the orchid species, it becomes attached to the bee's chest, back or abdomen. When this bee visits the next blossom of the same species of orchid, an even stickier part of the flower strips the pollinarium off the bee to deposit it on the female part of the flower for pollination. Many smaller species of orchid bees are common in the forest, and they are often bright metallic green or blue. You can identify them as they hover in front of a flower or tree trunk, rubbing their hind legs together.

Profiles

Leaf-cutter Ant, *Atta* sp., Plate 87b
Burchell's Army Ant, *Eciton burchelli*, Plate 87c
Conga Ant, *Paraponera clavata*, Plate 87d
Merian's Orchid Bee, *Eulaema meriana*, Plate 87e

10. Spiders

Probably the most maligned arthropods are the *spiders*. Although almost all the 35,000 species in the world have venom glands that they use together with their fangs to kill prey, only a very few species are dangerous to humans. The benefits spiders provide by controlling populations of insects more than outweighs the problems of a few bites and extra duties for fastidious house-cleaners. Most spiders are on land, but a few hunt underwater. Many spiders build webs to catch flying insects. These webs can be sticky, ornate orbs, flat sheets, funnel-shaped, or combinations thereof. Some spiders even use webbing like nets to throw onto prey. Most spiders catch small- to medium-sized insect prey, but some species are large enough to catch small birds in their webs. Waiting in a retreat at the side of the web, the spider detects a struggling prey by the vibrations transmitted along the strands of webbing. It then rushes out to inject the prey with poison and often wraps it in a cocoon of silk. Several large groups of spiders, however, do not use webs to catch prey but instead rely on ambush, stealth or stalking. All produce silk, however, which is a protein produced in the abdomen. It is released from the abdomen through finger-like holes called *spinnerets*. Young spiders often go to a high point in the habitat, spin out a line of silk and then let the wind take them, the silk serving as a balloon or parachute. This method of transportation can disperse spiders over long distances. Eggs are laid in a silk pouch near the web, on the female, or in a crevice. The young hatch out looking like miniature spiders, and they grow gradually.

Because they are completely predaceous and cannibalism is common, most spiders are solitary. Only during courtship and mating do they socialize, and then often to the detriment of the smaller male. Strangely, however, the spider you are most likely to see in the lowlands of Ecuador is one of 50 species in the world that is colonial or, more accurately, cooperative. The NEOTROPICAL COLONIAL SPIDER (Plate 87) builds communal webs that can be several meters (yards) long, the largest web of any spider in the world. The colony can range in numbers from one female and her offspring to more than 20,000 individuals. The immense webs follow the contour of vegetation along river and forest edges or in the understory of the forest itself. New colonies arise by a number of females moving some distance away from the parent colony and spinning their webs at a fresh site. Because these colonial spiders show no physical caste differences and have no subdivision of labor, their colonies are quite different from the highly organized ant and termite societies. In many ways the colonial spider social organization is more similar to that of communally breeding birds like anis (p. 121). Each male and each female spider builds and maintains its own orb web within the colony. This web is defended from other spiders, and prey captured in a web are not shared (at least voluntarily) with other spiders in the same colony.

One advantage to this colonial existence is that together the webs produce a more efficient trap for insects flying in the area. Each spider captures more prey in the colonial web than it would off by itself with only its own small web. Another advantage is that by using the support of other webs, each spider uses less silk to make its orb. Although predators and parasites can more easily locate the immense webs and the spiders living in them, the complex labyrinth of webs often makes it harder for enemies to enter. These immense webs have a disadvantage, however, in that disease, fungi and other microbes can easily be spread throughout the colony. More than 20% of these colonies become extinct every generation because of factors like this that are associated with crowding. Also, the complex arrangement of webs in a colony provides many hiding places for other species of spiders that make their living by stealing prey. They are called *klepto-parasites* and can have drastic effects on the amount of food the owners of the webs actually eat.

Profile

Neotropical Colonial Spider, *Anelosimus eximus*, Plate 87f

11. Crustaceans

The members of this group (Crustacea) include over 40,000 species of *crabs, crayfish, lobsters,* and *barnacles.* They include some that are predators, others that are herbivores or parasites and some that eat dead organisms. Many have the first leg modified into a claw or pincher (*cheliped*). A number of these species are important commercially as food. Several shrimp species are a mainstay of the Ecuadorean economy. Human-made shrimp ponds, however, have, in effect, destroyed much of the coastal mangrove habitat in Ecuador because mangroves are cleared to make way for these ponds. Although most crustaceans are found in oceans, several shrimp species are found in freshwater and a few crabs are common on the floor of moist Amazon forests. The young larval forms of crustaceans are tiny, swimming forms called *zoea*. They are important because they can disperse great distances on river and ocean currents.

Throughout the Indo-Pacific Ocean, one of the most widespread and obvious crabs at the water's edge is the SALLY LIGHTFOOT CRAB (Plate 87). In the Galápagos, the large size of the adults and their bright orange and red coloring make them unmistakable. The immature crabs are smaller and all dark. These crabs live just above the water level in moist areas as well as underwater. They forage mainly by using the front claws to scrape algae off rocks in the *intertidal zone* (the rocks and beach between high and low tide lines). They also commonly scavenge dead and decaying bodies of seals, birds and fish. In turn, the crabs often fall prey to herons and predatory fish. They get their name from their habit of quickly scampering across the surface of the water for short distances, usually to escape danger. The abdomen of crabs is a flat plate turned under the body between the bases of the legs. In females this plate is broad and protects the mass of fertilized eggs until the zoeal larvae hatch out and swim away in the ocean's currents. The larvae spend several months as *plankton* (floating organisms in the water) filtering tiny plant material from the water to eat and growing until, as small crabs, they return to land. Of course only a few of the thousands of zoea survive their oceanic cruise, as they are often the source of food for many fish and other invertebrates.

Profile
Sally Lightfoot Crab, *Grapsus grapsus*, Plate 87g

Chapter 10

GALÁPAGOS WILDLIFE

- *Introduction*
- *Group Profiles*
- *Environmental Close-Up 4: Darwin and the Theory of Evolution*

Introduction

As you first step onto one of the islands in the Galápagos archipelago, it is like entering a world of nature you thought existed only on educational TV or in some contrived outdoors film. Even if you have done lots of reading in advance and think you are prepared for what to expect, you will probably still be surprised by what you see and experience. The first thing that will strike you is that the animals are very tame. Not just the iguanas and crabs that you expect to be slow anyway, but lizards, snakes, hawks, herons, finches, albatrosses and seals tolerate incredibly close approach. Virtually the only species you have to sneak up on to get a close look at is the GREATER FLAMINGO (Plate 92), and it is a recent arrival to the islands that apparently hasn't yet acquired the more laid-back traits of longer-term residents. You may or may not become accustomed to species like mockingbirds so forward and arrogant that they will even perch on your telephoto lens in what seems some anthropomorphic parody of teasing. The second feature of the Galápagos wildlife that becomes more and more obvious as your experience and insight increase is the uniqueness of so many of these species. Most of them can be found nowhere else in the world, that is, they are *endemic*.

The standard explanation for the tameness is that the paucity of predators over millennia has made shyness and timidity unnecessary. In addition, boldness in investigating new sources of food and novel situations may often be a distinct advantage on these frequently harsh islands for survival and passing on genes to subsequent generations. The high degree of endemism has another explanation. Many species are not only limited to the Galápagos but are restricted to single islands within the archipelago. This is apparently caused by a combination of very long-term isolation and evolution of unique differences and specializations that, in many cases, confine species to narrow ways of life; they become adapted to the habitat and environment peculiar to one island (see Close-up, p. 246). The advantage is that extreme adaptations can make an individual very efficient at whatever it does. There is a dark side to this specialization, however. In cases such as the FLIGHTLESS CORMORANT (Plate 91) and MANGROVE FINCH, this confinement in ecological and behavioral specialization may end up condemning these species to extinction because habitats change or disappear so quickly and undoing or remolding specializations can never happen fast enough to keep up. In the case of the GALÁPAGOS TORTOISE (Plate 89), forms on three islands have already met this fate and become extinct.

Group Profiles

1. Reptiles

Compared with other *reptiles* in general and even with their relatives on mainland Ecuador (Chapter 6), the Galápagos reptiles exemplify a continuing theme for the native species on these islands – they have some of the most unusual adaptations, intriguing behavior and intricate distributions in the world. *Sea turtles, tortoises, snakes,* and *lizards* all have representative species on the Galápagos.

The GALÁPAGOS TORTOISES (Plate 89) are probably the most famous reptiles in Ecuador, and like all wildlife there are now protected by local law. Unfortunately, many decades of hunting wiped out four forms including large populations on the islands of Floreana and Fernandina. Other forms, such as on Pinta Island (only a single male, Lonely George, survives), are so reduced that they are not viable. Conservation and breeding programs are now underway to save those that remain. In total, about 15,000 individuals of all forms exist in the wild and in captivity. In the past, the 14 varieties of these huge (250 kg, 550 lb) tortoises were considered to be races of a single species. One form is or was present on each of the main islands except for Isabela. There five forms occur, one on each of the isolated volcanoes spread over the island. Recent studies, however, in which some were cross-bred to others and failed to produce viable offspring, strongly suggest that these forms or varieties may well prove to be distinct species.

Galápagos Tortoises eat grasses, cacti and other succulent plants, and other vegetation. They drink water from pools and ponds during the wetter parts of the year, but in the dry season, when surface water is scarce, all their water is obtained metabolically – as a by-product of the breakdown of the food they eat. They can go for more than a year without drinking or eating! One of the reasons that these tortoises were so sought after and decimated by 18th century sailors is that they provided fresh meat for long voyages. In the days before refrigeration, these animals were ideal. Placed upside down in the hold of a ship, a tortoise could survive for a year or more without food or water. This physiological ability to withstand long-term drought by metabolizing stored fat became part of their downfall.

These tortoises are usually day-active; they sleep at night under bushes, trees, or rock formations. The main difference in the various forms or species is in the size and shape of the shell over the body. The forms living on islands with sparse vegetation have narrow "saddle-backed" types of shells that permit them to reach with their long necks for leaves high overhead. The forms living on moister islands or at higher altitudes where low vegetation is common and easier to reach, have domed shells that more efficiently protect the body and neck from danger. Besides man, the only major predators these immense tortoises have are GALÁPAGOS HAWKS, which readily eat them as hatchlings. Galápagos Tortoises become sexually mature after about 20 years. The larger males rid themselves of lethargy each year for about a month when they begin courting females and ramming rival males. Females lay one or two clutches per year, usually with three to

12 eggs each. The hatchlings, about 6 cm (2.5 in) long, emerge from nests in the ground after 6 to 7 months of incubation.

All *sea turtles* (Plate 88) have front legs modified into oar-like flippers, which propel them through the water. Although they need air to breathe, they can remain submerged for long periods. At first, all sea turtles were assumed to have similar diets, probably sea plants. But some observations of natural feeding, as well as examinations of stomach contents, reveal a variety of specializations. GREEN SEA TURTLES eat bottom-dwelling sea grasses and algae, HAWKSBILL SEA TURTLES eat bottom sponges, LEATHERBACK SEA TURTLES eat mostly jellyfish, and OLIVE RIDLEY SEA TURTLES feed on crabs, mollusks, and jellyfish, as well as vegetation.

Mature males and females appear offshore during breeding periods. In the Galápagos, the common breeding species is the PACIFIC GREEN SEA TURTLE (November to January). Both males and females mate with numerous mates at the ocean's surface, with the smaller male riding the back of the female. After mating, females alone come ashore on sandy beaches to dig their nesting holes, apparently at the same beach on which they were born, and lay their eggs. Each female breeds probably every 2 to 4 years, laying from two to eight clutches of eggs in a season (each clutch being laid on a different day). For about 2 or 3 hours, and usually at night, a female drags herself up the beach to a suitable spot above the high-tide line, digs a hole with her rear flippers (a half meter, 2 ft, or more deep), deposits about 100 golfball-sized eggs, covers them with sand, tamps the sand down, and heads back to the ocean. Sometimes females emerge from the sea alone, but often there are mass emergences, with hundreds of females nesting on a beach in a single night. Eggs incubate for about 2 months, then hatch simultaneously. The hatchlings dig themselves out of the sand and make a dash for the water (if tiny turtles can be said to "dash"). Many terrestrial and ocean predators devour the hatchlings, and by some estimates only between 2% and 5% survive their first few days of life. The young float on rafts of sea vegetation during their first year, feeding and growing, until they reach a size when they can, with some safety, migrate long distances through the world's oceans. When sexually mature, in various species from 7 to 20+ years later, they undertake reverse migrations, returning to their birth sites to breed.

Three species of native terrestrial *snakes*, all *colubrids* (p. 72), are found in the Galápagos, two in the genus *Alsophis*, (Plate 89e) and one in the genus *Philodryas*. All are thin, small (less than 1 m, 3.3 ft, long), and brownish with stripes or spots. They are mildly venomous and use this venom together with squeezing to dispatch their prey. Each species has a different form or subspecies on two or three different islands. They feed mainly on small reptiles, nestling finches and large insects.

The Galápagos Islands are also home to several *iguanoid lizards* (p. 81). Some species are large and well known while others are smaller and less obvious. The most unique of them all is the MARINE IGUANA (Plate 89), probably evolved from castaway GREEN IGUANAS (Plate 11) from the mainland coast. This large black lizard with a chunky head and spiny backbone is so abundant along rocky shorelines in the Galápagos that it is sometimes difficult to find a place to walk without stepping on one. Marine Iguanas actually look like refugees from a Hollywood monster movie. They grow to 1.5 m (5 ft) in length, including the tail, but they have a 10-fold difference in size among islands. The smallest individuals are on Genovesa (maximum 900 g, 2 lb) and the largest on Santa Fe (3.5 kg, 7.7 lb).

The only ocean-going lizard on Earth, Marine Iguanas bask in the hot Galápagos sun on black volcanic rocks and sand at the water's edge. Once their bodies are sufficiently warmed by the sun, they dive into the chilly Pacific, where they feed on algae and perhaps other aquatic vegetation until their bodies cool and metabolisms slow; they then return to shore for more of the warming sun. This cycle of alternating sunning and swimming/feeding is repeated several times until they have found enough food for the day. However, they spend only about 5% of the day close to or in the water; the rest of the time they spend basking and resting on the shore. They are equipped with special "salt glands," which allow them to drink sea water and excrete the harmful salt from their bodies. Larger individuals (greater than 1800 g, 4 lb) can dive for 5 to 10 minutes and reach depths of 12 m (40 ft). Smaller individuals (less than 1200 g, 2.6 lb) find their algae in the intertidal zone or at much shallower parts of the inshore lagoons.

Marine Iguana males are about twice the size of females. The females on an island all become ready for mating at the same time and for only less than a month each year. At this time the largest males set up territories on small prominences above the beach. Here they show off and try to attract females to mate with them rather than the male on the next prominence – a type of lec behavior. During this time their body color becomes brighter and they chase other males from their territories. They mate promiscuously with females and do not defend a harem. On Genovesa, however, while the large males strut, the smallest males sneak around on the beach and mate with females unobtrusively. The females move to sandy areas in back of the beach and lay four eggs in a burrow, which is defended against other females trying to lay their eggs in it.

There are also two species of *land iguanas* (including the GALÁPAGOS LAND IGUANA; Plate 89) found on the islands – large tan to brown lizards with somewhat pointed snouts. You will see them in the drier interior parts of the islands. Here they feed mainly on *Opuntia* cactus (p. 19), seemingly immune from the sharp spines. Male land iguanas defend large territories that include several female's ranges. When males fight, it often is with vigor and spilled blood. After mating, the female retreats from the male's territory and lays her 10 or so eggs in a burrow, which she defends against other females.

Of all the Galápagos lizard species, only the land iguanas, owing to their small population sizes, are presently threatened. However, the Marine Iguana and the two species of Galápagos land iguanas, the BARRINGTON ISLAND and GALÁPAGOS LAND IGUANAS, are CITES Appendix II listed. The Santiago Island population of the Galápagos Land Iguana is extinct owing to human activity.

Seven species of small LAVA LIZARDS (Plate 89d) (a kind of dwarf iguana, p. 81) are common on all but a few of the Galápagos Islands. They are active by day on sandy or rocky shorelines, and in the interiors of the islands. Not only do their color patterns vary from island to island, but the territorial defensive behavior of males, which is a type of aggressive "push-up" motion with the front legs, also varies in pattern and sequence. They feed on insects and some plant material during the driest part of the year. Their enemies are many as hawk, herons, snakes and mockingbirds snatch them when they can. Five species of native *geckos* (p. 79) are also endemic to the Galápagos, and three additional species have been introduced there recently.

Profiles

Pacific Green Sea Turtle, *Chelonia mydas*, Plate 88a
Hawksbill Sea Turtle, *Eretmochelys imbricata*, Plate 88b
Leatherback Sea Turtle, *Dermochelys coriacea*, Plate 88c

Olive Ridley Sea Turtle, *Lepidochelys olivacea*, Plate 88d
Galápagos Tortoise, *Geochelone nigrita* and *G. hoodensis*, Plate 89a
Marine Iguana, *Amblyrhynchus cristatus*, Plate 89b
Galápagos Land Iguana, *Conolophus subcristatus*, Plate 89c
Galápagos Lava Lizard, *Tropidurus albemarlensis*, Plate 89d
Galápagos Snake, *Antillophis steindachneri*, Plate 89e

2. Penguin

The 18 species of the unique *penguin* family (Spheniscidae) are all restricted to the southern hemisphere, with one species in the Galápagos Islands. The largest species stands 1 m (3 ft) tall and the smallest stands only 30 cm (1 ft) tall. All are flightless and use their highly modified wings for propulsion underwater. These wings are unique in that, unlike in other birds, the bones are fused together and the wings cannot be folded. The feathers that cover the penguins' bodies and wings are small and dense, looking more like large scales than proper feathers. Their feet are placed far back on the body, and they have webbing between the toes and long sharp nails. The feet are used for steering and braking underwater and for clambering up steep and slippery slopes when going ashore. Most species are highly social, great numbers of individuals foraging together at sea and breeding in colonies.

The GALÁPAGOS PENGUIN (Plate 90) occurs farther north than any other penguin in the world. Standing only 40 cm (16 in) tall, it is one of the smallest species of penguins. On land, their black and white form and upright stance make them easy to recognize. In the water they lie low on the surface, looking like short-necked ducks. Sometimes they swim with only their heads exposed above the surface. Older chicks can be nearly the size of adults but are gray in color. This species is found only in the western sections of the archipelago, so on short cruises that do not include the northwestern islands of Isabela and Fernandina, your chances of seeing it are slim.

Natural History

Ecology and Behavior
The GALÁPAGOS PENGUIN is not as social as other penguins and normally occurs only in pairs or small groups of five to six. However, during times when the water is colder, 10 to 15 or more individuals gather together, perhaps because food is more concentrated. Their food includes fish, crustaceans and squid, all of which are captured in their strong, sharp bills during underwater pursuit. Their mouths are lined with rear-facing spines that help them hold onto and swallow slippery and wiggling prey. Although some large penguin species in the Antarctic can dive to depths of nearly 275 m (900 ft) and stay under for almost 20 minutes, the Galápagos Penguin seldom stays under for more than two minutes and feeds close to the surface. Parents feed young on shore by regurgitating food caught at sea.

Breeding
Breeding only on Isabela and Fernandina Islands, the GALÁPAGOS PENGUIN is monogamous and may mate for life. It can be found breeding almost any time of year, but usually only if there is an extended period of abundant prey. They lay one or two eggs in burrows in the ground or in protected areas under rocks, but usually only a single young survives. Both parents incubate the eggs and feed the

young for nearly two months, after which it begins to care for itself. Unlike almost all other penguin species, which nest only once a year, Galápagos Penguins can nest up to three times a year, again, depending on food abundance.

Notes
Fossil evidence and comparison of skull bones show that penguins likely evolved from flying albatross-like ancestors. Even today, the most primitive penguin species actually have tubular nostrils, a character otherwise restricted to albatrosses and petrels. The GALÁPAGOS PENGUIN is closely related to the HUMBOLDT and MAGELLANIC PENGUINS of coastal Perú and Chile, and probably arose from individuals of one or the other of these two species that strayed to the Galápagos on the cold Humboldt Current.

Status
The entire population of the GALÁPAGOS PENGUIN is between 2000 and 5000 individuals, and the species is listed as endangered (USA ESA). El Niño-induced changes in water temperature can drastically affect fish and squid populations which in turn directly affect penguin survival and chances for reproduction. Any time you are dealing with such a small population in a small area, major changes in the habitat, whether natural, caused by humans, or a deadly combination of both, create a potential for exterminating the species in a short time.

Profile
Galápagos Penguin, *Spheniscus mendiculus*, Plate 90a

3. Tubenose Birds

This order of *seabirds* (Procellariiformes) includes the *shearwaters, storm-petrels* and *albatrosses*. All of them are found only in *marine* (sea water) habitats, and they spend their entire lives at sea except for short periods of nesting on islands. They have peculiar tube-shaped nostrils and distinctly hooked upper bills. Like many seabirds, they have a large gland between and above their eyes, which permits them to drink seawater; it filters salt from the water and concentrates it. This highly concentrated salt solution is excreted in drops from the base of the bill and the nostril tubes direct the salt to the end of the bill where the drops can be easily discharged. In the Galápagos, species of the families of storm-petrels (Hydrobatidae) and albatrosses (Diomedeidae) are the tubenoses most frequently seen by eco-travellers. The WAVED, or GALÁPAGOS, ALBATROSS (Plate 90) is the largest bird in the Galápagos, with a wingspan of more than 2 m (6.5 ft). On the ground on the island of Española, where it breeds almost exclusively (a few pairs also breed on Isla de la Plata just off the coast of mainland Ecuador), it looks like a cross between a huge turkey and a gull. It is absent from the breeding colonies only from January to March, when it disperses far out into the Pacific Ocean. At sea in flight its straight, long and narrow wings are distinctive. At the other end of the size spectrum of tubenoses, the WHITE-VENTED STORM-PETREL (Plate 90) is only 15 cm (6 in) long.

Natural History

Ecology and Behavior
Members of the tubenoses have perhaps the best developed sense of smell of any birds, and they use this ability to locate young and nest sites when returning from

extended foraging trips. Tubenoses produce a vile-smelling stomach oil that they regurgitate and squirt at enemies. This oil makes an excellent sun tan lotion but wreaks havoc on your clothes and social life. Albatrosses use a type of flight that takes advantage of strong winds blowing across the ocean's surface. Their efficient but peculiar soaring flight takes them in huge loops from high above the ocean surface where the wind is fastest, down toward the surface, where friction slows the wind, and then up into the faster wind again to give them lift for the next loop – a kind of roller coaster flight that requires virtually no wing flapping. The storm-petrels, on the other hand, have a fluttering flight low over the water's surface that sometimes brings their long hanging legs in contact with the water, making it look like they are walking on water. Albatrosses feed on squid near the surface at night. Also, during both day and night, they eat fish and invertebrates near the surface, and they are not above eating garbage thrown overboard from ships, as well as floating carrion such as dead whales and seals. They often go out to sea for several days to bring food back to nestlings. Storm-petrels delicately pluck invertebrates and other prey items from the surface of the sea using their wings to flutter and hover just above the water. Most species feed during the day far out at sea and return to their nesting islands at night. In the Galápagos, however, the WEDGE-RUMPED STORM-PETREL (Plate 90) does just the opposite, and can be seen in large swarms during the day over its nesting islands. The other species of storm-petrels come to their nesting burrows only at night, and are more commonly seen feeding in the open ocean during the daytime.

Breeding

Albatrosses are monogamous and most breed with one mate for life. On the breeding islands, they have elaborate courtship dances in which, face to face, the wings are flicked, head and neck bounce up and down, and bills are clacked together like some dancing-fencing tournament. This behavior helps strengthen the pair-bond but it also coordinates hormone release and synchronizes mating readiness. The female lays one large egg in a scraping on the bare ground; incubation and brooding young is alternated with the male, each shift lasting several days to weeks. The other adult flies out to sea and searches for food. When it returns, it feeds the chick regurgitated food and stomach oil and takes over brooding again. When the chick's demand for food becomes overwhelming, both adults leave it alone for long periods as they search great distances over the ocean for enough food. After about 7 months, the chick is large enough to fledge and fly. Albatross take 5 to 7 years to mature and stay at sea this whole time before finally returning to their birth place to breed. Storm-petrels also lay a single egg, which is incubated by both mates. The nest is hidden in a tunnel or deep in a crevice of rocks and lava. Both parents regurgitate food – small fish, crustaceans and squid – to the young. In the Galápagos, SHORT-EARED OWLS often cruise the breeding areas of these storm-petrels to capture adults and chicks from burrows that are too shallow.

Notes

Like the WAVED ALBATROSS, most albatross species nest on only one or a few islands, and their survival can be precarious. In the case of the SHORT-TAILED ALBATROSS, the long wandering phase of the fledglings saved the species. Intense hunting, volcanic activity and a mid-20th century world war virtually wiped out the nesting population of this species on its single breeding island southeast of Japan. But a reservoir of younger individuals was at sea, and by the time they returned to the nesting island, the war was finished and the island was a preserve. The population is growing slowly now. Storm-petrels get their name from the Greek word *"petros,"* which refers to the biblical disciple Peter, who tried to walk on water, just like storm-petrels appear to be doing when feeding.

Status

Because of their often highly restricted nesting sites on small islands and vulnerability during the nesting period, many species of tubenoses are at risk. Albatrosses cannot become airborne readily from land and are easy victims for humans and introduced predators. Cats and rats, if carelessly released by humans, can wreak havoc on an entire island's population of storm-petrels.

Profiles

Waved Albatross, *Diomedea irrorata*, Plate 90b
White-vented Storm-petrel, *Oceanites gracilis*, Plate 90d
Wedge-rumped Storm-petrel, *Oceanodroma tethys*, Plate 90e

4. Galápagos Hawk

A general overview of hawks is available in the mainland section (p. 112), but the endemic GALÁPAGOS HAWK (Plate 90) is so special that it deserves additional details. As the only hawk in the islands, it is difficult to confuse with any other species. The only other regular predatory birds in the Galápagos, the SHORT-EARED OWL and the BARN OWL, have flat owl faces and look quite different. The hawk occurs on almost all the larger islands (except Genovesa and Floreana). It is extremely tame and easy to see as it perches low on a rock or tree snag or higher in the branches of live trees. It appears often to be curious and frequently will approach humans or follow them at a close distance. The hawk feeds on a wide variety of prey, from large insects to lizards and small birds, but it also scavenges dead carcasses. One of the most peculiar features of this bird, however, is its mating behavior. Like most other hawks of its size it makes a respectable nest of sticks, usually in a tree, but it is *polyandrous* – one female mates with up to four males. All the males help defend the territory, even during the nonbreeding season. The female does most of the incubating, but the males help with care and feeding of the young. This species is thought to have evolved from some individuals of the closely related SWAINSON'S HAWK, a migratory species that nests in northwestern North America and winters in northern Argentina. Individuals may have been blown west off their normal migratory course along the length of Central America to colonize the Galápagos.

Profiles

Galápagos Hawk, *Buteo galapagoensis*, Plate 90c

5. Pelicans and Allies

The *frigatebirds, pelicans, tropicbirds, boobies* and *cormorants* are all distinct families in the Order Pelecaniformes with representatives in the Galápagos. Except for the tropicbirds we have already covered these families in the mainland section (p. 93). The tropicbirds belong to the Family Phaethontidae, and all three species are restricted to tropical and subtropical oceans. They look like large, long-tailed terns. They plunge-dive into the ocean to catch fish and squid just below the surface. Their webbed feet and legs are very short, so when on land, they can hardly walk. Only one species, the RED-BILLED TROPICBIRD (Plate 90), is found in the Galápagos, where it nests year round. Their mating flights are spectacular, as courting pairs fly gracefully and noisily overhead, wheeling and diving. The nest is under a rock overhang or in a shallow but protected cavity or, in colonies, often on a cliff face. Both adults help guard and incubate the single egg and then feed the young regurgitated squid and fish. Unlike all other members of this order, tropicbird chicks are fully feathered when they hatch out of their eggs. Also unique among the group, the tropicbird chick does not bury its head down the throat and gullet of the adult during feeding, but instead, more daintily takes food from the parent's bill.

In addition to the BLUE-FOOTED BOOBY (Plates 14, 91), the MASKED BOOBY (Plate 91) and RED-FOOTED BOOBY (Plate 91) are common residents of the Galápagos. The two larger species, Blue-footed and Masked, are found on almost all the islands, where they nest in loose colonies on the ground. Unlike the Masked Booby, which nests on cliff edges, the Blue-footed Booby nests in flat, open areas and is thus the booby species you will most likely have a chance to watch. Its courting behavior is nothing less than spectacular as it "goose-steps" with its bright blue feet flashing like neon paddles. With tails raised, wings crooked, and bills straight up in the air, you have to admire the lengths these birds go to advertise their readiness to mate and then later to intensify their commitment to each other and to raising young together. The demands for food and care by the young are so much that neither adult alone can find enough food to feed them. The female is larger, has a bigger black pupil in the eye and honks like a goose. The male gives a screeching whistle that only another Blue-footed Booby could find attractive. Both parents incubate the one to three eggs for about 40 days. During this period, their defecation is squirted as they sit there and eventually forms a white ring about a meter and a half (5 ft) across around the nest scraped in the ground. The ring is also about as far as the booby sitting on the nest can reach with its bill to defend the site against other, nearby boobies, and thus defines its nesting territory. This area is the limit within which the young must remain when both parents are away from the nest searching for fish. Wandering young are likely to be skewered on the sharp bill of neighboring adults. The other booby species also have complex, if not so colorful, reproductive behavior. The Red-footed Booby makes a stick nest off the ground in bushes and low trees and lays only a single egg. They nest only on the islands where the GALÁPAGOS HAWK, a frequent predator on chicks, is absent. Most ecotravellers to the Galápagos will see this booby if they are visiting Genovesa Island. The Red-footed Booby comes in dark and white phases, but in the Galápagos over 90% of all individuals are the dark phase.

The BROWN PELICAN (Plate 14) is common throughout the Galápagos, as is the MAGNIFICENT FRIGATEBIRD (Plate 14). However, an additional species of frigatebird, the GREAT FRIGATEBIRD, nests on Genovesa and San Cristóbal Islands. It has a greenish sheen across the back while the Magnificent Frigatebird has a purplish sheen. The two species nest together in a mixed colony on North Seymour Island.

The only cormorant in the islands is the endemic FLIGHTLESS CORMORANT (Plate 91), found on Fernandina and the west coast of Isabela. Its dark brown color, bright turquoise eyes and stubby wings are unmistakable. It usually swims with only its head and neck out of the water, and it dives with a small leap from the surface to pursue bottom-living prey such as octopus. Like all other cormorants, but unlike the penguins, it uses its large and powerful feet for propulsion underwater. This species is monogamous, and after an intricate courtship dance on the water's surface, mates build a large nest on a rock near the beach. Two or three eggs are deposited in the seaweed nest, and incubation is shared by the mates for the next month. After fledging, the male alone continues to feed the young for another 6 to 7 months. The entire population of this species is made up of about 1200 individuals. As with any small, concentrated population, predation, pollution and other disturbances could have drastic effects on its survival.

Profiles

Red-billed Tropicbird, *Phaethon aethereus*, Plate 90f
Masked Booby, *Sula dactylatra*, Plate 91a
Red-footed Booby, *Sula sula*, Plate 91b
Blue-footed Booby, *Sula nebouxii*, Plate 91c
Flightless Cormorant, *Nannopterum harrisi*, Plate 91d

6. Gulls and Wading Birds

These groups of birds include families that have been detailed in the mainland portion of the text (pp. 96, 98). Here we highlight some species found near or on the water and that are either unique to the Galápagos or that you are more likely to see here than on the mainland. Among the common Galápagos herons and egrets, the GREAT EGRET (Plate 16), CATTLE EGRET (Plate 16) and a slaty gray form of the GREEN-BACKED HERON (Plate 17), sometimes considered a separate species called the LAVA HERON, are mainland species already profiled. The GREAT BLUE HERON apparently arrived on the archipelago from Central America or extreme northwestern Ecuador, where it is rare. It is similar in size and shape to the mainland COCOI HERON (Plate 17), but has a darker neck. The YELLOW-CROWNED NIGHT HERON (Plate 92) on the mainland is a shy and difficult-to-see bird of the coastal mangroves that is active only at night. But in the Galápagos, it is bold and active both day and night in open areas such as rocky coasts as well as in mangroves. It feeds mainly on crabs and insects.

The only flamingo on the islands is the GREATER FLAMINGO (Plate 92). A small population of about 500 individuals maintains a relatively tenuous presence in the saltwater lagoons of Floreana, Santa Cruz, Isabela and a few smaller islands. It is not known from mainland Ecuador and is evidently a relatively recent arrival from the Caribbean via Central America. Its nesting and feeding behavior and its colonial habits, are similar to that of other flamingo species (p. 95).

Numerous species of sandpipers and plovers (p. 104) pass through or winter on the Galápagos, but two obvious species are resident nesters. The tall and thin BLACK-NECKED STILT (Plate 20) is a regular in the saltwater lagoons throughout the archipelago, and it is also common on the mainland (p. 105). The AMERICAN OYSTERCATCHER (Plate 92) is also common on the coast of the mainland sandy beaches, but it is much more difficult to see there than on the rocky and sandy shores as well as saltwater lagoons of the Galápagos. Its bright red bill is flattened from the sides and used like a shucking knife to open clams and other mollusks. Its black and white plumage together with bold behavior make it easy to approach and identify.

Two species of gulls (p. 96) are unique or nearly unique to the Galápagos Islands. The dark gray LAVA GULL (Plate 92) occurs only in the bays and salt water lagoons of Santa Cruz, San Cristóbal and Isabela, where it nests in small and loose colonies. It scavenges dead organisms from the water, raids nestlings and eggs from seabird colonies, and eats freshly hatched lizards and turtles. With a total population of fewer than 1000 individuals, this may be the rarest gull on Earth. The attractive SWALLOW-TAILED GULL (Plate 92) is the only gull in the world that feeds completely at night. It catches fish and squid from the surface of the ocean 20 to 50 km (32 to 80 miles) from the nearest land, and it has many modifications for its nocturnal existence including night-adapted eyes. It nests in colonies on cliff faces, and unlike all other gulls, which lay two or three eggs, it lays only one egg. Its population of 25,000 breeds on all the Galápagos Islands except Fernandina and the west coast of Isabela. A small population of a few hundred individuals also breeds on a tiny island off the coast of Colombia.

Profiles

Yellow-crowned Night Heron, *Nyctanassa violacea*, Plate 92a
Greater Flamingo, *Phoenicopterus ruber*, Plate 92b
Swallow-tailed Gull, *Larus furcatus*, Plate 92c
Lava Gull, *Larus fuliginosus*, Plate 92d
American Oystercatcher, *Haematopus palliatus*, Plate 92e

7. Land Birds

Only about 25 species of land birds regularly occur on the Galápagos. Besides the Darwin's Finches (see the next section), the ones you are most likely to see and identify are: the GALÁPAGOS DOVE (Plate 93), which is a small (20 cm, 8 in) dove (p. 116) common in drier portions of all the major islands except Isabela. It nests on the ground or in abandoned nests of other similar-sized species and lays two eggs. It feeds on seeds and fruits, including those of cactus. Two flycatchers (p. 150) are common. The VERMILION FLYCATCHER (Plate 93), which is also common on the mainland of Ecuador, occurs in the highlands of most of the islands; the male's bright red and black plumage is unmistakable. The LARGE-BILLED or GALÁPAGOS FLYCATCHER (Plate 93) is a drabber flycatcher endemic to the Galápagos. It nests on all the islands except Genovesa, Darwin and Wolf and tends to be more restricted to drier lowland areas. The GALÁPAGOS MOCK-INGBIRD (Plate 93) is the most widespread of the four endemic mockingbird species found in the archipelago. These species are all very similar, separated by minor differences in size, eye color, and gray to brown body color. The young in nests are raised cooperatively by a group of helpers (usually close relatives) together with the parents. They feed on almost any kind of plant or animal material, and some populations are adept at plucking ticks from the skin of live iguanas. Unlike North American mockingbirds, none of the mockingbirds in the Galápagos is known to mimic the vocalizations of other species or foreign sounds. Because they are so bold and inquisitive, and not above a bit of larceny, you will have to guard your food and water with great diligence while hiking on islands where there are mockingbirds – they will steal you blind if you don't watch out. The YELLOW WARBLER (Plate 93) is one of the most widespread of all land bird species here, occurring on all islands, from shoreline to the tops of the highest mountains. It feeds mainly on small insects that it catches by gleaning them from the underside of leaves or by flycatching in the air. This is a distinct subpopulation of the same species that nests in the mangroves of the coast of mainland Ecuador and throughout North America.

Profiles

Galápagos Dove, *Zenaida galapagoensis*, Plate 93a
Vermilion Flycatcher, *Pyrocephalus rubinus*, Plate 93b
Large-billed Flycatcher, *Myiarchus magnirostris*, Plate 93c
Galápagos Mockingbird, *Nesomimus parvulus*, Plate 93d
Yellow Warbler, *Dendroica petechia*, Plate 93e

8. Darwin's Finches

Darwin's finches, drab black, brown and mottled birds, are initially rather unimpressive. Females and immatures tend to be lighter brown with more streaking and spotting than the darker males. There are 14 species, all of which except one are confined to the Galápagos (one occurs only on Cocos Island, 650 km, 400 miles, northeast toward Costa Rica and Panamá). When Darwin visited these islands, he also had a first impression of these birds being rather ordinary – he didn't even recognize them as finches until he returned to England and showed the preserved specimens to ornithologists. His second impression, however, helped blow the lid off the mystery of evolution. That small reassessment is probably the type of insight that separates most of us from genius. There is no way someone without a lot of insight and intelligence could have perceived such an important pattern from such a dull group of birds.

The array of bill sizes and shapes is especially important in understanding the natural history of these birds as well as how they helped formalize the theory of evolution (see Close-up, p. 246). Apparently, all of these species and bill shapes evolved from a single colonizing species from the mainland, perhaps the BLUE-BLACK GRASSQUIT (Plate 69), which is common in coastal areas of Central and South America. From the thin, insect-catching bill of the WARBLER FINCH (Plate 94) to the massive, seed-crushing bills of the LARGE GROUND FINCH (Plate 94) and the LARGE CACTUS FINCH, you begin to see how exciting these birds really are. On Genovesa, the SHARP-BEAKED GROUND FINCH (Plate 94) not only uses its bill to feed on fruits, insects and flower parts, but it also picks ticks off boobies and even makes puncture wounds at the base of boobies' tails to drink the blood that oozes out. The SMALL GROUND FINCH (Plate 94) has an intermediate bill size and shape that permits it to eat a wider variety of food types than any other of the Darwin's Finches. It also eats ticks off MARINE (Plate 89) and GALÁPAGOS LAND IGUANAS (Plate 89) (on some islands but not on others). The WOOD-PECKER FINCH (Plate 94) is one of two species of these finches that uses a tool to catch food. Preferring the highlands of several islands, it breaks off and shapes cactus spines or small twigs, which it then holds in its bill to probe for grubs and insects in tree holes or under rocks. The similar MANGROVE FINCH also uses a twig as a tool to extract insects, but this species is limited to coastal mangroves on the west side of Isabela. It is now extinct on Fernandina, and by some estimates no more than 300 individuals remain on Isabela. Human cutting of mangroves for fuel and the introduction of a mainland predatory wasp that competes for insects in this same habitat are probably the cause of this species' decline. All the other species of finches appear to be stable and, although several of them are vulnerable and have disappeared from parts of their former ranges, they are not considered endangered.

Profiles

Warbler Finch, *Certhidia olivacea*, Plate 94a
Woodpecker Finch, *Cactospiza pallida*, Plate 94b
Small Ground Finch, *Geospiza fuliginosa*, Plate 94c
Large Ground Finch, *Geospiza magnirostris*, Plate 94d
Sharp-beaked Ground Finch, *Geospiza difficilis*, Plate 94e

9. Seals

Seals are familiar marine mammals with hind and fore legs modified as flippers and noses adapted to balance large beach balls. The seals can be divided into three families: the *true* or *earless seals* (Family Phocidae), the *walrus* (Family Odobenidae), and the *eared seals* (Family Otariidae), all contained within the Order Pinnipedia. Most seal species are found in the Arctic and Antarctic areas, but two species, both *eared seals*, call the Galápagos home. Unlike the true seals, which have ears that are simply holes on each side of the head, and front legs that are held to their sides as the hind flippers propel them through the water, the eared seals have small external ears and powerful front flippers that are used to help with propulsion during swimming. The eared seals are in turn divided into two groups: *fur seals* (eight species worldwide), with dense, soft underfur, and *sea lions* (five species worldwide), with coarse hair.

The seal you will see most often in the Galápagos (and rarely on the mainland coast) is the GALÁPAGOS SEA LION (Plate 95). It is considered a smaller-sized sub-species of the CALIFORNIA SEA LION, and undoubtedly originated from stray individuals finding their way to the archipelago from the west coast of Mexico. You can tell the males from the females by their much larger size (up to 1.8 m, 6 ft, long) and also by the distinctively raised forehead "bump" and the thick neck, both of which are lacking in the more streamlined females. The much smaller GALÁPAGOS FUR SEAL (Plate 95) (males are up to 1.4 m, 4.5 ft, long) is related to the SOUTHERN FUR SEAL of coastal South America, but is considered a separate species. It is easy to confuse it with the sea lion, but its smaller size, shorter and more pointed nose, thicker fur and lower, softer voice (not the typical yelping and barking of the sea lion) distinguish it with a little study.

Natural History

Ecology and Behavior

Although considered marine mammals, seals spend a considerable proportion of their lives hauled ashore, usually for breeding and resting. They feed underwater by pursuing fish, squid and other invertebrates. The sea lion feeds largely during the day, but the fur seal feeds mainly at night. Each adult male defends a patch of beach as his territory and mates with females that come to visit him. Male sea lions tend to defend their territory against other males in the shallow water at the edge of the beach, usually sandy areas or gently sloping rocky areas. The fur seal, on the other hand, defends and fights on the beach itself, usually on gently sloping rocky stretches of the coast. Because there are always more males than territories to defend, a large proportion of the males of both species are left as bachelors without a territory and so without females to mate with. These unattached males form *bachelor herds* that spend time together hauled out on more inaccessible beaches and cruising the territorial males' beaches waiting for a lucky break. The dominant males defending territories are constantly challenged by more daring members of the bachelor herd, and this leaves the male with a territory virtually no time to feed or rest. Eventually he becomes worn down to the point of exhaustion, and some lucky bachelor inherits a territory, with its perks and problems, until he in turn is replaced by a fresher bachelor. The older pups gather together in groups, or *crèches* (nurseries), while the mothers go out to feed. Usually one female serves as a baby-sitter for the congregated pups.

Breeding
Male and female seals become sexually mature at about 4 to 5 years old. Females often live to be 15+ but males, because of their stressful lifestyle, rarely live that long. Pregnant females of both species cruise the various male territories, then choose the best territory (and the male that goes along with it) on which to give birth to a single pup. Less than a month after giving birth, the female becomes sexually receptive and mates with the male. Even though her gestation period is nine months, she will not give birth again until a year later. This three-month extension is due to delayed implantation of the fertilized egg onto the lining of her uterus (the same as for bears and some bats). The female suckles each pup for up to 2 or 3 years, and frequently you will see pups of obviously different years and sizes all suckling from the same mother.

Notes
You may have read about or even seen photos of tourists swimming with the Galápagos seals. Although laws now prohibit this kind of close approach, often the naturally curious seals approach swimming tourists. The law was made to protect seals, but also tourists: male seals, especially among sea lions, can be aggressive and their teeth are sharp; swimmers should stay away from active colonies with loud, territorial males.

Status
Because of their extremely fine, thick pelts, most species of fur seals were nearly wiped out by hunters in the 19th and early part of the 20th century. Only through a decline in the fur market and draconian conservation efforts were they saved. The Galápagos Fur Seal is CITES Appendix II listed.

Profiles
Galápagos Sea Lion, *Zalophus californianus wollebaeki*, Plate 95a
Galápagos Fur Seal, *Arctocephalus galapagoensis*, Plate 95b

10. Whales and Marine Dolphins

All *dolphins, porpoises* and *whales* belong to the Order Cetacea, and all but a few freshwater forms (see p. 200) are restricted to the *marine* environment (sea water). They never leave the water and generally come to the surface only to breathe. Their hind legs have been lost through evolution and their forelegs modified into paddle-like flippers. Their tails have become broad and flattened into what are called *flukes*. A single or double nostril, called a *blowhole*, is on top of the head. Up to a third of an individual's weight consists of a thick layer of fat (*blubber*) lying under the hairless skin. Although cetacean eyes are relatively small, hearing is well developed. Cetaceans are often divided into two broad categories, *baleen* and *toothed whales*. The baleen group consists of large whale species that have mouths that look like immense radiator grills, filled with long, vertical, brownish strands of baleen, or whalebone. The largest mammal, and probably the largest animal ever, the BLUE WHALE, is a member of this group. It reaches 30+ m (100 ft) in length and 150 tons in weight, but it is only rarely seen in the archipelago. The other group, which includes a few large whales and all the porpoises and dolphins, have mouths with short, sharp teeth instead of baleen.

In the Galápagos the baleen whales are represented most frequently by the large HUMPBACK WHALE (14.6 m, 48 ft, long) (Plate 96) and the medium-sized MINKE or PIKED WHALE (8 m, 26 ft, long) (Plate 96). The front flippers of the Humpback Whale are huge, white and wing-like. They usually equal a third of the whale's total body length. The dorsal fin is small and often shark-like. It is placed two-thirds of the way back on the body and mounted on a fleshy pedestal, a character that distinguishes it from all other baleen whales. When an individual initiates a deep dive (*sounds*), its scalloped flukes come well up off the water's surface to expose the underside of the flukes, which are variably mottled white and black (a character so variable and personalized that scientists use it to recognize and track the movements of individuals). The Minke Whale, besides being considerably smaller, is less streamlined than its relatives. It has a sharply pointed nose that is almost triangular. Most distinctive of all, however, is a bright white patch or band across the upper surface of each flipper. The flipper itself is relatively short and is only about 10% of the body length. Minke Whales are often attracted to boats and approach so close that more than one observer bending down over the bow to get a better look has received a cloud of damp, fish-smelling whale breath in the face. When sounding, the Minke rarely shows its flukes.

Among the toothed whales, there are four species that you are most likely to see around the Galápagos. The SPERM WHALE (Plate 96) is large (up to 20 m, 65 ft, long) and for anyone of the generation that was exposed to whales through reading *Moby Dick*, the species that first comes to mind. The squarish head forms more than one-third of its total weight, and there is a bump on the whale's back but no distinctive dorsal fin. Unlike the other members of this group, which have teeth on both upper and lower jaws, Sperm Whales only have teeth on the lower jaw. The flippers are short and stubby, but the flukes are large and prominent with a central notch. When sounding, the flukes are raised completely out of the water, but unlike in the Humpback, they are entirely dark below and without scalloping. From as great a distance as you can see the blow of water vapor from its blowhole, this species is distinctive. Its blowhole is situated forward and to the left, producing a spout unlike any other whale as it shoots forward and off to the left. The ORCA or KILLER WHALE (Plate 96) is the first whale that comes to mind for anyone in the generation that was first exposed to whales at theme parks and in the movies. It occurs in all oceans of the world, and males average 8 m (26 ft) in length. Their distinctive black and white coloring, heavy body, blunt round head and tall dorsal fin (almost 2 m, 6.5 ft, high in males) make them unmistakable. If all else fails, look for the white patch in back of the eye, as it is diagnostic. The SHORTFIN PILOT WHALE (Plate 96) occurs only in tropical and subtropical oceans of the world. It is relatively small, with males averaging 5.5 m (18 ft) in length, shiny black, with a prominent curved dorsal fin. It travels in groups, or *pods*, of 10 to 100 and usually ignores passing vessels.

In the same group as the toothed whales are the dolphins and porpoises. Two species, both of which occur worldwide in virtually all tropical and temperate seas, are seen regularly in the Galápagos on cruises between islands. The COMMON DOLPHIN (Plate 95) averages 2 m (6.5 ft) in length. You will usually see it in large groups across an expanse of the ocean's surface, leaping and rolling out of the water with breathtaking ease. They readily approach vessels to ride the bow pressure wave and may persist hitchhiking for 20 minutes or more. If you are close, the yellow patch on the side is obvious. The other commonly seen species here is the BOTTLENOSE DOLPHIN (Plate 95), the "Flipper" of TV and the movies. It averages 3 m (10 ft) in length and is uniformly light gray in color. It usually occurs in small groups and has a relatively long and prominent dorsal fin. This species also readily uses the pressure wave of a moving boat to take a free ride.

Natural History

Ecology and Behavior

Both MINKE and HUMPBACK WHALES migrate to feed in polar waters and return to equatorial waters to breed. Calves have no blubber and must remain in warmer waters until they have fed sufficiently to put on a layer of the fatty insulation for the cold polar waters. Minkes tend to be alone or in pairs, but Humpbacks are regularly found in family groups of three or four. Baleen whales, which are so large they can only be measured in tons and tens of meters, paradoxically feed mainly on planktonic crustaceans, small shrimp-like animals barely 5 to 10 cm (2 to 4 in) long. They swim through the food-rich layers of water, especially in polar regions, with their mouths wide open. Then they close their mouths and use their immense tongues (some weighing 4 tons) to push the water out through their 300-plus baleen plates, straining the small shrimp which stay in the mouth and are then swallowed in a monumental gulp. In tropical waters, both the Minke and Humpback Whales feed commonly on fish and squid using a similar method of feeding. The Humpback, however, has developed a special and spectacular modification for feeding on fish. Once a school of fish is located, the whale swims under and around the fish all the while releasing a stream of bubbles. This bubble stream serves as a *bubble net* that frightens and concentrates the fish and forces them to rise as the bubbles rise. The whale then dives and turns to swim vertically up through the bubble net, its wide-open mouth closing only as it reaches the surface to entrap and swallow large numbers of fish. If you are in an area where the humpbacks are using this method, just watch for the air bubbles to break the surface and the whale will soon rise at that very point, mouth first and several meters out of the water. Seabirds quickly learn about this behavior and many will concentrate to wait at the rising bubbles to catch escaping fish.

Humpback Whales also produce some of the most complex and fascinating songs of any animal in the world. Each geographical group has its own song, or *dialect*, that all the individuals there copy and use, but the song changes from year to year. By choosing the right layer of water by depth and temperature, the whale can have these songs travel hundreds of kilometers. Communication and social interactions across such large stretches of ocean give whole new meanings to territoriality, mate attraction and group behavior. Humpbacks also frequently jump completely out of the water, or *breach*, usually in an arching back flip. This behavior may be associated with mate attraction and courtship or it may be to knock off parasitic barnacles growing on the whales' skin.

SPERM WHALES feed on fish, lobsters and sharks, but most of all they feed on squid. An adult can eat up to a ton of squid a day. These whales regularly dive to depths of 1000 m (3300 ft) and individuals have been recorded descending to

2250 m (7400 ft). They use a sonar system at these dark depths to locate prey, and they can stay down for 45 minutes and descend at a speed of 8 kph (5 mph). Many individuals have scars produced by suckers on the tentacles of giant squid. By measuring the diameter of the sucker marks and extrapolating the body length, researchers have determined that some of these squid may be up to 45 m (150 ft) long (making you wonder if the whale in these interactions is the predator or the prey). Adult male and female Sperm Whales lead such different lives that it's amazing they ever get together. During June to September males leave tropical waters and live at the edge of the pack ice in polar regions, often in large bachelor groups. Females and young seldom get any farther than New Zealand or Hawaii. In November to February all individuals concentrate in tropical waters, and the biggest males (usually those over 25 years old) fight violently to gather harems of up to 25 females. Males can be very aggressive toward ships and people if provoked. Nursing females and their calves also form groups called *nursery schools*. These groups have been seen swimming in a circle to protect calves from predatory ORCA WHALES. Orcas normally travel in extended family groups of five to 20 members. When hunting their prey of squid, fish, sharks, seals, sea birds, polar bears, porpoises and other whales, the pod hunts cooperatively, much like a wolf-pack. There is no authenticated record, however, of Orcas attacking humans without provocation. This species produces a low-frequency sound unlike any other toothed whale or dolphin, likely used for echolocation. The SHORTFIN PILOT WHALE feeds mainly at night on squid. During the day these whales often float on the surface, bobbing with their heads up or lying on their backs, evidently sleeping. When disturbed they will investigate by *spyhopping*, rising vertically and extending their head high up out of the water. They are often found together with dolphins. This species is extremely vocal, and even from above the water you can hear the staccato popping noises of a passing pod. If you get the chance, put your ear against the inside of a boat's hull and listen for the higher pitched and bird-like twitters this species also produces. These sounds may help coordinate the pod, as well as serve as echolocation for hunting prey.

The COMMON DOLPHIN feeds at depths of 40 to 280 m (132 to 920 ft) below the surface on lantern fish and squid. It uses echolocation in dark and turbid water to locate prey. It also feeds at the surface on sardines, and occasionally will leap out of the water in pursuit of a flying fish. The large groups in which they travel usually have a hierarchy of leaders that direct movements and activities. The BOTTLENOSE DOLPHIN matures at 6 years and lives to be 25 years old. It feeds to depths of 600 m (2000 ft) and eats a broad range of prey, from bottom-dwelling fish, eels, sharks, rays, and hermit crabs to tuna. They have even learned to follow trawlers and shrimp boats to feed on the fish stirred up or discarded from nets. They produce clicks, pops and rasping sounds, sometimes at frequencies of 1000 per second, that function in echolocation of prey. The small groups in which this species travels often hunt cooperatively and defend themselves as a unit against enemies such as large sharks.

Breeding

MINKE WHALES live about 50 years and become sexually mature at 6 years old. The gestation period is 10 months and calves nurse for an additional 6 months. HUMPBACK WHALES reach sexual maturity at 9 to 10 years. Courtship is in shallow waters near the equator and involves a lot of splashing, churning and breaching. If you see a male breaching in courtship, watch for its sexual organ – often more than 2 m (6.5 ft) long and referred to as "Pink Floyd" by tour boat operators. Gestation is about a year and calves nurse for an additional year. A single male SPERM WHALE controls a harem of 20 or so females, but only a few are ready to mate in any one year. Gestation lasts 14 to 16 months, and the young whale suckles the mother's milk for another year or two. A single female may bear a young only once every 4 years. Several females serve as midwives and help after birth to nudge the calf to the surface. Little is known of the breeding behavior of ORCAS, but gestation is 12 months. The courtship of SHORTFIN PILOT WHALES, however, has been observed many times. It usually begins with loud head-butting underwater and then proceeds quickly to copulation. Gestation is 15 months, and the calf may be in the care of its mother for up to two years. COMMON DOLPHINS mate about 10 m (33 ft) under water and have a gestation period of 10 months. The young calf usually stays with its mother for about 16 months. BOTTLENOSE DOLPHINS mate near the surface, and their courtship involves elaborate stroking, nuzzling and posturing. Gestation lasts 12 months and the birth is often attended by several female "midwives." The calf accompanies its mother for about 2 years.

Notes
The whales of the Galápagos, especially concentrations of SPERM WHALES, attracted whalers in prodigious numbers throughout the 1800s. The American fleet alone in 1830 was made up of 729 ships. Whales were killed by the thousands for the thin, transparent oil they store in a reservoir in the forward part of their heads. This oil was used for lighting lamps. Sperm Whales also produce *ambergris*, a black and terrible-smelling residue found in the intestines, which was used in making expensive perfumes.

Status
As late as 1963, more than 30,000 SPERM WHALES were killed worldwide in a single year. However, this species has been slowly recovering ever since international controls and sanctions were placed on whaling. Populations of other species such as GRAY and MINKE WHALES also seem to have rebounded quickly with protection, but now the large numbers of Minke Whales are being used by whaling countries as an excuse to resume hunting. Part of the Minke's recovery, however, seems to be due to release from competition with BLUE WHALES, which have largely disappeared from much of their former range. Sadly for some species like the Blue Whale, the BOWHEAD WHALE and the GREAT RIGHT WHALE, over-hunting so reduced their numbers that they may never recover. Only a few countries like Japan, Norway and Iceland continue to hunt whales, but they also relentlessly pressure others to rescind or get around international laws. Subsistence hunting native peoples in the Arctic are also allowed permits to hunt whales. All cetaceans are CITES Appendix I or Appendix II listed.

Profiles
Common Dolphin, *Delphinus delphis*, Plate 95c
Bottlenose Dolphin, *Tursiops truncatus*, Plate 95d
Sperm Whale, *Physeter macrocephalus*, Plate 96a
Orca Whale, *Orcinus orca*, Plate 96d
Minke Whale, *Balaenoptera acutorostrata*, Plate 96b
Humpback Whale, *Megaptera novaengliae*, Plate 96c
Shortfin Pilot Whale, *Globicephala macrorhynchus*, Plate 96e

Environmental Close-up 4:
Darwin and the Theory of Evolution

Ecuador's Galápagos Islands are inextricably linked with the theory of evolution. In 1835, Charles Darwin spent five weeks exploring this archipelago and studying its peculiar animals and plants as a naturalist on board the HMS *Beagle*. When he left the Galápagos, he was impressed by the strange organisms on these islands, but he was then unaware of the significance of these creatures for evolutionary theory. He had even misidentified many of his specimens and put the wrong locality labels on others – after all, he initially assumed, the species had to be the same on all the islands, so why keep track of which island each specimen came from? Not until he returned to England did Darwin begin to have an inkling of just what he had seen on his trip – evidence for changes in animal and plant species over time. The thought of evolutionary change was an anathema to Darwin's culture, and he spent the next several decades honing his ideas as well as finding the courage to present such a heretical theory to colleagues and the public.

The importance of his Galápagos specimens became apparent to Darwin upon his return to England when ornithologists showed him that the small finch-like birds he had collected were not all the same. They represented numerous species, and they and other species from the islands appeared to be related to mainland forms. He then realized that each island had its own unique set of plants and animals but also that the island populations were all obviously closely related. How could these closely related species have become differentiated, presumably from a mainland ancestor species? In 1839 Darwin started the first of his notebooks and began to gather evidence for the creation of new species from ancestral ones. Darwin filled several notebooks with his thoughts and theories on what he called "descent with modification," but initially did not publish or even tell anyone of his ideas on this subject. Even after he did extensive studies of earthworms, barnacles, and selective breeding of racing pigeons, he still shared his earth-shattering theory with few others. Not until 1859, and then only when another naturalist, Alfred Russel Wallace, wrote him details about his independently discovered ideas of biological change over time, did Darwin write his now-famous book *On the Origin of Species*.

Although Darwin quickly convinced most biologists of his time of the importance of evolution, the primary mechanism driving evolution, *natural selection*, was not understood or appreciated until the 1930s. With this understanding, the full significance and power of his theory of evolution through natural selection began to be realized by the scientific community. This theory is the only unifying theory for all of biology and has guided studies from molecular biology and medicine to forestry management and conservation. Evolution and natural selection, however, are not the same thing. Evolution is *a change over time in the percent of the individuals of a species or population that share a certain character* (long bill, short hair, red color, etc.). Natural selection is one of several mechanisms by which this change is brought about. Natural selection is based on the *variation* nearly all species show, which means that not all individuals in a species are identical, and thus they will NOT be equally well adapted to survive changes in an environment such as cooler climate, less rain, or smaller prey items. Some individuals are more likely to survive and pass on the genes for their characters than are other individuals with different characters. The superior survival of the genes of certain individuals brings about a change, or evolution, in the species or population, with genes of successful types becoming increasingly common over time (survival of the fittest).

If populations of the same species are isolated from each other long enough, natural selection can result in so many changes in their genes that if individuals from these isolated populations were to come back together again, they could no longer interbreed – indeed, they may no longer recognize each other as similar organisms. When this happens, two species have formed from the ancestor. The Galápagos Islands were, and still are, a good laboratory for studying and understanding evolution. They are close enough to each other to be colonized, yet far enough apart to discourage constant immigration among them – the ideal isolating circumstances. Animals drifting on flotsam, birds blown off course by storms, plant seeds carried on the feathers of these birds or blown in on the wind, apparently arrived on the Galápagos from the South and Central American mainland to originally populate an island. As these populations of plants and animals grew, some individuals made it to other islands and were isolated long enough to become different from the population on the first island. Sometimes these individuals, now of a different species, made it back to the first island. Now there were two closely related but different species inhabiting that island, each species specialized by its bill size, leg length, or body mass to a special habitat or different resource on the island. Thus from a single invasion from the mainland, numerous species could evolve – and now occupy a single island. In this manner cacti, lizards, giant tortoises, mockingbirds, beetles, and, of course, Darwin's Finches themselves, "radiated," or formed, into new species or races on each island they colonized.

If this all seems obvious and logical now, try putting yourself in Darwin's shoes, that is, try imagining yourself, as you first step onto one of the Galápagos Islands and see these bizarre birds, lizards, tortoises and plants, as having no previous knowledge of evolution. Could you perceive the fundamental and underlying cause of the number and distribution of species from island to island? Would you even care enough to consider this important? Darwin's brilliance cannot be overstated; simply put, his contribution forever changed our world.

REFERENCES AND ADDITIONAL READING

If, in the course of your travels through Ecuador, you find yourself becoming more and more interested in the wildlife and plants around you, one of our major goals in writing this book will have been achieved. If you would like to satisfy your heightened natural history interest with additional reading, perhaps to find out about Ecuador's *other* wildlife (the 80% of it that we had not the space to cover in this book), we list below some of the best and most detailed reference books and articles that would assist you in these goals. We used these references ourselves as we wrote this book.

Bates, H. W. 1988. *The Naturalist on the River Amazonas*. Penguin Books, Baltimore, MD.

Best, B. J., T. Heijnen & S. R. Williams. 1996. *A Guide to Bird-watching in Ecuador and the Galápagos Islands*. Biosphere Publications, West Yorkshire, UK.

Boyce, B. 1994. *A Traveler's Guide to the Galápagos Islands,* 2nd ed. Galápagos Travel, San Juan Bautista, California.

Campbell, J. A. & W. W. Lamar. 1989. *The Venomous Reptiles of Latin America*. Cornell University Press/Comstock, Ithaca, NY.

Castro, I. & A. Phillips. 1996. *A Guide to the Birds of the Galápagos Islands*. Princeton University Press, Princeton, NJ.

Collins, M. (editor). 1990. *The Last Rain Forests*. Oxford University Press, Oxford, UK.

Constant, P. 1992. *Marine Life of the Galápagos – A Guide to the Fishes, Whales, Dolphins and other Marine Animals*. Pierre Constant Books, Paris, France.

Darwin, C. 1989. *The Voyage of the Beagle*. Penguin Books, Baltimore, MD.

Duellman, W. E. 1978. *The Biology of an Equatorial Herpetofauna in Amazonian Ecuador*. Misc. Publ. Mus. Nat. Hist. University Kansas 65:1–352.

Eisenberg, J. F. & K. H. Redford. 1999. *Mammals of the Neotropics: The Central Neotropics, vol. 3*. University of Chicago Press, Chicago, IL.

Emmons, L. H. 1997. *Neotropical Rainforest Mammals,* 2nd ed. University of Chicago Press, Chicago, IL.

Ernst, C. H. & R. W. Barbour. 1989. *Turtles of the World*. Smithsonian Institution Press, Washington, D.C.

Forsyth, A. & K. Miyata. 1987. *Tropical Nature*. Charles Scribner's Sons, New York.

Gentry, A. H. 1993. *A Field Guide to the Families and Genera of Woody Plants of Northwest South America (Colombia, Ecuador, Perú)*. University of Chicago Press, Chicago, IL.

Gill, F. B. 1994. *Ornithology,* 2nd ed. W. H. Freeman, San Francisco, CA.

Hairston, N. G. 1994. *Vertebrate Zoology: An Experimental Field Approach.* Cambridge University Press, Cambridge, UK.

Hilty, S. L. & W. L. Brown. 1986. *A Guide to the Birds of Colombia.* Princeton University Press, Princeton, NJ.

Hogue, C. L. 1993. *Latin American Insects and Entomology.* University of California Press, Los Angeles, CA.

IUCN 1996. 1996. *IUCN Red List of Threatened Animals.* The World Conservation Union (IUCN), Gland, Switzerland.

Jackson, M. H. 1993. *Galápagos: A Natural History.* University of Calgary Press, Calgary, Alberta, Canada.

Janzen, D. H. 1983. *Costa Rican Natural History.* University of Chicago Press, Chicago, IL.

Kricher, J. 1997. *A Neotropical Companion: An Introduction to the Animals, Plants, and Ecosystems of the New World Tropics,* 2nd ed. Princeton University Press, Princeton, NJ.

Moore, T. 1980. *Galápagos – Islands Lost in Time.* Viking Press, New York.

Pearson, D. L. & D. W. Middleton. 1999. *The New Key to Ecuador and the Galápagos,* 3rd ed. Ulysses Press, Berkeley, CA.

Perrins, C. M. & A. L. A. Middleton. 1985. *The Encyclopedia of Birds.* Facts on File Publications, New York.

Piñas Rubio, F. & P. Manzano. 1997. *Mariposas del Ecuador.* Catholic University of Ecuador Press, Quito, Ecuador.

Pough, F. H., R. M. Andrews, J. E. Cadle, M. L. Crump, A. H. Savitzky, & K. D. Wells. 1998. *Herpetology.* Prentice Hall, Upper Saddle River, NJ.

Rachowiecki, R., M. Thurber & B. Wagenhauser. 1997. *Climbing and Hiking in Ecuador,* 4th ed. Globe Pequot Press, Old Saybrook, CT.

Rodriguez, L. & W. Duellman. 1994. *Guide to the Frogs of the Iquitos Region, Amazonian Perú.* Natural History Museum, University of Kansas, Lawrence, KS.

Schofield, E. 1984. *Plants of the Galápagos Islands.* Universe Publishing, Englewood, NJ.

Stephenson, M. 1989. *The Galápagos Islands: The Essential Handbook for Exploring, Enjoying and Understanding Darwin's Enchanted Islands.* The Mountaineers, Seattle.

Stiles F. G. & A. F. Skutch. 1989. *A Field Guide to the Birds of Costa Rica.* Cornell University Press, Ithaca, NY.

Terborgh, J. 1992. *Diversity and the Tropical Rain Forest.* Scientific American Library, W. H. Freeman, San Francisco, CA.

Vaughn, T. A. 1997. *Mammalogy,* 4th ed. Saunders, Philadelphia, PA.

Watson, L. 1985. *Whales of the World.* Hutchinson, London, UK.

Weiner, J. 1994. *The Beak of the Finch: A Story of Evolution in Our Time.* Knopf, New York.

HABITAT PHOTOS

Cloud forest from the Old Road to Santo Domingo, western slope of the Andes, northern Ecuador. © N. Pearson

Cascading stream in cloud forest near Baeza, on the eastern slope of the Andes, northern Ecuador. © D. Middleton

Afternoon rain clouds forming below Papallacta on the eastern slope of the Andes, northern Ecuador. © D. Middleton

Typical plants growing as epiphytes on the branches of a cloud forest tree near Cosanga on the eastern slope of the Andes, northern Ecuador. © D. Middleton

Flooded lowland forest on the edge of Lake Limoncocha in the Oriente, northern Ecuador. © N. Pearson

The canopy of lowland forest from the observation tower at Sacha Lodge, northern Ecuador. © N. Pearson

Lowland forest along the upper Río Napo in the Oriente, near Misahuallí, central Ecuador. © D. Middleton

Stream flowing through lowland forest near Jatun Sacha in the Oriente, central Ecuador.
© D. Middleton

Tropical dry forest during the rainy season, from a ridge in the Cerro Blanco Reserve, near Guayaquil, in southern Ecuador. © Fundación Natura-Guayaquil

Coastal fog over tropical dry forest on the bluffs near Puerto Lopez, central Ecuador. © P. Enríquez

Bottle-trunk Ceiba tree in a tropical dry forest during the dry season near Machalilla National Park, southern coastal Ecuador. © P. Enríquez

ya plants in the highland Andes páramo near
lcán Chimborazo, central Ecuador.
© D. Middleton

Moist páramo in the highland Andes during the
rainy season along the Ibarra to San Lorenzo
Road, northern Ecuador. © D. Middleton

Agricultural fields in the highlands of Ecuador's Andes Mountains. © D. Middleton

Volcán Chimborazo, in central Ecuador, the country's highest peak at 6310 m (20,700 ft).
© D. Middleton

Rugged coastline of Española Island (Hood Island), Galápagos Islands. © N. Pearson

Open forest of Palo Santo trees on Santiago Island (James Island), Galápagos Islands.
© N. Pearson

Mangroves in an estuary on Fernandina Island, Galápagos Islands. © N. Pearson

emote bay on the barren coast of Santa Cruz
and, Galápagos Islands. © D. Middleton

Huge tree cactus on Santa Cruz Island,
Galápagos Islands. © D. Middleton

IDENTIFICATION PLATES

Plates 1–96

Abbreviations on the Identification Plates are as follows:

M;   male
F;   female
IM; immature
LF;   left front footprint
LH; left hind footprint

The species pictured on any one plate are not necessarily to scale.

Plate 1a

Ringed Blue Caecilian
Siphonops annulatus

ID: Resembles a large blue worm; legless; smooth skin with closely spaced lighter blue rings; caecilians can be distinguished from worms by the presence of jaws, and eyespots that are visible just under the skin; to 50 cm (20 in) long, 1.5 cm (0.6 in) wide, but most are smaller.

HABITAT: Lowland forests; normally found only underground, but occasionally seen on the surface, especially in swampy or river-floodplain areas after heavy rain.

REGION: AMA

Plate 1b

Ecuadorean Salamander
Bolitoglossa equatoriana

ID: Smooth-skinned with tail almost as long as body; hands and feet heavily webbed and paddle-like, obscuring separation of fingers and toes; upperparts dull gray to reddish brown; underparts gray with scattered clumped pale blotches; to 10 cm (4 in), but most are smaller.

HABITAT: Arboreal on vegetation 1 to 2 m (3 to 6.5 ft) above ground; open, river-floodplain forest and primary forest in eastern lowlands; fairly rare overall, but abundant at some sites; nocturnal.

REGION: AMA

Plate 1c

Río Pescado Stubfoot Toad
Atelopus balios

ID: Small with long, slender body and extremely long limbs; pale greenish-yellow with small black spots; palms of hands and soles of feet reddish-orange; reddish-orange patch on rump; underside light yellow; 3 to 3.5 cm (1.2 to 1.4 in).

HABITAT: Lowland rainforest, especially near streams, terrestrial but also active on low vegetation; day-active.

REGION: MCL, ACL

Plate 1d

Truando Toad
Bufo haematiticus

ID: Medium-sized with rough dry skin and obvious raised parotoid glands on shoulders behind eyes; brown with the sides of head and body a sharply distinct dark brown to black, separated by a faint yellow line; limbs reddish brown with darker bands; underside with purplish tinge on front half, gray on rear half and on limbs; 3.5 to 6 cm (1.5 to 2.5 in).

HABITAT: Found in a variety of sites in the western lowlands, especially near streams; also may be found in slope areas above 500 m (1600 ft); day- and night-active.

REGION: MCL

Plate 1e

Marine Toad (Giant Toad)
Bufo marinus

ID: Large with rough, "warted," dry skin and large parotoid glands on shoulders behind eyes; robust body and limbs grayish brown to deep brown, usually uniform but sometimes with darker spots on the raised "warts"; underside cream with variable brown spots and blotches; eyes yellow to green with fine black lines; to 20 cm (8 in).

HABITAT: Found in clearings, forest edge areas, and along edges of lakes and ponds; also near human dwellings and along roads.

REGION: MCL, ACL, AMA

Plate 1f

South American Common Toad
Bufo typhonius

ID: Medium-sized with rough dry skin; brown to dark brown; distinct raised bony crests between eyes which continue to shoulders; a line of small raised "warts" extends along the upper sides of the body, and some individuals have raised projections along the middle of the body above the backbone; underside cream speckled with gray; palms and soles bright orange-red; 4 to 8 cm (1.5 to 3.5 in).

HABITAT: Terrestrial in lowland forests on both sides of the Andes; primary forest near streams, forest edges; day-active.

REGION: MCL, AMA

Plate I 263

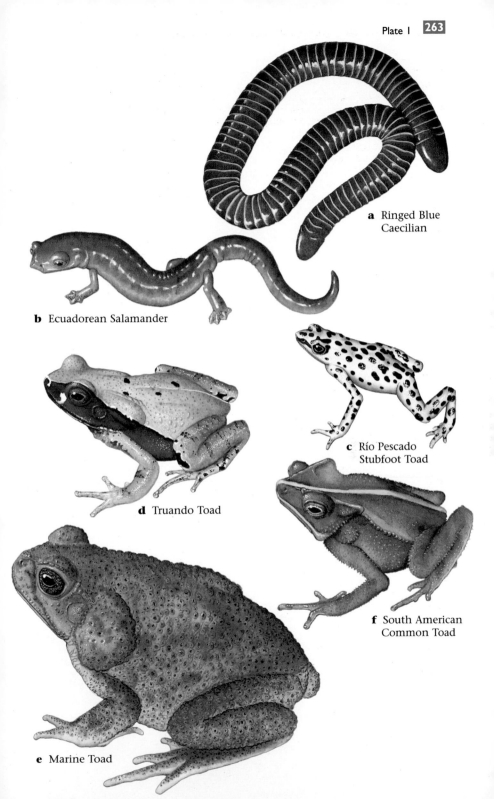

a Ringed Blue Caecilian

b Ecuadorean Salamander

c Río Pescado Stubfoot Toad

d Truando Toad

f South American Common Toad

e Marine Toad

Plate 2a

Western Lowlands Rainfrog
Eleutherodactylus achatinus

ID: Small, tan to light brown, with smooth skin and slender limbs and digits; no webbing between the fingers or toes; dark bands on limbs; dark stripe between nostril and eye; large eyes bronze to red; 2.5 to 4.5 cm (1 to 2 in).

HABITAT: Disturbed forest and agricultural patches in western lowlands and slopes up to 800 m (2600 ft); occasionally in primary rainforest; found on low bushes, grass, and ground near streams and waterfalls; nocturnal.

REGION: MCL, WSA

Plate 2b

Andean Slopes Rainfrog
Eleutherodactylus w-nigrum

ID: Medium-sized frog with smooth skin and slender limbs and digits; no webbing on hands or feet; variably colored with pale tan, olive-green, or brown lines, bands, or blotches; thick black bands curve down over prominent dark ear discs; black markings on sides of legs and in groin area; bronze to red eyes; 2.5 to 7.5 cm (1 to 3 in).

HABITAT: The most common rainfrog from 800 to 3200 m (2600 to 10,500 ft) on western and eastern slopes of the Andes; found on ground and low vegetation; nocturnal.

REGION: WSA, ESA

Plate 2c

Common Páramo Rainfrog
Eleutherodactylus unistrigatus

ID: Small with mostly smooth skin; scattered small "warts;" no webbing on hands or feet; yellowish tan to dark brown, with some individuals blotched and others with stripes running from head to rear of body; males with yellow throat; external ear disc barely visible; eyes gray to silver; 2 to 4 cm (1 to 1.5 in).

HABITAT: The most abundant highland rain frog, found in variety of habitats between 2500 and 3400 m (8200 to 11,200 ft); active at night on ground and low vegetation; hides during day under rocks, logs, trash.

REGION: HAP

Plate 2d

Orange-groin Rainfrog
Eleutherodactylus croceoinguinis

ID: Tiny with roughly sculptured skin and moderately slender limbs; no webbing on hands or feet; back gray to brown, sometimes with white or yellow flecks; underside lighter brown; yellow or orange spots where the legs meet body; eyes gray with fine black lines; 1.2 to 2.2 cm (0.5 to 1 in).

HABITAT: Primary forest, but also in more open forest, in eastern lowlands to 500 m (1600 ft); on low vegetation 1 to 2 m (3 to 6.5 ft) above ground, often near streams; nocturnal.

REGION: AMA

Plate 2e

Lance Rainfrog
(also called Metallic Robber Frog)
Eleutherodactylus lanthanites

ID: A small lance-shaped frog with rough skin on upper body; long, slender limbs; tan, brown, or dark brown with darker cross-bands (often chevron-shaped) on upper body; prominent skin folds on upper sides that form yellow or reddish stripes; underside of head gray to yellow with a pale center stripe; belly creamy white with dark flecks; eye bronze with fine black lines and a central red stripe; 3 to 5 cm (1 to 2 in).

HABITAT: Often the most common small rainfrog in the eastern lowlands; nocturnal and arboreal; found in both primary and open forests.

REGION: AMA

Plate 2f

Smoky Jungle Frog
Leptodactylus pentadactylus

ID: Large with a stout body and limbs; no webbing on hands, slight webbing on feet; prominent folds of skin on each side of upper body; patterned with bands of dark gray to brown; snout wide and rounded; dark bars on upper lip; underside cream to gray with bold black markings on belly; eye dark bronze; to 17 cm (6.5 in).

HABITAT: Lowland forests on both sides of the Andes; terrestrial.

REGION: MCL, AMA

Plate 2   265

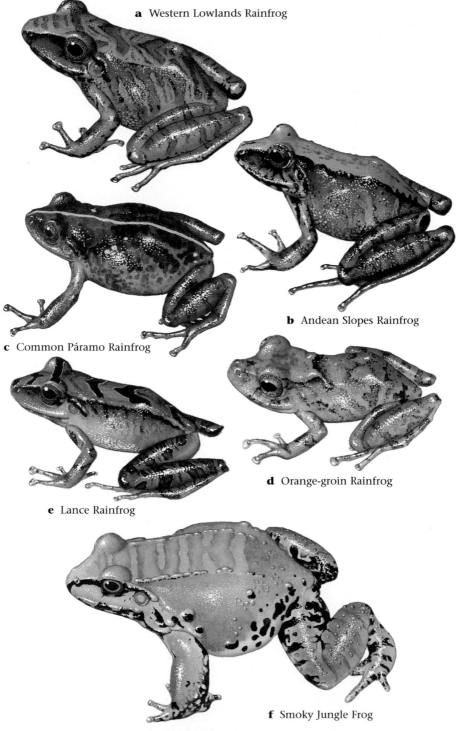

a Western Lowlands Rainfrog

b Andean Slopes Rainfrog

c Common Páramo Rainfrog

d Orange-groin Rainfrog

e Lance Rainfrog

f Smoky Jungle Frog

Plate 3a

Peter's Mudpuddle Frog
Physalaemus petersi
ID: Small, toad-like, with rounded body, short rounded snout, small hands and feet without webbing; skin on upper body rough, and usually dry, with tiny raised orange specks on a dull brown background; underside cream with black markings; bright orange in groin region; 2.5 to 4.0 cm (1 to 1.5 in).

HABITAT: Primary rainforest in eastern lowlands (a similar species of *Physalaemus* occurs in western lowlands); terrestrial; nocturnal.

REGION: AMA

Plate 3b

Horned Marsupial Treefrog
Gastrotheca cornuta
ID: Medium-sized, rust to pale brown with slight yellowish cast on upper surfaces of body, with brownish olive transverse bars; underside creamy yellow with whitish flecks, grading into yellowish brown on the throat and chin; fleshy "horns" protrude above each eye; female with brooding pouch opening on back; 4 to 6.5 cm (1.5 to 2.5 in).

HABITAT: Primary forest in western lowlands and slopes to 1000 m (3300 ft); on vegetation from eye level to higher; shuns disturbed forest; nocturnal.

REGION: MCL, WSA

Plate 3c

Two-lined Treefrog
Hyla bifurca
ID: Small, tan to dark brown; a yellowish band runs between eyes and continues along two-thirds of the length of body; markings of the same color on rump and heels; fingers webbed at the base, toes partly webbed; the webbing and concealed surfaces of limbs and body are orange to reddish brown; 2 to 3.5 cm (1 to 1.5 in). (A closely related species, *Hyla leucophyllata*, looks similar but is slightly larger and has yellow markings on the lower legs near knees.)

HABITAT: Open forest and clearings in eastern lowlands; on vegetation over temporary ponds, often in large numbers; nocturnal.

REGION: AMA

Plate 3d

Christmas Treefrog
Hyla punctata
ID: Medium-sized; at night, upper body with red flecks and spots, sometimes with larger yellow spots; distinct stripe, yellowish above, red below, runs along sides; limbs green with reduced red and yellow flecks; by day red is greatly reduced, with most of body and limbs green, but yellow and red stripe still visible; fingers webbed at the base; toes half-webbed; green throat and white belly; 3 to 4.5 cm (1 to 1.8 in).

HABITAT: Low vegetation in variety of open forests, clearings, swamps, and near temporary and more permanent ponds in the eastern lowlands; nocturnal.

REGION: AMA

Plate 3e

Miyata's Jeweled Treefrog
Hyla miyatai
ID: Tiny, metallic red over bright yellow, with the red forming a triangle or X on the head, neck and shoulders; unpigmented areas of upper body pink, as are the belly and all surfaces beneath body and limbs; fingers one-third webbed; toes three-quarters webbed; 1.5 to 2.5 cm (0.6 to 1 in).

HABITAT: Low vegetation in forests; often in or near shallow ponds or along slow moving, black-water streams in the eastern lowlands; nocturnal.

REGION: AMA

Plate 3f

Triangle Treefrog
Hyla triangulum
ID: Small, colors highly variable, usually with a single large, dark reddish brown spot on mid-body behind head; some with a pattern of bubble-like spots on rear surface of body; males most often have only a bubble-like pattern and lack the single large spot; webbing (fingers half, and toes three-quarters) and concealed surfaces of the limbs red; 2.5 to 4.5 cm (1 to 1.8 in).

HABITAT: Low vegetation in eastern lowlands; commonly found in brushy open forest and clearings, especially in the vicinity of temporary or small permanent ponds; nocturnal.

REGION: AMA

Plate 3 **267**

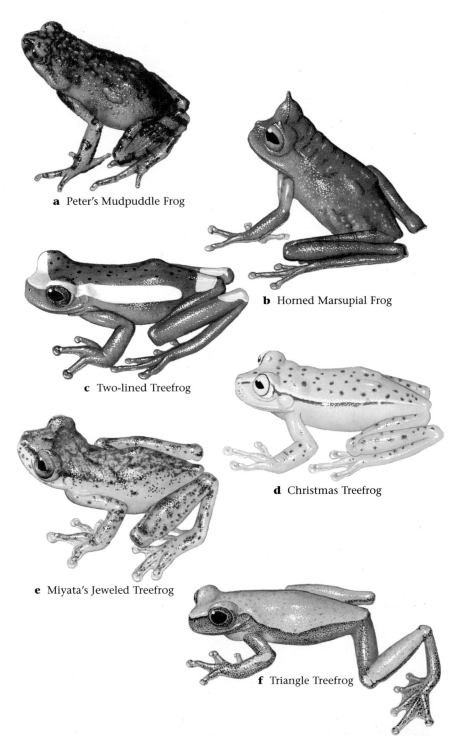

a Peter's Mudpuddle Frog

b Horned Marsupial Frog

c Two-lined Treefrog

d Christmas Treefrog

e Miyata's Jeweled Treefrog

f Triangle Treefrog

Plate 4a

Harlequin Poison-dart Frog
Dendrobates histrionicus
ID: Small, with highly variable colors; upper body usually with irregular blotched pattern ranging from orange to red over a background of dark brown to black; black underneath; 2 to 2.5 cm (1 in).

HABITAT: On ground and low vegetation in undisturbed forest in western lowlands, to 700 m (2300 ft); areas with thick layer of leaf litter, especially stream valleys; day-active.

REGION: MCL, WSA

Plate 4b

Amazonian Poison-dart Frog
Dendrobates ventrimaculatus
ID: Tiny, dark blue (yellow form) or black (red form), with brightly colored stripes; one stripe runs across the tip of the snout, over the eyes, and continues on either side of the upper body; a second runs from between the eyes down the center of the back; a third is on the upper lip; stripes can be metallic reddish or yellow; underside has a net or bubble-like pattern of bright blue over black; 1.5 to 2 cm (0.6 to 0.8 in).

HABITAT: Primary forest with ample leaf litter and in more disturbed forest, to 500 m (1600 ft), in eastern lowlands; on ground but also climbs into bromeliads; day-active.

REGION: AMA

Plate 4c

Spot-legged Poison-dart Frog
Epipedobates pictus
ID: Small; dark greenish gray to black with a thin cream stripe across the tip of snout, over eyes, and along uppersides; a second cream stripe runs along lower jaw, from just below eye to upper arm; groin region with two small, bright yellow spots; underside mottled with bright blue over black; 2 to 2.5 cm (0.8 to 1 in).

HABITAT: Terrestrial in open forests, forest edges, and swamps in eastern lowlands, to 500 m (1600 ft); day-active.

REGION: AMA

Plate 4d

Ruby Poison-dart Frog
Epipedobates parvulus
ID: Small, with bright red raised granular bumps against a background of dark brown to black; sides and upper surfaces of limbs gray to black; bright yellow spots where arms and legs join body; underside mottled with bright blue over black; 2 to 2.5 cm (0.8 to 1 in).

HABITAT: Terrestrial in primary forest in eastern lowlands, to 500 m (1600 ft); often the most abundant poison-dart frog on the forest floor; day-active.

REGION: AMA

Plate 4e

Red-armed Poison-dart Frog
Epipedobates erythromos
ID: Small, dark brown or blackish, usually with small, irregular, and faintly visible lighter or darker markings; sides gray to black; upper arms bright red; undersides of both body and limbs mottled with bright blue over black; 1.5 to 2.5 cm (0.6 to 1 in).

HABITAT: Steep, dark stream valleys with dense canopy cover and abundant leaf litter in primary forest, western lowlands, to 400 m (1300 ft); on ground near streams; day-active.

REGION: MCL

Plate 4f

Western Drab Poison-dart Frog
Colostethus infraguttatus
ID: Small, bronzy brown, with a slight metallic cast, and with scattered and faint irregular darker blotches or spots; pale cream to yellowish stripe from tip of snout, over the eyes, to along upper sides of body; a second smaller stripe along the lower jaw; underside spotted white (sometimes bluish) on gray to black background; 2 to 2.5 cm (0.8 to 1 in).

HABITAT: Primary but occasionally moist secondary forest, from 70 to 1500 m (200 to 5000 ft); terrestrial; day-active.

REGION: MCL, WSA

Plate 4 **269**

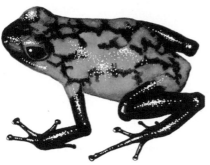

a Harlequin Poison-dart Frog

b Amazonian Poison-dart Frog

c Spot-legged Poison-dart Frog

d Ruby Poison-dart Frog

e Red-armed Poison-dart Frog

f Western Drab Poison-dart Frog

Plate 5a

Red-skirted Treefrog
Hyla rhodopepla

ID: Small, white to yellow (often lighter at night, darker by day), with red to brown flecks; wide red or reddish brown stripe from tip of snout to eyes, and continuing behind eyes on each side of body; underside yellow; fingers a third webbed, toes half webbed; 2 to 3 cm (0.8 to 1.2 in).

HABITAT: Low vegetation in eastern lowlands; in open forest, forest edges, and primary forest; often on vegetation over pools, ponds, swamps; nocturnal.

REGION: AMA

Plate 5b

Tiger-striped Leaf Frog
Phyllomedusa tomopterna

ID: Medium-sized, bright green, with short, blunt head and snout; concealed surfaces of limbs and body barred with orange and dark red/purple; throat and chest white; belly pale orange; very long limbs; fingers and toes with large terminal discs but no webbing; a fleshy triangular flap of skin protrudes from the heel tips of the legs; 3.5 to 6 cm (1.5 to 2.5 in).

HABITAT: Low vegetation in eastern lowlands; dense forest and near temporary ponds near forest edge; nocturnal.

REGION: AMA

Plate 5c

Fleischmann's Glass Frog
Hyalinobatrachium fleischmanni

ID: Tiny, delicate, with long slender limbs and broadly rounded snout; pale green with numerous pale yellow spots; underside transparent, revealing internal organs and bones; fingers and toes yellowish when viewed from below; fingers webbed at base, toes half webbed; 1.5 to 2.5 cm (0.6 to 1 in).

HABITAT: Undisturbed forest in western lowlands and slopes to 1500 m (4900 ft); near forest streams, often on vegetation over water; nocturnal.

REGION: MCL, WSA

Plate 5d

Regal Golden Glass Frog
Cochranella midas

ID: Tiny, delicate, with long slender limbs and short blunt snout; dark green with gold flecks along upper sides; underside transparent, revealing internal organs and bones; fingers webbed at base, toes a third webbed; 1.5 to 2.5 cm (0.6 to 1 in).

HABITAT: Lowland forest and lower cloud forest in eastern lowlands and slopes, to 600 m (2000 ft); primary and sometimes secondary forest; along small forest streams, often on vegetation over water; nocturnal.

REGION: ESA, AMA

Plate 5e

Amazon Bullfrog
Rana palmipes

ID: Large, with smooth skin, robust hind limbs, long pointed head and snout, and a distinct external ear disc (tympanum) as large as the eye; body patterned olive-tan to green with distinct skin folds along uppersides; rear surfaces of legs pale yellow with dense black mottling; underside cream to pale yellow; fingers not webbed, but toes fully webbed; to 13 cm (5 in).

HABITAT: Lowland forests, both sides of the Andes; in/near lakes, ponds, swamps, streams; day- and night-active.

REGION: MCL, AMA

Plate 5f

Bassler's Narrow-mouthed Frog
Chiasmocleis bassleri

ID: Small, with smooth skin, rotund body, fairly short limbs, small eyes and small pointed head and snout; body and hind limbs brown to dark brown; sides darker; upper surfaces of arms often pale tan; underside of body and hind limbs bluish white with large black spots; tips of fingers and toes not expanded into pads; fingers not webbed, toes webbed at base; 2 to 3 cm (0.8 to 1.2 in).

HABITAT: Primary and secondary forest, eastern lowlands; along forest edges, in leaf litter; also in/near temporary ponds after heavy rain; nocturnal.

REGION: AMA

Plate 5 **271**

a Red-skirted Treefrog

b Tiger-striped Leaf Frog

c Fleischmann's Glass Frog

d Regal Golden Glass Frog

e Amazon Bullfrog

f Bassler's Narrow-mouthed Frog

Plate 6a

Spectacled Caiman
Caiman crocodilus

ID: Large, brown or olive-brown, often with wide black bars on body and tail; to 2.5 m (8 ft), although most are 2 m (6.5 ft) or less. *Spectacled* refers to the bony ridges around the front of eyes, which crocodiles lack.

HABITAT: Lowland forests, both sides of the Andes, in or near streams, swamps, ponds, lakes, and rivers.

REGION: MCL, AMA

Note: Regulated for conservation purposes; CITES Appendix II listed.

Plate 6b

Black Caiman
Caiman niger

ID: Large, very dark olive, brown, or blackish; snout broad and rounded; to 6 m (19.5 ft) but most less than 4 m (13 ft); juveniles may have lighter bands on body and tail.

HABITAT: Large bodies of water, mostly large lakes, in eastern lowland forests; also large rivers and swampy areas near lakes, rivers; nocturnal; much less common than Spectacled Caiman.

REGION: AMA

Note: Endangered, CITES Appendix I listed (Appendix II listed for Ecuador).

Plate 6c

Dwarf Caiman
(also called Smooth-fronted Dwarf Caiman, Smooth-fronted Caiman)
Paleosuchus trigonatus

ID: Small, with a maximum length of 1 m (3 ft); moderately rounded snout; dark olive with darker bands on body and tail; lighter blotches often on sides of jaws.

HABITAT: Larger streams, small rivers, small ponds, and swamps of eastern lowland rainforest; nocturnal; also on forest floor, where it forages.

REGION: AMA

Note: Regulated for conservation purposes; CITES Appendix II listed.

Plate 6d

South American Yellow-footed Tortoise
Geochelone denticulata

ID: Large, with a moderately domed shell; distinctly textured, raised concentric "growth rings" on each upper shell plate; upper shell dull brown to black, usually with a pale tan to yellow area at the center of each plate; scales on front limbs yellow to orange; rear limbs have stubby, elephant-like feet; to 82 cm (32 in), but most smaller.

HABITAT: Terrestrial in variety of habitats in eastern lowland forests; day- and perhaps night-active; a similar species may occur in western lowlands.

REGION: AMA

Note: CITES Appendix II listed

Plate 6e

Yellow-spotted Amazon River Turtle
Podocnemis unifilis

ID: A large turtle, olive to brown, with a slightly domed, fairly smooth shell; limbs and head uniformly olive to light brown, except for several yellow spots on the head and snout; underside pale yellow; to 68 cm (27 in); males much smaller than females, to only half maximum size.

HABITAT: Ponds, lakes, rivers, and swamps, in eastern lowlands; diurnal; basks on logs, rocks in the water.

REGION: AMA

Note: CITES Appendix II listed

Plate 6f

Snapping Turtle
Chelydra serpentina acutirostris

ID: Large, olive to dark brown, with a fairly flattened but very rough-textured shell with three distinct, raised ridges; large head and tail as long as shell; bottom of shell small, revealing fleshy areas of limbs and neck; shell often covered with mud or algae; to 40 cm (16 in), but most are smaller.

HABITAT: Streams, rivers, ponds, lakes, and swamps in western lowlands; sometimes on land near water.

REGION: MCL, ACL

Plate 6 **273**

a Spectacled Caiman

b Black Caiman

c Dwarf Caiman

d South American Yellow-footed Tortoise

e Yellow-spotted Amazon River Turtle

f Snapping Turtle

Plate 7a

Catesby's Snail-eater
Dipsas catesbyi
ID: Small, reddish brown, fairly slender; large, paired, darker brown oval spots, each surrounded by a white border, run along sides; black head rounded with a white line across blunt snout; white belly with irregular black markings; lighter larger row of scales runs atop the backbone; 30 to 70 cm (12 to 28 in).

HABITAT: Lowland forest; on vegetation 1 to 2 m (3 to 6.5 ft) above ground; nocturnal.

REGION: AMA

Plate 7b

Amazon Snail-eater
Dipsas indica ecuadorensis
ID: Small gray to grayish brown snake; dark brown, triangular-shaped markings along sides, with bases of the triangles widest near the bottom and most pointed near the backbone; yellow chin; brown head; dark brown belly; lighter larger row of scales running atop backbone; 30 to 90 cm (12 to 36 in).

HABITAT: Lowland forest; on vegetation 1 to 2 m (3 to 6.5 ft) above ground; nocturnal.

REGION: AMA

Plate 7c

Blunt-headed Tree Snake
Imantodes cenchoa
ID: Long and slender with a bulbous, blunt head with large eyes and elliptical (cat-like) pupils; body noticeably flattened from side-to-side, with a larger row of scales running along the backbone; body with alternating bands of rich brown over tan; belly tan with brown flecks; to 110 cm (43 in). (This and a related species, *Imantodes lentiferus*, are the most slender snakes in Ecuador, resembling "living ropes.")

HABITAT: Lowland forests on both sides of the Andes; on vegetation 1 to 2 m (3 to 6.5 ft) above ground, where it is often the most abundant nocturnal tree snake.

REGION: MCL, ACL, AMA

Plate 7d

Lance-headed Vine Snake
Xenoxybelis argenteus
ID: Mid-sized, slender, with pointed head and snout; green and tan stripes run lengthwise down body; green and white stripes run lengthwise on belly; body rounded (not flattened) in cross-section; long tail, often 70% of body length; 50 to 100 cm (20 to 40 in).

HABITAT: Eastern lowland forests, where it is often the most abundant snake species (a similar species occurs in west); in vegetation by day, but sometimes on ground.

REGION: AMA

Plate 7e

Green Parrot Snake
Leptophis ahaetulla nigromarginatus
ID: Mid-sized, bright green; black edges around the outer margin of each scale on the upper body form a distinctive net-like pattern of black over green; rust-colored belly; 60 to 100 cm (24 to 40 in).

HABITAT: Arboreal in dense brushy vegetation; occurs in secondary and primary forest; day-active; at night sleeps in vegetation.

REGION: AMA

Plate 7f

Southern Cat-eyed Snake
Leptodeira annulata
ID: Small, tan to light brown, with a zig-zag, wavy dark brown stripe running lengthwise along upper body; the dark stripe is usually broken into unconnected blotches on the rear portion of body; creamy white to pinkish tan belly; 40 to 75 cm (16 to 30 in).

HABITAT: Arboreal in lowland forest in eastern lowlands, and eastern slopes to 1000 m (3300 ft); secondary and some primary forest; nocturnal.

REGION: ESA, AMA

Plate 7 **275**

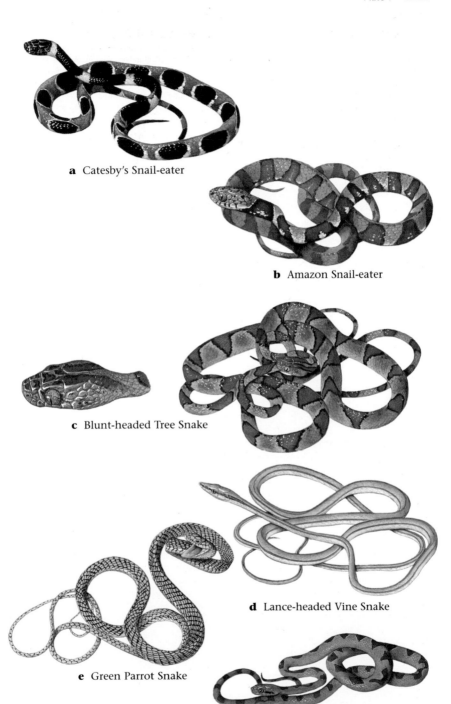

a Catesby's Snail-eater

b Amazon Snail-eater

c Blunt-headed Tree Snake

d Lance-headed Vine Snake

e Green Parrot Snake

f Southern Cat-eyed Snake

Plate 8a

South American Sipo
Chironius multiventris
ID: Long and slender with large, shiny scales on dark olive to almost black upper body; bright yellow belly; pink tongue with a gray tip; 1 to 2 m (3 to 6.5 ft).

HABITAT: Eastern lowland forests; terrestrial but sometimes in low vegetation; day-active.

REGION: AMA

Plate 8b

Chonta Snake
(also called Mussurana)
Clelia clelia
ID: Large, long, with large shiny scales; adults are black with cream-colored belly; juveniles (up to 50 cm, 20 in) are red (with black scale edges) with black snout and white neck-band; hatchlings are bright red; to 2+ m (6.5+ ft).

HABITAT: Lowland forests, both sides of the Andes, on ground; day- and night-active.

REGION: MCL, ACL, AMA

Note: CITES Appendix II listed

Plate 8c

Tropical Rat Snake
Spilotes pullatus
ID: Large, long, with large scales; alternating wide bands of black and yellow extend the length of the body; to 2+ m (6.5+ ft).

HABITAT: Lowland and slope forests, both sides of Andes; terrestrial but also in dense vegetation to 3 m (10 ft) up; day-active.

REGION: MCL, ACL, AMA

Plate 8d

Amazon Water Snake
Helicops angulatus
ID: Small but fairly stout-bodied; alternating bands of light brown (or olive) and dark brown on the upper body, the darker bands being slightly wider; pale yellow to orange belly with brown to black markings extending from the bands on the upper surface; small eyes; 40 to 60 cm (16 to 24 in).

HABITAT: Small ponds, streams in eastern lowland forests; nocturnal.

REGION: AMA

Plate 8e

Brown Ground Snake
Atractus major
ID: Small; light brown upper body with scattered dark brown spots and blotches; cream to pale yellow belly with scattered brown or black flecks; tongue gray with a white tip; 50 to 70 cm (20 to 28 in).

HABITAT: Eastern slopes and lowlands; on ground in leaf litter; primary forest but also secondary forest and clearings; day-active.

REGION: ESA, AMA

Plate 8f

Aesculapian False Coral Snake
Erythrolamprus aesculapii
ID: Small, with alternating bands of black, red, and yellowish white; the red and yellowish white scales have black in the rear-most area of the scale; the repeating band sequence, from just behind the head, is yellowish white, black, red, black; the front end of the head is black, the rear portion yellowish white with scattered black markings; colors on back extend onto belly; 50 to 70 cm (20 to 28 in).

HABITAT: Eastern lowland primary but sometimes secondary forests, on ground; day-active.

REGION: AMA

Plate 8 277

a South American Sipo

IM

b Chonta Snake

c Tropical Rat Snake

e Brown Ground Snake

d Amazon Water Snake

f Aesculapian False Coral Snake

Plate 9a

Boa Constrictor
Boa constrictor

ID: Large, stout-bodied; tan to light brown upper body with dark brown transverse markings that outline oval-shaped tan markings; triangular head with a wide, dark brown band running from nostril through eye and onto neck; cream-colored belly with scattered brown or black flecks and spots; tiny white bony spurs protrude from body near base of tail; to 5 m (16 ft), but most are much smaller.

HABITAT: Arboreal in lowland forests on both sides of Andes to 1000 m (3300 ft); nocturnal.

REGION: MCL, ACL, AMA

Note: CITES Appendix II listed

Plate 9b

Amazon Tree Boa
Corallus hortulanus

ID: Small, with body slightly flattened from side-to-side; cream, gray, or bright yellow with dark brown circular or oval-shaped markings; cream to tan belly with scattered darker markings; scales on upper and lower lips have obvious, deep, heat-sensing pits; to 1.25 m (4 ft).

HABITAT: Arboreal in eastern lowland forests; primary but also secondary forest; hangs from branches with the head positioned just above ground, waiting for prey; nocturnal.

REGION: AMA

Plate 9c

Rainbow Boa
Epicrates cenchria

ID: Small, with a rounded body (in cross-section); three dark lengthwise stripes on head; body tan to brown with roughly circular or oval markings that are pale tan or yellowish and outlined in black; under strong light, scales reflect a rainbow of iridescence; creamy white belly; 1 to 2 m (3 to 6.5 ft), but most are smaller.

HABITAT: Arboreal and on ground in many habitats in eastern lowland forests; probably active day and night.

REGION: AMA

Note: CITES Appendix II listed

Plate 9d

Anaconda
Eunectes murinus

ID: Very large, stout-bodied, yellowish to tan, with large dark brown blotches; lighter yellow or tan belly with scattered small dark markings; to 10+ m (33+ ft), but most are much smaller; the largest snake on Earth.

HABITAT: Mostly aquatic in large lakes, rivers, and swamps, but sometimes on land near water.

REGION: AMA

Plate 9e

Pelagic Sea Snake
Pelamis platurus

ID: Small; most specimens are black on the upper surface of the body and yellow on the sides and belly, with the black broken into blotches near the tail; some are almost all yellow; rear third of body is side-to-side flattened; 70 to 100 cm (28 to 40 in).

HABITAT: Marine; on ocean surface with floating debris but sometimes in more inland brackish waters; washes up on beaches along Pacific Coast; also in waters around Galápagos.

REGION: MCL, ACL, GAL

Plate 9f

Langsdorff's Coral Snake
Micrurus langsdorffi

ID: Small, with alternating bands of dull red, white, and black; red bands (formed by scales which have black pigment in their central areas) are the widest, followed by the black (half the width of the red), and narrow white rings; band sequence red – white – black – white – red; bands extend onto belly; white chin; to 70 cm (28 in).

HABITAT: Eastern lowlands and slopes to 1500 m (4900 ft); terrestrial; secretive, in leaf litter or under logs and vegetation; day-active.

REGION: ESA, AMA

Plate 9 **279**

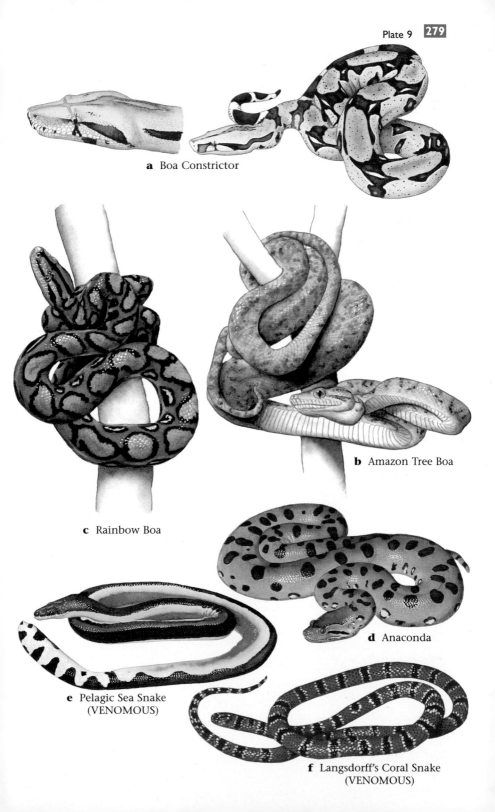

a Boa Constrictor

b Amazon Tree Boa

c Rainbow Boa

d Anaconda

e Pelagic Sea Snake
(VENOMOUS)

f Langsdorff's Coral Snake
(VENOMOUS)

Plate 10a
Fer-de-Lance
Bothrops atrox
ID: Large, medium-bodied, with very rough scales and distinctly lance-shaped head; dull olive or brown with a pattern of darker and lighter markings, which often form a series of "X" shapes; dark bands extend from behind each eye to the sides of head and neck; cream to tan belly with irregular darker markings; to 2 m (6.5 ft), but most are smaller.

HABITAT: Eastern lowlands and slopes to at least 1200 m (3900 ft); often near human habitations in lowland forests; terrestrial; active day and night; the most common pit-viper in eastern Ecuador.

REGION: ESA, AMA

Plate 10b
Speckled Forest Pit-viper
Bothriopsis taeniata
ID: Medium-sized, with lance-shaped head and complex coloration; upper body pale green to gray with yellow flecks; alternating square black blotches on top and sides; brown belly with pale yellow flecks; 50 to 120 cm (20 to 48 in).

HABITAT: Arboreal in eastern lowland forests and slopes to 2000 m (6500 ft); primary forest and along forest edges; nocturnal.

REGION: ESA, AMA

Plate 10c
Eyelash Palm Pit-viper
Bothriechis schlegelii
ID: Small, with lance-shaped head and highly variable coloration; bright yellow to green to rust-colored, with scattered small dark flecks and spots; distinct pointed scales project up above each eye; prehensile tail, used to hold onto branches; to 80 cm (32 in), but most are smaller.

HABITAT: Arboreal in forests in western lowlands and slopes to at least 2000 m (6500 ft); primary forest but also secondary forest and forest edges; the most common pit-viper in the western lowlands; nocturnal.

REGION: MCL, WSA

Plate 10d
Bushmaster
Lachesis muta
ID: Large, rough-scaled, with lance-shaped head; light brown with diamond-shaped, dark brown markings outlined by light tan; top of head is dark brown, sharply distinct from lighter lower portion (just below the eye); distinct raised ridge along backbone; cream-colored belly; to 3.6 m (12 ft); the longest viper on Earth.

HABITAT: Lowland forests and slopes on both sides of Andes to 1800 m (5900 ft); primary forest and forest edges; terrestrial; nocturnal.

REGION: MCL, ACL, ESA, AMA

Plate 10e
Collared Gecko
Gonatodes concinnatus
ID: Small, with fine granular scales; olive-green body with irregular pattern of thin black lines; orange or reddish brown head and neck; white collar on the back between front limbs; eyes covered by hard, transparent scales; no closeable eyelids; 7 to 9 cm (3 to 4 in).

HABITAT: Eastern lowland forests, both primary and secondary; often on tree trunks, but also on ground; day-active.

REGION: AMA

Plate 10f
Turniptail Gecko
Thecadactylus rapicauda
ID: Large gecko with large eyes (covered with non-closing, hard, transparent scales); gray to brown with irregular spots, blotches, and flecks; larger, slightly raised scales mixed with small granular scales on the back; hands and feet with thick webbing on fingers and toes, which each have expanded, ribbed pads underneath; large, thick tail; to 15 cm (6 in).

HABITAT: Lowland forests and slopes on both sides of Andes, to 1000 m (3300 ft); arboreal; nocturnal.

REGION: MCL, ACL, WSA, ESA, AMA

Plate 10 **281**

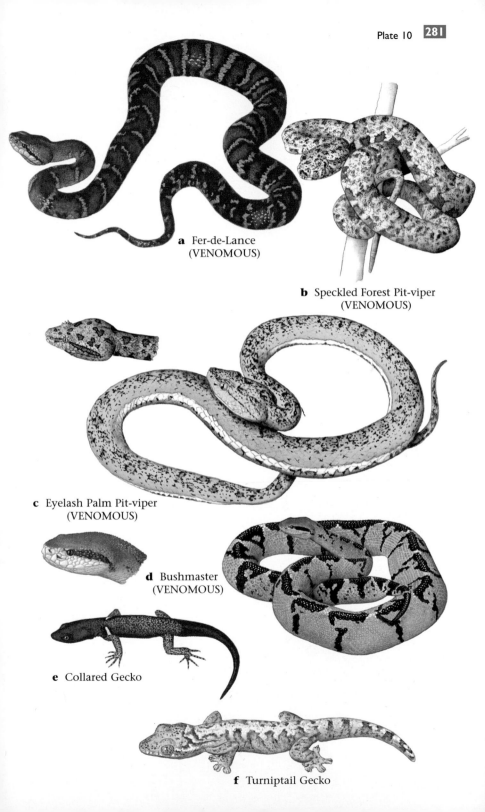

a Fer-de-Lance
(VENOMOUS)

b Speckled Forest Pit-viper
(VENOMOUS)

c Eyelash Palm Pit-viper
(VENOMOUS)

d Bushmaster
(VENOMOUS)

e Collared Gecko

f Turniptail Gecko

Plate 11a

Amazon Dwarf Gecko
Pseudogonatodes guianensis

ID: Tiny, with fine granular scales; eyes covered by non-closing, hard transparent scales; dull dark brown upper body with a pale yellow to rust-colored curved band behind the head and faint tan specks forming lines along upper sides; tan or gray belly; smallest lizard in the Amazon lowlands; 4 to 5 cm (1.5 to 2 in).

HABITAT: Eastern lowland forest; primary forest but also in secondary forest and forest edges; terrestrial, in leaf litter; day-active; similar species occur in western lowlands.

REGION: AMA

Plate 11b

Green Iguana
Iguana iguana

ID: Large, with prominent head crest and throat fan (especially males); bright green to dull olive with irregular darker crossbands; tail banded, extremely long; a distinctive, large round scale is present just below the ear opening; juveniles brightest in color, becoming darker with age; to 2 m (6.5 ft); largest mainland lizard in Ecuador.

HABITAT: Lowland forests and slopes to 1000 m (3300 ft); mostly arboreal but sometimes on ground; day-active.

REGION: MCL, ACL, WSA, ESA, AMA

Note: CITES Appendix II listed

Plate 11c

Basilisk (also called Jesus Christ Lizard, Common Basilisk)
Basiliscus basiliscus

ID: Large, dull olive to brown, with darker crossbands; long slender limbs, fingers, and toes; very long tail; prominent crest on top of head, running along backbone, and on top of tail (most prominent in males); crest often higher on head and tail, reduced on body; pale thin stripes on lips; to 1 m (3.3 ft), including tail much longer than body. (A similar species, also found in the western lowlands, is bright green and lacks the head crest.)

HABITAT: Western lowland forests; in low trees or bushes but also on ground; often near lakes, ponds, streams, rivers; day-active.

REGION: MCL

Plate 11d

Roof Anole
Anolis bitectus

ID: Slender with long tail and long, slender limbs, fingers, and toes; upper body olive to brown; pale yellow stripes run lengthwise from below eye to base of tail; dewlap (throat fan) orange with scattered yellow scales; belly brownish yellow; 10 to 12 cm (4 to 5 in).

HABITAT: Shaded areas in more open forests in western lowlands; in thick low brush or on tree trunks; day-active.

REGION: MCL, ACL

Plate 11e

Goldenscale Anole
Anolis chrysolepis scypheus

ID: Large, with a fairly robust body, large head, short snout, and long tail; upper body is tan to brown with variable darker markings such as diagonal bars or semi-circles; often with a narrow pale yellow to tan stripe running down center of back; dewlap (throat fan) of males blue with red edges; 20 to 25 cm (8 to 10 in).

HABITAT: Eastern lowland forests; on ground or on low vegetation, tree trunks; primary forest or more closed secondary forest; day-active.

REGION: AMA

Plate 11f

Orton's Anole
Anolis ortonii

ID: Small, moderately robust; upper body usually with a broad, pale tan stripe running lengthwise on the back bordered by narrower darker stripes; sides irregularly patterned with dull gray and brown; dark bar between eyes; pale tan belly; large male dewlap (throat fan) is orange with red streaks; 9 to 12 cm (3.5 to 5 in).

HABITAT: Eastern lowland forests, on ground and low vegetation in shady areas; day-active.

REGION: AMA

Plate 11   283

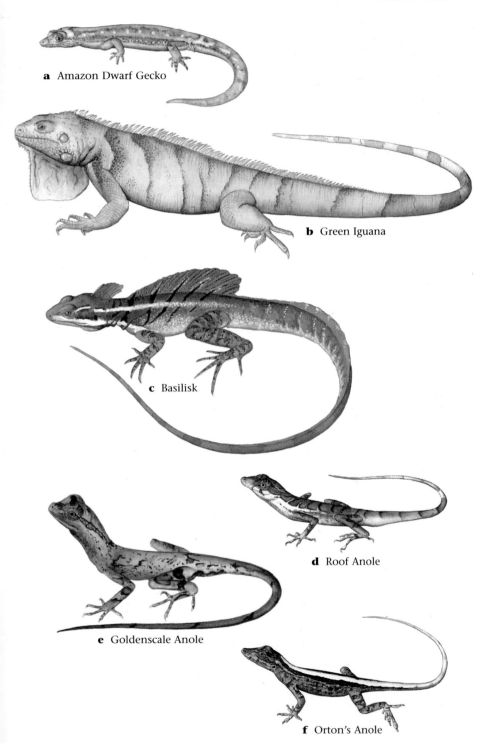

a Amazon Dwarf Gecko

b Green Iguana

c Basilisk

d Roof Anole

e Goldenscale Anole

f Orton's Anole

Plate 12a
Prince Anole
Anolis princeps
ID: Large, with long limbs and tail; upper body light green with fine yellowish-white lines and dark green and/or brown cross-bands; narrow line of enlarged scales atop backbone, alternates black and white; yellow line on head between eyes; dewlap (throat fan) white with pale gray scales, prominent in both sexes; to 25 cm (10 in).

HABITAT: Western lowlands and slopes to 1400 m (4600 ft); on small tree trunks 2 to 5 m (6 to 16 ft) above ground, in shade; prim rest but also more open areas, including banana groves; day-active.

REGION: MCL, ACL, WSA

Plate 12b
Amazon Forest Anole
Anolis trachyderma
ID: Small, slender, with long limbs and tail; upper body brown with darker brown, chevron-shaped markings on back; two distinct white markings on each side of lower jaw; belly cream to yellow with brown flecks; base of tail greatly swollen in males; male dewlap (throat fan) small, orange to red with black scales; 10 to 15 cm (4 to 6 in).

HABITAT: Eastern lowlands; on ground, but also on low vegetation, tree trunks; prefers shade, shuns clearings; the most common forest anole at many locations; day-active.

REGION: AMA

Plate 12c
Guichenot's Dwarf Iguana
Enyaliodes laticeps
ID: Largish, rough-scaled, long-tailed (tail longer than body), with a short, chunky head and snout; distinct row of large spiny scales run along the backbone; upper body bright green to pale brown with irregular black markings along back roughly forming cross-bars; dark band on lower jaw below eye; mouth slightly upturned, resembling a smile; 20 to 32 cm (8 to 13 in).

HABITAT: Primary forest in eastern lowlands; arboreal; basks head-up in the sun on trunks of small trees; day-active.

REGION: AMA

Plate 12d
Red-eyed Dwarf Iguana
Enyaliodes microlepis
ID: Moderately large, rough-scaled, long-tailed, with a short, chunky head and snout; upper body bright to dark green with turquoise spots; black band on throat; chin/dewlap area yellow to orange; bright red eye; yellowish green belly; 20 to 30 cm (8 to 12 in).

HABITAT: Primary forest in western lowlands; on branches and bushes within 2 m (6.5 ft) of ground; day-active.

REGION: MCL

Plate 12e
Iridescent Dwarf Iguana
Ophryoessoides iridescens
ID: Small, somewhat flattened, rough-scaled lizard with fairly short tail; upper body pale brown to olive with faint darker cross-bars; some also with a few black cross-bars; males with a stripe along back, pale yellow-green scales scattered along sides, and turquoise lips; some individuals show iridescence in strong light; 10 to 15 cm (4 to 6 in).

HABITAT: On ground and low vegetation, tree trunks in more open, sunny areas (especially clearings and forest edges) in western lowlands; day-active.

REGION: MCL, ACL

Plate 12f
Thornytail Canopy Iguana
Uracentron flaviceps
ID: Moderately large, stout-bodied, with short, wide, thorny-scaled tail; upper body and belly black; head pale orange with black flecks; pinkish white collar circles neck; 20 to 25 cm (8 to 10 in).

HABITAT: Primary forest in eastern lowlands; upper branches of large trees (but can be spotted with binoculars); day-active.

REGION: AMA

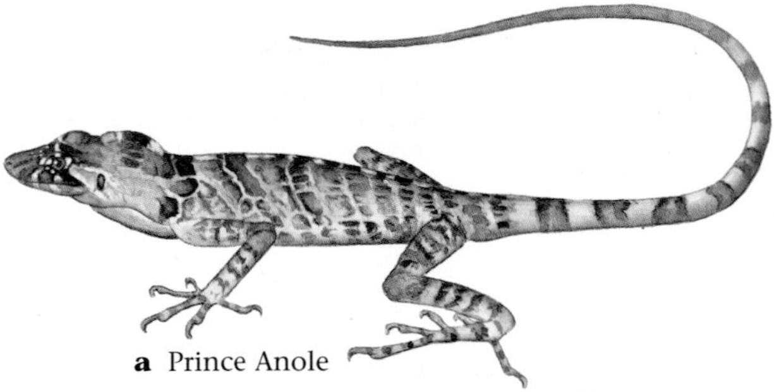

Plate 12 **285**

a Prince Anole

b Amazon Forest Anole

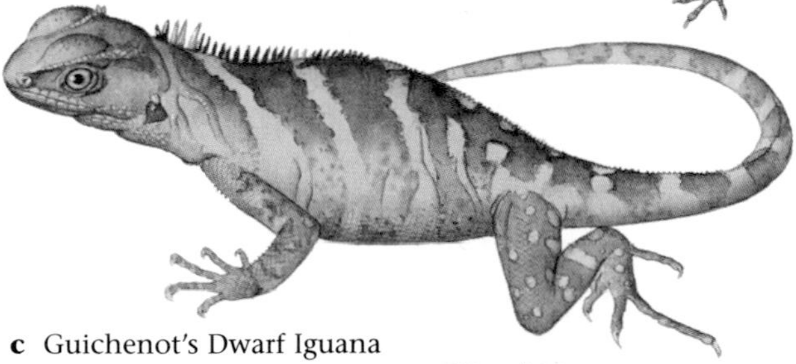

c Guichenot's Dwarf Iguana

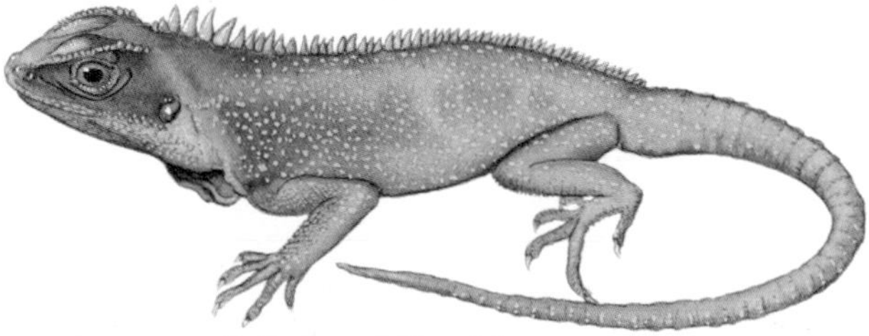

d Red-eyed Dwarf Iguana

e Iridescent Dwarf Iguana

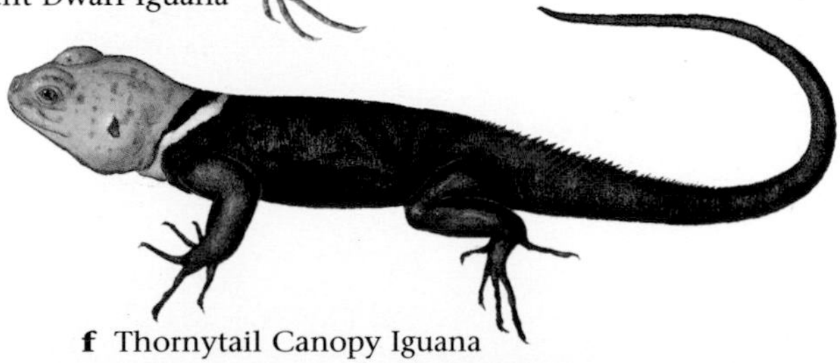

f Thornytail Canopy Iguana

Plate 13a
Common Neotropical Skink
Mabuya mabouya
ID: Small, with very shiny, glass-like smooth scales and long tail; upper body brown with bronzy sheen; sides darker and separated from upper body by narrow greenish bronze stripe; belly greenish bronze; underside of tail pale blue; 10 to 20 cm (4 to 8 in).

HABITAT: Open areas such as clearings and forest edges in eastern and western lowlands; terrestrial but also on low vegetation, tree trunks; basks in sun.

REGION: MCL, ACL, AMA

Plate 13b
Peter's Common Ameiva
Ameiva ameiva petersi
ID: Large, slender, with angular pointed head and snout, and long tail; body and sides patterned with bright green; light and dark stripes and spots run lengthwise along body; belly bluish white; 30 to 40 cm (12 to 16 in).

HABITAT: Eastern lowland forests; basks in sun on ground in clearings, forest edges; day-active; similar species occur in the western lowlands.

REGION: AMA

Plate 13c
Emerald-striped Teiid
Kentropyx pelviceps
ID: Moderately large, slender, with angular pointed head and snout, and long tail; wide, bright emerald green stripe runs from the tip of snout to mid-back, where it becomes reddish brown or tan; dark brown stripes border the green stripe on either side; throat grayish white; belly and undersides of limbs pale orange; 25 to 35 cm (10 to 14 in).

HABITAT: Secondary and primary forest in eastern lowlands; on ground but also in low vegetation; forest edges, treefall gaps in forest; basks in sun; day-active.

REGION: AMA

Plate 13d
Black Tegu
(also called Common Tegu)
Tupinambis teguixin
ID: Large, fairly stout-bodied, with angular pointed head and snout, and long tail; upper body with shiny scales patterned black and white, forming irregular narrow cross-bands that become wider on tail; to 80+ cm (32+ in).

HABITAT: Eastern lowlands; basks in sun on ground or on fallen logs; along forest edges, in clearings; day-active.

REGION: AMA

Note: CITES Appendix II listed

Plate 13e
Spiny Stream Teiid
Echinosaura horrida
ID: Small, dark mud-brown, resembling a tiny crocodile; upper body and neck covered with raised spiny scales projecting and curving to the rear, with remaining scales flat and irregular; thick tail with scales arranged to form four distinct ridges; lance-shaped head distinct from body; belly dull tan with scattered irregular brown spots and blotches; 12 to 17 cm (5 to 7 in).

HABITAT: Steep valleys in western lowland forests; primary forests but also in agricultural areas tucked into forests; along shaded streams, in leaf litter, beneath logs, in rock or root cavities; often covered with mud; day-active.

REGION: MCL, ACL

Plate 13f
Brown Ground Teiid
Alopoglossus festae
ID: Very small, slender, long-tailed, with raised ridges on each scale; upper body dull brown; belly dull yellow to reddish brown; 10 to 15 cm (4 to 6 in).

HABITAT: Western lowlands; terrestrial in areas with thick leaf-litter and scattered patches of sun; day-active; similar species found in western and eastern lowlands.

REGION: MCL, ACL

Plate 13 287

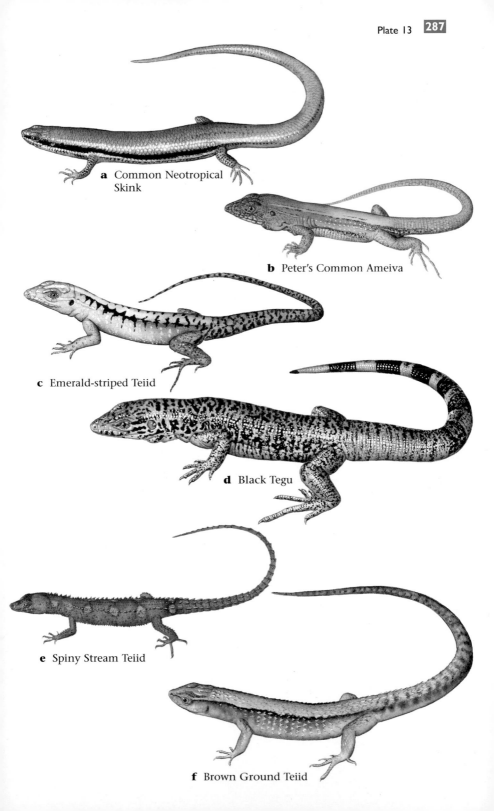

a Common Neotropical Skink

b Peter's Common Ameiva

c Emerald-striped Teiid

d Black Tegu

e Spiny Stream Teiid

f Brown Ground Teiid

Plate 14a

Brown Pelican
Pelecanus occidentalis

ID: Very large (1.3 m, 4 ft), brown and white (adult) or grayish (immature) seabird.

HABITAT: Coastal areas and estuaries where it flies in line or "V" formation low over water's surface or soars high over coastal hills and cliffs; rarely in freshwater lakes near coast.

REGION: MCL, ACL, GAL

Plate 14b

Blue-footed Booby
Sula nebouxii

ID: Large (86 cm, 2.8 ft); bright blue feet obvious only when standing on land (see Plate 91c); whitish breast and mottled dark back in flight.

HABITAT: Soaring low over ocean's surface and diving; seldom seen on land along coast of mainland but common on Galápagos Islands.

REGION: MCL, ACL, GAL

Plate 14c

Magnificent Frigatebird
Fregata magnificens

ID: Large (1 m, 3.3 ft); mostly dark; forked tail and immense narrow wings in flight (wingspan 2.2 m, 7 ft).

HABITAT: Soaring high over coast and chasing other birds to rob them of freshly caught fish.

REGION: MCL, ACL, GAL

Plate 14d

Neotropic Cormorant
Phalacrocorax brasilianus

ID: Large (69 cm, 2.3 ft); all black; long neck.

HABITAT: Swimming duck-like in water, sitting upright on dead branches in or near the water, or flying in flocks of long lines or "V" formation on or over coastal estuaries, freshwater reservoirs, rivers and cochas.

REGION: MCL, ACL, AMA

Plate 14e

Anhinga
Anhinga anhinga

ID: Large (86 cm, 2.8 ft); black with light upper wing patches and extremely long neck.

HABITAT: Singly or in pairs sitting on branches of trees near water; swimming with only head and neck exposed; or flying and even soaring eagle-like high overhead.

REGION: MCL, ACL, AMA

Plate 14f

Chilean Flamingo
Phoenicopterus chilensis

ID: Large (1 m, 3.3 ft); pink to whitish pink; yellow and black bill; adults with pale-colored legs and pink "knees." In flight with long neck extended and black flight feathers on trailing half of wings.

HABITAT: Small flocks winter in coastal mangrove estuaries, mudflats, salt lagoons.

REGION: ACL

Plate 14 289

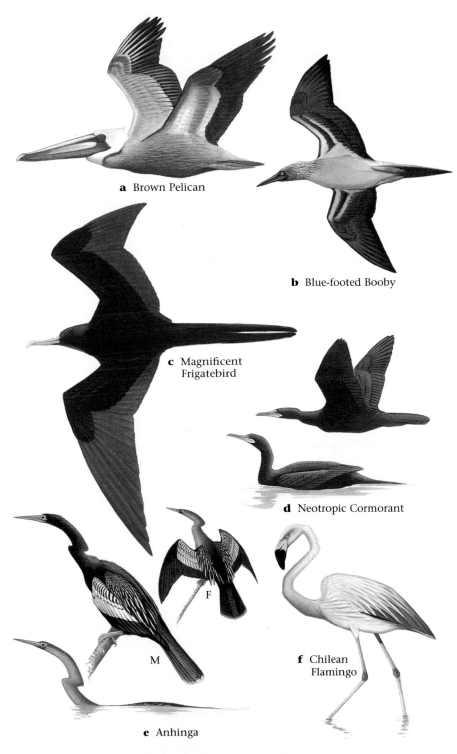

a Brown Pelican

b Blue-footed Booby

c Magnificent
Frigatebird

d Neotropic Cormorant

F

M

e Anhinga

f Chilean
Flamingo

Plate 15a
Gray-headed Gull
Larus cirrocephalus
ID: Medium-sized (45 cm, 1.5 ft); adults with light gray head, black wing tip with distinct white spots in flight. Similar wintering Laughing Gulls, *Larus atricilla*, with wing tips all black.

HABITAT: Coastal estuaries and river mouths.

REGION: ACL

Plate 15b
Gull-billed Tern
Sterna nilotica
ID: Medium-sized (36 cm, 1.2 ft); wings and body whitish with heavy all black bill. (Similar wintering Royal Terns, *Sterna maxima*, have orangish red bills.)

HABITAT: Coastal estuaries and river mouths.

REGION: ACL

Plate 15c
Andean Gull
Larus serranus
ID: Medium-sized (46 cm, 1.5 ft); breeding adults with black head. Only gull in the high Andes.

HABITAT: Páramo lakes and marshy areas.

REGION: HAP

Plate 15d
Large-billed Tern
Phaetusa simplex
ID: Medium-sized (38 cm, 1.3 ft); black, white and gray wings in flight; large greenish yellow bill.

HABITAT: Larger rivers and occasionally cochas of the Oriente lowlands.

REGION: AMA

Plate 15e
Yellow-billed Tern
Sterna superciliaris
ID: Medium-sized (25 cm, 10 in); white wings with black tips; slender yellow bill.

HABITAT: Larger rivers and occasionally cochas of the Oriente lowlands.

REGION: AMA

Plate 15f
Black Skimmer
Rynchops niger
ID: Medium-sized (44 cm, 1.4 ft); black on top and white below with an immense red and black bill. Peculiar low flight over water's surface with lower part of bill "skimming" the water.

HABITAT: Coastal estuaries and larger rivers of lowland Oriente.

REGION: ACL, AMA

Plate 15 291

c Andean Gull

a Gray-headed Gull

b Gull-billed Tern

f Black Skimmer

d Large-billed Tern

e Yellow-billed Tern

Plate 16a

Boat-billed Heron
Cochlearius cochlearius
ID: Large (49 cm, 1.6 ft), chunky, with monstrously wide bill.

HABITAT: Roosts by day in small group or alone in thick vegetation along water courses; feeds at night on beaches and vegetated water edges.

REGION: AMA

Plate 16b

Snowy Egret
Egretta thula
ID: Large (61 cm, 2 ft); adults all white with black bill, legs and bright yellow feet.

HABITAT: Coastal estuaries, river mouths, lowland lakes, marshes and rivers, usually solitary.

REGION: MCL, ACL, AMA

Playe 16c

Cattle Egret
Bubulcus ibis
ID: Large (51 cm, 1.7 ft); adults all white with orange-yellow bill and greenish legs. During the breeding season the back becomes pinkish orange and the legs and bill reddish.

HABITAT: Marshes, pastures and open areas along rivers and lakes from lowlands to 2600 m (8500 ft) elevation, often in flocks.

REGION: MCL, ACL, ESA, WSA, AMA

Plate 16d

Great Egret
(also called Common Egret)
Ardea alba
ID: Large (1 m, 3.3 ft); all white with yellow bill and black legs.

HABITAT: Coastal estuaries, river mouths, lowland lakes, marshes and rivers; usually solitary.

REGION: MCL, ACL, AMA

Plate 16e

Rufescent Tiger-heron
Tigrisoma lineatum
ID: Large (70 cm, 2.3 ft), chunky; adults chestnut, black and white; immatures buffy and white with barred back.

HABITAT: Solitary in thick vegetation along lowland watercourses.

REGION: MCL, AMA

Plate 16 **293**

b Snowy Egret

IM

a Boat-billed Heron

d Great Egret

IM

c Cattle Egret

IM

e Rufescent Tiger-heron

Plate 17a
Cocoi Heron
Ardea cocoi
ID: Large (1.2 m, 4 ft); white neck and throat, grayish body, top and sides of head all black. (Similar Great Blue Heron, *Ardea herodias*, on Galápagos and rarely in northwestern mainland has gray neck and only the sides of head black.)

HABITAT: Solitary in coastal estuaries, mangroves, and lowland river banks, marshes, cochas.

REGION: MCL, ACL, AMA

Plate 17b
Green Heron
(also called Striated Heron)
Buteroides striatus
ID: Medium-sized (40 cm, 1.3 ft); gray neck, greenish back. Gives loud high-pitched squawk when frightened into flight. The illustration is of the northern race that appears in the Oriente during the winter. The resident race is similar but has gray instead of rusty-coloured cheeks and chest. On the Galápagos this gray-necked race is also resident along with yet another form that is almost entirely gray, the Lava Heron. Some experts separate these forms into three seperate species.

HABITAT: Solitary low in vegetation near water's surface of mangroves, lowland swamps, small rivers and cochas.

REGION: MCL, ACL, AMA, GAL

Plate 17c
Capped Heron
Pilherodius pileatus
ID: Large (60 cm, 2 ft); white body, cream-colored neck, black cap and bare blue skin on face.

HABITAT: Solitary in vegetation and shallow water along forested lowland streams and lakes.

REGION: AMA

Plate 17d
Gray-necked Wood-rail
Aramides cajanea
ID: Large (37 cm, 15 in); bright red legs, long bill, gray neck contrasting with rust breast. (Replaced in coastal mangroves by similar Rufous-necked Wood-rail, *Aramides axillaris*.)

HABITAT: Forested swampy areas of lowlands.

REGION: AMA

Plate 17e
Wattled Jacana
Jacana jacana
ID: Medium-sized (25 cm, 10 in); adults with bright yellow bill, rust-colored body, yellow-green wings in flight and extremely long toes; immatures with white breast and bold white eyeline.

HABITAT: Grassy edges and lily pads of freshwater swamps and marshes of the lowands.

REGION: MCL, ACL, AMA

Plate 17　295

d Gray-necked Wood-rail

c Capped Heron

a Cocoi Heron

b Green Heron

IM

e Wattled Jacana

Plate 18a

Sunbittern
Eurypyga helias

ID: Medium-sized (47 cm, 1.5 ft); slender neck, small head with bold stripes; in flight or during display the spread wings with a distinctive "sunburst" pattern.

HABITAT: Along forested streams and lakes of lowlands.

REGION: MCL, AMA

Plate 18b

Sungrebe
Heliornis fulica

ID: Medium-sized (29 cm, 11 in); duck-like with bold white stripes on head and neck.

HABITAT: Swims under overhanging vegetation along lowland lakes and small rivers; escapes by flying low over water often hitting the surface with its running feet.

REGION: MCL, AMA

Plate 18c

Hoatzin
Opisthocomus hoazin

ID: Large (64 cm, 2.1 ft); rusty colored with buffy breast; crest on head and large wings and long tail.

HABITAT: In small family groups along forested swamps, cochas and small rivers.

REGION: AMA

Plate 18d

Horned Screamer
Anhima cornuta

ID: Very large (91 cm, 3 ft); dark back, white belly; white wing patch in flight obvious; call a deep, throaty gulp heard far away.

HABITAT: Swamps, marshes and nearby tree tops; individuals or pairs often soar high on broad wings.

REGION: ACL, AMA

Plate 18e

Silvery Grebe
Podiceps occipitalis

ID: Medium-sized (28 cm, 11 in); duck-like with pointed bill; light gray back; white underparts; silvery tufts on sides of head.

HABITAT: Páramo lakes above 2800 m (9000 ft) ringed with vegetation.

REGION: HAP

Plate 18 **297**

a Sunbittern

e Silvery Grebe

b Sungrebe

c Hoatzin

d Horned Screamer

Plate 19a

Muscovy Duck
Cairina moschata

ID: Large (84 cm, 2.8 ft); black with red bare face (male) and large white wing patches obvious in flight.

HABITAT: Mangroves, lowland forested swamps, rivers and cochas.

REGION: ACL, AMA

Plate 19b

Orinoco Goose
Neochen jubata

ID: Large (75 cm, 2.5 ft); buff and rusty colored; broad white band on inner half of wings obvious in flight.

HABITAT: Sand bars of remote lowland rivers.

REGION: AMA

Plate 19c

White-cheeked Pintail
Anas bahamensis

ID: Medium-sized (42 cm, 1.4 ft); all brown with strikingly white cheeks and throat; bill with bright red base.

HABITAT: Coastal estuaries and mangroves.

REGION: ACL, GAL

Plate 19d

Yellow-billed (Brown) Pintail
Anas georgica

ID: Large (66 cm, 2.2 ft); all pale brown with yellow bill. (The other common duck of páramo lakes, the Speckled Teal, *Anas flavirostris*, is smaller (43 cm, 1.4 ft), shorter-necked, and darker.)

HABITAT: Marshes and lakes of páramo.

REGION: HAP

Plate 19e

Torrent Duck
Merganetta armata

ID: Medium-sized (40 cm, 1.3 ft); long slender body with red bill; male with black and white head and neck stripes, white-breast with dark streaks; female with buffy breast and neck.

HABITAT: Rushing mountain streams and rivers between 1500 and 3500 m (5000 and 11,500 ft) elevation.

REGION: ESA, WSA

Plate 19　299

a Muscovy Duck

b Orinoco Goose

M

F

e Torrent Duck

c White-cheeked Pintail

d Yellow-billed Pintail

Plate 20a

Whimbrel
Numenius phaeopus
ID: Medium-sized (44 cm, 1.4 ft); long bill curved downwards; muted black and white stripes on head; brownish body. Nonbreeding and breeding plumage the same.

HABITAT: Outer sand beaches along the coast.

REGION: MCL, ACL, GAL

Plate 20b

Pied Lapwing
Vanellus cayanus
ID: Medium-sized (23 cm, 9 in); strikingly black and white-patterned with bright red legs. (The larger (33 cm, 1.1 ft) and slightly less-boldly patterned Andean Lapwing, *Vanellus resplendens*, is a common and noisy resident of wet grassy areas and marsh edges in páramo between 2500 and 4000 m, 8200 and 13,000 ft.)

HABITAT: Sandy beaches and islands on large rivers of the Oriente.

REGION: AMA

Plate 20c

Black-necked Stilt
Himantopus mexicanus
ID: Medium-sized (37 cm, 1.2 ft); tall, slender with striking black and white body and pinkish red legs.

HABITAT: Coastal estuaries and mangrove swamps.

REGION: MCL, ACL, GAL

Plate 20d

Andean Snipe
Gallinago jamesoni
ID: Medium-sized (30 cm, 1 ft); chunky, short-tailed and long-billed, its barred breast and distinctive eyestripes are difficult to see as it flies up from underfoot.

HABITAT: Grassy bogs, wet meadows and moist páramo above 3200 m (10,500 ft).

REGION: HAP

Plate 20e

Spotted Sandpiper
Actitis macularia
ID: Small (18 cm, 7 in); pale-breasted; bobs up and down while walking or resting; in flight a long, thin white stripe on upper wing surface; flies with a twittering, stiff-winged beat low over the water's surface; the breast spots only appear on individuals preparing (March to April) to migrate to northern nesting areas in North America.

HABITAT: Solitary on rocks, branches and sandy beaches along lowland rivers and lakes; some individuals present throughout the year.

REGION: MCL, AMA, GAL

Plate 20f

Sanderling
Calidris alba
ID: Medium-sized (20 cm, 8 in); light gray to whitish with short, black legs. Broad white wing stripe in flight. Turns rusty colored in preparation for migration north in April.

HABITAT: Small groups chase waves back and forth on sandy ocean beaches; present in Ecuador only in winter (July to April).

REGION: MCL, ACL, GAL

Plate 20 **301**

a Whimbrel

c Black-necked Stilt

d Andean Snipe

b Pied Lapwing

e Spotted Sandpiper

f Sanderling

Plate 21a

Black-bellied Plover
Pluvialis squatarola

ID: Medium-sized (30 cm, 1 ft); light gray nonbreeding plumage with black "wing pits" in flight; in breeding plumage in preparation for migration north (April) sides of face and belly become black.

HABITAT: Solitary on coastal estuaries, mudflats and sandy beaches.

REGION: MCL, ACL, GAL

Plate 21b

Rufous-bellied Seedsnipe
Attagis gayi

ID: Medium-sized (30 cm, 1 ft); dove- or quail-like with rusty colored breast, blackish back.

HABITAT: Dry, open páramo vegetation up to snow-line.

REGION: HAP

Plate 21c

Great Tinamou
Tinamus major

ID: Medium-sized (46 cm, 1.5 ft); short tail; whitish throat and belly; largest tinamou in lowland forests. Gives loud quavering whistles at dawn and late afternoon.

HABITAT: Floor of moist lowland forests.

REGION: MCL, AMA

Plate 21d

Little Tinamou
Crypturellus soui

ID: Medium-sized (23 cm, 9 in); whitish throat; no barring; smallest tinamou in Ecuador. Gives series of quavering whistles each rising in pitch.

HABITAT: Floor of lowland scrubby secondary forest, gardens and plantations.

REGION: MCL, ACL, AMA

Plate 21e

Undulated Tinamou
Crypturellus undulatus

ID: Medium-sized (28 cm, 11 in); whitish throat with distinctive barring on sides of lower belly. Gives low four-note whistle through the day, "ooh, oh-oh, ah," with last note rising.

HABITAT: Floor of lowland flooded forest, and moist secondary forest.

REGION: AMA

Plate 21 303

a Black-bellied Plover

b Rufous-bellied Seedsnipe

c Great Tinamou

d Little Tinamou

e Undulated Tinamou

Plate 22 (*See also*: Guans and Trumpeter, p. 108)

Plate 22a

Speckled Chachalaca
Ortalis guttata
ID: Large (53 cm, 1.7 ft); long tail; pheasant-like with obvious whitish spots on neck and breast. (It is replaced in the tropical dry forest of southwestern Ecuador by the similar-sized Rufous-headed Chachalaca, *Ortalis erythroptera*, which lacks the spots and has a rusty colored head.)

HABITAT: Family groups in trees of forest edge and along water courses; raucous calls between family groups at dawn.

REGION: AMA

Plate 22b

Spix's Guan
Penelope jacquacu
ID: Large (89 cm, 2.9 ft); long neck and tail, bare red skin on face and throat. Gives a wheezing whistle-like call when frightened and flies noisily through mid-levels of forest.

HABITAT: Solitary or in pairs in upper levels of moist lowland forest.

REGION: AMA

Plate 22c

Blue-throated Piping-Guan
Pipile cumanensis
ID: Large (69 cm, 2.3 ft); blackish body; white top of head; whitish blue bare throat and face; large white wing patch in flight. Gives wing-whirring sounds that travel considerable distance.

HABITAT: Tops of lowland forest trees, especially at forest edge or along rivers.

REGION: AMA

Plate 22d

Salvin's Curassow
Mitu salvini
ID: Large (89 cm, 3 ft); blackish; huge red bill; belly and tail tip white. Low humming sounds given at dawn.

HABITAT: Floor and lower branches of *tierra firme* forest and along river edges.

REGION: AMA

Plate 22e

Gray-winged Trumpeter
Psophia crepitans
ID: Large (53 cm, 1.7 ft); blackish; long legs; gray back.

HABITAT: Family groups of five to 15 on the floor of lowland primary forest; fly to mid-level branches to escape danger and roost at night.

REGION: AMA

Plate 22 **305**

a Speckled Chachalaca

b Spix's Guan

c Blue-throated Piping-Guan

d Salvin's Curassow

e Gray-winged
Trumpeter

Plate 23a
Turkey Vulture
Cathartes aura
ID: Large (75 cm, 2.5 ft); blackish with silverish underwings, long tail, and bright red head; in flight wings held in a broad "V," or dihedral, with little or no flapping (wingspan 1.8 m, 5.8 ft).

HABITAT: Solitary or in small groups soaring on rising warm air thermals in lowlands with open country and secondary forest, up to the intervalley highlands near Quito.

REGION: MCL, ACL, ESA, WSA, HAP, AMA

Plate 23b
Black Vulture
Coragyps atratus
ID: Large (62 cm, 2 ft); blackish with white patch on underside of wing, short tail, and all black head; in flight wings held flat and flap frequently (wingspan 1.4 m, 4.6 ft). On the ground runs like a huge chicken.

HABITAT: Small to large groups soaring on thermals or sitting gathered around garbage or offal; almost always associated with human settlements.

REGION: MCL, ACL, ESA, WSA, HAP, AMA

Plate 23c
Greater Yellow-headed Vulture
Cathartes melambrotus
ID: Large (80 cm, 2.6 ft); similar to Turkey Vulture but with a bright yellow head.

HABITAT: Solitary or in pairs over lowland primary forest.

REGION: AMA

Plate 23d
King Vulture
Sarcoramphus papa
ID: Large (80 cm, 2.6 ft); white with short, black tail and trailing edge of wings; colorful head is difficult to discern at a distance; soars with wings held flat (wingspan 2 m, 6.6 ft).

HABITAT: Solitary or in pairs over lowland forest usually away from human settlements.

REGION: MCL, ACL, AMA

Plate 23e
Andean Condor
Vultur gryphus
ID: Very large (1.3 m, 4.3 ft); black body; top of wings largely whitish; white ruff on neck; dull red head; in flight long, wide wings held flat with wing tip feathers spread (wingspan 3 m, 10 ft).

HABITAT: Páramo and open areas above 3000 m (10,000 ft).

REGION: HAP

Plate 23   **307**

a Turkey Vulture

b Black Vulture

d King Vulture

c Greater Yellow-headed
Vulture

e Andean
Condor

Plate 24 (*See also*: Kites, p. 112)

Plate 24a
Gray-headed Kite
Leptodon cayanensis
ID: Large (50 cm, 1.7 ft); white breast; long narrow tail with bold black and white bars; dark banded pattern on undersides of broad, rounded wings; soars in flight.

HABITAT: Near lowland forested streams, lakes and rivers.

REGION: MCL, AMA

Plate 24b
American Swallow-tailed Kite
Elanoides forficatus
ID: Large (60 cm, 2 ft), spectacular and beautiful; black and white with pointed wings and deeply forked tail; often soars over rivers and forest canopy in large groups.

HABITAT: Lowland secondary and primary forests.

REGION: MCL, AMA

Plate 24c
Snail Kite
Rostrhamus sociabilis
ID: Medium-sized (44 cm, 1.4 ft); male all gray with long squared tail, white rump, red bare skin on face; female similar but browner with streaked breast.

HABITAT: Always near or on extensive freshwater swamps of the lowlands, sitting on telephone wires or low bushes or flying low over marsh's surface.

REGION: MCL, ACL

Plate 24d
Double-toothed Kite
Harpagus bidentatus
ID: Medium-sized (35 cm, 1.1 ft); rusty colored breast, light throat with a dark center stripe.

HABITAT: Sits on branches in mid-level to canopy of secondary and primary lowland forest; often in association with monkey troop, catching insects scared up by the troop.

REGION: MCL, AMA

Plate 24e
Plumbeous Kite
Ictinia plumbea
ID: Medium-sized (36 cm, 1.2 ft); all gray with long pointed wings, which in flight reveal extensive rusty colored tips.

HABITAT: Sits at top of tall dead trees in lowlands; often soars alone or in pairs, especially along large rivers.

REGION: MCL, ACL, AMA

Plate 24 **309**

b American Swallow-tailed Kite

a Gray-headed Kite

d Double-toothed Kite

c Snail Kite

F

M

e Plumbeous Kite

Plate 25 (*See also*: Hawks and Eagles, p. 112)

Plate 25a

Mangrove Black Hawk
Buteogallus subtilis
ID: Large (50 cm, 1.6 ft); all black; extremely broad wings and broad tail with a single broad white band; varying amount of rusty color in flight feathers of wings.

HABITAT: Confined to mangroves and coastal estuaries.

REGION: MCL, ACL

Plate 25b

Roadside Hawk
Buteo magnirostris
ID: Medium-sized (35 cm, 1.1 ft); rusty barred breast; in flight a large rusty colored patch in each wing.

HABITAT: Common sitting alone in bushes and small trees in lowland open areas and secondary forest edge to 2550 m (8200 ft).

REGION: WCL, ACL, ESA, WSA, AMA

Plate 25c

Puna Hawk
(also called Variable Hawk)
Buteo poecilochrous
ID: Large (60 cm, 2 ft); body color varies from dark to white-breasted, but tail is usually white with a distinct black band on end; in flight soars with broad wings and broad tail.

HABITAT: Individuals soaring above 3000 m (10,000 ft) over páramo highlands.

REGION: HAP

Plate 25d

Harpy Eagle
Harpia harpyja
ID: Very large (1 m, 3.3 ft); crest; black chest; short, rounded wings; long banded tail.

HABITAT: Remote primary forest of lowlands.

REGION: AMA

Plate 25e

Ornate Hawk-eagle
Spizaetus ornatus
ID: Large (60 cm, 2 ft); rusty colored chest, face and neck; black crest; in flight soars to great heights and rounded wings are noticeably banded underneath; often calls while soaring, a loud series of whistles with every fifth note slurred up in pitch.

HABITAT: Lowland primary and tall secondary forest to 2000 m (6500 ft).

REGION: MCL, ACL, ESA, WSA, AMA

Plate 25 311

a Mangrove Black Hawk

b Roadside Hawk

d Harpy Eagle

e Ornate Hawk-eagle

c Puna Hawk

Plate 26a

Black Caracara
Daptrius ater
ID: Medium-sized (45 cm, 1.4 ft); all black with bold white patch at base of tail; bare skin of face bright orange; noisy, with a harsh scream given frequently. (Replaced in highland páramo by the larger (55 cm, 1.8 ft), more boldly black and white patterned, Carunculated Caracara, *Phalocoboenus carunculatus*.)

HABITAT: Seen in pairs in trees or on beaches of lowland rivers and lakes.

REGION: AMA

Plate 26b

Laughing Falcon
Herpetotheres cachinnans
ID: Large (52 cm, 1.7 ft); chunky body; buffy white underparts; black mask; often gives its loud falsetto "laughing" call in morning and afternoon.

HABITAT: Sits solitarily in secondary forest and plantations from lowlands to 2500 m (8200 ft).

REGION: MCL, ACL, ESA, WSA, AMA

Plate 26c

Collared Forest-falcon
Micrastur semitorquatus
ID: Large (50 cm, 1.6 ft); white breast; long banded tail; black back and top of head separated by a broad white band or collar at the nape of the neck.

HABITAT: Sits solitarily in lowland primary and secondary forest.

REGION: MCL, ACL, AMA

Plate 26d

Bat Falcon
Falco rufigularis
ID: Medium-sized (25 cm, 10 in); dark body with white and rusty colored breast; flies with a rapid wingbeat on long, pointed wings; seldom soars. (Replaced in highlands above 2500 m (8200 ft) by similar sized and shaped American Kestrel, *Falco sparverius*, which is lighter-breasted with a blue-gray and rusty back (male) or brownish back (female).)

HABITAT: Solitary or in pairs sitting at the top of tall, exposed trees.

REGION: MCL, ACL, AMA

Plate 26e

Osprey
Pandion haliaetus
ID: Large (60 cm, 2 ft); white underparts, dark upperparts; in flight long, slender wings held with a peculiar bow in the middle.

HABITAT: Always associated with freshwater lakes and rivers or coastal estuaries and river mouths where it hunts for fish. Nonbreeding in Ecuador but some individuals present year around.

REGION: MCL, ACL, ESA, WSA, AMA, GAL

Plate 26   313

b Laughing Falcon

a Black Caracara

c Collared Forest-falcon

e Osprey

d Bat Falcon

Plate 27a

Band-tailed Pigeon
Columba fasciata
ID: Medium-sized (36 cm, 1.2 ft); broad fan-shaped tail with gray band at end; white band on nape of neck.

HABITAT: Flocks fly high over mountain ridges and cloud forest tree tops between 2000 and 3000 m (6500 and 10,000 ft); low cooing sounds very owl-like.

REGION: ESA, WSA

Plate 27b

Pale-vented Pigeon
Columba cayennensis
ID: Medium-sized (30 cm, 1 ft); rusty back; light gray rump patch in flight.

HABITAT: Single or in pairs perched on trees or shrubs at edge of lowland swamps or flying over open wet areas.

REGION: MCL, ACL, AMA

Plate 27c

Ruddy Pigeon
Columba subvinacea
ID: Medium-sized (30 cm, 1 ft); dark brown with cinnamon-colored underwings evident in flight; best identified by its deep-whistled and four-noted call, with the third note higher and lengthened. (The similar-looking Plumbeous Pigeon, *Columba plumbea*, occurs side by side with it and is best distinguished by its three-note whistle with emphasis on the first and last notes.)

HABITAT: Solitary or in pairs in mid-level to canopy of lowland moist primary and tall secondary forest.

REGION: MCL, ACL, AMA

Plate 27d

Croaking Ground-dove
Columbina cruziana
ID: Small (18 cm, 7 in); gray-brown with bright yellow swelling at base of bill. Call given from the ground in dense vegetation a low growl. (Very similar to the co-occurring Ecuadorean Ground-dove, *Columbina buckleyi*, which lacks the yellow swelling at the base of the bill.)

HABITAT: Together in small flocks of five to 20 in low desert vegetation, open scrub, and gardens.

REGION: ACL

Plate 27e

Black-winged Ground-dove
Metriopelia melanoptera
ID: Medium-sized (23 cm, 9 in); grayish with black wings and tail; white patch on bend of upper wing in flight.

HABITAT: Small flocks on the ground in páramo grassy areas with low vegetation above 3000 m (10,000 ft).

REGION: HAP

Plate 27 315

c Ruddy Pigeon

a Band-tailed Pigeon

b Pale-vented Pigeon

d Croaking Ground-dove

e Black-winged Ground-dove

Plate 28a
Eared Dove
Zenaida auriculata
ID: Medium-sized (25 cm, 10 in); wedge-shaped tail; brown colored back with black spots; two black lines in back of eye.

HABITAT: Solitary or in pairs on ground in drier highlands above 1200 m (4000 ft), especially in agricultural areas, city parks and gardens.

REGION: WSA, ESA, HAP

Plate 28b
White-tipped Dove
Leptotila verreauxi
ID: Medium-sized (28 cm, 11 in); rounded tail with broad white tips; no spots on back or head.

HABITAT: On ground in secondary forests, scrubby vegetation, and forest edge from lowlands to 2000 m (6500 ft).

REGION: MCL, ACL, ESA, WSA, AMA

Plate 28c
Ruddy Quail-dove
Geotrygon montana
ID: Medium-sized (23 cm, 9 in); rusty upperparts; buffy underparts; rusty stripe on cheek; male brighter than female.

HABITAT: Solitary or in pairs on floor of moist secondary and primary forest from lowlands to 2500 m (8200 ft).

REGION: MCL, ESA, WSA, AMA

Plate 28d
Pacific Parrotlet
Forpus coelestis
ID: Small (13 cm, 5 in); all green and blue with short pointed tail.

HABITAT: Small flocks of five to 15 in primary and secondary tropical dry forest, gardens and parks in towns and cities of lowlands.

REGION: ACL

Plate 28e
Cobalt-winged Parakeet
Brotogeris cyanoptera
ID: Medium-sized (20 cm, 8 in); green with short pointed tail.

HABITAT: Flocks of five to 50 in primary and secondary lowland moist forest. The loud, shrill chattering of a flock can be heard long before it becomes visible flying high overhead.

REGION: AMA

Plate 28 317

b White-tipped Dove

c Ruddy Quail-dove

a Eared Dove

d Pacific Parrotlet

e Cobalt-winged Parakeet

Plate 29 (*See also*: Parrots, p. 118)

Plate 29a

Blue-and-yellow Macaw
Ara ararauna
ID: Large (84 cm, 2.8 ft); blue upperparts, yellow lower parts, long tail; deep resonating calls.

HABITAT: In pairs or flocks of up to 20 in moist lowland forest, Mauritia Palm swamps and flooded forest.

REGION: AMA

Plate 29b

Scarlet Macaw
Ara macao
ID: Large (89 cm, 3 ft); bright red with yellow patches on upperwing; long tail; loud, harsh calls.

HABITAT: In pairs or small flocks in moist lowland forest.

REGION: AMA

Plate 29c

Chestnut-fronted Macaw
Ara severa
ID: Medium-sized (46 cm, 1.5 ft); green body; red underwings; long tail; whitish bare face patch; harsh voice carries long distances.

HABITAT: In pairs or small flocks in moist lowland forest.

REGION: MCL, AMA

Plate 29d

White-eyed Parakeet
Aratinga leucopthalmus
ID: Medium-sized (36 cm, 1.2 ft); all green with bright red and yellow patches on underwings; long pointed tail.

HABITAT: Large flocks of 20 to 100 flying high overhead or in treetops in lowland moist forest and Mauritia Palm swamps.

REGION: AMA

Plate 29e

Red-masked Parakeet
Aratinga erythrogenys
ID: Medium-sized (33 cm, 1.1 ft); green with bright red cheeks; small red patches on underwings; long pointed tail.

HABITAT: Pairs and small flocks flying over the forest or in treetops of lowland tropical dry forest up to cloud forest clearings at 2000 m (6500 ft).

REGION: MCL, ACL, WSA

Plate 29f

Dusky-headed Parakeet
Aratinga weddellii
ID: Medium-sized (28 cm, 11 in); green and blue body and underwings; gray head; white eye; long pointed tail.

HABITAT: Flocks of 10 to 50 in trees along lowland rivers and swampy forest.

REGION: AMA

Plate 29 319

a Blue-and-yellow Macaw

b Scarlet Macaw

d White-eyed Parakeet

c Chestnut-fronted Macaw

f Dusky-headed Parakeet

e Red-masked Parakeet

Plate 30a

White-breasted Parakeet
Pyrrhura albipectus
ID: Medium-sized (25 cm, 10 in); green with brown and orange head; pinkish white breast; bright scarlet patches on upperwing; tail long with green and maroon upper surface.

HABITAT: Endemic to the lower slopes of southeastern Ecuador (between 450 and 1200 m, 1500 and 4000 ft); small flocks fly low through the canopy of primary and secondary forest.

REGION: ESA

Plate 30b

Black-headed Parrot
Pionites melanocephala
ID: Medium-sized (23 cm, 9 in); black crown; green back; creamy white breast; short tail; high-pitched squealing calls.

HABITAT: In small flocks flying through the canopy of lowland primary forest.

REGION: AMA

Plate 30c

Blue-headed Parrot
Pionus menstruus
ID: Medium-sized (25 cm, 10 in); green body with blue head and chest; red at base of short tail; deep wingbeats in flight; high-pitched call.

HABITAT: In small flocks flying high over moist lowland forests, rivers and lakes.

REGION: MCL, AMA

Plate 30d

Orange-winged Parrot
Amazona amazonica
ID: Medium-sized (33 cm, 1.1 ft); green body with yellow and blue on head and cheeks; bright orange patch on upperwing; short tail; "twittering" shallow wingbeats in flight.

HABITAT: Pairs and small flocks near swampy forests and cochas.

REGION: AMA

Plate 30e

Mealy Parrot
Amazona farinosa
ID: Medium-sized (41 cm, 16 in); all green with small yellow spot on crown; short tail; "twittering" shallow wingbeats in flight. In the Oriente (form illustrated in flight) this species has a yellow patch on the crown of the head and an additional red stripe on the leading edge of the wing. In the coastal northwestern lowlands (form illustrated perched) it has no yellow on the crown and lacks the thin red stripe on the leading edge of the wing.

HABITAT: Pairs seen in treetops or flying low over moist lowland forest.

REGION: MCL, AMA

Plate 30   **321**

a White-breasted Parakeet

b Black-headed Parrot

c Blue-headed Parrot

d Orange-winged Parrot

e Mealy Parrot

Plate 31a

Striped Cuckoo
Tapera naevia
ID: Medium-sized (29 cm, 11 in); buff and brown-streaked above with pale breast; often difficult to see but easily heard as it give its monotonous and loud two-noted whistle (second note higher than the first) throughout the day.

HABITAT: Lowland scrubby vegetation, grassy pastures where it perches on fence posts or low bushes in early morning and skulks on the ground in dense cover the rest of the day. (Becoming more common and widespread with deforestation; although not yet known from the Oriente, will likely move in there from Colombia and eastern Perú eventually as forest clearing continues.)

REGION: WCL, ACL

Plate 31b

Squirrel Cuckoo
Piaya cayana
ID: Medium-sized (43 cm, 17 in); chestnut upperparts, gray underparts; extremely long tail with white spots at tip.

HABITAT: Solitary or in pairs; often runs along branches and hops or flies clumsily from tree to tree in mid-level and canopy of secondary and primary forests in lowlands to 2500 m (8200 ft); frequently in mixed bird species foraging flocks.

REGION: MCL, ACL, WSA, ESA, AMA

Plate 31c

Smooth-billed Ani
Crotophaga ani
ID: Medium-sized (33 cm, 1.1 ft); all black; dark eye; large thin bill; long tail. Loose flight appears uncoordinated.

HABITAT: Family groups in lowland open grassy areas, clearings, pastures and along roads.

REGION: MCL, ACL, AMA, GAL

Plate 31d

Greater Ani
Crotophaga major
ID: Large (47 cm, 1.6 ft); all black with bluish sheen; white eye; long tail. Loud calls that can sound like a metal factory when an entire flock calls together.

HABITAT: Flocks in low vegetation along lowland streams, lakes and forested swamps.

REGION: MCL, ACL, AMA

Plate 31e

Oilbird
Steatornis caripensis
ID: Large (48 cm, 1.6 ft); rusty color with distinct silver spots; long tail; hooked bill.

HABITAT: Active at night around fruiting palms and trees; spend day-time in large breeding caves at isolated sites from the lowlands to 3000 m (10,000 ft).

REGION: ESA, AMA

Plate 31 | 323

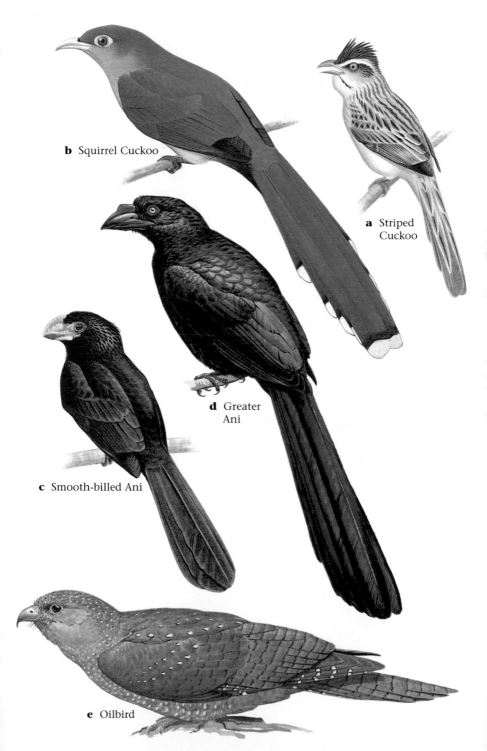

b Squirrel Cuckoo

a Striped Cuckoo

d Greater Ani

c Smooth-billed Ani

e Oilbird

Plate 32 (*See also*: Owls, p. 123)

Plate 32a

Tropical Screech-owl
Otus choliba

ID: Medium-sized (23 cm, 9 in); ear tufts; buffy white breast with dark streaks. Voice at night rising quavery whistle ending with two distinct, pure notes.

HABITAT: Active at night in secondary forest, forest edge, plantations and gardens from lowlands to 2500 m (8200 ft).

REGION: ESA, AMA

Plate 32b

Crested Owl
Lophostrix cristata

ID: Medium-sized (41 cm, 16 in); long white ear tufts; unstreaked buffy body.

HABITAT: Active at night high in trees of moist lowland forest.

REGION: AMA

Plate 32c

Spectacled Owl
Pulsatrix perspicillata

ID: Large (48 cm, 1.6 ft); lacks ear tufts; deep brown back and chest contrasting with white facial markings and white, unstreaked breast. Voice at night a loud series of resonating hoots resembling someone shaking a large piece of metal sheeting.

HABITAT: Active at night in moist lowland primary and secondary forest.

REGION: MCL, AMA

Plate 32d

Ferruginous Pygmy-owl
Glaucidium brasilianum

ID: Small (16 cm, 6 in); lacks ear tufts; relatively long tail; heavily streaked breast. Voice given commonly during day and night a series of high, whistled "whooks." (Replaced by the similar Andean Pygmy-owl, *Glaucidium jardinii*, above 2200 m (7200 ft) and by the Peruvian (Pacific) Pygmy-owl, *Glaucidium peruanum*, in tropical dry forests of southwestern coastal Ecuador.)

HABITAT: Active during day and at night in lowland secondary forest, forest edge and gardens.

REGION: AMA

Plate 32e

Black-banded Owl
Ciccaba huhula

ID: Medium-sized (36 cm, 1.2 ft); lacks ear tufts; black body with white bands. Voice given at night a loud scream ending with a distinct but low hoot.

HABITAT: Active at night in mid-level and canopy of moist lowland forest.

REGION: AMA

Plate 32   325

a Tropical Screech-owl

c Spectacled Owl

e Black-banded Owl

d Ferruginous Pygmy-owl

b Crested Owl

Plate 33a
Sand-colored Nighthawk
Chordeiles rupestris
ID: Medium-sized (22 cm, 9 in); buffy brown and white; in flight tail white except for black tip; long pointed wings white except for black tips and trailing edge. When disturbed from their roost during the day, they resemble a flock of terns flying.

HABITAT: Roosts during the day in flock of 10 to 100 on sand bars of large rivers in lowlands and in isolated trees in open flooded forest; night-active.

REGION: AMA

Plate 33b
Pauraque
Nyctidromis albicollis
ID: Medium-sized (28 cm, 11 in); mottled brown; usually seen in light of a flashlight when its orangish eyeshine reflects as it sits on the ground or in low vegetation along water courses. In flight, rounded wings have a bold white (male) or buffy (female) band, and outer tail feathers are white. Voice commonly heard at night is a low, down-slurring whistle-hum.

HABITAT: Solitary on forest edge, pastures, river beaches, open secondary forest and gardens in the lowlands.

REGION: MCL, ACL, AMA

Plate 33c
Lyre-tailed Nightjar
Uropsalis lyra
ID: Large (76 cm, 2.5 ft); spectacularly long tail of male obvious as it rises up from the road in the headlights of your vehicle; female more normally attired in brownish plumage.

HABITAT: Forest edge, roadsides of mid-elevation (1000 to 2500 m, 3300 to 8200 ft) cloud forest.

REGION: WSA, ESA

Plate 33d
Common Potoo
Nyctibius griseus
ID: Medium-sized (40 cm, 1.3 ft); gray-brown; long tail. Sits on exposed trees during the day with its bill pointing up, resembling a broken branch. Most often noticed by its mournful song of low whistles that descend slowly but deliberately in pitch, step-wise ever lower, especially on moonlit nights.

HABITAT: Lowland moist forest edge and along forested waterways.

REGION: MCL, ACL, AMA

Plate 33   327

b Pauraque

a Sand-colored Nighthawk

c Lyre-tailed Nightjar

M

M

c Lyre-tailed Nightjar

F

d Common Potoo

Plate 34a

White-collared Swift
Streptoprocne zonaris
ID: Medium-sized (20 cm, 8 in); black with bold white collar and slightly forked tail.

HABITAT: High overhead in swirling flocks of 10 to 200 individuals. Although they nest in the mid-elevations, they often descend to the lowlands to catch insects.

REGION: MCL, ACL, WSA, ESA, HAP, AMA

Plate 34b

Short-tailed Swift
Chaetura brachyura
ID: Small (10 cm, 4 in); all black; pale gray rump; almost tailless appearance.

HABITAT: In loose flocks overhead in lowland forest and cleared areas; sometimes mixed with other species of swifts.

REGION: AMA

Plate 34c

Fork-tailed Palm-swift
Tachornis squamata
ID: Small (13 cm, 5 in); slender, gray-brown with distinctively long and deeply forked tail.

HABITAT: Low over the canopy of lowland open forest or clearings, usually near Mauritia Palm stands, where they roost and nest; usually in small flocks of its own species or mixed in with other swift species.

REGION: AMA

Plate 34d

White-winged Swallow
Tachycineta albiventer
ID: Small (14 cm, 6 in); pure white underparts, blue-green upperparts; white patch on upperwing and on rump.

HABITAT: Perches on partially submerged poles and vegetation or flies low over lowland lakes and larger rivers.

REGION: AMA

Plate 34e

Southern Rough-winged Swallow
Stelgidopteryx ruficollis
ID: Small (13 cm, 5 in); brownish back with pale rump patch; gray-brown breast with contrasting light rusty throat.

HABITAT: Over rivers and nearby cleared areas, where it roosts together in small groups on exposed branches (lowlands to 2000 m, 6500 ft).

REGION: MCL, ACL, WSA, ESA, AMA

Plate 34 329

a White-collared Swift

b Short-tailed Swift

c Forked-tailed Palm-swift

d White-winged Swallow

e Southern Rough-winged Swallow

Plate 35a

Gray-breasted Martin
Progne chalybea

ID: Small (20 cm, 8 in); dark blue upperparts, grayish white underparts. (In the highlands replaced around human settlements by the smaller (13 cm, 5 in) and pure white-breasted and dark blue-backed Blue-and-white Swallow, *Notiochelidon cyanoleuca*.)

HABITAT: Lowland pastures, clearings, forest edge and over lakes and rivers; often abundant around human settlements, especially on the coast.

REGION: MCL, ACL, AMA

Plate 35b

White-banded Swallow
Atticora fasciata

ID: Small (15 cm, 6 in); completely bluish black with a bold white breast band; deeply forked tail.

HABITAT: Smaller forested rivers in the eastern foothills of the Andes between 400 and 1200 m (1300 and 4000 ft).

REGION: ESA, AMA

Plate 35c

Green Hermit
Phaethornis guy

ID: Small (13 cm, 5 in); long bill strongly curved down; greenish upperparts; long dark tail with long white tip; dark underparts; bright buffy head stripes and line down center of throat.

HABITAT: Moist secondary forest undergrowth of east slope foothills between 900 and 2000 m (3000 and 6500 ft); often in lecs.

REGION: ESA

Plate 35d

Long-tailed Hermit
Phaethornis superciliosus

ID: Small (13 cm, 5 in); long bill strongly curved down, brownish upperparts with contrasting buff rump; long dark tail with long white tip; buffy gray underparts; pale buffy head stripes and line down center of throat.

HABITAT: Moist secondary forest undergrowth of lowlands up to 1600 m (5200 ft) on the lower eastern slopes of the Andes; often in lecs.

REGION: ESA, AMA

Plate 35e

Little Hermit
Phaethornis longuemareus

ID: Small (9 cm, 3.5 in); long bill slightly curved down; coppery green upperparts with dirty brown rump; medium length tail with short white tip; buffy gray underparts; dirty white head stripes but no line down center of throat.

HABITAT: Moist undergrowth of secondary lowland forest up to 1000 m (3300 ft) elevation; often in lecs.

REGION: MCL, AMA

Plate 35 331

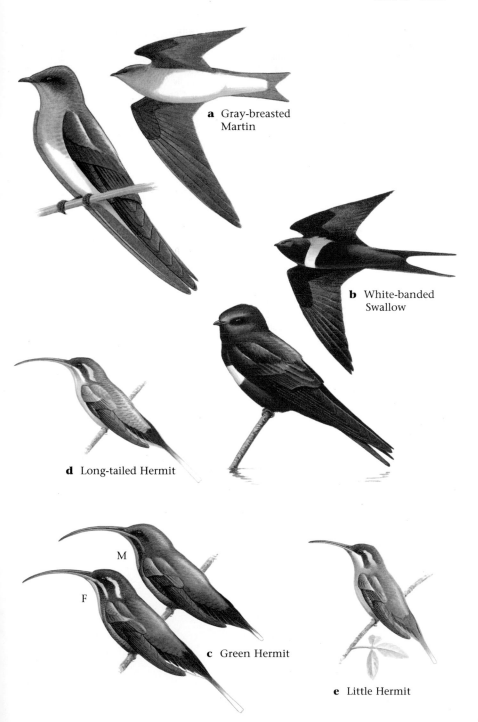

a Gray-breasted Martin

b White-banded Swallow

d Long-tailed Hermit

c Green Hermit

e Little Hermit

Plate 36 (*See also*: Hummingbirds, p. 129)

Plate 36a

White-tipped Sicklebill
Eutoxeres aquila
ID: Small (11 cm, 4.5 in); boldly streaked breast; sickle-shaped bill. (Largely replaced on east slope and lower eastern foothills by the similar Buff-tailed Sicklebill, *Eutoxeres condamini.*)

HABITAT: Moist undergrowth of mid-elevation secondary forest with patches of *Heliconia* plants between 1200 and 2000 m (4000 and 6500 ft).

REGION: WSA

Plate 36b

White-necked Jacobin
Florisuga mellivora
ID: Small (10 cm, 4 in); white lower belly, tail and crescent on neck of male contrast with an all-blue head and throat; scaly dark throat contrasts with the white lower belly of the female.

HABITAT: Undergrowth of moist lowland secondary forest, forest edge and gardens.

REGION: MCL, AMA

Plate 36c

Sparkling Violetear
Colibri coruscans
ID: Small (13 cm, 5 in); completely glittering green except for violet central breast and eye-mask that extends under bill; commonly heard singing its emphatic series of "sip" notes.

HABITAT: Open forest, clearings, gardens, city parks in the highlands above 2000 m (6500 ft).

REGION: HAP

Plate 36d

Green Thorntail
Popelairia conversii
ID: Tiny (8 cm, 3 in); bright green throat and long tail feathers of male; white band on rump of male and female.

HABITAT: Undergrowth of moist secondary lowland forest and at flowering trees.

REGION: MCL

Plate 36e

Fork-tailed Woodnymph
Thalurania furcata
ID: Small (10 cm, 4 in); purple breast and green throat of male; gray-breasted female similar to several other species. (Replaced by similar Crowned Woodnymph, *Thalurania colombica*, in moist forest of coastal lowlands.)

HABITAT: Undergrowth of moist lowland forest and forest edge.

REGION: AMA

Plate 36 333

b White-necked Jacobin

M

F

a White-tipped Sicklebill

M

F

d Green Thorntail

c Sparkling Violetear

e Fork-tailed Woodnymph

Plate 37a
Rufous-tailed Hummingbird
Amazilia tzacatl
ID: Small (9 cm, 3.5 in); straight reddish bill with black tip; greenish body with contrasting rusty colored tail.

HABITAT: Shrubby areas, forest edge, gardens in lowlands.

REGION: MCL, ACL

Plate 37b
Chimborazo (Ecuadorean) Hillstar
Oreotrochilus chimborazo
ID: Small (11 cm, 4.5 in); male with pure white breast with black line down center, violet head; female dull olive upperparts and white throat spotted green.

HABITAT: Rocky slopes and low vegetation of páramo.

REGION: HAP

Plate 37c
Ecuadorean Piedtail
Phlogophilus hemileucurus
ID: Tiny (8 cm, 3 in); white breast with green spots; clear white middle breast; rounded tail with broad white tips.

HABITAT: Mid-level of open primary forest in foothills.

REGION: ESA, AMA

Plate 37d
Green-crowned Brilliant
Heliodaxa jacula
ID: Small (13 cm, 5 in); male glittering green upper- and lowerparts, dark, deeply forked tail; female with distinct white spot in back of eye and white cheek stripe.

HABITAT: Openings and flowering bushes in mid-elevation cloud forest.

REGION: WSA

Plate 37e
Giant Hummingbird
Patagona gigas
ID: Medium-sized (19 cm, 7.5 in); largest of all hummingbirds; brown-buff breast; white rump.

HABITAT: Open dry highlands between 2000 and 3000 m (6500 and 10,000 ft) with flowering cactus and Century (*Agave*) plants.

REGION: HAP

c Ecuadorean
Piedtail

M

F

b Chimborazo
(Ecuadorean)
Hillstar

e Giant
Hummingbird

a Rufous-tailed Hummingbird

F

M

d Green-crowned
Brilliant

Plate 38a

Collared Inca
Coeligena torquata
ID: Small (11 cm, 4.5 in); striking white throat, breast, and large white tail contrast with dark green and black body.

HABITAT: Moist cloud forest undergrowth, flowering bushes between 2000 and 2500 m (6500 and 8200 ft).

REGION: WSA, ESA

Plate 38b

Sword-billed Hummingbird
Ensifera ensifera
ID: Small (11 cm, 4.5 in); bronze-green; enormous bill almost as long as body.

HABITAT: Forest edge, shrubby slopes and clearings in cloud forest between 2000 and 3000 m (6500 and 10,000 ft); often associated with the long, red and white flower of *Daytura*, or "huanto," bushes.

REGION: WSA, ESA, HAP

Plate 38c

Buff-tailed Coronet
Boissonneaua flavescens
ID: Small (11 cm, 4.5 in); green body; relatively short bill; bright cinnamon underwings; buffy tail.

HABITAT: Seen in cloud forest between 1500 and 2800 m (5000 and 9000 ft), in canopy, clinging to flowers with feet.

REGION: WSA

Plate 38d

Gorgeted Sunangel
Heliangelus strophianus
ID: Small (9 cm, 3.5 in); relatively short bill; shiny green upperparts; green breast with grayish buff lower belly; throat red with white crescent below it.

HABITAT: Bushes and undergrowth of cloud forest clearings between 2000 and 3000 m (6500 and 10,000 ft).

REGION: WSA

Plate 38e

Booted Racket-tail
Ocreatus underwoodii
ID: Tiny (8 cm, 3 in); male all green with long tail streamers ending in peculiar spatulate feathers; female with distinct white spot in back of eye, white underparts with green spots, and short white-tipped tail.

HABITAT: Flowering plants in undergrowth and canopy of cloud forest between 1500 and 2500 m (5000 and 8200 ft).

REGION: WSA, ESA

Plate 38 337

a Collared Inca

M

F

e Booted Racket-tail

b Sword-billed Hummingbird

d Gorgeted Sunangel

c Buff-tailed Coronet

Plate 39a

Black-tailed Trainbearer
Lesbia victoriae

ID: Medium-sized (25 cm, 10 in); green body; long black tail. Female's tail shorter than male's. (Similar but smaller (17 cm, 7 in) Green-tailed Trainbearer, *Lesbia nuna*, largely replaces it at lower elevations (2200 to 2800 m, 7000 to 9000 ft) and has an all-green tail.)

HABITAT: Bushy areas, forest edges and gardens of dry highlands (2600 to 4000 m, 8500 to 13,000 ft).

REGION: HAP

Plate 39b

Purple-backed Thornbill
Ramphomicron microrhynchum

ID: Tiny (7.5 cm, 3 in); male with extremely short bill, purple upperparts, green breast; female with short bill, green upperparts, buffy underparts with green spots.

HABITAT: Moist bushy fields of highlands and páramo up to snowline.

REGION: HAP

Plate 39c

Esmeraldas Woodstar
Acestrura berlepschi

ID: Tiny (6 cm, 2.5 in); male with green upperparts, white breast, bright red throat; female with white breast and buffy throat.

HABITAT: Endemic to coastal Ecuador in open areas, forest edge and gardens near moist forest patches.

REGION: MCL

Plate 39d

Golden-headed Quetzal
Pharomachrus auriceps

ID: Medium-sized (33 cm, 13 in); brilliant green upperparts; bright red breast; undertail black.

HABITAT: Cloud forest canopy, forest edge, and fruiting trees between 1500 and 2700 m (5000 and 9000 ft).

REGION: WSA, ESA

Plate 39 339

a Black-tailed Trainbearer

M

d Golden-headed Quetzal

F

M

b Purple-backed Thornbill

M

c Esmeraldas Woodstar

M

F

Plate 40a

White-tailed Trogon
Trogon viridis

ID: Medium-sized (28 cm, 11 in); male metallic greenish back and dark violet head and chest, bright yellow breast and mainly white undertail; female similar but with grayish head, chest and upperparts, black undertail with white barring, narrow but complete white eye-ring.

HABITAT: Mid-levels of humid primary and secondary lowland forest; often associated with mixed species foraging flocks.

REGION: MCL, AMA

Plate 40b

Collared Trogon
Trogon collaris

ID: Medium-sized (25 cm, 10 in); male dark metallic green upperparts, head and chest, red breast, black undertail with broad white barring; female brownish upperparts, head and chest, pinkish breast, grayish undertail, dark bill.

HABITAT: Mid-levels of humid secondary lowland forest.

REGION: MCL, AMA

Plate 40c

Violaceous Trogon
Trogon violaceus

ID: Medium-sized (24 cm, 9.5 in); male metallic green back, blue-violet head and chest, yellow breast, black undertail with fine white barring; female gray upperparts and chest, yellow breast, black undertail with white barring and small spots, incomplete white eye-ring.

HABITAT: Open secondary forest and forest edge of lowlands.

REGION: MCL, ACL, AMA

Plate 40d

Masked Trogon
Trogon personatus

ID: Medium-sized (25 cm, 10 in); male dark metallic green upperparts, head and chest, red breast, black undertail with fine white barring; female brownish upperparts, head and chest, pinkish breast, finely white-barred undertail, yellowish bill.

HABITAT: Mid-levels and edge of cloud forest between 1000 and 2000 m (3300 and 6600 ft).

REGION: WSA, ESA

Plate 40 **341**

a White-tailed Trogon

b Collared Trogon

d Masked Trogon

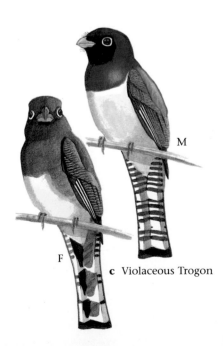

c Violaceous Trogon

Plate 41a

Ringed Kingfisher
Ceryle torquata

ID: Medium-sized (38 cm, 1.3 ft); blue-gray upperparts and white neck band; most of breast rusty (male) or blue-gray and rusty (female); crest on top of head.

HABITAT: Open vegetation along large rivers, lakes and mangroves; usually in lowlands but occasionally to 3000 m (10,000 ft).

REGION: MCL, ACL, AMA

Plate 41b

Amazon Kingfisher
Chloroceryle amazona

ID: Medium-sized (28 cm, 11 in); solid dark green upperparts; white underparts with rusty colored (male) or green (female) breast band.

HABITAT: Along open vegetation of large to medium-sized lowland rivers and lakes in the Oriente.

REGION: AMA

Plate 41c

Green Kingfisher
Chloroceryle americana

ID: Small (19 cm, 7.5 in); dark green upperparts; small white spots on upperwings; white underparts with single rusty colored breast band (male) or double green (female) breast bands.

HABITAT: Low in vegetation along small to medium-sized lowland streams, lakes and mangrove estuaries.

REGION: MCL, ACL, AMA

Plate 41d

Green-and-rufous Kingfisher
Chloroceryle inda

ID: Medium-sized (22 cm, 9 in); dark green upperparts; small white spots on wings and tail; entirely rusty (male) underparts or with spotted green and white band on chest (female).

HABITAT: Low in dense vegetation along small to medium streams and flooded forest ponds of lowlands.

REGION: MCL, AMA

Plate 41e

American Pygmy Kingfisher
Chloroceryle aenea

ID: Small (13 cm, 5 in); dark green upperparts; rusty colored chest (male) and white lower belly; narrow dark green chest band (female).

HABITAT: Low in dense vegetation of small streams and forest ponds of lowlands.

REGION: MCL, AMA

Plate 41 **343**

a Ringed Kingfisher

c Green Kingfisher

d Green-and-rufous Kingfisher

b Amazon Kingfisher

e American Pygmy Kingfisher

Plate 42a

White-eared Jacamar
Galbalcyrhynchus leucotis

ID: Medium-sized (20 cm, 8 in); dark rusty colored with blackish wings, tail and crown; long, narrow red bill and large white spot on cheek.

HABITAT: Solitary or in pairs at top of open *Cecropia* trees along small to medium streams of lowland forests.

REGION: AMA

Plate 42b

Coppery-chested Jacamar
Galbula pastazae

ID: Medium-sized (23 cm, 9 in); metallic coppery green upperparts and chest; long bill; belly and undertail rusty colored. (Replaced in coastal lowlands by similar Rufous-tailed Jacamar, *Galbula ruficauda*.)

HABITAT: Pairs seen in middle and lower parts of forest edge in foothills of eastern Andes between 600 and 2000 m (2000 and 6600 ft).

REGION: ESA

Plate 42c

White-necked Puffbird
Notharchus macrorhynchos

ID: Medium-sized (25 cm, 10 in); black upperparts and white underparts except for black breast band; large heavy bill.

HABITAT: Solitary high on exposed branches of tall trees of lowland primary and secondary forest.

REGION: AMA

Plate 42d

White-chested Puffbird
Malacoptila fusca

ID: Small (18 cm, 7 in); brown and white streaks, orange bill. (Replaced in northwestern lowland Ecuador by the similar White-whiskered Puffbird, *Malacoptila panamensis*.)

HABITAT: Solitary and unobtrusive in thick undergrowth of secondary and primary forest; easily overlooked as it sits quietly for long periods; only its high-pitched "seeeee" call makes it obvious.

REGION: AMA

Plate 42e

White-fronted Nunbird
Monasa morphoeus

ID: Medium-sized (25 cm, 10 in); dark gray; long bright red-orange bill; white forehead. (Replaced in lowland secondary forest and along river edges of Oriente by similar Black-fronted Nunbird, *Monasa nigrifrons*, which has a dark gray forehead.)

HABITAT: Canopy and primary forest edge of lowland *tierra firme* forest.

REGION: MCL, AMA

Plate 42f

Swallow-winged Puffbird
Chelidoptera tenebrosa

ID: Small (15 cm, 6 in); black upperparts, head and throat; rusty-colored belly; short tail and white rump obvious only in flight.

HABITAT: Sits in open branches at top of small trees along rivers and lowland forest edge looking like a husky swallow (both when perched or in its short sallying flights that usually return to the same perch).

REGION: AMA

Plate 42 **345**

a White-eared Jacamar

b Coppery-chested
Jacamar

M

F

c White-necked Puffbird

d White-chested
Puffbird

e White-fronted Nunbird

f Swallow-winged Puffbird

Plate 43a
Rufous Motmot
Baryphthengus martii
ID: Medium-sized (46 cm, 1.5 ft); bright rusty head, throat and breast; black mask; green upperparts and lower belly; long tail with peculiar rackets at end often swung from side to side; bill large but not broad; deep owl-like double-hoots usually before dawn and late afternoon.

HABITAT: Solitary or in pairs; mid-levels of primary and secondary lowland forest.

REGION: MCL, AMA

Plate 43b
Broad-billed Motmot
Electron platyrhynchum
ID: Medium-sized (33 cm, 1.1 ft); bright rusty head, throat and upper chest; black mask; green upperparts and lower belly extending fairly high up on the breast; long tail with or without peculiar rackets at end; bill large and extremely broad; high-pitched nasal call given at dawn and late afternoon.

HABITAT: Dense undergrowth and mid-levels of secondary and moist primary forest in lowlands.

REGION: MCL, AMA

Plate 43c
Blue-crowned Motmot
Momotus momota
ID: Medium-sized (39 cm, 15 in); head with blue and black crown, black mask; breast and throat dull rusty colored; upperparts greenish blue; long tail with peculiar rackets at end often swung from side to side; bill large but not broad; voice a low "BOO-boop" usually heard in morning and afternoon.

HABITAT: Solitary or pairs in mid-levels of secondary lowland forest. (The similar-appearing population in cloud forests on the eastern slopes of the Andes is considered by some to be a separate species, the Highland Motmot, *Momotus aequatorialis*.)

REGION: MCL, ACL, AMA

Plate 43d
Scarlet-crowned Barbet
Capito aurovirens
ID: Medium-sized (20 cm, 8 in); upperparts olive-brown; throat and chest orange; crown bright red (male) or gray-white (female); call commonly heard throughout the day, a series of rolling "brrrrp, brrrrp, brrrrp . . ."

HABITAT: Thick, low vegetation along lowland streams and lakes, moist secondary forest.

REGION: AMA

Plate 43e
Black-spotted Barbet
Capito niger
ID: Small (18 cm, 7 in); upperparts black with bright yellow spots and stripes; throat and upper breast clear orange-yellow (male) or orange with thick black streaks (female); call resembles deep, owl-like calls of Blue-crowned Motmot, but no hesitation between calls in a series, "BOO-boop, BOO-boop, BOO-boop . . ."

HABITAT: Canopy of lowland moist primary and secondary forests, often in mixed species foraging flocks.

REGION: AMA

Plate 43 **347**

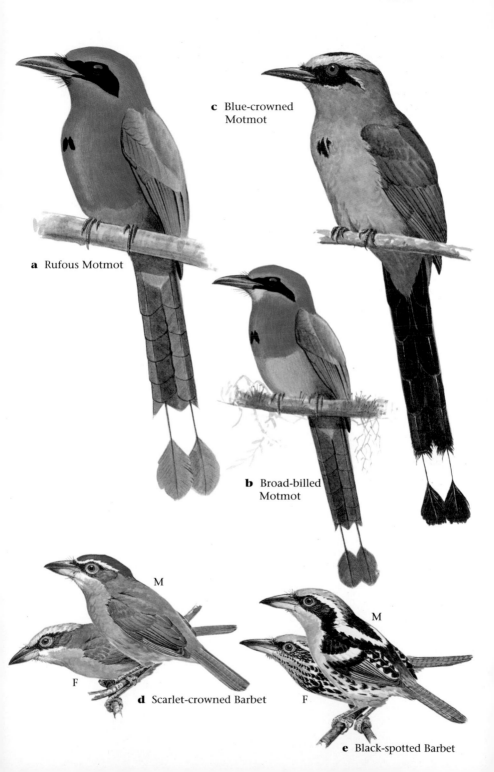

c Blue-crowned Motmot

a Rufous Motmot

b Broad-billed Motmot

M

F

d Scarlet-crowned Barbet

M

F

e Black-spotted Barbet

Plate 44a
Toucan Barbet
Semnornis ramphastinus
ID: Medium-sized (20 cm, 8 in); gray head; black mask; red belly; large light-colored bill with black ring near tip.

HABITAT: Pairs sing bell-like "tooks" in duet in cloud forest edges and canopy between 1000 and 2500 m (3300 and 8200 ft).

REGION: WSA

Plate 44b
Crimson-rumped Toucanet
Aulacorhynchus haematopygus
ID: Medium-sized (41 cm, 1.3 ft); green body with red rump; large dark red bill. (Replaced on the eastern slopes of Andes by similar Emerald Toucanet, *Aulacorhynchus prasinus*, which has largely yellow upper mandible and no red on rump.)

HABITAT: Cloud forest and moist forest edge between 1000 and 2000 m (3300 and 6600 ft).

REGION: WSA

Plate 44c
Chestnut-eared Aracari
Pteroglossus castanotis
ID: Medium-sized (46 cm, 1.5 ft); underparts yellow with one broad red breast band; head chestnut except for black crown.

HABITAT: Secondary and primary forest canopy of moist lowlands and along rivers.

REGION: AMA

Plate 44d
Many-banded Aracari
Pteroglossus pluricinctus
ID: Medium-sized (43 cm, 1.4 ft); underparts yellow with two black breast bands; upper bill mostly yellowish white.

HABITAT: Primary *tierra firme* forest canopy of lowlands.

REGION: AMA

Plate 44e
Pale-mandibled Aracari
Pteroglossus erythropygius
ID: Medium-sized (41 cm, 1.3 ft); underparts yellow with black spot in upper center of breast and red and black breast band lower down; bill largely ivory-white.

HABITAT: Endemic to tall secondary and primary forest canopy in lowland northwestern Ecuador.

REGION: MCL

Plate 44 **349**

a Toucan Barbet

b Crimson-rumped Toucanet

c Chestnut-eared Aracari

d Many-banded Aracari

e Pale-mandibled Aracari

Plate 45 (See also: Toucans, p. 138)

Plate 45a
Golden-collared Toucanet
Selenidera reinwardtii
ID: Medium-sized (33 cm, 1.1 ft); large red bill with black tip; green back, wings and tail; bright yellow cheek; black head and breast (male) or rusty head and breast (female); voice sounds like a loud frog croaking.

HABITAT: Mid-levels and canopy of lowland *tierra firme* forest.

REGION: AMA

Plate 45b
Plate-billed Mountain-Toucan
Andigena laminirostris
ID: Large (51 cm, 1.7 ft); blue-gray breast; large black bill with yellow square at base. (Replaced on eastern slopes of Andes by Gray-breasted Mountain-Toucan, *Andigena hypoglauca*, which has a mainly orange and yellow bill and a black crown and face.)

HABITAT: Cloud forest canopy and forest edge between 1500 and 2500 m (5000 and 8200 ft).

REGION: WSA

Plate 45c
White-throated Toucan
Ramphastos tucanus
ID: Large (61 cm, 2 ft); black body with white cheeks, throat and upper breast; huge black bill with yellow ridge and base; loud yelping calls distinguish it from the almost identical but smaller Yellow-ridged Toucan, *Ramphastos culminatus*, which gives a low croaking call. (Some experts consider the western Amazonian population of the White-throated Toucan, which occurs in Ecuador, to be a separate species, Cuvier's Toucan, *Ramphastos cuvieri*.)

HABITAT: Canopy and tops of isolated trees of primary lowland forest.

REGION: AMA

Plate 45d
Black-billed Mountain-Toucan
Andigena nigrirostris
ID: Large (50 cm, 1.7 ft); blue-gray breast and olive-brown back; throat startlingly pure white; all dark bill.

HABITAT: Northeastern slope cloud forest between 1600 and 3200 m (5250 and 10,500 ft). Pairs often sing their nasal calls loudly from tree tops in the early morning.

REGION: ESA

Plate 45e
Chestnut-mandibled Toucan
Ramphastos swainsonii
ID: Large (61 cm, 2 ft); black body with bright yellow throat and upper breast; huge dark brown bill with large yellow stripe covering most of top half; distinctive voice a loud yelping call distinguishes it from the very similar Chocó Toucan, *Ramphastos brevis*.

HABITAT: Lowland primary and tall secondary forest.

REGION: MCL

Plate 45 **351**

b Plate-billed Mountain-Toucan

M

F

a Golden-collared Toucanet

e Chestnut-mandibled Toucan

c White-throated Toucan

d Black-billed Mountain-Toucan

Plate 46a
Ecuadorean Piculet
Picumnus sclateri
ID: Small (9 cm, 3.5 in); upperparts brown with pale barring; underparts white with heavy barring; crown black with white and yellow dots.

HABITAT: Small branches of mid-level and undergrowth of lowland secondary forests.

REGION: ACL

Plate 46b
Spot-breasted Woodpecker
Chrysoptilus punctigula
ID: Medium-sized (20 cm, 8 in); yellow-green back with black bars; dotted black on breast; sides of head white.

HABITAT: Solitary on isolated trees in lowland clearings and pastures, secondary forest edge, and gardens.

REGION: AMA

Plate 46c
Crimson-mantled Woodpecker
Piculus rivolii
ID: Medium-sized (28 cm, 11 in); bright red upperparts; black and white-barred rump patch; scaled breast.

HABITAT: Solitary or pairs in short trees and bushes of upper cloud forest to lower páramo (2000 to 3500 m, 6500 to 11,500 ft); sometimes associates with mixed species foraging flocks.

REGION: WSA, HAP

Plate 46d
Cream-colored Woodpecker
Celeus flavus
ID: Medium-sized (23 cm, 9 in); crested; creamy yellow body, rusty wings and black tail; male with bright red stripe on cheek.

HABITAT: Solitary or pairs in dense undergrowth vegetation of lowland secondary forest.

REGION: AMA

Plate 46 **353**

a Ecuadorean Piculet

b Spot-breasted Woodpecker

d Cream-colored Woodpecker

c Crimson-mantled Woodpecker

Plate 47 (*See also*; Woodpeckers, p. 140)

Plate 47a

Lineated Woodpecker
Dryocopus lineatus
ID: Medium-sized (36 cm, 1.2 ft); crested; upperparts black with white lines on back forming an incomplete "V;" underparts barred brown and black.

HABITAT: Solitary or pairs in large trees in lowland secondary forest or forest edge.

REGION: MCL, ACL, AMA

Plate 47b

Yellow-tufted Woodpecker
Melanerpes cruentatus
ID: Medium-sized (19 cm, 7.5 in); black body with yellow eye-ring and nape of neck; crown red (male) or black (female); belly and lower breast red.

HABITAT: Family groups of four to eight on dead branches high in canopy of lowland primary forest; loud raucous calls obvious.

REGION: AMA

Plate 47c

Black-cheeked Woodpecker
Melanerpes pucherani
ID: Medium-sized (19 cm, 7.5 in); black mask; yellow forehead; red nape and crown (male) or white crown (female); upperparts black, white rump; underparts buffy with barring.

HABITAT: Large dead trees, at forest edge or in secondary forest, plantations and gardens of coastal lowlands.

REGION: MCL

Plate 47d

Crimson-crested Woodpecker
Campephilus melanoleucos
ID: Medium-sized (36 cm, 1.2 ft); crested; upperparts black with white lines on back forming a complete "V," underparts barred brown and black; head of male red except for white and black cheek spot. (Replaced in coastal lowlands by similar Guayaquil Woodpecker, *Campephilus quayaquilensis.*)

HABITAT: Pairs on large tree trunks of lowland primary forest and tall secondary forest.

REGION: AMA

Plate 47 355

a Lineated Woodpecker

d Crimson-crested Woodpecker

c Black-cheeked
Woodpecker

b Yellow-tufted
Woodpecker

Plate 48a

Olivaceous Woodcreeper
Sittasomus griseicapillus
ID: Small (16 cm, 6 in); no spots or obvious streaks; olive-gray head and underparts; rusty colored back, wings, and tail; straight bill short and thin.

HABITAT: Tree trunks and large branches of mid-levels of moist lowland primary forest and tall secondary forest; often associated with mixed species foraging flocks.

REGION: MCL, ACL, AMA

Plate 48b

Wedge-billed Woodcreeper
Glyphorynchus spirurus
ID: Small (14 cm, 5.5 in); brown head and underparts with buffy eyeline and breast streaks; rusty back, wings, and tail; bill short and wedge-shaped.

HABITAT: Lower parts of small and medium tree trunks in lowland primary and secondary forest; usually associated with mixed species foraging flocks.

REGION: MCL, AMA

Plate 48c

Long-billed Woodcreeper
Nasica longirostris
ID: Medium-sized (36 cm, 14 in); extremely long, thin, straight bill (7 cm, 2.7 in); rusty back, wings and tail; white throat, bold black and white stripes on crown, nape of head, lower breast; loud, low whistles given frequently.

HABITAT: Pairs seen on larger tree trunks in lowland flooded and swamp forest.

REGION: AMA

Plate 48d

Barred Woodcreeper
Dendrocolaptes certhia
ID: Medium-sized (27 cm, 11 in); thick straight bill; dark brown body with dark barring.

HABITAT: Lower trunks of *tierra firme* primary forest and tall secondary forest; frequently near army ant columns.

REGION: MCL, AMA

Plate 48e

Streak-headed Woodcreeper
Lepidocolaptes souleyetii
ID: Medium-sized (20 cm, 8 in); brown head and lower parts with bold buffy streaks; rusty back, wings and tail; slender bill slightly down-turned.

HABITAT: Medium and upper parts of tree trunks and large branches in lowland secondary forest and open dry scrub.

REGION: MCL, ACL

Plate 48   **357**

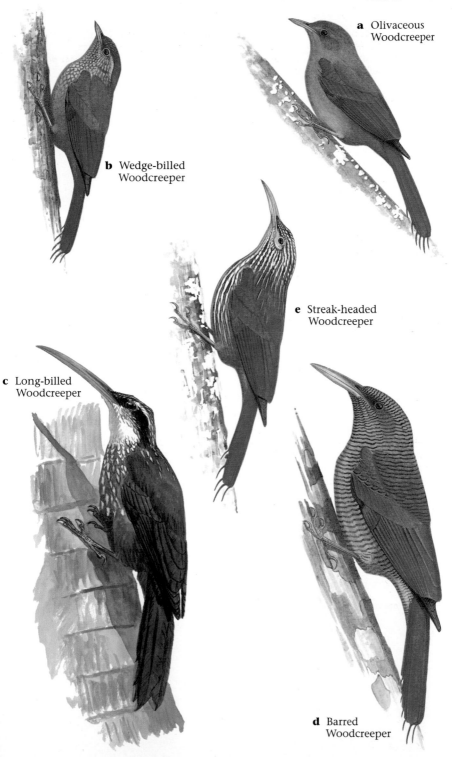

a Olivaceous
Woodcreeper

b Wedge-billed
Woodcreeper

e Streak-headed
Woodcreeper

c Long-billed
Woodcreeper

d Barred
Woodcreeper

Plate 49 (*See also*: Ovenbirds, p. 143)

Plate 49a

Bar-winged Cinclodes
Cinclodes fuscus
ID: Small (18 cm, 7 in); brown with white eyestripe; whitish throat; rusty wing stripe and rusty tail feathers obvious in flight.

HABITAT: Runs on ground in open páramo above 3500 m (11,500 ft) elevation, usually near clay banks and water.

REGION: HAP

Plate 49b

Pale-legged Hornero
Furnarius leucopus
ID: Small (17 cm, 6.5 in); bright buffy color with gray crown and white eyeline; black wings with bright rusty colored patch obvious in flight; short tail and light-colored legs; loud ringing trills given throughout the day.

HABITAT: Common on the ground in open areas, secondary forest floor, city parks and along roads in dry lowlands.

REGION: MCL, ACL

Plate 49c

Andean Tit-spinetail
Leptasthenura andicola
ID: Small (16 cm, 6 in); dark brown with white streaks on body and head; long dark tail with two distinctly longer feathers.

HABITAT: Low bushes and tall grass of páramo and *Polylepis* forest edge; in pairs or with mixed species foraging flocks.

REGION: HAP

Plate 49d

Pearled Treerunner
Margarornis squamiger
ID: Small (16 cm, 6 in); brown body; bold white eyeline; white throat and white teardrop spots on breast and side of neck; rusty back and tail.

HABITAT: Climbs like a woodcreeper along the tops and bottoms of large branches, usually in thick epiphyte cover of high-elevation cloud forest trees and *Polylepis* stands (above 2200 m, 7200 ft); almost always in large mixed species foraging flocks.

REGION: ESA

Plate 49e

Rufous-rumped Foliage-gleaner
Philydor erythrocercus
ID: Small (17 cm, 6.5 in); olive-brown upperparts; rusty colored tail; bold buffy streak through eye and buffy underparts.

HABITAT: In pairs rummaging through dead leaves and vine tangles at mid-levels of *tierra firme* forest; usually in mixed species foraging flocks.

REGION: AMA

Plate 49f

Streaked Xenops
Xenops rutilans
ID: Small (11 cm, 4 in); brown with buffy streaks on breast, back, and crown; bold whitish stripe over eye and another on cheek; peculiar upturned bill. (Replaced in the lowlands by the Plain Xenops, *Xenops minutus*, which lacks streaking on breast and back.)

HABITAT: Forages at the ends of tiny branches and twigs, often hanging upside down or moving along sideways in the mid-levels and canopy of cloud forest (1500 to 2500 m, 5000 to 8200 ft).

REGION: WSA, ESA

Plate 49 359

a Bar-winged Cinclodes

c Andean
Tit-Spinetail

b Pale-legged
Hornero

f Streaked
Xenops

e Rufous-rumped Foliage-gleaner

d Pearled Treerunner

Plate 50a

Great Antshrike
Taraba major
ID: Medium-sized (20 cm, 8 in); pure white underparts; black (male) or rusty colored (female) upperparts; red eye; voice commonly heard is an accelerating series of short whistled notes (bouncing ball) ending in a low growl.

HABITAT: Dense undergrowth and bushy secondary forest in moist lowlands.

REGION: MCL, ACL, AMA

Plate 50b

Barred Antshrike
Thamnophilus doliatus
ID: Small (15 cm, 6 in); male black and white barred upper- and underparts; female rusty colored upperparts and buffy underparts.

HABITAT: Thickets and secondary forest undergrowth of lowlands, in Ecuador mainly on river islands in the Río Napo and Río Aguarico.

REGION: AMA

Plate 50c

White-flanked Antwren
Myrmotherula axillaris
ID: Small (10 cm, 4 in); male blackish with white dots on upperwings and long white plumes on side of breast; female gray-brown with rusty colored dots on upperwings and long white plumes on side of breast; wings flicked often to expose the white feathers on the side of breast.

HABITAT: Undergrowth and lower levels of moist lowland primary and tall secondary forest; almost always in large mixed species foraging flocks.

REGION: MCL, AMA

Plate 50d

White-plumed Antbird
Pithys albifrons
ID: Small (13 cm, 5 in); spectacular white tufts on head and chin; rusty colored lower parts.

HABITAT: Forest floor and undergrowth of *tierra firme* forest at army ant columns.

REGION: AMA

Plate 50e

Black-faced Antthrush
Formicarius analis
ID: Small (18 cm, 7 in); dark brown upperparts; black throat; gray breast; rusty colored lower belly; walks on forest floor with black tail cocked up; voice commonly heard is a descending series of loud short whistles. (Replaced in coastal northwest by Black-headed Anththrush, *Formicarius nigricapillus*, which has a blackish head and upper breast.)

HABITAT: Solitary on floor of lowland moist primary and tall secondary forest.

REGION: AMA

Plate 50f

Tawny Antpitta
Grallaria quitensis
ID: Medium-sized (18 cm, 7 in); olive-brown upperparts; buff underparts; small light spot between base of bill and eye; long legs; very short tail.

HABITAT: Runs or hops on ground among scattered bushes and sings from tops of open shrubs and fence posts in páramo above 3000 m (8500 ft).

REGION: HAP

Plate 50   **361**

b Barred Antshrike

F

M

a Great
Antshrike

M

c White-flanked
Antwren

F

F

M

d White-plumed
Antbird

e Black-faced Antthrush

f Tawny Antpitta

Plate 51a
Blue-crowned Manakin
Pipra coronata
ID: Small (9 cm, 3.5 in); male all black with bright blue crown; female bright green upperparts and grayish yellow underparts.

HABITAT: Undergrowth and lower levels of moist primary and tall secondary forest in the lowlands; fruiting trees.

REGION: MCL, AMA

Plate 51b
Wire-tailed Manakin
Pipra filicauda
ID: Small (11 cm, 4 in); male with bright yellow underparts, black back, wings, and tail, bright red crown, and tail with thin, wire-like extensions; female with olive upperparts, greenish-yellow underparts, wire-like tail feather extensions shorter than in male.

HABITAT: Undergrowth of dense lowland flooded forest and moist secondary forest; fruiting trees.

REGION: AMA

Plate 51c
Golden-winged Manakin
Masius chrysopterus
ID: Small (11 cm, 4 in); male black except for peculiar bright yellow head feathers and some yellow in wings and tail in flight; female with olive upperparts, greenish yellow underparts.

HABITAT: Undergrowth of cloud forest between 1500 and 2500 m (5000 and 8200 ft).

REGION: WSA, ESA

Plate 51d
White-bearded Manakin
Manacus manacus
ID: Small (10 cm, 4 in); male with black upperparts and white underparts, orange legs; female with olive upperparts, greenish yellow underparts; fire-cracker-like snapping of wings heard commonly around male lecs.

HABITAT: Undergrowth of moist lowland secondary forest.

REGION: MCL, AMA

Plate 51e
Thrush-like Manakin
Schiffornis turdinus
ID: Small (17 cm, 7 in); olive-brown with dark eyes, bill, and legs; most commonly noticed by its clear four-note whistle; considered a flycatcher or cotinga by some experts.

HABITAT: Undergrowth of moist lowland secondary and edge of primary forest; often perches low on thin vertical saplings.

REGION: MCL, AMA

Plate 51 363

a Blue-crowned Manakin

F

M

b Wire-tailed Manakin

F

M

c Golden-winged Manakin

F

M

d White-bearded Manakin

F

M

e Thrush-like Manakin

Plate 52a
Black-necked Red-Cotinga
Phoenicircus nigricollis
ID: Medium-sized (24 cm, 9.5 in); male brilliant red except for black face, back, wings and tail tip; female upperparts maroon to olive-brown, underparts pink.

HABITAT: Mid-level to canopy of *tierra firme* primary forest; males in noisy lecs of three to five.

REGION: AMA

Plate 52b
Plum-throated Cotinga
Cotinga maynana
ID: Medium-sized (20 cm, 8 in); male strikingly turquoise blue with purple throat; female gray upperparts and buffy underparts spotted gray. (Similar Blue Cotinga, *Cotinga nattererii*, in northwestern lowland forests has more extensive purple extending to the breast.)

HABITAT: Canopy of moist lowland primary and tall secondary forest; fruiting trees.

REGION: AMA

Plate 52c
Red-crested Cotinga
Ampelion rubrocristata
ID: Medium-sized (23 cm, 9 in); dark gray with light-colored bill; white tail spots obvious in flight; dark red crest is obvious only when displayed.

HABITAT: Solitary perched on tall dead tree in cloud forest above 2500 m (8200 ft).

REGION: WSA, ESA

Plate 52d
Green-and-black Fruiteater
Pipreola riefferii
ID: Medium-sized (20 cm, 8 in); orange bill and legs; dark eye; green upperparts; yellowish breast; head black (male) or green (female).

HABITAT: Pairs or small family groups in cloud forest canopy, forest edge and fruiting trees between 1500 and 2500 m (5000 and 8200 ft).

REGION: WSA, ESA

Plate 52e
Screaming Piha
Lipaugus vociferans
ID: Medium-sized (28 cm, 11 in); all gray; most often noticed by the ear-splitting whistle-screams of lecking males.

HABITAT: Mid-level to canopy of primary *tierra firme* and flooded forest of the lowlands.

REGION: AMA

Plate 52 **365**

b Plum-throated Cotinga

a Black-necked
Red-Cotinga

M

F

F

M

c Red-crested
Cotinga

M

F

e Screaming Piha

d Green-and-black
Fruiteater

Plate 53a

Amazonian Umbrellabird
Cephalopterus ornatus

ID: Large (51 cm, 1.6 ft); black with permanent crest and hanging wattle on throat; flies in an undulating up-and-down pattern reminiscent of a large, crested woodpecker; males at lecs give low mooing sounds. (Replaced in the northwestern lowland forests by the similar Long-wattled Umbrellabird, *Cephalopterus penduliger*.)

HABITAT: Flooded forest edge and large river islands of the lowlands, usually associated with *Cecropia* trees.

REGION: AMA

Plate 53b

Purple-throated Fruitcrow
Querula purpurata

ID: Medium-sized (30 cm, 1 ft); all black; male with an indistinct purple throat; most readily noticed by its noisy slurred whistles.

HABITAT: Family groups of four to six in the canopy of moist lowland primary and tall secondary forest.

REGION: MCL, AMA

Plate 53c

Bare-necked Fruitcrow
Gymnoderus foetidus

ID: Medium-sized (34 cm, 1.2 ft); black and gray; small featherless head; in flight the wide wings of the male flash black and silver.

HABITAT: Canopy of lowland primary and secondary forest, fruiting trees; flying high overhead along rivers.

REGION: AMA

Plate 53d

Masked Tityra
Tityra semifasciata

ID: Medium-sized (20 cm, 8 in); bright red bill and bare area around eye; body white except for black wings and tail; male with black face; female with brown back, face and crown. (In the Oriente lowlands the similar Black-tailed Tityra, *Tityra cayana*, also occurs; it has an all-black crown.)

HABITAT: Tops of trees on forest edge, secondary and primary forest. Often noticed by its frog-like croaks and nasal grumbling.

REGION: MCL, AMA

Plate 53e

Andean Cock-of-the-Rock
Rupicola peruviana

ID: Medium-sized (32 cm, 1 ft); male bright red with crest, gray and black wings; female rusty orange with small crest and brownish wings and tail. Males in the east slope population are red-orange and considered a separate species (*aequatorialis*) by some experts.

HABITAT: Middle and low levels of cloud forest vegetation, especially near rocky streams.

REGION: WSA, ESA

Plate 53 **367**

a Amazonian Umbrellabird

b Purple-throated Fruitcrow

M

F

M

F

a

F

d Masked Tityra

M

M

F

c Bare-necked Fruitcrow   **e** Andean Cock-of-the-Rock

Plate 54a
Torrent Tyrannulet
Serpophaga cinerea
ID: Small (11 cm, 4 in); black head, tail and wings; rest of body light gray to white.

HABITAT: Pairs obvious on boulders along rushing mountain streams where they flick tails and give loud "chip" notes that can be heard over the roar of the stream.

REGION: WSA, ESA

Plate 54b
Common Tody-flycatcher
Todirostrum cinereum
ID: Small (10 cm, 4 in); long flat bill; white eye; gray crown, cheeks; olive-gray back; bright yellow underparts; thin tail often held angled up over the back. (Largely replaced in Oriente by Yellow-browed Todirostrum, *Todirostrum chrysocotaphum*, which is similar but has black crown and cheeks, yellow eyeline, white throat with bold black spots on the breast.)

HABITAT: Sits on open branches in undergrowth and mid-levels of lowland secondary forest.

REGION: MCL, ACL, AMA

Plate 54c
Black Phoebe
Sayornis nigricans
ID: Medium-sized (19 cm, 7.5 in); all blackish except for white lower belly and white flashes in opened wings.

HABITAT: Pairs perch on boulders, electric wires and buildings near mountain streams.

REGION: WSA, ESA

Plate 54d
Plain-capped Ground-tyrant
Muscisaxicola alpina
ID: Medium-sized (19 cm, 7.5 in); robin-like; all-black bill; gray-brown upperparts, whitish underparts, black tail; distinct white eyeline.

HABITAT: Pairs or small flocks run on the ground or perch on fence wires in páramo above 3300 m (10,800 ft).

REGION: HAP

Plate 54e
Masked Water-tyrant
Fluvicola nengeta
ID: Small (15 cm, 6 in); white with gray back; black wings, tail and eyeline.

HABITAT: Pairs seen on the ground or low vegetation near coastal lowland marshes, ponds, small streams and even swimming pools.

REGION: MCL, ACL

Plate 54f
Tropical Kingbird
Tyrannus melancholicus
ID: Medium-sized (22 cm, 8.5 in); gray head; olive back; brown tail with distinct notch; gray throat; olive-yellow upper breast, bright yellow lower breast.

HABITAT: Most common and easily seen flycatcher in open areas; perches alone on exposed branches and dead treetops in pastures, secondary forest edges and along rivers and lakes throughout lowlands and up to 2500 m (8200 ft). (The similar Snowy-throated Kingbird, *Tyrannus niveigularis*, is common near the coast and is distinguished by square-tipped tail and gray upper breast).

REGION: MCL, ACL, ESA, WSA, AMA

Plate 54 **369**

c Black Phoebe

b Common Tody-Flycatcher

a Torrent Tyrannulet

f Tropical Kingbird

e Masked Water-Tyrant

d Plain-capped Ground-Tyrant

Plate 55a

Great Kiskadee
Pitangus sulphuratus
ID: Medium-sized (22 cm, 8.5 in); chunky shape; black crown with bold white head band; brown back; rusty edges to wing feathers; bright yellow underparts; calls out its name in a loud voice throughout the day, "kis-ka-DEE."

HABITAT: High in secondary forest, forest edge, lake and river edges, gardens, city parks throughout Oriente lowlands.

REGION: AMA

Plate 55b

Lesser Kiskadee
Pitangus lictor
ID: Small (18 cm, 7 in); smaller replica of the Great Kiskadee, but more slender, less rusty in the wings; a nasal, wheezing voice completely unlike that of the Great Kiskadee.

HABITAT: Pairs seen on low, exposed vegetation along the water's edge of cochas and small, slow streams of lowland Oriente.

REGION: AMA

Plate 55c

Boat-billed Flycatcher
Megarynchus pitangua
ID: Medium-sized (23 cm, 9 in); larger replica of the Great Kiskadee, but much more massive bill, browner back, less rusty in the wings, and a long squeaking and nasal call.

HABITAT: Pairs seen in tops of tall secondary forest, dry wood lots and pasture edges often away from water in lowlands.

REGION: MCL, ACL, AMA

Plate 55d

Social Flycatcher
Myiozetetes similis
ID: Small (17 cm, 6.5 in); olive-gray back, tail and wings, with no rusty color in wings; small black bill; yellow breast and contrasting white throat; harsh staccato calls.

HABITAT: Pairs or small family groups perch together in mid to high levels of secondary forest, pasture edge and vegetation along water courses.

REGION: MCL, ACL, AMA

Plate 55e

Piratic Flycatcher
Legatus leucophaius
ID: Small (15 cm, 6 in); dark brown upperparts; bold white eyeline, cheek patch and throat; yellowish underparts with faint dark streaking; no rusty color in wings or tail.

HABITAT: Alone perched high on exposed treetop or dead branch of secondary forest, forest edge and clearings with scattered tall trees in moist lowlands.

REGION: MCL, ACL, AMA

Plate 55　371

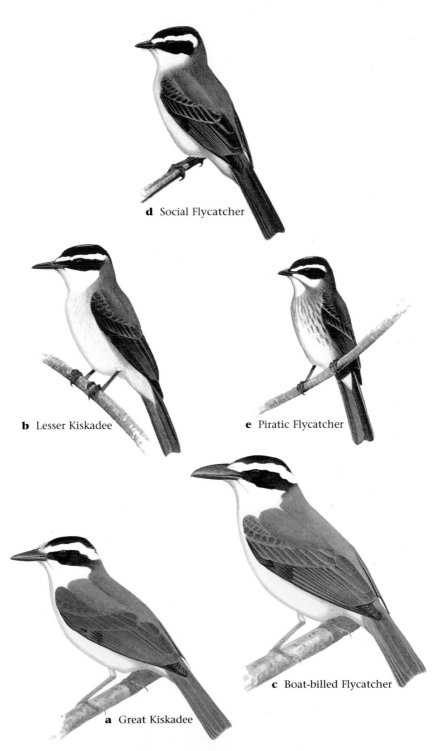

d Social Flycatcher

b Lesser Kiskadee

e Piratic Flycatcher

c Boat-billed Flycatcher

a Great Kiskadee

Plate 56a

Turquoise Jay
Cyanolyca turcosa

ID: Medium-sized (32 cm, 1 ft); turquoise-blue with black forehead, mask and narrow breast band; often shy and quiet but at other times bold and noisy.

HABITAT: Small family groups low in cloud forests undergrowth and alder forest edges between 2500 and 3000 m (8200 and 10,000 ft).

REGION: WSA, ESA

Plate 56b

Violaceous Jay
Cyanocorax violaceus

ID: Medium-sized (33 cm, 1.1 ft); pale blue-gray with black crown, face and upper breast; harsh, high-pitched calls.

HABITAT: Small family groups in moist lowland forest edge, flooded forests and small clearings throughout the Oriente.

REGION: AMA

Plate 56c

Green Jay
Cyanocorax yncas

ID: Medium-sized (30 cm, 1 ft); green above and yellow below; bold yellow outer tail feathers obvious in flight.

HABITAT: Small family groups in cloud forest undergrowth, clearings and pasture edges between 1400 and 2600 m (4500 and 8500 ft); usually first noticed by their nasal sounds and clicking calls.

REGION: ESA

Plate 56d

White-tailed Jay
Cyanocorax mystacalis

ID: Medium-sized (33 cm, 1.1 ft); blue back; pure white underparts, neck, cheek and outer tail feathers and tail tip; black face and throat.

HABITAT: Small family groups in arid scrub, dry forest and open areas of southwestern Ecuador; a Tumbesian endemic.

REGION: ACL

Plate 56e

White-capped Dipper
Cinclus leucocephalus

ID: Small (16 cm, 6 in); dark gray with strikingly white crown and throat.

HABITAT: Solitary or in pairs on rocks of mountain streams where they bob up and down on their legs and run or fly into the water.

REGION: WSA, ESA

Plate 56 **373**

b Violaceous Jay

d White-tailed Jay

c Green Jay

a Turquoise Jay

e White-capped Dipper

Plate 57a
Black-capped Donacobius
Donacobius atricapillus
ID: Medium-sized (22 cm, 9 in); brown back and wings; black tail, crown and cheeks; bright buffy underparts; long bill.

HABITAT: Family groups at the top of tall aquatic grass and low marsh vegetation of Oriente lowlands; loud voices are obvious.

REGION: AMA

Plate 57b
Thrush-like Wren
Campylorhynchus turdinus
ID: Medium-sized (21 cm, 8 in); brown upperparts; white underparts densely spotted; long tail.

HABITAT: Family groups in vine tangles, palm fronds and upper parts of forest edge and tall secondary forest of Amazonian lowlands; explosive and rollicking songs obvious.

REGION: AMA

Plate 57c
Fasciated Wren
Campylorhynchus fasciatus
ID: Medium-sized (19 cm, 7.5 in); upperparts banded black and brownish gray, underparts whitish with bold brownish gray spots.

HABITAT: Noisy family groups conspicuous in scrubby vegetation and open arid forest of coastal southwestern Ecuador. (Replaced in coastal northwest by the Band-backed Wren, *Campylorhynchus zonatus*, which is similar but has a buffy breast with spots.)

REGION: ACL

Plate 57d
White-breasted Wood-wren
Henicorhina leucosticta
ID: Small (10 cm, 4 in); short tail usually held up; dark rust upperparts; crown black; bold white eyestripe; white underparts. (Replaced in cloud forest undergrowth between 1000 and 2500 m (3200 and 8200 ft) by Gray-breasted Wood-wren, *Henicorhina leucophrys*, which is similar except for its gray breast.)

HABITAT: Undergrowth and ground of humid lowland forest.

REGION: MCL, AMA

Plate 57e
House Wren
Troglodytes aedon
ID: Small (11 cm, 4.5 in); brown upperparts, buffy underparts; buffy eyestripe; faint black barring on wings, tail.

HABITAT: Low vegetation and ground in clearings and dry open areas from the lowlands to páramo.

REGION: MCL, ACL, WSA, HAP, ESA, AMA

Plate 57f
Musician Wren
Cyphorhinus aradus
ID: Small (13 cm, 5 in); olive-brown upperparts; bright rusty underparts and eyeline; bright blue bare patch of skin around eye; often noticed by its flute-like whistled song, so uncoordinated it sounds like a young boy learning to whistle. (Replaced in moist coastal lowlands by similar-looking and sounding Song Wren, *Cyphorhinus phaeocephalus*.)

HABITAT: Ground and dense undergrowth of humid *tierra firme* forest in the Oriente.

REGION: AMA

Plate 57 **375**

b Thrush-like Wren

c Fasciated Wren

d White-breasted Wood-wren

a Black-capped Donacobius

e House Wren

f Musician Wren

Plate 58a

Long-tailed Mockingbird
Mimus longicaudatus
ID: Medium-sized (30 cm, 1 ft); brownish gray upperparts, light gray underparts; long tail with large white tips obvious in flight.

HABITAT: Solitary or in pairs on low shrubs in open areas, pastures, and arid secondary forest edge of southwestern coast.

REGION: ACL

Plate 58b

Great Thrush
Turdus fuscater
ID: Medium-sized (33 cm, 1.1 ft); dark gray-brown with bright orange legs and bill.

HABITAT: Common in pastures, open areas, city parks, gardens and Eucalyptus groves throughout the highlands above 2000 m (6500 ft).

REGION: HAP

Plate 58c

Lawrence's Thrush
Turdus lawrencii
ID: Medium-sized (23 cm, 9 in); gray-brown upperparts; olive underparts except for white lower belly and white throat with fine black streaks; bright yellow bill and eyering.

HABITAT: Feeds on ground and undergrowth of moist lowland primary forest, but sings its flute-like songs, mimicking other bird species, usually from high in the canopy.

REGION: AMA

Plate 58d

Black-billed Thrush
Turdus ignobilis
ID: Medium-sized (24 cm, 9.5 in); brown upperparts; olive underparts with white lower belly; black bill.

HABITAT: Thick scrub and low secondary vegetation of Amazonian lowlands, often around human habitation.

REGION: AMA

Plate 58e

Ecuadorean Thrush
Turdus maculirostris
ID: Medium-sized (23 cm, 9 in); olive-brown upperparts; olive underparts except for white lower belly and white throat with fine black streaks; olive-yellow bill; narrow yellow eyering.

HABITAT: On ground and undergrowth of lowland scrub and low secondary forest in coastal lowlands, often around human habitation.

REGION: MCL, ACL

Plate 58 **377**

b Great Thrush

a Long-tailed
Mockingbird

c Lawrence's Thrush

d Black-billed Thrush

e Ecuadorean Thrush

Plate 59a
Blackburnian Warbler
Dendroica fusca
ID: Small (13 cm, 5 in); unmistakable in March to April, just before migrating north to North American breeding grounds, with male's brilliant orange and black head; nonbreeding and female plumage recognized by yellow eyestripe, yellow throat and streaks on side of breast.

HABITAT: Common during northern winter in mixed species foraging flocks in mid-levels and canopy of open cloud forest between 1000 and 2500 m (3300 and 8200 ft).

REGION: WSA, ESA

Plate 59b
Canada Warbler
Wilsonia canadensis
ID: Small (13 cm, 5 in); gray upperparts; bright yellow underparts with "necklace" of short black stripes on chest; female and nonbreeding male with fainter necklace.

HABITAT: Winter resident in undergrowth of open cloud forest; during migration, in undergrowth of primary and secondary lowland forest.

REGION: WSA, ESA, AMA

Plate 59c
Spectacled Redstart
Myioborus melanocephalus
ID: Small (15 cm, 6 in); slate-gray upperparts, bright yellow underparts; short yellow eyeline and eyering forming "spectacles;" conspicuous white outer tail feathers often spread during foraging.

HABITAT: Undergrowth of cloud forest and low, thick bushes from 2000 m (6500 ft) to treeline; often in mixed species foraging flocks.

REGION: WSA, ESA

Plate 59d
Slate-throated Redstart
Myioborus miniatus
ID: Small (13 cm, 5 in); upperparts including head, throat and chest slate-gray; underparts bright yellow; conspicuous white outer tail feathers often spread during foraging.

HABITAT: Very active in undergrowth and cloud forest edge between 700 and 2500 m (2300 and 8200 ft); usually associated with mixed species foraging flocks.

REGION: WSA, ESA

Plate 59e
Gray-and-gold Warbler
Basileuterus fraseri
ID: Small (14 cm, 5.5 in); bluish gray upperparts; black and yellow crown; bright yellow underparts.

HABITAT: Pairs seen in thick undergrowth vegetation of secondary and dry scrub lowland forest; a Tumbesian endemic restricted to the coastal southwest.

REGION: ACL

Plate 59f
Three-striped Warbler
Basileuterus tristriatus
ID: Small (13 cm, 5 in); black head with three buffy stripes; olive upperparts, pale yellow-olive underparts.

HABITAT: Pairs forage in undergrowth of secondary cloud forest (1000 to 2000 m, 3300 to 6500 ft), often in mixed species foraging flocks.

REGION: WSA, ESA

Plate 59 **379**

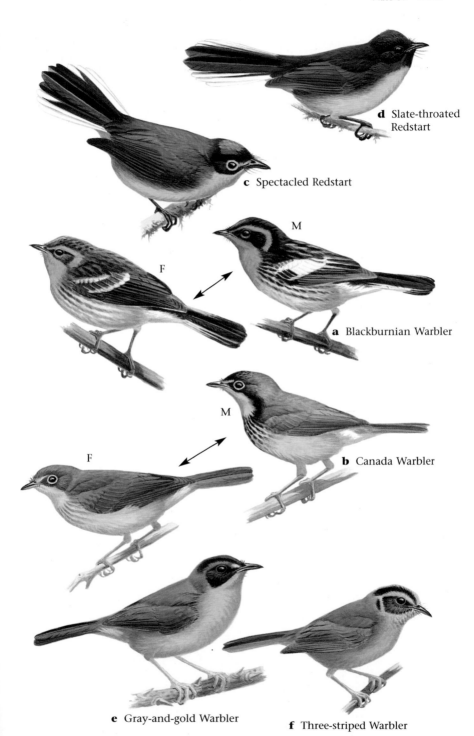

d Slate-throated Redstart

c Spectacled Redstart

F

M

a Blackburnian Warbler

M

b Canada Warbler

F

e Gray-and-gold Warbler

f Three-striped Warbler

Plate 60a

Buff-rumped Warbler
Phaeothlypis fulvicauda

ID: Small (14 cm, 5.5 in); olive-brown upperparts, buffy-white underparts; bright buffy tail and rump conspicuous in flight; loud series of musical "chew" notes often reveals its presence.

HABITAT: On ground or low vegetation along small lowland forested streams; fans its bright tail frequently.

REGION: MCL, ACL, AMA

Plate 60b

Masked Flower-piercer
Diglossa cyanea

ID: Small (15 cm, 6 in); dark blue; black mask; red eye; peculiarly curved and hooked bill.

HABITAT: Solitary or in mixed species foraging flocks around large flowers in the canopy of cloud forest between 2200 and 3000 m (7200 and 9800 ft).

REGION: WSA, ESA

Plate 60c

Glossy Flower-piercer
Diglossa lafresnayii

ID: Small (14 cm, 6 in); shiny black with blue shoulder patches; peculiarly curved and hooked bill.

HABITAT: Low bushes and lone trees near tree-line (2700 to 3700 m, 8800 to 12,000 ft).

REGION: HAP

Plate 60d

Giant Conebill
Oreomanes fraseri

ID: Small (17 cm, 7 in); gray upperparts, rusty colored underparts; whitish cheek patches and forehead; long pointed bill.

HABITAT: Almost exclusively restricted to groves of *Polylepis* forest between 3300 and 4500 m (10,800 and 14,800 ft), where it climbs up and down trunks and large branches.

REGION: HAP

Plate 60e

Cinereous Conebill
Conirostrum cinereum

ID: Small (12 cm, 5 in); dark gray upperparts, light gray underparts; cinnamon-colored patch under base of tail; bold white eyeline; white wing patch; sharp pointed bill.

HABITAT: Open forests, shrubby areas, gardens and city parks between 3000 and 3600 m (9800 and 11,800 ft).

REGION: HAP

Plate 60 **381**

b Masked Flower-piercer

d Giant Conebill

e Cinereous Conebill

c Glossy Flower-piercer

a Buff-rumped Warbler

Plate 61a

Bananaquit
Coereba flaveola
ID: Small (10 cm, 4 in); black crown and cheek; white eyeline; gray throat; underparts and rump bright yellow; rest of upperparts gray; wing with a small white patch; short bill thin and curved down.

HABITAT: Active in pairs around flowering and fruiting trees, bushes and shrubs in open secondary forest, gardens and city parks of the lowlands; usually absent from primary forest areas.

REGION: MCL, ACL, AMA

Plate 61b

Blue Dacnis
Dacnis cayana
ID: Small (13 cm, 5 in); male bright turquoise blue with small black throat patch, mainly black tail, wings; female green with blue-gray head.

HABITAT: Humid lowland secondary forest and shrubby clearings, flowering and fruiting trees; often in mixed species foraging flocks.

REGION: MCL, ACL, AMA

Plate 61c

Yellow-bellied Dacnis
Dacnis flaviventer
ID: Small (13 cm, 5 in); male with bright yellow underparts with black throat, mask, back, wings and tail; crown gray-green; female with pale brown-olive upperparts, buffy-yellow underparts.

HABITAT: Pairs seen in mid-levels to canopy of lowland *tierra firme* and flooded forest to moist tall secondary forest.

REGION: AMA

Plate 61d

Green Honeycreeper
Chlorophanes spiza
ID: Small (14 cm, 5.5 in); male shiny green with black face and crown, red eye, and bright yellow bill; female yellow-green with dark eye.

HABITAT: Pairs forage in mid-level to canopy of moist lowland primary and tall secondary forest; often in large mixed species foraging flocks.

REGION: MCL, ACL, AMA

Plate 61e

Purple Honeycreeper
Cyanerpes caeruleus
ID: Small (11 cm, 4 in); long slender bill curved down; short tail; male glistening purple with black throat, wings and tail, bright yellow legs; female with green upperparts, green to yellow underparts streaked white; legs dull yellow. (The similar Red-legged Honeycreeper, *Cyanerpes cyaneus*, occurs in the same areas and is distinguished by red legs in both sexes and a black back and blue crown in males.)

HABITAT: Canopy and upper levels of moist lowland primary and tall secondary forest; often in mixed species foraging flocks.

REGION: MCL, AMA

Plate 61 **383**

d Green Honeycreeper

M

F

b Blue Dacnis

M

F

a Bananaquit

F

c Yellow-bellied Dacnis

M

F

M

e Purple Honeycreeper

M

Plate 62a
Golden Tanager
Tangara arthus
ID: Small (14 cm, 5.5 in); bright golden head, rump and underparts; blackish back, wings and tail; small black "ear" patch.

HABITAT: Cloud forest canopy, forest edge, and fruiting trees between 1000 and 2500 m (3300 and 8200 ft); usually in mixed species foraging flocks.

REGION: WSA, ESA

Plate 62b
Blue-and-black Tanager
Tangara vassorii
ID: Small (13 cm, 5 in); shiny dark blue except for black wings and tail; dark eye; short straight bill.

HABITAT: High elevation cloud forest to tree-line (2000 to 3400 m, 6600 to 11,000 ft); usually in flocks of its own species or with mountain tanager flocks.

REGION: WSA, HAP, ESA

Plate 62c
Beryl-spangled Tanager
Tangara nigroviridis
ID: Small (14 cm, 5.5 in); breast flecked greenish blue and black; crown, neck and rump shiny pale green; face mask, back, wings and tail blackish.

HABITAT: Cloud forest edge, isolated treetops in pastures, and secondary forest at fruiting trees between 1500 and 2500 m (5000 and 8200 ft); usually in mixed species foraging flocks.

REGION: WSA, ESA

Plate 62d
Orange-eared Tanager
Tangara calliparaea
ID: Small (13 cm, 5 in); bright green upperparts, blue-green underparts; orange crown, "ear" and rump; black throat. (Replaced in northwest cloud forest by Glistening Green Tanager, *Tangara phoenicotis*, which is completely emerald green.)

HABITAT: Cloud forest canopy, forest edge, and fruiting trees between 1100 and 1700 m (3600 and 5600 ft); usually in mixed species foraging flocks.

REGION: ESA

Plate 62e
Bay-headed Tanager
Tangara gyrola
ID: Small (14 cm, 5.5 in); bright rusty head; blue-green underparts and rump; bright green back, wings, tail.

HABITAT: Canopy and mid-levels of lowland primary and tall secondary forest; usually in mixed species foraging flocks.

REGION: MCL, AMA

Plate 62 **385**

b Blue-and-black Tanager

c Beryl-spangled Tanager

a Golden Tanager

e Bay-headed Tanager

d Orange-eared Tanager

Plate 63a

Green-and-gold Tanager
Tangara schrankii

ID: Small (14 cm, 5.5 in); golden yellow crown, rump and center of breast shading into bright green on underparts; black forehead and side of face; back streaked black.

HABITAT: Canopy of humid lowland primary and tall secondary forest; usually in mixed species foraging flocks.

REGION: AMA

Plate 63b

Paradise Tanager
Tangara chilensis

ID: Small (14 cm, 5.5 in); bright yellow-green head; bright red rump; blue-green underparts; black tail, wings, back, and lower belly.

HABITAT: Canopy of humid lowland primary and tall secondary forest; usually in mixed species foraging flocks.

REGION: AMA

Plate 63c

Thick-billed Euphonia
Euphonia laniirostris

ID: Small (11 cm, 4 in); male with bright yellow underparts and crown, dark blue upperparts; female olive-green upperparts and gray-yellow underparts.

HABITAT: Open lowland forest, dry secondary scrub, gardens, city parks; often in mixed species foraging flocks.

REGION: MCL, ACL, AMA

Plate 63d

White-vented Euphonia
Euphonia minuta

ID: Small (10 cm, 4 in); male with bright yellow breast and crown, dark blue upperparts and throat, white lower belly and undertail; female olive upperparts, gray throat, olive-yellow breast and white lower belly. (The similar and equally widespread Orange-bellied Euphonia, *Euphonia xanthogaster*, has all yellow underparts except for white undertail; the Orange-crowned Euphonia, *Euphonia saturata*, is restricted to open forest of coastal lowlands and has all yellow-orange crown and underparts and a black undertail.)

HABITAT: Canopy of tall moist primary forest in lowlands.

REGION: MCL, AMA

Plate 63e

Chestnut-breasted Chlorophonia
Chlorophonia pyrrhophrys

ID: Small (12 cm, 5 in); green throat, face, back, wings and tail; bright yellow rump and breast with bright chestnut stripe up middle; crown blue.

HABITAT: Pairs seen in canopy of cloud forest at 1500 to 2500 m (5000 to 8200 ft).

REGION: WSA, ESA

Plate 63 **387**

a Green-and-gold Tanager

b Paradise Tanager

d White-vented Euphonia

M

M

c Thick-billed Euphonia

F

F

F

M

e Chestnut-breasted Chlorophonia

Plate 64a

Swallow Tanager
Tersina viridis

ID: Small (15 cm, 6 in); male shiny turquoise with black mask, faint barring on sides of breast, white lower belly; female all grass green with barring on sides of breast.

HABITAT: Small flocks or pairs perch high on exposed branches in lowland moist forest to lower reaches of cloud forest at 2000 m (6600 ft) elevation.

REGION: MCL, ESA, AMA

Plate 64b

Black-backed Bush-tanager
Urothraupis stolzmanni

ID: Small (15 cm, 6 in); black upperparts; white throat grading into gray underparts.

HABITAT: Small flocks in low forest and dense shrubs near treeline between 3000 and 4000 m (10,000 and 13,000 ft).

REGION: HAP

Plate 64c

Common Bush-tanager
Chlorospingus ophthalmicus

ID: Small (14 cm, 5.5 in); gray to brownish head; white eye; yelllow-olive upperparts; white throat and breast divided by yellowish breast band.

HABITAT: Noisy flocks of five to 10 in dense undergrowth and lower levels of cloud forest (800 to 2600 m, 2600 to 8500 ft) around which large mixed species foraging flocks form.

REGION: ESA

Plate 64d

Golden-crowned Tanager
Iridosornis rufivertex

ID: Small (17 cm, 7 in); dark violet-blue body with black head; startlingly bright orange crown; rusty lower belly.

HABITAT: Singly or pairs in canopy and on forest edge of upper elevation cloud forest (2500 to 3500 m, 8200 to 11,500 ft); often in mixed species foraging flocks.

REGION: WSA, ESA

Plate 64e

Grass-green Tanager
Chlorornis riefferii

ID: Medium-sized (21 cm, 8 in); bright green with rusty face and lower belly; bright orange legs and bill.

HABITAT: Small groups of three to six in canopy of cloud forest and forest edge between 2200 and 2800 m (7200 and 9000 ft); often in mixed species foraging flocks.

REGION: WSA, ESA

Plate 64 **389**

e Grass-green Tanager

d Golden-crowned Tanager

c Common
Bush-tanager

b Black-backed
Bush-tanager

M

F

a Swallow
Tanager

Plate 65a
Blue-winged Mountain-Tanager
Anisognathus somptuosus
ID: Small (18 cm, 7 in); black upperparts; bright yellow crown; pale blue in wings and tail; underparts bright yellow.

HABITAT: Small groups of two to eight in cloud forest edges, isolated trees in pastures, and secondary forest between 1500 and 2500 m (5000 and 8200 ft); often in mixed species foraging flocks.

REGION: WSA, ESA

Plate 65b
Scarlet-bellied Mountain-Tanager
Anisognathus igniventris
ID: Small (19 cm, 7.5 in); black upperparts with bright blue shoulders and rump; scarlet "ear" patch; underparts scarlet with black upper breast, throat.

HABITAT: Small groups in open cloud forest, scrubby bushes and scattered trees at high elevations (2500 to 3500 m, 8200 to 11,500 ft).

REGION: WSA, HAP, ESA

Plate 65c
Hooded Mountain-Tanager
Buthraupis montana
ID: Medium-sized (23 cm, 9 in); brilliant blue upperparts; black head; red eye; bright yellow underparts.

HABITAT: Groups of two to six in primary cloud forest canopy between 1500 and 3200 m (5000 and 10,500 ft); occasionally in mixed species foraging flocks.

REGION: WSA, ESA

Plate 65d
Palm Tanager
Thraupis palmarum
ID: Small (18 cm, 7 in); olive-gray; blackish tail; wings in flight show contrasting black and bright olive pattern.

HABITAT: Pairs seen in isolated trees in open scrub and agricultural areas, secondary forest, parks, gardens; often near or in palms.

REGION: MCL, ACL, AMA

Plate 65e
Blue-gray Tanager
Thraupis episcopus
ID: Small (17 cm, 7 in); pale blue-gray with either white (Amazonian) or blue (coastal) shoulders.

HABITAT: Pairs seen in open woodland, scrubby forest, secondary forest, gardens, and city parks.

REGION: MCL, ACL, AMA

Plate 65 391

b Scarlet-bellied
Mountain-Tanager

a Blue-winged
Mountain-Tanager

c Hooded
Mountain-Tanager

d Palm Tanager

Amazonian form

e Blue-gray Tanager

Coastal
form

Plate 66a
Silver-beaked Tanager
Ramphocelus carbo
ID: Small (18 cm, 7 in); male velvet black with deep red overtones, especially on head and upper breast; silvery white lower part of bill; female dark red-brown.

HABITAT: Noisy groups of four to eight in lowland scrubby areas, forest edge, and river edges.

REGION: AMA

Plate 66b
Masked Crimson Tanager
Ramphocelus nigrogularis
ID: Small (19 cm, 7.5 in); bright crimson head, upper breast; black mask, back, wings, tail and center of lower belly; silvery white lower part of bill.

HABITAT: Small groups in low vegetation and short trees along small rivers, cochas, and lakes of Amazonian lowlands.

REGION: AMA

Plate 66c
Flame-rumped Tanager
Ramphocelus flammigerus
ID: Small (19 cm, 7.5 in); male all black with striking yellow rump; female brownish black upperparts with yellowish rump and underparts.

HABITAT: Small groups in low vegetation, forest edge, gardens and pastures of coastal lowlands.

REGION: MCL, ACL

Plate 66d
White-shouldered Tanager
Tachyphonus luctuosus
ID: Small (13 cm, 5 in); male glossy black with large white shoulder patches; female with gray head, olive-green upperparts and bright yellow underparts.

HABITAT: Mid-levels and canopy of moist lowland primary and secondary forest; frequently in mixed species foraging flocks.

REGION: MCL, ACL, AMA

Plate 66e
Magpie Tanager
Cissopis leveriana
ID: Medium-sized (28 cm, 11 in); conspicuous with its long tail and striking black and white pattern.

HABITAT: Pairs seen in secondary lowland forest edge, shrubby areas, and vegetation along rivers and lakes.

REGION: AMA

Plate 66 **393**

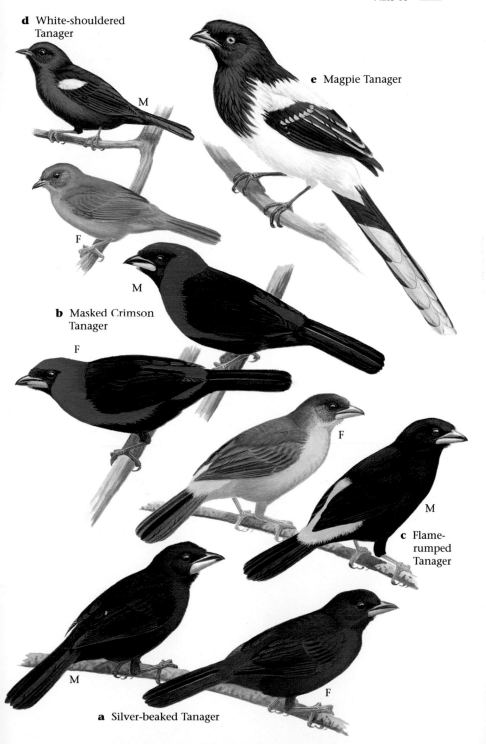

d White-shouldered Tanager

M

F

e Magpie Tanager

M

b Masked Crimson Tanager

F

F

M

c Flame-rumped Tanager

M

F

a Silver-beaked Tanager

Plate 67a

Peruvian Meadowlark
Sturnella bellicosa

ID: Medium-sized (21 cm, 8 in); upperparts black streaked with brown; thin white line over eye; throat and upper breast bright red; lower belly black; long, thin, pointed bill.

HABITAT: Sitting on the ground, low bushes or on telephone wires of open pastures, grassy fields and irrigated areas near coast.

REGION: MCL, ACL

Plate 67b

Scrub Blackbird
Dives warszewiczi

ID: Medium-sized (27 cm, 11 in); all glossy black; dark eye.

HABITAT: In groups on the ground or low vegetation of open farmland, city parks, and patches of secondary vegetation in coastal lowlands; loud ringing songs are obvious.

REGION: MCL, ACL

Plate 67c

Giant Cowbird
Scaphidura oryzivora

ID: Medium-sized (37 cm, 1.2 ft); male glossy black with conspicuous ruff on neck; female smaller, duller black, and little or no ruff on neck.

HABITAT: In pairs or small groups in open humid lowlands (rarely to 2000 m, 6600 ft); often along river sand bars; usually near oropendola colonies, the nests in which they lay their eggs.

REGION: MCL, ACL, AMA

Plate 67d

Oriole Blackbird
Gymnomystax mexicanus

ID: Medium-sized (28 cm, 11 in); black back, wings and tail contrasting with bright yellow head and underparts.

HABITAT: Pairs seen in top of small bushes in marshes and low, open vegetation along rivers, cochas in the Amazonian lowlands.

REGION: AMA

Plate 67e

White-edged Oriole
Icterus graceannae

ID: Medium-sized (21 cm, 8 in); yellow-orange with black throat; black wings and tail with conspicuous white patches. (Replaced in more humid shrubby areas of coastal lowlands by similar Yellow-tailed Oriole, *Icterus mesomelas*, which has yellow patches in the tail.)

HABITAT: Arid shrubby areas, secondary forest patches and desert scrub of coastal lowlands.

REGION: ACL

Plate 67 **395**

a Peruvian Meadowlark

b Scrub Blackbird

c Giant cowbird

e White-edged Oriole

d Oriole Blackbird

Plate 68a

Troupial
Icterus icterus
ID: Medium-sized (23 cm, 9 in); bright orange with black "bib" and face; black tail; black wings with small white patch; orange shoulder; its cheery song is a series of two- and three-noted loud piping whistles.

HABITAT: Moist forest edge and secondary vegetation along marshes and rivers in Amazonian lowlands.

REGION: AMA

Plate 68b

Great-tailed Grackle
Quiscalus mexicanus
ID: Medium-sized (44 cm, 1.4 ft); the all glossy black males have a light eye and a long tail peculiarly folded so that the edges are higher than the center; the smaller females (33 cm, 1.1 ft) have brown upperparts with buffy eyeline and underparts.

HABITAT: In small groups to large flocks walking on the ground in open moist areas close to coast; roost, often in large groups, in isolated groves of trees, mangroves.

REGION: MCL, ACL

Plate 68c

Yellow-rumped Cacique
Cacicus cela
ID: Medium-sized (30 cm, 1 ft); males are noticeably larger than females (23 cm, 9 in) but identical in their black color pattern with yellow wing patch, rump, and base of tail.

HABITAT: Usually in flocks of five to 25 in tall vegetation along lowland river and lake edges, open areas, and frequently near human habitation.

REGION: MCL, ACL, AMA

Plate 68d

Crested Oropendola
Psarocolius decumanus
ID: Medium-sized (47 cm, 1.5 ft); males are distinctly larger than females (37 cm, 1.2 ft) but both are glossy black with rusty rump and lower belly, bright yellow tail, and long, straight, whitish bills.

HABITAT: Large flocks in tall humid lowland forest edges or flying high across open rivers and marshes to their roosts.

REGION: AMA

Plate 68e

Russet-backed Oropendola
Psarocolius angustifrons
ID: Males are larger (49 cm, 1.6 ft) than females (35 cm, 1.2 ft), but both are rusty olive with bright outer tail feathers obvious in flight. The population east of the Andes occurs primarily in the lowlands and has an all-dark bill; west of the Andes it occurs at mid-elevations (400 to 2400 m, 1300 to 7900 ft) and has a yellow bill and forehead.

HABITAT: Large flocks in open secondary forest, isolated trees in pastures, and tall vegetation along rivers and lakes.

REGION: WSA, AMA

Plate 68 397

d Crested Oropendola

e Russet-backed Oropendola

c Yellow-rumped Cacique

a Troupial

F

M

b Great-tailed Grackle

Plate 69a

Slate-colored Grosbeak
Pitylus grossus

ID: Medium-sized (20 cm, 8 in); slate gray with thick red-orange bill and white throat patch.

HABITAT: Pairs seen in mid-level and canopy of moist lowland primary forest.

REGION: MCL, ACL, AMA

Plate 69b

Buff-throated Saltator
Saltator maximus

ID: Medium-sized (21 cm, 8 in); green-olive back, wings and tail; gray head with short white line over eye; small white throat patch with black border; the Amazon form (not illustrated) has a whiter chin, and the black border around the buffy throat patch is reduced to a short 'whisker' on either side; underparts buffy gray. (Occurs together in the Amazonian lowlands with Grayish Saltator, *Saltator coerulescens*, which has all gray upperparts; and in coastal lowlands with Streaked Saltator, *Saltator albicollis*, which has a streaked breast.)

HABITAT: Shrubby undergrowth, forest edge, and low secondary forest of lowlands.

REGION: MCL, ACL, AMA

Plate 69c

Red-capped Cardinal
Paroaria gularis

ID: Small (17 cm, 7 in); bright red head; black upperparts and throat patch; white underparts; immature with brown head.

HABITAT: Low in vegetation bordering cochas, lakes and small rivers in the Amazonian lowlands.

REGION: AMA

Plate 69d

Lesser Seed-finch
Oryzoborus angolensis

ID: Small (13 cm, 5 in); thick dark bill; male with black head and upperparts; underparts dark rusty (Amazon lowlands) or black (coastal lowlands); underwings and small patch in upperwing white, obvious in flight; female all brown.

HABITAT: Pairs in moist grassy areas and shrubby forest edge in the lowlands.

REGION: MCL, ACL, AMA

Plate 69e

Blue-black Grassquit
Volatinia jacarina

ID: Small (11 cm, 4 in); male all blue-black except for white underwings; female brown upperparts, buffy white underparts streaked brown.

HABITAT: Open fields, agricultural areas, and low shrubby patches throughout the lowlands.

REGION: MCL, ACL, AMA

Plate 69f

Variable Seedeater
Sporophila americana

ID: Small (12 cm, 4.5 in); male black above with gray rump patch and partial white collar; white underparts; female buffy brown.

HABITAT: Open fields, grassy areas and roadsides in lowlands.

REGION: MCL, ACL, AMA

Plate 69 **399**

b Buff-throated Saltator

a Slate-colored Grosbeak

f Variable Seedeater

F

M

c Red-capped Cardinal

M

IM

M

F

e Blue-black Grassquit

M

d Lesser Seed-finch

F

Plate 70a

Yellow-bellied Seedeater
Sporophila nigricollis
ID: Small (11 cm, 4 in); male olive-brown upperparts; black head and throat; pale yellow underparts; female olive-brown upperparts, yellowish brown underparts.

HABITAT: Open fields, grassy areas and roadsides in lowlands; especially common in coastal lowlands.

REGION: MCL, ACL, AMA

Plate 70b

Chestnut-bellied Seedeater
Sporophila castaneiventris
ID: Small (10 cm, 4 in); male all blue-gray except for deep rusty-colored center of throat, breast and lower belly; female olive-brown upperparts, buffy underparts.

HABITAT: Open fields, grassy areas, floating vegetation along edges of cochas and small rivers in the lowlands.

REGION: AMA

Plate 70c

Rufous-naped Brush-finch
Atlapetes rufinucha
ID: Small (17 cm, 7 in); dark gray upperparts; black face; bright rusty colored crown; yellow underparts.

HABITAT: Bushes and shrubs in open fields and low forest edge of mid-elevation slopes (1500 to 3000 m, 5000 to 10,000 ft).

REGION: WSA, ESA

Plate 70d

Plumbeous Sierra-finch
Phrygilus unicolor
ID: Small (15 cm, 6 in); male gray with dark bill; female with brown upperparts streaked dark brown and underparts whitish streaked brown.

HABITAT: Low bushes and on ground in open páramo between 3000 and 4500 m (10,000 and 14,800 ft).

REGION: HAP

Plate 70e

Band-tailed Seedeater
Catamenia analis
ID: Small (12 cm, 5 in); male gray with bright yellow bill, rusty colored lower belly, and blackish tail with conspicuous white band across center visible in flight.

HABITAT: Pastures, shrubby areas, and grasslands of upper western slopes (1000 to 3000 m, 3300 to 10,000 ft).

REGION: WSA, HAP

Plate 70f

Collared Warbling-finch
Poospiza hispaniolensis
ID: Small (14 cm, 5.5 in); tail black with large white patches obvious in flight; male upperparts gray, eyeline white, cheek black, underparts white with black breast band; female upperparts grayish brown with brown streaks, underparts whitish with buffy streaks.

HABITAT: Desert scrub, low bushes in the arid Santa Elena Peninsula of southwestern coast.

REGION: ACL

Plate 70 **401**

a Yellow-bellied Seedeater

b Chestnut-bellied Seedeater

M

F

c Rufous-
naped
Brush-
finch

M

d Plumbeous
Sierra-finch

F

M

F

M

M

F

F

e Band-tailed Seedeater

f Collared Warbling-finch

Plate 71a
Rufous-collared Sparrow
Zonotrichia capensis
ID: Small (15 cm, 6 in); upperparts brown with black streaks on back; rusty neck; gray head with prominent black lines; underparts whitish with black and rusty patch on side of upper breast.

HABITAT: Throughout open areas of highlands including pastures, low shrubby areas, gardens and city parks (1000 to 3700 m, 3300 to 12,000 ft).

REGION: HAP

Plate 71b
Saffron Finch
Sicalis flaveola
ID: Small (14 cm, 5.5 in); bright yellow with orange forehead.

HABITAT: Flocks on the ground or in low bushes and trees, open agriculture areas, arid scrublands, gardens and city parks of the lowland coast from Guayaquil south.

REGION: ACL

Plate 71c
Hooded Siskin
Carduelis magellanica
ID: Small (12 cm, 5 in); olive back; yellow rump patch; black tail; wings black with bold yellow stripes obvious in flight; breast bright yellow; head black (male) or olive-yellow (female).

HABITAT: Small flocks in open secondary forest, shrubby areas, agricultural fields, gardens and city parks mostly in highlands from 2000 to 3000 m (6600 to 10,000 ft), but also in southwestern coastal lowlands.

REGION: ACL, WSA, HAP, ESA

Plate 71d
Crimson Finch
Rhodospingus cruentus
ID: Small (11 cm, 4 in); long pointed bill; male upperparts black, underparts pinkish red; female upperparts light brown, underparts buffy yellow.

HABITAT: Secondary forest, low bushes and dry scrubby areas near coast.

REGION: MCL, ACL

Plate 71e
Southern Yellow Grosbeak
Pheucticus chrysogaster
ID: Medium-sized (22 cm, 9 in); thick bill; bright yellow with black streaks on back; black wings with white patches obvious in flight; black tail with white tips; female similar but not as bright yellow.

HABITAT: Secondary forest, open scrubby areas, forest edge, gardens, and city parks throughout highlands at 2000 to 3000 m (6600 to 10,000 ft), and into the arid lowlands of the coastal southwest.

REGION: ACL, HAP

Plate 71 403

e Southern Yellow Grosbeak

M

F

c Hooded Siskin

d Crimson Finch

M

F

M

F

a Rufous-collared Sparrow

IM

b Saffron Finch

Plate 72 (*See also*: Opossums, p. 177)

Plate 72a
Brown Four-eyed Opossum
Metachirus nudicaudatus
ID: Like a large brown rat (body length 27 cm, 10.5 in); distinctive buff spot above each eye; tail long (30 cm, 1 ft) and completely hairless.

HABITAT: Mature lowland forests and tall secondary forests with undergrowth; forages both in the trees and on the ground; active at night and shy.

REGION: MCL, ACL, AMA

Plate 72b
Common Opossum
Didelphis marsupialis
ID: Large (body length 40 cm, 15 in); black or gray; naked black ears and long, naked, black tail (40 cm, 15 in) with a white tip.

HABITAT: Common below 2000 m (6500 ft) around villages, secondary forests and river edge vegetation on the ground or in trees; night-active.

REGION: MCL, ACL, AMA

Plate 72c
Long-furred Woolly Mouse Opossum
Micoureus demerarae
ID: Small (body length 18 cm, 7 in); grayish brown; resembles more a rodent than a marsupial; long body fur and a tail whose first quarter is covered with short hairs. (Similar species of mouse opossums replace it at mid-elevations and on the coast of Ecuador.)

HABITAT: Primarily high above the ground in branches of trees in secondary and primary forests as well as in plantations and gardens in the eastern lowlands; occasionally forages on the ground and hisses actively if approached too closely; night-active.

REGION: AMA

Plate 72d
Water Opossum
Chironectes minimus
ID: Only medium-sized (body length 28 cm, 11 in) mammal with mottled black and light gray color pattern and webbed hind toes in lowland Ecuador.

HABITAT: Active at night swimming in water of lowland lakes and rivers; does not climb vegetation.

REGION: MCL, AMA

Plate 72   **405**

a Brown Four-eyed
Opossum

b Common Opossum

c Long-furred Woolly
Mouse Opossum

d Water Opossum

Plate 73a
Brown-throated Three-toed Sloth
Bradypus variegatus
ID: Medium-sized (body length 60 cm, 24 in); pale brown and gray but takes on distinctive green tinge during the rainy season when algae and fungi grow on the hairs; flat, black and white masked face and hooked claws.

HABITAT: Restricted to moist lowland forests, but most easily seen in open *Cecropia* forests along rivers; a docile and non-aggressive species active during the day.

REGION: MCL, AMA

Plate 73b
Hoffmann's Two-toed Sloth
Choloepus hoffmanni
ID: Medium-sized (body length 65 cm, 26 in); buffy colored with a long protruding snout; active mainly at night. (Replaced in the Amazon lowlands by the similar Southern Two-toed Sloth, *Choloepus didactylus*.)

HABITAT: Restricted mainly to moist primary forest high in the canopy; uses its two sharp toes on the front feet as effective weapons and can be quite aggressive when cornered.

REGION: MCL

Plate 73c
Giant Armadillo
Priodontes maximus
ID: Large (body length 90 cm, 35 in) with long scaled tail (52 cm, 20 in); incomplete armor plating; huge, curved central claw on the front feet.

HABITAT: Active at night in lowland primary forest and spends the daytime resting in large burrows dug into the forest floor.

REGION: AMA

Plate 73d
Nine-banded Armadillo
Dasypus novemcinctus
ID: Medium-sized (body length 40 cm, 16 in); long pointed tail (30 cm, 12 in); long nose; body armor plating covering the entire sides; six to 11 movable expansion bands across the back, most individuals with nine.

HABITAT: Active day and night in lowland forests, savannah and open areas.

REGION: MCL, ACL, WSA, ESA, AMA

Plate 73e
Giant Anteater
Myrmecophaga tridactyla
ID: Large (body length 1.6 m, 5 ft); striking and bold black, gray and white coloring; long, thin head and muzzle; long (75 cm, 30 in) and feather-like tail.
HABITAT: Active day or night, it is restricted almost entirely to primary lowland forest; found only on the ground; long claws on its front feet and a very aggressive nature when cornered can make it extremely dangerous.

REGION: MCL, AMA

Plate 73f
Southern Tamandua
Tamandua tetradactyla
ID: Medium-sized (body length 70 cm, 28 in); distinct yellowish and black pattern; long (50 cm, 20 in) furry tail is prehensile and used for climbing. (Replaced in coastal lowlands by the similar but smaller Northern Tamandua, *Tamandua mexicana*.)

HABITAT: Active both day and night either in trees or on ground of secondary and primary lowland forest.

REGION: AMA

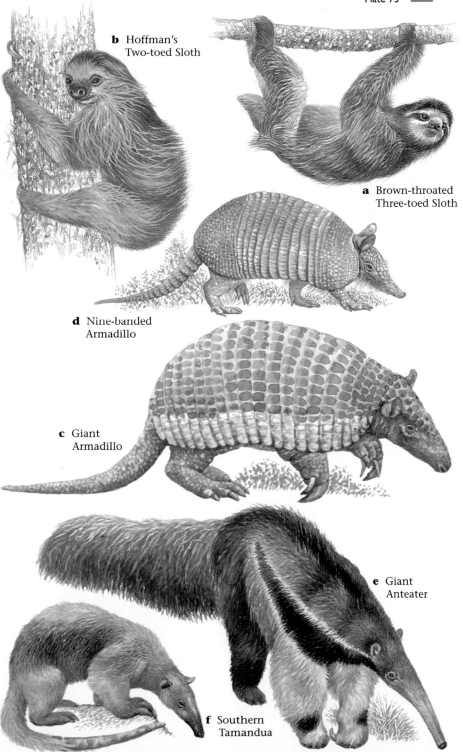

Plate 73   407

b Hoffman's
Two-toed Sloth

a Brown-throated
Three-toed Sloth

d Nine-banded
Armadillo

c Giant
Armadillo

e Giant
Anteater

f Southern
Tamandua

Plate 74a

Greater Fishing Bat
Noctilio leporinus

ID: Large (body length 9.7 cm, 4 in); brown to reddish brown with 60 cm (2 ft) wingspan; squared snout with no nose leaf.

HABITAT: Lowland lakes, estuaries, rivers, pastures and cleared areas; usually seen flying over water at night hunting for fish.

REGION: MCL, AMA

Plate 74b

Jamaican Fruit-eating Bat
Artibeus jamaicensis

ID: Large (body length 9 cm, 3.5 in; wingspan 40 cm, 16 in); brown to gray coloring; lack of a tail, prominent nose leaf and no white lines on the back are distinctive.

HABITAT: Low and middle elevation wet and dry forests; feeds at night mainly on fruit, especially figs.

REGION: MCL, ACL, WSA, ESA, AMA

Plate 74c

Common Vampire Bat
Desmodus rotundus

ID: Medium-sized (body length 7.5 cm, 3 in); triangular-shaped ears; razor-sharp front teeth; "thumb" on the wing twice as long as that of any other species of bat.

HABITAT: Nocturnal in lowland to mid-elevation forests and clearing; most common in pastures and agricultural areas where there are large domestic animals to supply its blood meal.

REGION: MCL, ACL, WSA, ESA, AMA

Plate 74d

False Vampire Bat
Vampyrum spectrum

ID: Largest bat in the New World (body length 15 cm, 6 in) with a huge wingspan (85 cm, 33 in); long snout with nose leaf and large rounded ears.

HABITAT: Nocturnal in lowland and mid-elevation forests and clearings; preys on small to medium-sized birds such as trogons and also other bats, rodents and occasionally fruit.

REGION: MCL, WSA, ESA, AMA

Plate 74e

White-lined Sac-winged Bat
Saccopteryx bilineata

ID: Small (body length 5 cm, 2 in); dark brown with two bold white lines running the length of the back; sharp-pointed nose lacking a nose leaf.

HABITAT: Nocturnal in lowland forest clearings and along forest paths where they pursue insects.

REGION: MCL, AMA

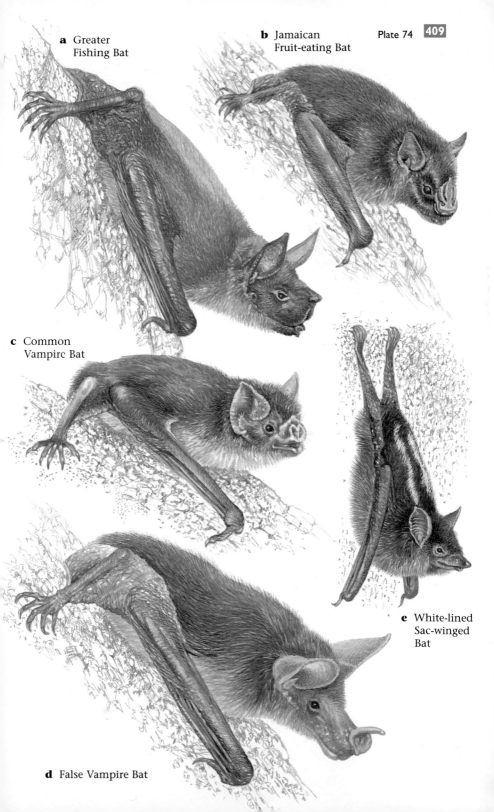

a Greater
Fishing Bat

b Jamaican
Fruit-eating Bat

Plate 74   409

c Common
Vampire Bat

e White-lined
Sac-winged
Bat

d False Vampire Bat

Plate 75a

Short-tailed Fruit Bat
Carollia perspicillata
ID: Small (body length 5.5 cm, 2 in); light brown; large nose leaf on nose.

HABITAT: Moist lowlands up to 1200 m (4000 ft) elevation; feed on the forest undergrowth fruits of *Piper* plants.

REGION: MCL, WSA, ESA, AMA

Plate 75b

Sucker-footed Bat
Thyroptera tricolor
ID: Small (body length 4 cm, 1.5 in); short muzzle lacking a nose leaf; silver-white breast contrasting with dark brown body upperparts.

HABITAT: Moist lowland forests, gardens and banana plantations; feed nocturnally on insects along forested rivers and clearings. Unique suction cups on ankles and thumbs attach to leaf surfaces while roosting during the day, especially inside young *Heliconia* and banana leaves that are still rolled into tubes before opening as mature leaves.

REGION: MCL, AMA

Plate 75c

Common Long-tongued Bat
Glossophaga soricina
ID: Medium-sized (body length 5.5 cm, 2 in); long snout with spear-shaped nose leaf.
HABITAT: Restricted to moist lowland forests; hovers while using its long tongue to reach flower nectar; also catches insects resting on plant leaves.

REGION: MCL, AMA

Plate 75d

Long-nosed Bat
Rhynchonycteris naso
ID: Small (body length 4 cm, 1.5 in); grizzly-white; distinctively long pointed snout lacking nose leaf.

HABITAT: Always in moist areas near lowland primary forest; hunts insects at night low over nearby water surfaces; several individuals roost together during the day on shaded logs along rivers and fly low over the water as a flock when frightened.

REGION: MCL, AMA

Plate 75e

Black Myotis
Myotis nigricans
ID: Small (body length 4 cm, 1.5 in); dark brown with a short nose and no nose leaf.

HABITAT: Common at night hawking for insects in the air over open areas of dry to moist forest from sea level to over 2000 m (6500 ft) elevation; also common around human habitation.

REGION: MCL, ACL, WSA, ESA, AMA

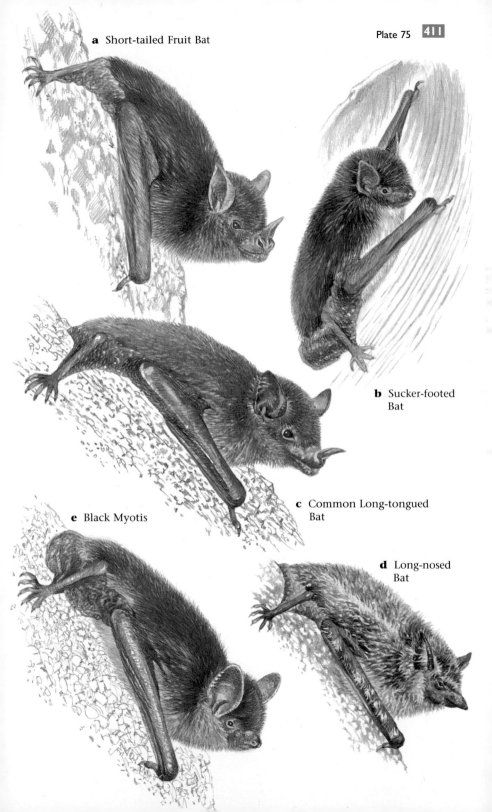

a Short-tailed Fruit Bat

Plate 75 411

b Sucker-footed Bat

c Common Long-tongued Bat

e Black Myotis

d Long-nosed Bat

Plate 76a

Dusky Titi Monkey
Callicebus moloch

ID: Small (body length 30 cm, 12 in); long (40 cm, 16 in) bushy tail; white forehead and rusty chest contrast with gray upperparts; often noticed by its whooping calls in early morning; moves little and is difficult to see when disturbed.

HABITAT: Active only during the day in dense vegetation and vine tangles of lowland secondary and primary forest.

REGION: AMA

Plate 76b

Golden-mantled Tamarin
Saguinus tripartitus

ID: Small (body length 23 cm, 9 in; tail 32 cm, 12 in); black head and contrasting golden shoulders.

HABITAT: Active only during the day; found in small troops in the mid levels of lowland *tierra firme* forests south of the Río Napo.

REGION: AMA

Plate 76c

Saddle-backed Tamarin
Saguinus fuscicollis

ID: Small (body length 24 cm, 9 in; tail 33 cm, 13 in); black head and feet; mostly chestnut body. The high chirping notes of the small family groups sound like a bird flock. It can be confused only with the rarer Black-mantled Tamarin, *Saguinus nigricollis*, which has all black foreparts, lacks the light speckling on the back, and often occurs in large troops of 40 or more.

HABITAT: Active only during the day in mid-levels of secondary and primary *tierra firme* forest with dense tangles of vines and branches.

REGION: AMA

Plate 76d

Pygmy Marmoset
Cebuella pygmaea

ID: Smallest primate in Ecuador (body length 14 cm, 5.5 in; tail 20 cm, 8 in); buffy gray; easily seen only at its sap-sucking sites low on tree trunks.

HABITAT: Primary *tierra firme* forest during the day.

REGION: AMA

Plate 76 413

a Dusky Titi Monkey

b Golden-mantled Tamarin

c Saddle-backed Tamarin

d Pygmy Marmoset

Plate 77a

Common Squirrel Monkey
Saimiri sciureus

ID: Medium-sized (body length 30 cm, 12 in); long non-prehensile tail (40 cm, 16 in); combination of black snout and white face and ears is unique.

HABITAT: Active during the day where its large, noisy troops move at mid- to upper levels of primary and secondary lowland forests.

REGION: AMA

Plate 77b

White-fronted Capuchin Monkey
Cebus albifrons

ID: Medium-sized (body length 40 cm, 16 in); long (45 cm, 18 in) prehensile tail usually carried coiled; combination of a dark cap and light-colored body and feet unique in Ecuador. Similar sized and shaped Brown Capuchin, *Cebus apella*, occasionally occurs in the same troops with the White-fronted Capuchin in Amazonian Ecuador, but it has dark legs and feet and darker brown body.

HABITAT: Active during the day; large and noisy troops move at all levels from the ground to canopy of primary and secondary forest.

REGION: MCL, WSA, ESA, AMA

Plate 77c

Common Woolly Monkey
Lagothrix lagotricha

ID: Medium-sized (body length 40 cm, 16 in); uniformly colored gray to black; long prehensile tail (70 cm, 28 in) carried coiled.

HABITAT: Travels during the day in noisy and often large troops through mid-levels to canopy of lowland *tierra firme* forest.

REGION: AMA

Plate 77d

White-bellied Spider Monkey
Ateles belzebuth

ID: Large (body length 50 cm, 20 in); all dark except for a light chest; long arms, legs and prehensile tail (78 cm, 31 in); distinctive screaming calls. The similar-sized and shaped, but brown and black, Central American Spider Monkey, *Ateles geoffroyi*, may be present in remote areas of extreme northwestern Ecuador.

HABITAT: Active day and night; small to large troops forage mainly in the canopy of primary lowland forest.

REGION: AMA

Plate 77 **415**

a Common Squirrel Monkey

b White-fronted Capuchin Monkey

c Common Woolly Monkey

d White-bellied Spider Monkey

Plate 78 (*See also*: Primates, p. 188))

Plate 78a

Noisy Night Monkey
Aotus vociferans

ID: Medium-sized (body length 33 cm, 13 in); black and white face pattern, dark ears; long non-prehensile tail (30 cm, 12 in) hanging straight down; often gives low owl-like hoots at night.

HABITAT: The small family groups rest during the day in dense vine tangles and forage at night in the upper canopy; occurs in Amazonian *tierra firme* and flooded forest up to cloud forest, where it regularly reaches elevations higher than any other monkey in Ecuador (3500 m, 11,500 ft).

REGION: WSA, AMA

Plate 78b

Monk Saki Monkey
Pithecia monachus

ID: Large (body length 40 cm, 16 in); shaggy gray and black body hair, naked face and long shaggy tail (45 cm, 18 in). Similar Equatorial Saki Monkey, *Pithecia aequatorialis*, differs in having a brownish rather than grayish chest. Immatures of these two species, however, are almost indistinguishable.

HABITAT: Both Saki species in Ecuador are active during the day and occur in the upper levels of primary forest in small family groups.

REGION: AMA

Plate 78c

Red Howler Monkey
Alouatta seniculus

ID: Large (body length 55 cm, 22 in); bright rusty color, long prehensile tail (60 cm, 24 in), and lion-like roars.

HABITAT: Small family groups sit quietly or move slowly during the day through the upper levels of primary forest of the Amazon; easiest to see along forested rivers.

REGION: AMA

Plate 78d

Mantled Howler Monkey
Alouatta palliata

ID: Largest monkey (body length 50 cm, 20 in) on the coast of Ecuador; black color, long prehensile tail (55 cm, 22 in), and loud roars.

HABITAT: Troops of five to 30 sit quietly or move slowly during the day in moist primary and secondary forests to tropical dry forest, especially along rivers.

REGION: MCL, ACL

Plate 78

b Monk Saki Monkey

a Noisy Night Monkey

c Red Howler Monkey

d Mantled Howler Monkey

Plate 79a

Spectacled Bear
Tremarctos ornatus
ID: Only bear in South America; huge size (body length 2 m, 6.5 ft) and black body; varying amount of white on face and chest.

HABITAT: Associated with the Andes Mountains primarily in cloud forest between 1500 and 3000 m (5000 to 10,000 ft), but occasionally higher into páramo or lower into upper Amazonian forest; active day and night.

REGION: WSA, HAP, ESA

Plate 79b

Kinkajou
Potos flavus
ID: Medium-sized (body length 52 cm, 20 in); large eyes, small ears, short hair and long, prehensile tail (48 cm, 29 in); active only at night; bright eyeshine reflected from a flashlight is the best way to find it.

HABITAT: Moist lowland forest, where it moves noisily through the upper levels of primary and secondary forest and even into plantations and gardens.

REGION: MCL, AMA

Plate 79c

Crab-eating Raccoon
Procyon cancrivorous
ID: Medium-sized (body length 60 cm, 24 in); black mask and prominently ringed tail (35 cm, 14 in) carried low to the ground.

HABITAT: Active only at night on the shores of streams, lakes and marshes of the Amazon lowlands.

REGION: AMA

Plate 79d

South American Coati
Nasua nasua
ID: Medium-sized (body length 50 cm, 20 in); long, tapered snout and long tail (48 cm, 19 in) often held up in the air. (The population of coatis in the coastal humid and dry lowlands of Ecuador is sometimes considered a separate species, the White-nosed Coati, *Nasua narica*. The Mountain Coati, *Nasua olivacea*, is also similar in shape but is half the size and restricted to cloud forests above 2000 m (6500 ft).)

HABITAT: Day-active; females travel in large groups on the ground and into the mid-levels of primary and secondary lowland forest; males travel solitarily.

REGION: AMA

Plate 79e

Andean Fox
(aslo called Culpeo Fox)
Dusicyon culpaeus
ID: Medium-sized (body length 71 cm, 28 in); orangish cast to a gray-brown coat and a dark back; long bushy tail (40 cm, 16 in) usually black but can be gray to orangish.

HABITAT: Active mainly at night in drier parts of páramo and highland Ecuador up to 4500 m (14,750 ft).

REGION: HAP

Plate 79 **419**

b Kinkajou

c Crab-eating Raccoon

d South American Coati

a Spectacled Bear

e Andean Fox

Plate 80a
Giant Otter
Pteronura brasiliensis
ID: Large size (body and tail together 1.5 m, 5 ft); dark fur with spotted throat and noisy calls. The smaller Neotropical Otter, *Lontra longicaudus*, also in Amazonian waterways, has an all-white breast.

HABITAT: Remote rivers and cochas of the Amazonian lowlands.

REGION: AMA

Plate 80b
Tayra
Eira barbara
ID: Large (body and tail 1 m, 3.3 ft); dark and short-legged; buffy throat and often an all-buffy head.

HABITAT: Active running on the ground or along branches of large trees, mainly during the day in moist and dry lowland forests up to cloud forests at 3000 m (10,000 ft).

REGION: MCL, ACL, WSA, ESA, AMA

Plate 80c
Grison
Galictis vittata
ID: Medium-sized (body and tail 55 cm, 22 in); distinctive black, gray and white color different than any other species in Amazonian Ecuador.

HABITAT: Active at night, often in family groups, on the floor of lowland primary and secondary forests.

REGION: AMA

Plate 80d
Long-tailed Weasel
Mustela frenata
ID: Small (body and tail 30 cm, 12 in), long and slender, this bold species is often easy to see and approach.

HABITAT: Active during the day near tree-line and up to low páramo as well as in open lowlands of coastal Ecuador.

REGION: MCL, ACL, HAP

Plate 80e
Striped Hog-nosed Skunk
Conepatus semistriatus
ID: Medium-sized (body length 40 cm, 16 in); black and white stripes, all white bushy tail (19 cm, 7 in), and distinctive smell.

HABITAT: Active at night; often bold in open areas at higher altitudes of the Andes but also down to the coast in tropical dry forest.

REGION: ACL, HAP, WSA, ESA,

Plate 80 421

a Giant Otter

e Striped Hog-nosed Skunk

b Tayra

c Grison

d Long-tailed Weasel

Plate 81a

Jaguarundi
Herpailurus yaguarondi

ID: Small (body length 60 cm, 24 in); uniformly gray, brown, or reddish; proportionately short legs; long tail (50 cm, 20 in).

HABITAT: Active mostly during the day, it is most often seen on the floor or clearings of primary and secondary forest, sometimes near human habitations.

REGION: MCL, ACL, AMA

Plate 81b

Ocelot
Leopardus pardalis

ID: Medium-sized (body length 80 cm, 32 in); distinctive spotting and proportionately short tail (36 cm, 14 in); most frequently noticed by its tracks.

HABITAT: Active day and night; occurs mainly on the ground in moist and dry lowland forests but often spends the day sleeping in trees.

REGION: MCL, ACL, AMA

Plate 81c

Margay
Leopardus wiedii

ID: Smaller (body length 60 cm, 24 in) than the similarly spotted Ocelot, but a longer tail (45 cm, 18 in); very shy, it is most likely to be noticed by its tracks.

HABITAT: Primarily nocturnal, it spends most of its time in trees of secondary and primary moist lowland forest.

REGION: MCL, AMA

Plate 81d

Jaguar
Panthera onca

ID: Largest (body length 1.5 m, 5 ft; tail 60 cm, 24 in) spotted cat in the New World. Its presence is most likely to be noted by its huge tracks along river beaches or lake banks.

HABITAT: Active day and night in lowland moist and dry forests; usually stays on the ground except to flee danger, when it will climb trees.

REGION: MCL, ACL, AMA

Plate 81e

Puma
Puma concolor

ID: Large (body length 1 m, 3.3 ft); uniformly colored with a long black-tipped tail (80 cm, 32 in); footprints smaller and different shape than Jaguar's.

HABITAT: Primarily on the ground in a wide range of habitats from coastal scrub and dry forest to moist lowland and mid-altitude cloud forest; occasionally into high elevation páramo.

REGION: MCL, ACL, WSA, HAP, ESA, AMA

Plate 81 423

brown form

red form

a Jaguarundi

LF

LH

c Margay

LF

LH

b Ocelot

LF

LH

d Jaguar

LF

LH

e Puma

Plate 82a

Collared Peccary
Tayassu tajacu

ID: Smaller (body length 90 cm, 35 in) than the White-lipped Peccary; brown with a grizzled collar; occurs mainly in small family groups.

HABITAT: Active during the day in lowland moist and dry forests.

REGION: MCL, ACL AMA

Plate 82b

White-lipped Peccary
Tayassu pecari

ID: Larger (body length 1 m, 3.3 ft), darker, and lacks the collar of the Collared Peccary; often forages in herds of up to 100 or more individuals.

HABITAT: Active during the day in moist lowland forests.

REGION: MCL, AMA

Plate 82c

Red Brocket Deer
Mazama americana

ID: Medium-sized (body length 1.2 m, 4 ft); rusty color distinguishes it from the slightly smaller and darker Gray Brocket Deer, *Mazama gouazoubira*, with which it occurs in the Amazonian portion of its range.

HABITAT: Active night and day in moist and dry lowland forests, swampy areas, secondary forests and plantations.

REGION: MCL, ACL, AMA

Plate 82d

White-tailed Deer
Odocoileus virginianus

ID: Large (body length 2 m, 6.5 ft); males with branching antlers; large white tail held up when running from danger.

HABITAT: Most common near tree-line and open areas above 3000 m (10,000 ft) in the Andes but also in open dry forests of the lowland coast.

REGION: ACL, HAP

Plate 82 425

LF
LH

a Collared Peccary

LF
LH

b White-lipped Peccary

c Red Brocket Deer

d White-tailed Deer

Plate 83a

Northern Amazon Red Squirrel
Sciurus igniventris

ID: Medium-sized (body length 27 cm, 11 in), noisy, brightly colored squirrel; large bushy tail as long as its body (30 cm, 12 in).

HABITAT: Active during the day on the ground and lower branches of lowland primary and secondary forest of the Amazon lowlands. (Replaced in the lowland coastal dry forest by the similar-sized but white-tailed Guayaquil Squirrel, *Sciurus stramineus*.)

REGION: AMA

Plate 83b

Amazon Bamboo Rat
Dactylomys dactylinus

ID: Large (body length 30 cm, 12 in); squared snout and long, naked tail (40 cm, 16 in); loud staccato calls at night are the easiest way to notice it.

HABITAT: Active at night; usually associated with bamboo stands, thick river edge vegetation, or the canopy of lowland moist forest.

REGION: AMA

Plate 83c

Amazon Dwarf Squirrel
Microsciurus flaviventer

ID: Small (body length 14 cm, 6 in) with short ears and a short (10 cm, 4 in) bushy tail. (Replaced by the similar Western Dwarf Squirrel, *Microsciurus mimulus*, in moist lowland forests of northern coastal Ecuador.)

HABITAT: Day-active from the ground to canopy of moist Amazonian lowland forests.

REGION: AMA

Plate 83d

Bicolor-spined Porcupine
Coendou bicolor

ID: Medium-sized (body length 42 cm, 17 in); all dark with distinctive prehensile tail as long as or longer than the body.

HABITAT: Night-active in mid-levels of lowland and mid-elevation primary and secondary forests. Several other rarer but lighter-colored porcupine species also occur in Ecuador.

REGION: MCL, WSA, ESA, AMA

Plate 83e

Black Agouti
Dasyprocta fuliginosa

ID: Medium-sized (body length 60 cm, 24 in); all dark and virtually tailless; resembles a small peccary.

HABITAT: Most often seen during the day foraging or running noisily through the forest undergrowth in Amazonian lowlands. (Replaced in the northern coastal lowland moist forest and western slope forests by the brownish Central American Agouti, *Dasyprocta punctata*.)

REGION: AMA

Plate 83f

Paca
Agouti paca

ID: Medium-sized (body length 70 cm, 28 in); chestnut color with several rows of white spots on its sides and virtually tailless.

HABITAT: Active at night along the banks of rivers and lakes or the undergrowth of lowland forests. (Between 2000 and 3000 m, 6500 to 10,000 ft, elevation, it is replaced by similar but longer-haired Mountain Paca, *Agouti taczanowskii*.)

REGION: MCL, AMA

Plate 83   **427**

a Northern Amazon Red
Squirrel

b Amazon Bamboo Rat

d Bicolor-spined
Porcupine

c Amazon
Dwarf Squirrel

e Black Agouti

f Paca

Plate 84 (*See also*: Rodents, p. 206; Dolphin, Manatee, Tapir, p. 200)

Plate 84a

Capybara
Hydrochaeris hydrochaeris
ID: Large (body length 1.2 m, 4 ft) brown rodent most likely to be confused with a pig.

HABITAT: Active during the day and almost always along Amazonian lowland lakes and rivers, into which they dive to escape danger.

REGION: AMA

Plate 84b

Brazilian Tapir
Tapirus terrestris
ID: Large (body length 2 m, 6.5 ft); dark; long snout is diagnostic; its huge tracks in muddy areas are also readily identified. (In cloud forests between 2000 and 3000 m, 6500 to 10,000 ft, it is replaced by the smaller Mountain Tapir, *Tapirus pinchaque*; and in the coastal moist lowland and lower west slopes by the larger Baird's Tapir, *Tapirus bairdii*).

HABITAT: Primarily active at night, they are almost always associated with swampy and moist areas in lowland Amazonian forests.

REGION: AMA

Plate 84c

Pink River Dolphin
Inia geoffrensis
ID: Medium-sized (body length 2.3 m, 7.5 ft); long snout and little or no dorsal fin. (The smaller Gray Dolphin, *Sotalia fluviatilis*, has a distinctive triangular dorsal fin and is also found in rivers of extreme eastern Amazonian Ecuador, but it is much rarer.)

HABITAT: Rivers and cochas of the Amazonian lowlands.

REGION: AMA

Plate 84d

Amazonian Manatee
Trichechus inunguis
ID: Large (body length 2.5 m, 8 ft) and seal-like; grayish black; found only in freshwater where they come to the surface only to breathe. Look for their round droppings floating on the water's surface.

HABITAT: Rivers and cochas of Amazonian lowlands.

REGION: AMA

Plate 84 **429**

LF

a Capybara

LH

LF

LH

b Brazilian Tapir

c Pink River Dolphin

d Amazonian Manatee

Plate 85 (*See also*: Arthropods, pp. 215–218)

Plate 85a

Helicopter Damselfly
Microstigma rotundatum
ID: Long, thin body; large wings flap slowly through the middle and upper levels of moist primary lowland forests on sunny days.

REGION: AMA

Plate 85b

Leaf-winged Katydid
(also called Leaf-mimicking Bush Katydid)
Cycloptera speculata
ID: Green or brown body and wings look just like a live or dead leaf; during the day sits on vegetation that matches its coloration; active at night, when it is often attracted to lights.

REGION: MCL, ACL, AMA

Plate 85c

Nasute Termite
Nasutitermes sp.
ID: Brown and white body; worker with mandibles and soldier with "nozzle head" for spraying enemies; forest undergrowth of lowlands; active during the day.

REGION: MCL, ACL, AMA

Plate 85d

Evening Cicada
Fidicina mannifera
ID: Delicate colors and wings held over back tent-like; usually seen during the day resting on vertical trunks of moist lowland forest; active at night feeding and calling.

REGION: MCL, ACL, AMA

Plate 85e

Peanut Bug
(also called Lantern Bug)
Fulgora laternaria
ID: Large, well-camouflaged; large "eyespots" on wings in flight; spends the day often in small groups roosting on vertical tree trunks in moist primary and tall secondary lowland forest; active at night.

REGION: MCL, AMA

Plate 85f

Antlion
Myrmeleon sp.
ID: Larvae at the bottom of inverted cones in dry sand in open lowland areas; also in shade of vegetation or buildings; dragonfly-like adult with long antennae with clubs at ends, attracted to lights at night.

REGION: MCL, ACL, AMA

Plate 85   431

a Helicopter Damselfly

b Leaf-mimicking Katydid

e Peanut Bug

c Nasute Termite

d Evening Cicada

f Antlion pits

f Antlion adult

Plate 86a

Chaudoir's Montane Tiger Beetle
Pseudoxycheila chaudoiri
ID: Velvet greenish blue with two bright yellow-orange spots on the back; active on sunny days above 1000 m (3300 ft) elevation, where it runs along near-vertical clay banks.
REGION: WSA, ESA

Plate 86b

Green Dung Beetle
Oxysternon conspicillatum
ID: Dark metallic green; male only with a prominent horn; commonly attracted to fresh dung in moist lowland primary and tall secondary forest; active during the day.
REGION: MCL, AMA

Plate 86c

Harlequin Long-horned Beetle
Acrocinus longimanus
ID: Huge and colorful beetle most often seen when attracted to lights at night in moist primary lowland forest; male's front legs are half again as long as those of the female.
REGION: MCL, AMA

Plate 86d

Menelaus' Morpho Butterfly
Morpho menelaus
ID: Huge bright blue male is unmistakable; the female is only a bit less garishly blue; flaps lazily along open corridors through forest or along river edges of lowland forest during sunny days; at rest, with wings folded, can be quite hard to see.
REGION: AMA

Plate 86e

Aurorina's Clear-winged Satyr
Cithaerias aurorina
ID: Brownish with clear forewings and reddish spots on hind wings; common during the day on forest floor and along shaded trails of moist lowland forest.
REGION: AMA

Plate 86f

Mechanitis Butterfly
Mechanitis sp.
ID: Bright orange, black, and yellow "tiger" pattern, this species is a poisonous and distasteful one that serves as a "model" to be mimicked by other, less dangerous, butterfly species; mid-levels of moist primary and tall secondary forest; active on sunny days.
REGION: AMA

Plate 86g

Dismorpha Butterfly
Dismorpha sp.
ID: Bright orange, black, and yellow "tiger" pattern, this species lacks toxins and is cheating by mimicking the distasteful and similar appearing model species, such as 86f; mid-levels of moist primary and tall secondary forest; active on sunny days.
REGION: AMA

Plate 86h

Lelius' Urania Moth
Urania lelius
ID: Brilliant green and black color; common on moist river beaches where males "puddle" to suck sodium and other essential chemicals from the sand; also often in large numbers migrating over the canopy of moist lowland forest; active on sunny days.
REGION: AMA

Plate 86   **433**

a Chaudoir's Montane Tiger Beetle

c Harlequin Long-horned Beetle

b Green Dung Beetle

d Menelaus' Morpho Butterfly

e Aurorina's Clear-winged Satyr

g Dismorpha Butterfly (mimic)

f Mechanitis Butterfly (model)

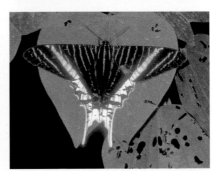

h Lelius' Urania Moth

Plate 87 (*See also*: Arthropods, p. 222–227)

Plate 87a

Robber Fly
Smeryngo sp.
ID: Brownish-yellow color; sits on ground or low vegetation in moist lowland forest waiting to pounce on small insects flying by on sunny days; wings produce loud buzzing in flight.
REGION: AMA

Plate 87b

Leaf-cutter Ant
Atta sp.
ID: Tan and brown; travel in long narrow columns carrying leaf or flower bits like open umbrellas; often create obvious well worn paths through leaf litter on the ground of lowland moist forest; several size castes in a colony; small caste often rides on leaf.
REGION: MCL, ACL, AMA

Plate 87c

Burchell's Army Ant
Eciton burchelli
ID: Tan to black and brown; travel in massive attack columns through moist lowland forest floor and lower vegetation searching for insect prey; several castes in a colony; soldiers have very impressive mandibles.
REGION: MCL, AMA

Plate 87d

Conga Ant
Paraponera clavata
ID: Large, all brownish black, and usually alone or in small groups; listen for their warning sounds and avoid at all costs being stung – an experience in pain you will not soon forget; lowland moist forests, canopy to forest floor.
REGION: MCL, AMA

Plate 87e

Merian's Orchid Bee
Eulaema meriana
ID: Large, bumblebee-like; black body with bright yellow and orange rings on the rear; listen for its deep humming during the day; a non-aggressive resident of moist lowland forest.
REGION: MCL, AMA

Plate 87f

Neotropical Colonial Spider
Anelosimus eximus
ID: Most easily recognized by the huge gossamer webs that stretch for meters (yards) high along riverside vegetation and forest borders. Hundreds of spiders can live together, each with its own small web united with those of its neighbors.
REGION: AMA

Plate 87g

Sally Lightfoot Crab
Grapsus grapsus
ID: Spectacular red, yellow and orange crab common on the beach edge of the Galápagos and on rocky points on the mainland coast. Young are smaller and all dark gray.
REGION: MCL, ACL, GAL

Plate 87   **435**

a Robber Fly

b Leaf-cutter Ant

soldier

workers

c Burchell's Army Ant

d Conga Ant (PAINFUL STING!)

e Merian's Orchid Bee

f Neotropical Colonial Spider

g Sally Lightfoot Crab

Plate 88a

Pacific Green Sea Turtle
Chelonia mydas

ID: Medium to large (to 1.5 m. 5 ft); dull olive to brown, with a flattened, roughly heart-shaped shell; underside yellowish white; front limbs formed into paddles, each with a single claw projecting from the outer edge.

HABITAT: Marine; feeds on vegetation in shallow coastal waters; lays eggs on sandy beaches at night along the Pacific Coast.

REGION: MCL, ACL, GAL

Note: Endangered, CITES Appendix I listed.

Plate 88b

Hawksbill Sea Turtle
Eretmochelys imbricata

ID: Small to mid-sized (to 90 cm, 35 in), with moderately flattened, oval-shaped shell, with shiny, translucent plates richly patterned with radiating colors of tan and dark brown; front limbs formed into paddles, each with two claws projecting from outer edge; upper jaw formed into hooked beak, like a hawk.

HABITAT: Marine; feeds mostly on sponges in shallow coastal waters, especially near reefs and rocks; lays eggs on sandy beaches at night along the Pacific Coast.

REGION: MCL, ACL, GAL

Note: Endangered, CITES Appendix I listed.

Plate 88c

Leatherback Sea Turtle
Dermochelys coriacea

ID: Very large (to 2.4 m, 7.5 ft), with shell formed of a thick, oily and leathery "skin;" blackish with scattered small white spots, with seven raised ridges running the entire length of shell; front limbs formed into paddles, with a single claw on each; the largest turtle on Earth.

HABITAT: Marine; feeds on jellyfish in open ocean, but occasionally in shallow coastal waters; lays eggs on sandy beaches at night along the Pacific Coast.

REGION: MCL, ACL, GAL

Note: Endangered, CITES Appendix I listed.

Plate 88d

Olive Ridley Sea Turtle
Lepidochelys olivacea

ID: Small (to 75 cm, 30 in); olive-colored, with a slightly flattened, heart-shaped shell; skin and scales on limbs and body olive above, lighter below; front limbs formed into paddles, with a single claw on each; the smallest sea turtle.

HABITAT: Marine; open ocean and shallow waters in coastal areas, especially near reefs; lays eggs on sandy beaches during the day along the Pacific Coast.

REGION: MCL, ACL, GAL

Note: Endangered, CITES Appendix I listed.

a Pacific Green Sea Turtle

b Hawksbill Sea Turtle

c Leatherback Sea Turtle

d Olive Ridley Sea Turtle

Plate 89a

Galápagos Tortoise (also called Galápagos Giant Tortoise)
Geochelone nigrita
Geochelone hoodensis

ID: Large, dark gray to black, with high, domed shell; unmistakable; *G. nigrita* to 130 cm (51 in); *G. hoodensis*, to 75 cm (30 in). *G. nigrita* is the largest species and is found only on Santa Cruz Island; *G. hoodensis* is the smallest and found only on Hood (Española) island. In the past, all Galápagos Tortoises were considered to comprise a single species; current classification considers each island's tortoise to be a distinct species, 12 in all.

HABITAT: Terrestrial in variety of inland habitats; day-active.

REGION: GAL

Note: Endangered, CITES Appendix I listed.

Plate 89b (also see book cover)

Marine Iguana
Amblyrhynchus cristatus

ID: Large (to 1.5+ m, 5 ft), stocky, dark brown to black, with a chunky, squared-off head; a row of large spiny scales runs atop the backbone along the neck and body.

HABITAT: Sun-basking; in great abundance along rocky shorelines; swim to feed on algae and seaweed; world's only marine lizard.

REGION: GAL

Plate 89c

Galápagos Land Iguana
Conolophus subcristatus

ID: Large (to 1.5 m, 5 ft), stocky, usually tan to dark brown; coloring varies among islands, but it is always much lighter in color than the Marine Iguana; like the Marine Iguana, it has a row of spiny scales atop the backbone, but its spines are shorter.

HABITAT: Inland, scrubby areas on Fernandina, Isabela, Santa Cruz, and South Plaza Islands; terrestrial; often near shoreline, but does not enter water. (A similar species, *C. pallidus*, more yellowish, is only on tiny island of Santa Fe.)

REGION: GAL

Plate 89d

Galápagos Lava Lizard
Tropidurus albemarlensis

ID: Small (to 20 cm, 8 in), rough-scaled, gray to tan or brown, with a distinct row of raised spiny scales running along the backbone; upper body variably patterned with lighter and darker lengthwise stripes and dark spots; throat and neck red, or black and yellow.

HABITAT: Along sandy shorelines and inland, in sun on sand, rocks, low vegetation. (Seven species, all similar, are found in Galápagos, some on only one island, others on two or more; this species is the most widespread.)

REGION: GAL

Plate 89e

Galápagos Snake
Antillophis steindachneri

ID: Four species of terrestrial snakes, all similar, are found on the various Galápagos Islands; They are all small and slender, and often have stripes (or spots that form stripes); to about 1 m (3 ft).

HABITAT: Common on San Cristóbal, Floreana, and Española Islands; terrestrial but also on low vegetation.

REGION: GAL

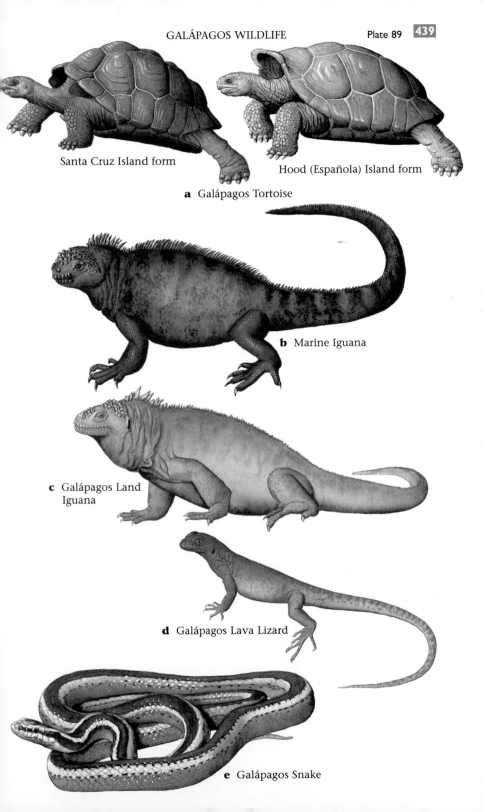

Santa Cruz Island form

Hood (Española) Island form

a Galápagos Tortoise

b Marine Iguana

c Galápagos Land Iguana

d Galápagos Lava Lizard

e Galápagos Snake

Plate 90a

Galápagos Penguin
Spheniscus mendiculus

ID: Large (55 cm, 1.8 ft), black upperparts, white underparts, white eyeline curving down and forward toward chest obvious both when standing upright onshore or swimming duck-like on the ocean's surface.

HABITAT: Beaches near ocean's edge or in water within site of land, Isabela and Fernandina only.

REGION: GAL

Plate 90b

Waved Albatross
(also called Galápagos Albatross)
Diomedea irrorata

ID: Large (90 cm, 3ft), upperparts dark brown, underparts finely barred brown, head and neck buffy white, huge bill; in flight long thin wings (wingspan 2.3 m, 7.5 ft) with whitish undersides and dark uppersides.

HABITAT: Nests and courts on flat grassy areas of Española and Isla de la Plata just off the coast of the mainland; during nonbreeding season (January to March) at sea off coast of northwestern South America.

REGION: ACL, GAL

Plate 90c

Galápagos Hawk
Buteo galapagoensis

ID: Large (56 cm, 1.8 ft), dark brown often with light shoulder patches, yellowish bill and feet; immature with light patches on underparts; in flight soaring on long (wingspan 1.2 m, 4 ft), broad wings.

HABITAT: Lowlands and highlands of most islands with the notable exceptions of Genovesa, San Cristóbal and Floreana.

REGION: GAL

Plate 90d

White-vented Storm-petrel
Oceanites gracilis

ID: Small (15 cm, 6 in), dark brown with white rump and white lower belly with black line up middle.

HABITAT: "Walking" on ocean's surface during the day usually within sight of land.

REGION: GAL

Plate 90e

Wedge-rumped Storm-petrel
Oceanodroma tethys

ID: Small (19 cm, 7.5 in); dark brown with large triangular-shaped white rump patch covering most of tail. The similar Band-rumped Storm-petrel (*Oceanodroma castro*) has a narrow white rump patch and feeds far out at sea during the daytime; it is also the species most likely to be seen close to shore in bays along the mainland.

HABITAT: Flying in huge flocks low over its flat rocky nesting areas on San Cristóbal and Genovesa during the daytime.

REGION: GAL

Plate 90f

Red-billed Tropicbird
Phaethon aethereus

ID: Large (48 cm, 1.6 ft); white with black eyestripe and outer wing patches; back barred gray; bill bright red and distinctive long tail streamers (50 cm, 1.6 ft) are about as long as the body.

HABITAT: Nests on cliffs and on the ground among rocks; often far out at sea flying high overhead or diving into the ocean.

REGION: GAL

a Galápagos Penguin

c Galápagos Hawk

b Waved Albatross

d White-vented Storm-Petrel

e Wedge-rumped Storm-Petrel

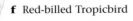

f Red-billed Tropicbird

Plate 91a

Masked Booby
Sula dactylatra

ID: Large (85 cm, 2.8 ft); all white except for black tail and black patches on wings; face dark; bill pinkish orange and feet yellowish gray. The population in the Galápagos is considered by some experts to be sufficiently different to be a separate species, the Nazca Booby, *Sula granti.*

HABITAT: Flat areas on nesting islands; soaring over ocean's surface and diving straight down into the water while feeding.

REGION: GAL

Plate 91b

Red-footed Booby
Sula sula

ID: Large, (70 cm, 2.3 ft); some individuals all white with dark wing patches and tails, others all brown; face pink and blue; feet bright red.

HABITAT: Nests in trees and feeds, often at night, well off-shore.

REGION: GAL

Plate 91c

Blue-footed Booby
Sula nebouxii

ID: Large (86 cm, 2.8 ft); bright blue feet obvious only when standing on land (see Plate 14b); whitish breast and mottled dark back in flight.

HABITAT: Soaring low over ocean's surface and diving; seldom seen on land along coast of mainland but common on Galápagos Islands.

REGION: MCL, ACL, GAL

Plate 91d

Flightless Cormorant
Nannopterum harrisi

ID: Large (92 cm, 3 ft); dark brown with torquoise eyes and short stubby wings often held out to dry when resting on shore; while swimming, the head and long neck are usually visible.

HABITAT: Shore and shallow coastline of Fernandina and western Isabela.

REGION: GAL

c Blue-footed Booby

d Flightless Cormorant

a Masked Booby

brown form

b Red-footed Booby

white form

Plate 92a

Yellow-crowned Night Heron
Nyctanassa violacea
ID: Large (60 cm, 2 ft); blue-gray; pale yellow crown and white cheeks contrast with rest of black head.

HABITAT: On rocky shore-line and in mangroves.

REGION: MCL, ACL, GAL

Plate 92b

Greater Flamingo
Phoenicopterus ruber
ID: Very large (1 m, 3.3 ft); pink with black wing patches and large black-tipped bill; in flight with long neck stretched out; long legs entirely pink.

HABITAT: Small flocks on saltwater estuaries and lagoons.

REGION: GAL

Plate 92c

Swallow-tailed Gull
Larus furcatus
ID: Large (58 cm, 1.9 ft); gray upperparts, white underparts; dark gray head (during breeding season) and black wing tips; forked tail in flight.

HABITAT: Rests during day on nesting cliffs and among rocks; feeds at night over ocean's surface.

REGION: GAL

Plate 92d

Lava Gull
Larus fuliginosus
ID: Large (53 cm, 1.7 ft); all dark gray with darker head and tail.

HABITAT: Estuaries and coastline of Santa Cruz, San Cristóbal and Isabela.

REGION: GAL

Plate 92e

American Oystercatcher
Haematopus palliatus
ID: Medium-sized (47 cm, 1.5 ft); black and white with long, straight orange bill.

HABITAT: Pairs seen on beaches of islands and in estuaries of mainland.

REGION: MCL, ACL, GAL

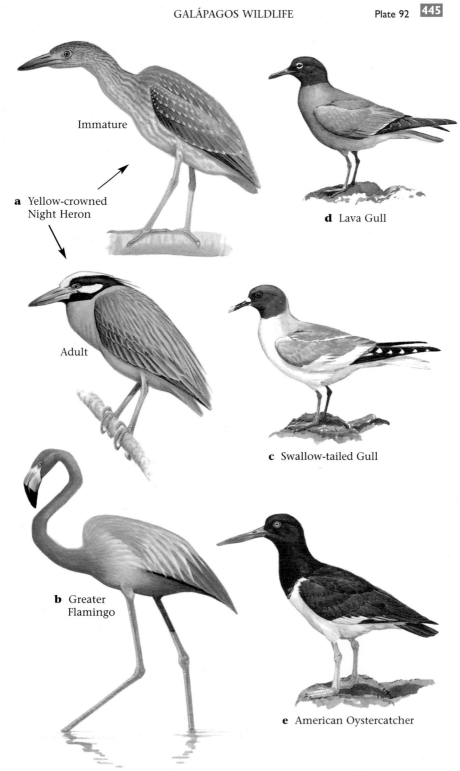

a Yellow-crowned Night Heron

Immature

Adult

b Greater Flamingo

c Swallow-tailed Gull

d Lava Gull

e American Oystercatcher

Plate 93a

Galápagos Dove
Zenaida galapagoensis

ID: Medium-sized (20 cm, 8 in); cinnamon-brown with black spots on upperparts, blue patch of bare skin around eye; legs red.

HABITAT: Pairs seen on ground in dry lowlands of most islands.

REGION: GAL

Plate 93b

Vermilion Flycatcher
Pyrocephalus rubinus

ID: Small (14 cm, 5.5 in); flat black bill; male upperparts and eye mask black, crown and underparts bright red; female upperparts pale brown, underparts whitish streaked pink on the sides.

HABITAT: Pairs seen on exposed branches in open areas in highlands and occasionally lowlands in the Galápagos; resident throughout drier shrubby areas of coastal mainland; Austral migrants in canopy and clearings of southern Oriente lowlands (June to September).

REGION: MCL, ACL, AMA

Plate 93c

Large-billed Flycatcher
Myiarchus magnirostris

ID: Small (16 cm, 6 in); upperparts brown-gray, throat and upper breast gray, belly pale yellow.

HABITAT: Perches in low bushes of open areas in dry lowlands; often very tame.

REGION: GAL

Plate 93d

Galápagos Mockingbird
Nesomimus parvulus

ID: Medium-sized (25 cm, 10 in); upperparts streaked gray-brown; underparts whitish; dark mask; tail long; bill long. Three other closely related and similar species are restricted to Champion-Gardner (Charles Mockingbird, *Nesomimus trifasciatus*), Española (Hood Mockingbird, *Nesomimus macdonaldi*), and San Cristóbal (Chatham Mockingbird, *Nesomimus melanotis*).

HABITAT: On the ground and low bushes primarily in the drier lowlands from shoreline to Palo Santo forests.

REGION: GAL

Plate 93e

Yellow Warbler
Dendroica petechia

ID: Small (12 cm, 5 in); upperparts olive-yellow, underparts yellow; male with rusty crown (resident population on Galápagos Islands and mangroves of mainland coast) or all yellow head (migratory wintering population in coastal lowlands and Amazonia) and streaks on breast.

HABITAT: Resident population in shrubs and trees from mangroves to highlands in Galápagos and mangroves on mainland coast; migratory population in tall lowland secondary forest of mainland (November to April).

REGION: MCL, ACL, AMA, GAL

a Galápagos Dove

b Vermilion Flycatcher

M   F

c Large-billed Flycatcher

d Galápagos Mockingbird

M

e Yellow Warbler

F

Plate 94a

Warbler Finch
Certhidia olivacea

ID: Small (10 cm, 4 in); upperparts olive-gray, underparts buffy white; long thin bill light-colored.

HABITAT: Feeds on insects and flower nectar in low bushes and trees from dry lowlands to moist highlands on almost all islands.

REGION: GAL

Plate 94b

Woodpecker Finch
Cactospiza pallida

ID: Small (13 cm, 5 in); upperparts olive-gray, underparts light olive; long, thick bill light-colored.

HABITAT: Clambers about on tree trunks, large branches and cactus searching for insects, often holds cactus spine or small twig in its bill as tool to excavate insect grubs from their tunnels in vegetation; most common in the highlands but can be found down to the coast on most islands.

REGION: GAL

Plate 94c

Small Ground Finch
Geospiza fuliginosa

ID: Small (12 cm, 5 in); males blackish, females and immatures streaked underparts; short conical bill yellow in nonbreeding season and black during breeding season.

HABITAT: Feeds on ground and low bushes on seed, insects, fruits; on some islands takes ticks from the skin of marine and land iguanas.

REGION: GAL

Plate 94d

Large Ground Finch
Geospiza magnirostris

ID: Small (17 cm, 6.5 in); males black, females and immatures brown above, streaked below; massive bill as deep as it is long.

HABITAT: Eats large seeds in arid areas of the lowlands. Found more in trees than on the ground. Occurs on all islands except Seymour, Baltra, San Cristóbal, Floreana, Santa Fé and Española.

REGION: GAL

Plate 94e

Sharp-beaked Ground Finch
Geospiza difficilis

ID: Small (13 cm, 5 in); males blackish with dark rusty lower belly, females and immatures streaked underparts; long conical bill yellow in nonbreeding season and black during breeding season.

HABITAT: Highlands except on northern islands of Genovesa, Darwin, and Wolf, where it occurs along the coast and is renowned for eating ticks from the feathers of boobies and occasionally pecking the booby's skin at the base of its tail to drink blood.

REGION: GAL

d Large Ground Finch

c Small Ground Finch

e Sharp-beaked Ground Finch

a Warbler Finch

b Woodpecker Finch

Plate 95a

Galápagos Sea Lion
Zalophus californianus wollebaeki
ID: Large (body length 1.8 m, 6 ft); blunt nose males (shown) much larger than females; makes barking or yelping sounds.

HABITAT: Hauls out on rock and pebble beaches of Galápagos but also rarely on the north coast of the mainland.

REGION: MCL, GAL

Plate 95b

Galápagos Fur Seal
Arctocephalus galapagoensis
ID: Medium-sized (body length 1.4 m, 4.5 ft); pointed snout males (shown) much larger than females; makes soft sounds.

HABITAT: Restricted to rocky beaches of the Galápagos and at sea where it often floats with a flipper up in the air.

REGION: GAL

Plate 95c

Common Dolphin
Delphinus delphis
ID: Medium-sized (body length 2 m, 6.5 ft); distinctive color patches on its sides.

HABITAT: Open ocean in large pods along the coast of mainland Ecuador and the Galápagos.

SYMBOLS: 8
REGION: MCL, ACL, GAL

Plate 95d

Bottlenose Dolphin
Tursiops truncatus
ID: Large (body length 3 m, 10 ft); uniform gray color.

HABITAT: Open ocean in small pods along the coast of mainland Ecuador and the Galápagos.

REGION: MCL, ACL, GAL

b Galápagos Fur Seal

a Galápagos Sea Lion

c Common Dolphin

d Bottlenose Dolphin

Plate 96a
Sperm Whale
Physeter macrocephalus
ID: Large (body length 20 m, 65 ft); blunt-headed; spout is angled forward and to the left. When sounding, its all dark flukes are raised completely out of the water.

HABITAT: Open ocean along the coast of mainland Ecuador and the Galápagos.

REGION: ACL, GAL

Plate 96b
Minke Whale
Balaenoptera acutorostrata
ID: Medium-sized (body length 8 m, 26 ft); distinctive white band across upper surface of each relatively short front flipper (but this white band is absent in Antarctic populations). Rarely shows its flukes when sounding.

HABITAT: Open ocean along the coast of mainland Ecuador and the Galápagos.

REGION: ACL, GAL

Plate 96c
Humpback Whale
Megaptera novaeangliae
ID: Large (body length 14.6 m, 48 ft); huge white front flippers. When sounding, raises its flukes, the undersides of which are mottled white, out of the water.

HABITAT: Open ocean along the coast of mainland Ecuador and the Galápagos.

REGION: ACL, GAL

Plate 96d
Orca Whale
(also called Killer Whale)
Orcinus orca
ID: Medium-sized (8 m, 27 ft); bold black and white pattern; white patch in back of each eye is distinctive; tall (2 m, 6.5 ft) dorsal fin of males can be seen at great distances.

HABITAT: Open ocean along the coast of mainland Ecuador and the Galápagos.

REGION: ACL, GAL

Plate 96e
Shortfin Pilot Whale
Globicephala macrorhynchus
ID: Small (body length 5.5 m, 18 ft); all black body; curved dorsal fin.

HABITAT: Open ocean along the coast of mainland Ecuador and the Galápagos; usually travels in large pods of 10 to 100 individuals.

REGION: GAL

a Sperm Whale

b Minke Whale

c Humpback Whale

e Shortfin Pilot Whale

d Orca Whale

SPECIES INDEX

GENERAL INDEX

Plate Key Symbols and Codes

Explanation of habitat symbols:

= Lowland wet forest.

= Lowland dry forest.

= Highland forest and cloud forest. Includes middle elevation and higher elevation wet forests and cloud forests.

= Highland páramo (wet, grassy areas above treeline).

= Forest edge and streamside. Some species typically are found along forest edges or near or along streams; these species prefer semi-open areas rather than dense, closed, interior parts of forests. Also included here: open woodlands, tree plantations, and shady gardens.

= Pastureland, non-tree plantations, savannah (grassland with scattered trees and shrubs), gardens without shade trees, roadside. Species found in these habitats prefer very open areas.

= Freshwater. For species typically found in or near lakes, streams, rivers, marshes, swamps.

= Saltwater/marine. For species usually found in or near the ocean or ocean beaches.

REGIONS (see Map 2, p. 29):

MCL	Moist coastal lowlands
ACL	Arid coastal lowlands
WSA	Western slope of the Andes
HAP	Highlands and páramo
ESA	Eastern slope of the Andes
AMA	Amazon lowlands (the Oriente)
GAL	Galápagos Island Archipelago